The

AUTHENTIC LIBRETTOS

of the

WAGNER OPERAS

The

AUTHENTIC

LIBRETTOS

of the

WAGNER OPERAS

FLYING DUTCHMAN	RHEINGOLD
TANNHÄUSER	WALKÜRE
LOHENGRIN	SIEGFRIED
TRISTAN AND ISOLDE	GÖTTERDÄMMERUNG
MEISTERSINGER	PARSIFAL

*Complete with English and German Parallel Texts
and Music of the Principal Airs*

CROWN PUBLISHERS

NEW YORK

Eleventh Printing

FOREWORD

Richard Wagner composed his operas not only of music but also of poetry. To him, music was, literally, the combination of the Muses' Arts.

He added a new dimension to Music, making "opera" no longer a synthetic art form of drama with a musical accompaniment, but rather a harmony of ideas and emotion.

So it is necessary to know the poetry to appreciate the music, for the poetry translates the music. Of course all operas are better enjoyed with a knowledge of the story. But Wagner's dramas are much more than mere stories. They are great epics informed with all the hope and the hopelessness, the victories and defeats, the pity and the courage of the eternal battle of Man against Fate.

For Wagner was the Composer of the People. He was moved by a great understanding of their struggle and his mind was occupied by that enormous drama. Its currents whirled in his brain and he had to tell of it. Words were too poor a language and music alone perhaps too grand.

Wagner tried to, and did, make his music more explicit by the splendid device of the leitmotive, a musical phrase that is associated with a character or a quality or an idea. When a mood or influence recurs in the drama, the leitmotive recurs. As the character changes, the leitmotives change in rhythm or mode and an entire pattern is woven of them. Brünnhilde's Farewell, Siegfried's Death March are examples of the ingenious blending of these motives and thus the music is considerably clarified.

7

But it is not enough. Wagner himself said that he "found it necessary to indicate a vast number of antecedent facts so as to put the main incidents in the proper light." That is why the conception of Götterdammerung, the saga of Siegfried's Death, led to the composition of "Siegfried" and that in turn to "Die Walküre" and "Das Rheingold." His conception was so large, his thought and feeling so deep and manifold that it is essential to know what was in his mind to get the full value and quality of his expression.

The libretto, then, is the thing. For these operas are really great poetry in words and music. The words must be read and known, they constitute the form, the structure. The music is the color whose magnificence is not fully realized until it is made glorious and brilliant in the light of the underlying poetry.

CONTENTS

CONTENTS

THE
FLYING DUTCHMAN
(Der Fliegende Holländer)

THE STORY OF THE OPERA.

In the legend of the Flying Dutchman we are told that a Dutch captain once tried to double the Cape of Good Hope in the teeth of a furious gale, and swore he would accomplish his purpose, even if he kept sailing on forever. The Devil heard the oath, and condemned the unhappy captain to sail the sea until the Day of Judgment, without aim, and without hope of release, unless he could find a woman to love him faithfully until death. The Devil allowed him to go ashore once in seven years to find such a woman; and this Opera opens with the appearance of the Flying Dutchman's ship, with her blood-red sails and black masts, on the coast of Norway, in a bay into which the ship of Daland, a Norwegian captain, had just before been driven by stress of weather. A seven years' term having then expired, the Dutchman goes on shore, and meets with Daland, from whom he asks for hospitality, offering him in return all his treasures. In conversation he finds out that Daland has a daughter, and he further asks for permission to woo her. Daland, anxious to secure a son-in-law so wealthy, agrees to both requests, and the two set sail for Daland's home, which is not far distant, with a moderate and favorable wind.

ACT II opens with a Spinning Chorus: Senta, Daland's daughter, Mary, her former nurse, and some Norwegian maidens, being discovered at work. On the wall of the room hangs the portrait of the Flying Dutchman, whose face has a fascination for Senta, and rouses in her a romantic attachment. In a ballad she relates his story to Mary and the maidens as they spin, and winds herself up to the highest pitch of excitement in relating it. Meanwhile, Erik, the huntsman, her lover, has come in to tell that he has seen her father's ship entering the port. The maidens wish to rush off at once to welcome the crew and hear their news, but they are kept by Mary to finish their household work, and prepare food for the hungry sailors. Senta also is eager to meet her father, but she is restrained by Erik, who, expecting that Daland will now fulfil his intention of finding a husband for Senta, earnestly pleads his suit with her once again. Senta listens as if in a trance, and Erik goes on to tell her a dream he has had, in which he saw her meeting her father and the sailor whose portrait hangs in the room, and promising to be the wife of the latter. Senta is greatly excited by the recital, and cries out that he in whose face and story she takes such an interest, is seeking for her, and that she will be his. Erik rushes away in horror and despair, and Senta, after her outbreak, remains in the room in deep thought, with her eyes fixed on the picture. Meanwhile, Daland and his guest have reached the house, and Senta starts from her reverie at the sight of the stranger, recognizing his likeness to the portrait. Daland asks Senta to receive him as a guest and a husband. A long scene between Senta and the Dutchman follows, in which Senta heroically vows to share his lot, and be faithful to him until death, he receiving her promise with transport. Daland, who had left them, returns, wishing to announce their betrothal to his crew, who are about to have their accustomed feast upon the successful completion of voyage.

ACT III opens with a chorus by the Norwegian sailors who are dancing and making merry on the deck of their vessel. They cease on seeing the maidens coming with food and drink for the crews of both ships. The maidens try in vain to attract the attention of the crew of the Flying Dutchman's ship, which shows no sign of life on board, and at length desist in surprise and alarm, leaving for the Norwegian sailors all that they have brought. While the Norwegian sailors are feasting, the crew of the Dutch ship rouse up, and sing in chorus the story of their captain. A dark bluish flame is seen, and the sound of a storm is heard. The Norwegian sailors look on and listen with wonder, and afterwards with affright, trying in vain to drown the noise with their own singing. At length they are silenced, and in horror quit the deck and go down to the cabin signing the cross. The crew of the Flying Dutchman's ship, seeing this, burst into shrill laughter. Their song ceases, the storm subsides, the flame goes out, and all is dark and silent as before.

Erik next appears, once more to try his fate with Senta. While he is making his final appeal, the Dutchman comes in, and immediately rushes off to his ship, as if again betrayed and forsaken, while Senta pleads her truth, and Erik implores her not to rush upon destruction. Erik cries out for help when he sees Senta follow the Dutchman, determined to link her fate with his; and, at the cry Daland, Mary, and the maidens hurry to the spot from the house, and the Norwegian sailors from the ship. The Flying Dutchman, after declaring who he is, goes hastily on board his ship, which at once puts to sea. Senta wishes to follow, but is held back by the others. She shakes herself free, and ascends a cliff overhanging the sea, whence she casts herself, calling to the Flying Dutchman and protesting her faithfulness until death. The Dutchman's ship with all her crew, sinks immediately. The sea rises high and sinks back in a whirlpool. In the glow of the sunset are seen, over the wreck of the ship, the forms of Senta and the Dutchman, embracing each other rising from the sea and floating upwards.

PERSONS REPRESENTED.

SENTA. DUTCHMAN. ERIK. DALAND. STEERSMAN. MARY.
Crew of the Norwegian Vessel. *Crew of the Flying Dutchman's Vessel.*
Chorus of Norwegian Maidens.

THE FLYING DUTCHMAN.

DER FLIEGENDE HOLLÄNDER.

ACT I.	ERSTER AKT.
### SCENE I.	### ERSTER AUFTRITT.
(Steep, rocky sea-shore. Gloomy weather; a violent storm. DALAND's ship has cast anchor close to the shore; the sailors are noisily employed in furling the sails, coiling ropes, etc. DALAND has gone on shore. He is standing on a rock and looking landwards, to find out in what place they are.)	(Steiles Felsenufer. Das Meer nimmt den grössten Theil der Bühne ein; weite Aussicht auf dasselbe. Finsteres Wetter; heftiger Sturm. Das Schiff DALANDS's hat so eben dicht am Ufer Anker geworfen; die Matrosen sind in geräuschvoller Arbeit beschäftigt die Segel aufzuhissen, Taue auszuwerfen, u. s. w.—DALAND ist an das Land gegangen; ersteigt einen Felsen und sieht landeinwärts, die Gegend zu erkennen.)
Chorus of Sailors. Yo-ho-eh! Hal-lo-yo! etc.	*Matrosen.* Hohoje! Hohoje! Halloho! etc.
Daland. On board with you—what cheer?	*Daland.* Am Bord bei Euch, wie steht's?
Steersman. Good, all is well! We have good holding ground.	*Steuermann.* Gut, Capitain! Wir sind auf sicherm Grund.
Daland. Sandwike it is! Right well I know the bay. Alas! There on the shore I saw my home. Senta, my child, ere now I should have met thee, If this unlook'd-for tempest had not come! Trust not the wind; in its grasp it will get thee! What good? But stay! The storm subsides; A storm that rages ceases soon. Ho, Sailors! See, she safely rides; Then take some rest—all fear is gone. Now, steersman, the turn is thine to take the watch; The risk is past, yet sleep not at thy post.	*Daland.* 's ist Sandwyk-Strand, genau kenn' ich die Bucht.— Verwünscht! schon sah am Ufer ich mein Haus, Senta, mein Kind, glaubt' ich schon zu umarmen. Da bläst er aus dem Teufels-Loch heraus. . . Wer baut auf Wind, baut auf Satans Erbarmen! Was hilft's? der Sturm läszt nach,— Wenn so er tobte, währt's nicht lang. He! Bursche! lange war't ihr wach; Zur Ruhe denn, mir ist's nicht bang! Nun, Steuermann! die Wache nimmst Du wohl für mich? Gefahr ist nicht, doch gut ist's wenn Du wachst.
Steersman. Depend on me! Sleep safely captain mine!	*Steuermann.* Seid auszer Sorg'! Schlaft ruhig, Capitain!

STEUERMANN.
Steersman. *Piu vivo.*

Through thun-der and storm from dis-tant seas, My maid - en, come I near! O - ver
Mit Ge - wit - ter und Sturm aus fer - nem Meer— Mein Mäd - el, bin dir nah'. Ue - ber

tow - er - ing waves, with south-ern breeze, My maid - en am I here! My
thurm - ho - he Fluth vom Süd - en her— Mein Mäd - el, ich bin da! Mein

maid - en, were there no south wind, I nev - er could come to thee; O
Mäd - el, wenn nicht Süd - wind wär, Ich nim - mer wohl käm' zu Dir;— Ach,

fair south wind, to me be kind! My maid - en, she longs for me!
lie - ber Süd - wind! blas' noch mehr, Mein Mäd - el ver - langt nach mir!

Ho - yo - ho! Hal - lo - ho, ho, hal - lo - ho, ho, ho! . . . .
Ho - ho - he! Jo - lo - he! Ho! Jo - lo - he! Ho! Ho! . . . .

Ho - yo - ho! Hal - lo - ho, ho, ho, ho, ho, ho, ... ho.
Ho - ho - he! Jo - lo - he! Ho - ho! Ho! Ho! Ho! . . . . Ho!

Steersman. From the shores of the south, in
 far-off lands,
 I oft on thee have thought;
Through thunder and waves, from Moor-
 ish strands,
 A gift I thee have brought.
My maiden, praise the sweet south wind—
 I bring thee a golden ring.
O fair south wind, to me be kind!
My maiden doth spin and sing.
 Ho-yo-ho! Hallo-ho!

(In the distance appears the ship of the Flying Dutchman, with blood-red sails and black masts. She quickly
nears the shore, over against the ship of the Norwegian.)

The Dutchman. The term is past,
And once again are ended the seven long
 years!
The weary sea casts me upon the land.
Ha, haughty ocean!
A little while, and thou again wilt bear me.
Though thou art changeful,

Steuermann. Von des Südens Gestad', au
 weitem Land'—
 Ich hab' an Dich gedacht;
 Durch Gewitter und Meer vom Mohren
 strand
 Hab' ich Dir was mitgebracht.
 Mein Mädel preis' den Südwind hoch,
 Ich bring' Dir ein gülden Band;—
 Ach, lieber Südwind, blase doch!
 Mein Mädel hätt gern' den Tand.
 Hoho! Ho jolobe! u. s. w.

(In der Ferne zeigt sich das Schiff der "fliegenden Ho
länder's" mit blutrothen Segeln und schwarzen Master
Es naht sich schnell der Küste nach der dem Schiffe de
Norweger's entgegengesetzten Seite.)

Holländer. Die Frist ist um, und abermal
 vers strichen
 Sind sieben Jahr!—Voll Ueberdrusz wirf
 mich
 Das Meer an's Land. . . Ha, stolzer Ocean
 In kurzer Frist sollst Du mich wieder tra
 gen!

Unchanging is my doom:
Release, which on the land I seek for,
Never shall I meet with.
True, thou heaving ocean,
Am I to thee,
Until thy latest billow shall break—
Until at last thou art no more.
Engulf'd in ocean's deepest wave,
Oft have I long'd to find a grave;
But, ah, a grave I found it not!
I oft have blindly rush'd along,
To find my death sharp rocks among;
But, ah, my death I found it not!
And oft, the pirate boldly daring,
My death I've courted from the sword:
"Here," cried I, "work thy deeds unspar-
    ing—
My ship with gold is richly stor'd."
Alas! the sea's rapacious son
But sign'd the cross, and straight was gone,
Nowhere a grave; no way of death!
Mine is the curse of living breath.
Thee do I pray, bright angel sent from
    heaven,
Thou, who for me didst win unlook'd-for
    grace—
Was there a fruitless hope to mock me
    given,
When thou didst tell me how to gain re-
    lease?
The hope is fruitless—freedom is in vain:
On earth a love unchanging none can gain!
A single hope with me remaineth,
A single hope still standeth fast:
Though earth its form long time retaineth,
In ruins it must fall at last.
Great day of judgment, nearing slow,
When wilt thou dawn, and chase my night?
When comes it, that o'erwhelming blow
Which strikes the world with crushing
    might?
When all the dead are rais'd again,
Destruction I shall then attain.
Ye worlds, your course continue not:
Endless destruction be my lot!

Chorus of the Crew of the Dutchman. End-
    less destruction be our lot.

Daland. Hey! Hallo, Steersman!

Steersman. 'T is nought—'t is nought!
    Ah, fair south wind, to me be kind,
    My maiden—

Daland. There is nought? What! Thou
    watchest well, my friend!

Dein Trotz ist beugsam—doch ewig meine
    Qual.
Das Heil, das auf dem Land ich suche,
    nimmer
Werd' ich es finden! Euch, des Welt-
    meers Fluthen,
Bleib' ich getreu, bis eure letzte Welle
Sich bricht und euer letztes Nasz versiegt!—
Wie oft in Meeres tiefsten Schlund
Stürzt' ich voll Sehnsucht mich hinab,—
Doch ach! den Tod, ich fand ihn nicht!
Da, wo der Schiffe furchtbar Grab,
Trieb mein Schiff ich zum Klippengrund,
Doch ach! mein Grab, es schlosz sich nicht!
Verhöhnend droht' ich dem Piraten,
Im wilden Kampfe hofft' ich Tod:—
"Hier—rief ich—zeige Deine Thaten!
Von Schätzen voll ist Schiff und Boot!"
Doch ach! des Meers barbar'scher Sohn
Schlägt bang' das Kreuz und flieht davon!
Nirgends ein Grab! Niemals der Tod!
Dies der Verdammnisz Schreck-Gebot.—
Dich frage ich, gepries'ner Engel Gottes,
Der meines Heils Bedingung mir gewann,
War ich Unseel'ger Spielwerk Deines
    Spottes,
Als die Erlösung Du mir zeigtest an?
—Vergebne Hoffnung! Furchtbar eitler
    Wahn!
Um ew'ge Treu' auf Erden ist's gethan!—
Nur eine Hoffnung soll mir bleiben,
Nur eine unerschüttert stehn!
So lang' der Erde Keim' auch treiben,
So musz sie doch zu Grunde gehn.
Tag des Gerichtes, jüngster Tag!
Wann brichst du an in meiner Nacht?
Wann dröhnt er, der Vernichtungschlag;
Mit dem die Welt zusammenkracht?
Wann alle Todten auferstehn,
Dann werde ich in Nichts vergehn!
Ihr Welten, endet euren Lauf.
Ew'ge Vernichtung, nimm mich auf!

Chor. Ew'ge Vernichtung, nimm uns auf!

Daland. He! Holla! Steuermann!

Steuermann. 's ist nichts! 's ist nichts!—
    Ach, lieber Südwind blas' noch mehr,—
    Mein Mädel. . .

Daland. Du siehst nichts? Gelt! Du wach
    est brav mein Bursch!

There lies a ship—How long thou must have slept!

Steersman. 'T is so, indeed.
Forgive me, captain mine!
Ahoy! Ahoy!

Daland. It seems that they are quite as bad as we.

Steersman. Give answer, ship and flag, there!

Daland. Forbear! I think I see the captain there!
Hey! Hallo, seaman! Tell thy name—thy country!

The Dutchman. Far have I come; wouldst thou in storm and tempest
Drive me from anchorage?

Daland. Nay, God forbid! Kind welcome do I give thee!
Who art thou?

The Dutchman. A Dutchman.

Dalana. God be with thee!
Hast thou as well been cast upon this
Bare and rocky shore?
I far'd no better; but a few short miles from here
My home awaits me, almost gained:
I must anew set forth to reach it.
Say, whence comest thou?
What damage hast thou suffered?

The Dutchman. My ship is safe; no damage have I suffered.
Through waves that rage and winds that bluster,
Over the wat'ry waste I rove.
What respite? That I cannot tell thee:
Scarce do I count how seasons move.
I cannot name, shouldst thou demand it,
The many seas I've wandered o'er:
The shore alone my heart doth long for—
Ne'er shall I reach my native shore.
Oh, grant to me a little while thy home,
And of thy friendship thou wilt not repent;
With treasure brought from every clime and country
My ship is richly laden: wilt thou bargain?
Thou mayest be sure that thou wilt gainer be.

Dort liegt ein Schiff! —Wie lange schliefs
Du schon?

Steuermann. Zum Teufel auch! — Verzeih
mir Capitain!
Werda! Werda!

Daland. Es scheint, sie sind gerad
So faul als wir.

Steuermann. Gebt Antwort! Schiff und
Flagge!

Daland. Lasz sein. Mich dünkt, ich seh den
Capitain.—
He! Holla! Seemann! Nenne Dich! Wesz
Landes?

Holländer. Weit komm' ich her. Verwehr
bei Sturm und Wetter
Ihr mir den Ankerplatz?

Daland. Behüt' es Gott!
Gastfreundschaft kennt der Seemann.—
Wer bist Du?

Holländer. Holländer.

Daland. Gott zum Grusz! —So trieb auch
Dich
Der Sturm an diesen nackten Felsenstrand
Mir ging's nicht besser, wenig Meilen nur
Von hier ist meine Heimath; fast erreicht
Muszt' ich auf's Neu' mich von ihr wen-
den.—Sag',
Woher kommst Du? Hast Schaden Du
genommen?

Holländer. Mein Schiff ist fest, es leidet kei-
nen Schaden.— —
Durch Sturm und bösen Wind verschlagen,
Irr' auf den Wassern ich umher;—
Wie lange? weisz ich kaum zu sagen,
Schon zähl' ich nicht die Jahre mehr.
Unmöglich dünkt mich's, dasz ich nenne,
Die Länder alle, die ich fand:
Das Einz'ge nur, nach dem ich brenne,
Ich find' es nicht; mein Heimathland!—
Vergönne mir auf kurze Frist Dein Haus,
Und Deine Freundschaft soll Dich nicht
gereu'n:
Mit Schätzen aller Gegenden und Zonen
Ist reich mein Schiff beladen :—willst Du
handeln,
So sollst Du sicher Deines Vortheils sein.

Daland. How wonderful! Can I indeed be-
believe thee?
A baleful star has followed thee till now.
To thee pleasure gladly would I try;
Yet may I ask thee what thy ship contains?

The Dutchman. A store of rarest treasures
shalt thou see—
Pearls rich and costly, stones beyond compare.
Behold, and so convince thyself how great
is their value.
All these for a friendly roof I give thee.

Daland. What? Amazement! All these
treasures!
Who has the wealth the price for them to
offer?

The Dutchman. The price? The price al-
ready have I named—
All these for shelter for a single night.
Nay, what is there is but the smallest part
Of that which in my vessel's hold is stored.
What good to me that have neither wife nor
child?
My native land I cannot find.
All these my riches give I thee
If thou wilt grant me now with thee to find
a home.

Daland. What am I hearing?

The Dutchman. Hast thou a daughter?

Daland. I have — a loving child.

The Dutchman. Let her be mine!

Daland. Wie wunderbar! Soll Deinem Wort
ich glauben?
Ein Unstern, scheint's, hat Dich bis jetzt
verfolgt.
Um Dir zu dienen, biet' ich, was ich kann;
Doch—darf ich fragen, was Dein Schiff
enthält?

Holländer. Die seltensten der Schätze sollst
Du sehn,
Kostbare Perlen, edelstes Gestein.
Blick' hin und überzeuge Dich vom Werthe
Des Preises, den ich für ein gastlich Dach
Dir biete!

Daland. Wie? Ist's möglich? Diese Schätze!
Wer ist so reich, den Preis dafür zu bieten?

Holländer. Den Preis? So eben hab' ich ihn
genannt:
Dies für das Obdach einer einz'gen Nacht!
Doch was Du siehst, ist nur der kleinste
Theil
Von dem, was meines Schiffes Raum ver-
schlieszt.
Was frommt der Schatz? Ich habe weder
Weib
Noch Kind, und meine Heimath find' ich
nie
All' meinen Reichthum biet' ich Dir wenn
be.
Den Deinen Du mir neue Heimath giebst.

Daland. Was musz ich hören?

Holländer. Hast Du eine Tochter?

Daland. Führwahr, ein theures Kind.

Holländer. Sie sei mein Weib!

DUTCHMAN.
HOLLÄNDER.

I have, a - las, nei - ther wife nor
Ach! oh - ne Weib, oh - ne Kind bin

ci - sion. Oh, say, am I dream - ing or
wan - ken. Wüsst' ich, ob ich wach' o - der

child, . . no tie on earth here to bind
ich, . . . nichts fes - selt mich an die Er

wak - ing? Could a son - in - law more . . wel - come
träu - me? Kann ein Ei - dam will - kom - me - ner

me; hope's cheer - ing ray on my life . . . . . . ne'er
de; rast - los ver - folg - te das Schick - sal

be? A fool if his for - tune not
sein? Ein Thor, wenn das Glück ich ver -

smil'd, the curse . is ev - er be - hind
mich, die Qual . . nur war mir Ge - fähr -

tak - ing! To his of - fer, charm'd, I a -
säu - me! Voll Ent - zü - cken schla - ge ich

me, no home shall I find to re - ceive . . . .
te. Nie werd' ich die Hei - math er - rei -

gree, oh, what for - tune! How! he doth ask for my
ein, voll Ent - zü - cken! Wie? Här' ich recht? mei - ne

me, ... of what . . . a - vail are jew - els and
chen, ... zu was . . . . frommt mir der Gü - ter Ge -

daugh - ter as bride! . . . . Is all this for - tune a
Tech - ter ein Weib? . . . . Er selbst spricht aus den Ge -

gold? Thy daugh-ter as bride on-ly give. . . . .
winn? *Lässt du zu dem Bund dich er-wei*

vi-sion, sure 't is but a dream! ah! my good for-tune I'll
dan-ken, er selbst sprich ihn aus. Fast, fürcht' ich, wenn un-ent-

me, then . . . take thou all my treas-ures un-
chen, oh! . . . so nimm mei-ne Schä-tze da-

take at the tide, . . . lest he may change his de-
schloss-en ich bleib', . . . er müsst' im Vor-sa-tze

told, oh, ... take thou all my treas-ures un-
hin! Oh, ... so nimm mei-ne Schä-tze da-

ci-sion, may change his de-ci-sion, yes, I'll take, lest he change his de-
wan-ken, im Vor-sa-tze wan-ken; fast,fürcht' ich, müsst' im Vor-sa-tze

told! as bride now thy daugh-ter, oh give me, and . . take
hin! Lässt du zu dem Bund dich er-wei-chen, oh! . . . so

ci-sion! oh, say, am I dream-ing or wak-ing? Could a
wan-ken. Wüsst' ich, ob ich wach' o-der träu-me! Kann ein

thou all my treas-ures un-told! as bride now thy daugh-ter, oh
nimm mei-ne Schä-tze da-hin! Lässt du zu dem Bund dich er-

son-in-law more wel-come be? a fool if his for-tune not
Ei-dam will-kom-me-ner sein? Ein Thor, wenn das Glück ich ver-

un poco stringendo.

give me, and . . take thou, ... and take thou all my
wei-chen, oh! . . so nimm, oh! so nimm mei-ne

tak-ing, to his of-fer, and take thou all my
säu-me! Voll Ent-zü-cken, to his of-fer
voll Ent-zü-cken

poco riten.

treas - ures   un - told,   oh! . . take   them   all, . .   my   treas - ures   un - told!
Schä - tze   da - hin,   oh! . . so   nimm   mei - ne   Schä - tze   da - hin!

charm'd, I   a - gree,   to . . his   of - - - fer,   charm'd, I   a - gree!)
schla - ge   ich   ein,   voll . . Ent - zü - - - cken schla - ge   ich   ein!)

Daland. Yes, stranger, true; I have an only daughter, Who gives her father all a daughter's love; She is my pride, the best of my possessions, In grief my comfort and in mirth my joy.	*Daland.* Wohl, Fremdling, hab' ich eine schöne Tochter, Mit treuer Kindeslieb' ergeben mir; Sie ist mein Stolz, das höchste meiner Güter. Mein Trost im Unglück, meine Freud' im Glück.
The Dutchman. Her father still receive her true affection! Love him, and she will love her husband too.	*Holländer.* Dem Vater stets bewahr' sie ihre Liebe, Ihm treu, wird sie auch treu dem Gatten sein.
Daland. Thou givest jewels, pearls of price-less value; A fairer jewel still, a faithful wife—	*Daland.* Du giebst Juwelen, unschätzbare Perlen, Das höchste Kleinod doch, ein treues Weib. . .
The Dutchman. Thou givest me?	*Holländer.* Du giebst es mir?
Daland. I give thee here my word. I mourn thy lot. As thou art bountiful, Thou showest me thy good and noble heart. My son I wish thou wert; And were thy wealth not half as great, I would not choose another!	*Daland.* Ich gebe Dir mein Wort. Mich rührt Dein Loos; freigebig, wie Du bist, Zeigst Edelmuth und hohen Sinn Du mir :- Den Eidam wünscht' ich so, und wär Dein Gut Auch nicht so reich, wählt' ich doch keinen Andern.
The Dutchman. I thank thee! Shall I thy daughter see to-day?	*Holländer.* Hab' Dank! Werd' ich die Tochter heut noch sehn?
Daland. The next propitious wind will bear us home; Thou'lt see her then, and if she pleases thee—	*Daland.* Der nächste günst'ge Wind führt uns nach Haus. Du sollst sie sehn, und wenn sie Dir gefällt—
The Dutchman. She shall be mine. Will she my angel be? Oft by unceasing torment driven, My heart has long'd for rest and peace; Oh, would the hope at last were given That I through her might find release! Dare I in that delusion languish, That through this angel pain shall cease? That after this tormenting anguish I shall attain to lasting peace? Ah! all but hopeless though I be, My heart still hopes that joy to see.	*Höllander.* So ist sie mein. . . Wird sie mein Engel sein? Wenn aus der Qualen Schreckgewalten Die Sehnsucht nach dem Heil mich treibt, Ist mir's erlaubt, mich fest zu halten An einer Hoffnung, die mir bleibt. Darf ich in jenem Wahn noch schmachten, Dasz sich ein Engel mir erweicht? Der Qualen, die mein Haupt umnachten, Ersehntes Ziel hätt' ich erreicht. Ach! ohne Hoffnung wie ich bin, Geb' ich mich docn der Hoffnung hin!

Daland. I thank the storm which me far has driven,
And on this rocky shore has cast:
In truth, good fortune freely given
I must not lose, but hold it fast.
Ye winds that to this coast have brought him,
To you my heartfelt thanks I pay;
No father but had gladly caught him;
His wealth and he are mine to-day!
Good fortune, freely given,
I must not lose, but hold it fast.
Yes! to one with wealth and noble heart,
With house and child I gladly part!

Steersman. South wind! South wind!
"Oh, fair south wind, to me be kind!"

Chorus of Sailors. Halloho! Yoo-ho-eh!

Daland. Gepriesen seid, des Sturms Gewalten
Die ihr an diesen Strand mich triebt.
Fürwahr! Blos brauch' ich festzuhalten.
Was sich so schön von selbst mir giebt
Die ihn an diese Küste brachten
Ihr Wind sollt gesegnet sein!
Ja, wonach alle Väter trachten,
Ein reicher Eidam, er ist mein.
Dem Mann mit Gut und hohem Sinn
Geb' froh ich Haus und Tochter hin!

Steuermann. —Südwind! Südwind!
"Ach! lieber Südwind blas' noch mehr!"

Matrosen. Holloje! Hollajo!

DALAND.
DALAND.

Thou seest how fate doth fa - vor thee, the sea is calm, and fair the breeze.
Du siehst, das Glück ist gün - stig dir; der Wind ist gut, die See in Ruh'.

We'll hoist the flow-'ng sails with glee, and reach my home to - day with ease.
So gleich die An - ker lich - ten wir, und se - geln schnell der Hei - math zu.

Sailors. Halloho! Ho! Halloho! etc.

The Dutchman. If I might ask thee, do thou first put to sea:
Though fair the wind, my crew are weary all;
So let them rest awhile, then follow thee.

Daland. Yes, but the wind?

The Dutchman. 'T is not a wind to fall.
My ship is swift, and thine will overtake.

Daland. Thy ship, if so, good speed will have to make.
Farewell! To-day thou wilt my daughter see!

The Dutchman. In truth?

Daland. Hey! quickly full the sails will be!
Hallo! Hallo!
Come, sailors, work away!

Matrosen. Hohone! Hohohe! Halloho! Jo! u.s.w.

Holländer. Darf ich Dich bitten, segelst Du voran;
Der Wind ist frisch, doch, meine Mann-schaft müd',
Ich gönn' ihr kurze Ruh, und folge dann.

Daland. Doch unser Wind?

Holländer. Er bläst noch lang' aus Süd',
Mein Schiff ist schnell, es holt' Dich sicher ein.

Daland. Du glaubst? Wohlan! Es möge denn so sein.
Leb' wohl! mögst heute Du mein Kind noch sehn!

Holländer. Gewisz!

Daland. Hei! Wie die Segel schon sich bläh'n!
Hallo! Hallo! Frisch, Jungen! Greifet an!

Sailors   Through thunder and storm from dis-
           tant seas,
      My maiden, come I near;
   Over towering waves, with southern breeze,
      My maiden, am I here!
   My maiden, were there no south wind,
      I never could come to thee;
   Oh, fair south wind, to me be kind!
      My maiden, she longs for me!
         Hoho! Halloho! etc.

Matrosen.   Mit Gewitter und Sturm aus fer-
             nem Meer.
      Mein Mädel, bin dir nah!
   Ueber thurmhohe Flutn, vom Süden her—
      Mein Mädel, ich bin da!
   Mein Mädel, wenn nicht Südwind wär',
      Ich nimmer wohl käm' zu dir!
   Ach, lieber Südwind, blas' noch mehr!
      Mein Mädel verlangt nach mir,
         Hohoje! Halloho! Hoho! Ho! Ho! Ho!

ACT II.

ZWEITER AKT.

(A room in DALAND's house. Marine views, maps, charts, etc., hung on the walls. On the wall at the back is hung the portrait of a man, pale, with dark beard, dressed in Spanish costume. MARY and the maidens are discovered spinning. SENTA is in contemplation of the portrait.)

(Ein grosses Zimmer im Hause DALAND's; an der Wand Bilder von Seegegenständen, Karten, u.s.w. An der Hinterwand das Bildniss eines bleichen Mannes mit dunklem Barte und in schwarzer spanischer Tracht. MARY und die Mädchen sitzen im den Kamin und spinnen. SENTA in einem Grossvaterstuhle zurückgelehnt, ist in träumerisches Anschauen des Bildnisses an der Hinterwand versunken.)

CHORUS OF MAIDENS.
CHOR DER MÄDCHEN.

Tra la ra la la la la la! Tra la ra la la la la la!
Tra la ra la la la la la! Tra la ra la la la la la!

spin,   maid - ens, maid - ens, spin,   sweet-hearts win - ning,
Spinnt,   *fleis - sig Mäd - chen! Brumm',*   *gu - tes Räd - chen!*

Tra la ra la la la la la la la la la la!
Tra la ra la la la la la la la la la la!

spin,   spin,   maid - ens spin - ning, sweet - hearts win - ning, spin!
Spinnt! Spinnt!   *fleis - sig Mäd - chen, fleis - sig Mäd - chen, spinn!*

Mary.   Ah, duly are they spinning!
Each girl a sweetheart would be winning!

The Maidens. Dame Mary, hush! for well you know
Our song as yet must onward go!

Mary.   Then sing—yet ply a busy wheel.
But wherefore, Senta, art thou still?

The Maidens. Hum, hum, hum—good wheel, be whirling!
Gaily, gaily turn thee round!
Spin, spin, spin—the threads be twirling!
Turn, good wheel, with humming sound!
On distant seas my love doth sail—
     In southern lands
     Much gold he wins;
Then turn, good wheel, nor tire, nor fail:
     The gold for her
     Who duly spins!
       Spin, spin,
     Spin we duly!
       Hum! hum!
     Wheel go truly!

Mary.   Thou careless girl! Wilt thou not spin?
Thy lover's gift thou wilt not win!

The Maidens. She has no need to work as we:
Her lover sails not on the sea—
He brings her game instead of gold;
One knows the worth of hunters bold.

Mary.   Ei! Fleiszig, fleiszig, wie sie spinnen!
Will jede sich den Schatz gewinnen.

Mädchen. Frau Mary, still! denn wohl Ihr wiszt,
Das Lied noch nicht zu Ende ist.

Mary.   So singt! dem Rädchen läszt's nicht Ruh.
Du aber, Senta, schweigst dazu?

Mädchen. Summ nnd brumm du gutes Räd-chen,
Munter, munter dreh' dich um!
Spinne, spinne tausend Fädchen,
Gutes Rädchen, summ und brumm!
Mein Schatz da drauszen auf dem Meer
Im Süden er
Viel Gold gewinnt.
Ach, gutes Rädchen, braus' noch mehr!
Er giebt's dem Kind,
Wenn's fleiszig spinnt.
Spinnt, spinnt!
Fleiszig, Mädchen!
Summ, brumm,
Gutes Rädchen!

Mary.   Du böses Kind, wenn Du nicht spinnst,
Vom Schatz Du kein Geschenk gewinnst!

Mädchen. Sie hat's nicht noth, dasz sie sich eilt.
Ihr Schatz nicht auf dem Meere weilt:
Bringt er nicht Gold, bringt er doch Wild,
Man weisz ja was ein Jäger gilt!

Mary. You see her still before that face!
Why wilt thou dream away thy girlhood
With gazing at that picture so?

Senta. Why hast thou told me of his sorrows?
His hapless fate why did I know?
The wretched man!

Mary. God help thee, girl!

The Maidens. Ei, ei! What's that she said?
Her sighs are for the ghostly man!

Mary. I fear that she will lose her head!

The Maidens. 'T is brooding makes her look
so wan.

Mary. No use for me to chide each day.
Come, Senta, wilt thou turn away?

The Maidens. She hears you not; she is in
love!
Ei, ei! No anger pray it move!
For Erik has a temper hot,
And if his heart will bear it not,
Say nought, lest in a rage he fall,
And shoot his rival on the wall!
Ha, ha, ha!

Senta. Be still with all your foolish jesting!
My temper are you bent on testing?

The Maidens. Hum, good wheel, etc.

Senta. Oh, make an end of all this singing!
Your hum, hum, hum, quite tires my ear.
If me you would your way be bringing,
Provide some better thing to hear!

The Maidens. Well, sing thyself!

Senta. Much would I rather
Dame Mary sing to us the ballad.

Mary. I'd rather not attempt the thing:
The Flying Dutchman, let him be!

Senta. The song I oft have heard you sing!
I'll sing myself!
Hark, then, to me—
A tale of sorrow I select you:
His wretched fate it must affect you.

Mary. Da seht ihr's! Immer vor dem Bild!—
Wirst Du Dein ganzes junges Leben
Verträumen vor dem Conterfei?

Senta. Was hast du Kunde mir gegeben,
Was mir erzählet, wei es sei!
Der arme Mann!

Mary. Gott sei mit Dir!

Mädchen. Ei, ei! Ei, ei! Was hören wir?
Sie seufzet um den bleichen Mann.

Mary. Den Kopf verliert sie noch darum.

Mädchen. Da sieht man, was ein Bild doch
kann!

Mary. Nichts hilft es, wenn ich täglich
brumm':
Komm', Senta! wend' Dich doch herum!

Mädchen. Sie hört Euch nicht,—sie ist ver-
liebt.
Ei, ei! Wenn's nur nicht Händel giebt!
Erik ist gar ein heiszes Blut,
Dasz er nur keinen Schaden thut!
Sagt nichts, er schieszt sonst wuthentbrannt
Den Nebenbuhler von der Wand.

Senta. O schweigt! Mit Eurem tollen Lachen,
Wollt ihr mich ernstlich böse machen?

Mädchen. Summ und brumm, du gutes Räd-
chen
Munter, munter dreh' dich um!
Spinne, spinne tausend Fädchen,
Gutes Rädchen brumm und summ!

Senta. O macht dem tollen Lied ein Ende,
Es summt und brummt mir vor dem Ohr!
Wollt ihr, dasz ich mich zu euch wende,
So sucht' was Besseres hervor!

Mädchen. Gut singe Du!

Senta. Hört, was ich rathe.
Frau Mary singt uns die Ballade.

Mary. Bewahre Gott! das fehlte mir!
Den fliegenden Holländer laszt in Ruh'.

Senta. Wie oft doch hört' ich sie von Dir!
Ich sing' sie selbst, hört, Mädchen, zu.
Laszt mich's euch recht zu Herzen führen
Des Aermsten Loos, es musz euch rühren

The Maidens. Well, let us hear.	*Mädchen.* Uns ist es recht.
Senta. Mark what I say.	*Senta.* Merkt auf die Wort'!
The Maidens. And we will rest.	*Mädchen.* Dem Spinnrad Ruh'!
Mary. I'll spin away.	*Mary.* Ich spinne fort.

SENTA (*seated in old arm chair*).
SENTA (*im Grossvaterstuhl*).

Yo ho - hoe! Yo - ho - ho - hoe! Yo - ho - hoe! Yo - - hoe! Saw
Jo ho hoe! Jo ho ho hoe! Jo ho hoe! Jo . . . . hoe! Traft

ye the ship on the rag - ing deep, blood - red the can - vas, black the mast? On
ihr das Schiff im Mee - re an, blut - roth die Se - gel, schwarz der Mast? Auf

board un - ceas - ing watch doth keep the ves - sel's mas - ter pale and ghast!
ho - hem Bord der blei - che Mann, des Schif - fes Herr, wacht oh - ne Rast.

Hui! How roars the wind! Yo - ho - hoe! . . . Yo - ho - hoe!
Hui! Wie pfeipft's im Tau! Jo ho he! . . . Jo ho he!

Hui! How bends the mast! Yo - ho - hoe! Yo - ho - hoe! Hui! Like an
Hui! Wie pfeit's im Tau! Jo ho he! Jo ho he! Hui! Wie ein

ar - row she flies, with-out aim, with-out goal, with-out rest! . . . . .
Pfeil fliegt er hin, oh - ne Ziel, oh - ne Rast, oh - ne Ruh'!

piu lento. (♩ = 100.)

Yet can the spec - tre sea - man be freed from the curse in - fer - nal, Find he a
Doch kann dem blei - chen Man - ne Er - lö - sung ein - stens noch wer - den, Fräud' er ein

wo - man on earth who'll pledge him her love e - ter - nal. Ah! that the poor spec - tre
Weib, das bis in den Tod ge - treu ihm auf Er - den. Ach! wann wirst du, blei - cher

sea - man may find her! Pray, pray, that Heav-en may soon in pit - y grant him this boon!
See - mann, sie fin - den? Be - tet zum Him-mel, dass bald ein Weib Treu - e ihm halt'!

Senta.   Against a tempest's utmost wrath,
Around a cape he once would sail;
He curs'd and swore a foolish oath:
"Befall what may, I will prevail!"
Hui!   And Satan heard!   Yo-ho-he!
Hui!   He marked his word,
And condemned him to sail on the sea,
without aim, without end.
Yet this the wretched man from his lifelong
curse may deliver,
Would but an angel show him the way his
bondage to sever.
Ah, mightest thou, spectral seaman, but
find it!
Pray ye that Heav'n may soon
At his need grant him this boon!
He lands at ev'ry seven year's end;
A wife to seek, he wanders round;
But wheresoe'er he bends
For him no faithful wife is found.
Hui!   "Unfurl the sails!"   Yo-ho-he!
Hui!   "The anchor weigh'd!"   Yo-ho he!
Hui!   "Faithless love, faithless troth!
To the sea, without aim, without end."

The Maidens.   Ah, where is she, to whose
loving heart the angel may guide thee?
Where lingers she, thine own unto death,
whatever betide thee?

Senta.   I am the one who through her love
will save thee!
Oh, may the angel hither guide thee!
Through me may new-found joy betide
thee!

Mary and the Maidens.   Heav'n help us!
Senta!

Erik.
(Has entered in time to hear the last exclamations of
SENTA.)
Senta, would'st thou, then, forsake me?

The Maidens.   Help, Erik, help!   This must
be madness.

Mary.   This outburst fills my heart with sad-
ness!
Abhorred picture, thou shalt burn!
Let but her father once return!

Erik.   Her father comes!

Senta   My father here?

Erik   From off the height I saw his sail.

Senta.   Bei bösem Wind und Sturmes Wuth
Umsegeln wollt' er einst ein Cap;
Er flucht' und schwur in tollem Muth;—
"In Ewigkeit lass' ich nicht ab!"—
Hui!—Und Satan hört's—Johohe!
Hui!—Nahm ihn bei'm Wort!—Johohe!
Hui!   Und verdammt zieht er nun durch
das Meer, ohne Rast, ohne Ruh'.
Doch, dasz der arme Mann noch Erlösung
fände auf Erden,
Zeigt Gottes Engel an, wie sein Heil ihm
einst könne werden:—
Ach!   mögtest Du, bleicher Seemann, es
finden!
Betet zum Himmel, dasz bald
Ein Weib Treue ihm halt'!—
Vor Anker alle sieben Jahr,
Ein Weib zu frei'n, ging er an's Land;
Er freite alle sieben Jahr,
Noch nie ein treues Weib er fand.—
Hui!   "die Segel auf!"—Johohe!
Hui!   "den Anker los!"—Johohe!
Hui!   falsche Lieb', falsche Treu'!   Auf in
See!   Ohne Rast, ohne Ruh!

Mädchen.   Ach, wo weilt sie, die dir Gottes
Engel einst könne zeigen?
Wo triffst Du sie, die bis in den Tod Dein
bliebe treueigen?

Senta.   Ich sei das Weib!   Meine Treu' soll
Dich erlösen!
Mög' Gottes Engel mich Dir zeigen;
Durch mich sollst Du das Heil erreichen!

Mary und die Mädchen.   Hilf Himmel!
Senta!   Senta!

Erik.
(Ist zur thüre hereingetreten und hat SENTA's Ausruf
vernommen.)
Senta, Senta!   Willst Du mich verderben?

Mädchen.   Hilf uns, Erik!   Sie ist von Sinnen!

Mary.   Vor Schreck fühl' ich mein Blut gerin-
nen!
Abscheulich Bild, Du sollst hinaus,
Kommt nur der Vater erst nach Haus!

Erik.   Der Vater kommt.

Senta.   Der Vater kommt?

Erik.   Vom Fels sah ich sein Schiff sich nahen.

The Maidens.   They are at home!

Mary.   Hold! hold! With me you ought to
            stay!
The sailors come with urgent hunger:
For food and wine they soon will ask.
Restrain yourselves a little longer,
Nor leave undone each needful task.

The Maidens.   We cannot stay at work much
            longer:
There is so much we want to ask.
Enough we satisfy their hunger,
Then have we done each needful task.

Erik.   Stay, Senta! Stay a single moment
            more,
And from my torture set me free!
Say, wilt thou, ah, wilt thou leave me
            quite?

Senta.   What is—what must?

Erik.   O Senta, speak—what will become of
            me?
Thy father comes; before he sails again
He will accomplish what he oft has pur-
            posed.

Senta.   What dost thou mean?

Erik.   And will a husband give thee—

Mädchen.   Sie sind daheim!—Auf, eilt hinaus.

Mary.   Halt! Halt! Ihr bleibet fein im Haus!
            Das Schiffsvolk kommt mit leerem Ma-
            gen:—
In Küch' und Keller!   Säumet nicht!
Laszt Euch nur brav die Neugier plagen,
Vor Allem geht an eure Pflicht!

Mädchen.   Ach, wie viel hab' ich ihn zu
            fragen!
Ich halte mich vor Neugier nicht.—
Schon gut: sobald nur aufgetragen,
Hält länger hier uns keine Pflicht!

Erik.   Bleib', Senta! Bleib' nur einen Augen-
            blick!
Aus meinen Qualen reisze mich! Doch
            willst Du—
Ach! so verdirb mich ganz!

Senta.   Was soll's, Erik . . .?

Erik.   O Senta, sprich, was aus mir werden
            soll?
Dein Vater kommt,—eh' wieder er verreist
Wird er vollbringen, was scho.. oft er
            wollte. . .

Senta.   Und was, Erik?

Erik.   Dir einen Gatten geben.—

ERIK.
A tempo, ma un poco ritenuto.

A heart, a hand, from ill to screen thee! A hun-ter's skill, a
Mein Herz voll Treu - e bis zum Ster - ben, Mein dürf - tig Gut, mein

fru - gal hut! Were I with these to seek to win thee,
Jä - ger-glück: Darf so um Dei - ne Hand ich wer - ben,

Would not thy fa - ther spurn my suit? Then let my heart with an - guish
Stöszt mich Dein nicht zu - rück? Wenn sich mein Herz in Jam - mer

break, Say, Sen - ta, who for me will speak? Then let my heart with an-guish
bricht, Sag', Sen - ta, wer dann für mich spricht? Wenn dann mein Herz im Jam - me,
molto rit.

break, Yes, let my heart with an - guish break, Say, Sen - ta, who for me will speak?
bricht, Wenn dann mein Herz im Jam - mer bricht: Sag', Sen - ta, wer dann für mich spricht?

Senta. Ah, ask not, Erik, now.
Let me begone:
My father I must welcome;
For if this once his daughter failed to come,
I fear he might be angry.

Erik. From me thou 'dst fly?

Senta. I must on board.

Erik. Thou shunnest me?

Senta. Oh, let me go!

Erik. And wilt thou leave the wound still
bleeding,
Which thou hast given my loving heart?
Ah, hear my fondest, latest pleading —
Hear what I ask, ere yet we part!
Say, let this heart with anguish break,
Will Senta care for me to speak?

Senta. What! dost thou doubt my heart's
devotion,
And question if I love thee still?
Oh, say, what makes this new emotion?
Why should mistrust thy bosom fill?

Erik. Thy father, ah, for wealth alone he
seeks;
And Senta, thou, how dare I on thee
reckon?
I pray thee grant but one of my petitions:
Grieve not my heart from day to day.

Senta. Thy heart?

Erik. What can I fancy? Yonder face.

Senta. The face?

Erik. Why not abandon all thy foolish
dreams?

Senta. Can I forbid my face to show compassion?

Erik. Then, too, the ballad thou hast sung
to-day!

Senta. I am a child, and know not what I 'm
singing.
But, say —What! fearest thou a song — a
face?

Erik. Thou art so pale; say, should I not be
fearful?

Senta. O schweige jetzt, Erik! Lasz mich
hinaus,
Den Vater zu begrüszen!
Wenn nicht, wie sonst, an Bord die Tochter kommt,
Wird er nicht zürnen müssen?

Erik. Du willst mich fliehn?

Senta. Ich musz zum Port.

Erik. Du weichst mir aus?

Senta. Ach! lasz mich fort!

Erik. Fliehst Du zurück vor dieser Wunde,
Die Du mir schlugst, den Liebeswahn?
O höre mich zu dieser Stunde,
Hör' meine letzte Frage an!
Wenn dieses Herz im Jammer bricht,
Wird's Senta sein, die für mich spricht?

Senta. Wie? zweifelst Du an meinem Herzen?
Du zweifelst, ob ich gut Dir bin?—
Doch sag', was weckt Dir solche Schmerzen?
Was trübt mit Argwohn Deinen Sinn?

Erik. Dein Vater—ach! nach Schätzen geizt
er nur . . .
Und Senta, Du! Wie dürst' auf Dich ich
zählen?
Erfülltest Du nur eine meiner Bitten?
Kränkst Du mein Herz nicht jeden Tag?

Senta. Dein Herz?

Erik. Was soll ich denken. Jenes Bild . . .

Senta. Das Bild?

Erik. Läszt Du von Deiner Schwermere[1]
wohl ab?

Senta. Kann meinem Blick Theilnahme ich
verwehren?

Erik. Und die Ballade, heut noch sangst Du
sie!

Senta. Ich bin ein Kind und weisz nicht was
ich singe . . . !
Erik, sag'! fürchtest Du ein Lied, ein Bild?

Erik. Du bist so bleich . . . sag', sollt' ich
es nicht fürchten?

Senta. Should, then, a fate so terrible not move me?

Erik. My sorrow, Senta, moves thee now no more!

Senta. Oh, vaunt it not!
What can thy sorrow be?
Know'st thou the fate of that unhappy man?
Look, canst thou feel the pain, the grief,
With which his gaze on me he bends?
Ah, when I think he has ne'er found relief,
How sharp a pang my bosom rends!

Erik. Woe's me! I think of my late hapless dream!
God keep thee safe! Satan would thee ensnare.

Senta. What affrights thee so?

Erik. Senta, hear what I tell!
A vision—heed thou its warning voice!
On lofty cliffs I lay, and, dreaming.
I watched the mighty sea below;
The sounding breakers white were gleaming,
And toward the shore came rolling slow.
A foreign ship off shore was riding:
I mark'd her—weird-like, strange to see.
Two men their steps to me were guiding;
The one I knew—thy father he.

Senta. The other?

Erik. Him, too, had I seen;
The garments black, the ghastly mien.

Senta. The gloomy look?

Erik. The seaman here.

Senta. And I?

Erik. From home thou didst appear,
And haste to give thy father greeting.
I saw thee to the stranger going,
And, as for his regard entreating,
Thyself at once before him throwing.

Senta. He rais'd me up—

Erik. Upon his breast:
I saw him close embraced by thee—
In kisses was thy love confessed.

Senta. And then?

Senta. Soll mich des Aermsten Schreckensloos nicht rühren?

Erik. Mein Leiden, Senta, rührt es Dich nicht mehr?

Senta. O! schweige doch. Was kann Dein Leiden sein?
Kennst jenes Unglücksel'gen Schicksal Du?
Fühlst Du den Schmerz, den tiefsten Gram,
Mit dem herab auf mich er sieht?
Ach, was die Ruh' ihm ewig nahm,
Wie schneidend Weh durch's Herz mir zieht!

Erik. Weh' mir! Es mahnt mich ein unsel'-ger Traum!
Gott schütze Dich! Satan hat Dich umgarnt.

Senta. Was schreckt Dich so?

Erik. Senta, lasz Dir vertrau'n :—
Ein Traum ist's,—höre ihn zur Warnung an!
Auf hohem Felsen lag ich träumend,
Sah unter mir des Meeres Fluth;
Die Brandung hört' ich, wie sich schäumend
Am Ufer brach der Wogen Wuth :—
Ein fremdes Schiff am nahen Strande
Erblickt' ich, seltsam, wunderbar :—
wei Männer nahten sich dem Lande,
Der Ein', ich sah's, Dein Vater war. . .

Senta. Der Andre?

Erik. Wohl erkannt' ich ihn :
Mit schwarzem Wams und bleicher Mien'

Senta. Und düst'rem Aug'. . .

Erik. Der Seemann, Er.

Senta. Und ich?

Erik. Du kamst vom Hause her,
Du flogst den Vater zu begrüszen;
Doch kaum noch fah' ich an Dich langer,
Du stürztest zu des Fremden Füszen-
Ich sah Dich seine Knie umfangen. . .

Senta. Er hob mich auf. . .

Erik. An seine Brust ;—
Voll Inbrunst hingst Du Dich an ihn,—
Du küsztest ihn mit heiszer Lust—

Senta. Und dann. . .?

Erik. I saw you put to sea.

Senta. He seeks for me, and I for him!
For him will I risk life and limb!

Erik. How frightful! Clearly I view
Her hapless end. My dream was true!

Senta. Ah, mightest thou, spectral seaman, but
find her!
Pray ye that Heav'n may soon,
At his need, grant him this boon!

(The door opens, DALAND and the DUTCHMAN enter.)

Daland. My child, thou seest me on the thresh-
old––
What? no embracing, not a kiss?
Thou standest fixed—nor word, nor mo-
tion?
My Senta, do I merit this?

Senta. God be thy guard! My father, say,
Who is this stranger?

Daland. Wouldst thou know?

Erik. Sah ich auf's Meer euch flieh'n.

Senta. Er sucht mich auf! Ich musz ihn sehn!
Mit ihm musz ich zu Grunde gehn!

Erik. Entsetzlich! Ha, mir wird es klar;
Sie ist dahin! Mein Traum sprach wahr

Senta. Ach, möchtest du, bleicher
Seemann, sie finden! Betet
Zum Himmel, das bald ein
Weib Trene ihm!

(Die Thür geht auf; der HOLLÄNDER und DALAND
zeigen sich.)

Daland. Mein Kind, du siehst nich auf der
Schwelle—
Wie? Kein Umarmen, Keinen Kuse?
Du bleibst gebannt an deiner Stelle?
Verdien' ich, Senta, solchen Gross?

Senta. Gott dir zum Gruse! Mein Vater.
sprich, war ist der Fremde?

Daland. Drängst du mich?

DALAND.

Wilt thou, my child, the stran-ger give a friend-ly wel-come? True sea-man
Mögst du, mein Kind, den frem-den Mann will-kom-mer heis-sen! See-mann ist

he, like me, our guest he would re-main. Long wand-'ring home-less, oft on
er, gleich mir, das Gast-recht spricht er an. Lang' oh-ne Hei-math, stets auf

dis-tant, dis-tant jour-neys, In for-eign lands he wealth and treas-ures vast did gain.
fer-nen, wei-ten Rei-sen, In frem-den Lan-den er der Schät-ze viel ge-wann.

From his own fa-ther-land ex-il'd he doth of-fer
Aus sei-nem Va-ter-land ver-wei-sen, für ei-nen

wealth our home to share. Say, wouldst ob-ject if hence-forth, child, he should join us
Heerd er reich-lich lohnt. Sprich, Sen-ta, würd' es dich ver-dries-sen, wenn die-ser

in our sim-ple fare? Should join us in our sim-ple fare?
Frem-de bei uns wohnt? Wenn die-ser Frem-de bei uns wohnt?

Daland. Say, have I gone too far in praising?
Look for thyself,—is she not fair?
Should not my praise be overflowing?
Confess her graces wondrous are!
Wilt thou, my child, accord our guest a
friendly welcome,
And wilt thou also let him share thy kindly
heart?
Give him thy hand, for bridegroom it is
thine to call him!
If thou but give consent, to-morrow his
thou art.
Look on these gems, look on the bracelets:
To what he owns trifles are these.
Dost thou, my child, not long to have
them?
And all are thine when thou art his!
Yet neither speaks;
What, then, if I were gone?
I see—'t were best that they were left alone.
May'st thou secure this noble husband!
Trust me such luck is given to few.
Stay here alone: and I will leave you.
Senta is fair, and she is true.

Daland. Sagt, hab' ich sie zu viel gepriesen
Ihr seht sie selbst,—ist sie Euch recht?—
Soll noch vom Lob' ich überflieszen?
Gesteht, sie zieret ihr Geschlecht!
Mögst Du, mein Kind, dem Manne freund
lich Dich erweisen!
Von Deinem Herzen auch spricht hold
Gab' er an.
Reich' ihm die Hand, denn Bräutigam solls
Du ihn heiszen;
Stimmst Du dem Vater bei, ist morgen e
Dein Mann.
Sieh' dieses Band, sieh' diese Spangen!
Was er besitzt, macht dies gering.
Musz, theures Kind, Dich's nicht verlangen
Dein ist es, wechselst Du den Ring!—
Doch—Keines spricht.—Sollt' ich hier läs
tig sein?
So ist's! Am Besten lasz ich sie allein.
Mögst Du den edlen Mann gewinnen!
Glaub' mir, solch Glück wird nimmer neu
Bleibt hier allein; ich geh' von hinnen. .
Glaubt mir, wie schön, so ist sie treu!

The Dutchman. Like to a vision, seen in
days long by-gone,
This maiden's face and form appear:
What I have sought thro' countless years of
sorrow
Am at I last beholding here!

Holländer. Wie aus der Ferne längst vergang
ner Zeiten
Spricht dieses Mädchens Bild zu mir;
Wie ich's geträumt seit langen Ewigkeite
Vor meinen Augen seh' ich's hier.

DUTCHMAN
HOLLÄNDER.

Oft 'mid the tor - ment of my night e - ter - nal, Long - ing I gaz'd up -
Wohl hub auch ich voll Sehn-sucht mei - ne Bli - cke Aus tie - fer Nacht em -

un poco riten.

on . . some be - ing fair! But I was driv'n by Sa - tan's pow'r in - fer - nal
por . . zu ein - em Weib! Ein schla - gend Herz liess, ach! mir Sa - tan's Tü - cke,

On my dread course, in an - guish and des - pair! The glow that warms my
Dass ein - ge - denk ich mei - ner Qua - len bleib'! Die dü - stre Gluth, die

heart with strange e - mo - tion, Can I, ac - curs'd one, call it love's de - vo - tion? Ah
hier ich füh - le bren - nen, Sollt' ich Un - se - li - ger sie Lie - be nen - nen? Ac

no, 'tis yearn - ing blest re - pose to gain, That such an an - gel
nein! Die Sehn - sucht ist es nach dem Heil.— Würd' es durch sol - chen

might for me ob - tain, That such an an - gel might for me ob - tain.
En - gel mir zu Theil, Würd' es durch sol - chen En - gel mir zu Theil!

Senta. And am I sunk in wondrous depths of dreaming?
Is this a vision which I see,
Or am I now set free from long delusion?
Has morning truly dawned on me?
See, there he stands, his face with sorrow clouding—
He tells me all his mingled hope and fear;
Is it the voice of sympathy that cheats me?
As he has oft in dreams, so stands he here!
The sorrow which within my breast is burning—
Ah, this compassion, what dare I call it?
Thy heart is longing after rest and peace,
And thou at last through me shall find release.

The Dutchman. Wilt thou, thy father's choice fulfilling,
Do what he said? Say, art thou willing?
Wilt thou, indeed, thyself forever give me?
Shall I in truth, a stranger, thus be blessed?
Say, shall I find the time of sorrow ended—
In thy true love my long-expected rest?

Senta. Whoe'er thou art, where'er thy curse may lead thee,
And me, when I thy lot mine own have made—
Whate'er the fate which I with thee may share in,
My father's will by me shall be obey'd.

The Dutchman. So full of trust? what? canst thou in thy gladness,
For these my sorrows deep compassion know?

Senta. Unheard-of sorrows! would I joy might bring thee!

The Dutchman. How sweet the sound that breaks my night of woe!
Thou art an angel, and a love angelic
Can comfort bring to one like me.
Ah, if redemption still be mine to hope for,
Heaven, grant that she my saviour be!

Senta. Ah, if redemption still be his to hope for,
Heaven, grant that I his saviour be!

Senta. Versank ich jetzt in wunderbares Träumen,
Was ich erblicke, ist es Wahn?—
Weilt' ich bisher in trügerischen Räumen,
Brach des Erwachens Tag heut an?—
Er steht vor mir mit leidenvollen Zügen,
Es spricht sein unerhörter Gram zu mir;
Kann tiefen Mitleids Stimme mich belügen?
Wie ich ihn oft geseh'n, so steht er hier.
Die Schmerzen, die in meinem Busen brennen,
Ach! dies Verlangen, wie soll ich es nennen?
Wonach mit Sehnsucht es ihn treibt—das Heil,

Holländer. Wirst Du des Vaters Wahl nicht schelten?
Was er versprach, wie? dürft' es gelten?—
Du könntest Dich für ewig mir ergeben,
Und Deine Hand dem Fremdling reichtest Du?
Soll finden ich nach qualenvollem Leben
In Deiner Treu' die lang ersehnte Ruh?—

Senta. Wer Du auch seist, und welches das Verderben,
Dem grausam Dich Dein Schicksal konnte weih'n;
Was auch das Loos, das ich mir sollt' erwerben:
Gehorsam stets werd' ich dem Vater sein.

Holländer. So unbedingt, wie? könnte Dich durchdringen
Für meine Leiden tiefstes Mitgefühl?

Senta. O, welche Leiden! Könnt' ich Trost Dir bringen!

Holländer. Welch holder Klang im nächtigen Gewühl!—
Du bist ein Engel!—Eines Engels Liebe
Verworf'ne selbst zu trösten weisz!—
Ach, wenn Erlösung mir zu hoffen bliebe.
Allewiger, durch diese sei's!

Senta. Ach! wenn Erlösung ihm zu hoffen bliebe,
Allewiger, durch mich nur sei's!

The Dutchman. Ah, thou, the certain fate
foreknowing,
Which must indeed with me be borne,
Wouldst not have made the vow thou
madest—
Wouldst not to be my wife have sworn!
Thou wouldst have shuddered ere devoting,
To aid me, all thy golden youth—
Ere thou hadst woman's joys surrendered.
Ere thou hadst bid me trust thy truth?

Senta. Well know I woman's holy duties;
O hapless man, be thou at ease!
Leave me to fate's unbending judgment—
Me, who defy its dread decrees.
Within the secret realm of conscience
Know I the high demands of faith:
Him, whom I chose, him I love only,
And loving e'en till death!

The Dutchman. A healing balm for all my
sorrows
From out her plighted word doth flow.

Senta. 'T was surely wrought by pow'r of magic
That I should his deliv'rer be.

The Dutchman. Hear this! Release at last
is granted!
Hear this, ye mighty:
Your power is now laid low!
Star of misfortune, thou art paling!
Hope's glorious light now shines anew!
Ye angels, ye who once forsook me,
Aid now my heart, and keep it true!

Senta. Here may a home at last be granted,
Here may he rest, from danger free!
What is the power within me working?
What is the task it bids me do?
Almighty, now that high Thou hast raised
me,
Grant me Thy strength, that I be true!

Daland.
(Returning.)
Your leave!
My people will no longer wait;
Each voyage ended, they expect a feast:
I would enchance it, so I come to ask
If your espousals forward can be press'd.
I think you must with courting be content.
Senta, my child, say, dost thou give consent?

Holländer. O könntest das Geschick Du ahnen,
Dem dann mit mir Du angehörst:
Dich würd' es an das Opfer mahnen,
Das Du mir bringst, wenn Treu Du
schwörst.
Es flöhe schaudernd Deine Jugend,
Dem Loose, dem Du sie willst weih'n:
Nennst Du des Weibes schönste Tugend,
Nennst heil'ge Treue Du nicht Dein!

Senta. Wohl kenn' ich Weibes hohe Pflich-
ten,—
Sei d'rum getrost, unsel'ger Mann!
Lasz über die das Schicksal richten,
Die seinem Spruche trotzen kann!
In meines Herzens höchster Reine
Kenn' ich der Treue Hochgebot:
Wem ich sie weih', schenk' ich die Eine;
Die Treue bis zum Tod!

Holländer. Ein heil'ger Balsam meinen Wunden,
Dem Schwur, dem hohen Wort entflieszt!

Senta. Von mächt'gem Zauber überwunden,
Reiszt mich's zu seiner Rettung fort:

Holländer. Hört' es: mein Heil hab' ich ge-
funden,
Mächte, die ihr zurück mich stiesz't!
Du Stern des Unheils, sollst erblassen!
Licht meiner Hoffnung leuchte neu.
Ihr Engel, die mich einst verlassen,
Stärkt jetzt dies Herz in seiner Treu'!

Senta. Hier habe Heimath er gefunden,
Hier ruh' sein Schiff im ew'gen Port!
Was ist's, das mächtig in mir lebet?
Was schliuszt berauscht mein Busen ein?
Allmächt'ger, was mich hoch erhebet,
Lasz es die Kraft der Treue sein!
(DALAND tritt wieder auf.)

Daland. Verzeiht, mein Volk hält drausze
sich nicht mehr;
Nach jeder Rückkunft, wisset, giebt's e
Fest:—
Verschönern möcht ich's, komme desha
her,
Ob mit Verlobung sich's vereinen läszt?—
Ich denk', Ihr habt nach Herzenswuns
gefreit?
Senta, mein Kind, sag', bist auch Du be
eit?—

Senta. Here is my hand! I will not rue,
 But e'en to death will I be true!

The Dutchman. She gives her hand! I conquer you,
 Dread powers of hell, while she is true!

Daland. You will this marriage never rue!
 The feast all will rejoice with you!

Senta. Hier meine Hand, und ohne Reu'
 Bis in den Tod gelob' ich Treu'!

Holländer. Sie reicht die Hand: gesprochen
 sei
 Hohn, Hölle Dir, durch ihre Treu'!

Daland. Euch soll dies Bündnisz nicht gereu'n!
 Zum Fest! heut musz sich Alles freu'n!

ACT III.

DRITTER AKT.

(A bay with a rocky shore. On one side, DALAND'S house
the foreground. The background is occupied by the two
ships, DALAND'S and the DUTCHMAN'S, lying near one an-
ther. The night is clear. The Norwegian ship is lighted
up; the sailors are making merry upon the deck. The appearance of the Dutch ship presents a strange contrast;
an unnatural darkness overspreads it; the stillness of death
reigns over it.)

(Seebucht mit felsigem Gestade, das Haus Daland's zu
Seite im Vordergrunde. Den Hintergrund nehmen, ziemlich nah bei einander liegend, die beiden schiffe das des
Norweger's und des Holländer's ein. Helle Nacht: das
norwegische Schiff ist erleuchtet; die Matrosen desselben
sind auf dem Verdeck—Jubel und Freude. Die Haltung
des holländischen Schiffes bietet einen unheimlichen Contrast: eine unnatürliche Finsterniss ist über dasselbe aus-
gebreitet; es herrscht Todtenstille auf ihm.)

Chorus of Norwegian Sailors. Steersman,
 leave the watch!
 Steersman, come to us!
 Ho! hey! Hey! ho!
 See the sails are in! Anchor fast!
 Steersman, come!
 Fearing neither storm nor rocky strand,
 We will all the day right merry be!
 Each one has a sweetheart on the land:
 We will smoke and drink, and quite forget
  the sea!
 Hus-sas-sa hey!
 Rock and storm, ho!
 Hal-lo-ho-hey!
 We let them go!
 Hu-sas-sa hey!
 Steersman, leave the watch!
 Come, drink with us!

Chor der norwegischen Matrosen. Steuer-
 mann, lasz die Wacht!
 Steuermann, her zu uns!
 Ho! He! Je! Ha!
 Hiszt die Segel auf! Anker fest!
 Steuermann, her!—
 Fürchten weder Wind noch bösen Strand,
 Wollen heute 'mal recht lustig sein!
 Jeder hat sein Mädel auf dem Land,
 Herrlichen Taback und guten Branntewein
 Hussassahe!
 Klipp' und Sturm draus—
 Jallolohe!
 Lachen wir aus!
 Hussassahe!
 Segel ein! Anker fest! Klipp' und Sturm
  lachen wir aus!
 Steuermann her, trink' mit aus!

Chorus of Maidens. Oh, do but look! They
 dance indeed!
 And maidens of course they do not need!

Chorus of Sailors. Ho, maidens! Stop!
 Where is 't you go?

The Maidens. What! think you this is all for
 you?
 Your neighbors there must have some also!
 Are food and drink for you alone?

Steersman. Of course they must, the wretched
 fellows!
 With thirst they seem to be struck down.

Mädchen. Nein! Seht doch an! Sie tanzen
 gar!
 Der Mädchen bedarf's da nicht fürwahr!

Matrosen. He! Mädel! Halt! wo geht ihr
 hin?

Mädchen. Steht euch nach frischem Wein der
 Sinn?
 Eu'r Nachbar dort soll auch was haben,
 Ist Trank und Schmaus für euch allein?

Steuermann. Fürwahr, tragt's hin den armen
 Knaben,
 Vor Durst sie scheinen matt zu sein.

The Sailors. How still they are!

Steersman. How strange a place
No light—of the seamen not a trace!

The Maidens. Ho, sailors—ho! a light we
bring!
Where have they gone? How strange a
thing!

The Sailors. Don't wake them up! Asleep
are they.

The Maidens. Ho, sailors—ho! Answer us,
pray!

The Sailors. Ha, ha! 'tis certain they are
dead,
No need have they for wine or bread!

The Maidens. Hey, sailors, and are you already asleep?
What! are you not meaning our feast-day
to keep?

The Sailors. They lie conceal'd within the
hold,
Like dragons, watching o'er their gold.

The Maidens. Hey, sailors, then will you
not have any wine?
Surely our offer you do not decline?

The Sailors. Both wine and songs disown
they quite;
Within their ship there burns no light.

The Maidens. Say, have you not got any
sweethearts on land?
Will you not dance with us here on the
strand?

The Sailors. They are all old, their hair is grey,
And all their sweethearts, dead are they!

Maidens and Sailors. Hey, sailors! waken up!
We bring you food and a cheering cup!
'T is certain, yes; they must be dead!
No need have they of wine or bread.

The Sailors. The Flying Dutchman you
surely know;
That ship does a likeness to his vessel show.

Matrosen. Man hört sie nicht?

Steuermann. Ei, seht doch nur!
Kein Licht! Von der Mannschaft kein
Spur.

Mädchen. He! Seeleut'! He! Wollt Fac-
eln ihr?
Wo seid ihr doch? Man sieht nicht hier.

Matrosen. Weckt sie nicht auf; sie schlafe
noch.

Mädchen. He! Seeleut'! He! Antwort
doch!

Steuermann und Matrosen. Haha! Wahrhaftig, sie sind todt.
Sie haben Speis' und Trank nicht noth.

Mädchen. Wie, Seeleute? Liegt ihr so fa
schon im Nest?
Ist heute für euch denn nicht auch ein Fest

Steuermann und Matrosen. Sie liegen fe
auf ihrem Platz,
Wie Drachen hüten sie den Schatz.

Mädchen. Wie, Seeleute? Wollt ihr nich
goldenen Wein?
Ihr müsset wahrlich doch auch durstig sein

Steuermann und Matrosen. Sie trinken nich
sie singen nicht,
In ihrem Schiffe brennt kein Licht.

Mädchen. Sagt, habt ihr denn nicht auch ei
Schätzchen am Land?
Wollt ihr nicht mit tanzen auf freundlicher
Strand?

Matrosen. Sie sind schon alt und bleich sta
roth,
Und ihre Liebsten, die sind todt.

Mädchen. He, Seeleut'! Seeleut'! wach
doch auf!
Wir bringen euch Speis' und Trank z
Hauf!
Matrosen. Sie bringen euch Speis' und Tran
zu Hauf!
Mädchen. Wahrhaftig! Ja, sie scheinen tod
Sie haben Speis' und Trank nicht noth.

Matrosen. Vom fliegenden Holländer wiss
ihr ja!
Sein Schiff, wie es leibt, wie es lebt, seht il
da.

The Maidens. To wake the crew we pray you spare,
For they are ghosts—we know they are!

The Sailors. For how many years have you been on the sea—
A terror the storm and the rock cannot be!

The Maidens. Both wine and songs disown they quite;
Within their ship there burns no light.

The Sailors. Have you not a letter or message for land,
To be carried safe to some ancestor's hand?

The Maidens. They all are old, their hair is grey,
And all their sweethearts, dead are they!

The Sailors. Hey! Sailors, your canvas spread out to the gale,
And show how the old Flying Dutchman can sail!

The Maidens. They hear us not! We shake with fear!
They want us not: why linger here?

The Sailors. Ye maidens let the dead have rest!
Let us who live your dainties taste!

The Maidens. Well, here—your neighbors quite refuse!

The Sailors. How? Come you not yourselves to us?

The Maidens. No, not just now; but later we may,
After a while. Now drink away,
And, if you will, go dance your best;
But let your weary neighbors rest!

The Sailors. Hurrah! We have abundance!
Good neighbors, thanks to you!

Steersman. Let each man fill and drink a bumper!
Good neighbors, thousand thanks to you!

The Sailors. Hal-lo-ho-ho!
Good neighbors, you can speak at least!
Come, waken up, and join our feast!

Mädchen. So wecket die Mannschaft ja nicht auf!
Gespenster sind's, wir schwören drauf!

Matrosen. Wie viel hundert Jahre schon seid ihr zur See?
Euch thut ja der Sturm und die Klippe nicht weh!

Mädchen. Sie trinken nicht, sie singen nicht!
In ihrem Schiffe brennt kein Licht!

Matrosen. Habt ihr keine Brief', keine Aufträg' für's Land?
Unsern Urgroszvätern wir bringen's zur Hand.

Mädchen. Sie sind schon alt und bleich statt roth;
Ach! ihre Liebsten, die sind todt.

Matrosen. Hei! Seeleute! Spannt eure Segel doch auf!
Und zeigt uns des fliegenden Holländers Lauf!

Mädchen. Sie hören nicht,—uns graust es hier!
Sie wollen nichts,—was rufen wir?

Matrosen. Ihr Mädel, laszt die Todten ruh'n!
Laszt's uns Lebend'gen glücklich thun!

Mädchen. So nehmt, Eu'r Nachbar hat's verschmäht!

Steuermann und Matrosen. Wie? Kommt ihr denn nicht selbst an Bord?

Mädchen. Ei, jetzt noch nicht, es ist nicht spät.
Wir kommen bald, jetzt trinkt nur fort.
Und, wenn ihr wollt, so tanzt dazu,
Nur laszt dem müden Nachbar Ruh'!

Matrosen. Juchhe! Juchhe! da giebt's die Fülle!
Ihr lieben Nachbarn, habet Dank!

Steuermann. Zum Rand sein Glas ein Jeder fülle!
Lieb Nachbar liefert uns den Trank!

Matrosen. Halloho! Halloho! Ho! ho! ho!
Lieb Nachbar'n. habt ihr Stimm' und Sprach',
So wachet auf, und macht's uns nach!

Steersman, leave the watch!
Steersman, come to us!
Ho, hey, hey, ha!
See the sails are in!   Anchor fast!
Steersman, come!
We have often watch'd 'mid howling storm;
We have often drunk the briny wave:
Watching takes to-day a fairer form—
Good and tasty wine our sweethearts let us
　　have!
　　Hus-sas-sa-hey!

The Crew of the Flying Dutchman.　Yo-ho-
　　ho!　Ho!　oh!
　　Huissa!
　To the land drives the storm.
　　Huissa!
　Sails are in!　Anchor down!
　　Huissa!
　To the bay hurry in!
Gloomy captain, go on land,
　Now that seven long years have flown,
Seek a faithful maiden's hand!
　Faithful maiden, be his own!
　　Joyful, hui!
　　　Bridegroom, hui!
　Winds be thy wedding song,
　Ocean rejoices with thee!
　Hui!　Hark!　He pipes!
　What!　captain, hast thou returned?
　Hui!　Spread the sails!
　And thy bride, say, where is she?
　Hui!　Off to sea!
　　As of old.
　No good fortune for thee!
　　Ha-ha-ha!
Blow, thou storm-wind, howl and blow!
What care we how fast we go?
We have sails from Satan's store,
Sails that last for evermore—ho-hoe!

Norwegian Sailors.　What a song!　Are they
　　ghosts?
　How I fear!　Let them hear!
　All unite in our song.
　Steersman, leave the watch! etc.

FINALE.

(SENTA comes from the house hurriedly; she is followed
by ERICK who is greatly excited.)

Erik.　Have I my senses?　Heavens! what do
　　I see?
　A vision?　Tell me—is it true?

Steuermann, lasz die Wacht!
Steuermann, her zu uns!
Ho!　He!　Je!　Ha!
Hiszt die Segel auf!　Anker fest!—
Steuermann, her!—
Wachten manche Nacht bei Sturm und
　　Graus,
Tranken oft des Meer's gesalz'nes Nasz;—
Heute wachen wir bei Saus und Schmaus,
Besseres Getränk giebt Mädel uns vom Fusz
Hussassahe!
Klipp' und Sturm draus!　u.s.w.

Chor der Mannschaft des fliegenden Holländ-
　　ers.　Johohe!　Johohohoe!　hohoh
　　hoe!　Hoe!　Hoe!　Hoe!
　Huissa.
　Nach dem Land treibt der Sturm—
　Huissa!
　Segel ein!　Anker los!
　Huissa!
　In die Bucht laufet ein!
　Schwarzer Hauptmann, geh' an's Land!
　Sieben Jahre sind vorbei;
　Frei' um blonden Mädchens Hand:
　Blondes Mädchen, sei ihm treu!
　　Lustig heut'
　　　Bräutigam!
　Sturmwind heult Brautmusik,
　Ocean tanzt dazu.
　Hui!—Horch, er pfeift!
　—Capitain, bist wieder da?—
　Hui!—"Segel auf."—
　—Deine Braut, sag', wo sie blieb?—
　Hui!　"Auf in See!"—
　Capitain!　Capitain!　Hast kein Glück
　　der Lieb'!
　Hahaha!
Sause, Sturmwind, heule zu!
Uns'ren Segeln läszt du Ruh':
Satan hat sie uns gefei't,
Reiszen nicht in Ewiakeit!

Norwegische Matrosen.　Welcher Sang!　I
　　es Spuk?　Wie mich's graut!
　Stimmet an unser Lied!　Singet laut!
　Steuermann, lasz die Wacht.　u.s.w.

FINALE.

(SENTA kommt bewegten Schrittes aus dem Hause; ih
folgt ERIK in der höchsten Aufregung.)

Erik.　Was muszt' ich hören?　Gott! wa
　　muszt ich sehen!
　Ist's Täuschung?　Wahrheit?　Ist es That

Senta. Oh, ask me not! Answer dare I not give thee.

Erik. O righteous Heaven! No question—it is true!
Oh, say what harmful pow'r led thee astray?
What is the spell constraining thee so soon
Coldly to rend in twain this faithful heart?
Thy father, ha! the bridegroom he did bring;
Him know I well: I fear'd what might befall!
Yet thou—amazing!—gavest him thine hand
When scarce across the threshold he had pass'd.

Senta. No further! Cease! I must!

Erik. Oh, this obedience, blind as in thy act!
Thy father's hint thou failest not to welcome;
A single blow destroys my loving heart!

Senta. No more! I may not see thee more,
Nor thee remember: higher calls are mine!

Erik. What higher calls? Thy highest is to render
What thou didst vow to give to me—love eternal.

Senta. What love eternal did I vow to give?

Erik. Senta! O Senta! Deniest thou—?

Senta. Frag' nicht, Erik! Antwort darf ich nicht geben.

Erik. Gerechter Gott! Kein Zweifel! Es ist wahr!
Welch unheilvolle Macht risz Dich dahin?
Welche Gewalt verführte Dich so schnell,
Grausam zu brechen dieses treuste Herz?
Dein Vater? ha, den Bräut'gam bracht er mit,—
Wohl kannt ich ihn,—mir ahnte, was geschieht.
Doch Du? Ist's möglich!—reichest Deine Hand
Dem Mann, der Deine Schwelle kaum betrat!

Senta. Nicht weiter! Schweig'! Ich musz! Ich musz!

Erik. O des Gehorsams, blind wie Deine That!
Den Wink des Vaters nanntest Du willkommen,
Mit einem Streich vernichtest Du mein Herz!

Senta. Nicht mehr! Nicht mehr! Ich darf Dich micht mehr seh'n!
Nicht an Dich denken. Hohe Pflicht gebeut's!

Erik. Welch hohe Pflicht? Ist's Höh're nicht zu halten,
Was Du mir einst gelobet, ew'ge Treue?

Senta. Wie? Ew'ge Treue hätt' ich Dir gelobt?

Erik. Senta! O Senta! Läugnest Du?

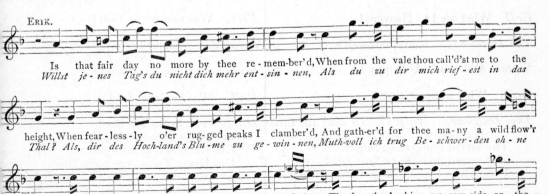

ERIK.

Is that fair day no more by thee re-mem-ber'd, When from the vale thou call'd'st me to the
Willst je-nes Tag's du nicht dich mehr ent-sin-nen, Als du zu dir mich rief-est in das

height, When fear-less-ly o'er rug-ged peaks I clamber'd, And gath-er'd for thee ma-ny a wild flow'r
Thal? Als, dir des Hoch-land's Blu-me zu ge-win-nen, Muth-voll ich trug Be-schwer-den oh-ne

bright? Re-member'st, as on rock-y sum-mit stand-ing, Thy fa-ther's ship we saw ride on the
Zahl? Gedenk'st du wie auf stei-lem Fel-sen-rif-fe Vom U-fer wir den Va-ter schei-den

tide? We watch'd the sails with favor'd breeze ex - pand - ing, Did he not thee un - to my care con
sah'n? Er zog da - hin auf weiss be-schwingtem Schif - fe, Und mei - nem Schutz ver - trau - te er dich

fide, Yea, to my care did he not thee con-fide, To my care . . did he not thee con-
an, Ja, mei - nem Schutz ver - trau - te er dich an, Mei - nem Schutz . ver - traut - te er dich

piu animato.

fide? Thy arm so sweet - ly round my neck en - twin - ing, Didst pledge thy love a - new, how hap - py
an. Als sich dein Arm um mei - nem Nacken schlang, Ges - tan - dest du mir Lie - be nicht auf's
animato.

both! Did'st press my hand, as on my breast re - clin - ing, Say, was not that the seal-ing of thy
Neu'? Was bei der Hän - de Druck mich hehr durch-drang, Sag', war's nicht die Ver - sich'rung dei - ner

troth? Say, was not that, in - deed, the seal - ing of thy troth? Did'st press my
Treu'? Sag', war es nicht, war's nicht Ver - sich-'rung dei - ner Treu'? Was bei der

hand as on my breast . . . . re - clin - ing, Say, was not that— that the
Hän - de Druck so hehr . . mich durch - drang, Sag', war es nicht die Ver -
ad lib.

seal - ing, that the seal - ing of . . . . . thy troth?
sich - 'rung, die Ver - sich - - 'rung dei . . . . ner Treu'?

The Dutchman. Abandon'd! Ah! Aban-don'd! All is forever lost!	*Holländer.* Verloren! Ach! verloren! Ewi verlor'nes Heil!
Erik What see I? Heavens!	*Erik.* Was seh' ich? Gott!
The Dutchman. Senta, farewell!	*Holländer.* Senta, leb' wohl!
Senta. Oh, stay! Unhappy!	*Senta.* Halt ein, Unsel'ger.
Erik. What meanest thou?	*Erik.* Was beginnst Du?
The Dutchman. To sea! To sea! till time is ended! Thy sacred promise be forgot. Thy sacred promise and my fate! Farewell! I wish not to destroy thee!	*Holländer.* In See. in See! In See für ewige Zeiten! Um Deine Treue ist's gethan, Um Deine Treue, um mein Heil. Lebwohl, ich will dich nicht verderben!
Erik Oh. horror! what a face!	*Erik.* Entsetzlich, dieser Blick!

Senta. Oh, stay!
From hence thou never more shalt flee!

The Dutchman. Set the sails! Anchor up!
Then bid farewell to land for ever!

Senta. Ha, canst thou doubt if I am faithful?
Unhappy, what has blinded thee?
Oh, stay, the vow we made forsake not!
What I have promised kept shall be.

Erik. What hear I? Heavens! and what be-
hold I?
Can I in ear, in eye believe?
Senta! Art thou then bent on ruin?
To me a spell doth Satan weave.

The Dutchman. Now hear, and learn the fate
from   which thou wilt be saved:
Condemn'd am I to bear a frightful for-
tune—
Ten times would death appear a brighter
lot.
A woman's hand alone the curse can lighten,
If she will love me, and till death be true.
Still to be faithful thou has vow'd,
Yet has not God thy promise:
This rescues thee; for know, unhappy,
what a fate is theirs
Who break the troth which they to me have
plighted:
Endless damnation is their doom!
Victims untold have fallen 'neath this curse
through me—
Yet, Senta, thou shalt escape.
Farewell! All hope is fled for evermore!

Erik. Oh, help her! let her not be lost!

Senta. Well do I know thee—well do I know
thy doom.
I knew thy face when I beheld thee first!
The end of thine affliction comes:
My love till death shall take thy curse away!

Erik, Daland, Mary, and Chorus. What
behold I?

The Dutchman. Thou knowest me not, nor
thinkest who I am;

Senta. Halt ein! Von dannen sollst Du nim
mer fliehn.

(Der Holländer gibt ein gellendes Zeichen auf seine
Pfeife und ruft der Mannschaft seines Schiffes zu.)

Holländer. Segel auf! Anker los! Sagt Lebwohl auf Ewigkeit dem Lande!

Senta. Ha zweifelst Du an meiner Treue?
Unseliger,—was verblendet Dich!
Halt ein! Halt ein!   Halt ein!
Das Bündnisz nicht bereue,
Was ich gelobte, halte ich.
Halt ein!   Halt ein!

Erik. Was hör' ich, Gott, was musz ich sehn!
Musz ich dem Ohr, musz ich dem Auge
traun!
Was hör' ich, Gott, Senta!
Willst Du zu Grunde geben?
Zu mir, zu mir: Du bist in Satans Klau'n!

Holländer. Erfahre das Geschick, vor dem ich
Dich bewahr!
Verdammt bin ich zum gräszlichsten der
Loose!
Zehnfacher Tod, wär mir erwünschte Lust.
Vom Fluch! ein Weib allein kann mich
erlösen,
Ein Weib, das Treue bis in den Tod mir
hält.
Wohl hast Du Treue mir gelobt,
Doch vor dem Ewigen noch nicht, diesz
rettet Dich!
Denn wisz'! Unselige, welches das Geschick,
Das Jene trifft, die mir die Treue brechen,
Ewige Verdammnisz ist ihr Loos!
Zahllose Opfer fielen diesem Spruch durch
mich.
Du aber sollst gerettet sein.
Lebwohl, fahr hin, mein Heil in Ewigkeit.

Erik. Zu Hülfe, rettet, rettet Sie!

Senta. Wohl kenn ich Dich! Wohl kenn ich
Dein Geschick;
Ich kannte Dich, als ich zuerst Dich sah!
Das Ende Deiner Qual ist da!
Ich bin's, durch deren Treu Dein Heil Du
finden sollst!

{ *Erik.* Helft Ihr, Sie ist verloren!
  Mary. Was erblicke ich?
  Daland. Was erblicke ich? Gott!

Holländer. Du kennst mich nicht, Du ahnst
nicht wer ich bin!

But ask the sea in ev'ry climate,
Or ask the seamen who the ocean wide have
cross'd:
They know my ship, of all good men the
terror—
The Flying Dutchman am I call'd.

Daland, Erik, Mary, and Chorus. Senta!
Senta! what wouldst thou do?

Senta. Praise thou thine angel for what he
saith:
Here stand I, faithful, yea, till death!

(She casts herself into the sea. The Dutchman's ship,
with all her crew, sinks immediately. The sea rises high,
and sinks back in a whirlpool. In the glow of the sunset
are clearly seen, over the wreck of the ship, the forms of
SENTA and the DUTCHMAN, embracing each other, rising
from the sea, and floating upwards.)

Befrage die Meere aller Zonen.
Befrage den Seemann, der den Oce
durchstrich;
Erkenn' diesz Schiff, der Schrecken all
Frommen,
Den: "Fliegenden Holländer" nennt m
mich.

*Die Mannschaft des Fliegenden Hollände
Jo ho, hoe!*

Mary, Erik, und Daland. Senta, Senta, w
willst Du thun?

Senta. Preis Deinen Engel und sein Gebot,
Hier steh' ich treu Dir bis zum Tod.

(Sie stürzt sich in das Meer;—vogleich versinkt d
Schiff des HOLLANDER's mit aller Mannschaft. Das Me
schwillt hoch auf und sinkt in einem Würbel wieder zurü
Im Glühroth der aufgehenden Sonne sieht man über d
Trümmern des Schiffec die verklärten Gestahen SENT
und des HOLLANDER's sich umhslungen haltend dem Mee
entsteigen und aufwärt's schweben.)

TANNHÄUSER

TANNHÄUSER, knight and minstrel, has in an evil hour sought refuge from the griefs of earth in the hill of Venus* (the Horselberg, in Thuringia), where, surrounded by her heathen train, the goddess is supposed to hold her court amid everlasting revels, destroying the souls of men who fall into her toils.

The opera opens when Tannhäuser, having dwelt with her a whole year, has become weary of monotonous joys, and in momentary returns of his better nature, longs for earthly life, with its mingled pains and pleasures. He implores the goddess to release him, and after a protracted struggle, regains his liberty. The scene now suddenly changes; he finds himself in a valley between the Wartburg and the Horselberg, and whilst he is still sunk in a prayer of gratitude at being restored to liberty, the Minstrel Knights, led by the Landgrave, enter, recognize him, and persuade him to rejoin them.

ACT II. — *The Tournament of Song.* — The theme of the contest is to be the Nature and Praise of Love, and the prize of the victor the hand of Elisabeth, whom Tannhäuser loves, and by whom he is beloved. During the contest Tannhäuser disputes all that the other minstrels say, and, having loved profanely, outrages the assembly by his revelations of what he conceives to be the Nature of Love. The minstrels challenge him, and would destroy him, but for the sudden interposition of Elisabeth. A train of Pilgrims is taking its way to Rome. Tannhäuser, who sees too late that an illusion had blinded him, despairingly joins them, whilst Elisabeth, on whom the discovery of his unworthiness has struck a mortal blow, conjures him to repent.

ACT III. — Wolfram, a man of noble and devoted nature, who vainly loves Elisabeth, awaits with her the return of the Pilgrims. They come, but Tannhäuser is not amongst them. Elisabeth now solemnly consecrates herself to the Virgin. When she has departed, Tannhäuser enters furtively, in pitiable plight, on his way to reenter the Hill of Venus. He tells Wolfram of his pilgrimage, of his self-tormenting remorse, of his humble appeal to the Pope, who, learning the nature of his sin, declared it as impossible for him to be absolved as for the staff he held in his hand again to put forth fresh leaves. Spurned and accused by all, nothing is left for him but to return to the joys he loathes. Wolfram's appeals are vain to dissuade him; he invokes the infernal train, which is becoming dimly visible, when a chant is heard, followed by the funeral procession of Elisabeth. A second band of Pilgrims appears on the heights announcing that a miracle has been wrought. During the night the staff of the Pope has put forth fresh green leaves, and he sends into all lands to declare the Almighty's pardon to the repentant sinner.

(With true medieval sternness, Tannhäuser is not redeemed in the old legend, but doomed to return to the domain of Venus, where, conscience-stricken, he finds everlasting wretchedness.)

*Early Christianity banished the Scandinavian as well as the classical divinities into mid-earth. Thus "Dame Holda," the young Shepherd in the third scene — the wise. gentle Holda, who brought the Spring, and was welcomed with triumphant processions throughout the German North.

TANNHÄUSER

<table>
<tr><td>

ACT I

—

SCENE I

</td><td>

AKT I

—

ERSTE SCENE

</td></tr>
</table>

<table>
<tr><td>

The Hill of Venus. The stage represents the interior of the Hill of Venus. A wide cave, bending at the back towards the right side, where it appears to be indefinitely prolonged. In the farthest visible background a bluish lake is seen in which Naiads are bathing; on its undulating banks Sirens are reclining. In the extreme foreground Venus is extended on a couch; before her, in a kneeling attitude, is Tannhäuser, his head sunk on her knees. The whole cave is illuminated by a rosy light. In the centre of the stage is a group of dancing Nymphs. There are mounds at the sides of the cave where tender couples are reclining, some of whom join the dances of the Nymphs in the course of the scene. A train of Bacchantes rushes from the back of the cave in a tumultuous dance; they wildly dart through the groups of Nymphs and under couples, inciting them to a frantic excitement.

</td><td>

Die Bühne stellt das Innere des Venusberges dar. Weit. Grotte, welche sich im Hintergrunde durch eine Bie. gung nach rechts wie unabsehbar dahinzieht. Im fern. sten sichtbaren Hintergrunde dehnt sich ein bläuliche. See aus; in ihm erblickt man die badenden Gestalte. von Najaden; auf seinen erhöhten Ufervorsprünge. sind Sirenen gelagert. Im äussersten Vordergrund. links liegt Venus auf einem Lager ausgestreckt, vo. ihr halb knieend Tannhäuser, das Haupt in ihre. Schoosse. Die ganze Grotte ist durch rosiges Lich. erleuchtet. Den Mittelgrund nimmt eine Gruppe tan. zender Nymphen ein; auf etwas erhöhten Vorsprünge. an den Seiten der Grotte sind liebende Paare gelager. von denen sich einzelne nach und nach in den Tan. der Nymphen mischen. Ein Zug von Bacchantinne. kommt aus dem Hintergrunde in wildem Tanz daher. gebraust, sie durchziehen mit trunkenen Gebärden di. Gruppen der Nymphen und liebenden Paare, welch. durch sie bald zu grösserem Ungestüme hingerisse. werden.

</td></tr>
<tr><td>

Chorus

    Come to these bowers,
    Radiant with flowers:
    Here love shall bless you—
        Here endeth longing;
    Soft arms shall press you,
    'Mid blisses thronging.

</td><td>

Gesang der Sirenen.

    Naht euch dem Strande,
    Naht euch dem Lande
    Wo in den Armen
    Glühender Liebe
    Selig Erwarmen
    Still' eure Triebe!

</td></tr>
<tr><td>

[The dancers suddenly pause from their wild tumult and listen to the singing, after which the dance recommences and rises to the wildest excitement. When the Bacchic frenzy is at its height, a sudden weariness is seen to spread amongst the dancers. The tender couples separate themselves from the dance and rest near the entrance of the cave. The train of Bacchantes disappears in the background, where a mist gathers and spreads in density. In the foreground also a thick mist gradually sinks, and envelops the groups of sleepers in rosy clouds, so that only a small space in the front of the stage remains visible, where Venus and Tannhäuser remain alone in their former attitude.

</td><td>

[Die Tanzenden halten in der leidenschaftlichste. Gruppe plötzlich an und lauschen dem Ge. sange, worauf sich der Tanz von Neuem beleb. und zu dem äussersten Grade wilden Unges. tümes gelangt. Mit dem Momente der trunken. sten bacchantischen Wuth tritt eine schne. um sich greifende Erschlaffung ein. Die lie. benden Paare scheiden sich allmählig vor. Tanze aus und lagern sich wie in angenehme. Ermattung auf den Vorsprüngen der Grotte. der Zug der Bacchantinnen verschwindet nac. dem Hintergrunde zu, vor welchem sich ei. immer dichter werdender Dunst ausbreite. Auch im Vordergrunde senkt sich allmähli. ein dichterer Duft herab und verhüllt di. Gruppen der Schlafenden wie in rosige Wol. ken, so dass endlich der sichtbare Theil de. frei gelass'nen Bühne sich nur noch auf eine. kleinen Raum beschränkt, in welchem Venu. und Tannhäuser in ihrer früheren Stellun. allein zurückbleiben.

</td></tr>
</table>

<table>
<tr><td>

SCENE II

</td><td>

ZWEITE SCENE

</td></tr>
<tr><td>

Venus. Oh, say my love, where stray thy thoughts?
Tann. No more, no more! O that I now might waken.
Venus. Say, what grief is thine?
Tann. I dreamt I heard upon the air
    Sounds that to me were long estrang'd
    The silv'ry chime of bells was borne on the breeze,
    Oh, say, how long has earth been lost to me?

</td><td>

Venus. Geliebter, sag', wo weilt dein Sinn?
Tann. Zu viel! Zu viel! O, dass ich nun Erwachte.
Venus. Sprich, was kümmert dich?
Tann. Im Traum war mir's, als hörte ich—
    Was meinem Ohr so lange fremd!—
    Als hörte ich der Glocken froh Geläute:—
    O, sag'! Wie lange hört ich's doch nicht mehr'

</td></tr>
</table>

Venus. What folly seizes thee? Why thus disturbed?
Tann. The time I dwelt here with thee
By days I cannot measure —
Seasons pass me, how I scarcely know:
The radiant sun I see no longer;
Strange hath become the heavens' starry splendor
The sweet verdure of spring,
The gentle token of earth's renewing life
The nightingale no more I hear
Who sings of hope and promise.
All these delights, are they for ever lost?

Venus. What! art thou wav'ring? Why these vain
lamentings?
Can'st thou so soon weary of the blisses
That love immortal hath cast round thee?
Can it be—dost thou now repent that thou'rt
divine?
Hast thou so soon forgotten how thy heart was
mourning,
Till by me thou wert consoled?
My minstrel, come, let not thy harp be silent;
Recall the rapture—sing the praise and bliss of
love
In tones that won for thee love's self to be thy
slave!
Of love sing only, for her treasures all are thine.

Venus. Wohin vierlierst du dich? Was ficht dich an?
Tann. Die Zeit, die hier ich weil', ich kann sie nicht
Ermessen:—Tage, Monde—giebt's für mich
Nicht mehr, denn nicht mehr sehe ich die Sonne,
Nicht mehr des Himmels freundliche Gestirne;
Den Halm seh' ich nicht mehr, der frisch
ergrünend
Den neuen Sommer bringt;—die Nachtigall
Nicht hör' ich mehr, die mir den Lenz
verkünde:—
Hör ich sie nie, seh' ich sie niemals mehr?

Venus. Ha! was vernehm' ich? welche thör'ge Klagen!
Bist du so bald der holden Wunder müde,
Die meine Liebe dir bereitet? Oder
Wie? Reut es dich so sehr, ein Gott zu sein?
Hast du so bald vergessen, wie du einst
Gelitten, während jetzt du dich erfreust?
Mein Sänger, auf! Ergreife deine Harfe!
Die Liebe fei're, die so herrlich du besingst,
Dass du der Liebe Göttin selber dir gewannst!
Die Liebe feire, da ihr höchster Preis dir ward!

No. 1.   ALL PRAISE BE THINE!

know. But while my sense thou hast en - chant - ed, by thy great love
hin. Doch ster - blich, ach! bin ich ge - blie - ben, und ü - ber - gross

my heart is daunt - ed; a god a - lone......... can dwell in
ist mir dein Lie - ben; wenn stets ein Gott........ ge - nie - ssen

joy to mor - tal frail,.......... its bliss - es cloy; I
kann, bin ich dem Wech - - sel un - ter - than; nicht

would be sway'd by...... pain and pleas - ure, in Na - ture's
Lust al - lein liegt.... mir am Her - zen, aus Freu - den

sweet al - ter - nate meas - ure, I must a - way from thee, or
sehn' ich mich nach Schmer - zen! Aus dei - nem Rei - che muss ich

die,.... Oh, Queen be - lov'd! God - dess, let.... me fly!
flieh'n. O Kö - ni - gin! Göt - tin, lass.... mich ziehn!

Venus. Ungrateful! What, shall thus my love be slighted By thee, in whom so dear my heart delighted? What praise is thine of joys thou yet would'st flee? My vaunted charms, alas! have wearied thee.	*Venus.* Treuloser! Weh! Was lässest du mich hören? Du wagest meine Liebe zu verhöhnen? Du preisest sie und willst sie dennoch fliehn, Zum Ueberdruss ist dir mein Reiz gediehn?
Tann. Oh, fair perfection! frown not on thy servant! Thy charms' excess, oh, goddess, have unmanned me!	*Tann.* O, schöne Göttin! Wolle mir nicht zürnen! Dein übergrosser Reiz ist's, den ich meide.
Venus. Traitor, beware, then? Serpent heart ungrateful! Ah! not thus we part. Ah, no, thou shalt not leave me.	*Venus.* Weh' dir! Verräther! Heuchler! Undankbarer! Ich lass' dich nicht! Du darfst von mir nicht ziehn!
Tann. But, reft of thy sweet presence, joy is hateful; But fate sternly impels me—for liberty I sigh.	*Tann.* Nie war mein Lieben grösser, niemals wahrer Als jetzt, da ich für ewig dich muss fliehn!
Venus. Beloved one, come! Soft dreams of wonder, Within yon grot shall wrap thee round; The purple shadows breaking yonder, With murmuring music shall resound. There joys unknown I'll shower upon thee: Within these arms thou shalt have rest, Until for mine again I've won thee— Till faith renewed thy lips have confess'd. The od'rous airs shall tell in dulcet voices That bliss divine once more our hearts rejoices. Love hath a solace for thy restless heart; 'Twere worse than dying, from sweet love to part. This day renew those tender vows we plighted— In joy immortal be our hearts united. Thou shalt no more adore the power of love, No! love itself to worship thou, belov'd, shalt move.	*Venus.* Geliebter, komm! Sieh dort die Grotte, Von ros'gen Düften mild durchwallt; Entzücken böt' selbst einem Gotte Der süss'sten Freuden Aufenthalt: Besänftigt auf dem weichsten Pfühle, Flieh' deine Glieder jeder Schmerz, Dein brennend Haupt umwehe Kühle, Wonnige Glut durchschwell' dein Herz. Aus holder Ferne mahnen süsse Klänge, Dass dich mein Arm in trauter Näh' umschlänge; Von meinen Lippen schlürfst du Göttertrank, Aus meinen Augen strahlt dir Liebesdank:— Ein Freudenfest soll unsrem Bund entstehen, Der Liebe Feier lass uns froh begehen! Nicht sollst du ihr ein scheues Opfer weihn,— Nein!—mit der Liebe Göttin schwelge im Verein!

Sireno.	Come to these bowers,
	Radiant with flowers, &c.
Venus.	My hero and my heart's love! Wilt thou fly?
Tann.	While I have life, alone my harp shall praise thee;
	No meaner thing shall e'er my song inspire.
	Nought can have grace or charm but it obeys thee,
	Of all that lives thou best and chief desire.
	The fire thou'st kindled in my longing spirits,
	An altar flame shall burn for thee alone;
	My song shall be divine, but by the merit
	That, as thy champion, harp and sword I own.
	And yet for earth I'm yearning.
	In thy soft chains with shame I'm burning,
	'Tis freedom I must win or die—
	For freedom I can all defy;
	To strife or glory forth I go,
	Come life or death, come joy or woe,
	No more in bondage will I sigh!
	Oh, queen, beloved goddess, let me fly!
Venus.	Then go, oh traitor heart! away,
	Thou madman! Go—I hold thee not!
	I set thee free! Away!
	Go forth—thy heart's desire shall be thy doom!
	Go to the cold and joyless earth,
	Where neither love nor life can bloom,
	Whence every smiling god hath flown,
	Where dark suspicion first had its birth:
	Go forth, thou madman!
	There seek thy joy, and seek in vain.
	Soon will this fever quit thy soul;
	Humbled and sorr'wing thou'lt return—
	Remore shall gnaw thee, naught will console:
	For joys remember'd thou shalt burn!
Tann.	Ah, fair enchantress, fare thee well!
	Never to thee I can return.
Venus.	Ah! If thou never shouldst return—
	If thou forget me—
	Oh, to lasting torments I doom
	Th' accurs'd and faithless race of man:
	For my delights they all shall vainly languish—
	The world a desert, and its lord a slave.
	Go forth, then—go, thy doom to brave!
Tann.	Love never more will bless thy slave.
Venus.	Go forth, then, till thy heart awake.
Tann.	Ah, love, I go, altho' it break.
Venus.	Thou'lt be received with hate and scorn.
Tann.	Repentance heals a heart forlorn.
Venus.	Never to thee will heaven ope;
	Return, then, if there is no hope.
Tann.	No hope! my hope resteth in heaven.

SCENE III

Tannhäuser — A Young Shepherd — Pilgrims, — Tannhäuser, who has not quitted his position, suddenly finds himself in a beautiful vale. Blue sky and sunshine; at the back the Wartburg. Through an opening in the valley the Horselberg is seen. Halfway up the ascent a path leads into the valley from the direction of the Wartburg, where it turns aside; in the foreground is a shrine of the Virgin on a small eminence, to which there is a practicable ascent. From the heights the sound of sheep-bells is heard. On a rocky eminence a young shepherd is reclining, turned towards the valley, playing on his pipe.

A Young Shepherd.
Dame Holda stepped from the mountain's heart,
To roam thro' wood and thro' meadow;
Sweet sounds and low around me did start—
I longed I might follow her shadow.
And there dreamt I a golden dream,
And when again the day did gleam.

Sirenen.	Naht euch dem Strande,
	Naht euch dem Lande, u. s. w.
Venus.	Mein Ritter! Mein Geliebter! Willst du flieh'n
Tann.	Stets soll nur dir, mein Lied ertönen!
	Gesungen laut sei nur dein Preis von mir!
	Dein süsser Reiz ist Quelle alles Schönen,
	Und jedes holde Wunder stammt von dir.
	Die Glut, die du mir in das Herz gegossen,
	Als Flamme lodre hell sie dir allein!
	Ja, gegen alle Welt will unverdrossen
	Fortan ich nun dein kühner Streiter sein.—
	Doch hin muss ich zur Welt der Erden,
	Bei dir kann ich nur Sklave werden;
	Nach Freiheit doch verlange ich,
	Nach Freiheit, Freiheit dürstet's mich;
	Zu Kampf und Streite will ich stehen,
	Sei's auch auf Tod und Untergehen:—
	Drum muss aus deinem Reich ich fliehn,
	O, Königin, Göttin? lass mich ziehn!—
Venus.	Zieh hin, Wahnsinniger, zieh hin!
	Verräther, sieh! nicht halt' ich dich.
	Ich geb' dich frei,—zieh hin! zieh hin
	Was du verlangst, das sei dein Loos,
	Hin zu den kalten Menschen flieh',
	Vor deren blödem, trübem Wahn
	Der Freude Götter wir entfloh'n
	Tief in der Erde wärmenden Schoos,
	Zieh hin, Bethörter! Suche dein Heil,
	Suche dein Heil—und find' es nie!
	Bald weicht der Stolz aus deiner Seel',—
	Demüthig seh' ich dich mir nahn,—
	Zerknirscht, zertreten suchst du mich auf
	Flehst, um die Wunder meiner Macht.
Tann.	Ach schöne Göttin, lebe wohl!
	Nie kehre ich zu dir zurück.
Venus.	Ha, kehrest du mir nie znrück! . . .
	Kehrst du nicht wieder, ha! so sei verfluchet!
	Von mir das ganze menschliche Geschlecht!
	Nach meinen Wundern dann vergebens suchet:
	Die Welt sei öde, und ihr Held ein Knecht!—
	Kehr' wieder! Kehre mir zurück!
Tann.	Nie mehr erfreu' mich Liebesglück!
Venus.	Kehr' wieder, wenn dein Herz dich zieht!—
Tann.	Für ewig dein Geliebter flieht.
Venus.	Wenn alle Welt dich von sich stösst!—
Tann.	Von Bann werd' ich durch Buss' erlöst.
Venus.	Nie wird Vergebung dir zu Theil,—
	Kehr' wieder, schliesst sich dir das Heil.
Tann.	Mein Heil! Mein Heil ruht in Maria!

DRITTE SCENE

Tannhäuser—Ein junger Hirt—Pilger.—Tannhäuser, der seine, Stellung nicht verlassen, befindet sich plötzlich in ein schönes Thal versetzt. Blauer Himmel, heitere Sonnenbeleuchtung. Rechts im Hintergrunde die Wartburg; durch die Thal öffnung nach links erblickt man den Hörselberg. Rechts führt auf der halben Höhe des Thales ein Bergweg von der Richtung der Wartburg her nach dem Vordergrunde zu, wo er dann seitwärts abbiegt; in demselben Vordergrunde ist ein Muttergottes-Bild, zu welchem ein niedriger Bergvorsprung hinauffürt. Von der Hohe links vernim man das Geläute von Herde-Glocken; auf einem hohen Vorsprunge sitzt ein junger Hirt mit der Schalmei.

Hirt.
Frau Holda kam aus dem Berg hervor,
Zu ziehen durch Flur und Auen;
Gar süssen Klang vernahm da mein Ohr,
Mein Auge begehrte zu schauen —
Da träumt' ich manchen holden Traum.
Und als mein Aug' erschlossen kaum.

The spell was gone that bound me:
'Twas May, sweet May, around me.
New songs of joy attune my lay,
For May hath come — the balmy May!

Chorus of Elder Pilgrims.

To Thee, O Lord, my steps I bend,
In Thee both joy and sorrow end!
Oh, Mary, pure and gracious one,
Bless thou the road we have begun!
Oh, see my heart, by guilt oppress'd —
I faint, I sink beneath my burden!
Nor will I cease, nor will I rest,
Till heav'nly mercy grants me pardon.
At thy august and holy shrine,
I go to seek the grace divine;
Thrice blessed who thy promise know,
Absolved by penance shall they go.

Shep.　God speed, God speed to Rome!
There for my soul, oh, breathe a prayer!
Tann.　Almighty, praise to Thee!
Great are the marvels of Thy mercy
Pil.　To Thee, O Lord, my steps I bend
In Thee both joy and sorrow end;
Oh, Mary, pure and gracious one,
Bless thou the road we have begun
Tann.　Oh, see my heart, by guilt oppress'd —
I faint, I sink beneath the burden!
Nor will I cease, nor will I rest,
Till heav'nly mercy grants me pardon.

SCENE IV

On the eminence the Landgrave and Minstrels, in hunting array, are seen to descend from a forest path.

Land.　Who is yon knight, so deep absorbed in prayer?
Walt.　A pilgrim, sure.
Bit.　By ev'ry sign, a noble.
Wolf.　Our lost one!
All.　Henry! Henry! is it thou?

Land.　Is't no delusion?
Dost thou, then, return to us,
Whom thou so rashly didst abandon?
Bit.　Say, what doth thy return this day forbode us?
Is't friendship? or a challenge, as of old?
Walt.　Com'st thou as friend, or scornful foe?
All except Wolfram.
As foe?
Wolf.　Oh, ask him not! His looks bespeak not scorning!
We welcome thee, thou gallant minstrel;
Alas! too long thou wert from us estrang'd.
Walt.　Yes, welcome, if thou com'st in peace!
Bit.　All hail! if we as friends can greet.
All.　All hail, all hail—we welcome thee!

Land.　I, too would welcome thy return;
But say, where tarry'st thou so long?
Tann.　In strange and distant realms I wandered far,
Where neither peace nor rest were ever found.
Ask not! at enmity I am with none;
We meet as friends—let me in peace depart.

Land.　Depart thou shalt not—for our own we claim thee.
Walt.　Thou must not go,
Bit.　From us thou shalt not part.
Tann.　I must! Onwards I'm driven ever,
Ne'er upon earth can I have rest.
The past to me is closed for ever,
I'm doomed to roam alone, unblest.

Da strahlte warm die Sonnen,
Der Mai, der Mai, war kommen.
Nun spiel' ich lustig die Schalmei:—
Der Mai ist da, der liebe Mai!

Gasang der älteren Pilger.

Zu dir wall' ich, mein Herr und Gott,
Der du des Sünders Hoffnung bist!
Gelobt sei, Jungfrau süss und rein,
Der Wallfahrt wolle günstig sein!—
Ach, schwer drückt mich der Sünden Last
Kann länger sie nicht mehr ertragen;
Drum will ich auch nicht Ruh' noch Rast,
Und wähle gern mir Müh' und Plagen.
Am hohen Fest der Gnadenhuld
In Demuth sühn' ich meine Schuld;
Gesegnet, wer im Glauben treu,
Er wird erlöst durch Buss' und Reu'.

Hirt.　Glück auf! Glück auf nach Rom!
Betet für meine arme Seele!
Tann.　Allmächt'ger, dir sei Preis!
Hehr sind die Wunder deiner Gnade.
Pilg.　Zu dir wall' ich, mein Herr und Gott,
Der du des Pilgers Hoffnung bist!
Gelobet sei, Jungfrau süss und rein,
Der Wallfahrt wolle günstig sein!
Tann.　Ach, schwer drückt mich der Sünden Last,
Kann länger sie nicht mehr ertragen;
Drum will ich auch nicht Ruh' noch Rast
Und wähle gern mir Müh' und Plagen.

VIERTE SCENE

Von der Anhöhe links herab, aus einem Waldwege treten der Landgraf und die Sänger in Jägertraeht einzelnd auf.

Land.　Wer ist der dort in brünstigen Gebete?
Walt.　Ein Büsser wohl.
Bit.　Nach seiner Tracht ein Ritter,
Wolf.　Er ist es!
Die Sanger und der Landgraf.
Heinrich! Heinrich! Seh' ich recht?
Land.　Du bist es wirklich? Kehrest in dem Kreis
Zurück, den du in Hochmuth stolz verliessest?

Bit.　Sag', was uns deine Wiederkunft bedewtet?
Versöhnung? Oder gilt's erneu'tem Kampf?
Walt.　Nah'st du als Freund uns oder Feind?
Die andern Sänger ausser Wolfram.
Als Feind?
Wolf.　O fraget nicht! Ist dies des Hochmuths Miene?
Gegrüsst sei uns, du kühner Sänger,
Der ach! so lang' in uns'rer Mitte fehlt!
Walt.　Willkommen, wenn du friedlich nah'st!
Bit.　Gegrüsst, wenn du uns Freund nennst!
Alle Sänger.
Gegrüsst! Gegrüsst! Gegrüsst sei uns!
Land.　So sei willkommen denn auch mir!
Sag' an, wo weiltest du so lang?
Tann.　Ich wanderte in weiter, weiter Fern',—
Da wo ich nimmer Rast noch Ruhe fand.
Fragt nicht! Zum Kampf mit euch nicht kam ich her.
Seid mir versöhnt und lasst mich weiter zieh'n!

Land.　Nicht doch! Der Uns're bist du neu geworden.
Walt.　Du darfst nicht zieh'n.
Bit.　Wir lassen dich nicht fort.
Tann.　Lasst mich! Mir frommet kein Verweilen,
Und nimmer kann ich rastend steh'n;
Mein Weg heisst mich nur vorwärts eilen,
Dennrückwärts darf ich niemals seh'n.

All.
Oh, stay, be ours; let us not sever
'Mid friends and home thou shalt find rest.
What dost thou seek with vain endeavor?
Why is thy soul with grief oppress'd?

Wolf. Here dwells Elisabeth.
Tann. Elisabeth! oh, ruth of Heaven!
That name ador'd once more I hear!
Wolf. He is no foe who doth that name to thee recall.
My sovereign lord, permit that I may tell him
of the prize he won.
Land. Tell him the marvel that his song hath wrought;
And keep him, Heav'n, in virtue, that nobly he
may own it.

Der Landgraf und die Sänger.
O bleib', bei uns sollst du verweilen,
Wir lassen dich nicht von uns gehn
Du suchtest uns, warum enteilen
Nach solchem kurzen Wiedersehn?

Wolf. Bleib' bei Elisabeth!
Tann. Elisabeth!—O Macht des Himmels,
Rufst du den süssen Namen mir?
Wolf. Nicht sollst du Feind mich schelten, dass ich ihn
Genannt!—Erlaubest du mir, Herr, dass ich
Verkünder seines Glücks ihm sei?
Land. Nenn ihm den Zauber, den er ausgeübt,
Und Gott verleih' ihm Tugend,
Das würdig er ihn löse!—

No. 2.   WHEN FOR THE PALM.

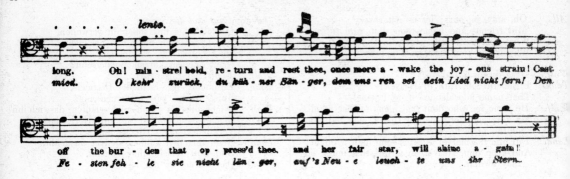

long. Oh! min-strel bold, re-turn and rest thee, once more a-wake the joy-ous strain! Cast
mied. O kehr' zurück, du küh-ner Sän-ger, dem uns-ren sei dein Lied nicht fern! Den.

off the bur-den that op-press'd thee, and her fair star, will shine a-gain!
Fe-sten feh-le sie nicht län-ger, auf's Neu-e leuch-te uns ihr Stern.

All. Return, oh, Henry, thou our brother! Anger and strife shall be no more; In joy and peace with one another Our strains united let us pour.	*Die Sänger.* Sei unser, Heinrich! Kehr' uns wieder! Zwietracht und Streit sei abgethan! Vereint ertönen unsre Lieder, Und Brüder nenne uns fortan!
Tann. What joy! what joy! oh, guide my steps to her! Ah, dost thou smile once more upon me, Thou radiant world that I had lost? Oh, sun of heav'n thou dost not shun me, By stormy clouds no longer crossed? 'T is May, sweet May, its thousand carols' Tender rejoicing set my sorrow free! A ray of new unwonted splendor My soul illumes. Oh, joy, 't is she!	*Tann.* Zu ihr! Zu ihr! O führet mich zu ihr! Ha, jetzt erkenne ich sie wieder, Die schöne Welt, der ich entrückt! Der Himmel blickt auf mich hernieder, Die Fluren prangen reich geschmückt. Der Lenz mit tausend holden Klängen Zog jubelnd in die Seele mir; In süssem, ungestümen Drängen Ruft laut mein Herz: Zu ihr! Zu ihr!
All. He doth return, no more to wander; Our lov'd and lost is ours again. All praise and thanks to those we render Who could persuade, and not in vain. Now let your harps indite a measure Of all that hero's hand may dare— Of all that poet's heart can pleasure, Before the fairest of the fair.	*Landgraf und die Sänger.* Er kehrt zurück, den wir verloren! Ein Wunder hat ihn hergebracht. Die ihm den Uebermuth beschworen, Gepriesen sei die holde Macht! Nun lausche { Euren / unsren } Hochgesängen Von Neuem der Gepries'nen Ohr! Est tön in frohbelebten Klängen Das Lied aus jeder Brust hervor!

[*During the foregoing, the whole hunting retinue of the Landgrave, with torchbearers, etc., have assembled on the stage. The huntsmen sound their bugles. The whole valley swarms with the train of the hunters. The Landgrave and Minstrels turn towards their retinue; the Landgrave sounds his bugle, and is answered by a loud peal from other hunters. While the Landgrave and Minstrels mount the horses that have been led down from the Wartburg, the curtain falls.*]

[*Das ganze Thal wimmelt jetzt vom immer noch stärker angewachsenem Jagdtross. Der Landgraf und die Sänger wenden sich den Jägern zu; der Landgraf stösst in sein Horn, lautes Hornschmettern und Rüdengebell antwortet ihm Während der Landgraf und die Sänger die Pferde, die ihnen von der Wartburg zugeführt worden sind, besteigen, fällt der Vorhang.*]

## ACT II	## AKT II
### SCENE I	### ERSTE SCENE

The Hall of Minstrels in the Wartburg. At the back an open prospect from the Valley.	*Die Sängerhalle auf der Wartburg; im Hintergrunde freie Aussicht auf dem Burghof und das Thal.*
Elisa. Oh, hall of song I give thee greeting! All hail to thee thou hallowed place! 'T was here that dream so sweet and fleeting, Upon my heart his song did trace. But since by him forsaken A desert thou dost seem— Thy echoes only waken Remembrance of a dream. But now the flame of hope is lighted, Thy vault shall ring with glorious war; For he whose strains my soul delighted No longer roams afar!	*Elisa.* Dich, theure Halle, grüss' ich wieder, Froh grüss' ich dich, geliebter Raum! In dir erwachen seine Lieder, Und wecken mich aus düst'rem Traum. Da er aus dir geschieden, Wie öd' erschienst du mir!— Aus mir entfloh der Frieden, Die Freude zog aus dir. Wie jetzt mein Busen hoch sich hebet, So scheinst du jetzt mir stolz und hehr; Der dich und mich so neu belebet, Nicht länger weilt er ferne mehr. Sei mir gegrüsst! sei mir gegrüsst!

SCENE II

Behold her! Naught your meeting shall disturb.
Oh Princess!
Heav'n! do not kneel! leave me
Here, thus we should not meet.
We may! oh, stay,
And let me kneel for ever here!
I pray thee rise!
'Tis not for thee to kneel where thou has
   conquer'd.
This hall is thy domain. Rise, I implore!
Thanks be to heaven that thou return'st to us!
So long where hast thou tarried?
Far away, in strange and distant regions—
And between yesterday and to-day oblivion's veil
   hath fallen.
Every remembrance hath for ever vanished,
Save one thing only, rising from the darkness—
That I then dared not hope I should behold thee,
Nor ever raise mine eyes to thy perfection.
How wert thou led now to return to us?
A marvel 'twas, by heaven wrought within my
   spirit.
I praise the power that wrought it
From out my heart's recesses!
Forgive— I scarcely know what I am saying:
Thy presence here; a vision doth it seem—
Strange dream of life, mysterious and alluring.
The world to me is changed. Canst thou declare
What this emotion to my heart betokens?
   In minstrels' lays delighting
   I mark'd and listened long and oft;
   Their subtle, sweet inditing
   To me seemed dalliance soft.
But now the past to me is darkened—
Repose and joy from me have flown;
Since fondly to thy lays I've hearken'd
The pangs and bliss of woe I've known.
Emotions that I comprehend not,
And longings never guess'd before—
Upon my bidding they depend not,
But fled are all delights of yore.
And when this land thou hadst forsaken
Repose and joy for me were fled;
No minstrel could my heart awaken—
To me their lays seem'd sad and dead.
In slumber oft near broken-hearted,
Awake, each pain fondly recalled
All joy hath from my life departed.
Henry, Henry, why thus am I enthrall'd!
All praise to love for this fair token!
Love touched my harp with magic sweet—
Love, through my song, to thee hath spoken,
And captive leads me at thy feet.

ZWEITE SCENE

Wolf. Dort ist sie; nahe dich ihr ungestört!
Tann. O Fürstin!
Elisa. Gott! Steht auf! Lasset mich! Nicht darf
Ich Euch hier seh'n!
Tann.   Du darf'st! O bleib' und lass
Zu deinen Füssen mich!
Elisa.   So stehet auf!
Nicht sollet hier Ihr knien, denn diese Halle
Ist Euer Königreich. O, stehet auf!
Nehmt meinen Dank, dass Ihr zuruckgekehrt!
Wo weiltet Ihr so lange?
Tann.   Fern von hier,
In weiten, weiten Landen. Dichtes Vergessen
Hat zwischen heut' und gestern sich gesenkt.—
All' mein Erinnern ist mir schnell geschwunden,
Und nur des Einen muss ich mich entsinnen,
Dass nie mehr ich gehofft Euch zu begrüssen,
Noch je zu Euch mein Auge zu erheben.
Elisa. Was war es dann, das Euch zurückgeführt?
Tann. Ein Wunder war's, ein unbegreiflich hohes
   Wunder!
Elisa. Gepriesen sei dies Wunder aus meines Herzens
   Tiefe!
Verzeiht, wenn ich nicht weiss, was ich beginne!
Im Traum bin ich und thör'ger als ein Kind,—
Machtlos der Macht der Wunder preisgegeben,
Fast kenn' ich mich nicht mehr; o, helfet mir,
Dass ich das Räthsel meines Herzens löse!
   Der Sänger klugen Weisen
   Lauscht' ich sonst gern und viel;
   Ihr Singen und ihr Preisen
   Schien mir ein holdes Spiel.
Doch welch' ein seltsam neues Leben
Rief Euer Lied mir in die Brust!
Bald wollt' es mich wie Schmerz durchbeben,
Bald drang's in mich wie jähe Lust:
Gefühle, die ich nie empfunden!
Verlangen, das ich nie gekannt!
Was einst mir lieblich, war verschwunden
Vor Wonnen, die noch nie genannt!—
Und als Ihr nun von uns gegangen,—
War Frieden mir und Lust dahin!
Die Weisen, die die Sänger sangen,
Erschienen matt mir, trüb' ihr Sinn;
Im Traume fühlt' ich dumpfe Schmerzen,
Mein Wachen ward trübsel'ger Wahn;
Die Freude zog aus meinem Herzen;—
Heinrich! Was thatet Ihr mir an?
Tann. Den Gott der Liebe sollst du preisen,
Er hat die Saiten mir berührt,
Er sprach zu dir aus meinen Weisen,
Zu dir hat er mich hergeführt!

No. 3.   OH ! BLESSED HOUR.

ELIZABETH.

Oh   bless - ed   hour............   of   meet - ing,   oh   bless - ed
Ge - prie - sen   sei............   die   Stun - de,   ge - prie - sen

TANNHÄUSER.

pow'r............ of love! At last......... I give........., thee
sei................. die Macht, die mir......... so hol - de

pow'r............ of love!
sei................. die Macht.

At
die

greet - ing! No long - er thou.................. wilt rove!
Kun - de von Eu - rer Näh'...................... ge - bracht!

last........ I give......... thee greet - ing, no more...... from hence to rove!
mir........ so hol - de Kun - de aus dei - nem Mund ge-bracht!

Oh bless - ed hour of meet - ing, oh bless - ed pow'r of love, At
Ge - prie - sen sei die Stun - de, ge - prie - sen sei die Macht, die

last I give thee greet - ing, no long - er thou wilt rove!
mir so hol - de Kun - de von Eu - rer Näh' ge - bracht!

last I give thee greet - ing, no more from hence to rove! Now
mir so hol - de Kun - de aus dei - nem Mund ge - bracht! Dem

Now life...... re
Von Won - ne

life...... re - new'd a - wak - eth the hope that once was mine,
neu...... er - kann - ten Le - ben darf ich mich zu thig weih'n,

wak - - - eth,   with - in this heart... ...... of
L - - ben   nenn'........ ich die Freu - de

break - - eth,   I know but joy di - vine.
Be - - ben,   sein schön - stes Wun - der mein.

mine, the cloud of sor - row break - eth, the cloud of sor - row break - eth the
mein; er-wacht zu neu - em Le - ben, er-wacht zu neu - em Le - ben nenn

Now life:.... re - new'd a - wak - eth, now life re-new'd a - wak - eth the
Dem neu.... er - kann - ten Le - ben. dem neu er - cann - ten Le - ben, darf

sun of joy doth shine,   the sun doth shine!...... Ah! thou
ich die Freu-de mein,   die Freu - de mein!...... Ach! Ge

hope that once was mine, the hope that once was mine!...... Ah! thou
ich mich mu - thig weih'n, darf ich mich mu - thig weih'n!.... Ach! Ge

WOLFRAM (at the back.)

All hope my heart for -
So flieht für die - ses

bless - ed hour of meet - ing, thou bless-ed pow'r of love!   At last I
prie - sen sei die Stun - de, ge - prie-sen sei die Macht,   die mir so

. sak - - eth,   ne'er will her heart be mine!
Le - - ben mir   je - der Hoff - nung Schein!

give thee greet - ing, no long - er thou wilt rove!......
hol - de Kun - de von Eu - rer Näh' ge - bracht!....

...... Oh bless - ed, oh bless - ed hour .... of
...... Ge - prie - sen! Ge - prie - sen sei............ die

meet - ing, oh bless - ed pow'r............ of love!........ Now
Stun - de, ge - prie - sen sei............ die Macht!...... Von

life...... re - new'd a - wak - eth with - in this heart of mine,
Won - ne - glanz um - ge - ben lacht mir der Son - ne Schein

Oh bless-ed pow'r of love! Now life...... . re -
Ge - prie - sen sei die Macht, Dem neu...... . er -

with - in this heart of mine; the cloud...... of sor - row
lacht mir der Son - ne Schein, er - wacht...... zu neu - em

new'd a - wak - eth the hope that once was mine, the cloud of
kann - ten Le - ben darf ich mich mu - thig weih'n, ich senn' in

stringendo.

break - eth the sun,.................................. the sun of oy doth
Le - ben... nenn' ich die Freu - - - de, nenn' ich die Freu - de

sor - row break - eth, I know........ but joy, yes, I know but joy di
freud' - gem Be - ben sein schön - stes Wun - der, sein schön - stes Wun - der

shine; Now life re-new'd a - wak - eth now life renew'd a - wak - eth with
mein: im neu er-wach - ten Le - ben, im neu er-wach - ten Le - ben nenn

vine; the cloud of sor - row break - eth, the cloud of sor - row break - eth, I
mein; ich nenn' in freud'-gem Be - ben, ich nenn' in freud'-gem Be - ben sein

- in this heart of mine, with - in this heart................ with - in
ich die Freu - de mein, nenn' ich die Freu - de,.... nenn'

know but joy di - vine, I know but joy,............. yes, I know
höch - stes Wun - der mein, sein höch - stes Wun - der, sein schön -

this glad heart.................................... of mine, with - in this
ich die Freu - - - - de mein, nenn' ich die

nought but joy, but joy.... di - vine, I know but joy, but
stes. sein schön - stes Wun - der.... mein, sein höch stes Wun - der

heart of mine, this heart................ of mine!
Freu - de mein, die Freu - - - de mein!

joy di - vine. but joy................................ di - vine!
nenn' ich mein. ich nenn'................................ es mein!

SCENE III

and.	Com'st thou at last to grace the contest?
	Wilt thou shun these walls no longer?
	What hath lur'd thee from thy solitude
	To come amongst us?
lisa.	My sov'reign, oh, my more than father!
and.	Wilt thou, then, at last reveal to me thy secret?
lisa.	Tell it I cannot; read my eyes, and know.
and.	This day it shall still be unspoken—
	Thy treasur'd thought thou need'st not own;
	The spell shall yet remain unbroken
	Till what the future brings is known
	So be't. .The wondrous flame that song hath
	kindled
	This day shall brightly soar;
	Thy joy, all hearts rejoicing,
	Shall on this day be crowned:
	What hath been sung shall spring to life for thee.
	This day will see our nobles all assembled—
	To grace the solemn feast they now approach;
	None will be absent, since they know
	That once again thy hand the victor's wreath
	bestows.

DRITTE SCENE

Land.	Dich treff' ich hier in dieser Halle, die
	So lange du gemieden? Endlich denn
	Lockt dich ein Sängerfest, das wir bereiten?
Elisa.	Mein Oheim! O, mein güt'ger Vater!
Land.	Drängt
	Es dich, dein Herz mir endlich zu erschliessen?
Elisa.	Blick' mir in's Auge! Sprechen kann ich nicht.
Land.	Noch bleibe denn unausgesprochen
	Dein süss Geheimniss kurze Frist,
	Der Zauber bleibe ungebrochen,
	Bis du der Lösung mächtig bist.—
	So sei's! Was der Gesang so Wunderbares
	Erweckt und angeregt, soll heute er
	Enthüllen auch und mit Vollendung krönen.
	Die holde Kunst, sie werde jetzt zur That!
	Schon nahen sich die Edlen meiner Lande,
	Die ich zum selt'nen Fest hieher beschied;
	Zahlreicher nahen sie als je, da sie
	Gehört, dass du des Festes Fürstin seist.

No. 4. ### HAIL BRIGHT ABODE.

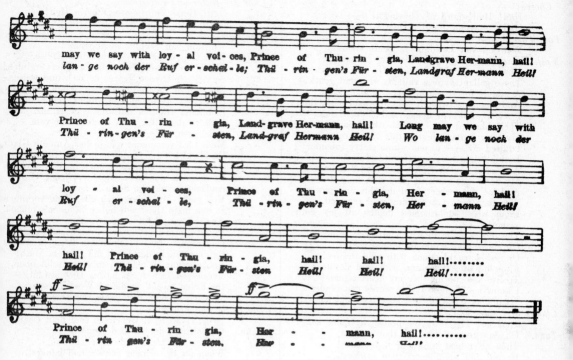

may we say with loy - al voi - ces, Prince of Thu - rin - gia, Landgrave Her-mann, hail!
lan - ge noch der Ruf er - schal-le; Thü - rin - gen's Für - sten, Landgraf Her-mann Heil!

Prince of Thu - rin - gia, Land- grave Her-mann, hail! Long may we say with
Thü - rin-gen's Für - sten, Land-graf Hermann Heil! Wo lan - ge noch der

loy - al voi - ces, Prince of Thu - rin - gia, Her - mann, hail!
Ruf er - schal - le, Thü - rin - gen's Für - sten, Her - mann Heil!

hail! Prince of Thu - rin - gia, hail! hail! hail!........
Heil! Thü - rin - gen's Für - sten Heil! Heil! Heil!........

Prince of Thu - rin - gia, Her - mann, hail!..........
Thü - rin gen's Für - sten, Her - mann, Heil!

Landgrave.	Der Landgraf.

Minstrels assembled here, I give you greeting.
Full oft within these walls your lays have
  sounded;
In veiled wisdom, or in mirthful measures
They ever gladdened every list'ning heart.
And though the sword of strife was loosed in
  battle,
Drawn to maintain our German land secure,
When 'gainst the southern foe we fought and
  conquer'd,
And for our country brav'd the death of heroes,
Unto the harp be equal praise and glory!
The tender graces of the homestead,
The faith in what is good and gracious—
For these you fought with word and voice:
The meed of praise for this is due.
Your strains inspiring, then, once more attune,
Now that the gallant minstrel hath to us returned
Who from our land too long was parted
To what we owe his presence here amongst us
In strange, mysterious darkness still is wrapp'd;
The magic power of song shall now reveal it,
Therefore hear now the theme you all shall sing.
Say, what is love? by what signs shall we know it?
This be your theme. Who so most nobly this can
  tell,
Him shall the Princess give the price.
He may demand the fairest guerdon:
I vouch that whatsoe'er he ask is granted.
Up, then, arouse ye—sing, oh, gallant minstrels!
Attune your harps to love—great is the price,
Ere ye begin, let all receive our thanks!
	Gar viel und schön ward hier in dieser Halle
	Von Euch, Ihr lieben Sänger, schon gesungen.
	In weisen Räthseln wie in heit'ren Liedern
	Erfreuet Ihr gleich sinnig unser Herz.—
	Wenn unser Schwert in blutig ernsten Kämpfen
	Stritt für des deutschen Reiches Majestät,
	Wenn wir dem grimmen Welfen widerstanden
	Und dem verderbenvollen Zwiespalt wehrten,
	So ward von Euch nicht mindrer Preis errungen.
	Der Anmuth und der holden Sitte,
	Der Tugend und dem reinen Glauben
	Erstrittet Ihr durch Eure Kunst
	Gar hohen, herrlich schönen Sieg.
	Bereitet heute uns denn auch ein Fest,
	Heut', wo der kühne Sänger uns zurück-
	Gekehrt, den wir so ungern lang' vermissten
	Was wieder ihn in unsre Nähe brachte,
	Ein wunderbar Geheimniss dünkt es mich;
	Durch Liedes Kunst sollt' Ihr es uns enthüllen.
	Deshalb stell' ich die Frage jetzt an Euch:
	Könnt Ihr der Liebe Wesen mir ergründen?
	Wer es vermag, wer sie am würdigsten
	Besingt, dem reich' Elisabeth den Preis:
	Er ford're ihn so hoch und kühn er wolle,
	Ich sorge, dass sie ihn gewähren solle.
	Auf, liebe Sänger! Greifet in die Saiten!
	Die Aufgab' ist gestellt, kämpft um den Preis
	Und nehmet all' im Voraus uns'ren Dank!

Chorus:
    Hail! Hail! Lord of Thuringia!
    Hail! protector thou of gentle song!
Four Pages.
    Wolfram von Eschinbach, begin thou?
Wolf. Gazing around upon this fair assembly,
    How doth the heart expand to see the scene!
    These gallant heroes, valiant, wise and gentle—
    A stately forest soaring fresh and green.
    And blooming by their side, in sweet perfection,
    I see a wreath of dames and maidens fair;
    Their blended glories dazzle the beholder—
    My song is mute before this vision rare.
    I raised my eyes to one whose starry splendor
    In this bright heaven with mild effulgence beams,
    And gazing on that pure and tender radiance,
    My heart was sunk in prayerful, holy dreams.
    And lo! the source of all delights and power
    Was then unto my list'ning soul revealed,
    From whose unfathomed depths all joy doth
       shower—
    The tender balm in which all grief is healed.
    Oh, never may I dim its limpid waters,
    Or rashly trouble them with wild desires!
    I worship thee kneeling, with soul devoted:
    To live and die for thee my heart aspires!
    I know not if these feeble words can render
    What I have felt of love both true and tender.
Chorus of Nobles and Ladies.
    They do! They do! We praise thy noble song!
Tann. Oh, minstrel, if 'tis thus thou singest,
    Thou ne'er hast known or tasted love!
    If cold and timid heart thou bringest,
    A weary lot thy joy must prove!
    If thou desire an unapproach'd perfection—
    Behold the stars—adore their bright reflection—
    They were not made to be belov'd:
    They ne'er by human pray'r were mov'd!
    But what can yield to soft caresses,
    And, fram'd with me in mortal mould
    Gentle persuasion's rule confesses,
    And in these arms I may unfold—
    This is for joy, and knows no measure,
    For love's fulfillment is pleasure!
Bit. To mortal combat I defy thee!
    Shameless blasphemer, draw thy sword!
    As brother henceforth we deny thee;
    Thy words profane too long we've heard!
    If I of love divine have spoken,
    Strength'ning in valor, sword and heart,
    Its glorious spell shall be unbroken
    Altho' from life this hour I part.
    For womanhood and noble honor
    Through death and danger I would go;
    But for the cheap delights that won thee
    I scorn them as not worth a blow!
Chorus of Nobles and Ladies.
    Hail Biterolf! Come, draw thy sword!
Tann. Yes, idle boaster, Biterolf!
    Shall love be sung by thee, grim wolf?
    Not thou hast e'er known aught of bliss—
    Its sweetness thy fierce heart must miss.
    Poor weary soul, what joy hath bless'd thee?
    What rapture couldst thou ever know?
    If any pale delight possess'd thee,
    That were indeed not worth a blow!
Nobles. We will not hear him, stay his daring madness.
Land. Put up your swords!—There must be peace be-
    tween ye.

Chor der Ritter und Edelfrauen.
    Heil! Heil! Thüringen's Fürstin Heil!
    Der holden Kunst Beschützer Heil!
Vier Edelknaben.
    Wolfram von Eschinbach, beginne!
Wolf. Blick' ich umher in diesem edlen Kreise,
    Welch' hoher Anblick macht mein Herz erglüh'n!
    So viel der Helden, tapfer deutsch und weise,—
    Ein stolzer Eichwald, herrlich, frisch und grün,
    Und hold und tugendsam erblick' ich Frauen,—
    Lieblicher Blüthen düftereichster Kranz.
    Es wird der Blick wohl trunken mir vom
       Schauen,
    Mein Lied verstummt vor solcher Anmuth Glanz,
    Da blick' ich auf zu einem nur der Sterne,
    Der an dem Himmel, der mich blendet, steht;
    Es sammelt sich mein Geist aus jeder Ferne,
    Andächtig sinkt die Seele in Gebet
    Und sieh! Mir zeiget sich ein Wunderbronnen,
    In den mein Geist voll hohen Staunen's blickt:
    Aus ihm er schöpfet gnadenreiche Wonnen,
    Durch die mein Herz er namenlos erquickt.
    Und nimmer möcht' ich diesen Bronnen trüben,
    Berühren nicht den Quell mit frevlem Muth:
    In Anbetung möcht, ich mich opfernd üben,
    Vergiessen froh mein letztes Herzensblut,—
    Ihr Edlen möcht' in diesen Worten lesen,
    Wie ich erkenn' der Liebe reinstes Wesen!
Die Ritter und Frauen.
    So ist's! So ist's! Gepriesen seid dein Lied!
Tann. O Wolfram, der du also sangest,
    Du hast die Liebe arg entstellt!
    Wenn du in solchem Schmachten bangest,
    Versiegte wahrlich wohl die Welt.
    Zu Gottes Preis in hoch erhab'ne Fernen,
    Blickt auf zum Himmel, blickt zu seinen Sternen
    Anbetung solchen Wundern zollt,
    Da ihr sie nicht begreifen sollt!
    Doch, was sich der Berührung beuget,
    Euch Herz und Sinnen nahe liegt,
    Was sich, aus gleichem Stoff erzeuget,
    In weicher Formung an euch mich schmiegt,—
    Dem ziemt Genuss in freud'gem Triebe
    Und im Genuss nur kenn ich Liebe!
Bit. Heraus zum Kampfe mit uns Allen!
    Wer bliebe ruhig, hört er dich?
    Wird deinem Hochmuth es gefallen,
    So höre, Lästrer, nun auch mich!
    Wenn mich begeistert hohe Liebe,
    Stählt sie die Waffen mir mit Muth;
    Dass ewig ungeschmäht sie bliebe,
    Vergöss ich stolz mein letztes Blut.
    Für Frauenehr' und hohe Tugend
    Als Ritter kämpf' ich mit dem Schwert;
    Doch, was Genuss beut' deiner Jugend,
    Ist wohlfeil, keines Streiches werth.
Die Zu. Heil, Biterolf! Hier unser Schwert!

Tann. Ha, thör'ger Prahler, Biterolf!
    Singst du von Liebe, grimmer Wolf?
    Gewisslich hast du nicht gemeint
    Was mir geniessenswerth erscheint.
    Was hast du Aermster wohl genossen?
    Dein Leben war nicht liebereich,
    Und was von Freuden dir entsprossen,
    Das galt wohl wahrlich keinen Streich!
Ritter. Lasst ihn nicht enden!—Wehret seiner Kühnheit
Land. Zurück das Schwert!—Ihr Sänger, halte Frieden

Wolf. Oh, Heaven! let me here implore thee!
Hallow my song to worthy praise!
Let sin crouch in the dust before thee,
Nor dare 'mongst us its head to raise!
Thou, noble love, inspire me,
Thy glory let me sing—
Thy flame immortal fire me,
Fann'd by an angel's wing!
Thou com'st, from Heav'n descended—
I follow thee afar;
By every joy attended
For ever shines thy star!

Wolf. O Himmel, lass dich jetzt erflehen,
Gieb meinem Lied der Weihe Preis
Gebannt lass mich die Sünde sehen
Aus diesem edlen reinen Kreis!
Dir hohe Liebe, töne
Begeistert mein Gesang,
Die mir in Engels-Schöne
Tief in die Seele drang!
Du nahst als Gottgesandte,
Ich folg' aus holder Fern',—
So führst du in die Lande,
We ewig strahlt dein Stern.

No. 5. THOU, GODDESS OF LOVE.

TANNHÄUSER *(in wildest exultation.)*

Thou goddess of love, shalt now in-spire my measure, in joyful
Dir Göt-tin der Lie-be, soll mein Lied er-tö-nen, ge-sun-gen

strains thy praise be ev-er song! Thou art the source of
laut sei jetzt dein Preis von mir! Dein sü-sser Reiz ist

all in life we treas-ure, thy sweet... de-lights are ev-er fair and
Quel-le al-les Schö-nen, und je-des hol-de Wun-der stammt von

young! Whose burn-ing soul once hath with ar-der embrac'd thee, can speak of
dir! Wer dich mit Gluth in sei-ne, Ar-me ge-schlo-ssen, was Lie-be

love, none... else its joys can prove! Dull mor-tals, who of love have nev-er
ist, kennt... er nur er al-lein! Arm-sel'-ge, die ihr Lie-be, nie ge-

tast-ed, Go forth! Ve-nus a-lone can show... ye love!
no-ssen, zieht hin! Zieht in den Berg der Ve-nus ein!

ll. Ah, hear the miscreant! hence away!
Hear him! he hath with Venus been!
dies. Away! away! nor near him stay!
*he Ladies quit the Hall with gestures of dismay and
horror; Elisabeth, who has heard the contest with growing alarm, alone remains, pale and trembling, supporting herself against one of the pillars of the royal
canopy. The Landgrave, the Minstrels and Nobles have
quitted their seats and stand together. Tannhäuser remains some time longer as in a trance.*

Alle. Ha, der Verruchte! Fliehet ihn!
Hört es! Er war im Venusberg!
Die Edelfrauen.
Hinweg! Hinweg aus seiner Näh'!
[*Die Frauen verlassen in grösster Bestürzung und mit
Gebärden des Abscheu's die Halle. Elisabeth, die dem
Streite der Sänger mit wachsender Angst zugehört
hatte, bleibt von den Frauen allein zurück,—bleich,
nur mit dem grössten aufwande ihrer Kraft an einer
der hölzernen Säulen des Baldachins sich aufrecht er-
haltend. Der Landgraf, alle Ritter und Sänger haben
ihre Sitze verlassen und treten zusammen. Tannhäuser,
zur äussersten Linken, verbleibt noch eine Zeit lang
wie in Verzückung.*

Landgrave, Knights and Nobles.
    Ye all have heard,
    His mouth hath confess'd
    That he hath shared the joys of hell,
    In Venus' dark abode that dwell.
    Disown him—curse him—banish him!
    Or let his traitor life-blood flow!
    Anathema, we call on thee:
    In hellish fires for ever glow!

[*All close round Tannhäuser, with drawn swords. Elisabeth throws herself between them.*

Elisa.   Stay your hands!
Landgrave, Knights and Nobles.
    On, wonder! thou, Elisabeth!
    The peerless maiden shields the guilty?
Elisa.   Stand back! or pierce this bosom with your
        swords!
    Death and its terrors cannot crush me
    Like to the deadly wound that he hath struck
    me here. .
Landgrave and Nobles.
    Oh, royal maid, can we believe thee?
    Let not thy guileless heart deceive thee,
    Nor let his fate accursed grieve thee:
    Thou more than all the wretch should scorn!
Elisa.   Think not of me! He must be saved!
    Ye would not rob his hope of heaven?
Landgrave and Nobles.
    For ever lost his hope of Heav'n—
    Madly his joy he cast aside!
    A crime like his is ne'er forgiven:
    The curse of Heav'n with him abide!
Elisa.   Away from him! 'Tis not for you to judge him!
    Shame on you! He is one against you all.
    Oh, let a spotless maid your grace implore!
    Let Heav'n declare through me what is its will—
    The erring mortal, who hath fallen
    Within the weary toils of sin,
    How dare ye close the heav'nly portal
    Where he on earth his shrift may win?
    If ye are strong in faith and honor,
    Why do ye not His word obey
    Who gave to us the law of mercy—
    Who ne'er from sinner turned away?
    On me, a maiden young and tender,
    Yon knight hath struck a cruel blow—
    I, who so deeply, truly lov'd him,
    Am hurl'd in dark abyss of woe!
    I pray for him—spare him, oh, I implore ye!
    Let not the hope of pardon be denied!
    To life renew'd his sinking faith restore ye.
    Think that for him, too, once the Saviour died.
Tann.   Oh! lost and for ever.
Landgrave, Knights and Nobles.
    An angel hath from Heav'n descended
    To bear us God's most high behest.
    Behold and see whom thou'st offended!
    Thy crime for ever haunt thy rest!
    Thou gav'st her death—she prays that life be
        spared thee!
    Who would not yield who heard the heav'nly
        maid?
    Though as accursed and guilty I declar'd thee,
    The voice of Heav'n by me shall be obey'd.
Tann.   Have mercy, Thou! I cry to thee despairing!
    Oh, from the gulf of error set me free!
Land.   A crime dark and unheard of hath befallen;
    In mask of loyal knight there treacherously
    Stole amongst us sin's accursed child.
    By us thou art disown'd;
    From this land thou art banish'd.

Landgraf, Ritter und Sänger.
    Ihr habt's gehört! Sein frevler Mund
    That das Bekenntniss schrecklich kund.
    Er hat der Hölle Lust getheilt,
    Im Venusberg hat er geweilt!—
    Entsetzlich! Scheusslich! Fluchenswerth!
    In seinem Blute netzt das Schwert!
    Zum Höllenpfuhl zurückgesandt!

[*Alle dringen mit gezücktem Schwerte auf Tannhäuse ein Elisabeth stürtzt dazwischen.*

Elisa.   Haltet ein!
Landgraf, Ritter und Sänger.
    Was seh' ich! Wie, Elisabeth!
    Die keusche Jungfrau für den Sünder?
Elisa.   Zurück! Des Todes achte ich sonst nicht!
    Was ist die Wunde Eures Eisen's gegen
    Den Todesstoss, den ich von ihm empfing?

Landgraf, Ritter und Sänger.
    Elisabeth! Was muss ich hören?
    Wie liess dein Herz sich so bethören,
    Von dem die Strafe zu beschwören,
    Der auch so furchtbar dich verrieth!
Elisa.   Was liegt an mir? Doch er,—sein Heil!
    Wollt Ihr sein ewig Heil ihm rauben?
Landgraf, Ritter und Sänger.
    Verworfen hat er jedes Hoffen.
    Niemals wird ihm des Heil's Gewinn!
    Des Himmels Fluch hat ihn getroffen!
    In seinen Sünden fahr' er hin!
Elisa.   Zurück von ihm! Nicht Ihr seid seine Richter
    Grausame! Werft von Euch das wilde Schwer
    Und gebt Gehör der reinen Jungfrau Wort!
    Vernehmt durch mich, was Gottes Wille ist!—
    Der Unglücksel'ge, den gefangen
    Ein furchtbar mächt'ger Zauber hält,
    Wie? sollt' er nie zum Heil gelangen
    Durch Reu' und Buss' in dieser Welt?
    Die Ihr so stark im reinen Glauben,
    Verkennt Ihr so des Höchsten Rath?
    Wollt Ihr sein ewig Heil ihm rauben?
    So sagt, was Euch er Leides that?
    Seht mich, die Jungfrau, deren Blüthe
    Mit einem jähen Schlag er brach,—
    Die ihn geliebt tief im Gemüthe,
    Der jubelnd er das Herz zerstach;—
    Ich fleh' für ihn, ich flehe für sein Leben,
    Zur Busse lenk' er reuevoll den Schritt!
    Der Muth des Glaubens sei ihm neu gegeben,
    Dass auch für ihn einst der Erlöser litt!
Tann.   Weh! Weh mir Unglücksel'gem.
Landgraf, Ritter and Sänger.
    Ein Engel stieg aus lichtem Aether,
    Zu künden Gottes heil'gen Rath.
    Blick hin, du schändlicher Verräther,
    Werd' inne deiner Missethat!
    Du gabst ihr Tod, sie bittet für dein Leben;
    Wer bliebe rauh, hört er des Engels Fleh'n?
    Darf ich auch nicht dem Schuldigen vergeber
    Dem Himmels Wort kann nicht ich widersteh'n
Tann.   Erbarm' dich mein, der ach! so tief in Sünde
    Schmachvoll des Himmels Mittlerin verkannt!
Land.   Ein furchtbares Verbrechen ward begangen:
    Es schlich mit heuchlerischer Larve sich
    Zu uns der Sünde fluchbelad'ner Sohn.
    Wir stossen dich von uns.—bei uns darfst du
    Nicht weilen; schmachbefleckt ist unser Herd

Thou with shame has stained this threshold pure:
The wrath of heav'n may strike the roof
That harbors thee, too long by guilt defil'd.
One path alone can save thee from perdition,
From everlasting woe—by earth abandon'd,
One way is left: that way thou now shalt know.
A band of pilgrims now assembled
From every part of my domain;
This morn the elders went before them,
The rest yet in the vale remain.
'Tis not for crimes like thine they tremble,
And leave their country, friends and home—
Desire for heav'nly grace is o'er them:
They seek the sacred shrine at Rome.

Landgrave, Knights and Nobles.
'Tis there repentant kneeling
Before the shrine of grace,
Thy heart in tears annealing,
Thy sin thou shalt efface.
In dust bow down before him
Who holds the keys of Heav'n.
But never more returning
Unless by him forgiven!
Our just revenge resign'd we,
Because an angel pray'd;
But yet this sword shall find thee
Unless thou seek heav'ns aid.

Elisa. Great Heav'n, repentant kneeling,
A sinner sues for grace:
Thy bounteous love revealing,
Turn not away thy face.
In dust bending before him
Who holds the keys of Heav'n!
Oh, let thy light restore him,
Oh, let him be forgiven!
All hope on earth resigning,
Thee I implore for aid;
My life, without repining,
I offer up, a maid!

Tann. Oh, where shall I find mercy?
Oh, where shall I find rest?
All hope from me hath vanish'd—
Despair within my breast!
I'll go repentant kneeling
Before the throne of grace;
If bitter tears are healing,
In dust I'll hide my face.
Oh, let me be forgiven,
By her, the heavenly maid
Whose heart by me was riven—
Whom basely I betray'd.

Chorus of Younger Pilgrims.
At thy august and holy shrine
I go to seek the grace divine.
Thrice blessed who thy promise know;
Absolv'd by penance shall they go.

Tann. To Rome!
All. To Rome!

Durch dich, und dräuend blickt der Himmel
   selbst
Auf dieses Dach, das dich zu lang schon birgt.
Zur Rettung doch vor ewigem Verderben
Steht offen dir ein Weg: von mir dich stossend
Zeig' ich ihn dir,—nütz' ihn zu deinem Heil!
Versammelt sind aus meinen Landen
Bussfert'ge Pilger, stark an Zahl:
Die ält'ren schon voran sich wandten,
Die jüng'ren rasten noch im Thal.
Nur um geringer Sünde willen
Ihr Herz nicht Ruhe ihnen lässt,
Der Busse frommen Drang zu stillen,
Ziehn sie nach Rom zum Gnadenfest.

Landgraf, Ritter und Sänger.
Mit ihnen sollst du wallen,
Zur Stadt der Gnadenhuld,
Im Staub dort niederfallen
Und büssen deine Schuld!
Vor ihm stürz' dich darnieder,
Der Gottes Urtheil spricht;
Doch kehre nimmer wieder,
Ward dir sein Segen nicht!
Musst' unsre Rache weichen,
Weil sie ein Engel brach:
Dies Schwert wird dich erreichen,
Harrst du in Sünd' und Schmach!

Elisa. Lass hin zu dir ihn wallen,
Du Gott der Gnad' und Huld!
Ihm, der so tief gefallen,
Vergieb der Sünden Schuld
Für ihn nur will ich flehen,
Mein Leben sei Gebet;
Lass ihn dein Leuchten sehen
Eh' er in Nacht vergeht!
Mit freudigem Erbeben
Lass dir ein Opfer weihn!
Nimm hin, o nimm mein Leben,
Nicht nenn' ich es mehr mein!

Tann. Wie soll ich Gnade finden,
Wie bussen meine Schuld?
Mein Heil sah' ich entschwinden,
Mich flieht des Himmels Huld.
Doch will ich bussend wallen,
Zerschlagen meine Brust,
Im Staube niederfallen,—
Zerknirschung sei mir Lust
O, dass nur er versöhnet,
Der Engel meiner Noth,
Der sich, so frech verhöhnet,
Zum opfer doch mir bot!

Gesang der jüngeren Pilger.
Am hohen Fest der Gnadenhuld
In Demuth sühnet Eure Schuld!
Gesegnet, wer in Glauben treu:
Er wird erlöst durch Buss und Reu'.

Tann. Nach Rom!
Alle. Nach Rom!

ACT III

—

SCENE I

[The Valley beneath the Wartburg, as in the first Act. It is near sunset. On the small eminence, Elisabeth is kneeling before the shrine in prayer. Wolfram comes down from a forest path; he stops when he has descended halfway, perceiving Elisabeth.

Wolf. By yonder shrine I'm ever sure to find her,
Kneeling in fervent prayer,
When my lonely and joyless way
Back to the valley leads me.
The death-blow struck by him within her—
She prays that Heaven may shrive the sinner,
His weal imploring day and night.
Oh, blessed love, how great thy might?
The pilgrims soon from Rome will be returning;
The year declines—ere long they must be here.
Will he return repentant and absolv'd?
This doth she pray for, Heav'n entreating.
Ye saints, oh grant their happy meeting,
Although my wound may never heal,
Oh, may she ne'er my anguish feel!

Elisa. The pilgrim's song! 'T is they! They have return'd!
Ye saints, oh let me know my task,
That I may worthily fulfil it!

Wolf. They come at last; it is the pious chant,
Telling of the sin absolv'd and pardon granted!
Oh! Heaven, let her heart be strong
If now her fate must be decided.

Chorus of Elder Pilgrims.
Once more with joy, oh, my home, I may meet thee;
Once more, ye fair flow'ry meadows, I greet ye;
My pilgrim staff henceforth may rest,
Since Heav'n's sweet peace is within my breast.
The sinner's plaint on high was heard,
Accepted by a gracious Lord;
The tears I laid before his shrine
Are turned to hope and joy divine.
Oh, Lord eternal praise be thine!
The blessed source of thy mercy o'erflowing
On souls repentant who seek Thee bestowing;
Of hell and death I have no fear,
My gracious Lord is ever near.
Hallelujah eternally.

Elisa. He will return no more!

AKT III

—

ERSTE SCENE

[Thal vor der Wartburg wie am Schlusse des erste Aktes, der Tag neigt sich zum Abend; auf dem kleine Bergvorsprunge rechts liegt Elisabeth vor dem Mu tergottesbilde betend ausgestreckt. Wolfram komm links von der waldigen Höhe herab, auf halber Höh hält er an als er Elisabeth gewahrt.

Wolf. Wohl wusst ich hier sie im Gebet zu finden,
Wie ich so oft sie treffe, wenn ich einsam
Aus wald'ger Höh' mich in das Thal verirre.—
Den Tod, den er ihr gab, im Herzen,
Dahin gestreckt in brünst'gen Schmerzen,
Fleht für sein Heil sie Tag und Nacht:—
O heil'ger Liebe ew'ge Macht!—
Von Rom zurück erwartet sie die Pilger.—
Schon fällt das Laub, die Heimkehr steht bevor:—
Kehrt er mit den Begnadigten zurück?
Dies ist ihr Fragen, dies ihr Flehen,—
Bleibt auch die Wunde ungeheillt,—
O, würd' ihr Lind'rung nur ertheilt!

Elisa. Dies ist ihr Sang,—sie sind's, sie kehren heim
Ihr Heil'gen, zeigt mir jetzt mein Amt,
Dass ich mit Würde es erfülle!

Wolf. Die Pilger sind's,—es ist die fromme Weise,
Die der empfang'nen Gnade Heil verkündet.—
O Himmel, stärke jetzt ihr Herz
Für die Entscheidung ihres Lebens.

Gesang der äteren Pilger.
Beglückt darf nun dich, o Heimath, ich schaue
Und grüssen froh deine lieblichen Auen;
Nun lass' ich ruhn den Wanderstab,
Weil Gott getreu ich gepilgert hab',
Durch Sühn' und Buss' hab ich versöhnt
Den Herren, dem mein Herze fröhnt,
Der meine Reu' mit Segen krönt,
Den Herren, dem mein Lied ertönt.
Der Gnade Heil ist dem Büsser beschieden,
Er geht einst ein in der Seligen Frieden!
Vor Höll' und Tod is ihm nicht bang',
Drum preis' ich Gott mein Lebenlang.
Halleluia in Ewigkeit!

Elisa. Er kehrt nicht zurück!—

No. 6.   **OH BLESSED VIRGIN.**

maid - en, pure and white, en - ter in - to thy king - dom bright! let me, a
rein und En - gel - gleich ein - ge - he in dein se - lig Reich, mach' das ick

a little more animated. ♩=72.

mai - den, pure and white, en - ter in - to thy king - dom bright! If
rein und En - gel - gleich, ein - ge he in dein se - lig Reich! Wenn

vain desires and earth - ly long - ing have turn'd my heart from thee a - way,
je, in thör'-gem Wahn be - fan - gen, mein Herz sich ab ge - wandt von dir,

the sin - ful hopes with - in me throng -ing, be - fore thy bless - ed feet I
wenn je ein sün - di - ges Ver-lan - gen, ein welt - lich Seh - nen keimt' in

slower.

lay; I'll wres - tle with the love I cher - ish'd, un - til in death its flame hath
mir; so rang' ich un - ter tau - send Schmerzen, dass ich es töd' in mei - nem

dim.

Tempo 1mo.

per - ish'd. If of my sin thou wilt not shrive me, yet in this hour, oh
Her - zen. Doch, konnt' ich je - den Fehl nicht bü - ssen, so nimm dich gnä - dig

pp

grant thy aid!...... In this hour, oh grant thy aid! Till thy e - ter - nal
mei - ner an!...... Nimm dich gnä - dig mei - ner an! Dass ich mit de - muth

p

peace thou give me, I vow to live and die thy maid. And on thy
vol - lem Grü - ssen, als würd' 'ge Magd dir na - hen kann. um dei - ne

boun ty I will call, that heav'n-ly grace on him may fall, yes, on thy
Gna - den reich - ste Huld, nur an - zu - flehn für sei - ne Schuld, um dei - ne

f *pp*

boun ty I...... will call, that.... heav'n-ly grace on him...... may fall.
Gna den reich - ste Huld nur.... an - zu - flehn für sei - - ne Schuld

SCENE II	ZWEITE SCENE
Wolf. Like Death's dark shadow, Night her gloom extendeth, Her sable wing o'er all the vale she bendeth; The soul that longs to tread yon path of light, Yet dreads to pass the gate of Fear and Night, I look on thee, oh, star in heaven the fairest, Thy gentle beam thro' trackless space thou bearest; The hour of darkness is by thee made bright, Thou lead'st us upward with pure kindly light.	*Wolf.* Wie Todesahnung Dämm'rung deckt die L Umhüllt das Thal mit schwärzlichem Gewa Der Seele, die nach jenen Höh'n verlangt. Vor ihrem Flug durch Nacht und Grausen h Da scheinest du, o lieblichster der Sterne, Dein sanftes Licht entsendest du der Fern Die nächt'ge Dämm'rung theilt dein lieber Strahl, Und freundlich zeigst den Weg du aus dem

No 7   O THOU SUBLIME, SWEET EV'NING STAR.

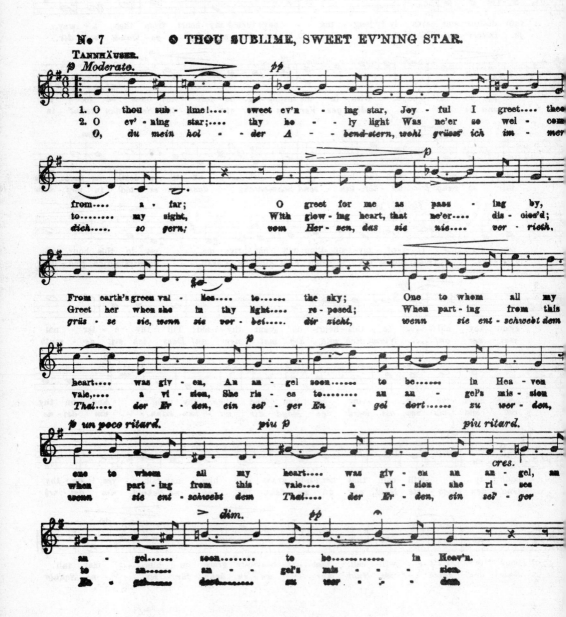

1. O thou sublime!.... sweet ev'n — ing star, Joy-ful I greet.... thee
2. O ev'-ning star;.... thy ho — ly light Was ne'er so wel-com
   O, du mein hol — der A — bend-stern, wohl grüss' ich im — mer

from.... a-far; O greet for me as pass-ing by,
to........ my sight, With glow-ing heart, that ne'er.... dis-cied'd,
dich..... so gern; vom Her-zen, das sie nie.... ver-rieth.

From earth's green val-lies.... to...... the sky; One to whom all my
Greet her whom she in thy light.... re-posed; When part-ing from this
grüs-se sie, wenn sie ver-bei..... dir zieht, wenn sie ent-schwebt dem

heart.... was giv-en, An an-gel seen........ to be........ in Hea-ven
vale,.... a vi-sion, She ris-es to........ an an-gel's mis-sion
Thal.... der Er-den, ein sel-ger En-gel dort....... zu wer-den,

one to whom all my heart.... was giv-en an an-gel,
when part-ing from this vale.... a vi-sion she ri-ses
wenn sie ent-schwebt dem Thal.... der Er-den, ein sel-ger

an-gel...... seen........ to be........ in Heav'n
to an-an........ an-gel's mis-sion
zu wer-den dort........ zu wer-den dem

SCENE III

nn. The sound of harp I heard: it spoke of sadness.
It was not she who sang.

lf. Who art thou, pilgrim,
Thy lonely path pursuing?

nn.   Who am I?
I who know thee so well! Wolfram thou art
The wise and skilful minstrel!

lf.   Henry? Thou?
What means thy coming thus dejected?
Speak! Tell me not that thou, unabsolv'd,
Hast dared to set thy foot within these precincts?

nn. Nay, have no fear, oh, sapient minstrel,
I seek thee not, nor yet thy proud companions
A path I seek, or one to guide my footsteps
To find a path erewhile I trod with ease.

lf. What path is that?
n.   It leads to Venus' hill.
lf. Thou godless man! Thy words defile my ear.
That is thy mission?

n.   Dost thou know the path?
f. Oh madman! Dread unknown thy words inspire.
Whence com'st thou? Hast thou not been in
Rome?

n. Speak not of Rome!
f. Hast thou not sued for pardon?
n. Speak not of that!
f. Thou wert not there?
Oh, I conjure thee, speak!

n. Yes, I have been in Rome.
f. Say on! oh, tell me all, unhappy man!
With deep compassion I will hear thy words.

n. What say'st thou, Wolfram? Say, art thou not my
foe?

f. No, never more, while thou art true to honor;
But tell—thy pilgrimage to Rome?

n. I will—I will.
Thou, Wolfram, shalt know what befell me.
Away from me! The refuge where I rest me
Is accursed! Now mark, Wolfram—mark well!
Contrite in spirit, as no pilgrim yet on earth
hath been,
I bent my steps to Rome.
An angel hath dispelled the pride of sin.
Its mad profaneness from my bosom;
For her sake I went forth a pilgrim,
To reconcile offended Heaven;
She who with tears for me had pleaded
Should know my sins had been forgiven.
When I beheld a heavy burden'd pilgrim
It seemed to me his load was all too light;
And if he sought a pathway o'er the meadow
I trod unshod amid the rock and thorns;
If he refreshed his lips by cooling fountain,
The brazen sun poured on my head forlorn;
When he besought the saints in murmured
prayers,
I shed my life-blood in the cause divine;
When in the hospice he sought rest and shelter,
On ice and snow it was that I sought mine;
Lest Italy's fair scenes my heart had gladdened,
I passed them blindfold, so my soul was
saddened;
I went, my wasted heart remorse was burning,
That for my sake an angel waited mourning.

DRITTE SCENE

Tann. Ich hörte Harfenschlag,—wie klang er traurig!
Der kam wohl nicht von ihr.—

Wolf. Wer bist du, Pilger,
Der du so einsam wanderst?

Tann.   Wer ich bin?
Kenn' ich doch dich recht gut;—Wolfram bist
du,
Der wohlgeübte Sänger.

Wolf.   Heinrich! du!
Was bringt dich her in diese Nähe?
Sprich!
Wagst du es, unentsündigt wohl den Fuss
Nach dieser Gegend hinzulenken?

Tann. Sei ausser Sorg' mein guter Sänger!—
Nicht such' ich dich, noch eurer Sippschaft
Einen.
Doch such' ich wen, der mir den Weg wohl zeige,
Den Weg, den einst so wunderleicht ich fand.

Wolf. Und welchen Weg?
Tann.   Den Weg zum Venusberg!
Wolf. Entsetzlicher! Entweihe nicht mein Ohr!
Treibt es dich dahin?

Tann.   Kennst du wohl den Weg?
Wolf. Wahnsinn'ger! Grauen fasst mich, hör ich dich?
Wo war'st du! Sag' zogst du denn nicht nach
Rom?

Tann. Schweig mir von Rom!
Wolf. War'st nich beim heil'gen Feste?
Tann. Schweig mir von ihm!
Wolf. So war'st du nicht?—Sag', ich
Beschwöre dich!

Tann. Wohl war auch ich in Rom.
Wolf. So sprich! Erzähle mir, Unglücklicher!
Mich fasst ein tiefes Mitleid für dich an.

Tann. Wie sag'st du, Wolfram? Bist du nicht mein
Feind?

Wolf. Nie war ich es, so lang' ich fromm dich
wähnte!—
Doch sprich! Du pilgertest nach Rom?

Tann. Wohl denn!
Hör' an! Du, Wolfram, du sollst es erfahren.
Bleib' fern von mir! Die Stätte, wo ich raste,
Ist verflucht! Hör' an, Wolfram, hör an!
Inbrunst im Herzen, wie kein Büsser noch
Sie je gefühlt, sucht' ich den Weg nach Rom.
Ein Engel hatte, ach! der Sünde Stolz
Dem Uebermüthigen entwunden!
Für ihn woll't ich in Demuth büssen,
Das Heil erfleh'n, das mir vernein't,
Um ihn die Thräne zu versüssen,
Die er mir Sünder einst geweint!
Wie neben mir der schwerstbedrückte Pilger
Die Strasse wallt', erschien mir allzuleicht;
Betrat sein Fuss den weichen Grund der Wiesen,
Der nackten Sohle sucht' sie Dorn und Stein;—
Liess Labung er am Quell den Mund geniessen
Sog' ich der Sonne heisses Glühen ein!—
Wenn fromm zum Himmel er Gebete schickte,
Vergoss mein Blut ich zu des Höchsten Preis;
Als der Hospiz die Wanderer erquickte,
Die Glieder bettet' ich in Schnee und Eis,
Verschloss'nen Aug's, ihr Wunder nicht zu
schauen,
Durchzog ich blind Italiens holde Auen.
Ich that's—denn in Zerknirschung wollt' ich
büssen
Um meines Engels Thränen zu versüssen!

Thus Rome I gained at last; with tears
  imploring,
I knelt before the rood in faith adoring.
When daylight broke, the silv'ry bells were
  pealing;
Through vaulted roof a song divine was stealing;
A cry of joy breaks forth from thousand voices—
The hope of pardon ev'ry heart rejoices.
There him I saw who holds the keys of Heav'n,
And prostrate fell they all before his face.
And thousands he forgave that day, and bless'd
  them,
And sent them forth, renew'd in heav'nly grace.
Then I drew near, my glances earthward
  bending;
I made my plaint, despair my bosom rending—
I told what mad desires my soul had darkened,
By sinful earthly pleasure long enslav'd—
To me it seem'd that he in mercy hearken'd—
A gracious word in dust and tears I crav'd.
Then he whom thus I prayed replied:
"If thou has shar'd the joys of Hell,
If thou unholy flames hast nurs'd
That in the hill of Venus dwell,
Thou art for evermore accurs'd!
And as this barren staff I hold
Ne'er will put forth a flow'r or leaf,
Thus shalt thou never more behold
Salvation or thy sin's relief!"
Then hopeless, dumb despair obscur'd my senses!
I sank down motionless. When I awoke
'Twas night, and I alone, by all forsook.
I heard afar the songs of praise and prayer:
With loathing I fled t' escape the sound.
What were to me the tidings of their joy,
An outcast, spurn'd, in whom all hope was dead?
With horror in my breast, I turn'd and fled.
Then long'd my soul those joys to taste again
Which once before my earthborn pains had slain.
To thee, fair Venus, I surrender—
Let thy sweet magic round me play;
I'll be thy slave, thou star of splendor:
Thou only canst these pangs allay!

Wolf. Oh, stay thy godless raving!

Tann. Oh, guide my steps that I may find thee:
How well erewhile the road I knew!
Behold! men have with curses spurn'd me—
Come, lovely goddess, guide me true!

Wolf. Thou godless one! Whom dost thou call?

Tann. Ah! dost thou not feel balmy breezes?

Wolf. Away! Oh, fly, or thou art lost!

Tann. My senses what ecstasy seizes!
Hear'st thou not rapturous music?

Wolf. O wert thou rather in thy grave!

Tann. In mazy dance the nymphs now are flying—
Come on—come on! Ye fair, come on, receive
  your slave!

Wolf. Woe? evil demons fill the air
That hell its victim may ensnare!

Tann. Oh, come on Pleasure's rosy pinion!
I feel thy breath ambrosial!
This is of love the sweet dominion—
Oh, Venus, on thee I will call!

Venus. I welcome thee, perfidious man;
Earth laid thee low beneath its ban.
Hast thou by all, then, been forsaken
In my arms blissfully to waken?

Tann. Sweet Venus, oh, in bliss receive me!
With thee, with thee, oh, let me fly!

Wolf. Ye hellish phantoms, leave him!
All hope is lost when ye are nigh!

Venus. Com'st thou on grace from me relying?
Thy rash resolve I will forgive,

Nach Rom gelangt' ich so zur heil'gen Stelle,
Lag betend auf des Heiligthumes Schwelle;
Der Tag brach an:—da läuteten die Glocken,
Hernieder tönten himmlische Gesänge;
Da jauchzt' es auf in brünstigem Frohlocken,
Denn Gnad' un Heil verhiessen sie der Men,
Da sah' ich ihn, durch den sich Gott verkündi
Vor ihm all' Volk im Staub sich niederliess;
Und Tausenden er Gnade gab, entsündigt
Er Tausende sich froh erheben hiess.
Da naht' auch ich; das Haupt gebeugt zur Er
Klagt' ich mich an jammernder Geberde
Der bösen Lust, die meine Sinn' empfanden,
Des Sehnens, das kein Büssen noch gekühlt;
Und um Erlösung aus den heissen Banden
Rief ich ihn an, von wildem Schmerz dur
  wühlt.—
Und er, den so ich bat, hub an:
"Hast du so böse Lust getheilt,
Dich an der Hölle Glut entflammt,
Hast du im Venusberg geweilt:
So bist nun ewig du verdammt;
Wie dieser Stab in meiner Hand
Nie mehr sich schmückt mit frischem Grün,
Kann aus der Hölle heissem Brand
Erlösung nimmer dir erblüh'n!"
Da sank ich in Vernichtung dumpf darnied
Die Sinne schwanden mir.—Als ich erwacht,
Auf odem Platze lagerte die Nacht,—
Von fern her tönten frohe Gnadenlieder—
Da ekelte mich der holde Sang,——
Von der Verheissung lügnerischem Klang,
Der eiseskalt mir durch die Seele schnitt,
Trieb Grauen mich hinweg mit wildem Schr
Dahin zog's mich, wo ich der Wonn' und L
So viel genoss an ihrer warmen Brust!
    Zu dir, frau Venus, kehr' ich wieder,
    In deiner Zauber holde Nacht,
    Zu deinem Hof steig' ich darnieder,
    Wo nun dein Reiz mir ewig lacht!

Wolf. Halt' ein! Halt' ein, Unseliger!

Tann. Ach, lass mich nicht vergebens suchen,
Wie leicht fand ich doch einstens dich!
Du hörst, dass mir die Menschen fluchen,
Nun, süsse Göttin, leite mich!

Wolf. Wahnsinniger, wen rufst du an?

Tann. Ha! fühlest du nicht milde Lüfte?

Wolf. Zu mir! Es ist um dich gethan!

Tann. Und athmest du nicht holde Düfte?
Hörst du nicht die jubelnden Klänge?

Wolf. In wildem Schauer bebt die Brust!

Tann. Das ist der Nymphen tanzende Menge.—
Herbei, herbei zu Wonn' und Lust!

Wolf. Weh, böser Zauber thut sich auf!
Die Hölle naht in wildem Lauf.

Tann. Entzücken dringt durch alle Sinne,
Gewahr' ich diesen Dämmerschein;
Dies ist das Zauberreich der Minne,
In Venusberg drangen wir ein!

Venus. Willkommen, ungetreuer Mann?
Schlug dich die Welt mit Acht und Bann?
Und findest nirgends du Erbarmen,
Suchst Liebe nun in meinen Armen?

Tann. Frau Venus, o, Erbarmungsreiche!
Zu dir, zu dir zieht es mich hin!

Wolf. Du Höllenzauber, weiche, weiche!
Berücke nicht des Reinen Sinn!

Venus. Nahst du dich wieder meiner Schwelle,
Sei dir dein Uebermuth verzeihn;

Come where joy is fed from source undying.
In pleasure's bright abode to live.

nn. Accurs'd of hope they have bereft me;
Now joys of hell alone are left me,

olf. Oh, mighty Lord! in mercy see!
Henry, one word and thou art free—
Repent!

nus.   O come belov'd!
For ever thou art mine.

nn. No more. Away from me!

olf. Yet canst thou gain thy soul's salvation.

nn. No, Wolfram, no; the Heavens are closed!

olf. It hears an angel's supplication,
Who now for thee its grace implores—
Elisabeth!

nn. Oh, maid divine!

orus of men.
Receive the soul, oh, bounteous Lord,
That now to Thee hath taken flight.

olf. Thy angel prays for thee before the throne,
And Heaven relents!
Henry, thou art absolv'd!

nus. Woe! I have lost him?

orus of men.
Hers be the angels' blest reward!
Bright be her glory in Thy sight!

olf. Oh, say, hear'st thou this strain?

nn. I hear it.

orus of Men.
Sainted forever thro' all the spheres,
She who thro' love thy salvation attain'd.
Blest is the sinner sav'd by her tears,
Now he the heav'nly gate hath gain'd

nn. Holy Saint Elisabeth, oh, pray for me!

olf. He is redeemed.

orus of Pilgrims.
The Lord Himself now thy bondage hath riven—
Go, enter in with the blest in His Heaven.

Ewig fliesst dir der Freuden Quelle,
Und nimmer sollst du von mir fliehn!

Tann. Mein Heil, mein Heil hab' ich verloren,
Nun sei der Hölle Lust erkoren!

Wolf. All mächt'ger, steh' dem Frommen bei!—
Heinrich,—ein Wort, es macht dich frei:—
Dein Heil—

Venus. Zu mir!
O komm! Auf ewig sei nun mein!

Tann.   Lass ab von mir!

Wolf. Noch soll das Heil dir Sünder werden.

Tann. Nie! Wolfram, nie! Ich muss dahin!

Wolf. Ein Engel bat für dich auf Erden—
Bald schwebt er segnend über dir,
Elisabeth!

Tann.   Elisabeth!

Pilger. Der Seele Heil, die nun entfloh'n
Dem Leib der frommen Dulderin!

Wolf. Dein Engel fleht für dich an Gottes Thron,
Er wird erhört! Heinrich, du bist erlöst!

Venus. Weh! Mir verloren!

Pilger. Ihr ward der Engel sel'ger Lohn,
Himmlischer Freuden Hochgewinn.

Wolf. Und hörst du diesen Sang?

Tann. Ich höre!

Pilger. Heilig die Reine, die nun vereint
Göttlicher Schaar vor dem Ewigen steht.
Selig der Sünder, dem sie geweint,
Dem sie des Himmels Heil erfleht!

Tann. Heilige Elisabeth, bitte für mich!

Wolf. Er ist erlöst!

Die Pilger.
Der Gnade Heil ward dem Büsser beschieden,
Er geht nun ein in der Seligen Frieden.

THE END

LOHENGRIN

HENRY I., King of Germany, surnamed the "Fowler," has arrived at Antwerp, with the intention of levying a force to assist in repelling the Hungarians, who have threatened his dominions with invasion. He finds Brabant in a state of anarchy. Godfrey, the young son of the late duke, has disappeared, and his sister Elsa is accused of murdering him by her guardian, Frederick, Count of Telramund, who has married Ortrud, daughter of Radbod, Prince of Friesland, and in right of his wife claims to be the ruler of the Duchy. Elsa, appearing before the King, asserts her innocence, and it is agreed that the cause should be decided by a judicial combat between Frederick and any champion who may appear on behalf of the accused. When her condition seems most hopeless, a knight appears ascending the river Scheldt, in a boat drawn by a single swan, which on landing he dismisses, and undertakes her defence, Elsa promising that if he is victorious she will bestow upon him her hand, and never question him as to his name or origin. In the combat that ensues Frederick is stricken to the ground by his unknown antagonist, and deprived of his title and estate.

Preparations are made for the immediate marriage of the stranger with Elsa; but while all are reveling in the Pallas, or abode of the knights, Frederick and Ortrud are without, plotting how they may be avenged and recover their lost honors. Presenting herself at the Kemenate or abode of the ladies, Ortrud moves the compassion of Elsa, who not only gains her admission, but promises to obtain the pardon of Frederick, and listens to the suggestion that she ought to inquire into the name and origin of her future husband, who, without the ducal title, has been appointed by the King, Protector of Brabant and leader of the Brabant contingent of the German army. As the nuptial procession approaches the cathedral, the conspirators reveal themselves in their true character, Ortrud opposing Elsa at the door, and Frederick declaring that the unknown knight, Lohengrin, is a sorcerer, who has gained his victory by unfair and unholy means.

The intruders are expelled by the King and people, and the marriage takes place; but, when the bride and bridegroom are left in the nuptial chamber, Elsa, roused by the evil suggestions of Ortrud, begins, in spite of her promise, to question the knight, who in vain endeavors to allay her suspicions. Frederick, who enters the room with the intention of assailing his former antagonist, is slain by him at once, and, on the following morning, the explanation unwisely solicited by Elsa, is given by the stranger in the presence of the King. He is the son of King Percival, keeper of the mysterious cup known as the "Holy Grail," to whose service he is attached, and whose name is Lohengrin. It is to the Grail that he is indebted for his invisible power, but now his name is revealed he must no longer remain in Brabant. The swan returns with the boat to bear him away, but he removes a gold chain from its neck, and in its stead appears the youth Godfrey, who has been changed to a swan by the sorceress Ortrud, and who is now declared rightful Duke of Brabant, while Lohengrin departs, to the intense grief of his bride and the King and people who have lost so valuable an ally.

LOHENGRIN

ACT I

SCENE I

[*A meadow on the banks of the Scheldt, by Antwerp,* KING HENRY *under the Oak of Justice, surrounded by Counts and Nobles of the Saxon Arriere-ban. Opposite to them the Counts and Nobles of Brabant, headed by* FREDERICK *of Telramund, with* ORTRUD *by his side. The Herald steps from the party of the King to the centre of the stage, and signs for the four Royal Trumpeters to play the call to muster.*

HERALD. Hark! Princes, nobles, freemen of Brabant!
    Henry, our German Sov'reign, calls ye forth
    This day to muster for the realm's defence.
    Will ye, as faithful vassals, serve your King?

MEN OF BRABANT.
    We will, as faithful vassals, serve our King.
    Be welcome, Henry, to Brabant!

KING. Heav'n shield ye, loyal lieges of Brabant!
    Not idly have I journeyed to your shores;
    I come to warn that danger is at hand.
    Ye know full well the tide of death and ruin
    That oft hath from the east swept o'er the land
    Upon our frontiers pray the wives and children
    "Lord, from th' Hungarian hordes protect our
        hearths!"
    For me, the nation's guardian, it was fitting
    To put an end to misrule and oppression.
    As conqueror, at last I gained a nine years'
        truce.
    That time I used to arm the land;
    With walls and towers I fortified the towns.
    And now against the foe I summon you. .
    The term is just o'erpast; the foe prepares;
    The wonted tribute I refuse to pay.
    Now is the time to guard our nation's honor.
    From east and west, all men of German blood
    Arise united; knights, your thralls assemble—
    No man shall dare deride my sov'reign rule.

SAXONS AND THURINGIANS. (*Striking their arms.*)
    'Tis well; we'll guard our German land!

KING. (*Reseating himself.*)
    Thus have I sought ye, freemen of Brabant
    To summon you to Mentz, nobles and vassals;
    Here, to my grief, I meet with nought but strife,
    All in disunion, from your chiefs estranged!
    Confusion, civil warfare meet we here.
    On thee I call, Frederick of Telramund!
    I know thee for a knight as brave as true,
    I charge thee, let me know this trouble's cause.

FRED. Thanks, gracious King, that thou to judge art
       come!
    The truth I'll tell thee, falsehood I disdain.
    When death was closing round our valiant Duke,
    'Twas me he chose as guardian of his children,

ERSTER AKT

ERSTE SCENE

[*Eine Aue am Ufer der Schelde bei Antwerpen. Kö* HEINRICH *unter der Gerichtseiche; zu seiner Se Grafen und Edle vom sächsischen Heerbann. Geg ülber brabantische Grafen und Edle an ihrer Sp* FRIEDRICH *von Telramund, zu dessen Seite* ORTR *Der Heerrufer ist aus des* KÖNIGS *Heerbann in Mitte geschritten; auf sein Zeichen blasen vier Tr peter des* KÖNIGS *den Aufruf.*

DER HEERRUFER. Hört! Grafen, Edle, Freie von Braba
    Heinrich, der Deutschen König, kam zur Sta
    Mit euch zu dingen nach des Reiches Recht
    Gebt ihr nun Fried' und Folge dem Gebot?

DIE BRABANTER.
    Wir geben Fried' und Folge dem Gebot.
    Willkommen! Willkommen! König, in Braba

KÖNIG HEINRICH.
    Gott grüss' euch, liebe Männer von Brabant!
    Nicht müssig that zu euch ich diese Fahrt;
    Der Noth des Reiches seid von mir gemahnt
    Soll ich euch erst der Drangsal Kunde sage
    Die deutsches Land so oft aus Osten traf?
    In fernster Mark hiess't Weib und Kind
       beten:
    "Herr Gott, bewahr' uns vor der Ungarn Wut
    Doch mir, des Reiches Haupt, musst' es ge
       men,
    Solch wilder Schmach ein Ende zu ersinnen
    Als Kampfes Preis gewann ich Frieden auf
    Neun Jahr' ihn nütz' ich zu des Reiches We
    Beschirmte Städt' und Burgen liess ich ba
    Den Heerbann übte ich zum Widerstand.
    Zu End' ist nun die Frist, der Zins versagt,
    Mit wildem Drohen rüstet sich der Feind.
    Nun ist es Zeit des Reiches Ehr, zu wahren
    Ob Ost, ob West, das gelte Allen gleich!
    Was deutsches Land heisst, stelle Kamp
       schaaren,
    Dann schmäht wohl Niemand mehr das deuts
       Reich!

DIE SACHSEN UND THÜRINGER.
    Mit Gott wohlauf für deutshen Reiches Ehr'

KÖNIG. Komm' ich zu euch nun, Männer von Brab
    Zur Heeresfolg' nach Mainz euch zu entbiet
    Wie muss mit Schmerz und Klagen ich erse
    Dass ohne Fürsten ihr in Zwietracht lebt!
    Verwirrung, wilde Fehde wird mir kund;
    Drum ruf' ich dich als aller Tugend Preis,
    Jetzt rede, dass der Drangsal Grund ich we

FRIED. Dank, König, dir, dass du zu richten kamst
    Die Wahrheit künd' ich, Untreu ist mir fre
    Zum Sterben kam der Herzog von Brabant,
    Und meinem Schutz empfahl er seine Kinde

ED. Elsa the maiden, and Gottfried her brother;
Whose dawning years with tender care I guarded
Whose welfare I have treasured as my honor
My sov'reign, mark now, if I'm aggrieved,
When of my honor's treasure I am robbed!
One day, when Elsa had with her brother
wandered forth,
Without the boy, trembling, she returned,
With feign'd lamenting, questioned of his safety,
Pretending she had been from him divided,
And in vain his traces she had sought.
Fruitless was every search we made to find him;
And when I questioned her with words severe,
Her pallor and her falt'ring tongue betray'd her,
Her crime in its guilty blackness stood confess'd
A horror fell upon me of the maid;
The claim upon her hand her father had
conferr'd
With willing heart I straight resigned,
And chose a wife full pleasant to my sense,
Ortrud, daughter of Radbod, true in death.
I here arraign her, Princess Elsa of Brabant;
Of fratricide be she charged.
I claim dominion o'er this land by right;
My nearest kinsman was the valiant duke,
My wife descendent of the race   [past
That gave this land their rulers thro' long ages
O king, give judgment! All now thou hast heard

LL THE MEN.
Ha! Telramund, what hast thou said?
I mark thee with dismay and dread!

ING. A dreadful accusation thou hast brought,
A crime so deadly, how can I believe?

RED. O king, listless and dreamy is the maid,
She who with scorn refused my proffer'd hand.
Some secret love her senses hath beguil'd; [ished
She deemed perchance, because the boy had per-
She'd reign secure as sov'reign of Brabant;
For that, her vassal she disdained as consort,
That openly she might her lover cherish.

ING. Summon the maid accused;
For judgment let all be prepared!
Heaven, let me deem aright!

ERALD. Dost thou decree, O king, to have a judgment
here?

ING. I will not rest beneath my shield
Until the truth hath been revealed!

LL THE MEN. No sword to scabbard shall return
Until thy will, O King, we learn.

ERALD. Where'er the royal shield ye see,
Know that the king doth there decree;
Resound, my cry, both far and near:
Elsa, thou royal maid, appear!

SCENE II

LSA *enters; she remains some time at the back of the
stage; then she slowly and very timidly comes forward
to the front (centre). The ladies of her train remain
during the first part of the scene in the extreme background, outside the circle where justice is given.*

LL THE MEN.
Behold! she comes, how grief o'er clouds her!
How like an angel of light her hue!
He who with base suspicion loads her
Must prove his dark surmise is true.

FRIED. Elsa, die Jungfrau, und Gottfried, den Knaben;
Mit Treue pfleg ich seiner grossen Jugend,
Sein Leben war das Kleinod meiner Ehre.
Ermiss nun König meinen grimmen Schmerz,
Als meiner Ehre Kleinod mir geraubt!
Lustwandelnd führte Elsa den Knaben einst
Zum Wald, doch ohne ihn kehrte sie zurück;
Mit falscher Sorge frug sie nach dem Bruder,
Da sie, von ohngefähr von ihm verirrt,
Bald seine Spur—so sprach sie—nicht mehr
fand.
Fruchtlos war all' Bemüh'n um den Verlor'nen!
Als ich mit Drohen nun in Elsa drang,
Da liess in bleichem Zagen und Erbeben
Der grässlichen Schuld Bekenntniss sie uns sehn.
Es fasste mich Entsetzen vor der Magd:
Dem Recht auf ihre Hand, vom Vater mir
Verliehn, entsagt' ich willig da und gern,—
Und nahm ein Weib, das meinem Sinn gefiel,
Ortrud, Radbod's, des Friesenfürsten, Spross.
Nun führ ich Klage wider Elsa von
Brabant: des Brudermordes zeih' ich sie.
Dies Land doch sprech' ich für mich an mit
Recht,
Da ich der Nächste von des Herzog's Blut,
Mein Weib jedoch aus dem Geschlecht, das
einst
Auch diesem Lande seine Fürsten gab.
Du hörst die Klage, König! Richte recht!

ALLE MÄNNER.
Ha! Schwerer Schuld zeiht Telramund!
Mit Grau'n werd' ich der Klage kund.

KÖNIG. Welch' fürchterliche Klage sprichst du aus!
Wie wäre möglich solche grosse Schuld?

FRIED. O Herr, traumselig ist die eitle Magd,
Die meine Hand voll Hochmuth von sich stiess
Geheimer Buhlschaft klag' ich drum sie an:
Sie wähnte wohl, wenn sie des Bruders ledig,
Dann könnte sie als Herrin von Brabant,
Mit Recht dem Lehnsmann ihre Hand
verwehren,
Und offen des geheimen Buhlen pflegen.

KÖNIG. Ruft die Beklagte her! Beginnen soll
Nun das Gericht! Gott lass' mich weise sein!

DER HEERRUFER. Soll hier nach Recht und Macht Gericht gehalten sein?

KÖNIG. Nicht eh'r soll bergen mich der Schild,
Bis ich gerichtet streng und mild!

ALLE MÄNNER.
Nicht eh'r zur Scheide kehr' das Schwert
Bis ihm durch Urtheil Recht gewährt!

HEERRUFER. Wo ihr des Königs Schild gewahrt,
Dort Recht durch Urtheil nun erfahrt!
Drum ruf' ich klagend laut und hell:
Elsa, erscheine hier zur Stell'!

ZWEITE SCENE

[ELSA *tritt langsam und verschämt auf; ein langer Zug
ihrer Frauen folgt ihr, sich zunächst an der äusserster.
Grenze des Gerichtskreises im Hintergrunde haltend.*

ALLE MÄNNER.
Seht hin! Sie naht, die hart Beklagte!
Ha, wie erscheint sie so licht und rein!
Der sie so schwer zu zeihen wagte,
Gar sicher muss der Schuld er sein.

KING. Art thou she, Elsa of Brabant?
Wilt thou be deemed by me, thy sov'reign Lord?
Then further I ask thee
If the charge to thee is known,
That darkly is alleged against thee?
Canst thou meet the accusation?

* * * *

KING. Then thy guilt thou dost confess?

ELSA. Oh, my poor brother!
ALL THE MEN. 'Tis wondrous strange—
Her words I cannot fathom.
KING. Speak, Elsa; in thy king thou may'st confide.

KÖNIG. Bist du es, Elsa von Brabant? Erkennst
Du mich als deinen Richter an? So frage
Ich weiter: ist die Klage dir bekannt,
Die schwer hier wider dich erhoben? Was
Entgegnest du der Klage?

* * * *

KÖNIG.   So bekenn
du deine Schuld?
ELSA. Mein armer Bruder!
ALLE MÄNNER. Wie wunderbar! Welch seltsames
Gebaren!
KÖNIG. Sag', Elsa! Was hast du mir zu vertrau'n?

OFT WHEN THE HOURS WERE LONELY.

ING AND ALL THE MEN.
 Oh, Heaven, in mercy be thou near,
  This day make truth from error clear!

ING. Frederick, bethink thee, while there's time,
  Could she enact so foul a crime?

RED. Her dreamy mood my mind hath ne'er deceiv'd
 Ye hear, she raves about a lover!
 I speak the truth, of that I'm well assur'd
 One do I know who can the deed attest.
 But if ye doubt my word as knight and noble
 No further proof or witness will I deign!
 For battle here I stand!
 Who dares attaint my honor—
 Let that man stand forth and fight!

HE BRABANTIANS. I am thy friend. I will not fight
 with thee.

RED. And thou, my king, recall to thy remembrances
 The day I saved thee from the murd'rous Dane?

ING. 'Twere ill if there were need of that to mind me!
 Thou'rt brave and true, all honors need be thine,
 As guardian of this land I'd fain appoint thee,
 Thou of my chiefs the noblest.
 Heav'n alone shall now for life or death decide
  between you!

LL THE MEN. A judgment of God! 'Tis well!

ING. Answer me, noble Count of Telramund:
 Wilt thou do battle here for life or death?
 Shall Heaven's ordeal decide if thou spok'st
  truly?

RED. Yea!

ING. And now I ask thee, Elsa of Brabant:
 Wilt thou count thy cause for life or death?
 As heaven's ordeal pronounceth, by thy cham-
  pion?

SA. Yea!

ING. Choose one who shall defend thee.

RD. Now ye shall know the name of her accomplice.

HE BRABANTIANS. Let us hear!

SA. My guardian, my defender,
  He shall my champion be!
 This is the prize I offer
  To him whom heaven shall send;
 The lands and crown I proffer,
  My sire to me did lend;
 As lord I will declare him,
  And glory in his fame,
 If in his heart he'll wear me
  I'll give him all I am!

LL THE MEN. A noble prize—who will the victor be?
 Who will contend? What will be Heaven's
  decree?

ING. The sun stands high; noon will not tarry.
 Call forth the warrior knights with trumpet's
  call!

*The Herald stands forward with the four Trumpeters
whom he places towards the four points of the compass at the extreme end of the circle, where they blow
the summons.*

ERALD. Who will do battle here on life or death
 For Elsa of Brabant, let him appear!

DER KÖNIG UND ALLE MÄNNER.
 Bewahre uns des Himmels Huld,
 Das klar wir sehen wer hier schuld!

KÖNIG. Friedrich, du ehrenwerther Mann,
 Bedenke wohl, wen klagst du an?

FRIED. Ihr hört, sie schwärmt von einem Buhlen!
 Wes' ich sie zeih' des' hab' ich sich'ren Grund:
 Glaubwürdig ward ihr Frevel mir bezeugt.
 Doch eurem Zweifel durch ein Zeugniss wehren,
 Das stünde wahrlich übel meinem Stolz!
 Hier steh' ich, hier mein Schwert! Wer wagt's
  von euch,
 Zu streiten wider meiner Ehre Preis?

DIE BRABANTISCHEN EDLEN.
 Keiner von uns! Wir streiten nur für dich.

FRIED. Und König, du! Gedenkst du meiner Dienste,
 Wie ich im Kampf den wilden Dänen schlug?

KÖNIG. Wie schlimm, liess' ich von dir daran mich
  mahnen:
 Gern geb' ich dir der höchsten Tugend Preis.
 In keiner and'ren Huth, als in der deinen,
 Möcht' ich die Lande wissen.
 Gott allein soll jetzt in dieser Sache noch ent-
  scheiden!

ALLE MÄNNER. Zum Gottesgericht! Zum Gottesgericht!
 Wohlan!

KÖNIG. Dich frag' ich, Friedrich, Graf von Telramund!
 Willst du durch Kampf auf Leben und auf Tod
 Im Gottesgericht vertreten deine Klage?

FRIED. Ja!

KÖNIG. Und dich nun frag' ich, Elsa von Brabant!
 Willst du, dass hier auf Leben und auf Tod
 Im Gottesgericht ein Kämpe für dich streite?

ELSA. Ja!

KÖNIG. Wen kiesest du zum Streiter?

FRIED. Vernehmet jetzt den namen ihres **Buhlen!**

DIE BRABANTISCHEN EDLEN. Merket auf!

ELSA. Des Ritters will ich wahren,
  Er soll mein Streiter sein!
 Hört was dem Gottgesandten
 Ich biete führ Gewähr:—
 In meines Vaters Landen
  Die Krone trage er;
 Mich glücklich soll ich preisen,
  Nimmt er mein Gut dahin,—
 Will er Gemahl mich heissen,
  Geb' ich ihm was ich bin!

DIE MÄNNER. Ein hoher Preis stünd' er in Hand!
 Wer um ihn stritt', wohl setzt' er schweres
  Pfand.

KÖNIG. Im Mittag hoch steht schon die Sonne;
 So ist es Zeit, dass nun der Ruf ergeh'.

*[Tritt mit vier Trompetern vor, die er, den Himmels-
gegenden zugewendet, an die äussersten Grenzen des
Gerichtskreises schreiten und blasen lässt.*

DIE HEERRUFER.
 Wer hier im Gotteskampf zu streiten kam
 Für Elsa von Brabant, der trete vor!

ALL THE MEN.
No champion to the call comes forth!
Ah, hapless maiden, hope resign!

FRED. Ye see what now her cause is worth,
Both right and power are justly mine!

ELSA. My gracious sov'reign, let me pray thee
Yet once again my knight to summon.
He dwells afar and heareth not.

THE KING. Once more, then, let the call go forth.

ALL THE MEN.
The heav'ns are silent, she is doomed!

ELSA. When in my grief I bent before Thee,
Thou sentest him who hath my vow;
Oh, Lord, hear me again implore Thee!
In my distress, oh, send him now!
Stainless and white, radiantly dight,
Let me behold that form of light!

CHORUS OF LADIES. Lord! Let Thy help be nigh!
Hear us, gracious Lord!

CHORUS OF MEN.

[*Standing nearest to the water's edge; they first perceive
the coming of* LOHENGRIN, *who is seen in the distance
approaching in a skiff drawn by a swan.*

Look! this is sure a marvel! see, a swan—
A fair swan, leading yonder pinnace on!
And lo, a knight,
A warrior full fair, standing on the prow!
Ha! his arms resplendent gleam!
A helm of light upon his brow!
Look there! he comes nearer, he hath gained
the shore,
And with a chain of gold the swan he reins:
Behold, he comes! Lo, he comes!

SCENE III

BOTH CHORUSES OF MEN.
A marvel wrought amongst us—
A great unheard-of marvel; yes, a marvel.

THE LADIES.
Thanks, oh, gracious Lord!
Thou our prayer hast granted.
All hail, thou hero from on high!
Be thou welcome, Heav'n itself sent thee here!
Yes Heav'n hath sent thee here!

[*The* KING *from his raised seat sees everything;* FREDER-
ICK *and* ORTRUD *are petrified with surprise and dread;*
ELSA, *who has listened to the previous exclamations
with rising delight, remains in her place in the centre
of the stage, as though she dared not look round. Here
the skiff drawn by the swan, reaches the shore in
the centre of the stage;* LOHENGRIN, *in a silver coat of
mail, with a shining helmet, his shield at his back a
little golden horn at his side, stands within it, leaning
on his sword.* FREDERICK *gazes on* LOHENGRIN *in
speechless amazement.* ORTRUD, *who during the pro-
ceeding had preserved a cold and haughty bearing, is
seized by a terrible consternation at the sight of the
swan. All deferentially bare their heads. Here* ELSA
has turned round and gives a cry of joy at the sight of
LOHENGRIN. *As* LOHENGRIN *moves to step out of the
skiff, all are silent in rapt expectancy.*

ALLE MÄNNER.
Ohn' Antwort ist der Ruf verhallt;
Um ihre Sache steht es schlecht.

FRIED. Gewahrt, ob ich sie fälschlich schalt?
Auf meiner Seite bleibt das Recht.

ELSA. Mein lieber König, lass dich bitten,
Noch einen Ruf an meinen Ritter!
Wohl weilt er fern und hört' ihn nicht.

KÖNIG. Noch einmal rufe zum Gericht!

ALLE MÄNNER. In düst'rem Schweigen richtet Gott.

ELSA. Du trugest zu ihm meine Klage,
Zu mir trat er auf dein Gebot:
O Herr, nun meinem Ritter sage,
Dass er mir helf' in meiner Noth!
Lass mich ihn sehn, wie ich ihn sah,
Wie ich ihn sah, sei er mir nah!

CHOR DER FRAUEN.
Herr! Sende Hülfe ihr!
Herr Gott, höre uns!

DIE MÄNNER.

[*Die auf einer Erhöhung dem Ufer am nächsten Stehe
den gewahren in der Ferne einen Nachen, von ein
Schwan gezogen, auf dem Flusse allmählich sich n
hern; in dem Nachen steht ein Ritter.*

Seht! Seht! Welch seltsam Wunder!
Wie? Ein Schwan?
Ein Schwan zieht einen Nachen dort heran!—
Ein Ritter drin hoch aufgerichtet steht!
Wie glänzt sein Waffenschmuck! Das Au
vergeht
Vor solchem Licht!—Seht, näher kommt
schon heran!
An einer goldnen Kette zieht der Schwan!

DRITTE SCENE

ALLE MÄNNER.
Ein Wunder! ein Wunder! ein Wunder i
gekommen!

DIE FRAUEN. Ha, unerhörtes, nie geseh'nes Wunder!
Gegrüsst, gegrüsst du gottgesandter Mann!
Dank, du Herr und Gott, der du die Schwac
beschirmet!
Sei gegrüsst du gottgesandter Mann!

[*Von seinem Platze aus übersieht der* KÖNIG *Alles.* FRI
RICH *und* ORTRUD *durch Schreck und Staunen g
fesselt.* ELSA, *in steigender Entzückung lauscher
wagt nicht umzublicken. Aller Augen wenden sich
wartungsvoll nach dem Hintergrunde.* LOHENGRIN,
*glänzender Silberrüstung, den Helm auf dem Haup
den Schild im Rücken, ein kleines goldenes Ho
zur Seite, steht auf sein Schwert gelehnt im Kal
FRIEDERICH *blickt in sprachlosem Erstaunen auf i
hin;* ORTRUD, *bisher in kalter, stolzer Haltung, gerä
bei des Schwanes Anblick in tödtlichen Schrec
Alles entblösst in höchster Ergriffenheit das Hau
ELSA, *sich wendend. schreit bei* LOHENGRIN'S *Anbli
laut auf. Sowie* LOHENGRIN *Bewegung macht den Ka
zu verlassen, gespanntestes Schweigen.*

I GIVE THEE THANKS, MY GENTLE SWAN.

LOHENGRIN.

I give thee thanks, my faith-ful swan! Turn thee a gain and breast.... the tide, Re
turn un-to that land of dawn Where joy-ous we did long...... a-bide
Well thy ap-point-ed task.... is done! Farewell! farewell! my trus-ty swan!

Chorus. pp

Doth he not seem...... from Heav'n descend-ed; His ra-diant
mien holds me enthrall'd! Val-or and grace in him are blend-ed, To deeds of glo-ry he is
call'd! Va-lor and grace in him are blend-ed, To deeds of glo-ry he is call'd!
Oh! sweet enchant-ment! Oh, sweet en-chant-ment! won-drous love! Deep in.... my
heart the spell I prove, Splen-dor di-vine.... a-round them plays!

pp

Splen-dor...... di-vine,.......... a-round their tress-es plays!

LOHENGRIN. Hail gracious sov'reign! Victory and honor be thy valor's meed! Thy glorious name shall from the land That chose thee ruler, ne'er depart.	LOHENGRIN. Heil König Heinrich! Segenvoll Mög' Gott bei deinem Schwerte steh'n! Ruhmreich und gross dein Name soll Von dieser Erde nie vergehn?
KING. Have thanks! Methinks I know the pow'r That sent thee here in this dread hour; On Heaven's mission thou art come.	KÖNIG. Hab' Dank! Erkenn' ich recht die Macht, Die dich in dieses Land gebracht, So kommst du uns von Gott gesandt?
LOHENGRIN. I came for yonder maid to fight, From dark surmise her name to clear: In quarrel true to guard her right, Who now my proffered vow shall hear! I ask thee, Elsa of Brabant, If thou the boon to me wilt grant As thy champion to fight this day— Wilt thou entrust thy cause to me?	LOHENGRIN. Zum Kampf für eine Magd zu steh'n, Der schwere Klage angethan. Bin ich gesandt: nun lasst mich seh'n, Ob ich zurecht sie treffe an!— So sprich denn, Elsa von Brabant! Wenn ich zum Streiter dir ernannt, Willst du wohl ohne Bang' und Grau'n Dich meinem Schutze anvertrau'n?
ELSA. My hope, my solace, hero mine, Do thou protect me, I am thine!	ELSA. Mein Held, mein Retter! Nimm mich hin, Dir geb' ich Alles, was ich bin!

LOHENGRIN. If in thy cause to-day I conquer,
 Wilt thou empledge thy faith to me?

ELSA. As here I lowly bend before thee,
 Thine will I now and ever be.

LOHENGRIN.
 Elsa, if thou thy troth wilt plight me,
 If from the foe this land I save;
 If nought from me shall disunite thee,
 A promise I of thee must crave:
 Never, as thou dost love me,
 Aught shall to question move thee,
 From whence to thee I came,
 Or what my race and name.

ELSA. Lord, at thy will thou shalt command me

LOHENGRIN. Say dost thou understand me?
 Never, as thou dost love me,
 Aught shall to question move thee;
 From whence to thee I came,
 Or what my race and name.

ELSA. Oh, thou, my hero, my defender,
 No doubt of thee is in my heart;
 I life and faith to thee surrender—
 How could I question what thou art?
 As thou wilt guard my name and land,
 Thus will I cherish thy command.

LOHENGRIN. Elsa, I worship thee!

THE KING AND CHORUS.
 Oh, sweet enchantment!
 Some magic pow'r my senses sways,
 Oh, sweet enchantment, wondrous love!
 Deep in my heart thy spell I prove,
 A light divine around them plays!

LOHENGRIN.
 Ye knights, nobles, and freeman of this land
 Guiltless and true is Elsa of Brabant!
 Thy tale was falsehood, Count Telramund,
 By Heav'n's assistance all thou shalt recant!

THE BRABANTIANS.
 Refrain, refrain, the fight forego—
 Thou wilt but win distress and woe.
 Oh, be advised!
 If it is Heaven that sent him here,
 What will avail thy sword or spear?
 Refrain, refrain! I warn thee as a friend;
 Go not forth to-day,
 Or in disaster thou wilt end!

FRED. If I must fall, I'll die!
 What spells so'er have brought thee here,
 Stranger, who dost my sword defy?
 No cause have I thy threats to fear,
 For all is truth my words imply.
 Behold me prepar'd for the fray,
 If right prevails, I'll win the day.

LOHENGRIN.
 Great sov'reign, now ordain the fight!

THE KING. Upon each side three knights the space
  shall measure.
 I here proclaim this place a fencéd field.

[*Three Saxon nobles stand forth for* LOHENGRIN, *and
three Brabantians for* FREDERICK: *they cross the stage
with solemn strides and measure the ground for the
combat; when the six have formed a complete circle
they cross spears into the ground.*

LOHENGRIN. Wenn ich im Kampfe für dich siege,
 Willst du, das ich dein Gatte sei?

ELSA. Wie ich zu deinen Füssen liege,
 Geb' ich dir Leib und Seele frei.

LOHENGRIN. Elsa, soll ich dein Gatte heissen,
 Soll Land und Leut' ich schirmen dir,
 Soll nichts mich wieder von dir reissen,
 Musst Eines du geloben mir:
 Nie sollst du mich befragen,
 Noch Wissen's Sorge tragen,
 Woher ich kam der Fahrt,
 Noch wie mein Nam' und Art!

ELSA. Nie, Herr, soll mir die Frage kommen.

LOHENGRIN. Elsa! Hast du mich wohl vernommen
 Nie sollst du mich befragen,
 Noch Wissen's Sorge tragen,
 Woher ich kam der Fahrt,
 Noch wie mein Nam' und Art!

ELSA. Mein Schirm! mein Engel! mein Erlöser,
 Der fest an meine Unschuld glaubt!
 Wie gäb' es Zweifels Schuld, die grösser,
 Als die an dich den Glauben raubt?
 Wie du mich schirmst in meiner Noth,
 So halt' in Treu' ich dein Gebot.

LOHENGRIN. Elsa, ich liebe dich!

DER KÖNIG, DIE MÄNNER UND FRAUEN.
 Welche holde Wunder muss ich seh'n?
 Ist's Zauber der mir angethan?
 Ich fühl' das Herze mir verge'hn,
 Schau' ich den wonniglichen Mann.

LOHENGRIN.
 Nun hört! Euch Volk und Edlen mach' ich kun
 Frei aller Schuld ist Elsa von Brabant.
 Dass falsch dein Klagen, Graf von Telramun
 Durch Gottes Urtheil werd' es dir bekannt!

BRABANTISCHE EDLE.
 Steh' ab vom Kampf! Wenn du ihn wagst,
 Zu siegen nimmer du vermagst!
 Ist er von höchster Macht geschützt,
 Sag', was dein tapf'res Schwert dir nützt?
 Steh' ab! wir mahnen dich in Treu'!
 Dein harret Unsieg, bittre Reu'!

FRIED. Viel lieber todt als feig!—
 Welch' Zaubern dich auch hergeführt,
 Fremdling, der mir so kühn erscheint,
 Dein stolzes Droh'n mich nimmer rührt,
 Da ich zu lügen nie vermeint.
 Den Kampf mit dir drum nehm' ich auf,
 Und hoffe Sieg nach Rechtes Lauf!

LOHENGRIN. Nun, König, ord'ne unsern Kampf.

KÖNIG. So tretet vor, zu drei für jeden Kämpfer,
 Und messet wohl den Ring zum Streite ab!

[*Drei sächsische Edle treten für* LOHENGRIN, *drei brab
tische für* FRIEDRICH *vor: sie messen mit feierlich
Schritte den Kampfplatz aus und stecken ihn, ein
vollständigen Ring bildend, durch ihre Speere ab.*

HERALD.
All here attend, and mark me well:
The fight no man shall seek to quell!
Let none within th' inclosure stand.
Who hinders aught that may befall,
If freeman, straight sha'l lose his hand,
And his base head shall forfeit the thrall!

ALL THE MEN.
The freeman straight shall lose his hand,
And his base head shall forfeit the thrall!

HERALD.
Mark me, ye combatants of might!
In fair and open quarrel fight;
By magic arts ye shall not win—
That were the judgment to deride.
Prosper as ye are free from sin,
Not in yourselves, in Heav'n confide.

LOHENGRIN AND FREDERICK.
Judge me as I am free from sin!
Not in myself, in Heaven I bide!

DER HEERRUFER.
Nun höret mich, und achtet wohl:
Den Kampf hier Keiner stören soll!
Dem Hage bleibet abgewandt,
Denn wer nicht wahrt des Friedens Recht,
Der Freie büss' es mit der Hand,
Mit seinem Haupt büss' es der Knecht!

ALLE MÄNNER.
Der Freie büss es mit der Hand,
Mit seinem Haupt büss' es der Knecht!

DER HEERRUFER.
Hört auch, ihr Streiter vor Gericht!
Gewahrt in Treue Kampfespflicht!
Durch bösen Zaubers List und Trug
Stört nicht des Urtheils Eigenschaft!
Gott richtet euch nach Recht und Fug,
Drum trauet ihm, nicht eurer Kraft!

LOHENGRIN UND FRIEDRICH.
Gott richte mich nach Recht und Fug,
So trau' ich ihm, nicht Meiner Kraft!

OH KING OF KINGS, ON THEE I CALL.

THE KING.

Oh, King of kings, on Thee I call; Look down on us in this dread hour! Let him in this or-de-al fall, Whom Thou know'st guil-ty, Lord of pow'r! To stain-less knight give strength and might, With cra-ven heart the false one smite.... Do Thou, O Lord, to hear us deign, For all our wis-dom is but vain, For all our wis-dom is but vain.

ELSA AND LOHENGRIN.
Now, Lord, make known Thy just decree,
I have no fear, I trust in Thee!

ORTRUD. In his strong arm I trust alone,
That nor defeat nor fear hath known.

D. I here await thy just decree!
Great Lord, let not my honour tarnished be!

ELSA UND LOHENGRIN.
Du kündest nun dein wahr Gericht,
Mein Herr und Gott, drum zag, ich nicht!

ORTRUD. Ich baue fest auf seine Kraft,
Die, wo er kämpft, ihm Sieg verschafft.

FRIED. Ich geh' in Treu' vor dein Gericht!
Herr Gott, verlass' mein' Ehre nicht!

ALL THE MEN.
>To stainless knight give strength and might,
>With craven heart the false one smite,
>Now, Lord, make known Thy just decree,
>Protect the right—we trust in Thee!

THE LADIES.
>My gracious Lord! O bless Thy true knight!

[*In rapt excitement all resume their places, the six witnesses remain standing beside the spears of the inclosure, the other men form a wider circle round them, ELSA and her ladies in the foreground under the oak beside the KING. On a sign from the Herald, the Trumpeters blow the call to battle! LOHENGRIN and FREDERICK make final preparations. The KING draws his sword out of the ground and strikes it three times on the shield that hangs on the oak. First stroke: LOHENGRIN and FREDERICK step into the circle. Second stroke: they advance their shields and draw. Third stroke: they begin to fight. LOHENGRIN attacks. LOHENGRIN with a great stroke fells FREDERICK to the earth. FREDERICK tries to raise himself, staggers a few steps backwards, then falls.*

LOHENGRIN.
>Heav'n's behest to me has vict'ry lent;
>Thy life I spare: may'st thou in peace repent.

CHORUS. Hail! hail! hail! great hero!

ELSA.
>Oh joy, that my tongue thy name could praise,
>The songs of the angels for thee I would upraise;
>My lord here I confess thee
>I'll live for thee alone!
>Wilt thou divinely bless me,
>Oh, take me for thine own.

LOHENGRIN. Heav'n lent me strength to right thee,
>That truth might stand confess'd;
>But now I will requite thee
>For all thy sorrow past.

FREDERICK. Woe! Heav'n itself hath doom'd me,
>And brought my trusted sword to nought.
>Oh earth, hadst thou entombed me,
>Ere I to this was brought!

ORTRUD. Who is't that thus hath doomed us—
>Who brings my power to nought?
>Oh, had the earth entomb'd us,
>Ere we to shame were brought!

THE KING AND CHORUS.
>Hail! blest be the power that brought them
>Valiant knight! hail great in glory, great in fame!
>Ye minstrels sing of pleasure,
>Intone a loud triumphant measure!
>Great be thy power, glorious thy name,
>Great be thy fame! blest be thy name!
>Hail to thy coming! blest be thy name!
>All praise to thee is due,
>Thy name shall live in story!
>Ne'er will a knight so true
>Fulfil the land with glory!
>Blest be the hour that hither brought thee!
>Long live in glory,
>Prais'd be thy name,
>All hail to thee.

ALLE MÄNNER.
>Des Reinen Arm gieb Heldenkraft,
>Des Falschen Stärke sei erschlafft;
>So künde uns dein wahr Gericht,
>Du Herr und Gott, nun zög're nicht!

ALLE FRAUEN.
>Mein Herr und Gott, segne ihn!

[*Alle treten in grosser, feierlicher Aufregung an ihre Plätze zurück. ELSA und die Frauen unter der Eiche beim KÖNIG. Auf das Zeichen des Heerrufers fallen die Heerhörner mit einem langen Kampfrufe ein. LOHENGRIN und FRIEDRICH vollenden ihre Waffenrüstung. Der KÖNIG zieht sein Schwert aus der Erde und schlägt damit dreimal auf seinen Schild. Die Kämpfer treten in den Ring, legen die Schilder vor und ziehen das Schwert. LOHENGRIN greift zuerst an und streckt dann mit weitausgeholtem Streich FRIEDRICH nieder. Dieser versucht sich wieder zu erheben, taumelt zurück und stürzt zu Boden. LOHENGRIN setzt das Schwert auf seinen Hals.*

LOHENGRIN.
>Durch Gottes Sieg ist jetzt dein Leben mein:
>Ich schenk' es dir, mög'st du der Reu' es weih'n!

CHOR. Sieg! Sieg! Sieg! Heil dir, Heil!

ELSA.
>O fänd' ich Jubelweisen,
>Die deinem Ruhme gleich,
>Die, würdig dich zu preisen,
>An höchstem Lobe reich!
>In dir muss ich vergehen,
>Vor dir schwind' ich dahin!
>Soll ich mich selig sehen,
>Nimm alles was ich bin!

LOHENGRIN. Den Sieg hab ich erstritten
>Durch deine Rein' allein!
>Nun soll was du gelitten,
>Dir reich vergolten sein!

FRIED. Weh', mich hat Gott geschlagen,
>Durch ihn ich sieglos bin!
>Am Heil muss ich verzagen,
>Mein Ruhm' und Ehr' ist hin!

ORTRUD. Wer ist's, der ihn geschlagen,
>Durch den ich machtlos bin?
>Sollt' ich vor ihm verzagen,
>Wär' all' mein Hoffen hin?

DER KÖNIG, DIE MÄNNER UND FRAUEN.
>Ertöne, Siegeweise,
>Dem Helden laut zum Preise!
>Ruhm deiner Fahrt!
>Preis deinem Kommen!
>Heil deiner Art,
>Schützer der Frommen!
>Dich nur besingen wir,
>Dir schallen uns're Lieder!
>Nie kehrt ein Held gleich dir
>In diesen Landen wieder!
>Wo fand' ich Jubelweisen,
>Seinem Ruhme gleich?
>Ihr würdig zu preisen,
>An höchstem Lobe reich.
>Du hast gewahrt
>Das Recht der Frommen,
>Heil deiner Fahrt',
>Heil deinem Kommen!

FREDERICK, crushed, falls at the feet of ORTRUD. *Youths raise* LOHENGRIN *upon his shield, and* ELSA *upon the shield of the* KING, *upon which several have spread their mantles, thus both are borne away amid general rejoicing.*

ACT II

SCENE I

The Fortress at Antwerp. At the back of the Palace (residence of Knights); in the foreground the Kemmenate (dwelling of women); R. H., the Minster. It is night. ORTRUD *and* FREDERICK—*both in dark, servile garments—are seated on the steps of the Minster.* FREDERICK *is musing gloomily;* ORTRUD *gazing fixedly at the windows of the Palace, which is brightly illuminated. Festive music is heard from the Palace.*

FRED. Arouse thyself, companion of my shame!
The dawning day we here may not await.

ORTRUD. I cannot flee; some spell holds me enchained.
Yon festive hall, where joy triumphant reigneth,
Within my soul distils the deadly bane
That shall avenge our cruel wrongs and end them!

FRED. What dark, mysterious spell binds me to thee,
Unholy woman?
Ah, why can I from thee not fly,
Where I might find some rest, some peace,
Where my distracted soul could be at rest?
'Tis thou whose spells have cost me
My honor and my fame;
Thou hast my knighthood lost me,
Thou'st led me on to shame!
My sword lies stained and broken,
My shield is cast to earth;
My name with curses spoken,
I'm reft of home and hearth!
Where'er for rest I turn me,
Abhorr'd from me they fly;
The vilest wretch may spurn me,
None is so vile as I!
Oh, had but death o'ertaken me,
I had my honour saved;
But thus, as miscreant to arraign me
My sword, my name disgraced!

ORTRUD. Why dost thou thus in idle grief thy heart consume?

FRED. Because I have no sword with which to strike thee dead!

ORTRUD. Well art thou named the peaceful one—
Why dost thou doubt in me?

FRED. Why doubt?
Was't not thy showing, thy beguiling,
That led me on t' accuse yon spotless maiden?
When in thy dismal forest home,
Didst thou not say that from its ruin'd tower
Thou saw'st how Elsa did the foul and murdrous deed?
Then didst thou lie, or in the castle moat
Did she not her brother drown?
To lure my heart with wily spells

[FRIEDRICH *sinkt zu* ORTRUDS *Füssen ohnmächtig zusammen.* LOHENGRIN *auf seinem und* ELSA *auf des* KÖNIGS *Schild werden von jungen Männern jauchzend hinweg getragen.*]

ZWEITER AKT

ERSTE SCENE

[*Burg zu Antwerpen. In Mitte des Hintergrundes der Palast (Ritterwohnung); Seitwärts rechts das Thurmthor. Links vorn die Kemenate (Frauenwohnung) gegenüber die Pforte des Münsters.—Nacht.—*FRIEDRICH, *finster in sich gekehrt, und* ORTRUD, *unverwandt nach den hellerleuchteten Fenstern des Palais, aus denen jubelnde Musik ertönt, starrend, in dunkler, knechtischer Tracht auf den Stufen des Münsters.*]

FRIED. Erhebe dich, Genossin meiner Schmach!
Der junge Tag darf hier uns nicht mehr seh'n.

ORTRUD. Ich kann nicht fort: hierher bin ich gebannt.
Aus diesem Glanz des Festes uns'rer Feinde
Lass, saugen mich ein furchtbar tödtlich Gift,
Das uns're Schmach und ihre Freuden ende!

FRIED. Du fürchterliches Weib, was bannt mich noch
In deine Nähe? Warum lass ich dich nicht
Allein, und fliehe fort, dahin, dahin,—
Wo mein Gewissen Ruhe wieder fände?
Durch dich musst' ich verlieren
Mein' Ehr', all' meinen Ruhm:
Nie soll mich Lob mehr zieren,
Schmach ist mein Heldenthum!
Die Acht ist mir gesprochen,
Zertrümmert liegt mein Schwert;
Mein Wappen ward zerbrochen,
Verflucht mein Vaterherd!
Wohin ich nun mich wende,
Gefloh'n, gefehmt bin ich:
Dass ihn mein Blick nicht schände,
Flieht selbst der Räuber mich.
O hätt' ich Tod erkoren,
Da ich so elend bin!
Mein Ehr' hab' ich verloren,
Mein' Ehr', mein Ehr' ist hin!

ORTRUD. Was macht dich in so wilder Klage doch Vergeh'n?

FRIED. Dass mir die Waffe selbst geraubt,
Mit der ich dich erschlüg'!

ORTRUD. Friedreicher Graff von Telramund!
Wesshalb misstrau'st du mir?

FRIED. Du fragst? War's nicht dein Zeugniss, deine Kunde,
Die mich bestrickt, die Reine zu verklagen?
Die du im düst'ren Wald zu Haus, logst du
Mir nicht, von deinem wilden Schlosse aus
Die Unthat habest du verüben sehn?
Mit eig'nem Aug', wie Elsa selbst den Bruder
Im Weiher dort ertränkt?—Umstricktest du
Mein stolzes Herz durch die Weissagung nicht,

Thou didst falsely predict Radbod's renown'd
And ancient house ere long should
Rise anew and give princes to Brabant!
'Twas thus enticed by thee, that Elsa's hand,
The peerless, I renounc'd,
And took thee for my consort,
As the last of Radbod's race!

ORTRUD. Oh, how deadly is his scorn!
I grant it, yea, all this I prov'd to thee.

FRED. Thou mad'st me, whose name was well renown'd
Whose knighthood was untainted by a flaw,
Of lying arts a dupe and an accomplice!

ORTRUD. Who lied?

FRED. Thou! Was not the judgment clear?
Heav'n hath declar'd against me!

ORTRUD. Heav'n?

FRED. Oh, horror!
That wonted word of hope,
On thy lips how dreadful!

ORTRUD. Ha! is thy hope the coward's Heav'n?

FRED. Ortrud!

ORTRUD. What means thy threat?
Would'st thou assail thy wife? Oh, craven!
If thou hadst but threatened him like this
Who dooms us to this bitter woe,
Well hadst thou won,
And glorious were thy name.
Ah, if thou wouldst but hearken now,
There is a spell can lay him low!

FRED. No spell avails,
All heav'nly powers on his side are rang'd!

ORTRUD. Heav'nly powers? Ha, ha!
Mark but my word, and I will show to thee
How weak those heav'nly pow'rs
That fight for him.

FRED. Thou godless prophetess!
And dost thou think thy subtle spells
Again to weave around me?

ORTRUD.
Of feasting weary, they are slumb'ring now
Come seat thee here by me!
The hour is nigh when yonder stars
Reveal their lore to me!
Know'st thou who is yon knight,
Who by a swan was guided to our land?

FRED. No!

ORTRUD. Shall I reveal to thee a secret?
Mark what I say;   [and name,
If aught compel him to answer what his race
His vaunted power is paralys'd,
The spell that lends him strength dissolv'd.

FRED. Ha! was't for that he forbade?

ORTRUD. For that.
No one here hath the pow'r
From him to draw the fatal secret
But she whom he so sternly bade
That she the question ne'er should ask

FRED. To ask him Elsa must be tempted,
'Tis she alone can break the spell.

Bald würde Radbod's alter Fürstenstamm
Von neuem grünen und herrschen in Brabant?
Bewogst du so mich nicht, von Elsa's Hand,
Der reinen, abzusteh'n und dich zum Weib
Zu nehmen, weil du Radbod's letzter Spross?

ORTRUD. Ha, wie tödtlich du mich kränkst!—
Dies alles, ja! ich sagt' und zeugt' es dir!

FRIED. Und machtest mich, des' Name hochgeehrt,
Des' Leben aller höchsten Tugend Preis,
Zu deiner Lüge schändlichem Genossen?

ORTRUD. Wer log?

FRIED. Du!—Hat nicht durch sein Gericht
Gott mich dafür geschlagen?

ORTRUD. Gott?

FRIED.   Entsetzlich!
Wie tönt aus deinem Mund furchtbar de
Name!

ORTRUD. Ha, nennst du deine Feigheit Gott?

FRIED. Ortrud!

ORTRUD. Willst du mir droh'n? Mir einem Weib
—droh'n?
O Feiger! Hättest du so grimmig ihm
Gedroht, der jetzt dich in das Elend schickt,
Wohl hättest Sieg statt Schande du erkauft!—
Ha, wer ihm zu entgegnen wüsst,' der fänd'
Ihn schwächer als ein Kind!

FRIED.   Je schwächer er,
Desto gewalt'ger kämpfte Gottes Kraft!

ORTRUD. Gottes Kraft? Ha! ha!—
Gieb mir die Macht, und sicher zeig' ich dir,
Welch' schwacher Gott es ist, der ihn beschütz

FRIED. Du wilde Seherin! Wie willst du doch
Geheimnissvoll den Geist mir neu berücken!

ORTRUD. Die Schwelger strecken sich zur üpp'gen Ruh
Setz' dich zur Seite mir! Die Stund' ist da,
Wo dir mein Seherauge leuchten soll.—
Weisst du wer dieser Held, den hier
Ein Schwan gezogen an das Land?

FRIED. Nein!

ORTRUD. Was gäbst du drum es zu erfahren?
Ich sage dir: ist er gezwungen
Zu nennen wie sein Nam' und Art,
All seine Macht zu Ende ist,
Die müh'voll ihm ein Zauber leiht.

FRIED. Ha! Dann begreif' ich sein Verbot!

ORTRUD. Nun hör', Niemand hat hier Gewalt,
Ihm das Geheimniss zu entreissen,
Als die, der er so streng verbot,
Die Frage je an ihn zu thun.

FRIED. So gält' es Elsa, zu verleiten,
Dass sie die Frag' ihm nicht erliess'?

Ortrud. Ha! thou art swift to understand.

Fred. How can she be persuaded?

Ortrud. Mark!
Above all else, from hence we must not fly
Then nerve thee to the task;
Her just suspicion we must kindle.
Go forth—say that by sorcery
He triumphed o'er a righteous cause.

Fred. Ha! yea, 'twas sorcery.

Ortrud. At worst,
If that should fail, she must be forc'd.

Fred. Be forc'd?

Ortrud. Not all in vain.
The secret lore of old to me's familiar;
Store in thy mind what now I tell thee;
Strength that is lent by magic art fails
If of him bewitch'd one drop of blood be shed
His native helplessness and frailty then is shown.

Fred. Oh, were that true!
Oh, thou who dost the pow'rs of darkness know,
If thou speak falsely now, woe on thee!

Ortrud. Nay, thou art raving.
Temper wrath with measure;
And I will teach thee vengeance,
Godlike pleasure.

Both. For dread revenge here I implore ye,
Oh, pow'rs that rule our earthly lot.
Ye, who now dream that joy's before ye,
Know that our vengeance slumbers not.

SCENE II

Elsa, *in white garments, appears on the balcony, she steps forward to the parapet and leans her head on her hand.*

Ortrud. She's yonder!

Fred. Elsa!

Ortrud. Be near, ye pow'rs of darkness,
May she for ever rue this hour!
Away! thou must awhile from hence depart.

Fred. But why?

Ortrud. Ha, wie begreifst du schnell und wohl!

Fried. Doch wie soll das gelingen?

Ortrud. Hör'!
Vor allem gilt's, von hinnen nicht
Zu flieh'n: drum schärfe deinen Witz!
Gerechten Argwohn ihr zu wecken,
Tritt vor, klag' ihn des Zaubers an,
Durch den er das Gericht getäuscht!

Fried. Ha! Trug und Zauber's List!

Ortrud. Missglückt's,
So bleibt ein Mittel der Gewalt!

Fried. Gewalt?

Ortrud. Umsonst nicht bin ich in
Geheimsten Künsten tief erfahren;
Drum achte wohl was ich dir sage:
Jed' Wesen, das durch Zauber stark,
Wird Ihm des Leibes kleinstes Glied
Entrissen nur, muss sich alsbald
Ohnmächtig zeigen, wie es ist.

Fred. Ha, sprächst du wahr!
O Weib, das in der Nacht ich vor mir seh'!
Betrügst du jetzt mich noch, dann weh' dir, weh'!

Ortrud. Ha, wie du rasest!—Ruhig und besonnen!
So lehr' ich dich der Rache süsse Wonnen.

Beide. Der Rache Werk sei nun beschworen
Aus meines Busens wilder Nacht!
Die ihr in süssem Schlaf verloren,
Wisst, dass für euch das Unheil wacht!

ZWEITE SCENE

[Elsa *in weissem Gewande erscheint auf dem Balcon, tritt an die Brüstung und lehnt den Kopf in die Hand.*

Ortrud. Sie ist es!

Fried. Elsa!

Ortrud. Der Stunde soll sie fluchen,
In der sie jetzt mein Blick gewahrt!—Hinweg!
Entfern' ein Kleines dich von hier!

Fried. Warum?

YE WANDERING BREEZES.

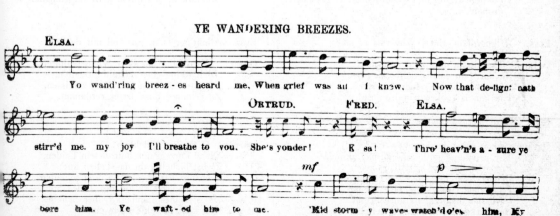

Elsa.
Ye wand'ring breez-es heard me, When grief was all I knew. Now that de-light: hath stirr'd me, my joy I'll breathe to you. She's yonder! Elsa! Thro' heav'n's a-zure ye bore him. Ye waft-ed him to me. 'Mid storm-y waves watch'd o'er him, My

guide, my love to be. Where'er thy pin - ion rush - eth, The mourner's tears are dried, My cheek that burns and flush - eth with love, Oh, cool and hide' My cheek that burns and flush - eth with love.... Oh,.... cool thou, oh, cool thou oh, cool and hide, Oh, cool thou!

ORTRUD.
    Leave her for me; her knight shall be for thee
    Elsa!
	ORTRUD. Sie ist für mich,—ihr Held gehöre d
	    Elsa!

ELSA. Who calls? How drearily and strangely
    My name resoundeth thro' the night.
	ELSA. Wer ruft?—Wie schauerlich und klagend
	    Ertönt mein Name durch die Nacht.

ORTRUD. Elsa! Hast thou forgotten e'en my voice?
    Wilt thou disown me in my sorrow,
    Who am by thee of all bereft?
	ORTRUD. Elsa! Ist meine Stimme dir so fremd?
	    Willst du die Arme ganz verleugnen,
	    Die du in's fernste Elend schick'st?

ELSA. Ortrud! 'tis thou? What dost thou here,
    Woman unblest?
	ELSA. Ortrud! bist du's?—was machst du hier,
	    Unglücklich Weib?

ORTRUD. "Woman unblest!"
    Yea, thou hast cause unblest to call me!
    I dwell in solitude protected,
    My home the deep and silent wood:
    I harm'd thee not, I harm'd thee not.
    Joyless I mourn'd the evil fortune
    That long hath rested on my race.
	ORTRUD. "Unglücklich Weib!"
	    Wohl hast du recht, so mich zu nennen!
	    In ferner Einsamkeit des Waldes,
	    Wo still und friedsam ich gelebt,—
	    Was that ich dir? was that ich dir?
	    Freudlos, das Unglück nur beweinend,
	    Das lang belastet meinen Stamm,—
	    Was that ich dir? was that ich dir?

ELSA. Ah, why speak to me of this?
    Thy sorrow was not caused by me!
	ELSA. Um Gott, was klagest du mich an?
	    War ich es, die dir Leid gebracht?

ORTRUD. 'Twere strange indeed if thou didst envy my
    lot.
    To be the wife of him whom scornfully thy heart
    disclaim'd.
	ORTRUD. Wie könntest du fürwahr mir neiden
	    Das Glück, das mich zum Weib erwählt
	    Der Mann, den du so gern verschmäht?

ELSA. Ye guardian saints! Why this to me?	ELSA. Allgüt'ger Gott, was soll mir das?

ORTRUD. The victim of a wild delusion,
    He dared to cast a doubt on thee;
    Since then he by remorse is riven,
    The ban is spoken o'er his head.
	ORTRUD. Musst' ihn unsel'ger Wahn bethören,
	    Dich Reine einer Schuld zu zeih'n,—
	    Von Reu' ist nun sein Herz zerrissen,
	    Zu grimmer Buss' ist er verdammt.

ELSA. Have mercy, Heav'n.	ELSA. Gerechter Gott!

ORTRUD. Thou canst be happy;
    Thy grief and guileless morn of promise
    Prepared thee for a radiant noon.
    Depart from my unholy presence.
    From thee I may not crave a boon.
    I will not haunt thy future bright.
    Nor darken thy undimm'd delight!
	ORTRUD. O du bist glücklich!
	    Nach kurzem unschuldsüssem Leiden,
	    Siehst lächelnd du das Leben nur;
	    Von mir darfst selig du dich scheiden,
	    Mich schickst du auf des Todes Spur,—
	    Dass meines Jammers trüber Schein
	    Nie kehr in deine Feste ein.

ELSA. So blest I am, oh, bounteous Heaven:
So great the boon I owe to thee—
Ne'er from my side be sorrow driven,
When in the dust it sues to me!
Oh, never! Ortrud, wait thou there!
Ere long again I shall be near.

ORTRUD. Ye gods forsaken, grant me your vengeance!
Declare your pow'r benign in this dread hour!
Strike them with death who profane your altars
And strengthen my soul to avenge your wrongs
Odin! thou strong and mighty one!
Freya! Oh, Queen, bend down to me!
Prosper my cause with deadly guile,
Immortals, on my vengeance smile!

ELSA. Ortrud! where art thou?

ORTRUD. Here, before thee kneeling!

ELSA. Oh, Heav'n! How sorely art thou stricken,
Whom I in pride and splendor saw!
My heart's compassion it doth quicken,
Heav'n's dark decree I mark with awe.
Arise! Oh, do not thus entreat me!
Wert thou my foe, I pardon thee;
And if through me thy heart hath sorrow'd
I humbly ask thou pardon me.

ORTRUD. My grateful thanks for all thy goodness!

ELSA. Of him whom I shall wed at morn,
Grace I'll crave for thee and thy husband
A boon to me he'll not refuse.

ORTRUD. Oh, hold my heart in grateful bondage!

ELSA. By morning's dawn be thou prepar'd;
Attire thyself in royal raiment,
With me before the altar go!
Then I shall meet my hero-guide,
In face of Heav'n to be his bride!
His bride to be!

ORTRUD. How can I e'er for this requite thee,
Since I henceforth am poor and lone?
Though as thy friend thou dost invite me,
I must myself thy vassal own
One gift alone the gods have lent me,
None silence to me hath ordain'd!
With that perchance
I may prevent thee from treason,
And thy life's attaint.

ELSA. What say'st thou?

ORTRUD. As thy friend I warn thee,
Lest thou in love too blindly trust;
Lest cruel fortune change and spurn thee,
For its decrees are often unjust. .

ELSA. What fortune?

ORTRUD. May he never leave thee,
Who was by magic hither brought!
And may the glamour ne'er deceive thee
That in thy soul his words have wrought!

ELSA. Oh, that thy heart could know the treasure
Of love that knows not fear or doubt!
No child of earth that bliss can measure
Who doth not dwell in faith devout.
Rest thee with me!

ELSA. Wie schlecht ich deine Güte priese,
Allmächt'ger, der mich so beglückt,
Wenn ich das Unglück von mir stiesse,
Das sich im Staube vor mir bückt!—
O nimmer!—Ortrud, harre mein!
Ich selber lass dich zu mir ein.

ORTRUD. Entweihte Götter! Helft jetzt meiner Rache!
Bestraft die Schmach, die hier euch angethan!
Stärkt mich im Dienste eurer heil'gen Sache,
Vernichtet der Abtrünn'gen schnöden Wahn!
Wodan! Dich Starken rufe ich!
Freia! Erhab'ne, höre mich!
Segnet mir Trug und Heuchelei,
Dass glücklich meine Rache sei!

ELSA. Ortrud! wo bist du?

ORTRUD. Hier, zu deinen Füssen!

ELSA. Hilf Gott! So muss ich dich erblicken,
Die ich in Stolz und Pracht nur sah!
Es will das Herze mir ersticken,
Seh' ich so niedrig dich mir nah.—
Steh' auf! o spare mir dein Bitten!
Trug'st du mir Hass' verzeih' ich dir;
Was du schon jetzt durch mich gelitten.
Das, bitte ich, verzeih' auch mir!

ORTRUD. O habe Dank für so viel Güte!

ELSA. Der morgen nun mein Gatte heisst,
Anfleh, ich sein liebreich Gemüthe,
Dass Friedrich auch er Gnad' erweist.

ORTRUD. Du fesselst mich in Dankes Banden!

ELSA. In Früh'n lass mich bereit dich seh'n!
Geschmückt mit prächtigen Gewanden
Sollst du mit mir zum Münster geh'n:—
Dort harre ich des Helden mein,
Vor Gott sein Eh'gemahl zu sein.

ORTRUD. Wie kann ich solche Huld dir lohnen,
Da machtlos ich und elend bin?
Soll ich in Gnaden bei dir wohnen,
Stets bleib' ich nur die Bettlerin.
Nur eine Kraft ist mir gegeben,
Sie raubte mir kein Machtgebot;
Durch sie vielleicht schütz ich dein Leben,
Bewahr' es vor der Reue Noth.

ELSA. Wie meinst du?

ORTRUD. Wohl, dass ich dich warne,
Zu blind nicht deinem Glück zu trau'n,
Dass nicht ein Unheil dich umgarne,
Lass mich für dich zur Zukunft schau'n.

ELSA. Welch Unheil?

ORTRUD. Könntest du erfassen,
Wie dessen Art so wundersam,
Der nie dich möge so verlassen,
Wie er durch Zauber zu dir kam!

ELSA. Du Aermste kannst wohl nie ermessen,
Wie zweifellos mein Herze liebt!
Du hast wohl nie das Glück besessen,
Das sich uns nur durch Glauben giebt?
Kehr' bei mir ein!

O LET ME TEACH THEE.

FRED. The powers of darkness enter'd there.
Thou godless one! thy fell resolve fulfil thou;
No pow'r have I to hinder thy intent!
The ruin that began with my disaster
Downward shall hurl those who abased me thus;
Come life or death, my purpose shall not fail,
The cause of my dishonor shall not live.

FRIED. So zieht das Unheil in dies Haus!
Vollführe, Weib, was deine List ersonnen,
Dein Werk zu hemmen fühl' ich keine Macht!
Das Unheil hat mit meinem Fall begonnen,
Nun stürzet nach, die mich dahin gebracht!
Nur eines seh' ich mahnend vor mir stehn:
Der Räuber meiner Ehre soll vergeh'n!

SCENE III

[*Gradual daybreak. Two Warders blow the Reveille from the turret, which is answered from another turret in the distance. FREDERICK having spied about for the spot most favorable for concealing himself from the populace, steps behind one of mural projections of the Minster. While the Warders descend from the turret and unlock the gates, Servitors of the Castle enter from various directions; they salute each other and proceed quietly on their several ways. The nobles and retainers of the royal domain enter from various quarters more and more numerously.*

CHORUS. The call that summon'd us betimes,
Great deeds this day to us doth bode;
Ere high the sun in heaven climbs
Will much be wrought fo

DRITTE SCENE

[*Der Tag bricht vollends an. Zwei Wächter blasen vo Thurme das Morgenlied, von einem entfernten Thurm wird geantwortet.—Dann schreiten die vier Heerhor bläser aus dem Palais und blasen den Königsru worauf sie wieder zurückgehen.—Von verschiedene Richtungen Dienstmannen, die sich begrüssen un ruhig an ihre Verrichtungen gehen.—FRIEDRICH sich hinter einem Mauervorsprung am Münster verbo gen.—Aus dem Burghofe und durch das von den Wäc tern erschlossene Thurmthor kommen nun brabantisch Edle und Mannen vor dem Münster zusammen.*

DIE EDLEN UND MANNEN.
In Früh'n versammelt uns der Ruf,
Gar viel verheisset wohl der Tag!
Der hier so hehre Wunder schuf,
Der theure Held, manch neue That

THE HERALD.
Our King's august decree through all the lands
I here make known—mark well what he commands:
Beneath a ban he lays Count Telramund
For tempting Heav'n with traitrous intent.
Whoe'er shall harbor or companion him,
By right shall share his doom with life and limb.

CHORUS OF MEN.
Cursed, accursed be the traitor!
By us and Heav'n unblest,
He shall be held abhorred!

HERALD. This further doth the King make known
through me:
The noble stranger sent by Heav'n's decree,
Who Elsa's hand as consort doth request,
With crown and sceptre doth the King invest.
The knight doth not as Duke to reign consent,
But takes for title—Guardian of Brabant.

CHORUS. Hail to the valiant knight!
Whom Heav'n its power doth grant;
We vow allegiance to the Guardian of Brabant.
Hail, hail, thou knight of Heav'n!
Long reign thou o'er Brabant.

THE HERALD.
The knight through me doth furthermore declare:
All to th' espousals shall this day repair.
Then straight be under arms by morning's dawn,
And follow him till glory's meed be won;
In dalliance soft to linger he disdaineth,
While foe or danger to the land remaineth.

CHORUS. We follow where he leads,
Till glory's meed be won,
Mighty and gallant deeds
Thro' him shall yet be done.
Come, come! we follow him,
Till glory's meed be won;
Blessed are our shores,
For glory wi'l be ours—
Oh, blest our happy shores!

FOUR PAGES.
Make way! make way! Our lady Elsa comes
Unto the Minster she goes forth.

SCENE IV

CHORUS. May every joy attend thee,
Who long in grief wert bound:
May Heav'n its blessings lend thee,
And angels guard thee round!
She comes with blushes glowing,
On holy thoughts intent!
All hail! thine be a bliss o'erflowing!
Hail, Elsa of Brabant!

ORTRUD. Stand back Elsa! no longer will I bear it,
That I like any slave must follow thee!
'Tis I precede, to all I here declare it,
And thou shalt humbly bow thy head to me!

THE EIGHT PAGES AND CHORUS
What does she mean?

ELSA. Great Heav'n, what does she mean?
How chang'd thy tone, who late to me did steal!

DER HEERRUFER.
Des Königs Wort und Will' thu' ich euch kund,
Drum achtet wohl, was euch durch mich er sagt!
In Bann und Acht ist Friedrich Telramund,
Weil untreu er den Gotteskampf gewagt:
Wer sein noch pflegt, wer sich zu ihm gesellt,
Nach Reiches Recht derselben Acht verfällt.

DIE MÄNNER.
Fluech ihm, dem Ungetreuen,
Den Gottes Urtheil traf!
Ihn soll der Reine scheuen,
Es flieh' ihn Ruh' und Schlaf!

DER HEERRUFER.
Und weiter kündet euch der König an,
Dass er den fremden gottgesandten Mann,
Den Elsa zum Gemahle sich ersehnt,
Mit Land und Kröne von Brabant belehnt.
Doch will der Held nicht Herzog sein genannt,
Ihr sollt ihn heissen: Schützer von Brabant!

DIE MÄNNER.
Hoch der ersehnte Mann!
Heil ihm, den Gott gesandt!
Treu sind wir unterthan
Dem Schützer von Brabant.

DER HEERRUFER.
Nun hört, was er durch mich euch künden lässt:
Heut feiert er mit euch sein Hochzeitsfest;
Doch morgen sollt ihr kampfgerüstet nah'n,
Zur Heeresfolg' dem König unterthan.
Er selbst verschmäht der süssen Ruh' zu pflegen,
Er führt euch an zu hehren Ruhmes Segen!

DIE MÄNNER.
Zum Streite säumet nicht,
Fürht euch der Hehre an!
Wer muthig mit ihm ficht,
Dem lacht des Ruhmes Bahn.
Von Gott ist er gesandt
Zur Grösse von Brabant!

EDELKNABEN.
Macht Platz für Elsa, uns're Frau!
Die will in Gott zum Münster gehn.

VIERTE SCENE

DIE EDLEN UND MANNEN.
Gesegnet soll sie schreiten,
Die lang' in Demuth litt!
Gott möge sie geleiten
Und hüten ihren Schritt!—
Sie naht, die Engelgleiche,
Von keuscher Gluth entbrannt!
Heil dir, du Tugendreiche!
Heil Elsa von Brabant!

ORTRUD. Zurück, Elsa! Nicht länger will ich dulden,
Dass ich gleich einer Magd dir folgen soll!
Den Vortritt sollst du überall mir schulden,
Vor mir dich beugen sollst du demuthvoll!

DIE EDELKNABEN UND DIE MÄNNER.
Was will das Weib?

ELSA. Um Gott! Was muss ich sehen?
Welch jäher Wechsel ist mit dir geschehen?

ORTRUD.
    If I one hour was of my worth unmindful,
    Think thou not that I before thy feet will cow'r!
    An ample vengeance thy disdain doth owe me
    My rightful rank I will assert this hour!

ELSA. Woe! was it nought but falsehood to mislead me
    Last night that brought thee wailing to my
      door?
    Now thou wouldst fain attempt to supersede me,
    Thou mate of one whom God and man forswore?

ORTRUD.. Through doom unjust o'er him the ban was
      spoken.
    But his renown was great throughout the land;
    His name of virtue's self was held the token,
    Both fear and honor did his sword command.
    Your stranger, say, as what dost thou proclaim
      him?
    If I have heard aright, thou canst not name him.

ELSA. Thou slanderer, taunt me no more,
    Let my reply all doubts assure——
    So pure and noble is his nature,
    As none can match in high renown.
    Oh, can there live so vile a creature
    As to asperse all honor's crown?
    Hath not as victor Heav'n declar'd him,
    When he the recreant knight o'erthrew?
    Ye saw his triumph, yet he spar'd him,
    Say, lieges, can ye doubt him true?

THE MEN.
    Make way! the King is near—our sov'reign!

SCENE V

[*The* KING, LOHENGRIN, *and the Saxon nobles have issued
from the Palace in stately procession; the commotion
in front interrupts the train; the* KING *and* LOHENGRIN
come forward hastily.

CHORUS. Hail, hail, oh, sov'reign! hail, oh, Guardian
    of Brabant!

THE KING. Why is this strife?

ELSA. My lord! Oh, my defender!

LOHENGRIN. What is't?

THE KING.
    Who dares to clamor here with words unseemly?

THE TRAIN OF THE KING.
    We have heard the voice of anger.

LOHENGRIN.
    Oh! horror! Why this evil one with thee?

ELSA. My champion! shelter me against her wrath!
    Blame me, if I obey'd not thy command;
    I heard her weeping sore by yonder portal,
    And in compassion harbour'd her this night,
    And now with harsh and bitter words of hatred
    She taunts me for my boundless trust in thee.

LOHENGRIN.
    Away from her, thou fiend! In vain thy arts—
    Thou hast no part in her!
    Elsa, oh, say, hath she had power
    To taint thy heart with doubting?
    Come where in joy thy tears shall dissolve and
    vanish!

ORTRUD.
    Weil eine Stund' ich meines Werth's vergesse
    Glaubst du, ich müsste dir nur kriechend nah'n
    Mein Leid zu rächen will ich mich vermessen
    Was mir gebührt, das will ich nun empfahn.

ELSA. Weh! liess ich durch dein Heucheln mic
    verleiten,
    Die diese Nacht sich jammernd zu mir stahl?
    Willst du nun in Hochmuth vor mir schreiten
    Du, eines Gottgerichteten Gemahl?

ORTRUD. Wenn falsch Gericht mir den Gemahl ve
    bannte,
    War doch sein Nam' im Lande hochgeehrt;
    Als aller Tugend Preis man ihn nur nannte,
    Gekannt, gefürchtet war sein tapf'res Schwert
    Der Deine, sag', wer sollte hier ihn kennen,
    Vermagst du selbst den Namen nicht zu nennen

ELSA. Du Lästerin! Ruchlose Frau!
    Hör', ob ich Antwort mir getrau'!—
    So rein und edel ist sein Wesen,
    So tugendreich der hehre Mann,
    Dass nie des Unheils soll genesen,
    Wer seiner Sendung zweifeln kann!
    Hat nicht durch Gott im Kampf geschlagen
    Mein theurer Held den Gatten dein?
    Nun sollt nach Recht ihr alle sagen,
    Wer kann da nur der Reine sein?

MÄNNER. Macht Platz! Macht Platz! Der König nah

FUENFTE SCENE

[*Der* KÖNIG, LOHENGRIN, *die sächsischen Grafen un
Edlen sind in feierlichen uuge aus dem Palais g
schritten. Da durch die Verwirrung vorn der un
unterbrochen wird, treten der* KÖNIG *und* LOHENGR
lebhaft vor.

DIE MÄNNER. Heil! Heil dem König!
    Heil dem Schützer von Brabant!

KÖNIG. Was für ein Streit?

ELSA. Mein Herr! O mein Gebieter!

LOHENGRIN. Was giebt's?

KÖNIG.
    Wer wagt es hier, den Kirchengang zu stören

DES KÖNIGS GEFOLGE.
    Welcher Streit, den wir vernahmen?

LOHENGRIN.
    Was seh' ich! Das unsel'ge Weib bei dir?

ELSA. Mein Retter! Schütze mich vor dieser Frau
    Schilt mich, wenn ich dir ungehorsam war!
    In Jammer sah ich sie vor dieser Pforte,
    Aus ihrer Noth nahm ich sie bei mir auf:—
    Nun sieh', wie furchtbar sie mir lohnt d
    Güte,—
    Sie schilt mich, dass ich dir zu sehr vertrau'!

LOHENGRIN.
    Du fürchterliches Weib, steh' ab von ihr!
    Hier wird dir nimmer Sieg!—Sieg', Elsa, mit
    Vermocht ihr Gift sie in dein Herz zu giesser
    Komm, lass in Freude dort die Thränen fliesse

RED.

Great Henry! Oh deluded Princess! Nay, desist!

LL THE MEN.

Hence, or beware, thou traitor! Hence! I warn
thee! Avaunt, or of thy life beware!

HE KING. What seeks he here?

RED. Oh, King, give ear.

HE KING. Avaunt; hence, thou accurs'd one!

RED.

Hear me, ye all have done me grievous wrong
Heav'n's dread ordeal hath he profan'd, derided,
Thro' sorc'ry vile its judgment was misguided!

CHORUS. Seize the accurs'd one! Hark! how he
blasphemes!

RED.

Yon shining knight, my sword defying
I here accuse of sorc'ry vile!
His station, name, I ask him,
Let these be heard in light of day!
Who is he that the billows tided——
A swan leading him in pinnace frail?
With such familiars, whoso bideth
All honest men may well assail!
Justice he now shall foil no more.
Condemn me, if he prove his cause;
If not, on him let vengeance fall——
A knight dishonor'd by our laws!

THE KING, CHORUS OF MEN.

What dread aspersion! How will he refute it?

LOHENGRIN.

Not thou, base knight, may'st impeach me,
Whose craven falsehood Heav'n hath shown;
No doubts of evil men can reach me,
Nor can it tarnish my renown!

FRED.

I hurl thee back the vile suggestion.
And upon thee, oh, King, I call!
Will he presume thy right to question,
If me he scorns as base-born thrall?

LOHENGRIN.

Yea, e'en the King shall not command me,
Nor any Prince that rules on earth!
None shall constrain or reprimand me:
They saw my deed and know my worth.
There's one alone she can to speak compel me
Elsa—
Elsa! Why thus disturb'd and trembling?

THE KING.

Brave knight, put him to shame who dares defy
thee;
We know thee true, ne'er shall a doubt come
nigh thee.

CHORUS. We trust in thee, though doubt and danger
try thee;
To thee we give the prize of high renown.
Here, take my hand. No danger shall come
nigh thee;
Tho' thy name be still unknown, no danger shall
befall thee.

LOHENGRIN.

Ye valiant hearts, tho' doubt and danger try me,
Ye ne'er shall rue the trust this hour hath shown.

FRIED. O König! Trugbethörte Fürsten! Haltet ein!

DIE MÄNNER.

Was will der hier? Verfluchter, weich' von
hinnen!
Hinweg, du bist des Todes, Mann!

KÖNIG. Wag'st du zu trotzen meinem Zorn?

FRIED. O hört mich an!

KÖNIG. Zurück! Weiche von dannen!

FRIED. Hört mich, dem grimmes Unrecht ihr gethan!
Gottes Gericht, es ward entehrt, betrogen,
Durch eines Zaub'rers List, seid ihr belogen!

DIE MÄNNER.

Greift den Verruchten! Hört, er lästert Gott!

FRIED.

Den dort im Glanz ich vor mir sehe,
Den klage ich des Zaubers an!
Nach Namen, Stand und Ehren
Frag' ich ihn laut vor aller Welt.—
Wer ist er, der an's Land geschwommen,
Geführt von einem wilden Schwan?
Wem solche Zauberthiere frommen,
Des' Reinheit achte ich für Wahn.
Nun soll der Klag' er Rede steh'n;
Vermag er's, so geschah mir Recht,
Wenn nicht, so sollet ihr erseh'n,
Um seine Tugend steht es schlecht!

DER KÖNIG UND DIE MÄNNER.

Welch harte Klage! Was wird er ihm entgegnen?

LOHENGRIN. Nicht dir, der so vergass der Ehren,
Hab' Noth ich Rede hier zu steh'n!
Des Bösen Zweifel darf ich wehren,
Vor ihm wird Reine nie vergeh'n.

FRIED. Darf ich ihm nicht als würdig gelten,
Dich ruf' ich, König, hochgeehrt!
Wird er auch dich unadlig schelten,
Dass er die Frage dir verwehrt?

LOHENGRIN. Ja, selbst dem König darf ich wehren,
Und aller Fürsten höchstem Rath!
Nicht darf sie Zweifels Last beschweren,
Sie sahen meine gute That.
Nur eine ist's,—der muss ich Antwort geben:
Elsa—
Elsa!—wie seh' ich sie erbeben!

DER KÖNIG.

Mein Held, entgeg'ne kühn dem Ungetreuen!
Du bist zu hehr, um, was er klagt, zu scheuen!

DIE MÄNNER. Wir steh'n zu dir, es soll uns nie ge-
reuen,
Dass wir der Helden Preis in dir erkannt.
Reich' uns die Hand! Wir glauben dir in
Treuen,
Dass hehr dein Nam', auch wenn er nicht ge-
nannt.

LOHENGRIN.

Euch Helden soll der Glaube nimmer reuen,
Werd' euch mein Nam' und Art auch nie genannt!

FRED. Confide in me. Let me a secret tell thee, hear and convince thyself.	**FRIED.** Vertraue mir! Lass dir ein Mittel heissen, Das dir Gewissheit schafft!
ELSA. Away from me!	**ELSA.** Hinweg von mir!
FRED. Give me but leave the smallest limb to maim him; One drop of life-blood, and I swear to thee, What now he hides he freely shall declare, Nor ever from thy side to wander dare.	**FRIED.** Lass mich das kleinste Glied ihm nur entreissen Des Fingers Spitze, und ich schwöre dir, Was er dir hehlt, sollst frei du vor dir sehn,— Dir treu, soll nie er dir von hinnen gehn.
ELSA. Ah, tempt me not!	**ELSA.** Ha, nimmermehr!
FRED. This night I shall be near— Call me, and straight I'll come all doubt to clear.	**FRIED.** Ich bin dir nah' zur Nacht— Ruf'st du, ohn' Schaden ist es schnell vollbracht
LOHENGRIN. Elsa, with whom dost thou converse? Away from her, thou cursed ones! On peril of my wrath, dare ye to cross her path Elsa, arise my love; in thy command, In thy good faith my ev'ry hope doth stand, Doth any doubt thy heart inspire? Dost thou to question me desire?	**LOHENGRIN.** Elsa, mit wem verkehrest du? Zurück von ihr, Verfluchte! Dass nie mein Auge je Euch wieder bei ihr seh'! Elsa, erhebe dich!—In deiner Hand, In deiner Treu' liegt alles Glückes Pfand! Lässt nicht des Zweifels Macht dich ruh'n? Willst du die Frage an mich thun?
ELSA. My champion, my deliverer dear! Oh, thou who dost my soul sustain! High o'er the reach of doubt and fear, Love over all shall reign.	**ELSA.** Mein Retter, der mir Heil gebracht! Mein Held, in dem ich muss vergeh'n! Hoch über alles Zweifels Macht Soll meine Liebe stehn!
LOHENGRIN. Come, then, Elsa, let us plight our faith.	**LOHENGRIN.** Heil dir, Elsa! Nun lass vor Gott uns gehen!
THE MEN. Lo! he is from heav'n sent! Hail, Elsa of Brabant! Go forth with blessings laden! Hail, thou royal maiden! Oh hail, royal Elsa of Brabant!	**DIE MÄNNER UND FRAUEN.** Seht! seht! Er ist von Gott gesandt!— Heil ihm! Heil Elsa von Brabant! Gesegnet sollst du schreiten! Heil dir, Tugendreiche! Gott möge dich geleiten! Heil dir, Elsa von Brabant!

[*Here the* KING, *with the bridal pair, has reached the highest step of the Minster;* ELSA *with deep emotion turns to* LOHENGRIN, *who clasps her in his arms. From this embrace she looks up with a startled expression, and on the foot of the steps perceives* ORTRUD, *who lifts an arm against her with an expression of certain triumph.* ELSA, *terrified, turns away her face.*

[*Als der* KÖNIG *mit dem Brautpaare die höchste Stu erreicht, kehrt sich* ELSA *in grosser Ergriffenheit z dem sie in den Armen auffangenden* LOHENGRIN. *A dieser Umarmung wirft sie mit scheue Besorgniss de Blick auf* ORTRUD, *die siegesgewiss den Arm gege sie erhebt, sie wendet erschreckt ihr Gesicht ab.*

ACT III
SCENE I

[*The Bridal Chamber; to the right an oriel casement, which is open. Music behind the stage, at first heard quite in the distance, and gradually approaching nearer; at the middle of the strain, doors at the back of the stage are opened: the Ladies enter leading in* ELSA, *the* KING *and Nobles leading in* LOHENGRIN; *Pages with lights go before them.*

DRITTER AKT
ERSTE SCENE

[*Wenn der Vorhang aufgeht, stellt die Bühne das Brautg mach dar. Rechts ein Erkerthurm mit offenem Fe ster. Der Gesang erst entfernt, nähert sich. In Mitt des Liedes werden die Thüren geöffnet. rechts trete Frauen mit* ELSA, *links Männer mit* LOHENGRIN un *dem* KÖNIG *ein. Edelknaben mit Lichtern gehe voraus.*

EIGHT LADIES. As solemn vows unite ye,
We hallow ye to joy!
This hour shall still requite ye,
When bliss hath known alloy!

ACHT FRAUEN. Wie Gott euch selig weihte,
Zu Freuden weih'n euch wir;
In Liebesglück's Geleite
Denkt lang' der Stunde hier!

CHORUS. Faithful and true, &c..

CHOR. Treulich bewacht bleibet zurück, u. s. w.

SCENE II

LOHENGRIN.

The blissful strain is o'er; we are alone,
The first and only time since we have met.
Now ev'ry pent-up thought our hearts may own,
No rash intruder this sweet hour shall fret.
Elsa, my love! my own, my gentle wife!
If thou art blest as I, oh, say, sweet life!

ELSA. Words can not tell the rapture sweet and tender
That floods my soul with joy divine.
When thou dost bend o'er me thy glance of
splendor—
When thou art near the bliss of heaven is mine.

LOHENGRIN.
Thy words, oh, fairest, well thy transports
render,

ZWEITE SCENE

LOHENGRIN.

Das süsse Lied verhallt; wir sind allein,
Zum ersten Mal allein, seit wir uns sah'n.
Nun sollen wir der Welt entronnen sein,
Kein Lauscher darf des Herzens Grüssen nah'n.—
Elsa, mein Weib! du süsse, reine Braut,
Ob Glücklich du, das sei mir nun vertrawt!

ELSA. Wie wär' ich kalt, mich glücklich nur zu nennen,
Besitz' ich aller Himmel Seligkeit!
Fühl' ich zu dir so süss mein Herz entbrennen,
Athme ich Wonnen, die nur Gott verleiht!

LOHENGRIN.
Vermagst du, Holde! glücklich dich zu nennen,

FAITHFUL AND TRUE.

If thou art blest, thy joy is doubly mine.
Oh, bend those eyes soft and tender,
Oh, let me breathe with thee this joy divine.
With charmed links did Heav'n to thee unite me
Ere yet we met thy heart had dreamt of me;
And if as champion I was call'd to right thee,
'Twas love alone that led my way to thee.
I knew thee pure from ev'ry taint of wrong:
To thee my heart and homage true belong.

ELSA.   I saw thee first from azure heights descending,
'Twas in a dream thy form I first beheld:
When o'er my waking eyes I saw thee bending,
I knew thee sent as angels were of old.
My heart with joy would fain dissolve before
    thee
I'd trace my steps as brooks thro' flow'ry mead
Like od'rous roses' sweetness I'd waft o'er thee
Dying for thy dear sake were blessed indeed!
Say, do I love thee?
By what blissful token is shown that pow'r so
    dread
And yet so blest? or, like thy name, ah, may
    it not be spoken?
Must what I prize the most be ne'er expressed?

LOHENGRIN.   Elsa!

ELSA.
How sweet my name, as from thy lips it glided
Canst thou deny to me the sound of thine?
In blissful hour thou'lt to my heart confide it,
That of thy love shall be the sign and seal!

LOHENGRIN.   Oh, my sweet wife!

ELSA.   Softly when none are nigh, whisper the word,
None e'er shall hear but I.

ELSA.   Ah, could I show my deep devotion—
Do some good deed, worthy of thee!
Nought have I but my fond emotion:
Never can I thy equal be!
Were doubt and danger low'ring o'er thee,
As once they threaten'd me with woe,
And I could to thy right restore thee,
Then might my heart some comfort know.
Haply thy secret's fraught with danger,
Therefore thy lips to all are clos'd!
It shall ne'er be known to friend or stranger,
If thou in me thy trust repose.
Doubt me not! Oh, let me share it—
Oh, let me know thy faith complete!
Not death itself from me shall tear it,
And torture borne for thee were sweet.

LOHENGRIN.   My loved one!

ELSA.   Oh, make me glad with thy reliance;
Humble me not that bend so low!
Ne'er shalt thou rue thy dear affiance—
Him that I love, oh, let me know!

LOHENGRIN.   No more, oh, Elsa!

ELSA.   Tell, oh, tell me!
Reveal thy name ador'd to love—
Thy race and name—all that befell thee!
My pow'r of silence thou shall prove!

LOHENGRIN.
Greatest of trusts, oh, Elsa, I have shown thee.
When I believ'd thee true from ev'ry stain;
Wav'ring in faith if thou shouldst ever own thee

Giebst du auch mir des Himmels Seligkeit!
Fühl' ich zu dir so süss mein Herz entbrenner
Athme ich Wonnen, die nur Gott verleiht!—
Wie hehr erkenn' ich unsrer Liebe Wesen!
Die nie sich sah'n, wir hatten uns geahnt:
War ich zu deinem Streiter auserlesen,
Hat Liebe mir zu dir den Weg gebahnt.
Dein Auge sagte mir dich rein von Schuld,
Mich zwang dein Blick zu dienen deiner Huld

ELSA.   Doch ich zuvor schon hatte dich gesehen,
In sel'gem Traume warst du mir genaht:
Als ich nun wachend dich sah vor mir stehen
Erkannt' ich, dass du kamst auf Gottes Rath,
Da wollte ich vor deinem Blick zerfliessen.
Gleich einem Bach umwinden deinen Schritt.
Als eine Blume, duftend auf der Wiesen,
Wollt' ich entzückt mich beugen deinem Tritt.
Ist dies nur Liebe?—Wie soll ich es nennen,
Dies Wort, so unaussprechlich wonnevoll,
Wie, ach! dein Name, den ich nie darf kennen
Bei dem ich nie mein Höchstes nennen soll!

LOHENGRIN.   Elsa!

ELSA.   Wie süss mein Name deinem Mund entgleitet
Gönnst du denn deinen holden Klang mir nicht
Nur, wenn zur Liebesstille wir geleitet,
Sollst du gestatten, dass mein Mund ihn spricht

LOHENGRIN.   Mein süsses Weib!

ELSA.   —Einsam, wenn Niemand wacht;
Nie sei der Welt er zu Gehör gebracht!

ELSA.   Ach könnt' ich deiner werth erscheinen!
Müsst' ich vor dir nicht bloss vergeh'n!
Könnt' ein Verdienst mich dir vereinen,
Dürft' ich in Pein für dich mich seh'n,
Wie du mich traf'st vor schwerer Klage!
O! wüsste ich auch dich in Noth!
Dass aller Welt verschweigt dein Mund?
Kennt' ich ein Sorgen, das dir droht!
Wär das Geheimniss so geartet,
Dass aller Welt verschweight dein Mund?
Vielleicht, dass Unheil dich erwartet,
Würd es den Menschen offen kund?
Wär' es so! und dürft' ich's wissen,
Dürft' ich in meiner Macht es sehn,
Durch keines Droh'n sei mir's entrissen,
Für dich wollt' ich zum Tode gehn!

LOHENGRIN.   Geliebte!

ELSA.   O mach' mich stolz durch dein Vertrauen,
Dass ich in Unwerth nicht vergeh'!
Lass dein Geheimniss mich erschauen,
Dass, wer du bist, ich offen seh'!

LOHENGRIN.   Ach, schweige, Elsa!

ELSA.   Meiner Treue
Enthülle deines Adels Werth!
Woher du kamst, sag, ohne Reue,—
Durch mich sei Schweigens Kraft bewährt!

LOHENGRIN.
Höchstes Vertrau'n hast du mir schon zu danken,
Da deinem Schwur ich Glauben gern gewährt
Wirst nimmer du vor dem Gebote wanken,

SAY, DOST THOU BREATHE THE INCENSE.

Say, dost thou breathe the in - cense sweet of flow'rs. Bear - ing a tide of deep mysterious joy! And would'st thou know from whence this rap - ture show - ers, Ask not.. lest thou the won - drous charm destroy; Such is the mag - ic that to thee hath bound me, When I first be - held thy beau - ty past com - pare, Know - ing thee not, I worshipp'd and re - nown'd thee, I felt thy glance, And knew thee true as fair; And as the o - d'rous gales with rap - ture fire me, Borne on the dark, un - fath-om'd gloom of night, Thus thou to trust un - meas - ur'd did'st in - spire me. When thou wert crush'd by dark sus - pic-ion's blight.

Thy empire o'er thy heart thou'lt ne'er regain	Hoch über alle Frau'n dünkst du mich werth!—
Oh, let my arms in love enfold thee!	An meine Brust, du süsse, Reine!
Come, rest thee here, my love, my life!	Sei meines Herzens Glühen nah!
Let me in radiant joy behold thee—	Dass mich dein Auge sanft bescheine,
Far from our hearts be thought of strife	In dem ich all' mein Glück ersah!
Come, to my heart let me press thee;	O; gönne mir, dass mit Entzücken
Let me inhale thy od'rous breath!	Ich deinen Athem sauge ein!
Angels might glory to possess thee—	Lass' fest, ach! fest an mich dich drücken,
Oh, turn to me in loving faith!	Dass ich in dir mög' glücklich sein!
Thy love alone for all consoles me	Dein Lieben muss mir hoch entgelten
That I for thy dear sake have lost;	Für das, was ich um dich verliess;
A high and glorious fate controls me:	Kein Loos in Gottes weiten Welten
The fate true knight must prize the most	Wohl edler als das meine hiess;
As when the king desired to crown me,	Böt' mir der König seine Krone,
My heart disdain'd the proffer'd boon,	Ich dürfte sie mit Recht verschmäh'n:
No earthly glory can renown me,	Das einz'ge, was mein Opfer lohne,
I glory in thy love alone!	Muss ich in deiner Lieb' erseh'n!
Let not a doubt thy spirit borrow;	Drum wolle stets den Zweifel meiden,
Thy love is all the world to me.	Dein Lieben sei mein stolz Gewähr;
I came not here from night and sorrow,	Denn nicht komm' ich aus Nacht und Leiden,
From blest delights I came to thee.	Aus Glanz und Wonne' komm' ich her.

ELSA.	Help, Heav'n! What dost thou tell me—	ELSA.	Hilf Gott, was muss ich hören!
	What must thy lips relate!		Welch' Zeugniss gab dein Mund!
	With glamour tho'udst beguile me:		Du wolltest mich bethören,
	I know my wretched fate.		Nun wird mir Jammer kund!
	The lot thou hast forsaken		Dass Loos, dem du entrounen,
	Is still thy heart's desire		Es war dein höchstes Glück:
	One day I shall awaken,		Du kamst zu mir aus Wonnen,
	When thou of me shalt tire!		Und sehnest dich zurück!
	Oh, how can I believe thee?		Wie soll ich Aermste glauben,

I know that we must part;
Of joy thy words bereave me,
Hope fades within my heart.

LOHENGRIN. No more, oh, I beseech thee

ELSA. On thee I yet may gaze!
Until despair shall reach me
Oh, must I count my days?
In dread my soul shall languish,
Lest from my sight thou fly;
Thou'lt leave me in my anguish—
Of sorrow I shall die.

LOHENGRIN. Thou ne'er for me shalt sorrow,
While thou from doubt art free.

ELSA. What magic can I borrow
To bind thy heart to me?
A spell is cast around thee—
By magic thou art here—
What ties so'er have bound thee,
Thou by a spell canst tear!
Hark, there are sounds! oh, bend thy ear and
listen!

LOHENGRIN. Elsa!

ELSA. Alas!
'Tis there, the swan! as when I first beheld his
pinions glisten.
For thee he comes! oh must thou now be gone?

LOHENGRIN.
Elsa, oh, hush! what fancies vain are these?

ELSA. No, thou shalt not compel me to trust by words
of blame—
No, not unless thou tell me thy country and thy
name!

LOHENGRIN. Elsa, oh, I conjure thee!

ELSA. What fatal spell is thine?
In vain wouldst thou assure me—
Declare thy race and name!

LOHENGRIN. Forbear!

ELSA. Declare thy name.

LOHENGRIN. Woe's me!

ELSA. Where is thy home!

[ELSA perceives FREDERICK and his four associates, who
break in with drawn swords through a door at the
back.

LOHENGRIN. Elsa! oh, misery!

ELSA. Save thyself! Thy sword!

[She hands him his sword, which was by the side of the
couch, so that while she holds the sheath he quickly
draws it out, and with one blow strikes FREDERICK,
whose arm is uplifted against him, dead. The four
nobles let fall their swords, and kneel before LOHEN-
GRIN. ELSA, who has sunk on LOHENGRIN's breast,
faints and slowly sinks to the ground. Long silence.

LOHENGRIN. Woe! all our joy now is fled for aye!

ELSA. Eternal One, have mercy. Thou!

Dir g'nüge meine Treu'?
Ein Tag wird dich mir rauben
Durch deiner Liebe Reu'!

LOHENGRIN. Halt' ein, dich so zu quälen!

ELSA. Was quälest du mich doch?
Soll ich die Tage zählen,
Die du mir bleibest noch?
In Sorg' um dein Verweilen
Verblüht die Wange mir;
Dann wirst du mir enteilen,
Im Elend bleib' ich hier!

LOHENGRIN. Nie soll dein Reiz entschwinden,
Bleib'st du von Zweifel rein!

ELSA. Ach! dich an mich zu binden,
Wie sollt' ich mächtig sein?
Voll Zauber ist dein Wesen,
Durch Wunder kamst du her:
Wie sollt' ich da genesen?
Wo fand ich dein Gewähr?—
Hörtest du nichts? vernahmest du kein Kom-
men?

LOHENGRIN. Elsa!

ELSA. Ach nein!—doch dort! der Schwan, der Schwan!
Dort kommt er auf der Wasserfluth geschwom-
men. . .
Du rufest ihm,—er zieht herbei den Kahn!—

LOHENGRIN.
Elsa, halt' ein! Beruh'ge deinen Wahn!

ELSA. Nichts kann mir Ruhe geben,
Dem Wahn mich nichts entreisst,
Als—gelt' es auch mein Leben!—
Zu wiessen—wer du seist!

LOHENGRIN. Elsa, was willst du wagen?

ELSA. Unselig holder Mann,
Hör'! was ich dich muss fragen!
Den Namen sag' mir an!

LOHENGRIN. Halt' ein!

ELSA. Woher die Fahrt?

LOHENGRIN. Weh' dir.

ELSA. Wie deine Art?

[FRIEDRICH und die vier brabantischen Edlen brechen
mit gezicktem Schwerte herein.

LOHENGRIN. Weh' uns, was thatest du!

ELSA. Rette dich! dein Schwert! dein Schwert!

[Sie reicht das am Ruhebette angelehnte Schwert.
LOHENGRIN streckt FRIEDRICH, da er nach ihm aus-
holt, mit einem Streiche todt zu Boden. Den entsetzten
Edlen entfallen die Schwerter, sie stürzen zu LOHEN-
GRIN's Füssen au fdie Kniee. ELSA, die sich an seine
Brust geworfen, sinkt ohnmächtig langsam an ihm zu
Boden.—Langes Schweigen.

LOHENGRIN. Weh'! nun ist all unser Glück dahin!

ELSA. Alleweiger! erbarm' dich mein!

LOHENGRIN.

Bear hence the corpse into the King's judgment
   hall,
Into the royal presence lead her,
Array'd as fits so fair a bride;
There all she asks I will concede her,
Nor from her knowledge aught will hide.

SCENE III

*When the curtain is drawn aside, the scene presents
the banks of the Scheldt, as in Act 1.; a brilliant dawn
gradually brightens into full daylight. Enter from
different sides the Brabantian Nobles. When they
are all on the stage, the* KING, *with the Saxon Arriere-
ban enters.*

ALL THE MEN. Hail, royal Henry!
   Royal Henry, hail!

THE KING.

Have thanks, good lieges of Brabant:
Glory in arms may fortune grant!
Great is my pride, that hearts so brave
Go forth our German land to save.
Now 'gainst the wild Hungarian foe,
All are resolv'd at morn to go.
Henceforth his dreary eastern plain
Let him not dare to quit again;
For German land draw German sword!
Then ye the realm shall surely guard.

ALL THE MEN.

For German land draw German sword!
Thus we the land shall surely guard.

KING. Where lingers he, the heav'n-sent knight,
   Who ev'ry virtue doth unite?

MEN. What do they bear? What would they hear?
   Of Telramund they vassals are.

KING. Whom do ye bear? What shall I hear?
   Some dire event doth bring you here.

FOUR NOBLES.

E'en by the Guardian of Brabant,
Our liege and lord, we here are sent.

MEN. Lo, Elsa comes, that lady peerless!
   Her mien is sad, her eye is tearless!

KING. Why do I see thee mourning thus?
   Canst thou not bear thy Lord to lose?

A PORTION OF THE CHORUS.

Make way! The Guardian of Brabant!

ALL THE CHORUS.

Hail! hail, thou Guardian of Brabant!

KING. Hail, heav'n-sent hero, welcome here!
   Thy loyal vassals all are near,
   Waiting for thee to give the word,
   And fight by thy all-conq'ring sword.

ALL THE MEN.

We wait for thee to give the word,
To fight by thy all-conq'ring sword.

LOHENGRIN.

My gracious sov'reign, bear me blameless,
Reasons have I that must be nameless,
The destin'd campaign I suspend!

LOHENGRIN.

Tragt den Erschlag'nen vor des KÖNIGS Gericht!
Sie vor den KÖNIG zu geleiten,
Schmückt Elsa, meine süsse Frau!
Dort will ich Antwort ihr bereiten,
Dass sie des Gatten Art erschau'.

DRITTE SCENE

*[Wenn der Vorhang in die Höhe gezogen wird, stellt die
Bühne wieder die Aue am Ufer der Schelde, wie im
ersten Aufzuge, dar.—Glühende Morgenröthe; der
Tag bricht voll an. Von verschiedenen Seiten gelangt
nach und nach der brabantische Heerbann auf die
Scene. Als die Brabanter alle eingetroffen sind, zieht*
KÖNIG HEINRICH *mit seinem Heerbann ein.*

ALLE MÄNNER. Hoch König Heinrich!
   König Heinrich, Heil!

DER KÖNIG.

Habt Dank, ihr Lieben von Brabant!
Wie fühl ich stolz mein Herz entbrannt,
Find' ich in jedem deutschen Land
So kräftig reichen Heerverband!
Nun soll des Reiches Feind sich nahn,
Wir wollen tapfer ihn empfahn:
Aus seinem öden Ost daher
Soll er sich nimmer wagen mehr!
Für deutsches Land das deutsche Schwert!
So sei des Reiches Kraft bewährt!

ALLE MÄNNER.

Für deutsches Land das deutsche Schwert!
So sei des Reiches Kraft bewährt!

KÖNIG. Wo weilt nun der, den Gott gesandt
   Zum Ruhm, zur Grösse von Brabant?

ALLE. Was bringen die? Was thun sie kund?
   Die Mannen sind's des Telramund.

KÖNIG. Wen führt ihr her? Was soll ich schau'n?
   Mich fasst bei eurem Anblick Grau'n!

DIE VIER EDLEN.

So will's der Schützer von Brabant:
Wer dieser ist, macht er bekannt!

DIE MÄNNER. Seht! Elsa naht, die tugendreiche!
   Wie ist ihr Antlitz trüb und bleiche!

DER KÖNIG. Wie muss ich dich so traurig seh'n?
   Will dir so nah die Trennung geh'n?

STIMMEN. Macht Platz dem Helden von Brabant!

ALLE MÄNNER. Heil! Heil dem Helden von Brabant!

DER KÖNIG. Heil deinem Kommen, theurer Held!
   Die du so treulich rief'st in's Feld,
   Die harren dein im Streites Lust,
   Von dir geführt, des Sieg's bewusst.

ALLE MÄNNER. Wir harren dein in Streites Lust,
   Von dir geführt, des Sieg's bewusst.

LOHENGRIN.

Mein Herr und König, lass dir melden:
Die ich berief, die kühnen Helden,
Zum Streit sie führen darf ich nicht!

MEN.   Alas! what can his words portend!

LOHENGRIN.
  To lead ye forth to battle here I came not;
  But judge me, for your leniency I claim not.
  Then, firstly, do ye hold that I am guilty?
  Your just decree to me is due.
  He sought my life despite honor and fealty—
  Say, did I right when him I slew?

KING AND MEN.
  E'en as thy sword in earth has laid him,
  The saints will sure refuse to aid him!

LOHENGRIN.
  And further, I declare in face of Heav'n,
  Though bitter grief to me it bode,
  That from her fair allegiance hath been driven
  The wife that Heav'n on me bestow'd.

MEN.   Elsa! say, oh, what hast thou done?
  Sentence so stern how hast thou won?

LADIES.   Woe is thine, Elsa!

LOHENGRIN.
  Ye all have heard her give her word in token
  That she my name and country ne'er would ask
  That promise her impatient heart hath broken—
  Vainly I hop'd she would fulfil her task!
  Now mark me well, I will no more with-hold it.
  Nor have I cause to shrink from any test;
  When I my name and lineage have unfolded
  Ye'll know that I am noble as the best!

CHORUS.
  What is this secret he so well hath guarded?
  Oh, that this fatal hour had been retarded!

LOHENGRIN.
  In distant land, by ways remote and hidden,
  There stands a burg that men call Monsalvat;
  It holds a shrine, to the profane forbidden:
  More precious there is nought on earth than that,
  And thron'd in light it holds a cup immortal,
  That whoso sees from earthly sin is cleans'd;
  'Twas borne by angels thro' the heav'nly portal—
  Its coming hath a holy reign commenc'd.
  Once every year a dove from Heav'n descendeth,
  To strengthen it anew for works of grace;
  'Tis called the Grail, the pow'r of Heav'n attendeth
  The faithful knights who guard that sacred place.
  He whom the Grail to be its servant chooses
  Is armed henceforth by high invincible might;
  All evil craft its power before him loses,
  The spirits of darkness where he dwells take flight.
  Nor will he lose the awful charm it blendeth,
  Although he should be called to distant lands,
  When the high cause of virtue he defendeth:
  While he's unknown, its spell he still commands.
  By perils dread the holy Grail is girded,
  No eye rash or profane its light may see;
  Its champion knight from doubtings shall be warded,
  If known to man, he must depart and flee. .
  Now mark, craft or disguise my soul disdaineth,
  The Grail sent me to right yon lady's name;
  My father, Percival, gloriously reigneth,
  His knight am I, and Lohengrin my name.

ALLE MÄNNER.
  Hilf Gott! welch' hartes Wort er spricht!

LOHENGRIN.
  Als Streitgenoss bin nicht ich hergekommen,
  Als Kläger sei ich jetzt von euch vernommen
  Zum ersten klage laut ich vor euch Allen,
  Und frag' um Spruch nach Recht und Fug:
  Da dieser Mann mich nächtens überfallen,
  Sagt, ob ich ihn mit Recht erschlug?

DER KÖNIG UND ALLE MÄNNER.
  Wie deine Hand ihn schlug auf Erden,
  Soll dort ihm Gottes Strafe werden!

LOHENGRIN.
  Zum and'ren aber sollt ihr Klage hören:
  Denn aller Welt nun klag' ich laut,
  Dass zum Verrath an mir sich liess bethören
  Das Weib, das Gott mir angetraut.

ALLE MÄNNER.   Elsa! wie mochte das gescheh'n?
  Wie konntest so du dich vergeh'n?

DIE FRAUEN.   Wehe dir, Elsa!

LOHENGRIN.
  Ihr hörtet Alle, wie sie mir versprochen,
  Dass nie sie woll' erfragen, wer ich bin?
  Nun hat sie ihren theuren Schwur gebrochen
  Treulosem Rath gab sie ihr Herz dahin!
  Jetzt merket wohl, ob ich den Tag muss scheuen
  Vor aller Welt, vor König und vor Reich
  Enthülle mein Geheimniss ich in Treuen.
  So hört, ob ich an Adel euch nicht gleich!

ALLE MÄNNER UND FRAUEN.
  Welch' Unerhörtes muss ich nunerfahren!
  O könnt er die erzwung'ne Kunde sparen!

LOHENGRIN.
  In fernem Land, unnahbar euren Schritten,
  Liegt eine Burg, die Monsalvat genannt;
  Ein lichter Tempel stehet dort in Mitten,
  So kostbar, wie auf Erden nichts bekannt:
  Drin ein Gefäss von wunderthät'gem Segen
  Wird dort als höchstes Heiligthum bewacht,
  Es ward, dass sein der Menschen reinste pflegen
  Herab von einer Engelschaar gebracht;
  Alljährlich naht vom Himmel eine Taube,
  Um neu zu stärken seine Wunderkraft;
  Es heisst der Gral, und selig reinster Glaube
  Ertheilt durch ihn sich seiner Ritterschaft.
  Wer nun dem Gral zu dienen ist erkoren,
  Den rüstet er mit überird'scher Macht;
  An dem ist jedes Bösen Trug verloren,
  Wenn ihn er sieht, weicht dem des Todes Nacht
  Selbst wer von ihm in ferne Land' entsendet,
  Zum Streiter für der Tugend Recht ernannt,
  Dem wird nicht seine heil'ge Kraft entwendet,
  Bleibt als sein Ritter dort er unerkannt.
  So hehrer Art doch ist des Grales Segen;
  Enthüllt muss er des Laien Auge flieh'n;—
  Des Ritter's drum sollt Zweifel ihr nicht hegen
  Erkennt ihr ihn,—dann muss er von euch ziehn.—
  Nun hört, wie ich verbot'ner Frage lohne!
  Vom Gral ward ich zu euch daher gesandt:
  Mein Vater Parsifal trägt seine Krone,
  Sein Ritter ich—bin Lohengrin genannt.

LADIES AND MEN.

While I hear him the wondrous tale revealing,
The holy tears adown my cheek are stealing!

ELSA. 'Tis dark around me! Give me air!
Oh, help, help! oh, me, most wretched!

LADIES AND MEN.

The swan! the swan! the swan!
The stream he floateth down.
The swan! ah, he comes!

ELSA. Oh, horror! ah, the swan!

LOHENGRIN.

Too long I stay—I must obey the Grail!
My trusty swan! O that this summons ne'er
    had been!
Oh, that this day I ne'er had seen!
I thought the year would soon be o'er
When thy probation would have pass'd;
Then by the Grail's transcendent pow'r,
In thy true shape we'd meet at last!
Oh, Elsa, think what joys thy doubts have ended.
Couldst thou not trust in me for one short year?
Then thy dear brother, whom the Grail defended,
In life and honor thou hadst welcom'd here.
If he returns, when our sweet ties are broken,
This horn, this sword, and ring give him in
    token:
This horn succor on battle-field shall send him,
And with this sword he'll conquer ev'ry foe;
This ring shall mind him who did most befriend
    him—
Of me who sav'd thee from the depths of woe!
Farewell, my love! my wife, farewell!
Henceforth the Grail commands my life!

ORTRUD.

Go forth! Go forth! thou knight audacious!
Thy bride shall hear a tale veracious!
All now upon my mind doth dawn;
'Twas I that wound the golden band
Around the neck of yonder swan;
He is the true heir of Brabant!

CHORUS. Ha!

ORTRUD.

Oh, joy! my magic was the stronger!
Now thou afar from here must roam!
But if thy knight had tarried longer,
His spells had call'd thy brother home!

CHORUS.

Thou witch accurs'd, dost thou compass it?
Thou shall atone for crime so vile!

ORTRUD.

Stand back, I do myself confess it,
On me the gods of vengeance smile!

ALLE MÄNNER UND FRAUEN.

Hör' ich so seine höchste Art bewähren,
Entbrennt mein Aug' in heil'gen Wonnezähren.

ELSA. Mir schwankt der Boden! Welche Nacht!
O Luft! Luft der Unglücksel'gen!

DIE MÄNNER UND DIE FRAUEN.

Der Schwan! der Schwan!
Seht dort ihn wieder nahn!
Der Schwan! Weh, er naht!

ELSA. Entsetzlich! Ha! der Schwan! der Schwan!

LOHENGRIN.

Schon sendet nach dem Säumigen der Gral.—
Mein lieber Schwan!
Ach! diese letzte traur'ge Fahrt,
Wie gern hätt' ich sie dir erspart!
In einem Jahr, wenn deine Zeit
Im Dienst zu Ende sollte geh'n—
Dann, durch des Grales Macht befreit,
Wollt' ich dich anders wiederseh'n!
O Elsa! Nur ein Jahr an deiner Seite
Hätt' ich als Zeuge deines Glücks ersehnt!
Dann kehrte, selig in des Gral's Geleite,
Dein Bruder wieder, den du todt gewähnt—
Kommt er dann heim, wenn ich ihm fern im
    Leben,
Dies Horn, dies Schwert, den Ring sollst du ihm
    geben.
Dies Horn soll in Gefahr ihm Hülfe schenken,—
In wildem Kampf dies Schwert ihm Sieg verleiht;
Doch bei dem Ringe soll er mein gedenken,
Der einstens dich aus Schmach und Noth befreit!
Leb wohl! Leb wohl! Leb wohl! mein süsses
    Weib!
Leb wohl! Mein zürnt der Gral, wenn ich noch
    bleib'!

ORTRUD.

Fahr' heim! Fahr' heim, du stolzer Helde,
Dass jubelnd ich der Thörin melde,
Wer dich gezogen in dem Kahn;
Am Kettlein, das ich um ihn wand,
Mit dem das Kind ich schuf zum Schwan:
Das war der Erbe von Brabant!

ALLE. Ha!

ORTRUD.

Dank, dass den Ritter du vertrieben!
Nun giebt der Schwan ihm Heimgeleit!
Der Held, wär' länger er geblieben,
Den Bruder hätt' er auch befreit.

ALLE. Abscheulich Weib! Ha, welch' Verbrechen
Hast du in frechem Hohn bekannt!

ORTRUD.

Erfahrt, wie sich die Götter rächen,
Von deren Huld ihr euch gewandt!

[*She remains standing with an expression of wild despair.* LOHENGRIN, *standing on the bank, has heard all that* ORTRUD *said; he now sinks on his knees in mute prayer. All eyes turn with anxious expectancy to him. The white dove of the Grail flies slowly down, and hovers over the skiff;* LOHENGGRIN *perceives it, and with a grateful look rises quickly, and loosens the chain from the swan, who immediately sinks. In its place* LOHENGRIN *raises Gottfried, a fair boy in shining silver garment, from the river, and places him on the bank.*

LOHENGRIN.   Behold the ruler of Brabant,
            The rightful heir of this fair land.

[*With a shriek* ORTRUD *falls at the right of Gottfried.* LOHENGRIN *springs into the skiff, and the dove, having seized the chain, draws it along.* ELSA, *with a last look of joy, gazes on Gottfried, who advances to the* KING *and makes his obeisance to him. All contemplate him with astonishment and joy, the Brabantians sinking on their knees in homage. Gottfried rushes into* ELSA's *arms, who for a moment of joyous transport, turns her eyes again towards the river where* LOHENGRIN *has vanished.*

ELSA.   My consort! My consort!

[LOHENGRIN *is seen once more in the distance; he stands with head bent, sorrowfully leaning on his shield in the skiff; at the sight of him all break into loud lamentation.* ELSA *sinks lifeless to the ground, supported by Gottfried.*

[*Bleibt in wilder Verzweiflung hoch aufgerichtet stehen.* LOHENGRIN, *der vernommen, was sie sprach, sinkt jetzt, dicht am Strande, zu stummen Gebet feierlich auf die Kniee. Aller Blicke richten sich in gespannter Erwartung auf ihn. Plötzlich erblickt er die weisse Grals-Taube über den Nachen herabschwebend; mit lebhafter Freude springt er auf und löst dem Schwane die Kette, worauf dieser sogleich untertaucht. An seiner Stelle hebt* LOHENGRIN *einen schönen Jüngling in glänzendem Silbergewande—Gottfried—aus dem Flusse an's Ufer.*

LOHENGRIN.   Seht da den Herzog von Brabant!
            Zum Führer sei er euch ernannt!

[*Er springt schnell in den Nachen, welchen die Taube an der Kette fasst und sogleich fortzieht.* ORTRUD *sinkt bei Gottfried's Anblick mit einem Schrei zusammen.* ELSA *blickt mit letzter freudiger Verklärung auf den nun vorschreitenden Gottfried, der sich vor dem* KÖNIG *verneigt und nor dem die Brabanter huldigend auf die Kniee sinken. Dann eilt er in ihre Arme.*

ELSA.   Mein Gatte! Mein Gatte!

[*Sie erblickt* LOHENGRIN *bereits in der Ferne; von der Taube im Nachen gezogen. Er steht mit gesenktem Haupt, traurig auf seinem Schild gelehnt. Alles bricht bei diesem Anblicke in einen jähen Wehruf aus.* ELSA *gleitet in Gottfried's Armen entseelt langsam zu Boden.*

THE END

THE RHINEGOLD

THE RING OF THE NIBELUNG.

THE cycle to which this general title is given consists of the four music dramas — *Rhinegold, The Valkyr, Siegfried*, and *The Dusk of the Gods*. Wagner was occupied with this monumental work, with extended periods of interruption, during twenty-six years; for, as early as 1848, he made a prose sketch of the Nibelung myth, followed a year later by the dramatic poem *Siegfried's Death*, which subsequently became *The Dusk of the Gods*. Curiously enough, the books these four dramas were written in inverse order, the reason for which Wagner gives fully in a letter to Liszt, dated 1851. Briefly stated, he found that so many important facts leading to the death of Siegfried must, in his drama, either be narrated or taken for granted, that he wrote a preparatory drama, *Young Siegfried*, which, in turn, seemed incomplete without the presentation the events which are set forth in *The Valkyr*. Thus the cycle assumed its final shape as we now possess it; *Rhinegold*, which was written last, forming an introductory drama to the whole.

Wagner found the material for his colossal project in the saga of the Northern Mythology; but required the hand of the master-dramatist to weld the disconnected legends into a logically developed and unified whole, to trace the relation cause and effect; and by eliminating what was irrelevant to his purpose, and emphasizing the important facts of the narrative, to give to the mass of incident life and action, leading to overpowering climaxes. In the light of his genius the simple legends acquired a deeper significance; the rape of the Rhinegold, and the curse which was thereafter visited upon its possessors, crafty or innocent, became symbolic of the lust for wealth and power, with all its attendant evil — a curse which could be removed only thro' the expiation and triumphing love of Brünnhilde, whose self-immolation, while marking the end of the reign of the gods, brought the dawn of a new era — that of human love — upon the earth.

A thorough comprehension of *Rhinegold*, both musically and dramatically, is essential, in order to enjoy with understanding the other dramas of the cycle. Not only are the fundamental motives of all future action made clear, but most of the musical themes, which are used so significantly and frequently throughout the entire work, are heard for the first time in their original form and application in *Rhinegold;* for, tho' the book was written last, Wagner undertook the musical composition of the four dramas in their natural order, and accumulated his musical material as the action progressed.

C. F. M.

THE STORY OF "RHINEGOLD."

IN the prologue, or "fore-evening," to the cycle Wagner introduces us to the supernatural beings the Northern Mythology — Wotan, the chief the gods, and his spouse, Fricka, who, like Juno, was the guardian of domestic virtue; Loge, the god of Flame, crafty and cunning; Freia, the goddess of Youth and Beauty; her two brothers, Donner and Froh; the giants, Fasolt and Fafner; the Nibelungs, Alberich and Mime; the three Rhinedaughters, Woglinde, Wellgunde, and Flosshilde, who guarded the treasure in the depths of the Rhine; and the all-wise Erda, goddess of primeval wisdom, who later bore to Wotan the nine Valkyrs.

The first scene shows the rocky bed of the Rhine, with its flowing waters, filling the entire height of the stage, the daylight scarcely filtering through from above. The three Rhinedaughters disport themselves merrily, swimming about, and diving from rock to rock, while in its pristine innocence the Rhinegold slumbers securely. Their play is interrupted by the approach of

Alberich of the tribe of Nibelungs, a race of cunning, demoniacal gnomes, who inhabit Nibelheim
in the bowels of the earth. Hideous and
uncouth, he seeks to win the pleasures of love
from the nymphs. But though tantalizing him
by their banter, they elude their awkward pur-
suer, who slips about on the slimy rocks until his
gaze is attracted by an increasing brilliance
which glows from a rocky eminence. It is the
Rhinegold, which presently shines forth daz-
zlingly in the rays of the rising sun, and around
which the maidens circle with joyous shouts.
They jeeringly betray to Alberich that he alone
who is willing to renounce the pleasures of love,
can possess himself of the gold; but that by its
possession in the shape of a magic ring he may
make himself ruler and lord of the world. Seized
with new desire, the Nibelung curses love, which
for him is but lust, and scrambling madly up the
rock, tears the gold from its bed and disappears
in the depths. Night falls again upon the waters,
and the Rhinedaughters break forth into wild
lamentation. The billows sink, giving way to
veils of mist, which, as they clear away, disclose
Scene II.

The rising sun lights up the spires and turrets
of a castle on a rocky cliff at the back. Between
this and the foreground the Rhine is supposed to
flow thro' a deep valley. Wotan and Fricka are
lying asleep at one side; but Fricka awakes and
arouses her spouse, who rapturously greets the
shining castle. Fricka reproaches him, however,
that in order to recompense the giants, Fasolt
and Fafner, for building his new abode, he has
promised them her sister Freia, the goddess of
Youth and Beauty, to bring light and love into their
cold home. Wotan responds that he never really
intended to give up Freia, when the latter enters
in hasty flight, pursued by the giants who, the
work finished, have come to claim their reward.
Froh and Donner seek to protect their sister, but
this Wotan, as god of justice, may not permit; and
the giants, deaf to his parleying, are about to
carry off Freia when the arrival of Loge induces
them to pause. The latter had been sent thro'
the world by Wotan to discover something which
the giants would accept as a substitute for Freia;
but he confesses that nowhere could he find aught
for which men were willing to renounce the
pleasures of love. With great diplomacy Loge
then tells of his visit to Alberich, of the gold the
Nibelung had won thro' renouncing love, and of
the power which dwelt in the magic ring. Forthwith the giants agree to relinquish Freia if Wotan
will get and give them the gold. This Wotan is

unwilling to do, for he is already plotting to w
the ring for himself; but the giants, giving hi
until nightfall to comply, drag Freia away
hostage. Soon the greyness of age settles upo
the features of the gods, for Freia, the conserv
of eternal youth, is no longer with them. The
need is so urgent that Wotan at once accor
panies Loge to Nibelheim to wrest the ring fro
Alberich.

SCENE III. The abode of the Nibelung
Alberich now is master of all the gnomes, an
drives them unceasingly at the task of piling hig
his hoarded treasure. Mime has been set
forge the Tarnhelm, which can render its weare
invisible, or enable him to assume any shape
please. Unsuccessfully Mime tries to conce
from Alberich the finished work; Alberich seize
the Tarnhelm, and, to demonstrate its powe
changes into a column of vapor, in which for
he gives the cowed Mime a severe drubbing, an
then departs, still invisible, urging his slaves
their labor. Wotan and Loge descend thro'
cleft of the rock, and Mime, who is nursing h
wounds, tells how Alberich has become all-po
erful thro' the Ring and the Tarnhelm, made
Rhinegold. Alberich, once more in his natur
form, returns; and Loge craftily gets him to di
play his power — first, by changing into an enc
mous serpent, and later into a toad. This bei
their chance, Wotan puts his foot on the toa
Loge secures the Tarnhelm, and Alberich, aga
in his own form, is securely bound, and dragge
away to the upper world.

SCENE IV shows again the meadows befo
Wotan's castle, still veiled by pale mists as at t
end of Scene II. Wotan and Loge return wi
the fettered Alberich, who, as the price of h
freedom, is forced to give up his golden hoar
The Tarnhelm also is taken from him, but whe
the Ring is torn from him his rage and ha
are unbounded, and he curses with fatal effect t
Ring. He is then freed, and disappears. No
as Freia is brought back by the giants, the mis
begin to disappear, for her presence restores you
to the gods, who all enter to greet Wotan. T
giants demand the ransom — a pile of gold
great as the height and breadth of Freia. Wota
seeks to withhold the Ring, but is warned by t
apparition of Erda not to retain in his possessio
that which was obtained by a double theft, ar
bring down the Nibelung's curse upon the god
Upon gaining the Ring the two giants quarr
and Fasolt is slain; whereat Wotan, struck by t

wful power of the curse, bends his thoughts upon averting the menace of fate. Donner clears the air with a thunderstorm, and Walhalla is seen in he bright light with a rainbow bridge leading to t across the Rhine. As the gods start over the bridge, the Rhinedaughters are heard imploring Wotan to restore the gold to the depths; but, bidding Loge silence the wailing, Wotan leads the gods into their new abode.

PUBLISHERS' NOTE.

FOR the use of those who wish to familiarize hemselves with the musical framework of *Rhine-old*, the following list of themes (*Leitmotiven*) has een prepared. The themes are numbered for convenience; corresponding reference numerals are placed in the margin of the poem, opposite the place or line where each one occurs for the first time, or with especial significance.

LEADING MOTIVES (LEITMOTIVEN) OF THE DRAMA.

No. 1.   MOTIVE OF THE RHINE (MOTIV DES URELEMENTES).

No. 2.   MOTIVE OF THE RHINEDAUGHTERS (MOTIV DER RHEINTÖCHTER).

Wei - a, wa - ga, Wan - der, ye wa - ters; wa - ver and waft me!

wa - ga - la wei - a! wal - la - la, wei - a - la wei a! . .

No. 3. MOTIVE OF THE NIBELUNG'S SERVITUDE (MOTIV EINER KNECHTUNG)

No. 4.   RHINEGOLD MOTIVE (MOTIV DES RHEINGOLDES).

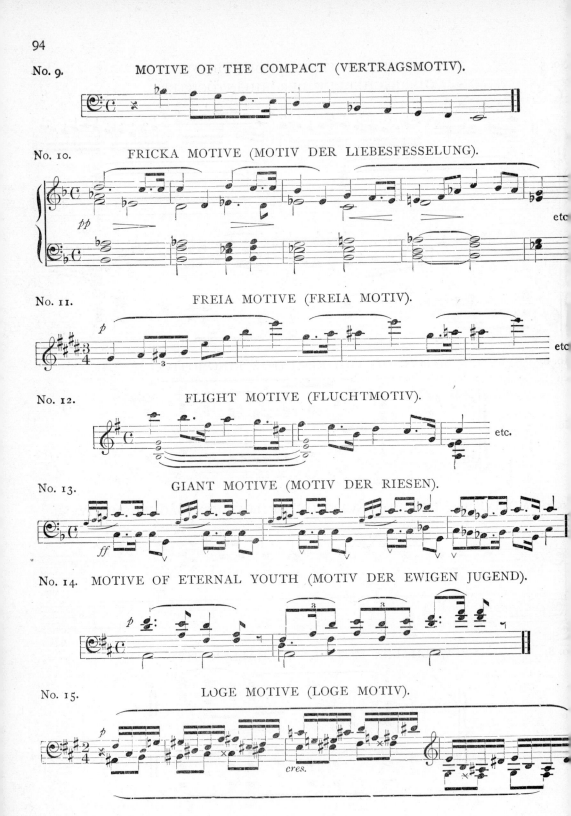

No. 9. MOTIVE OF THE COMPACT (VERTRAGSMOTIV).

No. 10. FRICKA MOTIVE (MOTIV DER LIEBESFESSELUNG).

No. 11. FREIA MOTIVE (FREIA MOTIV).

No. 12. FLIGHT MOTIVE (FLUCHTMOTIV).

No. 13. GIANT MOTIVE (MOTIV DER RIESEN).

No. 14. MOTIVE OF ETERNAL YOUTH (MOTIV DER EWIGEN JUGEND).

No. 15. LOGE MOTIVE (LOGE MOTIV).

No. 16.   MAGIC FIRE MOTIVE (MOTIV DES FEUERZAUBERS).

No. 17.   NIBELUNG MOTIVE (SCHMIEDEMOTIV DER NIBELUNGEN).

No. 18.   MOTIVE OF THE TARNHELMET (MOTIV DES TARNHELMS).

No. 19.   MOTIVE OF THE RISING HOARD (MOTIV DES AUFSTEIGENDEN HORTES).

No. 20.   MOTIVE OF THE CURSE (FLUCH MOTIV).

As   at   first   by   curse 'twas reach'd,   hence forth curs'd   be   this Ring!

No. 21. MOTIVE OF THE NIBELUNGS' HATRED (VERNICHTUNGSARBEIT DER NIBELUNGEN).

No. 22. ERDA MOTIVE (MOTIV DER NORNEN).

No. 23. RAINBOW MOTIVE (MOTIV DES REGENBOGENS).

No. 24. THE SWORD MOTIVE (SCHWERTMOTIV).

THE RHINEGOLD.

FIRST SCENE.

At the bottom of the Rhine.

Greenish twilight, lighter above, darker below. The upper part of the scene is filled with moving water which restlessly streams from R to L. Towards the ground the waters resolve themselves into a fine mist, so that the space to a man's height from the stage seems free from water, which flows like a train of clouds over the gloomy depths. Everywhere are steep points of rock jutting up from the depths and enclosing the whole stage; all the ground is broken up into a wild confusion of jagged pieces, so that there is no level place, while on all sides darkness indicates other deeper fissures.

Round a rock, in the center of the stage, whence its peak rises high into the lighter water, one of the *Rhine-nymphs* is seen merrily swimming.

Woglinde. Weia! Waga!
　　　Wander ye waters,
　　　waver and waft me!
　　　Wagalaweia!
　　　Wallala weiala weia!

Wellgunde's
　　　　(voice from above).
　　　Woglinde, watch you alone?

Woglinde. Till Wellgunde wends to my side.

Wellgunde
　　　　(diving down to the rock).
　　　How fares with your watch?
　　　　(She tries to seize *Woglinde*.)

Woglinde
　　　　(avoiding her by swimming).
　　　Far from your reach!
　　(They tease, and seek playfully to catch one another.)

Flosshilde's
　　　　(voice from above).
　　　Heiala weia!
　　　Whimsical sisters!

Wellgunde. Flosshilde, swim!
　　　Woglinde flies:
　　help me to foil her in fleetness.

Flosshilde
　　(dives down and comes between the playmates).
　　　The sleeping gold
　　　badly ye guard:
　　　better begird
　　　the gleaming one's bed;
　　such banter both may regret.

With merry cries the two separate: *Flosshilde* chases first one and then the other; they evade her and then unite to pursue her in turn. Thus they dart about like fish from rock to rock, laughing and sporting.

From a dark chasm *Alberich* clambers up to one of the rocks. He halts in the shadow and watches the gambols of the nymphs with growing delight.

ERSTE SCENE.

Auf dem Grunde des Rheines.

Grünliche Dämmerung, nach oben zu lichter, nach unten zu dunkler. Die Höhe ist von wogendem Gewässer erfüllt, das rastlos von rechts nach links zu strömt. Nach der Tiefe zu lösen sich die Fluthen in einen immer feineren feuchten Nebel auf, so dass der Raum der Manneshöhe vom Boden auf gänzlich frei vom Wasser zu sein scheint, welches wie in Wolkenzügen über den nächtlichen Grund dahin fliesst. Ueberall ragen schroffe Felsenriffe aus der Tiefe auf, und grenzen den Raum der Bühne ab; der ganze Boden ist in ein wildes Zackengewirr zerspalten, so dass er nirgends vollkommen eben ist und nach allen Seiten hin in dichtester Finsterniss tiefere Schlüffte annehmen lässt.

Um ein Riff in der Mitte der Bühne, welches mit seiner schlanken Spitze bis in die dichtere, heller dämmernde Wasserfluth hinaufragt, kreis't in anmuthig schwimmender Bewegung eine der *Rheintöchter*.

Woglinde. Weia! Waga!
　　　Woge, du Welle,
　　　walle zur Wiege!
　　　Wagalaweia!
　　　Wallala weiala weia!

Wellgunde's
　　　　(Stimme, von oben).
　　　Woglinde, wach'st du allein?

Woglinde. Mit Wellgunde wär' ich zu zwei.

Wellgunde
　　　　(taucht aus der Fluth zum Riff herab).
　　　Lass' seh'n, wie du wach'st.
　　　　(Sie sucht *Woglinde* zu erhaschen.)

Woglinde
　　　　(entweicht ihr schwimmend).
　　　Sicher vor dir.
　　　（Sie necken sich und suchen sich spielend zu fangen.)

Flosshilde's
　　　　(Stimme, von oben).
　　　Heiala weia!
　　　Wildes Geschwister!

Wellgunde. Flosshilde, schwimm'!
　　　Woglinde flieht:
　　hilf mir die Fliessende fangen!

Flosshilde
　　(taucht herab und fährt zwischen die Spielenden)
　　　Des Goldes Schlaf
　　　hütet ihr schlecht;
　　　besser bewacht
　　　des schlummernden Bett,
　　sonst büss't ihr beide das Spiel!

Mit munt'rem Gekreisch fahren die beiden auseinander; *Flosshilde* sucht bald die eine, bald die andere zu erhaschen; sie entschlüpfen ihr und vereinigen sich endlich, umgemeinschaftlich auf Flosshilde Jagd zu machen: so schnellen sie sich gleich Fischen von Riff zu Riff, scherzend und lachend.

Aus einer finstern Schlufft ist währenddem *Alberich*, an einem Riffe klimmend, dem Abgrunde entstiegen. Er hält, noch vom Dunkel umgeben an, und schaut dem Spiele der Wassermädchen mit steigendem Wohlgefallen zu.

Alberich.　Ho, ho! ye nixies!
　　Are ye not nimble,
　　nice to behold!
　　From Nibelheim's night
　　now would I fain
　　near you, if ye be kind.
(The girls, when hearing *Alberich's* voice, leave off playing.)

Woglinde.　Hey! who is there?

Wellgunde.　A thing with a voice.

Flosshilde.　Look, who is below!
(They dive deeper and perceive the Nibelung.)

Woglinde and Wellgunde.　Faugh! the gruesome one.

Flosshilde
(swiftly diving upwards).
　　Look to the gold!
　　Father warned us
　　from such a foe.
(The others follow her, and all three collect quickly round the central rock.)

Alberich.　List! aloft there!

The Three Nymphs.　What want you, below there?

Alberich.　Spoilt were your sport
　　if 'stonished I stand here still?
　　Near to me dive then;
　　a poor Niblung
　　longs dearly to dally with you!

Woglinde.　He offers to join us?

Wellgunde.　Is it his joke?

Alberich.　How sweet and soft
　　in this light ye seem!
　　Gladly I'd seek
　　to encircle one of your waists,
　　should you kindly descend.

Flosshilde.　I laugh at our fears;
　　the foe is in love!
(They laugh.)

Wellgunde.　The languishing calf!

Woglinde.　Let us accost him.
(She descends to the point of the rock at the base of which *Alberich* is.)

Alberich.　She's coming below!

Woglinde.　Climb closer to me.

Alberich
{clambers with gnome-like rapidity, but with difficulty, to the summit of the rock).
　　Smooth with slime
　　the slippery stone is!
　　How slide my steps!
　　My hands and my feet
　　cannot fasten or hold on
　　the steepness unsteady!
(Sneezes.)

Alberich.　He, he! Ihr Nicker!
　　Wie seid ihr niedlich,
　　neidliches Volk!
　　Aus Nibelheim's Nacht
　　naht' ich euch gern,
　　neiget ihr euch zu mir.
(Die Mädchen halten, als sie *Alberich's* Stimme hören, mit ihrem Spiele ein.)

Woglinde.　Hei! wer ist dort?

Wellgunde.　Es dämmert und ruft.

Flosshilde.　Luget, wer uns belauscht!
(Sie tauchen tiefer herab und erkennen den Nibelung.)

Woglinde und *Wellgunde.*　Pfui! der Garstige!

Flosshilde
(schnell auftauchend).
　　Hütet das Gold!
　　Vater warnte
　　vor solchem Feind.
(Die beiden andern folgen ihr, und alle drei versammeln sich schnell um das mittlere Riff.)

Alberich.　Ihr da oben!

Die Drei.　Was willst du da unten?

Alberich.　Stör' ich e'ur Spiel,
　　wenn staunend ich still hier steh'?
　　Tauchtet ihr nieder,
　　mit euch tollte
　　und neckte der Niblung sich gern!

Woglinde.　Mit uns will er spielen?

Wellgunde.　Ist ihm das Spott?

Alberich.　Wie scheint im Schimmer
　　ihr hell und schön?
　　Wie gern umschlänge
　　der Schlanken eine mein Arm,
　　schlüpfte hold sie herab!

Flosshilde.　Nun lach 'ich der Furcht:
　　der Feind ist verliebt.
(Sie lachen.)

Wellgunde.　Der lüsterne Kauz!

Woglinde.　Lasst ihn uns kennen?
(Sie lässt sich auf die Spitze des Riffes herab, an dessen Fusse *Alberich* angelangt ist.)

Alberich.　Die neigt sich herab.

Woglinde.　Nun nahe dich mir!

Alberich
(klettert mit koboldartiger Behendigkeit, doch wiederholt aufgehalten der Spitze des Riffes zu).
　　Garstig glatter
　　glitschriger Glimmer!
　　Wie gleit' ich aus!
　　Mit Händen und Füssen
　　nicht fasse noch halt' ich
　　das schlecke Geschlüpfer!
(Er pruhstet.)

Clamminess
creeps up my nostrils :
accursed sneezing !

(He has approached *Woglinde*.)

Woglinde

(laughing).

See how nicely
my beau can sneeze !

Alberich. O be but mine,
my beautiful child !

(He seeks to embrace her.)

Woglinde

(eluding him).

Would you make court,
then follow me here !

(She flies up to another rock. The others laugh.)

Alberich

(scratching his head).

Alas ! you are lost !
Come but lower !
Far too hard
'tis for me so to fly.

Woglinde

(swinging down to a third rock in the depths).

Clamber down here ;
your hand may then clasp me.

Alberich

(hastily scrambling down).

Much better down lower !

Woglinde

(darting quickly upwards to a high peak at the side).

But look, I uplift me !

(The Nymphs all laugh.)

Alberich. How follow and take
this timid fish ?
Wait a bit. false one !

Wellgunde

(has descended to a lower rock on the other side).

Heia ! my hero !
hear what I say !

Alberich

(turning round).

Call you to me ?

Wellgunde. I caution you well ;
to me wend your way :
mind not Woglinde !

Feuchtes Nass
füllt mir die Nase :
verfluchtes Niesen !

(Er ist in der Nähe *Woglinde's* angelangt.)

Woglinde

(lachend).

Pruhstend naht
meines Freiers Pracht !

Alberich. Mein Friedel sei,
du fräuliches Kind !

(Er sucht sie zu umfassen.)

Woglinde

(sich ihm entwindend).

Willst du mich frei'n,
so freie mich hier !

(Sie ist auf einem andern Riffe angelangt. Die Schwestern lachen.)

Alberich

(kratzt sich den Kopf).

O weh : du entweich'st ?
Komm' doch wieder !
Schwer ward mir,
was so leicht du erschwing'st.

Woglinde

(schwingt sich auf ein drittes Riff in grösserer Tiefe).

Steig' nur zu Grund :
da greifst du mich sicher !

Alberich

(klettert hastig hinab).

Wohl besser da unten !

Woglinde

(schnellt sich rasch aufwärts nach einem hohen Seitenriffe).

Nun aber nach oben !

(Alle Mädchen lachen.)

Alberich. Wie fang' ich im Sprung'
den spröden Fisch ?
Warte, du Falsche !

(Er will ihr eilig nachklettern.)

Wellgunde

(hat sich auf ein tieferes Riff auf der andern Seite gesenkt).

Heia ! Du Holder !
hör'st du mich nicht ?

Alberich

(sich umwendend).

Ruf'st du nach mir ?

Wellgunde. Ich rathe dir gut :
zu mir wende dich,
Woglinde meide !

Alberich

(hastily clambering over the rocks towards her).

More fair are you
than she who but flies me ;
for she's less sparkling,
too sleek and sly.
But dive yet deeper
if you would dally !

Wellgunde

(descending a little nearer to him).

So now am I near ?

Alberich.   No, not enough !
With tender arms
entwine me around,
that I may fondle
that form so bewitching :
in passionate bliss
to my panting embrace let me press thee.

Wellgunde.   Are you in love
and longing for favors ?
Let's see what semblance,
my beauty can show. —
Faugh'! you hairy
and horrible imp !
Swarthy, stunted,
and shrivelled up dwarf !
Seek as a fellow
one of like form !

Alberich

(trying to detain her by force).

Though fair I am not,
I'll fetter you fast !

Wellgunde

(quickly darting up to the central rock).

Quite fast, for fear I should flow !

(All three laugh.)

Alberich

(Calling angrily after her).

Fickle chit !
Chilly, slippery fish !
Seem I not shapely,
tender, enticing,
glib and gay —
Go ! let eels be your lovers,
if so loathsome am I !

Flosshilde.   Why scold thus, imp ?
Does your heart sink ?
But two have been sought ;
try now the third one .
soft reward
surely awaits you there !

Alberich

(kle.tert hastig über den Bodengrund zu *Wellgunde*).

Viel schöner bist du
als jene Scheue,
die minder gleissend
und gar zu glatt. —
Nur tiefer tauche,
willst du mir taugen !

Wellgunde

(noch etwas mehr zu ihm sich herabsenkend).

Bin nun ich dir nah' ?

Alberich.   Noch nicht genug !
Die schlanken Arme
schlinge um mich,
dass ich den Nacken
dir neckend betaste,
mit schmeichelnder Brunst
an die schwellende Brust mich dir schmiege.

Wellgunde.   Bist du verliebt
und lüstern nach Minne ?
Lass' seh'n, du Schöner,
wie du bist zu schau'n ? —
Pfui, du haariger,
höck'riger Geck !
Schwarzes, schwieliges
Schwefelgezwerg !
Such' dir ein Friedel,
dem du gefällst !

Alberich

(sucht sie mit Gewalt zu halten).

Gefall' ich dir nicht,
dich fass' ich doch fest !

Wellgunde

(schnell zum mittleren Riffe auftauchend).

Nur fest, sonst fliess' ich dir fort !

(Alle Drei lachen.)

Alberich

(erbos't ihr nachzankend).

Falsches Kind !
Kalter, grätiger Fisch !
Schein' ich nicht schön **dir**,
niedlich und neckisch,
glatt und glau —
hei ! so buhle mit Aalen,
ist dir eklig mein Balg !

Flosshilde.   Was zank'st du, Alp ?
Schon so verzagt ?
Du frei'test um zwei !
früg'st du die dritte,
süssen Trost
schüfe die Traute dir !

Alberich. Music sweet
sing'st thou to me : —
what joy that all
are not alike !
'Mid many I must delight one,
though all be chary to choose me.
Ere I believe thee
still lower descend.

Flosshilde
(diving down to Alberich).
How foolish are
my sisters' hearts
to see no symmetry here !

Alberich
(approaching her hastily)
Both dull and hideous
do I now hold them,
since I've beheld thee, my sweet.

Flosshilde
(cajolingly).
O warble still
thy wondrous song ;
it filleth sweetly mine ears !

Alberich
(caressing her).
I flush, flame
and flutter at heart,
homage so flatt'ring to hear.

Flosshilde
(gently repulsing him).
Thy beauty's glory
makes glad mine eyes :
and thy loving smile
doth assuage my alarms !
(Draws him tenderly to her.)
Sweetest of men !

Alberich. Softest of maids !

Flosshilde. Wert thou but mine !

Alberich. Might I e'er hold thee !

Flosshilde
(holding him quite in her arms).
O ! thy staring-eyed brow,
thy straggle-haired beard,
to see them and handle them still !
That thy stubbly grey hair,
in streaming elf locks,
might float round Flosshild' for ever !
And thy toad-allied stature.
thy stridulous tones,
O might I astonish and still,
sate with these ev'ry sense !

(*Woglinde* and *Wellgunde* have dived down to them and now
raise a peal of laughter.)

Alberich. Holder Sang
singt zu mir her. —
Wie gut, dass ihr
eine nicht seid !
Von vielen gefall' ich wohl einer :
von einer kies'te mich keine ! —
Soll ich dir glauben,
so gleite herab !

Flosshilde
(taucht zu *Alberich* hinab).
Wie thörig seid ihr,
dumme Schwestern,
dünkt euch dieser nicht schön !

Alberich
(hastig ihr nahend).
Für dumm und lässlich
darf ich sie halten,
seit ich dich Holdeste seh'.

Flosshilde
(schmeichelnd).
O singe fort
so süss und fein ;
wie hehr verführt es mein Ohr !

Alberich
(zutraulich sie berührend).
Mir zagt, zuckt
und zehrt sich das Herz,
lacht mir so zierliches Lob.

Flosshilde
(ihn sanft abwehrend).
Wie deine Anmuth
mein Aug' erfreut,
deines Lächelns Milde
den Muth mir labt !
(Sie zieht ihn zärtlich an sich.)
Seligster Mann !

Alberich. Süsseste Maid !

Flosshilde. Wär'st du mir hold !

Alberich. Hielt'ich dich immer !

Flosshilde
(ihn ganz in ihren Armen haltend).
Deinen stechenden Blick,
deinen struppigen Bart,
o säh' ich ihn, fasst' ich ihn stets !
Deines stachlichen Haares
strammes Gelock,
umflöss' es Flosshilde ewig !
Deine Krötengestalt,
deiner Stimme Gekrächz,
o dürft' ich staunend und stumm,
sie nur hören und seh'n !

(*Woglinde* und *Wellgunde* sind nah herabgetaucht und schlagen
jetzt ein helles Gelächter auf.)

Alberich

(starting timidly from Flosshilde's arms).

Are you laughing at me?

Flosshilde

(suddenly darting from him).

Your love-song thus merrily ends.

(She darts quickly up to her sisters and joins in their laughter.

Alberich

(with a screaming voice).

Woe's me! Ah, woe's me!
Alas! Alas!
The third of my trust
betraying me thus!
Most shocking, shifty,
wicked and shameless of wantons!
know you no truth,
you treacherous, nondescript brood?

The Three Rhine-Nymphs.

Walala! Lalaleia! Lalei!
Heia! Heia! Haha!
Fie on you, gnome,
in fury thus gnashing!
Take the rede that we tender.
How was it, calf,
you could not have kept
the lady of your love?
True are we,
firm is our troth
toward him who bravely holds.
Seize on us then,
and cease to reproach:
we can fly not fast in the wave.

(They swim about, hither and thither, high and low, to incite
Alberich to chase them.)

Alberich. How through my frame
there rages a fire
with radiance fierce!
Wrath and passion,
rude and pow'rful,
rouse up my pulses.
Though ye may laugh and lie,
lusting I long for one;
I'll win her, too, for my leman!

(He chases them with desperate exertions; with frightful activity
he clambers from rock to rock, springing from one to the other and
striving to reach first one nymph and then another; they always avoid
him with mocking laughter. He staggers and falls below, then
clambers aloft again — till at last his patience is exhausted: foaming
with rage, he pauses breathless and shakes his clenched fist at the
nymphs.)

Alberich

(nearly beside himself).

Were I but to catch one!

He remains in speechless rage, gazing upwards, when suddenly he
is rivetted to the spot by the following sight.
Through the water above breaks an ever-increasing glow, which on
the summit of the central rock kindles gradually to a blinding yellow
gleam; a magical golden light then streams from thence through the
water.

Alberich

(erschreckt aus Flosshilde's Armen auffahrend).

Lacht ihr Bösen mich aus?

Flosshilde

(sich plötzlich ihm entreissend).

Wie billig am Ende vom Lied.

(Sie taucht mit den Schwestern schnell in die Höhe und stimmt in
ihr Gelächter ein.)

Alberich

(mit kreischender Stimme).

Wehe! ach wehe!
O Schmerz! O Schmerz!
Die dritte, so traut,
betrog sie mich auch? —
Ihr schmählich schlaues,
lüderlich schlechtes Gelichter!
Nährt ihr nur Trug,
ihr treuloses Nickergezücht?

Die drei Rheintöchter.

Wallala! Lalaleia! Lalei!
Heia! Heia! Haha!
Schäme dich, Albe!
Schilt nicht dort unten!
Höre, was wir dich heissen!
Warum, du, Banger,
bandest du nicht
das Mädchen, das du minnst?
Treu sind wir
und ohne Trug
dem Freier, der uns fängt. —
Greife nur zu
und grause dich nicht!
In der Fluth entflieh'n wir nicht leicht.

(Sie schwimmen aus einander, hierher und dorthin, bald tiefer, bald
höher, um *Alberich* zur Jagd auf sie zu reizen.)

Alberich. Wie in den Gliedern
brünstige Gluth
mir brennt und glüht!
Wuth und Minne
wild und mächig
wühlt mir den Muth auf! —
Wie ihr auch lacht und lugt,
lüstern lechz' ich nach euch,
und eine muss mir erliegen!

Er macht sich mit verzweifelter Anstrengung zur Jagd auf: m
grauenhafter Behendigkeit erklimmt er Riff für Riff, springt von eine
zum andern, sucht bald dieses bald jenes der Mädchen zu erhasche
die mit höhnischem Gelächter stets ihm entweichen; er strauchel
stürzt in den Abgrund hinab, klettert dann hastig wieder zur Höhe, —
bis ihm endlich die Geduld entführt: vor Wuth schäumend hält e
athemlos an und streckt die geballte Faust nach den Mädchen hinauf.

Alberich

(kaum seiner mächtig).

Fing' eine diese Faust! . . .

Er verbleibt in sprachloser Wuth, den Blick aufwärts gerichtet, w
er dann plötzlich mit folgendem Schauspiele angezogen und gefesse
wird.
Durch die Fluth ist von oben her ein immer lichterer Schein g
drun en, der sich nun an einer hohen Stelle des mittleren Riffes z
einem blendend hell strahlenden Goldglanze entzündet; ein zauberisc
goldenes Licht bricht von hier durch das Wasser.

Woglinde.   Look, sisters !
  The wakener laughs in the deep.

Wellgunde.   Through the dark green surge
  it wooeth the sleeper adored.

Flosshilde.   Now kissing its eyelids
    striving to ope them.
    Look, 'tis smiling
    in silvery light !
    Through the flood around
  flows a stream as of stars.

All Three
    (swimming joyously around the rock).

    Heiajaheia !
    Heiajaheia !
  Wallala lalala leia jahei !
    Rhinegold !
    Rhinegold !
    Lustrous delight ;
  thou laughest in radiance rare !
    Glistening gleams
  outglow from thee wide o'er the waves.
    Heiajahei !
    Heia·aheia !
    Waken friend,
    waken, fain !
    Winsome the games
    we'll gambol with thee :
    flashes the foam
    flames all the flood ;
    we float around dancing,
    diving and singing,
  as sweetly we bathe in thy bed.
    Rhinegold !
    Rhinegold !
    Heiajaheia !
  Walalaleia jahei !

Alberich
  (whose eyes, fascinated by the light, are fixed on the gold).

    What is't, ye gliders,
  that there doth gleam and glow ?

The Three Nymphs
    (severally).

  Whence do you, rugged one, hail,
  of the Rhinegold ne'er to have heard ?
    You wot not, imp,
    of the gold's bright eyes then,
  the which now wake, now sleep ?
    Of the wondrous star
    of waters profound
  whose light illumines the wave ? —

Woglinde.   Lugt, Schwestern !
  Die Weckerin lacht in den Grund.

Wellgunde.   Durch den grünen Schwall
  den wonnigen Schläfer sie grüsst.

Flosshilde.   Jetzt küsst sie sein Auge
    dass er es öff'ne ;
    schaut, es lächelt
    in lichtem Schein ;
    durch die Fluthen hin
  fliesst sein strahlender Stern.

Die Drei
    (zusammen das Riff anmuthig umschwimmend).

    Heiajaheia !
    Heiajaheia !
  Wallala lalala leia jahei !
    Rheingold !
    Rheingold !
    Leuchtende Lust,
  wie lach'st du so hell und hehr !
    Glühender Glanz
  entgleisst dir weihlich im Wag !
    Heiajahei
    Heiajaheia !
    Wache, Freund,
    wache froh,
    Wonnige Spiele
    spenden wir dir :
    flimmert der Fluss,
    flammet die Fluth,
    Umfliessen wir tauchend,
    tanzend und singend,
  im seligen Bade dein Bett.
    Rheingold !
    Rheingold !
    Heiajaheia !
  Wallalaleia jahei !

Alberich
  (dessen Auge, mächtig vom Glanze angezogen, starr an dem Golde
      haftet).

    Was ist's, ihr Glatten,
  das dort so gleisst und glänzt ?

Die Drei Mädchen
    (abwechselnd).

  Wo bist du Rauher denn heim,
  dass vom Rheingold nie du gehört ? —
    Nichts weiss der Alp
    von des Goldes Auge,
  das wechselnd wacht und schläft ?
    von der Wassertiefe
    wonnigem Stern,
  der hehr die Wogen durchhellt ? —

See how sweetly
we ride in its radiance !
Would you, laggard, then
seek to lave there,
come sport and swim by our side.
(They laugh.)

Alberich.   Is the gold ye dive around
good but for play ?
' twould please me but little.

Woglinde.   The golden prize
precious you'd deem,
wist you but all of its wonder.

Wellgunde.   The world's kingdom
that one can encompass
who from the Rhinegold
shapeth the Ring,
which measureless might can secure.

Flosshilde.   Our father said it,
and bade us firmly
keep the treasure
in careful trust,
that no foeman should forcibly filch it :
so peace, ye prattling crew !

Wellgunde.   O prudent sister,
reproving us both !
Bear you in mind
but unto whom
'tis given to fashion the gold ?

Woglinde.   But he who passion's
pow'r forswears,
and from delights
of love forbears, —
but he the magic commandeth,
the prize to mould to a ring.

Wellgunde.   Full safe from such
must we surely be :
for none may live and love not :
parteth no man from the passion.

Woglinde.   He least of them all ;
the libertine imp,
with lustful rage
mortally racked.

Flosshilde.   I fear not him :
for my part I found
in his bestial warmth
well nigh I burned.

Wellgunde.   A brimstone brand
to the water brought !
in heat of love-rage
hissing loud.

Sieh', wie selig
im Glanze wir gleiten !
Willst du Banger
in ihm dich baden,
so schwimm' und schwelge mit **uns** !
(Sie lachen.)

Alberich.   Eu'rem Taucherspiele
nur taugte das Gold ?
Mir gält' es dann wenig !

Woglinde.   Des Goldes Schmuck
schmähte er nicht,
wüsst' er all' seine Wunder !

6 *Wellgunde.*   Der Welt Erbe
gewänne zu eigen,
wer aus dem Rheingold
schüfe den Ring,
der masslose Macht ihm verlieh'.

Flosshilde.   Der Vater sagt' es,
und uns befahl er
klug zu hüten
den klaren Hort,
dass kein Falscher der Fluth ihn entführte :
d'rum schweigt, ihr schwatzendes Heer !

Wellgunde.   Du klügste Schwester !
Verklag'st du uns wohl ?
Weisst du denn nicht,
wem allein
das Gold zu schmieden vergönnt ?

7 *Woglinde.*   Nur wer der Minne
Macht versagt,
nur wer der Liebe
Lust verjagt,
nur der erzielt sich den Zauber,
zum Reif zu zwingen das Gold.

Wellgunde.   Wohl sicher sind wir
und sorgenfrei :
denn was nur lebt will lieben ;
meiden will keiner die Minne.

Woglinde.   Am wenigsten er,
der lüsterne Alp :
vor Liebesgier
möcht' er vergeh'n !

Flosshilde.   Nicht fürcht' ich den,
wie ich ihn erfand :
seiner Minne Brunst
brannte fast mich.

Wellgunde.   Ein Schwefelbrand
in der Wogen Schwall :
vor Zorn der Liebe
zischt er laut.

All Three (together).	**Die Drei** (zusammen).

All Three (together).   **2**

Walalaleia! Lahei!
  Loveliest earth-gnome,
  laugh too with us!
  In the golden shimmer
  how lordly you seem!
Come, lovely one, laugh with us too!

(They laugh.)

Alberich

(his eyes still rivetted on the gold, has listened closely to the sisters' talk).

  The world's kingdom   **6**
at once could I compass through this?
  If love is denied me,
  a newer delight I may know!

(Terribly loud.)

  Twit as ye will;
the Nibelung neareth your toy!

Raging, he springs to the central rock and clambers with terrible haste to its summit. The nymphs separate screaming, and dart upwards at different sides.

The Three Nymphs.
  Heia! Heia! Heiahahei!
  Save us all!
  Insane is the imp!
  How the water spurts
  where he has sprung.
  A madman made by his love.

(They laugh in wild excitement.)

Alberich

(on the summit of the peak, stretching out his hand toward the gold).

  Fear ye not now?
  Then fondle in darkness,
  dark that ye are!   **4**
The light's luster I quench;
and rend from the rock the gold,   **6**
vengeance to wreak with a Ring:
  for, hear me ye floods —
Love I forswear forever!

With terrible strength he tears the gold from the rock and, hastily descending, disappears quickly below. Sudden darkness overspreads the scene. The nymphs dive down after the robber.

The Three Nymphs
(screaming).

  Hinder the robber!
  Rescue the gold!
  Help us! Help us!
  Woe! Woe!

The flood falls with them into the deep. Far below is heard Alberich's mocking laughter.—The rocks disappear in the thickest darkness, the whole stage is completely filled with black waves of water which seem for some time continually to sink.   **7 6**

Die Drei (zusammen).   **2**

Wallalalleia! Lahei!
  Lieblicher Albe,
  lach'st du nicht auch!
  In des Goldes Schein
  wie leuchtest du schön!
Komm', Lieblicher, lache mit uns!

(Sie lachen.)

Alberich

(die Augen starr auf das Gold gerichtet, hat dem hastigen Geplaude der Schwestern wohl gelauscht).

  Der Welt Erbe   **6**
gewänn' ich zu eigen durch dich?
  Erzwäng' ich nicht Liebe,
  doch listig erzwäng' ich mir Lust?—

(Furchtbar laut.)

  Spottet nur zu!
Der Nibelung naht eu'rem Spiel!

Wüthend springt er nach dem mittleren Riff hinüber und klettert in grausiger Hast nach dessen Spitze hinauf. Die Mädchen fahren kreischend auseinander und tauchen nach verschiedenen Seiten hin auf.

Die drei Rheintöchter.
  Heia! Heia! Heiahahei!
  Rettet euch!
  es raset der Alp!
  in den Wassern sprüht's
  wohin er springt:
  die Minne macht ihn verrückt!

(Sie lachen im tollsten Uebermuth.)

Alberich

(auf der Spitze des Riffes, die Hand nach dem Golde ausstreckend).

  Bangt euch noch nicht?
  So buhlt nun im Finstern,
  feuchtes Gezücht!
Das Licht lösch' ich euch aus;
das Gold entreiss' ich dem Riff,
schmiede den rächenden Ring:
  denn hör' es die Fluth—
so verfluch' ich die Liebe!

Er reisst mit furchtbarer Gewalt das Gold aus dem Riffe und stürzt damit hastig in die Tiefe, wo er schnell verschwindet. Dichte Nacht bricht plötzlich überall herein. Die Mädchen tauchen nach dem Räuber in die Tiefe nach.

Die drei Rheintöchter
(schreiend).

  Haltet den Räuber!
  Rettet das Gold!
  Hülfe! Hülfe!
  Wehe! Wehe!

Die Fluth fällt mit ihnen nach der Tiefe hinab: aus dem untersten Grunde hört man Alberich's gellendes Hohngelächter. — In dichtester Finsterniss verschwinden die Riffe; die ganze Bühne ist von der Höhe bis zur Tiefe von schwarzem Wassergewoge erfüllt, das eine Zeit lang immer noch abwärts zu sinken scheint.

SECOND SCENE.

Gradually the waves give place to clouds which clear off in fine mist, showing

An open space on a mountain top

first by the faint light of night.—The dawning day lights up with increasing luster a castle with glittering pinnacles, which stands on a cliff at the back : between this and the foreground is a deep valley through which the Rhine is supposed to flow.—At one side *Wotan* and *Fricka* are lying asleep in a flowery meadow.

Fricka

(wakes, and her eyes fall on the castle ; she starts in surprise).

Wotan ! my lord ! awaken !

Wotan

(still dreaming).

The wondrous heavenly hall
is warded with gate and gulf.
Mortal honor,
infinite might,
fly to the acme of fame !

Fricka

(shaking him).

Wake from thy visions
rosy and vain !
Awake now, spouse, and arouse thee !

Wotan

(wakes and raises himself slightly. His eyes are at once attracted and riveted by the sight of the castle).

'Tis ended — the infinite work !
A heavenly mansion
on mountain heights ;
proudly peer
my prosperous halls
as in visions I viewed,
as I ordered it erst ;
strong and sound
stands it in sight :
grand and glorious pile.

Fricka. So welcome deem'st thou
what I but dread ?
Though fair thy tow'r
I tremble for Freia.
Mindless one, pause and remember
the mentioned price to be paid !
the castle finished,
now falleth the bond.
Forgettest then what thou must give ?

Wotan. I mind well all they demanded,
my men who built me this burg ;
their grim race I
by agreement o'erawed,
whereby this hallowed
home they should build me.

ZWEITE SCENE.

Allmählig gehen die Wogen in Gewölke über, das sich nach u nach abklärt, und als es sich endlich, wie in feinem Nebel, gänzli verliert, wird eine

freie Gegend auf Bergeshöhen

sichtbar, anfänglich noch in nächtlicher Beleuchtung.—Der herv brechende Tag beleuchtet mit wachsendem Glanze eine Burg mit blir enden Zinnen, die auf einem Felsgipfel im Hintergrunde steht ; zw chen diesem burggekrönten Felsgipfel und dem Vordergrunde c Scene ist ein tiefes Thal, durch welches der Rhein fliesst, anzunehme —Zur Seite auf blumigem Grunde liegt *Wotan*, neben ihm *Fric* beide schlafend.

Fricka

(erwacht : ihr Blick fällt auf die Burg ; sie staunt und erschrickt).

Wotan ! Gemahl ! erwache !

Wotan

(im Traume leise).

Der Wonne seligen Saal
bewachen mir Thür' und Thor :
Mannes Ehre,
ewige Macht,
ragen zu endlosem Ruhm !

Fricka

(rüttelt ihn).

Auf, aus der Träume
wonnigen Trug !
Erwache, Mann, und erwäge !

Wotan

(erwacht und erhebt sich ein wenig : sein Auge wird sogleich vc Anblick der Burg gefesselt).

Vollendet das ewige Werk :
auf Berges Gipfel
die Götter-Burg,
prunkvoll prahlt
der prangende Bau !
Wie im Traum ich ihn trug,
wie mein Wille ihn wies,
stark und schön
steht er zur Schau ;
hehrer, herrlicher Bau !

Fricka. Nur Wonne schafft dir
was mich erschreckt ?
Dich freut die Burg,
mir bangt es um Freia.
Achtloser, lass dich erinnern
des ausbedungenen Lohn's !
Die Burg ist fertig,
verfallen das Pfand :
vergiss'st du, was du vergab'st ?

Wotan. Wohl dünkt mich's, was sie bedangen,
die dort die Burg mir gebaut ;
durch Vertrag zähmt'ich
ihr trotzig Gezücht,
dass sie die hehre
Halle mir schlüfen ;

It prospers——thanks to their prowess !
For the price pray have no heed.

icka. Alas ! thy fatuous lightness !
lacking love is thy folly.
Had I but known of this bond
the baseness might have been helped :
but pleased were ye wise ones
to part from the women ;
no jot confiding in us,
alone ye conferred with the giants.
So, without shame,
ye shrink not to forfeit
Freia, my glorious sister,
for this scandalous cause.
Nought may your hard hearts
of holiness know,
when you pant but for power.

otan. Like longings
did Fricka not feel,
when she herself bade me to build ?

icka. Of my husband's truth ill assured,
in trouble I considered
how to hold him beside me
when he was seeking to stray :
halls bright and gleaming,
glorious homestead,
such might surely allure thee
to linger and seek in them rest.
But thou in this fortress thought'st
of fence and force alone :
power and might
'twas to augment thee :
this ravishing castle but rises
to cause yet more riotous strife.

otan
(smiling).
If with these walls
thou, O wife, shouldst enwind me,
yet grant but this to my godhood ;
while in the castle's
confines I yet
may outside it win me the world.
Wand'ring at will
all love who live :
my sport I cannot dispense with.

icka. Light, unloving,
low-natured man !
For such mere conceits
as might and control
wouldst trample in lawless contempt
love and a woman's worth ?

die steht nun — Dank den Starken :—
um den Sold sorge dich nicht.

Fricka. O lachend frevelnder Leichtsinn !
Liebelosester Frohmuth !
Wusst' ich um eu'ren Vertrag,
dem Truge hätt' ich gewehrt ;
doch muthig entferntet
ihr Männer die Frauen,
um taub und ruhig vor uns
allein mit den Riesen zu tagen.
So ohne Scham
verschenktet ihr Frechen
Freia, mein holdes Geschwister,
froh des Schächergewerb's. —
Was ist euch Harten
doch heilig und werth,
giert ihr Männer nach Macht !

Wotan. Gleiche Gier
war Fricka wohl fremd,
als selbst um den Bau sie bat ?

Fricka. Um des Gatten Treue besorgt
muss traurig ich wohl sinnen,
wie an mich er zu fesseln,
zieht's in die Ferne ihn fort :
herrliche Wohnung,
wonniger Hausrath,
sollten mit sanftem Band
dich binden zu säumender Rast.
Doch du bei dem Wohnbau sannst
auf Wehr und Wall allein :
Herrschaft und Macht
soll er dir mehren ;
nur rastlosern Sturm zu erregen
erstand die ragende Burg.

Wotan
(lächelnd).
Wolltest du Frau
in der feste mich fangen,
mir Gotte musst du schon gönnen,
dass, in der Burg
gebunden, ich mir
von aussen gewinne die Welt.
Wandel und Wechsel
liebt wer lebt :
das Spiel drum kann ich nicht sparen.

Fricka. Liebeloser,
leidigster Mann !
Um der Macht und Herrschaft
müssigen Tand
verspielst du in lästerndem Spott
Liebe und Weibes Werth ?

Wotan

(earnestly).

When I for wife sought to win thee,
my other eyeball
in a wager I risked;
thou blamest blindly, methinks!
Women I lean to
E'en more than thou lik'st.
I'll let not our fairest
Freia be ta'en:
my thoughts ne'er turned to such thing.

Fricka. Then save her at once:—
in sorest alarm
hither she hastens for help.

Freia

(entering hastily).

Help me, Fricka!
fail me not, father!
From mountain fastness
Fasolt gives menace:
he comes too surely to catch me.

Wotan. Let him rage!—
Saw'st thou not Loki?

Fricka. That belief thou shouldst still
to that liar accord!
Much wrong already he's wrought,
yet sets new snares for thee ever.

Wotan. Where simple might serves
let none seek to assist me;
but to shape the fraud
of foes to serve me,
I can learn by such arts
as only Loki employs.
He this agreement advised,
and vowed to extricate Freia:
on him I firmly rely.

Fricka. And he fails in his faith.—
The giants hast'ning
hither behold:
where lurks thy juggling ally?

Freia. Why hasten not my brothers
with help they should bring me,
now my father refuses defence?
O help me, Donner!
hither! hither!
rescue Freia, my Froh!

Fricka.
Those who basely bargained to wrong thee
have all abandoned thee now.

Wotan

(ernst).

Um dich zum Weib zu gewinnen,
mein eines Auge
setzt' ich werbend daran:
wie thörig tadelst du jetzt!
Ehr' ich die Frauen
doch mehr als dich freut!
Und Freia, die gute,
geb' ich nicht auf:
nie sann dies ernstlich mein Sinn.

Fricka. So schirme sie jetzt:
in schutzloser Angst
11   läuft sie nach Hülf' dort her!
12 *Freia*

(hastig auftretend).

Hilf mir, Schwester!
Schütze mich, Schwäher!
Vom Felsen drüben
drohte mir Fasolt,
mich Holde käm' er zu holen.

Wotan. Lass' ihn droh'n!—
Sah'st du nicht Loge?

Fricka. Dass am liebsten du immer
dem Listigen trau'st!
Manch Schlimmes schuf er uns schon,
doch stets bestrickt er dich wieder.

Wotan. Wo freier Muth frommt
allein, frag' ich nach keinem;
doch des Feindes Neid
zum Nutz' sich fügen,
lehrt nur Schlauheit und List,
wie Loge verschlagen sie übt.
Der zum Vertrage mir rieth,
versprach Freia zu lösen:
auf ihn verlass' ich mich nun.

Fricka. Und er lässt dich allein.—
Dort schreiten rasch
die Riesen heran:
wo harrt dein schlauer Gehülf?

11 *Freia.* Wo harren meine Brüder,
12   dass Hülfe sie brächten,
da mein Schwäher die Schwache verschenkt
Zu Hülfe, Donner!
Hieher! hieher!
Rette Freia, mein Froh!

Fricka.
Die in bösem Bund dich verriethe,
sie alle bergen sich nun.

asolt and Fafner	*13* *Fasolt* und *Fafner*
(men of gigantic stature, armed with strong staves, enter).	(beide in riesiger Gestalt, mit starken Pfählen bewaffnet, treten auf).

asolt. Soft sleep
      sealed thine eyes :
      while we in wakeful
labor wove thy walls.
      Tedious toil
      tired us not ;
      heap'd we huge
      and heavy stones.
      High with dome,
      donjon, door,
      we have formed
a fortress fair and fast.
      There bideth
      our building,
      bright'ning in
      the beams of day.
      Pass within,
but pay our wage.

otan. Name, workmen, your wage.
What forfeit have ye fixed on ?

asolt. 'Twas fixed beforehand,
      what we deemed fit :
thy mem'ry is remiss !
      Freia the holy —
      Holda the free one —
      agreed it is,
she goes with us home.

otan. Are ye engrossed
      on what was agreed ?
other guerdon ask :
Freia I must refuse.

asolt
(remaining awhile speechless with wrathful surprise).
      What say'st thou — Ha !
      seek'st to betray —
      betray a contract ?
      On thy spear writ,
      serve but for sport
those compelling runes of power ?

fner
            (ironically).
      My faithful brother !
Deem'st thou, fool, he is false ?

asolt. Son of light,
      swayed so lightly,
hear and heed thyself !
Thy treaties hold in truth)
      What thou art,
art thou only by treaties ;

Fasolt. Sanft schloss
      Schlaf dein Aug' :
      wir beide bauten
Schlummers bar die Burg.
      Mächt'ger Müh'
      müde nie,
      stau'ten starke
      Stein' wir auf ;
      steiler Thurm,
      Thür' und Thor,
      deckt und schliesst
8 im schlanken Schloss den Saal.
      Dort steht's,
      was wir stemmten ;
      schimmernd hell
      bescheint's der Tag :
      zieh' nun ein,
uns zahl' den Lohn !

Wotan. Nennt, Leute, den Lohn :
      was dünkt euch zu bedingen ?

9 *Fasolt.* Bedungen ist's,
      was tauglich uns dünkt :
      gemahnt es dich so matt ?
11   Freia, die holde,
      Holda, die freie —
      vertragen ist's —
sie tragen wir heim.

Wotan. Seid ihr bei Trost
      mit eurem Vertrag ?
Denkt auf andern Dank :
Freia ist mir nicht feil.

Fasolt
(vor wüthendem Erstaunen einen Augenblick sprachlos).
      was sagst du, ha !
      Sinnst du Verrath ?
      Verrath am Vertrag ?
      Die dein Speer birgt,
      sind sie dir Spiel,
des berath'nen Bundes Runen ?

Fafner
            (höhnisch).
      Getreu'ster Bruder !
Merkst du Tropf nun Betrug ?

Fasolt. Lichtsohn du,
      leicht gefügter,
hör' und hüte dich :
Verträgen halte Treu' !
      Was du bist,
bist du nur durch Verträge :

Conformable,
well defined was thy might.
 More wise art thou
 than we are wary,
 binding us free ones
 in friendly peace:
cursed be thy wisdom futile,
far shall wane peace before thee,
 when no more open,
 honest and free,
thou breakest thy warrant and bond!—
 A simple giant
 judges so:
Be warned, thou wise one, by him!

Wotan. How sly to take for truth
what only in sport we had settled!
 The beauteous goddess,
 light and bright,
what use to you are her charms?

Fasolt. Flout'st thou us?
 Fie! how evil!—
You who in radiance sway,
regal, sorrowless race,
 like fools ye strive
 for a fortress of stone;
setting 'gainst it, sooth,
a wondrous woman in pledge.
We, blockheads, bother us,
toiling with toughness of hand
 to win us a woman,
 who, winning and sweet,
should go gladly with us.—
From the bond now wilt thou back?

Fafner. Check thy foolish chatter;
no luck look we to gain.
 Freia's self
 serves little;
 but 'twere good
to get her away from the Æsir:
 golden apples
grow in her orchard garden;
 none else can
grasp the art of their culture:
 this grateful fruit
 grants to her kindred
 eternal youth
 time cannot ravage;
 weak and blighted
 waneth their beauty,—
 old and worn
 will they pass hence,
fareth e'er from them Freia:
let her forthwith be torn from them all.

bedungen ist,
wohl bedacht deine **Macht.**
 Bist weiser du
 als witzig wir sind,
 bandest uns Freie
 zum Frieden du:
all deinem Wissen fluch' ich,
fliehe weit deinen Frieden,
 weisst du nicht offen,
 ehrlich und frei,
Verträgen zu wahren die **Treu'!**—
 Ein dummer Riese
 räth' dir das:
du Weiser, wiss' es von ihm!

Wotan. Wie schlau für Ernst du achtest,
was wir zum Scherz nur beschlossen!
 Die liebliche Göttin,
 licht und leicht,
was taugt euch Tölpeln ihr Reiz?

Fasolt. Höhn'st du uns?
 Ha! wie unrecht!—
Die ihr durch Schönheit herrscht,
schimmernd hehres Geschlecht,
 wie thörig strebt ihr
 nach Thürmen von Stein
setzt um Burg und Saal
Weibes Wonne zum Pfand!
Wir Plumpen plagen uns
schwitzend mit schwieliger **Hand,**
 ein Weib zu gewinnen,
 das wonnig und mild
bei uns Armen wohne:—
und verkehrt nennt ihr den Kauf?

Fafner. Schweig' dein faules Schwatzen,
Gewinn werben wir nicht:
 Freia's Haft
 hilft wenig;
 doch viel gilt's
den Göttern sie zu entführen.
 Gold'ne Aepfel
wachsen in ihrem Garten;
 sie allein
weiss die Aepfel zu pflegen:
 der Frucht Genuss
 frommt ihren Sippen
 zu ewig nie
 alternder Jugend;
 siech und bleich
 doch sinkt ihre Blüthe,
 alt und schwach
 schwinden sie hin,
müssen Freia sie missen:
ihrer Mitte drum sei sie entführt!

14

14
13

Wotan (aside). Loki stays too long !	*Wotan* (für sich). Loge säumt zu lang !
Fasolt. Straight tell thy resolve.	*Fasolt.* Schlicht gieb nun Bescheid !
Wotan. Fix on other spoil.	*Wotan.* Sinnt auf andern Sold !
Fasolt. No other : Freia alone !	*Fasolt.* Kein andrer : Freia allein !
Fafner. Thou there ! follow us ! (They press towards *Freia*.)	*Fafner.* Du da, folg' uns fort ! (Sie dringen auf *Freia* zu.)
Freia (seeking to fly). Help ! Help from these harsh ones !	*Freia* (fliehend). Helft ! helft vor den Harten !
Donner and *Froh* (enter hastily).	*Donner* und *Froh* (kommen eilig).
Froh (clasping *Freia* in his arms). To me, Freia ! — Miscreant, fall back ! Froh guards the goddess !	*Froh* (*Freia* in seine Arme fassend). Zu mir, Freia ! — Meide sie, Frecher ! Froh schützt die Schöne.
Donner (planting himself before the two giants). Fasolt and Fafner — felt ye the blow of my hammer's head before ?	*Donner* (sich vor die beiden Riesen stellend). Fasolt und Fafner, fühltet ihr schon meines Hammers harten Schlag ?
Fafner. What means thy threat ?	*Fafner.* Was soll das Droh'n ?
Fasolt. Why thrust in here ? we want not to fight — expect nought else but our pay.	*Fasolt.* Was dringst du her ? Kampf kies'ten wir nicht, verlangen nur unsern Lohn.
Donner (swinging his hammer). I've paid many giants their meed; rascals e'er I'm ready to pay. Come here ! I'll deal your due, helped with a generous hand.	*Donner* (den Hammer schwingend). Schon oft zahlt' ich Riesen den Zoll; schuldig blieb' ich Schächern nie : kommt her ! des Lohnes Last wäg' ich mit gutem Gewicht !
Wotan (stretching out his spear between the disputants). Hold ! thou fierce one ! Nought booteth force. This bond the shaft of my spear doth shield : spare then thy hammer's helve.	*Wotan* (seinen Speer zwischen den Streitenden ausstreckend). Halt, du Wilder ! Nichts durch Gewalt ! Verträge schützt meines Speeres Schaft : spar' deines Hammers Heft !
Freia. Woe's me ! Woe's me ! Wotan forsakes me !	*Freia.* Wehe ! Wehe ! Wotan verlässt mich !
Fricka. Thou meanest it then, merciless man ?	*Fricka.* Begreif' ich dich noch, grausamer Mann ?

9

Wotan

(turns away and perceives *Loge* coming).

Here is Loge !
Hastest thou so
when thou shouldst straighten
the sorry bargain thou struckest ?

Loge

(who has climbed up from the valley at back).

Why ! what bargain
bad have I struck you ?
Was't what you conjointly
with the giants did work ?
To depths and to heights
I drive at my heed.
House and hearth
can hold me not ;
Donner and Froh
they dote on a dwelling fair :
fain would they woo ;
a house then must they find :
a bright abode,
a bulwark brave,
thereto bends Wotan's wish ;
roof and room, —
house and hall, —
the heavenly pile, —
behold it in its pride.
The towering walls
I tried myself,
examined all
if it were firm.
Fasolt and Fafner
failed not in faith :
each stone fits where it stands.
Not idle was I
like all the rest :
who styles me sluggard, he lies.

Wotan.   Artfully
slippest thou out :
look to thee, traitor,
if thou betrayest me now !
Of all th' immortals
thine only friend,
I took thee up
to our over-credulous crew : —
now speak, and spae us well.
When they who built us the burg
For meed Freia demanded,
thou'rt 'ware that solely
would I consent
when word thou plightedst at last
to deliver the glorious pledge.

Loge.   With greatest pains
th' affair to ponder

Wotan

(wendet sich ab und sieht *Loge* kommen).

15
—
16

Endlich Loge !
Eiltest du so,
den du geschlossen,
den schlimmen Handel zu schlichten ?

Loge

(ist im Hintergrunde aus dem Thale aufgetreten).

Wie ? welchen Handel
hätt' ich geschlossen ? .
Wohl was mit den Riesen
dort im Rathe du dangst ? —
In Tiefen und Höh'n
treibt mich mein Hang ;
Haus und Herd
behagt mir nicht :
Donner und Froh,
die denken an Dach und Fach ;
wollen sei frei'n,
ein Haus muss sie erfreu'n :
ein stolzer Saal,
ein starkes Schloss,
danach stand Wotan's Wunsch. —
Haus und Hof,
Saal und Schloss,
die selige Burg,
sie steht nun stark gebaut ;
das Prachtgemäuer
prüfte ich selbst ;
ob alles fest,
forscht' ich genau :
Fasolt und Fafner
fand ich bewährt ;
kein Stein wankt im Gestemm'.
Nicht müssig war ich,
wie mancher hier :
der lügt, wer lässig mich schilt !

Wotan.   Arglistig
weichst du mir aus :
mich zu betrügen
hüte in Treuen dich wohl !
Von allen Göttern
dein einz'ger Freund,
nahm ich dich auf
in der übel trauenden Tross. —
Nun red' und rathe klug !
Da einst die Bauer der Burg
zum Dank Freia bedangen,
du weisst, nicht anders
willigt' ich ein,
als weil auf Pflicht du gelobtest
zu lösen das hehre Pfand.

Loge.   Mit höchster Sorge
drauf zu sinnen.

how we might save her
that — did I swear.
But to discover
what ne'er occurred —
what ne'er took place —
how possibly could I promise?

Fricka
(to *Wotan*).
See what traitorous
scamp thou didst trust!

Froh. Loge art thou,
but better called " liar."*

Donner. Accursed glist'ner,
thy gleam I'll quench.

Loge. But to screen your blunder
ye scold me, blockheads.
(*Donner* and *Froh* are about to set on him.)

Wotan
(restraining them).
I pray you leave him in peace!
Ye know not Loge's knacks.
Value high
his advice e'er has,
when we wait for it long.

Fafner. No more waiting:
quick! — the wage!

Fasolt. Pay fails to appear.

Wotan
(to *Loge*).
Now hark, strategist!
hold thee still.
Why strayedst thou here and there?

Loge. Evil is ever
Loge's lot.
Alone for thy sake
I sallied out,
and stormily strode
to the ends of the earth
to seek for Freia a substitute,
which for the giants were just.
Success slipped me:
I see now full well
in the world around
nought is so rare
to replace in mind of a man
a woman's wonderful worth.
(All exhibit surprise and emotion.)

*The pun in the original, between " Loge " and " Lüge," cannot
be preserved in translation.

---

wie es zu lösen,
das — hab' ich gelobt:
doch dass ich fände,
was nie sich fügt,
was nie gelingt,
wie liess sich das wohl geloben?

Fricka
(zu *Wotan*).
Sieh, welch' trugvollem
Schelm du getraut!

Froh. Loge heisst du,
doch nenn' ich dich Lüge!

Donner. Verfluchte Lohe,
dich lösch' ich aus!

Loge. Ihre Schmach zu decken
schmähen mich Dumme.
(*Donner* und *Froh* wollem ihm zu Leibe.)

Wotan
(wehrt ihnen).
In Frieden lasst mir den Freund!
Nicht kennt ihr Loge's Kunst:
reicher wiegt
seines Rathes Werth,
zahlt er zögernd ihn aus.

13 *Fafner.* Nichts gezögert:
rasch gezahlt!

Fasolt. Lang währt's mit dem Lohn.

Wotan
(zu *Loge*).
Jetzt hör', Störrischer!
halte mir Stich!
Wo schweiftest du hin und her?

Loge. Immer ist Undank
Loge's Lohn!
Um dich nur besorgt
sah ich mich um,
durchstöbert' im Sturm
alle Winkel der Welt,
Ersatz für Freia zu suchen,
wie er den Riesen wohl recht:
Umsonst sucht' ich
und sehe nun wohl,
in der Welten Ring
nichts ist so reich,
als Ersatz zu muthen dem Mann
für Weibes Wonne und Werth.
(Alle gerathen in Erstaunen und Betroffenheit.)

Where life ebbeth and floweth	So weit Leben und Weben,
in flood, and earth, and air,	in Wasser, Erd' und Luft,
all asked I,	viel frug ich,
ever inquiring	forschte bei allen,
where sinew doth reign,	wo Kraft nur sich rührt
and seedlings are rooted,	und Keime sich regen:
what well a man	was wohl dem Manne
could mightier deem	mächtiger dünk',
than woman's wonderful worth.	als Weibes Wonne und Werth?
But where life ebbeth and floweth,	Doch so weit Leben und Weben,
I only found myself	verlacht nur ward
laughed at by all.	meine fragende List:
In flood and earth and air	in Wasser, Erd' und Luft
everything hath	lassen will nichts
for aim but love.	von Lieb' und Weib. —
Yet one I met with	Nur einen sah ich,
had made against love his oath;	der sagte der Liebe ab:
for ruddy gold	um rothes Gold
bereft him of woman's grace.	entrieth er des Weibes Gunst.
The Rhine's indignant daughters	Des Rheines klare Kinder
dismal tidings announced:	klagten mir ihre Noth:
The Nibelung,	der Nibelung,
Night-Alberich,	Nacht-Alberich,
failed from the girls	buhlte vergebens
amorous favors to gain;	um der Badenden Gunst;
the Rhinegold he	das Rheingold da
robbed in his raging revenge:	raubte sich rächend der Dieb:
and values now	das dünkt ihm nun
its worth over all, —	das theuerste Gut,
greater than woman's grace.	hehrer als Weibes Huld.
For their glittering toy,	Um den gleissenden Tand,
thus torn from the deep,	der Tiefe entwandt,
the maidens with tears are mourning.	erklang mir der Töchter Klage:
To thee, Wotan,	an dich, Wotan,
wailing they turn,	wenden sie sich,
that thy wrath may fall on the robber:	dass zu Recht du zögest den Räuber,
the gold to the waves	das Gold dem Wasser
be once more given,	wieder gebest,
their own to continue for ever. —	und ewig es bliebe ihr Eigen. —
This to mention	Dir's zu melden
I swore to the maidens:	gelobt' ich den Mädchen:
now staunch I stand to my word.	nun lös'te Loge sein Wort.

11

4
7
5

2

4
6

Wotan.   Senseless art thou   *Wotan.*   Thörig bist du,
          if not designing!   wenn nicht gar tückisch!
          Myself suffering ruth   Mich selbst siehst du in Noth;
          for others what help have I?   wie hülf' ich andren zum Heil?

Fasolt   *Fasolt*
   (who has been listening attentively -- to *Fafner*).   (der aufmerksam zugehört. zu *Fafner*).
   This gold I begrudge the Niblung.   Nicht gönn' ich das Gold dem Alben,
   Much wrong he's hatched us already: viel Noth schuf uns der Niblung,
   but slily slipped the dwarf   doch schlau entschlüpfte immer
   unhindered out of our hold.   unsrem Zwange der Zwerg.

Fafner.   Now the gnome   *Fafner.*   Neue Neidthat
          will shape new annoyance,   sinnt uns der Niblung,

mighty made by gold.
   Thou there, Loge ;
   say without lies
what greatness giveth this gold,
that the dwarf doth hold it dear ?

Loge.   A toy 'twas
   ere from waters taken,
serving gay maidens for sport :
   but when to a Ring
   'tis rounded and fashioned
marvellous might it grants,
and wins its grasper the world.

Wotan.   Many rumors tell
   of the Rhinegold :
   runes of riches
run in its ruddy light ;
   might and wealth
'twould win were it made a ring.

Fricka.   Boots as well
   the golden bauble's
   glittering dross
for women to deck and adorn ?

Loge.   A wife could fix
   the faith of her spouse,
   found she the rare
   and radiant mass
whose metal pigmies moulded,
ruled by the pow'r of the ring.

Fricka.   O might but my husband
   gain me the hoard !

Wotan.   To win me that circlet
seemeth wise to my thinking. —
   But how, Loge,
   light on the means ?
how make the dwarf's treasure mine ?

Loge.   A rune of magic
makes the gold a ring ;
   none may know it ;
but he its hold hath learned,
who sweets of love forswears.
     (Wotan turns away discouraged.)
   That likes you not ;
   too late you are too :
Alberich paused not in doubt !
   promptly he conquered
   the potent spell,
and rightly fashioned the ring.

Donner.   Placed were all of us
   in his power,
were not the ring from him ravished.

giebt das Gold ihm Macht. —
   Du da, Loge !
   Sag' ohne Lüg :
was Grosses gilt denn das Gold,
dass es dem Niblung genügt ?

5 *Loge.*   Ein Tand ist's
   In des Wassers Tiefe,
lachenden Kindern zur Lust :
   doch, ward es zum runden
   Reife geschmiedet,
hilft es zu höchster Macht,
Gewinnt dem Manne die Welt.

Wotan.   Von des Rheines Gold
   hört' ich raunen :
   Beute-Runen
berge sein rother Glanz,
   Macht und Schätze
schüf' ohne Mass ein Reif.

Fricka.   Taugte wohl auch
   des gold'nen Tandes
   gleissend Geschmeid
Frauen zu schönem Schmuck ?

Loge.   Des Gatten Treu'
   ertrotzte die Frau,
   trüge sie hold
   den hellen Schmuck ?
den schimmernd Zwerge schmieden
rührig im Zwange des Reif's.

11 *Fricka.*   Gewänne mein Gatte
   wohl sich das Gold !

Wotan.   Des Reifes zu walten,
räthlich will es mich dünken. —
   Doch wie, Loge,
   lernt' ich die Kunst ?
wie schüf' ich mir das Geschmeid ?

6 *Loge.*   Ein Runenzauber
   zwingt das Gold zum Reif :
   keiner kennt ihn ;
doch einer übt ihn leicht,
der sel'ger Lieb' entsagt.
     (Wotan wendet sich unmuthig ab.)
   Das spar'st du wohl ;
   zu spät auch käm'st du :
Alberich zögerte nicht ;
   zaglos gewann er
   des Zaubers Macht :
7 gerathen ist ihm der Ring.

Donner.   Zwang uns allen
   schüfe der Zwerg,
würd' ihm der Reif nicht entrissen.

Wotan.   That ring I must seize on.

Froh.   Lightly now,
   without love forswearing, 'twere gained.

Loge.   Quite lightly ;
   scant knowledge you need require.

Wotan.   Bethink us, how?

Loge.   By theft !
   What a thief stole,
   that steal from the thief .
were anything done with more ease ?
   But with artful foils
   fighteth Alberich ;
   shrewd and wileful
   be your workings
that the robber be o'er-reached :
   to the river-sisters
   their ruddy toy,
   the gold, once more be given ;
   for therefore cry they to thee.

Wotan.   The river-sisters !
   What serves me thy rede ?

Fricka.   Of that watery race
   mention I wish not,
   for many men
   — more's my pain —
   have perished, allured by their love.

Wotan stands silently struggling with himself, while the other
gods all look expectantly on him. Meanwhile *Fafner* has consulted
aside with *Fasolt*.

Fafner.   Trust me, more than Freia
   fits us treasure so true,
   nor need we yearn long for youth
with the gold's all-mastering might.

(They again advance.)

   Hear, Wotan,
   our hasty last words !
Free from our hands be Freia :
   let a less
   forfeit release thee ;
   th'ungentle giants will need
   but Nibelheim's gems and gold.

Wotan.   Where are your wits ?
   How can I award ye
what is not mine yet, ye miscreants ?

Fafner.   Work 'twas
   to raise yonder tow'rs ;
   thou canst, though, do
   with thoughtfuller craft
what ne'er our needs could bring through :
   the Nibelung fetter fast.

Wotan.   Den Ring muss ich haben !

Froh.   Leicht erringt
   ohne Liebesfluch er sich jetzt.

Loge.   Spott-leicht,
   ohne Kunst wie im Kinder-Spiel !

Wotan.   So rathe, wie ?

Loge.   Durch raub !
   Was ein Dieb stahl,
   das stiehlst du dem Dieb :
   ward leichter ein Eigen erlangt ? —
   Doch mit arger Wehr
   wahrt sich Alberich ;
   klug und fein
   musst du verfahren,
   ziehst du den Räuber zu Recht,
   um des Rheines Töchtern
   den rothen Tand,
   das Gold, wieder zu geben :
   denn darum bitten sie dich.

Wotan.   Des Rheines Töchter ?
   Was taugt mir der Rath ?

Fricka.   Von dem Wassergezücht
   mag ich nichts wissen :
   schon manchen Mann
   — mir zum Leid —
   verlockten sie buhlend im Bad.

Wotan steht stumm mit sich kämpfend ; die übrigen Götter heften
in schweigender Spannung die Blicke auf ihn. — Währenddem hat
Fafner bei Seite mit *Fasolt* berathen.

Fafner.   Glaub' mir, mehr als Freia
   frommt das gleissende Gold :
   auch ew'ge Jugend erjagt,
   wer durch Goldes Zauber sie zwingt.

(Sie treten wieder heran.)

   Hör', Wotan,
   der Harrenden Wort :
   Freia bleib' euch in Frieden ;
   leichter'n Lohn
   fand ich zur Lösung :
   uns rauhen Riesen genügt
   des Niblungen rothes Gold.

Wotan.   Seid ihr bei Sinn ?
   was nicht ich besitze,
   soll ich euch Schamlosen schenken ?

Fafner.   Schwer baute
   dort sich die Burg :
   leicht wird's dir
   mit list'ger Gewalt
   (was im Neidspiel nie uns gelang,
   den Niblungen fest zu fah'n.

Wotan. For *you* shall I
    show myself yielding?
    For *you* fetter a foe?
    Shame-devoid
    and shockingly covetous
such conduct I call!

Fasolt
    (suddenly seizing *Freia* and drawing her with *Fafner* aside).
    Come here, maid!
    With us remain.
    In pledge placed art thou now
    till our forfeit be paid.
    (*Freia* cries aloud: all the gods are in the greatest perturbation.)

Fafner. Far from hence
    shall she be forced:
    till night-fall — note me well —
    placed is she as a pledge·
    then once more come we,
    and when we call
    should we not find as the forfeit
    the Rhinegold fair and red —

Fasolt. At end is the friendship,
    Freia is forfeit;
    for ever fallen to us.

Freia. Sisters! Brothers!
    save me! Help!
She is borne off by the hastily retreating giants; the troubled gods
    hear her cries of distress dying away in the distance.)

Froh. Up! on their track!

Donner. Perish now all things!
    (They look enquiringly towards *Wotan*.)

Loge
    (looking after the giants).
    Over stock and stone they tramp
    straight down the vale;
through the Rhine's befriending ford
    flounder the ruffians:
    'frightedly
    now Freia
must ride the back of the rascals.—
    Heia! hei!
How stumble the stupids along!
Past the steep stride they amain;
    but in Riesenheim's bounds
    they first will take rest.
    (He turns to the gods.)
What dreameth Wotan so wild?
What dread hath gotten the gods?

A pale mist, increasing in density, fills the stage; in it the gods
 em to take an aged and haggard appearance: all stand in alarm
 oking towards *Wotan*, who thoughtfully casts his eyes on the
 ound.

Wotan. Für euch müht' ich
    mich um den Alben?
    für euch fing' ich den Feind?
    Unverschämt
    und überbegehrlich
macht euch Dumme mein Dank!

Fasolt
    (ergreift plötzlich *Freia* und führt sie mit *Fafner* zur Seite).
    Hieher, Maid!
    in uns're Macht!
    Als Pfand folgst du jetzt,
    bis wir Lösung empfahn.
    (*Freia* schreit laut auf: alle *Götter* sind in höchster Bestürzung.)

Fafner. Fort von hier
    sei sie entführt!
    Bis Abend, achtet's wohl,
    pflegen wir sie als Pfand:
    wir kehren wieder;
    doch kommen wir,
    und bereit liegt nicht als Lösung
    das Rheingold roth und licht —

Fasolt. Zu End' ist die Frist dann,
    Freia verfallen:
    für immer folge sie uns!

Freia. Schwester! Brüder!
    Rettet! helft!
(Sie wird von den hastig enteilenden Riesen fortgetragen: in der Ferne
    hören die bestürzten Götten ihren Wehruf verhallen.)

Froh. Auf, ihnen nach!

Donner. Breche denn alles!
    (Sie blicken *Wotan* fragend an.)

Loge
    (den Riesen nachsehend).
    Ueber Stock und Stein zu Thal
    stapfen sie hin;
    durch des Rheines Wasserfurth
    waten die Riesen:
    fröhlich nicht
    hängt Freia
den Rauhen über den Rücken!—
    Heia! hei!
Wie taumeln die Tölpel dahin!
Durch das Thal talpen sie schon:
    wohl an Riesenheim's Mark
    erst halten sie Rast!
    (Er wendet sich zu den Göttern.)
Was sinnt nun Wotan so wild?
Den seligen Göttern wie geht's?

Ein fahler Nebel erfüllt mit wachsender Dichtheit die Bühne, in
ihm erhalten die Götter ein zunehmend bleiches und ältliches Aussehen: alle stehen bang und erwartungsvoll auf *Wotan* blickend, der
sinnend die Augen an den Boden heftet.

Loge.   Dupes me a vapor?
      Veils me a dream?
      How fast your features'
      fairness hath fled!
From your cheeks the bloom is chased;
the spark of your eyes hath expired!—
      Flag not, Froh;
      day hath not fled!
      Doth thy hand, Donner,
      relax from the hammer?
      What aileth Fricka?
      Finds she displeasing
her spouse's grayness and gloom,
which o'er him gather like age?

Fricka.   Woe's me! Woe's me!
      What is it all?

Donner.   My hand doth sink!

Froh.   My heart doth stop!

Loge.   I've found it — hear what's befall'n!
      Of Freia's fruit
no atom to-day did ye eat.
      The golden apples
      from out her garden
preserved you from dwindling with age,
eating them every day.
      The garden's keeper
      now bideth a captive;
      'mong the foliage rests
      and rots the fruit:
full soon spoiled it will fall.
      My case is milder;
      for me, unkindly,
      Freia has e'er
kept from the coveted fruit;
      in me but half
the pow'r ye immortal ones have.
      But all leaned ye on the
      apples' youth-giving aid:
this wotted the giants well;
      against your lives
      a league is begun,
and how find ye defense?
      If without apples,
      old and grim —
      gray and gruesome,
waning to sport of the world,
the stock of gods would cease

Fricka.   Wotan! My lord!
      Hapless and lost!
      Look how thy heedless
      hastiness now
our shunless shame hath shaped!

Loge.   Trügt mich ein Nebel?
      neckt mich ein Traum?   **14**
      Wie bang und bleich
      verblüht ihr so bald!
Euch erlischt der Wangen Licht,
der Blick eures Auges verblitzt!—
      Frisch, mein Froh,
      noch ist's ja früh!—
      Deiner Hand, Donner,
      entfüllt ja der Hammer!—
      Was ist's mit Fricka?
      freut sie sich wenig
ob Wotan's grämlichem Grau,
das schier zum Greisen ihn schafft?

Fricka.   Wehe! Wehe!
      Was ist geschehen?

Donner.   Mir sinkt die Hand.

Froh.   Mir stockt das Herz.

Loge.   Jetzt fand ich's: hört was euch fehlt!
      Von Freia's Frucht
genosset ihr heute noch nicht:
      die gold'nen Aepfel
      in ihrem Garten,   **14**
sie machten euch tüchtig und jung
ass't ihr sie jeden Tag.
      Des Gartens Pflegerin
      ist nun verpfändet;
      an den Aesten darbt
      und dorrt das Obst:
bald fällt faul es herab. —
      Mich kümmert's minder;
      an mir kargte
      Freia von je
knausernd die köstliche Frucht:
      denn halb so ächt nur
bin ich wie, Herrliche, ihr!
      Doch ihr setztet alles
      auf das jüngende Obst:
das wussten die Riesen wohl;
      auf euer Leben
      legten sie's an:
nun sorgt, wie ihr das wahrt!
      Ohne die Aepfel
      alt und grau,
      greis und grämlich,
welkend zum Spott aller Welt,
erstirbt der Götter Stamm.

Fricka.   Wotan, Gemahl,
      unsel'ger Mann!
      Sieh wie dein Leichtsinn
      lachend uns allen
Schimpf und Schmach erschuf!

Wotan

(starting up with sudden resolution).

Up! Loge,
and off with me!
Beneath, to the home of the Nibelungs.
I'll surely seize on this gold.

Loge.   The Rhine-maidens
raised their complaint:
so may they then hope for a hearing?

Wotan

(violently).

Peace! thou prattler!
Freia the noble —
Freia needs our assistance.

Loge.   Swiftly I'll guide,
go where you will:
steeply down
shall we descend through the Rhine?

Wotan.   Not through the Rhine.

Loge.   We'll swing ourselves then
through the sulphur cleft:
so slip with me down it thus!

He goes first and disappears at the side down a crevice from which
immediately a sulphurous vapor rises.

Wotan.   Ye others halt
till evening here:
our youth departed
I'll purchase me yet with the gold.

He clambers after *Loge* into the sulphur cleft: the vapor stealing
out of which spreads over the whole stage with a thick cloud, concealing the rest of the characters.

Donner.   Fare thee well, Wotan!

Froh.   Good luck! Good luck!

Fricka.   O, soon return
my trouble to soothe!

The sulphurous vapor thickens to a quite black cloud which rises
upwards; this then changes to a firm, gloomy, rocky chasm which also
continually rises, giving the stage the appearance of sinking deeper and
deeper into the earth.

THIRD SCENE.

Presently from various quarters ruddy light gleams out; and there
extends farther than eye can reach

A Subterranean Cavern

which on all sides seems to lead to other and narrower passages.

Alberich enters, dragging the shrieking *Mime* forth by the ear from
left at one side.

Alberich.   Hello! Hello!
Come here! Come here!
Rascally imp!

Wotan

(mit plötzlichem Entschluss auftanrend).

Auf, Loge!
hinab mit mir.
Nach Nibelheim fahren wir nieder:
gewinnen will ich das Gold.

Loge.   Die Rheintöchter
riefen dich an:
so dürfen Erhörung sie hoffen?

Wotan

(heftig).

Schweige, Schwätzer!
Freia, die gute,
Freia gilt es zu lösen.

Loge.   Wie du befiehlst
führ' ich dich gern:
steil hinab
steigen wir denn durch den Rhein?

Wotan.   Nicht durch den Rhein!

Loge.   So schwingen wir uns
durch die Schwefelkluft:
dort schlüpfe mit mir hinein!

Er geht voran und verschwindet seitwärts in einer Kluft, aus der
sogleich ein schwefliger Dampf hervorquillt.

Wotan.   Ihr andren harrt
bis Abend hier:
verlor'ner Jugend
erjag' ich erlösendes Gold!

Er steigt *Loge* nach in die Kluft hinab: der aus ihr dringende
Schwefeldampf verbreitet sich über die ganze Bühne und erfüllt diese
schnell mit dickem Gewölk. Bereits sind die Zurück-bleibenden unsichtbar.

Donner.   Fahre wohl, Wotan!

Froh.   Glück auf! Glück auf!

Fricka.   O kehre bald
zur bangenden Frau!

Der Schwefeldampf verdüstert sich bis zu ganz schwarzem Gewölk,
welches von unten nach oben steigt; dann verwandelt sich dieses in
festes, finstres Steingeklüft, das sich immer aufwärts bewegt, so dass es
den Anschein hat, als sänke die Scene immer tiefer in die Erde hinab.

DRITTE SCENE.

Endlich dämmert von verschiedenen Seiten aus der Ferne her,
dunkelrother Schein auf: eine unabsehbar weit sich dahinziehende

unterirdische Kluft

wird erkennbar die nach allen Seiten hin in enge Schachte auszu-
münden scheint.

Alberich zerrt den kreischenden *Mime* an den Ohren aus einer
Seitenschlufft herbei.

Alberich.   Hehe! hehe!
hieher! hieher!
Tückischer Zwerg!

Rarely your ear
now will I nip,
should you not weld me
straight on the spot
the special work I have shown.

Mime

(howling).

Oho! Oho!
Oh! Oh!
Let me alone!
Made it is
at your command,
with moil and toil
moulded by me.
Nick not your nails in me so!

Alberich

(letting him go).

Why hesitate then
to hand it out?

Mime.   I apprehended
lest aught were failing —

Alberich.   Where was it unfinished?

Mime

(hesitating).

Here — and there —

Alberich.   How "here and there"?
hand me the work!

He threatens to seize again the ear of *Mime* who, in terror, lets fall a piece of metal work that he has held concealed in his hand. *Alberich* hastily picks it up and examines it.

See, you scamp!
All has been smithied
and welded, I ween,
after my word.
You, idiot, would seek
so to deceive me,
and save the wonderful
work for yourself?
when by my lore
you could shape it alone!
Read are your thoughts, my thief?

(He sets the metal work on his head as a "Tarnhelm.")

The helm fits to the head;
now will it act as it ought?
    — "Night annul me.
Nought be seen!" —

(He vanishes, and a column of smoke takes his place.)

Brother, d'ye see me?

Mime

(gazing about in astonishment).

Where stand you?   I see you no jot!

---

tapfer gezwickt
sollst du mir sein.
schaffst du nicht fertig,
wie ich's bestellt,
zur Stund' das feine Geschmeid!

Mime

(heulend)

Ohe! Ohe!
Au! Au!
Lass' mich nur los!
Fertig ist es,
wie du befahlst;
mit Fleiss und Schweiss
ist es gefügt:
nimm nur die Nägel vom Ohr!

Alberich

(loslassend).

Was zögerst du dann
und zeigst es nicht?

Mime.   Ich Armer zagte,
dass noch was fehle.

Alberich.   Was wär' noch nicht fertig?

Mime

(verlegen)

Hier . . . und da . . .

Alberich.   Was hier und da?
Her das Gewirk!

Er will ihm wieder an das Ohr fahren: vor Schreck lässt *Mime* ein metallenes Gewirke, das er krampfhaft in den Händen hielt sich entfallen. *Alberich* hebt es hastig auf und prüft es genau.

Schau' du Schelm!
Alles geschmiedet
und fertig gefügt,
wie ich's befahl!
So wollte der Tropf
schlau mich betrügen?
für sich behalten
das hehre Geschmeid,
das meine List
ihn zu schmieden gelehrt?
kenn' ich dich dummen Dieb?

(Er setzt das Gewirk als "Tarnhelm" auf den Kopf.)

Dem Haupt fügt sich der Helm
ob sich der Zauber auch zeigt?
    — "Nacht und Nebel,
Niemand gleich!" —

(Seine Gestalt verschwindet; statt ihrer gewahrt man eine Nebelsäule.

Siehst du mich, Bruder?

Mime

(blickt sich verwundert um).

Wo bist du? ich sehe dich nicht.

18

*`erich's`
(voice).
Then feel me instead,
you faithless scamp;
take this for your thievish tricks!

me
hes and cries under the blows which are heard to fall on him from
an invisible scourge).

`erich's`
(voice, laughing).
I thank you, thickhead:
the work is well performed.
Hoho! Hoho!
Nibelung elves,
kneel all to Alberich!
Everywhere wanders he
over you watching;
reign of rest
is from you riven;
aye must you serve him
who lurketh unseen:
when you least of all note him
haply he's nigh you!
Unto him slaves are ye ever.
Hoho! Hoho!
hear him; he nears,
the Nibelung's head!

The column of vapor disappears towards the back; *Alberich's* **3**
ings are heard retreating in the distance; howls and cries—
ond from lower passages, finally the sounds are lost in the **17**
nce. *Mime* has cowered down in pain. His groans and whim-
gs are heard by *Wotan* and *Loge* who descend from above by a
cleft.

e. Nibelheim's here.
What glare I notice
that glows from yon varying vapors?

tan. Who groans so loud?
what lies on the ground?

e
(bending down to *Mime*).
What whining whimperer's here?

ne. Oho! Oho!
Oh! Oh!

e. Hey, Mime, merry gnome!
what nips and knocks you like this?

ne. Leave me in quiet!

e. Yes without question;
and more yet, hark —
help I'll give to you, Mime.

ne
(partially rising).
What help for me?
I have for master
a hard-hearted brother
who makes me bondsman to him!

Alberich's
(Stimme).
So fühle mich doch,
du fauler Schuft!
Nimm' das für dein Diebsgelüst!

Mime
(schreit und windet sich unter empfangenen Geisselhieben, deren **Fall**
man vernimmt ohne die Geissel selbst zu sehen).

Alberich's
(Stimme, lachend).
Dank, du Dummer!
Dein Werk bewährt sich gut. —
Hoho! Hoho!
Niblungen all,
neigt euch Alberich!
Ueberall weilt er nun,
euch zu bewachen;
Ruh' und Rast
ist euch zerronnen;
ihm müsst ihr schaffen,
wo nicht ihr ihn schaut;
wo ihr nicht ihn gewahrt,
seid seiner gewärtig:
unterthan seid ihr ihm immer!
Hoho! Hoho!
hört ihn: er naht,
der Niblungen-Herr!

Die Nebelsäule verschwindet dem Hintergrunde zu: man hört
in immer weiterer Ferne *Alberich's* Toben und Zanken; Geheul und
Geschrei antwortet ihm aus den untern Klüften, das sich endlich in
immer weitere Ferne unhörbar verliert — *Mime* ist vor Schmerz
zusammengesunken; sein Stöhnen und Wimmern wird von *Wotan*
und *Loge* gehört, die aus einer Schlufft von oben her sich hera-
blassen.

Loge. Nibelheim hier:
durch bleiche Nebel
wie blitzen dort feurige Funken?

Wotan. Hier stöhnt es laut:
was liegt im Gestein?

Loge
(neigt sich zu *Mime*).
Was Wunder wimmerst du hier?

Mime. Ohe! Ohe!
Au! Au!

Loge. Hei, Mime! Muntrer Zwerg!
was zwingt und zwackt dich denn so?

Mime. Lass' mich in Frieden!

Loge. Das will ich freilich,
und mehr noch, hör':
helfen will ich dir, Mime!

Mime
(sich etwas aufrichtend).
Wer hälfe mir?
Gehorchen muss ich
dem leiblichen Bruder,
der mich in Bande gelegt.

Loge.   But, Mime, what brought him
          the pow'r to command ?

Mime.   With evil craft
          lately Alberich
          hath wrought from Rhinegold
          a ruddy ring
          and its spell of magic
          masters our spirits ;
with this he moves to serve him
the night-loving Niblung race.
          Once at our anvils
          ornaments all made,
          only our wives to deck ;
          worked from the ore
nice little Nibelung toys :
we lightly laughed as we toiled.
          This wretch now compels us
          deep caverns to pierce to :
          for him alone
          to heavily toil.
          Through the ring of gold
          he redes in his greed
          where unknown splendor
          is spread in the earth.
          Then must we all trace it,
          track it and dig it ;
          extract the metal
          and melt it in bars.
          With no peace nor pause,
to heap up the hoard for him.

Loge.   His lash has chastised
          your laziness then ?

Mime.   Most ill-starred I !
          my thraldom is endless.
          I had a forged
          helmet to fashion :
          exact commands
          he gave for its making.
          My wit surmised
          the wondrous might
          possess'd by the work
          that from steel I wove :
          the helm I sorely
          wanted myself,
          that its enchantment
Alberich's chiding might check ;
          maybe -— yes, maybe
the bully himself 'twould bamboozle.
That he might be placed in my power —
the ring be from him ravished :
then I who bend as his bondsman,
as master henceforth should command.

Loge.   Dich, Mime, zu binden
          was gab ihm die Macht ?

Mime.   Mit arger List
          schuf sich Alberich
          aus Rheines Gold
          einen gelben Reif :
          seinem starken Zauber
          zittern wir staunend ;
mit ihm zwingt er uns alle,
der Niblungen nächtiges Heer. —
          Sorglose Schmiede,
          schufen wir sonst wohl
          Schmuck unsren Weibern,
          wonnig Geschmeid,
niedlichen Niblungentand :
wir lachten lustig der Müh'.
          Nun zwingt uns der Schlimme
          in Klüfte zu schlüpfen,
          für ihn allein
          uns immer zu müh'n.
          Durch des Ringes Gold
          erräth seine Gier,
          wo neuer Schimmer
          in Schachten sich birgt :
          da müssen wir spähen,
          spüren und graben,
          die Beute schmelzen
          und schmieden den Guss,
          ohne Ruh' und Rast
den Hort zu häufen dem Herrn.

Loge.   Den Trägen so eben
          traf wohl sein Zorn ?

Mime.   Mich Armen, ach !
          mich zwang er zum ärgsten :
          ein Helmgeschmeid
          hiess er mich schweissen ;
          genau befahl er
          wie es zu fügen.
          Wohl merkt' ich klug
          welch' mächt'ge Kraft
          zu eigen dem Werk,
          das aus Erz ich wirkte :
          für mich drum hüten
          wollt' ich den Helm,
          durch seinen Zauber
Alberich's Zwang mich entzieh'n —
          vielleicht, ja vielleicht
den Lästigen selbst überlisten,
in meine Gewalt ihn zu werfen.
den Ring ihm zu entreissen,
dass, wie ich Knecht jetzt dem Kühnen,
mir Freien er selber dann fröhn' !

17

3

6

Loge. And why, my trickster, triumph'd you not?	*Loge.* Warum, du Kluger, glückte dir's nicht?
Mime. Ah! though the work I welded, the magic to which 'twas made, that magic I read not aright. He who from me robbed the work I wrought, I learned of him now, — too late though, alas! — what good luck lay in the helm. From my eyes he faded, but finely his arm my fool's back furrowed with stripes Through foolishness thus I found my thanks. (He rubs his back, howling. The gods laugh.)	*Mime.* Ach, der das Werk ich wirkte, den Zauber, der ihm entzuckt, den Zauber errieth ich nicht recht! Der das Werk mir rieth, und mir's entriss, der lehrte mich nun — doch leider zu spät! — welche List läg' in dem Helm: meinem Blick entschwand er, doch Schwielen dem Blinden schlug unschaubar sein Arm. Das schuf ich mir Dummen schön zu Dank! (Er streicht sich heulend den Rücken. Die Gotter lachen.)
Loge (to *Wotan*). Admit, not easy is our task.	*Loge* (zu *Wotan*). Gesteh', nicht leicht gelingt der Fang.
Votan. Ere our end's attained thy cunning must aid.	*Wotan.* Doch erliegt der Feind, hilft deine List.
Mime struck by the laughter of the gods, observes them more attentively). Who are ye before me that question so freely?	*Mime* (vom dem Lachen der Götter betroffen, betrachtet diese aufmerk- samer). Mit eurem Gefrage wer seid denn ihr Fremde?
Loge. Friends to you: from their annoys we'd free all the Nibelung folk. (*Alberich's* threats and scourgings again approach.)	*Loge.* Freunde dir; von ihrer Noth befrei'n wir der Niblungen Volk. (*Alberich's* Zanken und Züchtigen nähert sich wieder.)
Mime. Keep a look out! Alberich comes.	*Mime.* Nehmt euch in Acht! Alberich naht.
Votan. For him we wait here.	*Wotan.* Sein harren wir hier.
He quietly seats himself on a stone. *Loge* leans by his side.— *Alberich*, who has now removed the Tarnhelm and wears it in his rdle, drives with brandished whip from the caves below a crowd of belungs before him. They are laden with gold and silver jewelry ich under *Alberich's* continual scolding and urging, they pile up in e heap.	Er setzt sich ruhig auf einen Stein; *Loge* lehnt ihm zur Seite.— *Alberich*, der den Tarnhelm vom Haupte genommen und in den Gürtel gehängt hat, treibt mit geschwungener Geissel aus der unteren, tiefer gelegenen Schlucht, aufwärts eine Schaar *Nibelungen* vor sich her; diese sind mit goldenem und silbernem Geschmeide beladen, das sie, unter *Alberich's* stetem Schimpfen und Schelten all auf einen Haufen speichern und so zu einem Horte häufen.
Alberich. Hither! Thither! Hallo! Hallo! Lazy hounds! There in heaps pile up the hoard! You there, get up! Will you move on? Indolent pack, down with the ingots. Shall I then help you? drag it all here. (He suddenly perceives *Wotan* and *Loge*.) Hey! who are these who thus intrude?	17 *Alberich.* Hieher! Dorthin! Hehe! Hoho! Träges Heer, dort zu Hauf schichtet den Hort! Du da, hinauf! Willst du voran? Schmähliches Volk, ab das Geschmeide! Soll ich euch helfen? Alles hieher! (Er gewahrt plötzlich *Wotan* und *Loge*.) He! wer ist dort? Wer drang hier ein? —

Mime, to me!
pestilent patch!
pratest thou here
with this promising pair?
Off, thou idler!
Back to thy pickaxe and pincers!

(With uplifted scourge he drives *Mime* into the midst of the crowd of Nibelungs.)

Hey! to your labor!
Look that ye hasten!
Hurry below!
From the new found shafts
now shovel the gold!
Who grubs not gaily
getteth the whip!
If any be idle
Mime shall answer,
or make his escape
from the sting of my scourge!
That I everywhere wander
where no one doth ween
who wotteth better than he?
Tarrying still?
Take ye no heed?

(Draws the ring from his finger, kisses it and stretches it commandingly out.)

Tremble in terror,
Down-trodden race:
heed his rule
who holds the Ring!

With howls and shrieks the Nibelungs — *Mime* among them — separate and slip into crevices on all sides down to their shafts again.

Alberich

(advancing wrathfully to *Wotan* and *Loge*).
What want you here?

Wotan.   From Nibelheim's night-bound land
strange news to our notice rang,
of rarest wonders
worked here by Alberich:
to witness these marvels
makes us guests at thy gate.

Alberich.   Nought gnaws you
but envy, I know:
and why you greet me,
guests, well I guess.

Loge.   Do you know *me*,
mis'rable dwarf?
Who is't? now say,
at whom you would snarl?
In frigid lair
where freezing you lay,
where were your light
and warming illume
if on Loge you had not looked?

Mime! Zu mir,
schäbiger Schuft!
Schwatztest du gar
mit dem schweifenden Paar?
Fort! du Fauler!
Willst du gleich schmieden und schaffen?

(Er treibt *Mime* mit Geisselhieben unter den Haufen der Nibelunge hinein.)

Hie! an die Arbeit!
Alle von hinnen!
Hurtig hinab?
Aus den neuen Schachten
schafft mir das Gold!
Euch grüsst die Geissel,
grabt ihr nicht rasch!
Dass keiner mir müssig
bürge mir Mime,
sonst birgt er sich schwer
meines Armes Schwunge:
dass ich überall weile,
wo Niemand es wähnt,
das weiss er, dünkt mich, genau. —
Zögert ihr noch?
Zaudert wohl gar?

(Er zieht seinen Ring vom Finger, küsst ihn und streckt ihn drohen aus.)

Zittre und zage,
gezähmtes Heer:
rasch gehorcht
des Ringes Herrn!

Unter Geheul und Gekreisch stieben die Nibelungen (unter ihn *Mime*) auseinander, und schlüpfen nach allen Seiten in die Schach hinab.

Alberich

(grimmig auf *Wotan* und *Loge* zutretend).
Was sucht ihr hier?

Wotan.   Von Nibelheim's nächt'gem Land
vernahmen wir neue Mähr':
mächt'ge Wunder
wirke hier Alberich;
daran uns zu weiden
trieb uns Gäste die Gier.

Alberich.   Nach Nibelheim
führt euch wohl Neid:
so kühne Gaste,
glaubt, kenn' ich gar gut.

Loge.   Kennst du mich gut,
kindischer Alp?
Nun sag': wer bin ich,
dass du so bell'st?
Im kalten Loch,
da kauernd du lag'st
wer gab dir Licht
und wärmende Lohe,
wenn Loge nie dir gelacht?

What aid were your hammer
if I ne'er heated the forge?
  Cousin you may be,
  once friend of mine;—
no more than these are your thanks?

Alberich. To light-elves
  belongs now Loge,
  deluding rogue!
Art as fairly their friend
as my friend thou wert once?
  Haha! that'st fine!—
nought need I fear from their hands.

Loge. I'm surely worthy your trust.

Alberich. In thy untruth trust I;
  not in thy truth!
But entrenched I triumph o'er all.

Loge. Power has brought you
  spirit brave:
  grimly great
  waxes your force.

Alberich. Seest thou the hoard
  that my host
  heaps for me there?

Loge. So noble a sight I ne'er knew.

Alberich. That's for to-day,
  the merest driblet:
  much more metal
shall augment it to-morrow.

Wotan. But what can boot you the hoard
here in baleful Nibelheim,
where nought by riches is bought?

Alberich. Riches to raise me,
  and riches to furnish,
I need Nibelheim's night.
  But with the hoard
  that in hollows I heap
wonders I count to accomplish:
  the world my cunning
can by its might overmaster.

Wotan. How, my worthy, wilt thou do that?

Alberich. Ye aloft, who lapped in airs
  ambrosial, live,
  laugh and love,
  with gilded fist
I'll grasp you and fetter all to me!
As I have loving aye forsworn,
  all they that live
  shall eke forswear it:

Was hülf' dir dein Schmieden,
heizt' ich die Schmiede dir nicht?
  Dir bin ich Vetter,
  und war dir Freund:
nicht fein drum dünkt mich dein Dank!

Alberich. Den Lichtalben
  lacht jetzt Loge,
  der listige Schelm:
bist du Falscher ihr Freund,
wie mir Freund du einst warst
  haha! mich freut's!
von ihnen fürcht' ich dann nichts.

Loge. So denk' ich, kannst du mir trau'n?

Alberich. Deiner Untreu' trau' ich,
  nicht deiner Treu'!—
Doch getrost trotz' ich euch allen.

Loge. Hohen Muth
  verleiht deine Macht:
  grimmig gross
  wuchs dir die Kraft.

Alberich. Siehst du den Hort,
  den mein Heer
  dort mir gehäuft?

Loge. So neidlichen sah' ich noch nie.

Alberich. Das ist für heut',
  ein kärglich Häufchen:
  kühn und mächtig
soll es künftig sich mehren.

Wotan. Zu was doch frommt dir der Hort,
da freundlos Nibelheim,
und nichts um Schätze hier feil?

Alberich. Schätze zu schaffen
  und Schätze zu bergen,
nützt mir Nibelheim's Nacht;
  doch mit dem Hort,
  in der Höhle gehäuft,
denk' ich dann Wunder zu wirken.
  die ganze Welt
gewinn' ich mit ihm mir zu eigen.

Wotan. Wie beginnst du, Gütiger, das?

Alberich. Die in linder Lüfte Weh'n
  da oben ihr lebt,
  lacht und liebt:
  mit gold'ner Faust
euch Göttliche fang' ich mir alle!
Wie ich der Liebe abgesagt,
  Alles was lebt
  soll ihr entsagen:

15

19

11

allured by my gold,
for gold alone shall they languish.
   On radiant heights,
   in visions of rapture
   rocked are ye:
   the black dwarfs
ye look down upon, deathless debauchees.
   Beware!
   Beware!—
   For first ye men
   shall work to my might,
   then your sprightly women,
   who my wooing despise,
the gnome shall lure to his needs;
love lacking, withal.
   Ha, ha, ha, ha!
   Have ye now heard?
   Beware!
Beware of the night-begot host,
when the Niblung hoard shall upheave
from night and darkness to day!

Wotan
                    (starting).
   Aroint! miserable wretch!

Alberich.   What says he?

Loge
            (stepping between them:—to *Wotan*).
   Subdue thy spirit!
                (To *Alberich*.)
What can hinder our wonder,
beholding Alberich's work?
If safely your tricks can assure
what you attract with the treasure,
the mightiest must I then hail you·
   for moon and stars
   and the sun in its splendor
surely thus must regard you:
they, too, must be your thralls.
But 'twe·e of primal importance
   that the host who heap up
   the Nibelung hoard
nought of hatred nurse.
You have well wielded a ring
which puts your people in awe:—
   think if in sleep
   a thief to you slipped,
the ring slyly to wrest!
What, wise one, would warrant you then?

Alberich.   Delightfully deep is Loge:
   e'er he deems
   all others are dull.

mit Golde gegirrt,
nach Gold nur sollt ihr noch **gieren.**
   Auf wonnigen Höh'n
   in seligem Weben
   wiegt ihr euch,
   den Schwarz-Alben
verachtet ihr ewigen Schwelger:—
   habt Acht!
   habt Acht!—
   denn dient ihr Männer
   erst meiner Macht,
   eure schmucken Frau'n—
   die mein Frei'n verschmält—
sie zwingt zur Lust sich der Zwerg,
lacht Liebe ihm nicht.—
   Hahahaha!
   hört ihr mich recht?
   Habt Acht!
Habt Acht vor dem nächtlichen **Heer,**
entsteigt des Niblungen Hort
aus stummer Tiefe zu Tag!

Wotan
                    (auffahrend).
   Vergeh', frevelnder Gauch!

Alberich.   Was sagt der?

Loge
            (ist dazwischen **getreten**).
   Sei doch bei Sinnen!
                (Zu *Alberich*.)
Wen doch fasste nicht Wunder,
erfährt er Alberich's Werk?
Gelingt deiner herrlichen List,
Was mit dem Hort du heischest,
Den Mächtigsten muss ich dich **rühmen:**
   denn Mond und Stern'
   und die strahlende Sonne,
sie auch dürfen nicht anders,
dienen müssen sie dir.—
Doch wichtig acht'ich vor allem,
   dass des Hortes Häufer,
   der Niblungen Heer,
neidlos dir geneigt.
Einen Ring rührtest du kühn,
dem zagte zitternd dein Volk:
   doch wenn im Schlaf
   ein Dieb dich beschlich,
den Ring schlau dir entriss',
wie wahrtest du Weiser dich dann?

Alberich.   Der Listigste dünkt sich **Loge;**
   andre denkt er
   immer sich dumm:

That I were indebted
to him, indeed,
for service deft
would seem to the dog right good. —
The helmet that hides
myself I designed:
the skillfullest smith,
Mime, I make to shape it:
swiftly to waft me,
or, at my will,
to assume other semblance
serves the helm.
None may see me,
much as he seek;
but hidden from all men
I everywhere am.
So, undisturbed,
by aught, I stand safe e'en from thee,
thou fond sedulous friend!

Loge.   Much I've looked at —
lighted on marvels;
but lacked to witness
such wonders yet.
This work without fellow
I have no faith in:
were but this only possible,
your power would be unending.

Alberich.   Pray do I lie
and prattle like Loge?

Loge.   Till it is proved,
good dwarf, I doubt your word.

Alberich.   With cunning, blockhead,
thou'lt finish by bursting.
Confusion I'll cause!
Now say, before thee what shape
shall my figure assume?

Loge.   Whatever you will;
but make me mute with amaze!

Alberich
(putting on the Tarnhelm).
" Draw thee here,
hugest of dragons."

He instantly disappears and in his place there writhes a huge
monster serpent which bends and opens its outstretched jaws at *Wotan*
and *Loge*.

Loge
(affecting extreme fear).
Oho! Oho!
Sinister serpent,
pray swallow me not!
Spare but life to poor **Loge**!

---

dass sein' ich bedürfte
zu Rath und Dienst
um harten Dank,
das hörte der Dieb jetzt gern! —
Den hehlenden Helm
ersann ich mir selbst;
der sorglichste Schmied,
Mime, musst' ihn mir schmieden:
schnell mich zu wandeln
nach meinem Wunsch,
die Gestalt mir zu tauschen,
taugt mir der Helm;
niemand sieht mich,
wenn er mich sucht;
doch überall bin ich,
geborgen dem Blick.
So ohne Sorge
bin ich selbst sicher vor dir,
du fromm sorgender Freund!

8
15

Loge.   Vieles sah' ich,
Seltsames fand ich:
doch solches Wunder
gewahrt' ich nie.
Dem Werk ohne Gleichen
kann ich nicht glauben;
wäre diess einz'ge möglich,
deine Macht währte dann ewig.

Alberich.   Meinst du, ich lüg',
und prahle wie Loge?

Loge.   Bis ich's geprüft,
bezweifl' ich, Zwerg, dein Wort.

Alberich.   Vor Klugheit bläht sich
zum platzen der Blöde:
nun plage dich Neid!
Bestimm', in welcher Gestalt
soll ich jach vor dir stehn?

Loge.   In welcher du willst:
nur mach' vor Staunen mich stumm!

Alberich
(hat den Helm aufgesetzt).

18

" Riesen-Wurm
winde dich ringelnd! "

Sogleich verschwindet er: eine ungeheure Riesenschlange windet
sich statt seiner am Boden; sie bäumt sich und streckt den aufgesperrten
Rachen nach *Wotan* und *Loge* hin.

Loge
(stellt sich von Furcht ergriffen).
Ohe! Ohe!
schreckliche Schlange!
verschling' mich nicht!
Schone Logen das Leben!

Wotan

(laughing).

Good, Alberich !
Good — and artful !
So soon canst turn
to terrible serpent thy form ?

The dragon disappears and instead Alberich is seen in his own figure.

Alberich.   Haha ! you deep ones,
do ye believe ?

Loge.   My trembling surely attests it.
From you the serpent
swiftly was shaped :
When I have witnessed,
well I credit the wonder.
But as you waxed great
can you not wane too,
becoming smaller ?
More cunning seems to me
from dangers so to withdraw :
that, truly, I think too stiff.

Alberich.   Too stiff ? yes,
for such as ye !
How small shall I seem ?

Loge.   That a tiny slit may contain you,
as timidly slinketh a toad.

Alberich.   Pah ! nought simpler !
Spy at me now.

(He puts on the helm again.)

"Crooked toad,
creep from cranny."

He disappears. The gods perceive a toad crawling on the rocks.

Loge

(to *Wotan*).

There ! that creature !
grasp it in haste.

Wotan sets his foot on the toad and Loge, putting his hand to its head, seizes the Tarnhelm.

Alberich

(who is then seen in his own form writhing under *Wotan's* foot).

Oho ! Accurst !
I am a captive.

Loge.   Hold him close,
till he is tied.

He brings forward a bast-rope and binds ...erich hand and foot with it; the two then seize their prisoner, who furiously struggles to escape, and drag him with them to the shaft from which they descended.

Loge.   With speed above ;
there he's our bondsman !

(They disappear, mounting upwards.)

Wotan

(lacht).

Gut, Alberich !
gut, du Arger !
Wie wuchs so rasch
zum riesigen Wurme der Zwerg !

Die Schlange verschwindet, und statt ihrer erscheint sogle Alberich wieder in seiner wirklichen Gestalt.

Alberich.   Hehe ! Ihr Klugen,
glaubt ihr mir nun ?

Loge.   Mein Zittern mag dir's bezeugen.
Zur grossen Schlange
schuf'st du dich schnell :
weil ich's gewahrt,
willig glaub' ich das Wunder.
Doch, wie du wuchsest,
kannst du auch winzig
und klein dich schaffen ?
Das Klügste schiene mir das,
Gefahren schlau zu entflieh'n :
das aber dünkt mich zu schwer !

Alberich.   Zu schwer dir,
weil du zu dumm !
Wie klein soll ich sein ?

Loge.   Dass die engste Klinze dich fasse,
wo bang die Kröte sich birgt.

Alberich.   Pah ! nichts leichter !
Luge du her !

(Er setzt den Tarnhelm wieder auf.)

" Krumm und grau
krieche Kröte ! "

Er verschwindet: die Götter gewahren im Gestein eine Kröte sich zukriechen.

Loge

(zu *Wotan*).

Dort die Kröte,
greife sie rasch !

Wotan setzt seinen Fuss auf die Kröte: Loge fährt ihr nach d Kopfe und hält den Tarnhelm in der Hand.

Alberich

(wird plötzlich in seiner wirklichen Gestalt sichtbar, wie er sich un *Wotan's* Fusse windet)

Ohe ! Verflucht !
ich bin gefangen !

Loge.   Halt' ihn fest,
bis ich ihn band.

Er hat ein Bastseil hervorgeholt, und bindet Alberich damit Ar und Beine; den Geknebelten, der sich wüthend zu wehren suc fassen dann Beide, und schleppen ihn mit sich nach der Kluft, aus sie herabkamen.

Loge.   Schnell hinauf !
dort ist er unser.

(Sie verschwinden, aufwärts steigend.)

FOURTH SCENE.

The scene changes in the same manner as before, but the reverse way, till there appears again the

Open space on a mountain top

in the second Scene; it is, however, still veiled in a pale mist, as after *Freia's* abduction.

Wotan and *Loge*, dragging the pinioned *Alberich* with them, mount from the cleft.

Loge.   Be seated,
coz, I beseech!
Look, belovèd,
there lies the world
that you long so to win to your will.
What station, say,
assign you there for myself?

Alberich.   Scandalous scoundrel!
Thou scamp! thou scum!
Loosen these bonds!
Bind not my limbs!
else, rogue, thou shalt bitterly rue it.

Wotan.   I've caught thee now,
my cords bind thee closely.
While thou didst ween
the living world
already thy will had won thee,
in bonds thou liest at my feet:
now blenching must thou allow it.
Ere letting thee run
a ransom we look for.

Alberich.   What a block —
a booby I've been!
To trust blindly
to traitors so black!
Fearful revenge
I'll vent for my fault.

Loge.   Ere vengeance you foster
you'd better view yourself free:
to a fettered man
no freeman answers for evil.
So, pant you for vengeance,
verily pause not
in paying the tax we demand.

Alberich
            (harshly).
Then state what I must give.

Wotan.   The store, and thy sparkling gold.

Alberich.   Griping and gluttonous thieves!
            (Aside.)
So I hold for myself the Ring,
the hoard I can readily yield:

VIERTE SCENE.

Die Scene verwandelt sich, nur in umgekehrter Weise, wie zuvor; schliesslich erscheint wieder die

freie Gegend auf Bergeshöhen,

wie in der zweiten Scene; nur ist sie jetzt noch in einem fahlen Nebelschleier verhüllt, wie vor der zweiten Verwandlung nach *Freia's* Abführung.

Wotan und *Loge*, den gebundenen *Alberich* mit sich führend, steigen aus der Kluft herauf.

Loge.   Hier, Vetter,
sitze du fest!
Luge, Liebster,
dort liegt die Welt,
die du Lung'rer gewinnen dir willst:
welch Stellchen, sag',
bestimmst du mir drin zum Stall?

Alberich.   Schändlicher Schächer!
du Schalk! du Schelm!
Löse den Bast,
binde mich los,
den Frevel sonst büssest du Frecher!

Wotan.   Gefangen bist du,
fest mir gefesselt,
wie du die Welt,
was lebt und webt,
in deiner Gewalt schon wähntest.
In Banden liegst du vor mir,
du Banger kannst es nicht läugnen.
zu ledigen dich
bedarf's nun der Lösung.

Alberich.   O, ich Tropf!
ich träumender Thor!
Wie dumm traut' ich
dem diebischen Trug!
Furchtbare Rache
räche den Fehl!

Loge.   Soll Rache dir frommen,
vor allem rathe dich frei:
dem gebund'nen Manne
büsst kein Freier den Frevel.
Drum sinn'st du auf Rache,
rasch ohne Säumen
sorg' um die Lösung zunächst!

Alberich
            (barsch).
So heisst, was ihr begehrt!

Wotan.   Den Hort und dein helles Gold.

Alberich.   Gieriges Gaunergezücht!
            (Für sich.)
Behalt' ich mir nur den Ring,
des Hortes entrath' ich dann leicht:

for I know that to make
and augment it anew
for the spell of the Ring were a sport.
And a warning it were
my wits to remind ;
the lesson I deem is not dear,
if this is all I must lose. —

Wotan.   Dost offer the hoard ?

Alberich.   Untie my hand ;
     I'll summon it here.

       (*Loge* releases his right hand.)

Alberich
   (touches the ring with his lips and murmurs a command).
     — Now then, I've called up
     the Nibelung crew.
     Of their master mindful,
     mark how they mount
   to the light with the hoard from below ! —
   Unbind now these burdensome cords.

Wotan.   No whit till we have been paid.

   Tne Nibelungs climb up from the crevice laden with the treasure of the hoard.

Alberich.   O sharpest of shame,
     that my shrinking vassals
   should view me shackled and shorn ! —
     There let it rest
     as I direct ;
     in a heap
     pile up the hoard !
     Help must I offer ? —
     Hie hence with your eyes !
     Quick there — quick !
     then quit for your hollows.
     Off to your tasks !
     Back to the tunnels !
   Woe, if idlers there be !
   I'm about your backs in a trice.

   The Nibelungs, having piled up the hoard, slip back timidly into the cleft.

Alberich.   I've paid duly !
     let me depart !
     And the helmet there
     that Loge doth hold
   your goodness will give it me back ?

Loge
       (throwing the Tarnhelm on the heap).
   We place it as part of the plunder.

Alberich.   Accursed wolf !
     wait but awhile !
     He who forged it for me
   naketh a fresh one :

---

denn von neuem gewonnen
und wonnig genährt
ist er bald durch des Ringes Gebot.
Eine Witzigung wär's,
die weise mich macht :
zu theuer nicht zahl' ich die Zucht,
lass' ich für die Lehre den Tand. —

Wotan.   Erlegst du den Hort ?

Alberich.   Lös't mir die Hand,
     so ruf' ich ihn her.

       (*Loge* löst ihm die rechte Hand.)

Alberich
   (rührt den Ring mit den Lippen und murmelt den Befehl).
     — Wohlan, die Niblungen
     rief ich mir nah :
     dem Herrn gehorchend
     hör' ich den Hort
   aus der Tiefe sie führen zu Tag. —
   Nun lös't mich vom lästigen Band !

Wotan.   Nicht eh'r, bis alles gezahlt.

   Die Nibelungen steigen aus der Kluft herauf, mit den Geschmeider des Hortes beladen.

Alberich.   O schändliche Schmach,
     dass die scheuen Knechte
   geknebelt selbst mich erschau'n ! —
     Dorthin geführt,
     wie ich's befehl' !
     All zu Hauf
     schichtet den Hort !
     Helf' ich euch Lahmen ? —
     Hieher nicht gelugt ! —
     Rasch da ! rasch !
     dann rührt euch von hinnen :
     dass ihr mir schafft,
     fort in den Schachten !
   Weh' euch, find' ich euch faul !
   Auf den Fersen folg' ich euch nach.

   Die Nibelungen, nachdem sie den Hort aufgeschichtet, schlüpfen ängstlich wieder in die Kluft hinab.

Alberich.   Gezahlt hab' ich :
     lasst mich nun ziehn !
     Und das Helmgeschmeid,
     das Loge dort hält,
   das gebt mir nun gütlich zurück !

Loge
       (den Tarnhelm zum Horte werfend).
   Zur Busse gehört auch die Beute.

Alberich.   Verfluchter Dieb ! —
     Doch nur Geduld !
     Der den alten mir schuf,
     schafft einen andern .

6

17

3
17

still 'bideth the might
that Mime obeys.
Hard, indeed,
that hated foes
should seize on my subtle defence !
Now then, Alberich's
spoiled of all things:
ye'll sure release him at length ?

Loge

(to *Wotan*).

Are you contented ?
shall I untie ?

Wotan.　A golden ring
rests on thy finger —
hear'st thou, imp ? —
that also must heighten the hoard.

Alberich

(horrified).

The ring !

Wotan.　Ere we release thee
that must be left us.

Alberich.　My life take — but not the ring !

Wotan.　The ring, I look for :
with thy life then do what thou wilt.

Alberich.　If life and limbs you leave me,
the ring, too, must be allowed me.
Eye and ear, —
hand and head,
are not mine more wholly
than is this ruddy ring.

Wotan.　Thine own thou callest the ring !
Ravest thou, impudent earth-gnome ?
Tell me now,
whence was taken the gold
from which thou hast hammered the hoop ?
was't thine own then,
which thine arm
from the water's depth tore away ?
By the river-maidens
be thou arraigned
if their gold
for thine own they have given,
which thou hast robbed for thy ring.

Alberich.　Shameful contrivance !
Scandalous trick !
Rogue, dost cast
in my teeth the crime
that thou wert dying to do ?
Hadst robbed gladly
thyself the gold from the Rhine,

noch halt' ich die **Macht**,
der Mime gehorcht.
Schlimm zwar ist's,
dem schlauen Feind
zu lassen die listige Wehr ! —
Nun denn ! Alberich
liess euch alles :
jetzt löst ihr Bösen, das Band !

Loge

(zu *Wotan*).

Bist du befriedigt ?
bind' ich ihn frei ?

Wotan.　Ein gold'ner Ring
ragt dir am Finger :
hörst du, Alp ?
der, acht' ich, gehört mit zum **Hort**.

Alberich

(entsetzt).

Der Ring ?

Wotan.　Zu deiner Lösung
musst du ihn lassen.

Alberich.　Das Leben — doch nicht den **Ring** !

Wotan.　Den Reif verlang' ich :
mit dem Leben mach' was du willst !

Alberich.　Lös' ich mir Leib und Leben,
den Ring auch muss ich mir lösen :
Hand und Haupt,
Aug' und Ohr,
ist nicht mehr mein Eigen
als hier dieser rothe Ring !

Wotan.　Dein Eigen nennst du den Ring ?
Rasest du, schamloser Albe ?
Nüchtern sag',
wem entnahmst du das Gold,
daraus du den schimmernden schuf'st ?
War's dein Eigen,
was du Arger
der Wassertiefe entwandt ?
Bei des Rheines **Töchtern**
hole dir Rath,
ob sie ihr Gold
dir zu eigen gaben,
das du zum Ring dir geraubt.

Alberich.　Schmähliche Tücke !
schändlicher Trug !
Wirfst du Schächer
die Schuld mir vor,
die dir so wonnig erwünscht ?
Wie gern raubtest
du selbst dem Rheine das **Gold,**

couldst but as well
the art of its forging have won!
    So, hypocrite,
    how happy thou art
    that the Niblung, here,
    in torturing need,
    in a maddened moment,
_e terrible magic did win ;
whose work now gladdens thy glance.
    The unhallowed one's
    anguish-harried,
    bliss-banishing,
    bitterest deed
shall boot but for dazzle
and thy brilliant adornment?
Shall bliss then be brought by my ban? —
    Mighty god
    mind what thou dost!
    Say I have sinned ;
the sin on myself but falls :
but on all things that were,
    are, and will be,
strikes this evil of thine,
if rashly thou seizest my ring.

Wotan.   Yield the ring !
    No right to that
prov'st thou by prating, methinks.

    (He tears the ring from *Alberich's* finger by force.)

Alberich

        (screaming horribly)

Ha ! I'm vanquished ! — destroyed !
A vassal to vilest of slaves !

Wotan

(donning the ring and contemplating it with satisfaction).

My own 'tis, making me aye
the mightiest monarch of all.

Loge.   Is he released ?

Wotan.   Set him loose.

Loge

        (undoing *Alberich's* bonds).

Slip away home :
  no more shackles hold you :
fare freely from hence !

Alberich

(raising himself from the ground in raging laughter).

    Am I now free ? —
    really free ?
    Then listen, friends,
to my freedom's first salute ! —
As at first by my curse 'twas reached,
henceforth cursed be this ring !

    war nur so leicht
die List, es zu schmieden, erlangt?
    Wie glückt' es nun
    dir Gleissner zum Heil,
    dass der Niblung ich
    aus schmählicher Noth,
    in des Zornes Zwange,
den schrecklichen Zauber gewann,
dess' Werk nun lustig dir lacht ?
    Des Unseligsten,
    Angstversehrten
    fluchfertige,
    furchtbare That,
    zu fürstlichem Tand
soll sie fröhlich dir taugen ?
zur Freude dir frommen mein Fluch ? —
    Hüte dich,
    herrischer Gott !
    Frevelte ich,
so frevelt' ich frei an mir ?
doch an allem, was war,
    ist und wird,
frevelst, Ewiger, du,
entreissest du frech mir den Ring !

Wotan.   Her den Ring !
    Kein Recht an ihm
schwört dein Schwatzen dir zu.

    (Er entzieht *Alberich's* Finger mit heftiger Gewalt den Ring.)

Alberich

        (grässlich aufschreiend).

Weh ! Zertrümmert ! Zerknickt !
Der Traurigen traurigster Knecht !

Wotan

(hat den Ring an seinen Finger gesteckt und betrachtet ihn wohlge-
    fällig).

Nun halt' ich, was mich erhebt,
der Mächtigen mächtigsten Herrn !

Loge.   Ist er gelöst ?

Wotan.   Bind' ihn los !

Loge

        (löst *Alberich* die Bande).

Schlüpfe denn heim !
  Keine Schlinge hält' dich :
frei fahre dahin !

Alberich

(sich vom Boden erhebend, mit wüthendem Lachen),

    Bin ich nun frei ?
    wirklich frei ? —
    So grüss' euch denn
meiner Freiheit erster Gruss ! —
Wie durch Fluch er mir gerieth,
verflucht sei dieser Ring !

21

20

Gold which gave me measureless might, now may its magic deal each owner death! No man shall e'er own it in mirth, and to gladden no life shall its lustre gleam. May care consume each sev'ral possessor, and envy gnaw him who neareth it not! all shall lust after its delights, but none shall employ them to profit him. To its master giving no gain, aye the murd'rer's brand it shall bring. To death he is fated. its fear on his fancy shall feed; though long he live shall he languish each day, the treasure's lord and the treasure's slave: till within my hand I in triumph once more behold it! — So — stirred by the hardest need, the Niblung blesses his ring! — I give it thee guard it with care — but my curse can'st thou not flee!	Gab sein Gold mir — Macht ohne Mass, nun zeug' sein Zauber Tod dem — der ihn trägt! Kein Froher soll seiner sich freu'n; keinem Glücklichen lache sein lichter Glanz; wer ihn besitzt, den zehre Sorge, und wer ihn nicht hat, nage der Neid! Jeder giere nach seinem Gut, doch keiner geniesse mit Nutzen sein'; ohne Wucher hüt' ihn sein Herr, doch den Würger zieh' er ihm zu! Dem Tode verfallen, fessle den Feigen die Furcht; so lang' er lebt, sterb' er lechzend dahin, des Ringes Herr als des Ringes Knecht: bis in meiner Hand den geraubten wieder ich halte! — So — segnet in höchster Noth der Nibelung seinen Hort! — Behalt' ihn nun, hüte ihn wohl: meinem Fluch fliehest du nicht!

(He vanishes swiftly in the crevice.)	(Er verschwindet schnell in der Kluft.)

Loge. Did you hear
      his adieu of love?

Wotan
    (absorbed in contemplation of the ring).
Let him give loose to his dole.

   The vapor in the foreground now gradually clears.

Loge
    (looking off, R.).
Fasolt and Fafner
hitherward fare.
Freia follows their steps.

(From the other side enter *Fricka, Donner* and *Froh.*)

Froh. The gods have returned!

Donner. We greet thee, brother!
    (anxiously advancing to *Wotan*).

Fricka. Bring'st thou news to glad us?

Loge. Lauschtest du
      seinem Liebesgruss?

Wotan
    (in die Betrachtung des Ringes verloren).
Gönn' ihm die geifernde Lust!

   Der Nebelduft des Vordergrundes klärt sich allmählig auf.

Loge
    (nach rechts blickend).
Fasolt und Fafner
nahen von fern;
Freia führen sie her.

(Von der andern Seite treten *Fricka, Donner* und *Froh* auf.)

Froh. Sie kehrten zurück.

Donner. Willkommen, Bruder!
    (Besorgt auf *Wotan* zueilend.)

Fricka. Bringst du mir gute Kunde?

Log.

      (pointing to the hoard)

  With power of wit
    the prize was won:
  yon pile is Freia's price.

Donner. From the giants' hold
    now doth she hasten.

Froh. What exquisite air
    wafteth this way!
    wondrous the feeling
    that steals o'er each frame!
    Hard 'twould go with the Æsir,
    withheld for aye from their own,
    who lends them ecstatic youth's
    unyielding and lasting delights.

The foreground is now quite clear again, the renewed light restoring to the gods their first aspect: the background, however, is still shrouded in mists, so that the distant castle is invisible.

Fasolt and *Fafner* enter leading *Freia* between them.

Fricka

   (hastening joyfully towards her sister, to embrace her).

  Loveliest sister,
    sweetest delight!
  look we again on our goddess?

Fasolt

      (stopping her).

  Halt! stand from her side!
  Still we hold her ours.—
    On Riesenheim's
    rugged confines
    rest did we take:
    the contract's forfeit
    with careful truth
    treated we.
    So, sorely loth,
    I lead her hither.
    I prythee hand us
    the price agreed.

Wotan. At hand rests the ransom:
    the golden mass
  must be guardedly measured.

Fasolt. To lose the maiden,
    look you, will make me forlorn·
  so, from my soul to unseat her,
    be the sparkling hoard
    heaped in a stack,
    so as to hide
  the heavenly maid from our sight.

Wotan. Then fix a gauge
    like Freia in form.

Fafner and *Fasolt* place *Freia* in the middle of the stage and stick their staves into the ground on each side, so as to give her height and breadth.

Loge

      (auf den Hort deutend).

  Mit List und Gewalt
    gelang das Werk:
  dort liegt, was Freia lös't.

Donner. Aus der Riesen Haft
    naht dort die Holde.

Froh. Wie liebliche Luft
    wieder uns weht,
    wonnig Gefühl
    die Sinne füllt!
    Traurig ging' es uns allen,
    getrennt für immer von ihr,
    die leidlos ewiger Jugend
    jubelnde Lust uns verleiht.

Der Vordergrund ist wieder hell geworden; das Aussehen der Götter gewinnt durch das Licht wieder die erste Frische: über dem Hintergrunde haftet jedoch noch der Nebelschleier, so dass die ferne Burg unsichtbar bleibt.

Fasolt und *Fafner* treten auf, *Freia* zwischen sich führend.

Fricka

   (eilt freudig auf die Schwester zu, um sie zu umarmen).

  Lieblichste Schwester,
    süsseste Lust!
  Bist du mir wieder gewonnen?

Fasolt

      (ihr wehrend).

  Halt! Nicht sie berührt!
  Noch gehört sie uns.—
    Auf Riesenheim's
    ragender Mark
    rasteten wir:
    mit treuem Muth
    des Vertrages Pfand
    pflegten wir;
    so sehr mich's reut,
    zurück doch bring' ich's
    erlegt uns Brüdern
    die Lösung ihr.

Wotan. Bereit liegt die Lösung:
    des Goldes Mass
  sei nun gütlich gemessen.

Fasolt. Das Weib zu missen,
    wisse, gemuthet mich weh:
  soll aus dem Sinn sie mir schwinden,
    des Geschmeides Hort
    häufe denn so,
    dass meinem Blick
  die Blühende ganz er verdeck'!

Wotan. So stellt das Mass
    nach Freia's Gestalt.

Fafner und *Fasolt* stossen ihre Pfähle vor *Freia* hin so in den Boden, dass sie gleiche Höhe und Breite mit ihrer Gestalt messen.

9

7

Fafner. Our poles we have planted in proper form : to hide them pile up the hoard.	*Fafner.* Gepflanzt sind die Pfähle nach Pfandes Mass : gehäuft füll' es der Hort.
Wotan. Haste with the task; 'tis to me hateful.	*Wotan.* Eilt mit dem Werk : widerlich ist mir's!
Loge. Help me, Froh!	*Loge.* Hilf mir, Froh!
Froh. Freia's shame I'll make an end of.	*Froh.* Freia's Schmach eil' ich zu enden.
(*Loge* and *Froh* quickly heap up the treasure between the poles.)	(*Loge* und *Froh* häufen hastig zwischen den Pfählen die Geschmeide.)
Fafner. Not so light and loose in the form; firm and close fill up the gauge.	*Fafner.* Nicht so leicht und locker gefügt : fest und dicht füll' er das Mass!
He roughly presses the ornaments close together and stoops to peer about for crevices. Through here I see day. — All chinks must be hidden.	Mit roher Kraft drückt er die Geschmeide dicht zusammen; **er** beugt sich, um nach Lücken zu spähen. Hier lug' ich noch durch : verstopft mir die Lücken!
Loge. Away, you lubber! Let it alone!	*Loge.* Zurück, du Grober! greif' mir nichts an!
Fafner. Look here, this cleft must be closed!	*Fafner.* Hieher! die Klinze verklemmt!
Wotan (turning away moodily). Deep in my breast burneth this shame. (His eyes are fixed on *Freia*.)	*Wotan* (unmuthig sich abwendend). Tief in der Brust brennt mich die Schmach. (Den Blick auf *Freia* geheftet.)
Fricka. See how distressed sadly the fair one stands! for release the mute suff'rer looketh a pray'r. Perjured man! our maid thou hast placed in this strait.	*Fricka.* Sieh, wie in Scham schmählich die Edle steht : um Erlösung fleht stumm der leidende Blick. O böser Mann! Der Minnigen botest du das!
Fafner. Still more must be piled!	*Fafner.* Noch mehr hierher!
Donner. This passes all! hot is my rage roused by so hardened a rogue! — Come here thou hound! wouldst thou measure, then match thyself against me!	*Donner.* Kaum halt' ich mich : schäumende Wuth weckt mir der schamlose Wicht! — Hierher, du Hund! willst du messen, so miss dich selber mit mir!
Fafner. Rest thee, thund'rer, rumble not thus; we heed thy rolling not here.	*Fafner.* Ruhig, Donner! Rolle wo's taugt : hier nützt dein Rasseln dir nichts!
Donner (menacing him). I will first crush thee to fragments!	*Donner* (holt aus). Nicht dich Schmählichen zu zerschmettern?
Wotan. Friend, withhold. Sure, wholly Freia is hid?	*Wotan.* Friede doch! Schon dünkt mich Freia verdeckt.
Loge The hoard gives out.	*Loge.* Der Hort ging auf.

Fafner
          (measuring with his eye).
     Still shines on me Holda's hair:
          throw me that wove-
          work on the heap.

Loge.   What! e'en the helm?

Fafner.   Hither haste with it.

Wotan.   Let it go freely.

Loge
          (throwing the Tarnhelm on the heap).
     So surely 'tis finished;
          seek ye aught further?

Fasolt.   Freia the glorious
          glads me no more,
          O is she released?
          Must I then lose her?
     (Goes nearer and peeps through the hoard.)
          Ah! her glance
          yet gleams on me here;
          her eyes like stars,
          stream to my own;
          yes, I can spy them
          still through this space:
     so while I gaze on her features
     from the goddess can I not fare.

Fafner.   Ha! you hear me?
          that chink must be hidden.

Loge.   Never sated!
          See ye then not,
          quite spent is the hoard?

Fafner.   By no means, friend.
          On Wotan's finger
          gleams a glittering ring:
          that give to rest in the fissure.

Wotan.   What! give the ring?

Loge.   Let me rede you —
          to Rhine-maidens
          this gold belongs.
          Wotan looks still to restore it.

Wotan.   What pratest thou there?
          The prize so hardly come by
          I shall keep, unawed, for myself.

Loge.   Poorly paid
          then is the promise
          I gave the sorrowing nymphs.

Wotan.   But thy promise bindeth not me:
          my booty 'bideth the ring.

Fafner
          (mit dem Blicke messend).
     Noch schimmert mir Holda's **Haar**:
          dort das Gewirk
          wirf auf den Hort!

Loge.   Wie, auch den Helm?

Fafner.   Hurtig her mit ihm!

Wotan.   Lass ihn denn fahren!

Loge
          (wirft den Helm auf den Haufen).
     So sind wir fertig. —
          Seid ihr zufrieden?

Fasolt.   Freia, die schöne,
          schau' ich nicht mehr:
          ist sie gelös't?
          muss ich sie lassen?
     (Er tritt nahe hinzu und späht durch den **Hort**.)
          Weh! noch blitzt
          ihr Blick zu mir her;
          des Auges Stern
          strahlt mich noch an.
          durch eine Spalte
          muss ich's erspäh'n! —
     Seh' ich dies wonnige Aug',
     von dem Weibe lass ich nicht ab.

Fafner.   He! euch rath' ich,
          verstopft mir die Ritze!

Loge.   Nimmer-Satte!
          seht ihr denn nicht,
          ganz schwand uns das Gold?

Fafner.   Mit nichten, Freund!
          An Wotan's Finger
          glänzt von Gold noch ein Ring,
          den gebt, die Ritze zu füllen!

Wotan.   Wie! diesen Ring?

Loge.   Lasst euch rathen!
          Den Rheintöchtern
          gehört dies Gold:
          ihnen giebt Wotan es wieder.

3 *Wotan.*   Was schwatzest du da?
          Was schwer ich mir erbeutet,
          ohne Bangen wahr' ich's für mich.

Loge.   Schlimm dann steht's
          un mein Versprechen,
          das ich den Klagenden gab.

Wotan.   Dein Versprechen bindet mich nicht:
          als Beute bleibt mir der Reif.

fner. But here for ransom
　　　must it be rendered.

otan. Make demand as ye will:
　　　all I'll award you;
　　　but all the world shall not
move this ring from my hand.

solt
　　　(wrathfully pulling *Freia* from behind the hoard).
　　　All is off!
　　　as erst it stands,
　　　and Freia's forfeit for ever.

eia. Help me! Help me!

icka. Haughty god!
　　　give them their way.

oh. Hold not the gold back.

nner. Hand them the ring too.

otan. Leave me at rest;
　　　the ring I retain.

Fafner holds back the departing *Fasolt* all stand perplexed.
e Wotan turns away in wrath. The stage has again become
*; from the rocky cleft at the side shines out a bluish glow in
h Wotan suddenly perceives *Erda*, who rises from below to half
height. She is of noble presence and enveloped in a mass of
k hair.

da.
　　　(stretching out her hand warningly towards *Wotan*).
　　　Waver, Wotan, waver!
　　　quit the ring accursed.
　　　Ruin
　　　and dismallest downfall
wait thee in its wealth.

tan. Who speaks such menacing words?

da. What ever was, wis I;
　　　what is, as well —
　　　what ages shall work —
　　　all I show:
　　　the endless world's
　　　All-wise one,
Erda — opens thine eyes.
　　　Three the daughters
　　　born to me
　　　e'er the world was made;
　　　all I notice
nightly thou know'st from the Nornir.
　　　But hither in dire
　　　danger haste I
　　　to thy help.
Hear me! hear me! hear me!
All that exists, endeth!
　　　A dismal day
　　　dawns for the Æsir:
O render wisely the ring!

She sinks slowly to the breast and the bluish glow begins to

Fafner. Doch hier zur Lösung
　　　musst du ihn legen.

Wotan. Fordert frech was ihr wollt:
　　　alles gewähr' ich,
　　　um alle Welt
　　　nicht fahren doch lass' ich den Ring!

Fasolt
　　　(zieht wüthend *Freia* hinter dem Horte hervor).
　　　Aus denn ist's,
　　　beim Alten bleibt's:
　　　nun folgt uns Freia für immer!

Freia. Hülfe! Hülfe!

Fricka. Harter Gott,
　　　gieb ihnen nach!

Froh. Spare das Gold nicht!

Donner. Spende den Ring doch!

Wotan. Lasst mich in Ruh'!
　　　Den Reif geb' ich nicht.

Fafner hält den fortdrängenden *Fasolt* noch auf; Alle stehen
bestürzt; *Wotan* wendet sich zürnend von ihnen zur Seite. Die
Bühne hat sich von Neuem verfinstert; aus der Felskluft zur Seite
bricht ein bläulicher Schein hervor: in ihm wird *Wotan* plötzlich
Erda sichtbar, die bis zu halber Leibeshöhe aus der Tiefe aufsteigt:
sie ist von edler Gestalt, weithin von schwarzem Haare umwallt.

Erda
　　　(die Hand mahnend gegen *Wotan* ausstreckend).
　　　Weiche, Wotan, weiche!
　　　flieh' des Ringes Fluch!
　　　Rettungslos
　　　dunklem Verderben
weiht dich sein Gewinn.

Wotan. Wer bist du, mahnendes Weib?

Erda. Wie alles war, weiss ich;
　　　wie alles wird,
　　　wie alles sein wird,
　　　seh' ich auch:
　　　der ew'gen Welt
　　　Ur-Wala,
　　　Erda mahnt deinen Muth.
　　　Drei der Töchter,
　　　ur-erschaff'ne,
　　　gebar mein Schoss:
　　　was ich sehe,
　　　sagen dir nächtlich die Nornen.
　　　Doch höchste Gefahr
　　　führt mich heut'
　　　selbst zu dir her:
　　　höre! höre! höre!
　　　Alles, was ist, endet.
　　　Ein düsterer Tag
　　　dämmert den Göttern:
　　　dir rath' ich, meide den Ring!

Sie versinkt langsam bis an die Brust, während der bläulich
Schein zu dunkeln beginnt.

Wotan.   A secret spell
               speaks in thy words :
         wait, and impart more wisdom.

Erda
                    (disappearing).
            I've warned thee now,
            thou wott'st enough ;
         pause and ponder truth.
                (She completely disappears.)

Wotan.   Pain and peril attending —
            I must detain thee.
            All thou must tell me !

He tries to go to the crevass in order to detain *Erda*. *Donner*, *Froh*, and *Fricka* throw themselves in his way and hold him back.

Fricka.   What wouldst thou wildly do ?

Froh.   Take heed, Wotan ;
           seek not to hold her :
           hark to her words !

Donner
                    (to the giants).
            Here — you monsters,
            remain and harken !
         the gold Wotan will give you.

Freia.   Dared I but hope it !
            Deem ye Holda
         were such a ransom worth ?
                (All look anxiously at *Wotan*.)

Wotan
(who has been absorbed in deep thought, now musters his strength to
                    a decision).
            Return, Freia !
            I set thee free.
            Purchased again
         gladly in youth we rejoice !
         Ye giants, there is your gem.
                (He throws the Ring on the heap.)
   The giants release *Freia* : she hastens joyfully to the gods who
embrace her in turn during some time, with greatest delight.

Fafner
meanwhile spreads out a huge sack and goes to the hoard preparing to
pack it all up.

Fasolt
                    (opposing his brother).
            Halt, thou greedy one,
            give me some also !
            Equally, surely,
            should we share it.

Fafner.   More on the maid than the gold,
             amorous ape, thou gloat'st.
             My might could scarcely
             make thee resign her :
             as, without sharing,

Wotan.   Geheimniss-hehr
            hallt mir dein Wort :
         weile, dass mehr ich wisse !

Erda
                    (im Verschwinden).
            Ich warnte dich —
            du weisst genug :
         sinne in Sorg' und Furcht !
                (Sie verschwindet gänzlich.)

Wotan.   Soll ich sorgen und fürchten —
            dich muss ich fassen,
            alles erfahren !

Er will in die Kluft, um *Erda* zu halten : *Donner*, *Froh* *Fricka* werfen sich ihm entgegen, und halten ihn auf.

Fricka.   Was willst du, Wüthender ?

Froh.   Halt' ein, Wotan !
           Scheue die Edle,
           achte ihr Wort !

Donner
                    (zu den Riesen).
            Hört, ihr Riesen !
            zurück, und harret :
         das Gold wird euch gegeben.

Freia.   Darf ich es hoffen ?
            dünkt euch Holda
         wirklich der Lösung werth ?
                (Alle blicken gespannt auf *Wotan*.)

Wotan
(war in tiefes Sinnen versunken und fasst sich jetzt mit Gewalt
                    Entschluss).
            Zu uns, Freia !
            du bist befreit :
            wieder gekauft
         kehr' uns die Jugend zurück ! —
         Ihr Riesen, nehmt euren Ring !
                (Er wirft den Ring auf den Hort.)
   Die Riesen lassen *Freia* los : sie eilt freudig auf die Götter z
sie abwechselnd längere Zeit in höchster Freude liebkosen.

Fafner
breitet sogleich einen ungeheuren Sack aus und macht sich übe
            Hort her, um ihn da hinein zu schichten.

Fasolt
                    (dem Bruder sich entgegenwerfend)
            Halt, du Gieriger !
            gönne mir auch 'was !
            Redliche Theilung
            taugt uns beiden.

Fafner.   Mehr an der Maid als am Gold
             lag dir verliebtem Geck :
             mit Müh' zum Tausch
             vermocht' ich dich Thoren.
             Ohne zu theilen

9

Holda thou wouldst have wooed :
    so of the hoard,
    justly I'll hold back
the greater half for myself.
	hättest du Freia gefreit :
	    theil' ich den Hort,
	    billig behalt' ich
	die grösste Hälfte für mich.

olt. Swindler and thief !
    Thus am I served ?
         (To the gods.)
Ye jointly shall judge us :
    should not the jewels
    justly be halved ?
  (*Wotan* turns contemptuously away.)
	Fasolt. Schändlicher du !
	    Mir diesen Schimpf ? —
	         (Zu den Göttern.)
	Euch ruf' ich zu Richtern :
	    theilet nach Recht
	    uns redlich den Hort !
	  (*Wotan* wendet sich verächtlich ab.)

e. Let him take the jewels :
  hold thou the ring, and rejoice !
	Loge. Lass' den Hort ihn raffen :
	  halte du nur auf den Ring !

olt
  (throws himself on *Fafner* who is packing up busily).
    Aroint, defrauder !
    mine is the ring :
it veiled me from Freia's view.
    (He snatches hastily at the ring.)
	Fasolt
	  (stürzt sich auf *Fafner*, der während dem mächtig eingesackt hat).
	    Zurück, du Frecher !
	    mein ist der Ring :
	  mir blieb er für Freia's Blick.
	    (Er greift hastig nach dem Ring.)

ner. Fold not thy fist ;
    the ring is mine.
  (They struggle : *Fasolt* wrests the ring from *Fafner*.)
	Fafner. Fort mit der Faust !
	    der Ring ist mein.
	  (Sie ringen mit einander ; *Fasolt* entreisst *Fafner* den Ring.)

olt. I have it — I shall hold it !	*Fasolt.* Ich halt' ihn, mir gehört er !

ner. Hold it fast, or it may fall !
  urious, he hits out at *Fasolt* with his staff and with one blow fells
  o the ground ; then he wrests the ring from his dying hand.
Now feast upon Freia's face !
  for the ring's rent from thy grasp !
Ie puts the ring in the sack and proceeds coolly to collect the rest
  e gold.
  (All the gods stand horrified. Long, solemn silence.)
	Fafner. Halt' fest, dass er nicht fall' !
	  Er holt wüthend mit seinem Pfahle nach *Fasolt* aus, und streckt
	  ihn mit einen Schlage zu Boden, dem Sterbenden entreisst er dann
	  hastig den Ring.
	    Nun blinzle nach Freia's Blick :
	  an den Reif rühr'st du nicht mehr !
	  Er steckt den Ring in den Sack, und rafft dann gemächlich
	  vollends den Hort ein.
	  (Alle *Götter* stehen entsetzt. Langes, feierliches Schweigen.)

tan. Fearful pow'r
  I find in the fatal curse !
	Wotan. Furchtbar nun
	  erfind' ich des Fluches Kraft !

e. What luck, Wotan,
    were to thine likened ?
    Much it was
    when the ring thou didst win ;
    but it still better serves thee
    since it was lost :
    for thy foemen — see :
    felling themselves
for the gold thou hast let go.
	Loge. Was gleicht, Wotan,
	    wohl deinem Glücke ?
	    Viel erwarb dir
	    des Ringes Gewinn ;
	    dass er nun dir genommen,
	    nützt dir noch mehr :
	    deine Feinde, sieh,
	    fällen sich selbst
	um das Gold, das du vergabst.

tan
      (deep shocked).
How doth horror o'erhang me !
    sickly fear
    fetters my soul ;
    only to heal it
    Erda can help me :
to her forth will I hie.
	Wotan
	      (tief erschüttert).
	Wie doch Bangen mich bindet !
	    Sorg' und Furcht
	    fesseln den Sinn ;
	    wie sie zu enden
	    lehre mich Erda :
	zu ihr muss ich hinab !

Fricka

      (approaching him cajolingly).
Why wait'st thou, Wotan?
Wondrously fair
the fortress shines;
doth it not surely
genial shelter afford?

Wotan.   A shameful price
pays for this shrine.

Donner

   (pointing to the back which is still hidden in clouds).
Vaporous mist
veileth the scene;
sick am I
of the mournful mask!
I'll liven these thin
clouds with some lightning and thunder,
and clear the air for us all.

He mounts an overhanging rock and swings his hammer during the
following.

Halloa! halloa!
To me all ye dews!
come down to me, mists!
Donner is here,
calling his hosts.
At his hammer's swing
swoop to his side!
Halloa! halloa!
Drizzle and damp,
Donner calleth his hosts!

The mist has collected round him; he disappears in an ever thick-
ening and darkening thunder-cloud. Then his hammer-stroke is heard
to fall heavily on the rocks: a vivid flash of lightning breaks through
the clouds, followed by a violent clap of thunder.

Brother, come here!
show what a bridge we can shape!

Froh has also disappeared in the clouds. Suddenly these separate; *Donner* and *Froh* are visible; from their feet stretches, in blinding radiance, a rainbow-bridge over the valley to the castle, which now
gleams with utmost brilliance, illumined by the evening sun.

Fafner, who, beside the body of his brother, has collected the
whole hoard during *Donner's* magic thunder-storm, puts the huge sack
on his back and quits the stage.

Froh.   This bridge home will bring you;
light but hardy of hold.
So tread undaunted
its terrorless height!

Wotan

   (absorbed in contemplation of the castle).
See how at eve
the eye of sunlight
with glorious touch
gilds turret and tow'r!
In the morning glamour,
manful and glad,
it bided masterless,
mildly beck'ning to me.

Fricka

      (schmeichelnd sich an ihn schmiegend).
Wo weilst du, Wotan?
Winkt dir nicht hold
die hehre Burg,
die des Gebieters
gastlich bergend nun harrt?

Wotan.   Mit bösem Zoll
zahlt' ich den Bau!

Donner

(auf den Hintergrund deutend, der noch in Nebelschleier gehüllt
Schwüles Gedünst
schwebt in der Luft,
lästig ist mir
der trübe Druck:
das bleiche Gewölk
samml' ich zu blitzendem Wetter;
das fegt den Himmel mir hell.

Er hat einen hohen Felsstein am Thalabhange bestiegen,
schwingt jetzt seinen Hammer.

He da! He da!
Zu mir, du Gedüft!
ihr Dünste, zu mir!
Donner, der Herr,
ruft euch zu Heer.
Auf des Hammers Schwung
schwebet herbei:
he da! he da!
duftig Gedünst'
Donner ruft euch zu Heer!

Die Nebel haben sich um ihn zusammen gezogen; er verschwi
völlig in einer immer finsterer sich ballenden Gewitter-wolke. D
hört man seinen Hammerschlag schwer auf den Felsstein fallen:
starker Blitz entführt der Wolke; ein heftiger Donnerschlag folgt.

Bruder, zu mir!
weise der Brücke den Weg!

Froh ist mit Gewölk verschwunden. Plötzlich verzieht sich
Wolke; *Donner* und *Froh* werden sichtbar: von ihren Füssen aus z
sich, mit blendendem Leuchten, eine Regenbogenbrücke über
Thal hinüber bis zur Burg, die jetzt, von der Abendsonne beschie
im hellsten Glanze erstrahlt.

Fafner, der neben der Leiche seines Bruders endlich den gar
Hort eingerafft, hat den ungeheuren Sack auf dem Rücken, wäh
Donner's Gewitterzauber die Bühne verlassen.

Froh.   Zur Burg führt die Brücke,
leicht, doch fest eurem Fuss:
beschreitet kühn
ihren schrecklosen Pfad!

Wotan

   (in den Anblick der Burg versunken).
Abendlich strahlt
der Sonne Auge;
in pr cht'ger Gluth
prangt glänzend die Burg:
in des Morgens Scheine
muthig erschimmernd,
lag sie herrenlos
hehr verlockend vor mir.

23

8

From morning till evening thro' mighty ills I won no way to its wonders! The night is nigh; from all annoy shelter it shows us now. So — hailed be the fort; sorrow and fear it heals. — (To *Fricka*.) Wend with me, wife, in " Valhall' " vast we will dwell. (He takes her by the hand.)	Von Morgen bis Abend in Müh' und Angst nicht wonnig ward sie gewonnen! Es naht die Nacht: vor ihrem Neid biete sie Bergung nun. So — grüss' ich die Burg, sicher vor Bang und Grau'n. — (Zu *Fricka*.) Folge mir, Frau: in Walhall wohne mit mir! (Er fasst ihre Hand.)

6

24

8

Fricka. Why so dost thou name it?
 Ne'er such a title was known of.

Fricka. Was deutet der Name?
 Nie, dünkt mich, hört' ich ihn nennen.

Wotan. What might 'gainst our fears
 my mind may have found
 if proved a success
 soon shall explain the name.

Wotan. Was, mächtig der Furcht,
 mein Muth mir erfand,
 wenn siegend es lebt —
 leg' es den Sinn dir dar!

Wotan and *Fricka* go towards the bridge; *Froh* and *Freia* follow mediately, then *Donner*.

Wotan und *Fricka* schreiten der Brücke zu: *Froh* und *Freia* folgen zunächst, dann *Donner*.

Loge
(pausing in the foreground and looking after the gods).

To their end they even now haste,
while esteeming their strength overwhelming.
  Ashamed am I
  their acts to have share in.
  A feverish fancy
  doth woo me to wander
forth in flickering fire:
  to burn and waste them
  who bound me erewhile,
  rather than be
  thus blindly engulfed —
e'en were they of gods the most godlike —
  there seems sense in the scheme!
  I'll study on it!
  Who asks what I do?

Loge
(im Vordergrunde verharrend und den Göttern nachblickend).

Ihrem Ende eilen sie zu,
die so stark im Bestehen sich wähnen.
  Fast schäm' ich mich
  mit ihnen zu schaffen;
  zur leckenden Lohe
  mich wieder zu wandeln
spür' ich lockende Lust.
  Sie aufzuzehren,
  die einst mich gezähmt,
  statt mit den Blinden
  blöd zu vergeh'n —
und wären's göttlichste Götter —
  nicht dumm dünkte mich das!
  Bedenken will ich's:
  wer weiss was ich thu'!

He follows the gods as if unconcerned.

Er geht, um sich den Göttern in nachlässiger Haltung anzuschliessen.

From the valley the song of the *Rhine-nymphs* is heard to peal.

Aus der Tiefe hört man den Gesang der *Rheintöchter* herauf schallen.

The three Rhine-nymphs.

Die drei Rheintöchter.

5

Rhinegold!
Rarest gold!
How wondrously bright
once didst thou beam on us!
  For thee, our plaything!
  now implore we:
  Give us our gold!
O give us our glory again!

Rheingold!
Reines Gold,
wie lauter und hell
leuchtest hold du uns!
  Um dich, du klares,
  nun wir klagen!
  Gebt uns das Gold,
o gebt uns das reine zurück!

Wotan
(in the act of setting his foot on the bridge pauses and returns)

What mournful sounds do I hear?

Wotan
(im Begriff, den Fuss auf die Brücke zu setzen, hält an und wendet sich um)

Welch Klagen klingt zu mir her?

Loge.   The river-maidens
  who mourn, of their gold bereaved.

Wotan.   Accursed Nixies !—
  Quell their clamorous noise.

Loge
                 (calling down the valley).
  Ye in the water !
  why worry us yet ?
Hear what Wotan doth wish !
  Gleams no more
  on you maidens the gold,
in the gods' augmented grandeur
henceforth happily bask.

  The gods laugh loudly and once more turn towards the bridge.

The Rhine-nymphs
                 (from below).
  Rhinegold !
  Rarest gold !
  O might but again
in the wave thy pure magic awake !
  What is of worth,
  dwells but in the waters !
  base and bad
those who are thronèd above.

As the gods slowly cross the bridge to the castle, the curtain falls.

Loge.   Des Rheines Kinder
  beklagen des Goldes Raub.

Wotan.   Verwünschte Nicker !—
  Wehre ihrem Geneck !

Loge
                 (in das Thal hinabrufend).
  Ihr da im Wasser !
  was weint ihr herauf ?
Hört, was Wotan euch wünscht.
  Glänzt nicht mehr
  euch Mädchen das Gold,
in der Götter neuem Glanze
sonnt euch selig fortan !

  Die *Götter* lachen laut und beschreiten **nun die Brücke**

Die Rheintöchter
                 (aus der Tiefe).
  Rheingold !
  Reines Gold !
  O leuchtete noch
in der Tiefe dein laut'rer Tand !
  Traulich und Treu
  ist's nur in der Tiefe :
  falsch und feig
ist was dort oben sich freut !

Als alle Götter auf der Brücke der Burg zuschreiten, fällt **Vorhang.**

8

5

4

8

23

DIE WALKÜRE

For a better understanding of "Der Walküre," the
[read]er should have some knowledge of the *Nibelung*
[sa]g, from which mythical story Wagner's great Trilogy
[—Die] *Walkure*, *Siegfried*, and *Gotterdammerung*—is
[deriv]ed. In the prologue to the Trilogy (*Rhinegold*),
[the] story of the *Nibelung* is told, as follows:

Under the waves of the Rhine, unthought-of and
[unca]red-for, rested purest gold in beautiful masses.
Naiads of the stream—the Rhine-daughters—were
[guar]dians of this treasure. Suddenly, out of the depths
[of t]he earth, there comes into the waters an avaricious
[Nibe]lung, a descendant of the dwarfs, who are born of
[Night] and Darkness. The mischievous water-sprites en-
[tic]e him and tell him of the great worldly power he
[coul]d gain by becoming possessor of the gold. To do
[so] he must utterly renounce Love. The avaricious
[Nibe]lung is bewitched by the gleam of gold, and, curs-
[ing] Love and beauty, tears the treasure from its rock.

[W]otan, king of the gods, is longing for greater
[pow]es. The adventure of Alberich (the Nibelung), be-
[known to] him and his companion, Loge, they de-
[scen]d to the mines where the dwarfs hoard their trea-
[sure], and where Alberich has made a Ring from the
[gold], which gives him power. Wotan and Loge easily
[cap]ture the Nibelung and his treasure. Alberich puts
[a cu]rse upon the Ring.

Wotan, having returned to his castle, would retain
[the] Ring, but the goddess, Erda, "the all-knowing
[prop]hetess," rises and reminds Wotan of the curse at-
[tach]ed to the Ring, and the destruction it will bring
[to t]he power of the gods. Wotan flings the Ring to
[the] giants, and there is strife and blood-shed between
[them].

Wotan resolves to create beings (the Walküre) who
[will] mitigate the sufferings which the greed of gold—
[the] Ring—has brought to those on earth! and so he
[nam]es his new castle "Walhalla."

And now follows the story of

DIE WALKÜRE

To protect the heroes whom the gods loved (but
[who]m Alberich, the Nibelung, continually lurking to
[reco]ver the Ring, threatened with destruction by incit-
[ing] them to battle and blood-shed), Wotan and Erda
[creat]ed the knightly daughters Walküre to bring to
[Wal]halla those warriors who should lose their lives up-
[on] the battle-field. But these were of little use to
[Wot]an, unless he could create a being who, free from
[greed?], could through self-sacrifice, redeem the world

from the annihilation which the love of gold (the possession of the Ring) had brought upon earth. His
children, Siegmund and Sieglinde, born of an earthly
mother, he determined to devote to the work of redemption. Sieglinde was stolen away from her kindred by
the robber Hunding, and Siegmund, parted from Sieglinde, grew to manhood in a stranger land. At the wedding feast of Sieglinde and Hunding, Wotan appeared,
and thrusting a sword in the trunk of an oak-tree which
grew in the centre of the dwelling, he told the guests
that this god-like sword should belong to him who could
draw it from the oak. To Sieglinde he confided the
secret that no one but her lost brother Siegmund would
obtain possession of the sword.

Years pass by, and one stormy night Sieglinde finds
a weary warrior sleeping before the fire on her hearth.
He, awakened by her expressions of pity and compassion, tells her that he seeks refuge from Hunding; he
does not know that he is under his enemy's roof. In
the absence of her husband, Sieglinde learns to love
this stranger; their love is mutual, and not until he
has drawn the sword from the oak, does she recognize
him as her brother Siegmund.

The wife of Wotan, goddess and protector of marriage, compels her husband to withdraw his protection
from the sinful hero Siegmund; but the work of annihilation must go on, and Wotan consecrates as heir of
this work (*Vernichtung*), Hagen of Gabich, born of
Alberich and the wife of the Rhine king, whose favors
the Nibelung bought with gold.

Brünnhilde, Wotan's favorite Walküre, is intrusted
with the mission of telling Siegmund of his approaching death; but as she sees him flying from the rage of
Hunding with the poor woman whom he so dearly loves,
her heart feels god-like pity for him. The fight with
Hunding begins, and Brünnhilde protects Siegmund, but
Wotan stretches his spear between them, and Siegmund,
striking his sword upon the spear, it breaks, god-like
sword although it is, and he falls, killed by a blow from
Hunding.

Brünnhilde has disobeyed Wotan by protecting
Siegmund; she further disobeys him by aiding Sieglinde; she gives her the broken sword "Nothung," and
placing her upon Grane, her own Walküre horse, indicates a place of safety.

For this disobedience Wotan banishes Brünnhilde
from among the Walküre, and condemns her to slumber on the Walküre Rock surrounded with flame, so
that no one but "a hero who knows no fear" will dare
to penetrate the fire and awaken her. He covers her
with helm and shield, and calls Loge, who surrounds
these heights with the blazing *Waberlohe* (fire).

DIE WALKÜRE

ACT I

SCENE I

Interior of a dwelling, built round the stem of a great ash-tree, which forms its centre. To the right, in the foreground, is the hearth; behind it, the storeroom; at back, a great entrance door. To the left, at back, steps lead up to an inner room; lower down, same side, a table, with a broad seat let into the wall behind it, and wooden stools before it. (The stage remains awhile empty; storm without, just subsiding.)

(SIEGMUND opens the entrance-door from without and enters. He still holds the latch in his hand, and looks all round the room; he seems exhausted by over-exertion; his dress and appearance indicate that he is in flight. Perceiving no one, he closes the door behind him, staggers with the last effort of an exhausted man to the hearth, and throws himself down there on a rug of bear-skin.)

(He sinks back, and remains stretched out motionless.)

SIEGMUND.
 Whose hearth this may be, here I must rest me.
(SIEGLINDA enters from the inner room, thinking her husband has returned. Her earnest look changes to surprise on seeing a stranger lying on the hearth.)

SIEGLINDA *(still at back).*
 Whence came this man? I must accost him.

 (She advances.)
 Who enters here and lies on the hearth?

(As SIEGMUND does not move, she comes nearer and inspects him.)
 Tired is he with the way's fatigue.
 Seems he insensible? Can he be sick?

 (She bends down to him and listens.)
 Still active his breathing, though bound are his eyelids;
 Dauntless seems he, indeed, though so drooping now.
SIEGMUND *(lifting his head up suddenly).*
 A draught! a draught!
SIEGLINDA. I'll draw thee water.

ERSTE AKT

ERSTE SCENE

Das Innere eines Wohnraumes. In der Mitte steht Stamm einer mächtigen Esche, dessen starkerhab Wurzeln sich weithin in den Erdboden verliere von seinem Wipfel ist der Baum durch ein gez mertes Dach geschieden, welches so durchschnit ist, dass der Stamm und die nach allen Seiten sich ausstreckenden Aeste durch genau entsprecher Oeffnungen hindurch gehen; von dem belaubten W fel wird angenommen, dass er sich über dieses De uusbreite. Um den Eschenstamm, als Mittelpun ist nun ein Saal gezimmert; die Wände sind aus behauenem Holzwerk, hie und da mit geflochter und gewebten Decken behangen. Rechts im V dergrunde steht der Herd, dessen Rauchfang se wärts zum Dache hinausführt; hinter dem Her befindet sich ein innerer Raum, gleich einem V rathsspeicher, zu dem man auf einigen hölzern Stufen hinaufsteigt; davor hängt halb zurück schlagen, eine geflochtene Decke. Im Hintergru eine Eingangsthüre mit schlichtem Holzriegel. Lir die Thüre zu einem inneren Gemache, zu dem glei falls Stufen hinaufführen; weiter vornen auf desell Seite ein Tisch mit einer breiten, an der Wa angezimmerten Bank dahinter, und hölzernen Schem davor.

Ein kurzes Orchestervorspiel von heftiger, stürmisc Bewegung leitet ein. Wenn der Vorhang aufge öffnet SIEGMUND von aussen hastig die Eingangstl und tritt ein; es ist gegen Abend; starkes Gewitt im Begriff sich zu legen.

SIEGMUND. Wess' Herd dies auch sei
 Hier muss ich rasten.
(Er sinkt zurück und bleibt einige Zeit regungslos a gestreckt, SIEGLINDE tritt aus der Thür des inner Gemaches. Dem vernommenen Geräusche nach glau sie ihren Mann heimgekehrt; ihre ernste Miene ze sich dann verwundert als sie einen Fremden am Her ausgestreckt findet.)

SIEGLINDE *(noch im Hintergrunde).*
 Ein fremder Mann!
 Ihn muss ich fragen.
 (Sie tritt ruhig einige Schritte näher.)
 Wer kam in's Haus
 Und liegt dort am Herd?
(Da SIEGMUND sich nicht regt, tritt sie noch etwas nä und betrachtet ihn.)
 Müde liegt er
 Von Weges Müh'n;
 Schwanden die Sinne ihm?
 Wäre er siech?
  (Sie neigt sich näher zu ihm.)
 Noch schwillt ihm der Athem;
 Das Auge nur schloss er;—
 Muthig dünkt mich der Mann,
 Sank er müd' auch hin.
SIEGMUND *(jäh das Haupt erhebend.)*
 Ein Quell! ein Quell!
SIEGLINDE. Erquickung schaff' ich.

She quickly takes a drinking horn and goes out with it. She returns and hands the filled horn to SIEGMUND.)

SIEGLINDA.
Lift but this to thy lips dry and parching:
Water, what thou dost wish!

SIEGMUND *drinks and hands her back the horn. As he signs his thanks with his head, his gaze rests with growing interest on her features.)*

SIEGMUND.
Freshening liquid here I have found.
My weary load. weigheth more light;
Aroused are my wits, my hopes arise,
The sense of sight is relit.
Who is't restores me to life?

SIEGLINDA.
The house and the wife of Hunding serve thee:
Guestful greeting he'll give:
Tarry but till he come!

SIEGMUND.
Weaponless am I: a wounded guest,
Would thy goodman not wile me.

SIEGLINDA (*with anxious haste*).
A wound! Oh, where is the hurt?

SIEGMUND (*shaking himself and springing up from the couch to a sitting position*).
'Tis well, trust me, unworthy of words;
I feel as ere while my sinews are firm.
Had but half as strong as mine arm shield
And spear been for havoc, ne'er from foes had
I fled;
But they shivered my spear and shield.
The foe, pursuing, pressed on me sore,
And tempest bruit broke o'er my head;
But swifter than I from hunters, speeds my
heaviness hence:
Sank on my lids dismal night,
But sunlight laughs on me now.

SIEGLINDA *goes to the pantry, fills a horn with mead, and hands it to* SIEGMUND *with friendly alacrity.)*

SIEGLINDA.
A freshening horn of foamy mead haply
Thou'lt not refuse.

SIEGMUND. First wilt taste it thyself?

SIEGLINDA *sips from the horn and returns it to him.* SIEGMUND *takes a long draught, while his gaze rests on her with growing warmth. Then he removes the horn, and sets it down slowly, while the expression of his features shows strong emotion.)*
He sighs deeply and lowers his gaze gloomily to the ground.)

SIEGMUND (*with quivering voice*).
An unfriended mortal tendest thou;
Fortune ward my woe from thee!
(*He starts away.*)
Now strengthened am I and well restored;
Farther fareth my step.
(*He goes up.*)

(*Sie nimmt schnell ein Trinkhorn, geht aus dem Hause und kommt mit demselben, gefüllt, zurück, das sie* SIEGMUND *reicht.*)

Labung biet' ich
Dem lechzenden Gaumen:
Wasser, wie du gewollt!

(SIEGMUND *trinkt und reicht ihr das Horn zurück. Nachdem er ihr mit dem Kopfe Dank zugewinkt, haftet sein Blick länger und mit steigender Theilnahme an ihren Mienen.*)

SIEGMUND. Kühlende Labung
Gab mir der Quell,
Des Müden Last
Machte er leicht;
Erfrischt ist der Muth,
Das Auge erfreut
Des Sehens selige Lust:—
Wer ist's, der so mir es labt?

SIEGLINDE. Dies Haus und dies Weib
Sind Hundings Eigen;
Gastlich gönn' er dir Rast:
Harre bis heim er kehrt!

SIEGMUND. Waffenlos bin ich:
Dem wunden Gast
Wird dein Gatte nicht wehren.

SIEGLINDE (*besorgt*).
Die Wunden weise mir schnell!

SIEGMUND (*schüttelt sich und springt lebhaft vom Lager zum Sitz auf*).
Gering sind sie,
Der Rede nicht werth;
Noch fügen des Leibes
Glieder sich fest.
Hätten halb so stark wie mein Arm
Schild und Speer mir gehalten,
Nimmer floh ich dem Feind;
Doch zerschellten mir Speer und Schild.
Der Feinde Meute
Hetzte mich müd',
Gewitter-Brunst
Brach meinen Leib:
Doch schneller als ich der Meute,
Schwand die Müdigkeit mir:
Sank auf die Lider mir Nacht,
Die Sonne lacht mir nun neu.

SIEGLINDE (*hat ein Horn mit Meth gefüllt und reicht es ihm.*)
Des seimigen Methes
Süssen Trank
Mög'st du mir nicht verschmäh'n.

SIEGMUND. Schmecktest du mir ihn zu?
(SIEGLINDE *nippt am Horne und reicht es ihm wieder;* SIEGMUND *thut einen langen Zug; dann setzt er schnell ab und reicht das Horn zurück. Beide blicken sich, mit wachsender Ergriffenheit, eine Zeit lang stumm an.*)

SIEGMUND (*mit bebender Stimme*).
Einen Unseligen labtest du:—
Unheil wende
Der Wunsch von dir!
(*Er bricht schnell auf, um fortzugehen.*)
Gerastet hab' ich
Und süss geruh't:
Weiter wend' ich den Schritt.

SIEGLINDA (*quickly turning*).
    Who dost follow, that thou must flee?
SIEGMUND. Ill fortune follows fast on my footsteps,
    Ill fortune tracks me where'er I tarry:
    That from this thou may be free,
    Forth shall my foot remove.
(*He walks quickly to the door and lifts the latch.*)

SIEGLINDA (*involuntarily and hastily calls to him.*)
    Nay, bide thee here! Thou'llt bring no ill-hap,
    Methinks, where ill-hap hath harboured long.

SIEGMUND (*deeply agitated, remains; he searches SIEG-
LINDA's features; she casts down her eyes shyly and
sadly. SIEGMUND returns*).
    Woeful have I been called:
    Hunding will I await here.
(*He stands leaning on the hearth; his gaze turns with
calm and steady sympathy on SIEGLINDA; she slowly
raises her eyes again to his; they look into one
another's eyes, during a long silence, with an expression of intense emotion.*)

SCENE II

(*SIEGLINDA suddenly starts, listens, and hears HUNDING,
who is leading his horse to its stable without. She
goes hastily up and opens the door. HUNDING, armed
with shield and spear, enters, and pauses on the
threshold, perceiving SIEGMUND. HUNDING turns to
SIEGLINDA with a look of stern enquiry.*)
SIEGLINDA (*meeting HUNDING's gaze*).
    He—this guest—sank on our hearth,
    Rest seeking to gain.
HUNDING. His needs supplied?
(*SIEGMUND quietly and steadily watches HUNDING.*)
SIEGLINDA.
    I gave him nourishment; gladly harboured him.
SIEGMUND. Aid and rest I have had:
    Choose you to chide the woman?

HUNDING.
    Holy is my hearth: haven find in my house!
(*He doffs his weapons and gives them to SIEGLINDA.*)
(*To SIEGLINDA*) Haste our suppers to serve!

(*SIEGLINDA hangs the weapons on branches of the ash-
tree; then fetches provisions and drink from the
pantry; and lays the table for supper.*)
(*Involuntarily she turns her eyes on SIEGMUND again.*)

(*HUNDING scans sharply and with surprise SIEGMUND's
features, comparing them with those of his wife.*)

HUNDING (*aside*).
    How like is their seeming!
    That look of a snake likewise gleams in his
      glances.
(*He conceals his surprise, and turns as if unconcerned
to SIEGMUND.*)
    Sure from far thy way was shaped?
    No horse had he who sheltered here:
    What rugged path hath wrought thee such pain?

SIEGLINDE (*lebhaft sich unwendend*).
    Wer verfolgt dich, dass du schon flieh'st?
SIEGMUND (*von ihrem Rufe gefesselt, wendet sich wieder
      langsam und düster*).
    Misswende folgt mir
    Wohin ich fliehe;
    Misswende naht mir
    Wo ich mich neige:
    Dir Frau doch bleibe sie fern!
    Fort wend' ich Fuss und Blick.
(*Er schreitet schnell zur Thür und hebt den Riegel.*)
SIEGLINDE (*in heftigem Selbstvergessen ihm nachrufend*)
    So bleibe hier!
    Nicht bringst du Unheil dahin,
    Wo Unheil im Hause wohnt!
SIEGMUND (*bleibt tief erschüttert stehen und forscht :
SIEGLINDE's Mienen; diese schlägt endlich verschä?
und traurig die Augen nieder. Langes Schweige
SIEGMUND kehrt zurück und lässt sich, an den Her
gelehnt, nieder*).
    Wehwalt hiess ich mich selbst:—
    Hunding will ich erwarten.
(*SIEGLINDE verharrt in betretenem Schweigen; dan?
fährt sie auf, lauscht, und hört HUNDING, der se?
Ross aussen zu Stall führt; sie geht hastig zur Thür
und öffnet.*)

ZWEITE SCENE

(*HUNDING, gewaffnet mit Schild und Speer, tritt ei?
und hält unter der Thür, als er SIEGMUND gewahrt.*
SIEGLINDE (*dem ernst fragenden Blicke, den HUNDIN?
auf sie richtet, entgegnend*).
    Müd' am Herd
    Fand ich den Mann:
    Noth führt' ihn in's Haus.

HUNDING. Du labtest ihn?

SIEGLINDE. Den Gauman letzt' ich ihm,
    Gastlich sorgt' ich sein'.
SIEGMUND (*der HUNDING fest und ruhig beobachtet*).
    Dach und Trank
    Dank ich ihr:
    Willst du dein Weib drum schelten?
HUNDING. Heilig ist mein Herd:—
    Heilig sei dir mein Haus!
(*Zu SIEGLINDE, indem er die Waffen ablegt und i?
      übergiebt.*)
    Rüst' uns Männern das Mahl!

(*SIEGLINDE hängt die Waffen am Eschenstamme auf, ho?
Speise und Trank aus dem Speicher und rüstet a?
dem Tische das Nachtmahl.*)

(*HUNDING misst scharf und verwundert SIEGMUND?
Züge, die er mit denen seiner Frau vergleicht; f?
sich:*)
    Wie gleicht er dem Weibe!
    Der gleisende Wurm
    Glänzt auch ihm aus dem Auge.

(*Er birgt sein Befremden und wendet sich unbefange?
    an SIEGMUND.*)
    Weit her, traun!
    Kamst du des Weg's;
    Ein Ross nicht ritt,
    Der Rast hier fand:
    Welch' schlimme Pfade
    Schufen dir Pein?

SIEGMUND.
    Through thorn and thicket, forest and field,
    I was pursued by storm and stress:
    I trow not the way that I took.
    Whither I've wandered wist I no better;
    Tidings I'd willingly learn.

HUNDING (*at table, signing* SIEGMUND *to a seat*).
    This resting roof, this harb'ring house,
    Hunding holds for wealth;
    Wendest thou hence to the west thy way, in homesteads
    Rich hordes of my kinsmen uphold the honour of Hunding;
    Grant the favour, my guest,
    That thy name may not stay unknown.

SIEGMUND, *who has taken his place at the table, gazes thoughtfully before him;* SIEGLINDA, *seated beside* HUNDING, *opposite* SIEGMUND, *fixes her eyes on the latter with strange interest and expectancy.*)

HUNDING (*observing them both*).
    Care or trouble hast to disclose,
    My wife would gladly listen:
    See, how greedily she waits!

SIEGLINDA. Guest, who thou art I would glean.

SIEGMUND *looks up, gazes into her eyes and begins earnestly.*)
    "Peaceful" may I not call me;
    "Joyful" would I had been;
    But "Woeful" must be my title,
    "Wolfing," he was my father;
    As twins entered the world
    My tender sister and I.
    Full soon I lost mother and maid;
    The parent fond and the playfellow fair,
    Nay, they have scarcely been known.
    Warlike and strong was Wolfing.
    And foes he won not a few.
    Through forest fared we in forage together;
    When home from the hunt one even we hied,
    The Wolfing's nest lay waste.
    To cinders burnt the building so strong,
    To stumps the oak trees' blossoming stem,
    And slaughter'd the mother motionless lay;
    No trace of my sister the cinders showed.
    This shameful deed we knew the Neidings had done, for sure.
    Then, friendless, fled my father with me.
    Lapsed my youth while living for years with Wolfing in woodlands wild;
    Onsets yet against us were aimed,
    But ever warded the wolves themselves.

SIEGMUND. Durch Wald und Wiese,
    Haide und Hain,
    Jagte mich Sturm
    Und starke Noth:
    Nicht kenn' ich den Weg, den ich kam.
    Wohin ich irrte
    Weis ich noch minder:
    Kunde gewänn' ich dess gern.

HUNDING (*am Tische und* SIEGMUND *den Sitz bietend*).
    Dess' Dach dich deckt,
    Dess Haus dich hegt,
    Hunding heisst der Wirth;
    Wendest von hier du
    Nach West den Schritt,
    In Höfen reich
    Hausen dort Sippen,
    Die Hunding's Ehre behüten.
    Gönnt mir Ehre mein Gast,
    Wird sein Name nun mir genannt.

(SIEGMUND, *der sich am Tische niedergesetzt, blickt nachdenklich vor sich hin.* SIEGLINDE *hat si h neben* HUNDING, SIEGMUND *gegenüber, gesetzt, und heftet mit auffallender Theilnahme und Spannung ihr Auge auf diesen.*)

HUNDING (*der beide beobachtet*).
    Trägst du Sorge,
    Mir zu vertrau'n,
    Der Frau hier gieb doch Kunde:
    Sieh', wie sie gierig dich frägt!

SIEGLINDE (*unbefangen und theilnahmvoll*).
    Gast, wer du bist,
    Wüsst' ich gern.

(SIEGMUND *blickt auf, sieht ihr in das Auge, und beginnt ernst*).
    Friedmund darf ich nicht heissen;
    Frohwald möcht' ich wohl sein:
    Doch Wehwalt muss ich mich nennen.
    Wolfe, der war mein Vater;
    Zu Zwei kam ich zur Welt,
    Eine Zwillingsschwester und ich.
    Früh schwanden mir
    Mutter und Maid;
    Die mich gebar,
    Und die mit mir sie barg,
    Kaum hab' ich sie je gekannt.—
    Wehrlich und stark war Wolfe!
    Der Feinde wuchsen ihm viel.
    Zum Jagen zog
    Mit dem Jungen der Alte;
    Von Hetze und Harst
    Einst kehrten sie heim:
    Da lag das Wolfsnest leer;
    Zu Schutt gebrannt
    Der prangende Saal,
    Zum Stumpf der Eiche
    Blühender Stamm;
    Erschlagen der Mutter
    Muthiger Leib,
    Verschwunden in Gluthen
    Der Schwester Spur:
    Uns schuf die herbe Noth
    Der Neidinge harte Schaar.
    Geächtet floh
    Der Alte mit mir;
    Lange Jahre
    Lebte der Junge
    Mit Wolfe im Wald:
    Manche Jagd
    Ward auf sie gemacht;
    Doch muthig wehrte
    Das Wolfspaar sich.

(Turning to HUNDING.)
A Wolfing now relates this;
And as Wolfing I am well known.

HUNDING.
Wild and unwonted stories tell'st thou, intrepid
    guest.
Woeful the Wolfing!
I've heard of that warrior pair, full of unholy
    stories,
I myself neither have known till now.

SIEGLINDA. Yet, stranger, tell us further;
Where stays thy father now?

SIEGMUND.
An onslaught mighty of aim ordered the Neid-
    lings on us;
But many foemen fell by the Wolfings;
Their flight thro' the wood others did wing;
Like chaff we chas'd them afar.
I stray'd from my father by chance;
He, my chief, was wanting, though wearily
    watched for.
But alone a wolfskin lay in the wood, toss'd
    tenantless there; my father found I not.
After this, shunning the woods,
I shelter'd with heroes and women.
But far and near, where'er I fared,
If for a friend or fair I wished,
I could not win what I asked for; ill luck lay
    on me.
When recking I was right, wrong to others I
    wrought; and things ill, as I thought, others
    hotly upheld.
I fell in feud wherever I fared;
Strife came wherever I strayed.
Did I seek pleasure, pain but appeared:
They call me then "Woeful" rightly;
Unwitting, woe I must wreck.

HUNDING. Sure the Norn who knitted thy fate
Had naught of love for thee!
Neither hails thee the man
Who now the host must play!

SIEGLINDA.
Foolish 'twere, fear to hod of one o'erta'en by
    defeat!
Tell us now, guest, in what attack of late, thy
    weapons were lost?

SIEGMUND *(with more vigor).*
For succor a maid loudly besought,
Whom chiding kin would have chained
And wed to a churl whom the child did not
    choose.
Swift to her aid I urged my way,
The heartless crew crushing in flight:
Before my force they sank.
I slew the brethren relentless;
Their bodies the sister embraced;
Her panic yielded to pain.
In floods of wildest tears,
She wailed the fiat of fate;
For her brothers' inhuman murder,
Loudly to heaven she moaned.

(Zu HUNDING *gewendet.)*
Ein Wölfing kündet dir das,
Den als Wölfing mancher wohl kennt.

HUNDING. Wunder und wilde Märe
Kündest du, kühner Gast,
Wehwalt—der Wölfing!
Mich dünkt, von dem wehrlichen Paar
Vernahm ich dunkle Sage,
    Kannt' ich auch Wolfe
    Und Wölfing nicht.

SIEGLINDE. Doch weiter künde, Fremder,
Wo weilt dein Vater jetzt?

SIEGMUND. Ein starkes Jagen auf uns
Stellten die Neidinge an:
    Der Jäger viele
    Fielen den Wölfen,
    In Flucht durch den Wald
    Trieb sie das Wild:
Wie Spreu zerstob uns der Feind.
Doch ward ich vom Vater versprengt!
    Seine Spur verlor ich,
    Je länger ich forschte;
    Eines Wolfes Fell
    Nur traf ich im Forst:
Leer lag das vor mir,
Den Vater fand ich nicht.—
Aus dem Wald trieb es mich fort;
Mich drängt' es zu Männern und Frauen:
    Wie viel ich traf,
    Wo ich sie fand,
    Ob ich um Freund,
    Um Frauen warb,
Immer doch war ich geächtet,
Unheil lag auf mir.
Was rechtes je ich rieth,
Andern dünktes es arg;
Was schlimm immer mir schien,
Andre gaben ihm Gunst.
    In Fehde fiel ich,
    Wo ich mich fand;
    Zorn traf mich
    Wohin ich zog;
    Gehrt' ich nach Wonne,
    Weckt' ich nur Weh':—
Drum musst' ich mich Wehwalt nennen;
Des Wehes waltet' ich nur.

HUNDING. Die so leidig Loos dir beschied,
Nicht liebte dich die Norn:
Froh nicht grüsst dich der Mann,
Dem fremd als Gast du nah'st.

SIEGLINDE. Feige nur fürchten den,
Der waffenlos einsam fährt!—
    Künde noch Gast,
    Wo du im Kampf
Zuletzt die Waffe verlor'st!

SIEGMUND *(immer lebhafter).*
    Ein trauriges Kind
    Rief mich zum Trutz:
    Vermählen wollte
    Der Magen Sippe
Dem Mann ohne Minne die Maid.
    Wider den Zwang
    Zog ich zum Schutz;
    Der Dränger Tross
    Traf ich im Kampf:
Dem Sieger sank der Feind.
Erschlagen lagen die Brüder:
Die Leichen umschlang da die Maid;
Den Grimm verjagt' ihr der Gram.
Mit wilder Thränen Fluth

Then the slain men's servants swooped to the spot,
Crowding on me cried they for punishment;
Pouring around me panted the rabble;
Yet from the mourned moved not the maid:
My shield and spear shelter'd her long,
Till spear and shield were hewn from my hands.
Weak and weaponless standing,
Soon I saw her expire.
Still menaced the furious mob,
But the maiden moved no more.

(with a glance of vainful ardor towards SIEGLINDA.)

So, mistress, knowest thou now,
Why I may name me not "Joyful"!

(he rises and crosses the hearth; SIEGLINDA, *pale and deeply moved, casts down her eyes.)*

HUNDING *(rising).*
I trow, a truculent race! Our holiest laws ye lightly hold;
      (With violence.)
The hatred of all ye have earned.
They sought but now my assistance.
Vengeance to render for vassal's blood.
They sent too late: returning now home,
The flying foe himself upon my hearth do I see.

    *(*HUNDING *crosses to the right.)*

HUNDING.
My house holds thee, Wolfing, from harm;
For this night know thou art safe;
But arms redoubtable don with the morning;
At dawn of day shalt thou fall,
My fellows' cause to requite.

*(*SIEGLINDA *steps between the two men with anxious looks.)*
    (Harshly, to SIEGLINDA.)
Forth from the hall! Hence without pause!
Prepare my evening draught,
And wait for me within.

*(*SIEGLINDA *stands awhile undecided and reflecting, then turns slowly and with trembling steps towards the pantry; there she again pauses and remains motionless, deep in thought, with averted face. With calm resolution she opens the cupboard, fills a drinking horn and shakes in spices from a box. Then she again turns her eyes on* SIEGMUND *so as meet his fixed gaze. On the steps she once more turns, looks yearningly at* SIEGMUND, *and indicates with her eyes persistently and with eloquent earnestness a particular spot in the ash-tree stem.)*
*(*HUNDING *starts and orders her by a commanding gesture to leave the room. With a last look at* SIEGMUND *she exits into the bed-chamber and shuts the door behind her.)*

HUNDING *(taking his weapons from the tree).*
Beware these weapons of mine.
    (Going, turns to SIEGMUND.)

Betroff sie weinend die Wal:
Um des Mordes der eig'nen Brüder
Klagte die unsel'ge Braut.—
    Der Erschlag'nen Sippen
    Stürmten daher;
    Uebermächtig
    Aechzten nach Rache sie,
    Rings um die Stätte
    Ragten mir Feinde.
    Doch von der Wal
    Wich nicht die Maid:
    Mit Schild und Speer
    Schirmt' ich sie lang',
    Bis Speer und Schild
    Im Harst mir zerhau'n.
Wund und waffenlos stand ich—
Sterben sah ich die Maid:
Mich hetzte das wüthende Heer—
Auf den Leichen lag sie todt.
(Mit einem Blicke voll schmerzlichen Feuers auf SIEG-LINDE.)
Nun weisst du, fragende Frau,
Warum ich—Friedmund nicht heisse!
(Er steht auf und schreitet auf den Herd zu. SIEGLINDE *blickt erbleichend und tief erschüttert zu Boden.)*

HUNDING *(erhebt sich).*
Ich weis ein wildes Geschlecht,
    Nicht heilig ist ihm,
    Was andern hehr:
Verhasst ist es Allen und mir.
Zur Rache ward ich gerufen,
    Sühne zu nehmen
    Für Sippen-Blut:
    Zu spät kam ich,
    Und kehre nun heim,
Des flücht'gen Frevlers Spur
Im eig'nen Haus zu erspäh'n.—
    *(*HUNDING *sehr finster.)*

HUNDING. Mein Haus hütet,
    Wölfing, dich heut';
Für die Nacht nahm ich dich auf:
    Mit starker Waffe
    Doch wehre dich morgen;
Zum Kampfe kies' ich den Tag:
Für Todte zahlst du mir Zoll.
(zu SIEGLINDE, *die sich mit besorgeter Geberde zwischen die beiden Männer stellt.)*
    (Barsch.)
    Fort aus dem Saal!
    Säume hier nicht!
Den Nachttrunk rüste mir drin,
Und harre mein' zur Ruh'.

*(*SIEGLINDE *nimmt sinnend ein Trinkhorn vom Tisch, geht zu einem Schrein, aus dem sie Würze nimmt, und wendet sich nach dem Seitengemache; auf der obersten Stufe bei der Thüre angelangt, wendet sie sich noch einmal um und richtet auf* SIEGMUND—der mit verhaltenem Grimme ruhig am Herde steht, und einzig sie im Auge behält—einen langen, sehnsüchtigen Blick, mit welchem sie ihn endlich auf eine Stelle im Eschenstamme bedeutungsvoll auffordernd hinweist.* HUNDING, *der ihr Zögern bemerkt, treibt sie dann mit einem gebietenden Winke fort, worauf sie mit dem Trinkhorn und der Leuchte durch die Thüre verschwindet.)*

HUNDING *(nimmt seine Waffen vom Baume).*
Mit Waffen wehrt sich der Mann.—

Thou, Wolfing, diest to-morrow.
My words hearken to; heed thyself weil!
(*He goes into the chamber; the bolt is heard to shut
within.*)

SCENE III

(SIEGMUND *alone. It is now quite night; the room is
only lit by the faint fire on the hearth.*)
(SIEGMUND *reclines on the couch by the fire and broods
silently for awhile in great inward agitation.*)
SIEGMUND.

A sword once promised my father to furnish in
    pressing need.
Weaponless fall'n into foemen's lair,
As a hostage doomed, here do I lie.
A wife saw I, wondrously fair,
And strange emotion stirred my frame!
To her do my longings stray,
Who hath lured my soul toward love,
In servance holds her this man,
Who mocks my swordless hand.
Volsung! Volsung! where is thy sword?
Thy sturdy sword, that in strife should serve
    me?
Breaks madly forth from my breast the frenzy
    my heart would hide!

(*The fire falls together; from the up-springing glow a
bright ray strikes on that spot of the ash-tree stem
indicated by* SIEGLINDA's *look, and where a buried
sword-hilt is now plainly visible.*)

What gleam from out the glow doth shoot?
What a star breaks from the ash-tree stem?
Before mine eyes a lightning doth flash;
It laughs in my face!—
How the sunny glow doth glad my soul!
Is it the look the lovely one threw,
Which yet lingers alluringly there,
Though from the hall she hied?

(*Here the fire on the hearth gradually begins to fade.*)
Deepening shadow shrouded mine eyes,
But on me her glance gloriously shone:
Wondrous the warmth that it shed.
Gleamed in grandeur the golden sun,
His glittering halo encircled my head
Till he retired to rest.

(*Another faint glare from the fire.*)
Yet once more, ere he left, kindled evening's
    soft light;
E'en the aged ash-tree's stem
He gladdened with golden glow.
The flush is fading, the light sinks low;
Deep'ning shadow shroudeth my eyelids:

Dich Wölfing treff' ich morgen:
Mein Wort hörtest du—
Hüte dich wohl!
(*Er geht mit den Waffen in das Gemach ab.*)

DRITTE SCENE
SIEGMUND (*allein*).

(*Es ist vollständig Nacht geworden; der Saal ist n
noch von einem matten Feuer im Herde erhellt. Si
MUND lässt sich, nahe beim Feuer, auf das Lag
nieder, und brütet in grosser Aufregung eine veit la
schweigend vor sich hin.*)
Ein Schwert verhiess mir der Vater,
Ich fänd' es in höchster Noth.—
Waffenlos fiel ich
In Feindes Haus:
Seiner Rache Pfand
Rast' ich hier:—
Ein Weib sah' ich,
Wonnig und hehr;
Entzückendes Bangen
Zehret mein Herz:—
Zu der mich nun Sehnsucht zieht,
Die mit süssem Zauber mich zehrt—
Im Zwange hält sie der Mann,
Der mich—Wehrlosen höhnt.—
Wälse! Wälse!
Wo ist dein Schwert?
Das starke Schwert,
Das im Sturm ich schwänge,
Bricht mir hervor aus der Brust
Was wüthend das Herz noch hegt?

(*Das Feuer bricht zusammen; es fällt aus der aufsp
henden Gluth ein greller Schein auf die Stelle a
Eschenstammes, welche* SIEGLINDE's *Blick bezeichr
hatte, und an der man jetzt deutlicher einen Schwe
griff haften sieht.*)
Was gleisst dort hell
Im Glimmerschein?
Welch' ein Strahl bricht
Aus der Esche Stamm?—
Des Blinden Auge
Leuchtet ein Blitz:
Lustig lacht da der Blick.
Wie der Schein so hehr
Das Herz mir sengt!
Ist es der Blick
Der blühenden Frau,
Den dort haftend
Sie hinter sich liess,
Als aus dem Saal sie schied?

(*Von hier an verglimmt das Herdfeuer allmälig.*)
Nächtiges Dunkel
Deckte mein Aug';
Ihres Blickes Strahl
Streifte mich da:
Wärme gewann ich und Tag.
Selig schien mir
Der Sonne Licht,
Den Scheitel umgliss mir
Ihr wonniger Glanz—
Bis hinter Bergen sie sank.

(*Ein neuer, schwacher aufschein des Feuers.*)
Noch einmal, da sie schied,
Traf mich Abends ihr Schein,
Selbst der alten Esche Stamm
Erglänzte in goldener Gluth:
Da erbleicht die Blüthe—
Das Licht verlischt—
Nächt'ges Dunkel

Deep in my heart lies hid a faint
But yet smouldering fire.

he fire is quite extinguished; complete night. The
loor at side opens softly. SIEGLINDA, *in a white*
obe, comes out and goes lightly, but quickly towards
he hearth.)

GLINDA.   Sleep'st thou, guest?

GMUND (*in joyful surprise*).
    Who steals toward?

GLINDA (*with secrecy and haste*).
    See me, hear what I say:
    In deepest sleep lies Hunding;
    I mingled a drug with his drink.
    Haste from this house without fear!

GMUND (*ardently interrupting*).
    Fear drivest thou hence!

GLINDA.   To a goodly weapon I'll guide thee;
    A glorious prize to gain!
    As highest hero then I might hail thee:
    The strongest alone bears off that steel.
    Oh, ponder well what I repeat thee!
    His people Hunding had in this hall,
    With wassail his wedding to honour;
    He wedded a maid whom ne'er he wooed;
    Ravishers wrought her this woe.
    Mis'ry filled me while all were merry;
    When sudden marked I a man,
    In garments gray and full old;
    Low hung was his hat, and one of his eyes 'twas
       over;
    But the other's flash, awe forced on all men.
    Ev'ry heart felt its haughty pow'r:
    Howbeit I gleaned from that look a sweet solace
       and pain,
    Gladness and grief in one.
    On me smiling, he scowled at the others,
    As a sword he solemnly swung;
    Then struck it deep in the ash-tree's stem,
    With a blow buried it there.
    To none should the prize be fated,
    But who could pluck it forth.
    Then valiant heroes bestirr'd them all vainly,
    The wondrous steel none might win;
    Warriors came here and warriors wended,
    The stoutest laboured and strove,
    But they loosed it not from the stem;
    Yet bides the sword in its sheath.
    Ah! well I wist who 'twas that so gravely me
       did greet;
    His name, too, I know well, for whom that
       sword is withheld.
    Oh! found I in need but now that friend;
    Came he, from far my distress to find.
    What e'er I had suffered in anguish of soul,

    Deckt mir das Auge:
    Tief in des Busens Berge
    Glimmt nur noch lichtlose Gluth!
(*Das Feuer ist gänzlich verloschen; volle Nacht.—Das*
Seitengemach öffnet sich leise: SIEGLINDE, *in weissem*
Gewande, schreitet auf SIEGMUND *zu.*)

SIEGLINDE.   Schläfst du, Gast?

SIEGMUND (*freudig überrascht aufspringend*).
    Wer schleicht daher?

SIEGLINDE (*mit geheimnissvoller Hast*).
    Ich bin's, höre mich an!—
    In tiefem Schlaf liegt Hunding;
    Ich würzt' ihm betäubenden Trank.
    Nütze die Nacht dir zum Heil!

SIEGMUND (*hitzig unterbrechend*).
    Heil macht mich dein Nah'n!

SIEGLINDE.   Eine Waffe lass mich dir weisen—
    O wenn du sie gewänn'st!
    Den hehrsten Helden
    Dürft' ich dich heissen:
    Dem Stärksten allein
    Ward sie bestimmt.
    O merke was ich dir melde!—
    Der Männer Sippe
    Sass hier im Saal,
    Von Hunding zur Hochzeit geladen:
    Er freite ein Weib,
    Das ungefragt
    Schächer ihm schenkten zur Frau.
    Traurig sass ich
    Während sie tranken:
    Ein Fremder trat da herein—
    Ein Greis in grauem Gewand;
    Tief hing ihm der Hut,
    Der deckt' ihm der Augen eines;
    Doch des andren Strahl,
    Angst schuf er allen,
    Traf die Männer
    Sein mächt'ges Dräu'n:
    Mir allein
    Weckte das Auge
    Süss sehnenden Harm,
    Thränen und Trost zugleich.
    Auf mich blickt' er,
    Und blitzte auf Jene,
    Als ein Schwert in Händen er schwang;
    Das stiess er nun
    In der Esche Stamm,
    Bis zum Heft haftet' es drin:
    Dem sollte der Stahl geziemen,
    Der aus dem Stamm' es zög'.
    Der Männer Alle,
    So kühn sie sich müh'ten,
    Die Wehr sich keiner gewann:
    Gäste kamen
    Und Gäste gingen,
    Die stärksten zogen am Stahl—
    Keinen Zoll entwich er dem Stamm:
    Dort haftet schweigend das Schwert.—
    Da wusst' ich, wer der war,
    Der mich Gramvolle gegrüsst:
    Ich weiss auch
    Wem allein
    Im Stamm das Schwert er bestimmt.
    O fänd' ich ihn heut'
    Und hier, den Freund;
    Käm' er aus Fremden
    Zur ärmsten Frau:
    Was je ich gelitten
    In grimmigem Leid,

Howe'er I had pined in penance and pain,
Sweet consolation surely would follow!
Then all losses should I have retrieved,
What erst I bewailed well might be won me,
Found I this help-giving friend,
And folded him in these arms!

Was je mich geschmerzt
In Schand' und Schmach,—
Süsseste Rache
Sühnte dann Alles!
Erjagt hätt' ich
Was je ich verlor,
Was je ich beweint
Wär' mir gewonnen—
Fänd ich den heiligen Freund,
Umfing' den Helden mein Arm!

SIEGMUND (*ardently embracing* SIEGLINDA).
Thou'rt now, mistress fair,
Held by that friend, who weapon and wife doth
claim!
Warm in this heart hidden doth lie the thought
that links me to thee.
Whate'er I have sought I see here in thee;
In thee liveth whate'er I have lacked!
Wept thou for wrongs: I writhed, too, in woe:
I was degraded, thou also disgraced;
Loudly revenge's voice now delights me!
I laugh out with triumph elate,
Holding thee, highest and fairest,
Feeling the beat of thy heart!

SIEGMUND (*umfasst sie mit feuriger Gluth*).
Dich selige Frau
Hält nun der Freund,
Dem Waffe und Weib bestimmt!
Heiss in der Brust
Brennt mir der Eid,
Der mich dir Edlen vermählt.
Was je ich ersehnt,
Ersah' ich in dir;
In dir fand ich,
Was je mir gefehlt!
Littest du Schmach,
Und schmerzte mich Leid;
War ich geächtet,
Und warst du entehrt;
Freudige Rache
Ruft nun den Frohen!
Auf lach' ich
In heiliger Lust,
Halt' ich dich Hehre umfangen,
Fühl' ich dein schlagendes Herz!

(*The great door springs open.* SIEGLINDA *starts in alarm
and tears herself loose.*)

SIEGLINDA. Ha! Who pass'd?
Who entered here?

(*The door remains open; without is a lovely spring
night; the full moon shines in and throws its bright
light on the pair, who can now suddenly and plainly
behold each other.*)

SIEGMUND (*in soft ecstasy*).
No one passed—but one draws nigh;
Lo, now; where spring spreads o'er the land!

(SIEGMUND *draws* SIEGLINDA *towards him on the bench
with tender force, so that she sits beside him.*)
(*Increasing brilliance of the moonlight.*)

(*Die hintere Thüre ist aufgesprungen und bleibt we
ken zusammen und reisst sich los.*)

SIEGLINDE. Ha, wer ging? wer kam herein?

(*Die hintere Thür ist aufgesprungen und bleibt we
geöffnet; aussen herrliche Frühlingsnacht; der Vol
mond leuchtet herein und wirft sein helles Licht au
das Paar, das so sich plötzlich in voller Deutlichke
wahrnehmen kann.*)

SEIGMUND (*in leiser Entzückung*).
Keiner ging—
Doch einer kam:
Siehe, der Lenz
Lacht in den Saal!

(*Er zieht sie mit sanftem Ungestüm zu sich auf da
Lager.*)
(*Wachsende Helligkeit des Mondscheines.*)

No 1   SIEGMUND'S LOVE SONG.

Win-ter storms have wan'd to the winsome moon, .n mild as-cendance smil-eth the Spring, and,
Win - ter stür - me wi-chen dem Wonne - mond, in mil - dem Lich-te leuchtet der Lenz; auf

swayed by Zeph - yrs, soft and sooth - ing, weav-ing won-ders lo! he wends; throughf
lin - den Lüf ten leicht und lieb - lich, Wun-der we-bend er sich wiegt; durch

wood and broad - land wafts his breath-ing, wide-ly beam his eyes with bliss;.... in
Wald und Au en weht sein A - them weit ge-öff - net lacht sein Aug'.... au

songs of birds re-sounds his sil -v'ry voice,.... pleas - ant o -dors pours he forth, from his
sel' - ger Vög - lein San - ge süss er tönt,...... hol - de Düf - te haucht er aus; sei - nem

liv - ing blood out-burst the love-li - est blos - soms, ver-dant sprays upspring at his voice, With
war-men Blut ent -blü -hen won-ni - ge Blu - men, Keim und Spross ent springt seiner Kraft, Mit

soft - ly wield - ed scep - tre sways he the world; Winter and storm wane as his strength awakes, Oh,
zar - ter Waf - fen Zier be - zwingt er die Welt; Winter und Sturm wichen der starken Wehr; wohl

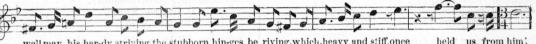

well may his har-dy striving the stubborn hin-ges be riving, which, heavy and stiff once held us from him!
muss-te den tapfern Streichen die strenge Thü re auch weichen die trotzig und starr uns trenn - te von ihm

SIEGMUND.
Winter storms have waned to the winsome
  moon;
In mild ascendance smileth the spring,
And swayed by zephyrs,
Soft and soothing, weaving wonders, lo! he
  wends;
Through wood and broadland wafts his breath-
  ing.
Widely beam his eyes with bliss;
In songs of birds resounds his silvery voice.
Pleasant odours pours he forth;
From his living blood outburst the loveliest
  blossoms;
Verdant sprays upspring at his voice.
With softly wielded sceptre sways he the world;
Winter and storm wane as his strength awakes:
Oh, well may his hardy striving the stubborn
Hinges be riving, which, heavy and stiff,
Once held us from him!
Towards his sister swiftly he flies;
Thus longing Love spring allures,
Within our bosoms buried she slept;
Now leaps she forth to the light.
The bride and the sister is freed by the brother
Lie prone the walls that held them apart:
Hail each other the happy pair!
Now spring at last holds his Love!

SIEGMUND. Winterstürme wichen
  Dem Wonnemond,
  In mildem Lichte
  Leuchtet der Lenz;
  Auf lauen Lüften,
  Lind und lieblich,
  Wunder webend
  Er sich wiegt;
  Ueber Wald und Auen
  Weht sein Athem,
  Weit geöffnet
  Lacht sein Aug'
Aus sel'ger Vöglein Sange
  Süss er tönt,
  Holdeste Düfte
  Haucht er aus;
Seinem warmen Blut entblühen
  Wonnige Blumen,
  Keim und Spross
  Entspriesst seiner Kraft.
Mit zarter Waffen Zier
  Bezwingt er die Welt.
Winter und Sturm wichen
  Der starken Wehr:—
Wohl musste den tapfern Streichen
Die strenge Thüre auch weichen,
  Die trotzig und starr
Uns—trennte von ihm.—
  Zu seiner Schwester
  Schwang er sich her;
Die Liebe lockte den Lenz;
  In uns'rem Busen
  Barg sie sich tief:
Nun lacht sie selig dem Licht.
  Die bräutliche Schwester
  Befreite der Bruder!
  Zertrümmert liegt
  Was sie getrennt;
  Jauchzend grüsst' sich
  Das junge Paar:
Vereint sind Liebe und Lenz!

SIEGLINDA. Thou art the spring;
For thee have I sighed 'neath the
Frost-fettered winter's frown.
Tow'rd thee leapt my heart

SIEGLINDE. Du bist der Lenz,
  Nach dem ich verlangte
In frostigen Winter's Frist;
  Dich grüsste mein Herz

With heavenly thrill, when thy radiant
Glance on me rested.
Foreign seemed all until now;
Friendless I, and forsaken;
I counted strange and unknown
Each and all that came near.
But thee now I thoroughly knew,
When these eyes fell on thee.
Wert thou mine own one,
What my heart long had held,
What was hid.
Clear as the day dawned on my eyes,
The dulcet refrain fell on my ear,
When in winter's frosty wildness a friend first
    awaited me.

*(She hangs in rapture on his neck and looks close into
his face.)*

SIEGMUND *(with transport)*.
    O wondrous vision!
    Woman divine!

SIEGLINDA *(close to his eyes)*.
    Oh, let me closer embracing clasp thee,
    That I may look on the angel light,
    Which from thine eyes in ardour breaks,
    And so sweetly swayeth my sense!

SIEGMUND.
    The spring's fair moon streams on thy head,
    Hanging a wreath o'er thy rippling hair;
    What 'twas bewitched me well now I feel;
    I feast in fervour mine eyes.

*(SIEGLINDA pushes back his locks from his brow and
gazes at him astonished.)*
    How fair and broad thy open brow!
    The varying veins in thy temples I trace!
    I tremble with emotion resting entranced!
    A memory masters my spirit;
    Though but to-day met we first
    I deem not strange thy face!

SIEGMUND. Such fairy dreams my fancy filled;
    Thy form I viewed in visions of bliss!

SIEGLINDA. In streams my semblance I often saw;
    Again it floateth before me
    As erst from river it rose,
    Mildly 'tis mirrored in thee!

SIEGMUND.
    Thine was the picture to me that appeared.

SIEGLINDA *(suddenly turning away her gaze)*.
    O hush! let me unhindered listen;
    Thy voice seems to peal out from the past.
    Yet hold! more lately I heard it.

Mit heil'gem Grau'n,
Als dein Blick zuerst mir erblühte.—
Fremdes nur sah ich von je,
Freundlos war mir das Nahe;
Als hätt' ich nie es gekannt
War was immer mir kam.
    Doch dich kannt' ich
    Deutlich und klar:
    Als mein Auge dich sah,
    Warst du mein Eigen:
    Was im Busen ich barg,
    Was ich bin,
    Hell wie der Tag
    Taucht er mir auf,
    Wie tönender Schall
    Schlug's an mein Ohr,
Als in frostig öder Fremde
Zuerst den Freund ich ersah.

*(Sie hängt sich entzückt an seinen Hals, und blickt
nahe in's Gesicht.)*

SIEGMUND *(mit Hingerissenheit)*.
    O süsseste Wonne!
    Seligstes Weib!

SIEGLINDE *(dicht an seinen Augen)*.
    Lass in Nähe
    Zu dir mich neigen,
    Dass deutlich ich schaue
    Den hehren Schein,
    Der dir aus Augen
    Und Antlitz bricht,
    Und so süss die Sinne mir zwingt!

SIEGMUND. Im Lenzesmond
    Leuchtest du hell;
    Hehr umwebt dich
    Das Wellenhaar;
    Was mich berückt
    Errath' ich nun leicht—
    Denn wonnig weidet mein Blick.

SIEGLINDE *(schlägt ihm die Locken von der Stirn zur
    und betrachtet ihn staunend)*.
    Wie dir die Stirn
    So offen steht,
    In den Schläfen der Adern
    Geäst sich schlingt;
    Mir zagt's vor der Wonne,
    Die mich entzückt—
    Ein Wunder will mich gemahnen:
    Den heut' zuerst ich erschaut,
    Mein Auge sah dich schon!

SIEGMUND. Ein Minnetraum
    Gemahnt auch mich:
    In heissem Sehnen
    Sah ich dich schon!

SIEGLINDE. Im Bach erblickt' ich
    Mein eigen Bild—
    Und jetzt gewahr' ich es wieder:
    Wie einst dem Teich es enttaucht,
    Bietest mein Bild mir nun du!

SIEGMUND. Du bist das Bild—
    Das ich in mir barg.

SIEGLINDE *(den Blick schnell abwendend)*.
    O still! las mich
    Der Stimme lauschen:—
    Mich dünkt, ihren Klang
    Hört' ich als Kind——
    Doch nein! ich hörte sie neulich.

(In emotion.)
When through the waving woods
The echo came of my own.

GMUND. O loveliest lute to which now I listen!

EGLINDA *(again gazing into his eyes)*.
Well I know the light that lurks in thine eyes
So once the strange guest greeting bestowed,
When he solemnly soothed my grief.
In that glance my father I felt;
His name had I fain uttered fondly!
(Pausing.)
"Woeful" calls thee the world?

GMUND. Ne'er call me so, since thou art mine!
I rest now in highest rapture!

GLINDA.
Now "Joyful" may be justly thy title?

GMUND.
Name me thyself as thou judgest my nature
I'll take my title from thee!

GLINDA. Then truly was Wolfing thy father?

GMUND. A wolf he to fearful foxes!
But he whose eye on thee is beaming,
As flashes, O fair one! thine own, avers!
Voisung his name.

GLINDA *(transported)*.
Was Volsung thy father,
Art thou too a Volsung?
Struck he for thee yon sword in the stem?
So let me then name thee,
As I do love thee:
Siegmund,—so be thou called!

GMUND *(springs up)*.
Siegmund hight—I—and Siegmund am I!
A witness this sword,
Unwav'ring I seize it!
Volsung assured me in sorest need
Mine it should be:
I'll make it so!
Holy affection, highest need,
Passionate longing, pressingest need,
Brightly flame in my breast,
Drive to deeds and death;
Needful! Needful!
I name so this sword.
Needful! Needful!
Notable steel,
Prove me thy sharpness,
Show me thy point!
Leap forth from thy scabbard to me!

ith a mighty effort SIEGMUND *plucks the sword from
he tree and shows it to the astonished and enraptured
IEGLINDA.)*
Siegmund, the Volsung stands revealed!
For Bridegift he brings thee this sword;
And fearless woes a wife sweet and fair!

(Aufgeregt)
Als meiner Stimme Schall
Mir wiederhallte der Wald.

SIEGMUND. O lieblichste Laute,
Denen ich lausche!

SIEGLINDE *(ihm wieder in die Augen spähend)*.
Deines Auges Gluth
Erglänzte mir schon:—
So blickte der Greis
Grüssend auf mich,
Als der Traurigen Trost er gab.
An dem kühnen Blick
Erkannt' ihn sein Kind—
Schon wollt' ich beim Namen ihn nennen—
(Sie hält inne und fährt dann leise fort.)
Wehwalt heiss'st du fürwahr?

SIEGMUND. Nicht heiss' ich so
Seit du mich liebst:
Nun walt' ich der hehrsten Wonnen!

SIEGLINDE. Und Friedmund darfst du
Froh dich nicht nennen?

SIEGMUND. Heisse mich du
Wie du liebst dass ich heisse:
Den Namen nehm' ich von dir!

SIEGLINDE. Doch manntest du Wolfe den Vater?

SIEGMUND. Ein Wolf war er feigen Füchsen!
Doch dem so stolz
Strahlte das Auge,
Wie, Herrliche, hehr dir es strahlt,
Der war—Wälse genannt.

SIEGLINDE *(ausser sich)*.
War Wälse dein Vater,
Und bist du ein Wälsung,
Stiess er für dich
Sein Schwert in den Stamm?—
So lass mich dich heissen
Wie ich dich liebe:
Siegmund—
So nenn' ich dich.

SIEGMUND *(springt auf und fasst den Schwertgriff)*.
Siegmund heiss' ich,
Und Siegmund bin ich:
Bezeug' es dies Schwert,
Das zaglos ich halte!
Wälse verhiess mir,
In höchster Noth
Sollt' ich es finden:
Ich fass' es nun!
Heiligster Minne
Höchste Noth,
Sehnender Liebe
Zehrende Noth,
Brennt mir hell in der Brust,
Drängt zu That und Tod:
Nothung! Nothung!—
So nenn' ich dich Schwert—
Nothung! Nothung!
Neidlicher Stahl!
Zeig' deiner Schärfe
Schneidenden Zahn:
Heraus aus der Scheide zu mir!
*(Er zieht mir einem gewaltigen Zuck das Schwert aus
dem Stamme, und zeigt es der von Staunen und
Entzücken erfassten* SIEGLINDE.)*
Siegmund den Wälsung
Siehst du, Weib!
Als Brautgabe
Bringt er dies Schwert;
So freit er sich
Die seligste Frau:

From foeman's house he flies with his bride,
Far from hence follow his steps,
Forth in the smiling softness of spring;
There shields thee Needful, my sword,
And Siegmund but lives in thy love.

SIEGLINDA (*in wild intoxication tears herself away and
            stands before him*).
(*He has clasped her to lead her away with him.*)
    Art thou Siegmund, standing beside me?
    Sieglinda am I. For thee I've sighed:
    Thou'st won thy sister, I tell thee,
    As well as the sword.
        (*She throws herself upon his breast.*)
SIEGMUND. Bride and sister be to thy brother,
    So blest may the Volsungs abound.
    (*He draws her to him in a frenzy of passion.*)
        (*The curtain falls quickly.*)

ACT II

SCENE I

(*A wild and rocky pass. At the back a gorge slopes
    downwards from a high peak, the ground sinking
    again gradually from this towards the foreground.*)
(*WOTAN, in warlike array, with spear and shield; be-
    fore him stands BRYNHILDE as a Valkyrie, also fully
    armed.*)
WOTAN. Make ready thy steed, stalwartest maid,
    Battle's brawl breaketh out soon:
    Brynhilde, spur to the fray,
    The Volsung favour and aid!
    Hunding vainly sues;
    Void are his hopes, in Valhall'
    He has no place;
    So headlong in haste, hie to the field.

BRYNHILDE (*springing from rock to rock up the height
            to the right and shouting*).
    Ho-yo-to-ho! ho-yo-to-ho!
    Heiaha! heiaha!
    Hoyotoho! hoyotoho—heiaha—heiaha!
    Hoyotoho—hoyotoho—hoyotoho—hoyotoho!
    Heiaha—ha! Hoyotoho!
(*She pauses on a high peak of rock, looks down into the
    valley at back, and calls back to WOTAN.*)
    But listen, father! look to thyself! thou wilt
        soon
    Suffer a storm. Watchful Fricka, thy wife,
    Arriveth in her ram-impelled car.
    Ha! how she grasps her golden scourge!
    The foolish beasts are fainting with fear.
    Wheels rattling and rolling whirl her here to the
        war,
    In such disputes no part would I take,
    Though I am happy when heroes fight;
    Take heed that thou find not defeat,
    For lightly I leave thee to fate!

Dem Feindeshaus
Entführt er dich so.
Fern von hier
Folge ihm nun,
Fort in des Lenzes
Lachendes Haus:
Dort schützt dich Nothung das Schwert,
Wenn Siegmund dir liebend erlag!
    (*Er erfasst sie um sie mit sich fortzuziehen.*)
SIEGLINDE. Bist du Siegmund,
    Den ich hier sehe—
    Sieglinde bin ich,
    Die dich ersehnt:
    Die eig'ne Schwester
    Gewann'st du zueins mit dem Schwert!
        (*Sie wirft sich ihm an die Brust.*)
SIEGMUND. Braut und Schwester
    Bist du dem Bruder—
    So blühe denn Wälsungen-Blut!
(*Er zieht sie mit wüthender Gluth an sich; sie sinkt m
    einem Schrei an seine Brust.*)

ZWEITER AKT

ERSTE SCENE

(*Wildes Felsengebirg.*)
(WOTAN, *kriegerisch gewaffnet, und mit dem Speer; v
    ihm* BRÜNNHILDE, *als Walküre, ebenfalls in voll
    Waffenrüstung.*)

WOTAN. Nun zäume dein Ross,
    Reisige Maid!
    Bald entbrennt
    Brünstiger Streit:
    Brünnhilde stürme zum Kampf,
    Dem Wälsung kiese sie Sieg!
    Hunding wähle sich
    Wem er gehört:
    Nach Walhall taugt er mir nicht.
    Drum rüstig und rasch
    Reite zur Wal!

BRÜNNHILDE (*jauchzend von Fels zu Fels die Höh
    rechts hinaufspringend*).
    Hojotoho! Hojotoho!
    Heiaha! Heiaha!
    Hahei! Hahei! Heiaho!

(*Auf einer hohen Felsspitze hält sie an, blickt in d
    hintere Schlucht hinab, und ruft zu* WOTAN *zurück.*)
    Dir rath' ich, Vater,
    Rüste dich selbst;
    Harten Sturm
    Sollst du besteh'n:
    Fricka naht, deine Frau,
    Im Wagen mit dem Widdergespann.
    Hei! wie die gold'ne
    Geissel sie schwingt;
    Die armen Thiere
    Aechzen vor Angst;
    Wild rasseln die Räder;
    Zornig fährt sie zum Zank!
    In solchem Strausse
    Streit' ich nicht gern,
    Lieb' ich auch muthiger
    Männer Schlacht.
    Drum sieh', wie den Sturm du bestehst;
    Ich Lustige lass dich im Stich!—

Hoyotoho! hoyotoho! heiaha!
Heiaha! hoyotoho! hoyotoho!
Heiaha! Heiaha! hoyotoho!
Hoyotoho! hoyotoho! hoyotoho!
Hoyotoho! heiaha—ha—(*dying away*).

RYNHILDE *disappears behind the mountain heights at side*.)

RICKA *comes up from the ravine in a car drawn by two rams; on reaching the ridge she stops suddenly and dismounts; she advances hastily towards* WOTAN *in the foreground*.)

TAN (*aside, observing* FRICKA's *approach*).
   The old complaint, the old annoys!
   No peace! needs I must meet them!

RICKA (*as she advances, moderates her pace and places herself before* WOTAN *with dignity*).
   Where thou wand'rest in these wilds thy very
      wife to avoid,
   Even here I seek thee out,
   That right to me thou may'st render.

TAN. Thy harass, Fricka, fain would I hear.

CKA. Well I know Hunding's need;
   His voice for vengeance is raised;
   The queen of Wedlock hath weighed his guest,
   And wends straight to stir thee to scourge
   Those rash recreants twain who wrought a hus-
      band this wrong.

TAN. What hath wrought of wrong this pair.
   Allured by Spring into love?
   Their passion's fury that frenzied them:
   Who mastereth Love by law?

CKA. How foolish and fond are thy words!
   As knewest thou not, forsooth, that for the
      blessed conjugal bond,
   Discarded thus, I'm complaining!

TAN. Unholy are to me oaths which oust Love
      from his own;
   And prithee expect not from me that my might
      should hold
   Where thine own is helpless;
   For when strong spirits are rampant.
   I rouse them ever to strife.

CKA. Deemest thou righteous adult'rous love?
   Extend then thy license and treat as holy
   The troth plighted between a twin-born, licen-
      tious pair!
   My heart and my sense with horror consume;
   Bridal embrace of sister and brother!
   When was it allowed, that love should
   Exist 'twixt relations?

TAN. Now know it at last!
   Accept the shame which hath shaped itself,
   Though ne'er seen was the like till to-day.
   That these are true lovers learn well from me:
   To milder views then revert!

Hojotoho! Hojotoho!
Heiaha! Heiaha!
Hahei! Hahei! Hojohei!

(*Sie verschwindet, während aus der Schlucht herauf*
(FRICKA *je näher sie kommt, mässigt sie den Schritt.
auf dem Joch anlangt: dort steigt sie schnell ab und
schreitet auf* WOTAN *zu*.)

WOTAN (*indem er sie kommen sieht*).
   Der alte Sturm!
   Die alte Müh'!
   Doch Stand muss ich ihr halten.

(FRICKA *je näher sie kommt, mässigt sie den Schritt
und stellt sich mit würds vor* WOTAN *hin*).
   Wo in Bergen du dich birgst
   Der Gattin Blick zu entgeh'n,
   Einsam hier such' ich dich auf,
   Dass Hilfe du mir verhiessest.

WOTAN. Was Fricka kümmert
   Künde sie frei.

FRICKA. Ich vernahm Hunding's Noth,
   Um Rache rief er mich an:
   Der Ehe Hüterin hörte ihn,
   Verhiess streng
   Zu strafen die That
   Des frech frevelnden Paar's,
   Das kühn den Gatten gekränkt.

WOTAN. Was so Schlimmes
   Schuf das Paar,
   Das liebend einte der Lenz?
   Der Minne Zauber
   Entzückte sie:
   Wer büsst mir der Minne Macht.

FRICKA. Wie thörig und taub du dich stellst,
   Als wüsstest fürwahr du nicht,
   Dass um der Ehe
   Heiligen Eid,
   Den hart gekränkten, ich klage!

WOTAN. Unheilig
   Acht' ich den Eid,
   Der Unliebende eint;
   Und mir wahrlich
   Muthe nicht zu,
   Dass mit Zwang ich halte
   Was dir nicht haftet:
   Denn wo kühn Kräfte sich regen,
   Da rath' ich offen zum Krieg.

FRICKA. Achtest du rühmlich
   Der Ehe Bruch,
   So prahle nun weiter
   Und preis' es heilig,
   Dass Blutschande entblüht
   Dem Bund eines Zwillingspaar's.
   Mir schaudert das Herz,
   Es schwindelt mein Hirn:
   Bräutlich umfing
   Die Schwester der Bruder.
   Wann—ward es erlebt'
   Dass lieblich Geschwister sich liebten.

WOTAN. Heut'—hast du's erlebt:
   Erfahre so
   Was von selbst sich fügt,
   Sei zuvor auch nie es gescheh'n.
   Dass jene sich lieben,
   Leuchtet dir hell:
   Drum höre redlichen Rath!

If aught of bliss follows e'er on thy blessing,
Then smile in lenient love on Siegmund and
    Sieglinda's troth.

FRICKA (*bursting out into violent wrath*).
    Dawn on us the end of the Æsir eternal,
    When thou these vagrant Volsungs begatest!
    I speak straightly—touched is thy soul?
    Esteem'st thou no more thy mightiest subjects?
    Disdained are all things that once were exalted,
    Unloosened the ties thine own wisdom estab-
        lished,
    Lightly leav'st thou thy hold of heav'n,
    That unheld and haughty may flourish
    This froward and sinful pair,
    Thine unfaithfulness' sensual fruit!
    Oh, why mourn thus o'er virtue and vows
    Thou hast vilely slighted thyself?
    Thine own true wife full oft hast thou wronged;
    Never a depth and never a height
    Where thy heart longed not lustful to rove,
    While of change there lacked not to charm
        thee;
    Thou gav'st no heed to my grief,
    Sorrow I bore when thou didst forsake me,
    Leading to battle the barb'rous maidens,
    Of shameless mother born to thy blood;
    For avoided so was thy wife, that this Valkyrie
        set,
    With Brynhilde herself who obeys thy voice,
    At my potent disposal were placed.
    But now that another name takes thy fancy,
    Thou wand'rest wolf-like thro' woodlands as
        "Volsung."
    Now basely deigning to such degradation,
    A pair of pitiful mortals to get thee,
    With these whelps of a wolf
    Thou wishest to humble thy wife!
    O finish thy work! Fill up the cup!
    Let them trample me in their triumph!

WOTAN.
    Thou tak'st me not when I would teach thee.
    Nor may'st thou conceive a case
    Demanded never till now.
    Statutes only canst thou understand;
    But my full thoughts must heed
    The things hitherto strange.
    One thing mark thou!
    We need a man who finds not heaven's protec-
        tion,
    Who flieth from heavenly ties;
    Then a change he alone may effect,
    Which, though fain to the Godhead,
    The gods to effect are refused.

        Soll süsse Lust
        Deinen Segen dir lohnen,
    So seg'ne, lachend der Liebe,
    Siegmund's und Sieglinde's Bund!

FRICKA (*in höchste Entrüstung ausbrechend*).
        So istes denn aus
        Mit den ewigen Göttern,
        Seit du die wilden
        Wälsungen zeugtest?
        Heraus sagt' ich's—
        Traf ich den Sinn?
        Nichts gilt dir der Hehren
        Heilige Sippe;
        Hin wirfst du Alles,
        Was einst du geachtet;
        Zerreissest die Bande,
        Die selbst du gebunden:
        Lösest lachend
        Des Himmels Haft—
    Dass nach Lust und Laune nur walte
    Dies frevelnde Zwillingspaar,
    Deiner Untreue zuchtlose Frucht!
        O, was klag' ich
        Um Ehe und Eid!
    Du zuerst, du selbst sie versehrt!
        Die treue Gattin
        Trogest du stets:
        Wo eine Tiefe,
        Wo eine Höhe,
        Dahin lugte lüstern dein Blick,
    Wie des Wechsels Lust du gewännst',
    Und höhnend kränktest mein Herz!
        Trauernden Sinnes
        Musst' ich's ertragen,
        Zog'st du zur Schlacht
    Mit den schlimmen Mädchen,
        Die wilder Minne
        Bund dir gebar;
    Denn dein Weib noch scheutest du so,
        Dass der Walküren Schaar,
        Und Brünnhilde selbst,
        Deines Wunsches Braut,
    In Gehorsam der Herrin du gab'st.
        Doch jetzt, da dir neue
        Namen gefielen,
        Als "Wälse" wölfisch
        Im Walde du schweiftest;
        Jetzt, da zu niedrigster
        Schmach du dich neigtest,
        Gemeiner Menschen
        Ein Paar zu erzeugen:
    Jetzt dem Wurfe der Wölfin
    Wirfst du zu Füssen dein Weib!—
        So führ' es denn aus,
        Fülle das Mass:
    Die Betrog'ne lass auch zertreten!

WOTAN.   Nichts lerntest du,
        Wollt' ich dich lehren,
    Was nie du erkennen kannst,
    Eh' nicht ertagte die That.
        Stets Gewohntes
        Nur magst du versteh'n;
    Doch was noch nie sich traf,
    Darnach trachtet mein Sinn!—
        Eines höre!
        Noth thut ein Held,
    Der, ledig göttlichen Schutzes,
    Sich löse vom Göttergesetz:
        So nur taugt er
        Zu wirken die That,
    Die, wie noth sie den Göttern,
    Dem Gott doch zu wirken verwehrt.

CKA. With lying spirit wouldst thou delude me.
What help divine could heroes e'er shape us,
Which to the gods themselves were gainsaid,
By whose grace alone they may speed?

TAN.
And their courage fearless count'st thou for naught?

CKA. Who breathes this courage in them?
Who brightens the face of the faint?
Beneath thy shield strong do they seem,
By thee bestirr'd they strive in the fight,
Thou prickest these mortals whom thus to me thou applaud'st:
Again with falsehood wouldst thou befool me,
With new contrivance seeking to trick me.
But for this Volsung in vain dost thou plead;
Through him I strike at thee,
For through thee only he dares.

TAN (with emotion).
In sorrow drooping deserted he lived:
My shield sheltered him ne'er.

CKA. Then shelter now withhold!
Have back the sword upon him bestowed.

TAN. The sword?

CKA.
Yes, the sword, the marvellous, magical sword,
Which the God his son hath giv'n.

TAN. Siegmund has won it himself in his need.

(With suppressed tremor.)
om this point WOTAN's whole demeanor-expresses an ever increasing deep distress.)

CKA (continuing violently).
Thou'st shaped him the need and the notable sword,
Dar'st thou deny it, when night and day I have followed thy feet?
For him struckest thou the sword in the stem;
Thou didst guard for him the glorious blade;
Be this gainsaid not, that but by thy subtle schemings
She found the prize.

(WOTAN starts up with a gesture of wrath.)
RICKA, still more earnestly, on seeing the impression she has made on WOTAN.)
With bondsmen no sovereign does battle;
The monarch scourges his minion.
Against thine my strength properly strives,
But Siegmund I punish as slave.

OTAN makes another angry gesture and then sinks down, feeling his impotence.)

FRICKA. Mit tiefem Sinne
Willst du mich täuschen!
Was Hehres sollten
Helden je wirken,
Das ihren Göttern wäre verwehrt,
Deren Gunst in ihnen nur wirkt?

WOTAN. Ihres eigenen Muthes
Achtest du nicht?

FRICKA. Wer hauchte Menschen ihn ein?
Wer hellte den Blöden den Blick?
In deinem Schutz
Scheinen sie stark,
Durch deinen Stachel
Streben sie auf:
Du—reizest sie einzig
Die so mir Ew'gen du rühmst.
Mit neuer List
Willst du mich belügen,
Durch neue Ränke
Jetzt mir entrinnen;
Doch diesen Wälsung
Gewinnst du dir nicht:
In ihm treff' ich nur dich,
Denn durch dich trotzt er allein.

WOTAN (ergriffen).
In wilden Leiden
Erwuchs er sich selbst:
Mein Schutz schirmte ihn nie.

FRICKA. So schütz' auch heut' ihn nicht;
Nimm ihm das Schwert,
Das du ihm geschenkt!

WOTAN. Das Schwert?

FRICKA. Ja—das Schwert,
Das zauberstark
Zuckende Schwert,
Das du Gott dem Sohne gab'st.

WOTAN. Siegmund gewann es sich
Selbst in der Noth.
(Mit unterdrücktem Beben.)
(WOTAN drückt in seiner ganzen Haltung von hier an einer immer wachsenden unheimlichen, tiefen Unmuth aus.)

FRICKA (heftig fortfahrend.)
Du schuf'st ihm die Noth;
Wie das neidliche Schwert:
Willst du mich täuschen,
Die Tag und Nacht
Auf den Fersen dir folgte?
Für ihn stiessest du
Das Schwert in den Stamm;
Du verhiessest ihm
Die hehre Wehr;
Willst du es leugnen,
Dass nur deine List
Ihn lockte wo er es fänd'?
(WOTAN fährt mit einer grimmigen Geberde auf.)

(FRICKA, immer sicherer, da sie den Eindruck gewahrt, den sie auf WOTAN hervor gebracht hat.)
Mit Unfrieden
Streitet kein Edler,
Den Frevler straft nur der Freie:
Wider deine Kraft
Führt ich wohl Krieg;
Doch Siegmund verfiel mir als Knecht.
(WOTAN wendet sich unmuthig ab.)

This slave thou holdest wholly and closely,
To his caprice must thy consort submit?
Shall he this shame and infamy shape me,
To varlets a scoff, to villains a scorn?
Sure ne'er my husband could suffer so heinous
A slight to his queen!

WOTAN. What requir'st thou?

FRICKA. Cast off the Volsung!

WOTAN. I give him his vent.

FRICKA. But thou favour him not,
When to fight calls th' avenger's voice.

WOTAN. I'll favour him not.

FRICKA. Look on me fairly; lie not to me;
The Valkyrie vow to recall!

WOTAN. The war-maiden works untaught.

FRICKA. Not so! 'tis thy will she accomplishes now,
Recall her from Siegmund's side!

WOTAN. I cannot defeat him: he found my sword.

FRICKA. Remove then its magic,
Or bid it to break!
Shieldless send him to fight!
(BRYNHILDE's *call is heard from the heights.*)
Heiaha! Heiaha! Hoyotoho!

FRICKA. Here wendeth thy warlike maid;
Comes her call to my ears.

BRYNHILDE (*on perceiving* FRICKA, *she suddenly ceases
and leads her horse quietly and silently down the
path during the following, then she hides it in a cave*).
Heiaha! Heiaha! Hoyoho! toyotoyo—ha!

WOTAN. I made her for Siegmund to mount.

FRICKA. Thy eternal spouse's high reputation
To-day she holdeth dear!
If laughed at in scorn,
Unscreened and forlorn,
Gone were the glory of gods.
Let to-day my dues with daring and wit
Be won by the mettlesome maid.
This Volsung, fey to my honour,
Confirm as my victim by oath.

WOTAN (*throwing himself down upon a rocky seat in
terrible dejection*).
Take my oath!

(FRICKA *strides towards the back, there she meets
BRYNHILDE and pauses a moment before her.*)

FRICKA (*to* BRYNHILDE).
Wot an doth wait for thee;
Let him inform thee how the lot is to fall.

Der dir als Herren
Hörig und eigen
Gehorchen soll ihm
Dein ew'ges Gemahl?
Soll mich in Schmach
Der Niedrigste schmäh'n,
Dem Frechen zum Sporn,
Dem Freien zum Spott?
Das kann mein Gatte nicht wollen,
Die Göttin entweiht es nicht so!

WOTAN. Was verlangst du?

FRICKA. Lass' von dem Wälsung!

WOTAN. Er geh' seines Weg's.

FRICKA. Doch du—schütze ihn nicht,
Wenn zur Schlacht der Rächer ihn ruft.

WOTAN. Ich—schütze ihn nicht.

FRICKA. Sieh' mir in's Auge,
Sinne nicht Trug!
Die Walküre wend' auch von ihm!

WOTAN. Die Walküre walte frei.

FRICKA. Nicht doch! Deinen Willen
Vollbringt sie allein:
Verbiete ihr Siegmund's Sieg!

WOTAN. Ich kan ihn nicht fällen:
Er fand mein Schwert!

FRICKA. Entzieh' dem den Zauber,
Zerknick' es dem Knecht:
Schutzlos schau' ihn der Feind!
(*Sie vernimmt von der Höhe her den jauchzenden W
kürenruf* BRÜNNHILDE's: *diese erscheint dann se
mit ihrem Ross auf dem Felspfade rechts.*)
Dort kommt deine kühne Maid:
Jauchzend jagt sie daher.

WOTAN. Ich rief sie für Siegmund zu Ross.

FRICKA. Deiner ew'gen Gattin
Heilige Ehre
Schirme heut' ihr Schild!
Von Menschen verlacht,
Verlustig der Macht,
Gingen wir Götter zu Grund,
Würde heut' nicht zehr
Und herrlich mein Recht
Gerächt von der muthigen Maid.—
Der Wälsung fällt meiner Ehre:—
Empfah' ich von Wotan den Eid?

WOTAN (*in furchtbarem Unmuth und innerem Grin
auf einen Felsensitz sich werfend*).
Nimm den Eid!

(*Als* BRÜNNHILDE *von der Höhe aus* FRICKA *gewah
brach sie schnell ihren Gesang ab, und hat nun
Ross am Zügel den Felsweg herabgeleitet; sie bi
dieses jetzt in einer Höhle, als* FRICKA, *zu ihr
Wagen sich zurückwendend, an ihr vorüberschreite*)

FRICKA (*zu* BRÜNNHILDE).
Heervater
Harret dein:
Lass' ihn dir künden,
Wie er das Loos gekies't!

(*She drives away.*) BRYNHILDE, *surprised, advances with anxious looks towards* WOTAN, *who, leaning back on his rocky seat, is absorbed in gloomy brooding.*)	(*Sie besteigt den Wagen und fährt schnell davon.*) (BRÜNNHILDE *tritt mit verwunderter und besorgter Miene vor* WOTAN, *der, auf dem Feldsitz zurückgelehnt, das Haupt auf die Hand gestützt, in finsteres Brüten versunken ist.*)

## SCENE II	## ZWEITE SCENE

BRÜNNHILDE. Sure luckless was the strife;
    Fricka laughs at the fiat.
    Father, what must thy child fulfill thee?
    Sad and downcast thou seemest!

WOTAN. My own the fetters fast'ning me!
    I, less free than the earth-born!

BRÜNNHILDE.
    I saw thee thus ne'er; what gnaws at thy heart?

WOTAN. O, greatest of shame!
    O, shunless disgrace!
    God's distress! God's distress!
    Endless regret! Infinite grief!
    The saddest am I among all men!

BRÜNNHILDE (*alarmed, drops her spear and helmet and sinks down at his feet with anxious affection*).
    Father! Father! Teil me; what ails thee?
    See how trembles with terror thy child!
    Oh, trust in me, thy daughter true!
    Lo, Brünnhilde beggeth!

(*She lays her head and hands confidingly and anxiously on his knee and breast.* WOTAN *gazes into her eyes for a long while, then strokes her hair with unconscious tenderness, as if awaking from a deep reverie; he at last begins in a low voice:*)
WOTAN. If it were uttered
    I should lay bare ev'ry secret hold of my heart.

BRÜNNHILDE (*whispering*).
    To Wotan's will thou speakest;
    Tell me then what thou wilt.
    What am I when I'm away from thee?

WOTAN (*softly*).
    What lies in my breast unrelated,
    It must remain unspoken forever;
    Myself I talk with, telling to thee.

    (*With choked and suppressed voice.*)
    When youthful love's illusions
    Had fled, then lusted my soul for sway;
    Impelled by wildest wishes for pow'r,
    I won to me the world.
    Scarce witting ill, I stooped to deception;
    Covenants ordered that stretched to crime:
    Loki allured me with lying,
    Then faithlessly he fled,
    And yet, love I would fain not relinquish;

BRÜNNHILDE. Schlimm, fürcht' ich,
    Schloss der Streit,
    Lachte Fricka dem Loose!—
    Vater, was soll
    Dein Kind erfahren?
    Trübe scheinst du und traurig!

WOTAN. In eig'ner Fessel
    Fing ich mich:—
    Ich unfreiester Aller!

BRÜNNHILDE. So sah ich dich nie!
    Was nagt dir das Herz?

WOTAN. O heilige Schmach!
    O schmählicher Harm!
    Götternoth!
    Endloser Grimm!
    Ewiger Gram!
    Der Traurigste bin ich von Allen!

BRÜNNHILDE (*wirft erschrocken Schild, Speer und Helm von sich, und lässt sich mit besorgter Zutraulichkeit zu* WOTAN's *Füssen nieder*).
    Vater! Vater!
    Sage, was ist dir?
    Wie erschreck'st du mit Sorge dein Kind!
    Vertrau mir:
    Ich bin dir treu;
    Sieh', Brünnhilde bittet!
(*Sie legt traulich und ängstlich Haupt und Hände ihm auf Knie und Schooss.*)
WOTAN (*blickt ihr sehr lange in's Auge, und streichelt ihr dann die Locken: wie aus tiefem Sinnen zu sich kommend, beginnt er endlich mit sehr leiser Stimme*).
    Lass' ich's verlauten,
    Lös' ich dann nicht
    Meines Willens haltenden Haft?

BRÜNNHILDE (*ihm eben so leise erwidernd*).
    Zu Wotan's Willen sprichst du,
    Sagst du mir was du willst:
    Wer—bin ich,
    Wär' ich dein Wille nicht?

WOTAN (*leise*).
    Was Keinem in Worten ich künde,
    Unausgesprochen
    Bleib' es ewig:
    Mit mir nur rath' ich,
    Red'ich zu dir.— —
(*Mit noch gedämpfterer, schauerlicher Stimme während er* BRÜNNHILDEN *in das Auge blickt.*)
    Als junger Liebe
    Lust mir verblich,
    Verlangte nach Macht mein Muth:
    Von jäher Wünsche
    Wüthen gejagt,
    Gewann ich mir die Welt.
    Unwissend trugvoll
    Uebt' ich Untreue,
    Band durch Verträge,
    Was Unheil barg:
    Listig verlockte mich Loge,
    Der schweifend nun verschwand.
    Von der Liebe doch
    Mocht' ich nicht lassen;

Through all fame I longed for affection.
In night's abode the baleful Nibelung,
Alberic, broke from its bonds:
He cursed at love's passion, and won by that
  curse
The Rhine nymph's glittering gold,
And mastered measureless might.
The ring which he shaped ravished by cun-
  ning,
But ne'er I rendered it to the Rhine;
It was the handsel of Valhalla,
The burg that giants had built me,
From which now all kingdoms I bend.
That able witch who all things wist,
Erda, most wise and wondrous of women,
Read me ill of the ring,
Warned me of awfullest ending.
Then this ending I longed more to learn of,
But silent the seer took leave.
So departed my peace of mind,
And wisdom I strove to possess;
To the depths of earth diving in my search,
By love I won the witch to my purpose.
Mastered her potent might,
That to me she ope'd her mind,
Sooth sayings plainly she spoke,
In payment bearing my pledge;
The world's wonder of women bore thee,
Brünnhilde, to me.
With eight sisters wert thou b ought up,
In these Valkyries' valiant virt ie
Viewed I a vent from impending doom.
A dolorous end to the Æsir,
That foes might thus stror g for the strife.
Heroes I bade ye select me
The bravest of hearts we he d in bondage,
Those mortals whom in th ir might
We had checked,
Who by guileful agreeme t's
Glamour and baseness obediently
Served us truly and blindly;
These should ye bestir to stormiest striving
Ev'ry force guiding to grimmest fight,
That flocks of fearless heroes might
Hail me in Valhall's hall.

In der Macht gehrt' ich nach Minne:
  Den Nacht gebar,
  Der bange Nibelung.
Alberich brach ihren Bund
  Er fluchte der Liebe,
  Und gewann durch den Fluch
Des Rheines glänzendes Gold
Und mit ihm masslose Macht.
  Den Ring, den er schuf,
  Entriss ich ihm listig:
  Doch nicht dem Rhein
  Gab ich ihn zurück;
  Mit ihm bezahlt' ich
  Walhall's Zinnen,
Der Burg, die Riesen mir bauten,
Aus der ich der Welt nun gebot.
  Die Alles weiss,
  Was einstens war,
  Erda, die weihlich
  Weiseste Wala
Rieth mir ab von dem Ring,
Warnte vor ewigem Ende.
  Von dem Ende wollt' ich
  Mehr noch wissen;
Doch schweigend entschwand mir das Weib.
Da verlor ich den leichten Muth;
Zu wissen begehrt' es den Gott:
  In den Schooss der Welt
  Schwang ich mich hinab,
  Mit Liebes-Zauber
  Zwang ich die Wala,
Stört' ihres Wissens Stolz,
Dass sie nun Rede mir stand.
Kunde empfing ich von ihr:
Von mir doch barg sie ein Pfand:
Der Welt weisestes Weib
Gebar mir, Brünnhilde, dich.
  Mit acht Schwestern
  Zog ich dich auf:
  Durch euch Walküren
  Wollt' ich wenden,
  Was mir die Wala
  Zu fürchten schuf—
Ein schmähliches Ende der Ew'gen.
  Dass stark zum Streit
  Uns fände der Feind,
Hiess ich euch Helden mir schaffen:
  Die herrisch wir sonst
  In Gesetzen hielten,
  Die Männer, denen
  Den Muth wir gewehrt,
  Die durch trüber Verträge
  Trügende Bande
  Zu blinden Gehorsam,
  Wir uns gebunden—
  Die solltet zu Sturm
  Und Streit ihr nun stacheln,
  Ihre Kraft reizen zu rauhem Krieg,
Dass kühner Kämpfer Schaaren
Ich sammle in Walhall's Saal.

BRÜNNHILDE.
    And thy hall mightily filled we:
    Many a man have I brought;
    Whence comes thy depression?
    We never have paused.

WOTAN.   Another's ache: earnestly weigh
    What more the witch hath forewarned!
    Through Alberic's host threatens our ending:
    Still nourishing wrath, rages the Nibelung;

BRÜNNHILDE.
    Deinen Saal füllten wir weidlich;
    Viele schon führt' ich dir zu.
    Was macht dir nun Sorge,
    Da nie wir gesäumt?

WOTAN.   Ein Andres ist's:
    Achte es wohl,
    Wess' mich die Wala gewarnt!—
    Durch Alberich's Heer
    Droht uns das Ende:
    In neidischem Grimm
    Grollt mir der Nibelung;

I shrink not, though, now from his nation of
    shadows
By my heroes sheltered and safe.
But if e'er the wretch the ring should recover,
Our high Valhalla were lost then:
He who love surrendered,
He alone evil ends by the ring can wreck,
And to all of us unending disgrace.
My heroes' might were ravished from me,
My friends themselves were turned into foes,
Whom he would force to fight against me.
So I set to myself to keep the ring from his
    clutches.
The craftsman huge, to whom as a hire the
Accursed gold my compact gave—
Fafnir holdeth the hoard,
To gain which his brother he felled.
From him must the ring be wrested.
Although for wage 'twas awarded,
But my treaty with him restrains me from
    harming;
Nerveless and weak 'gainst him is my might.
These are the chains which gall and chafe me;
I, who by treaty have reigned,
To my treaties now become slave.
But one may compass what I must leave:
A hero helped by none of our number,
Who finds no guide or friend in the gods,
Unawares, under no stress, from out his need,
By his own design works out the deed
Which I would have done,
Of which my tongue ne'er told,
Though ever first in my thoughts!
He, who 'gainst every god,
Fights yet for me,
This friendliest foe, how find him indeed?
How shall I affect one whom ne'er I shielded,
Who in his defiance is faithful to me?
How master another, who, not mine own,
From out his will for my ends shall work?
O, goldly distress!
Grievous reproach!
Abhorrent to my heart have I found
Each hazard wild I have worked for!
Another end I have sighed for,
That other I seek in vain;
Unswayed must a free man assist me;
Near me are nothing but slaves.

Doch scheu' ich nun nicht
Seine nächtlichen Schaaren—
Meine Helden schüfen mir Sieg.
    Nur wenn je den Ring
    Zurück er gewänne—
Dann wäre Walhall verloren:
    Der der Liebe fluchte,
    Er allein Nützte neidisch
    Des Ringes Runen
    Zu aller Edlen
    Endloser Schmach;
    Der Helden Muth
    Entwendet er mir;
    Die Kühnen selber
    Zwäng' er zum Kampf,
    Mit ihrer Kraft
    Bekriegte er mich.
Sorgend sann ich nun selbst
Den Ring dem Feind zu entreissen:
    Der Riesen einer,
    Denen ich einst
    Mit verfluchtem Gold
    Den Fleiss vergalt,
Fafner hütet den Ort,
Um den er den Bruder gefällt.
Ihm müsst' ich den Reif entringen,
Den selbst als Zoll ich ihm zahlte:
    Doch mit dem ich vertrug,
    Ihn darf ich nicht treffen;
    Machtlos vor ihm
    Erläge mein Muth.
    Das sind die Bande,
    Die mich binden:
Der durch Verträge ich Herr,
Den Verträgen bin ich nun Knecht.
    Nur Einer dürfte
    Was ich nicht darf:
    Ein Held, dem helfend
    Nie ich mich neigte;
    Der fremd dem Gotte
    Frei seiner Gunst,
    Unbewusst,
    Ohne Geheiss,
    Aus eig'ner Noth
    Mit der eig'nen Wehr
    Schüfe die That,
    Die ich scheuen muss.
Die nie mein Rath ihm rieth,
Wünscht sie auch einzig mein Wunsch!—
    Der entgegen dem Gott
    Für mich föchte,
    Den freundlichen Feind,
    Wie fänd' ich ihn?
    Wie schüf ich den Freien,
    Den nie ich schirmte,
    Der in eig'nem Trotze
    Der Trauteste mir?
    Wie macht' ich den And'ren,
    Der nicht mehr ich,
    Und aus sich wirkte.
    Was ich nur will?—
    O göttliche Schmach!
    O schmähliche Noth!
    Zum Ekel find' ich
    Ewig nur mich
In Allem was ich erwirke!
Das And're, das ich ersehne,
Das And're erseh' ich nie;
Denn selbst muss der Freie sich schaffen—
Knechte erknet' ich mir nur!

RÜNNHILDE.
    But the Volsung, Siegmund, works by himself.

BRÜNNHILDE. Doch der Wälsung, Siegmund?
    Wirkt er nicht selbst?

WOTAN. Wildly roving with him thro' woodlands,
      'Gainst ev'ry godly rede roused I ever his hate,
      'Gainst ev'ry godly rancour shields him
      Now only the sword,
      That, as a grace, a God has bestowed.
      How to myself my craft was deceptive!
      So swiftly hath Fricka found out the lie;
      She looked me through and thrust on me shame:
      I perforce must shape to her fiat.

BRÜNNHILDE.
      The victory from Siegmund thou'lt snatch?

WOTAN. I have wrested Alberic's Ring,
      Grasped the coveted gold!
      The curse I incurred
      Doth cling to me yet:
      What I love best I must relinquish,
      Slay him I hold most sacred;
      Trusting belief foully betray;
      Glory and fame fade from my sight!
      Heavenly splendour, smiling disgrace!
      Be laid in ruins all I have reared;
      Over is my work;
      But one thing waits me now:
      The Ending—the Ending!
      And for that ending looks Alberic!
      Now I measure the meaning mute
      Of what the witch spake in wisdom:
      "When that Love's defiant foe
      Grimly getteth a son,
      The sway of gods full soon shall end."
      The Nibelung dwarf I now understand
      To have won to him a woman,
      By gold gaining his hopes.
      The love-scorner well can work such wonders,
      But he I long for fondly—the free one—doth
        lack to me yet.
              (*Fiercely.*)
      Then now take my blessing,
      Nibelung babe!
      What thus I fling from me hold as thy fortune:
      Valhalla's sumptuous halls
      Shall sate thy unhallowed desires!

BRÜNNHILDE.
      O speak, father! what should I perform?

WOTAN (*bitterly*).
      Fight duly for Fricka;
      Champion her virgin vows!

WOTAN. Wild durchschweift' ich
      Mit ihm die Wälder;
      Gegen der Götter Rath
      Reizte kühn ich ihn auf—
      Gegen der Götter Rache
      Schütz ihn nun eitnzig das Schwert,
      Das eines Gottes
      Gunst ihm beschied—
      Wie wollt' ich listig
      Selbst mich belügen?
      So leicht entfrug mir
      Ja Fricka den Trug!
      Zu tiefster Scham
      Durchschaute sie mich:
      Ihrem Willen muss ich gewähren!

BRÜNNHILDE.
      So nimmst du von Siegmund den Sieg?

WOTAN. Ich berührte Alberich's Ring—
      Gierig hielt ich das Gold!
      Der Fluch, den ich floh,
      Nicht flieht er nun mich:—
      Was ich liebe, muss ich verlassen,
      Morden, was je ich minne,
      Trügend verrathen
      Wer mir vertraut!—
      Fahre denn hin,
      Herrische Pracht,
      Göttlichen Prunkes
      Prahlende Schmach!
      Zusammen breche
      Was ich gebaut!
      Auf geb' ich mein Werk,
      Eines nur will ich noch,
      Das Ende — —
      Das Ende!—
        (*Er hält sinnend ein.*)
      Und für das Ende
      Sorgt Alberich!—
      Jetzt versteh' ich
      Den stummen Sinn
      Des wilden Wortes der Wala:—
      "Wenn der Diebe finst'rer Feind
      Zürnend zeugt einen Sohn,
      Der Seligen Ende
      Säumt dann nicht!"—
      Vom Nibelung jüngst
      Vernahm ich die Mähr',
      Dass ein Weib der Zwerg bewältigt,
      Dess' Gunst Gold ihm erzwang.
      Des Hasses Frucht
      Hegt eine Frau;
      Des Neides Kraft
      Kreiss't ihr im Schooss:
      Das Wunder gelang
      Dem Liebelosen:
      Doch der in Liebe ich frei'te,
      Den Freien erlang' ich mir nie!—
        (*Grimmig.*)
      So nimm meinen Seger
      Nibelungen-Sohn!
      Was tief mich ekelt,
      Dir geb' ich's zum Erbe,
      Der Gottheit nichtigen Glanz;
      Zernage sie gierig dein Neid?

BRÜNNHILDE. O sag', künde!
      Was soll nun dein Kind?

WOTAN (*bitter*).
      Fromm streite für Fricka,
      Hüte ihr Ehe und Eide!

What she commands is my bidding too;
How fruitless is my volition,
Since a free man ne'er I may light on,
For Fricka's vassal victory shape!

BRÜNNHILDE.
Woe! retract, I entreat, thy word!
Thou lov'st Siegmund: for this love
I wot well, should I o'erwatch him.

WOTAN. Vanquish Siegmund surely;
To Hunding the victory assign!
Heed thyself well and hold thyself strong;
Bring all thy bravery duly to bear:
A sooth-sword swings Siegmund;
Scarcely canst thou o'ercome.

BRÜNNHILDE.
One thou hast bade me ever to bless,
Whose unwonted firmness awakes
Thy affection,
From his side moves me never thy mandate
constrained.

WOTAN. Ha, froward child! floutest thou me?
Siegmund falleth!
Brünnhilde must work out my will.

(He rushes away and disappears in the Mountains.)

(BRÜNNHILDE stands a long time terrified and bewildered.)
So spake my sire nee'r before,
Though stirred and shaken oft by strife.

(She bends down sadly and takes up her weapons, which
she again dons.)
How waxes my weapon's weight!
When I love the fight how lightly they lift!
I fear to seek such an evil fray!
Ha! my hero!
In grievous strait thy defender must falsely
forsake thee!

(She turns slowly away.)

BRÜNNHILDE, looking down into the valley, perceives
SIEGMUND and SIEGLINDA; she watches their approach
awhile; then she turns into the cave to her horse, so
that she disappears from view of the audience.)

SCENE III

(SIEGMUND and SIEGLINDA appear.)

SIEGMUND. Pause here awhile; take some repose!

SIEGLINDA. Farther! farther!
(He clasps her with gentle force.)

SIEGMUND.
No farther now! O linger, sweet one, at last
From loving embraces brok'st thou away,
With sudden haste sallying forth;

Was sie erkor,
Das kiese auch ich.
Was frommte mir eig'ner Wille?
Einen Freien kann ich nicht wollen—
Für Fricka's Knechte
Kämpfe du nun!

BRÜNNHILDE. Weh! nimm reuig
Zurück das Wort!
Du liebst Siegmund:
Dir zu Lieb'—
Ich weiss es—schütz' ich den Wälsung.

WOTAN. Fällen sollst du Siegmund,
Für Hunding erfechten den Sieg!
Hüte dich wohl
Und halte dich stark;
All deiner Kühnheit
Entbiete im Kampf:
Ein Sieg-Schwert
Schwingt Siegmund—
Schwerlich fällt er dir feig.

BRÜNNHILDE. Den du zu lieben
Stets mich gelehrt,
Der in hehrer Tugend
Dem Herzen dir theuer—
Gegen ihn zwingt mich nimmer
Dein zwiespältig Wort.

WOTAN. Ha, Freche, du!
Frevelst du mir?
Besorge was ich befahl:—
Siegmund falle!—
Dies sei der Walküre Werk.
(Er stürmt fort, und verschwindet schnell links im
Gebirge.)
(BRÜNNHILDE steht lange betäubt und erschrocken.)
So—sah ich
Siegvater nie,
Erzürnt' ihn sonst auch ein Zank!
(Sie neigt sich betrübt und nimmt ihre Waffen auf, mit
denen sie sich wieder rüstet.)
Schwer mir
Der Waffen Wucht:—
Wenn nach Lust ich focht,
Wie waren sie leicht!—
Zu böser Schlacht
Schleich' ich heut' sobang!—
Weh', mein Wälsung!
Im höchsten Leid
Muss dich treulos die Treue verlassen!
(Sie wendet sich langsam dem Hintergrunde zu.)
(Sie wendet sich nach hinten und gewahrt SIEGMUND
und SIEGLINDE, wie sie aus der Schlucht herauf stei-
gen: sie betrachtet die Nahenden einen Augenblick,
und wendet sich dann in die Höhle zu ihrem Ross,
so dass sie dem Zuschauer gänzlich verschwindet.)

DRITTE SCENE

(SIEGMUND und SIEGLINDE treten auf.)

SIEGMUND. Raste nun hier:
Gönne dir Ruh'!

SIEGLINDE. Weiter! weiter!

SIEGMUND (umfasst sie mit sanfter Gewalt).
Nicht weiter nun!
Verweile, süssestes Weib!—
Aus Wonne-Entzücken
Zucktest du auf,
Mit jäher Hast
Jagtest du fort;

Scarce found I thy way of flight,
Through wood and field, over fell and steep,
Speechless, silent, speeding along;
My voice lured thee in vain.
    (*She stares wildly before her.*)
Onward no more:
Open thy lips!
End me this silent awe!
See, thy brother holdeth his bride:
Siegmund's guarding thee safe!

(*She gazes with growing rapture into his eyes; then
mournfully throws her arms around his neck. Alarmed,
she starts up in sudden terror.*)

SIEGLINDA. Away! away! flee from the wanton!
Unholily fold thee my arms.
Disgraced, polluted, life ebbeth
Forth. Shun the foul one,
Fly from her face! Her dust tempests
Shall drive, who, soiled, gave
Herself to thine arms!
When in thy loving embrace,
With hallowed delight I brimmed,
My only husband was he
Who all my heart had awaked.
From this heavenly rapture's
Glorious radiance which all
My soul and senses o'erwhelmed,
Shudder and trembling and shamefullest terror
Grimly o'ertook the traitorous woman,
Who to a bridegrom belonged,
Whom she obeyed without love!
Leave the accurs'd one; let her escape!
I rest degraded, bereft of grace!
The pearl of manhood must I depart from;
For ne'er may I link me with one so noble.
Shame I bring to my brother;
Shape my rescuer's ruin!

SIEGMUND. Who erst shaped for thee shame
Shall bring me his felon blood!
So fly me no farther; halt for the
Foeman; here shall I defeat him.
When "Needful" at his heart shall
Gnaw, then revenge hast thou attained!

SIEGLINDA. Hark! the horn calls;
Hearest thou not?
Nearer still waxes the sound;
From wood and vale voices arise!
Hunding hath wakened from heavy sleep!
Sleuth hounds and hunters bids he assemble
Roused by his hail howls the rabble;
All crying to heaven for the breaking
Of conjugal bonds!

(*She stares before her as if demented.*)

Where art thou, Siegmund?
Still art thou near?

Kaum folgt' ich der wilden Flucht:
Durch Wald und Flur,
Ueber Fels und Stein,
Sprachlos schweigend
Sprangst du dahin;
Zur Rast hielt dich kein Ruf.
    (*Sie starrt wild vor sich hin.*)
Ruhe nun aus:
Rede zu mir!
Ende des Schweigens Angst!
Sieh, dein Bruder
Hält seine Braut:
Siegmund ist dir Gesell!

(*Er hat sie unvermerkt nach dem Steinsitze geleitet.*)
(*Blickt* SIEGMUND *mit wachsendem Entzücken in
Augen; dann umschlingt sie leidenschaftlich sein
Hals. Dann fährt sie mit jähem Schreck auf.*)

SIEGLINDE. Hinweg! hinweg! flieh die Entweihte!
Unheilig umfängt dich ihr Arm,
Entehrt, geschändet, schwand
Dieser Leib; flieh' die Leiche, lasse
Sie los; der Wind mag sie
Verwehn', die ehrlos dem Edlen
Sich gab!
    Da er sie liebend umfing,
Da seligste Lust sie fand,
Da ganz sie minnte der Mann,
Der ganz ihr Minne geweckt,
Von der süssesten Wonne
Heiligster Weihe, die ganz
Ihr Sinn und Seele durch
Drang, Grauen und
Schauder ob grässlichster
Schande musste mit Schreck
Die Schmähliche fassen,
Die je dem Manne
Gehorcht, der ohne Minne
Sie hielt!
    Lass' die Verfluchte,
Lass' sie dich flieh'n!
Verworfen bin ich, der Würde
Bar; dir reinstem Manne
Muss ich entrinnen, dir herrlichem
Darf ich nimmer gehören:
Schande bring ich dem Bruder,
Schmach dem freienden Freund!

SIEGMUND. Was je Schande dir schuf, das büsst
Nun des Frevlers Blut! Drum
Fliehe nicht weiter; harre des
Feindes; hier soll er mir fallen:
Wenn Nothung ihm das Herz
Zernagt, Rache dann hast du erreicht!

SIEGLINDE. Horch! die Hörner!
Hörst du den Ruf?—
Ringsher tönt
Wüthend Getös';
Aus Wald und Gau
Gellt es herauf.
Hunding erwachte
Von hartem Schlaf;
Sippen und Hunde
Ruft er zusammen:
Muthig gehetzt
Heult die Meute,
Wild bellt sie zum Himmel
Um der Ehe gebrochenen Eid!

(*Sie lacht wie wahnsinnig auf:— dann schrickt s
ängstlich zusammen.*)
Wo bist du, Siegmund?
Seh' ich dich noch?

Bridegroom beloved, lordliest brother!
Let thy starlike eyes yet but stream light upon
   me:
Wend not away from a woeful woman's kiss:
Hark! oh hark! that is Hunding's horn!
And his men approach in mighty force.
No sword that pack of hounds can scare:
Cast it forth, Siegmund!
Siegmund, where art thou?
Ha, there!
I see thee now! sinister sight!
Dogs are mouthing and gnashing for meat:
No heed they take of thy hero glance;
In thy feet they bury their furious teeth!
Thou fall'st; to splinters doth spring thy sword;
The ash-tree splits both branch and stem!
Brother! my brother! Siegmund, ha!
(*She sinks fainting in* SIEGMUND's *arms.*)

Brünstig geliebter
Leuchtender Bruder!
Deines Auges Stern
Lass noch einmal mir strahlen:
Wehre dem Kuss
Des verworf'nen Weibes nicht!—
Horch! o horch!
Das ist Hunding's Horn!
Seine Meute naht
Mit mächtiger Wehr.
Kein Schwert frommt
Vor der Hunde Schwall:—
Wirf es fort, Siegmund!—
Siegmund—wo bist du?—
Ha dort—ich sehe dich—
Schrecklich Gesicht!—
Rüden fletschen
Die Zähne nach Fleisch;
Sie achten nicht
Deines edlen Blick's;
Bei den Füssen packt dich
Das feste Gebiss—
Du fällst—
In Stücken zerstaucht das Schwert:—
Die Esche stürzt—
Es bricht der Stamm!—
Bruder! mein Bruder!
Siegmund—ha!—
(*Sie sinkt ohnmächtig in* SIEGMUND's *Arme.*)

SIEGMUND. Sister! Belov'd one!
(*He listens to her breathing and satisfies himself that she still lives. He allows her to sink down with himself, so that when he is in a sitting posture her head rests upon his lap. In this position both remain until the end of the following scene.)
(Long silence, during which* SIEGMUND *bends in tender care over* SIEGLINDA, *and imprints a long kiss upon her brow.*)

SIEGMUND. Schwester! Geliebte!
(*Er lauscht ihrem Athem, und überzeugt sich, dass sie noch lebe. Er lässt sie an sich herabgleiten, so dass sie, als er sich selbst zum Sitze niederlässt, mit ihrem Haupt auf seinem Schooss zu ruhen kommt. Langes Schweigen, während dessen* SIEGMUND *mit zärtlicher Sorge über* SIEGLINDE *sich hinneigt.*)

SCENE IV

VIERTE SCENE

(BRÜNNHILDE, *leading her horse by the bridle, enters from the cave and advances slowly and solemnly to the front; she pauses and observes* SIEGMUND *from a distance. She again slowly advances; she bears her spear and shield in one hand, rests the other on her horse's neck, and thus gazes earnestly at* SIEGMUND.)

BRÜNNHILDE. *Siegmund—
vornen geschritten, und hält nun,* SIEGMUND *zur Seite, in geringer Entfernung von ihm. Sie trägt Schild und Speer in der einen Hand, lehnt sich mit der andren an den Hals des Rosses, und betrachtet so, in ernstem Schweigen, eine Zeit lang* SIEGMUND.)

BRÜNNHILDE. Siegmund! See'st thou me?
   I come to call thee hence!
   (SIEGMUND *turns his eyes upon her.*)

BRÜNNHILDE. Siegmund—
   Sieh' auf mich!
   Ich—bin's,
   Der gald du folgst.

SIEGMUND. Declare thy name,
   Who dost stand so beauteous and stern.

SIEGMUND (*richtet den Blick zu ihr auf*).
   Wer bist du, sag',
   Die so schön und ernst mir erscheint?

BRÜNNHILDE. But fated men my form may look on;
   To whom 'tis shown full shortly must lose his
     life,
   On the war-plain alone the warrior sees me:
   Well then he weens, away must he with me!

BRÜNNHILDE. Nur Todgeweihten
   Taugt mein Anblick:
   Wer mich erschaut,
   Der scheidet vom Lebens-Licht.
   Auf der Walstatt allein
   Erschein' ich Edlen:
   Wer mich gewahrt,
   Zur Wal kor ich ihn mir.

(SIEGMUND *gazes long with firmness and enquiry into her eyes, then thoughtfully droops his head, and presently turns to her resolutely again.*)

(SIEGMUND *blickt ihr lange in das Auge, senkt dann sinnend das Haupt, und wendet sich endlich mit feierlichem Ernste wieder zu ihr.*)

SIEGMUND.
   But firstly tell—Whither tak'st thou the hero?

SIEGMUND. Der dir nun folgt.
   Wohin führst du den Helden?

BRÜNNHILDE. To Wotan, for such is his will;
    Hence with me:
    Awaits Valhall' for thee.

SIEGMUND. In Valhall's bright vault
    Shall I find him alone?

BRÜNNHILDE.
    The fallen heroes' hallowed band shall flock,
    With hand and heart hailing thy sight.

SIEGMUND. Fareth in Valhall'
    Volsung, my noble father?

BRÜNNHILDE.
    Thy father findest thou, Volsung, there!

SIEGMUND. Shall I in Valhall' welcome a wife?

BRÜNNHILDE. Wish maidens wait on thee there;
    Wotan's daughter faithfully deals thee the
    drink!

SIEGMUND. High art thou and holy;
    I ween thou art Wotan's child:
    Yet tell me one thing, and truly!
    Attendeth her brother my bride
    And my sister? Shall there
    Siegmund Sieglinda find?

BRÜNNHILDE. Lone on earth must she still linger:
    Siegmund will see Sieglind' no more.

(SIEGMUND *bends softly over* SIEGLINDA, *kisses her gently*
    on the brow, and again turns tranquilly to BRÜNN-
    HILDE.)

SIEGMUND.
    Then greet for me Valhall', greet for me Wotan!
    Greet for me Volsung and all the heroes;
    Greet, too, the highborn wishing maidens.
    To them I'll follow thee not.

BRÜNNHILDE.
    Thou'st looked on the Valkyrie's life-quelling
    face:
    With her must thou away!

SIEGMUND. Where Sieglinda bides, in bliss or bane,
    There will Siegmund too sojourn:
    Not yet hath thy sight weakened my spirit;
    'Twill stir me never away!

BRÜNNHILDE.
    While life doth last, dauntless thou art:
    'Gainst Death 'twere foolish to fight;
    And to announce him now I come.

SIEGMUND. What hero is he by whom I fall?

BRÜNNHILDE. Hunding fells thee in strife.

SIEGMUND.
    Bring stronger menace than Hunding's struggle
    Swoopest thou here seeking thy prey,
    Choose my foeman for spoil;
    I purpose to slay him in fight!

BRÜNNHILDE. Thou, Volsung, hark to my voice:
    Thou art to death consigned.

SIEGMUND. See'st thou this sword?
    By one 'twas sent who'll shape success,
    I defy thee, firm in its strength!

BRÜNNHILDE. Zu Walvater,
    Der dich gewährt,
    Führ' ich dich:
    Nach Walhall folgst du mir.

SIEGMUND. In Walhall's Saal
    Walvater find' ich allein?

BRÜNNHILDE. Gefall'ner Helden
    Hehre Schaar
    Umfängt dich hold
    Mit hoch-heiligem Gruss.

SIEGMUND. Fänd' ich in Walhall
    Wälse, den eig'nen Vater?

BRÜNNHILDE. Den Vater findet
    Der Wälsung dort.

SIEGMUND. Grüsst mich in Walhall
    Froh eine Frau?

BRÜNNHILDE. Wunschmädchen
    Walten dort hehr:
    Wotan's Tochter
    Reicht dir traulich den Trank.

SIEGMUND. Hehr bist du:
    Heilig gewahr' ich
    Das Wotanskind:
    Doch Eines sag' mir, du Ew'ge!
    Begleitet den Bruder
    Die bräutliche Schwester?
    Umfängt Siegmund
    Sieglinde dort?

BRÜNNHILDE. Erdenluft
    Muss sie noch athmen:
    Sieglinde
    Sieht Siegmund dort nicht!

(SIEGMUND *neigt sich sanft über* SIEGLINDE, *küsst s*
    leise auf die Stirn und wendet sich ruhig wieder
    BRÜNNHILDE.)

SIEGMUND. So grüsse mir Walhall,
    Grüsse mir Wotan,
    Grüsse mir Walse
    Und alle Helden—
    Grüss' auch die holden
    Wunschesmädchen:
    Zu ihnen folg' ich dir nicht.

BRÜNNHILDE.
    Du sahest der Walküre Sehrenden Blick:
    Mit ihr musst du nun zieh'n!

SIEGMUND. Wo Sieglinde lebt in Lust und Leid,
    Da will Siegmund auch säumen:
    Noch machte dein Blick nicht mich
    Erbleichen, vom Bleiben zwingt er mich nie!

BRÜNNHILDE.
    So lang du lebst, zwäng' dich wohl nichts:
    Doch zwingt dich Thoren den Tod:—
    Ihn dir zu künden kam ich her.

SIEGMUND. Wo wäre der Held dem heut' ich fiel?

BRÜNNHILDE. **Hunding fällt dich im Streit.**

SIEGMUND.
    Mit Stärk'rem drohe als Hunding's Streiche
    Lauerst du hier lüstern auf Wal.
    Jenen kiese zum Fang;
    Ich denk'ihn zu fällen im Kampf!

BRÜNNHILDE. Dir, Wälsung höre mich Wohl:
    Dir ward das Loos gekies't.

SIEGMUND. Kennst du dies Schwert?
    Der mir es schuf,
    Beschied mir Sieg:
    Deinem Drohen trotz' ich mit ihm!

BRÜNNHILDE (*with emphasis*).
> He who bestowed it shapes thee now death:
> He withdraws the charm from the sword.

SIEGMUND. Soft! Disturb not my slumbering love!

In an outburst of pain he bends tenderly over SIEG-
LINDA.)
> Woe! Woe! Loveliest one!
> Thou saddest and faithfullest sister!
> 'Gainst thy peace wantonly warreth the world:
> And I, on whom only thou lean'st,
> For whom thou hast ev'rything left,
> I may not shield nor seek thee a shelter.
> But fail thee, alas! in the fight.
> O shame on him who bestowed the sword,
> To shape me such shifting shield!
> If I must perish, I'll pass not to Valhall;
> Hella hold me her prey!
> (*He bends low over* SIEGLINDA.)

BRÜNNHILDE.
> Celestial splendours then spurn'st thou so
> lightly?
> Is this woman thy only wealth,
> Who, faint and ailing, feebly reclines in thy
> arms?
> Naught else deemest thou dear?

SIEGMUND (*looking bitterly up at her*).
> So youthful and fair thy features appear,
> But how cold and hard accounts thee my heart!
> Canst thou not help me, then hie thee away,
> Thou harsh, unwav'ring maid!
> If moved not to pity by my despair,
> Then freely feast on my woe:
> Let my pangs flatter thy pitiless heart,
> But of Valhall's paltry virtues,
> Prythee, vaunt not to me!

BRÜNNHILDE.
> I see the distress of thy heart at this strait,
> I feel for the hardy hero's illhap!
> Siegmund, to me trust thy wife;
> I'll shield her much as I may!

SIEGMUND.
> No other than I shall in life defend my beloved:
> If fate will it so,
> I will slay her slumbering first!

BRÜNNHILDE. Volsung! Reckless man!
> Hark to my rede:
> Assign me thy bride!

SIEGMUND (*drawing the sword*).
> This sword, which a traitor for true man de-
> signed; this sword,
> Which falsely in fight shall betray,
> Falls it to slaughter my foe,
> More fatal 'twill prove to my friend!
> (*He holds the sword over* SIERLINDA.)

BRÜNNHILDE (*sehr stark betont*).
> Der dir es schuf, beschied dir jetzt Tod;
> Seine Tugend nimmt er dem Schwert.

SIEGMUND. Schweig' und schrecke
> Die Schlummernde nicht!
> (*Er beugt sich mit hervorbrechendem Schmerze zärtlich
> über* SIEGLINDE.)
> Weh! Weh! süssestes Weib!
> Du traurigste aller Getreuen!
> Gegen dich wüthet in Waffen die Welt:
> Und ich, dem du einzig vertraut,
> Für den du ihr einzig
> Getrotzt; mit meinem Schutz
> Nicht soll ich dich schirmen,
> Die Kühne verrathen im Kampf?
> O Schande ihm, der das Schwert
> Mir schuf, beschied er mir Schimpf
> Für Sieg! Muss ich denn fallen,
> Nicht fahr' ich nach Walhall:
> Hella halte mich fest!
> (*Er neigt sich tief zu* SIEGLINDE.)

BRÜNNHILDE (*erschüttert*).
> So wenig achtest du
> Ewige Wonne?
> Alles wär' dir
> Das arme Weib,
> Das müd' und harmvoll
> Matt auf dem Schoosse dir hängt?
> Nichts sonst hieltest du hehr?

SIEGMUND (*bitter zu ihr aufblickend*).
> So jung und schön
> Erschimmerst du mir:
> Doch wie kalt und hart
> Kennt dich mein Herz!—
> Kannst du nur höhnen,
> So hebe dich fort.
> Du arge, fühllose Maid!
> Doch musst du dich weiden
> An meinem Weh',
> Mein Leid letze dich denn;
> Meine Noth labe
> Dein neidvolles Herz:—
> Nur von Walhall's spröden Wonnen
> Sprich du wahrlich mir nicht!

BRÜNNHILDE. Ich sehe die Noth,
> Die das Herz dir nagt;
> Ich fühle des Helden
> Heiligen Harm——
> Siegmund, befiehl mir dein Weib:
> Mein Schutz umfange sie fest!

SIEGMUND. Kein andrer als ich
> Soll die Reine lebend berühren;
> Verfiel ich dem Tod,
> Die Betäubte tödt' ich zuvor!

BRÜNNHILDE. Wälsung! Rasender!
> Hör' meinen Rath:
> Befiehl mir dein Weib
> Um des Pfandes willen,
> Das wonnig von dir es empfing!

SIEGMUND (*sein Schwert ziehend*).
> Dies Schwert—
> Das dem Treuen ein Trugvoller schuf;
> Dies Schwert—
> Das feig vor dem Feind mich verräth:—
> Frommt es nicht gegen den Feind,
> So Fromm' es denn wider den Freund!—
> (*Das Schwert auf* SIEGLINDE *zückend.*)

Two lives here lie before thee;
Take them, Needful, terrible steel!
Take them with one fell stroke!

BRÜNNHILDE (*in a violent gust of sympathy*).
Forbear, Volsung! List to my voice!
Sieglinda shall live still,
And Siegmund leave not her side:
'Tis so ordained.
The death lot cancelled; thou, Siegmund,
Doubt not, safely shalt speed!
Mark'st thou that horn?
Now hold thyself manned;
Take up thy sword and swing it with trust;
'Twill surely prevail,
For the Valkyrie tenders aid.
Farewell, Siegmund, stalwartest man!
At the combat seek for my coming!

(*She rushes away and disappears with her horse in a ravine: SIEGMUND looks after her with joy and relief. The stage has grown dark: heavy storm clouds descend gradually, veiling the cliffs, ravine and high peak completely from view.*)

SCENE V

SIEGMUND (*bending over SIEGLINDA*).
Slumber's charm has soothed my fair one's
Wild and frenzied woe.
Did the Valkyrie's heedful care
This quiet divine o'er her cast?
Would not the tidings of war
Her womanly terrors awake?
Lifeless seems she, but yet she lives;
Her dread is allayed by loveliest dreams;
So slumber in peace till the strife is o'er
And peril shall be past.

(*He lays her softly on the rocky seat and kisses her brow as a farewell. Hearing HUNDING's horn-call he starts up resolutely.*)
The coming foe firmly must stand;
What he demands mine to give:
Needful deals him his due!
(*He hastens to meet HUNDING; on reaching the mountain top disappears in the black clouds, from which breaks a flash of lightning.*)

SIEGLINDA (*dreaming*).
Hies not my father yet home?
Still he hunts with the boy in the woods.
Mother! Mother! I tremble much!
These strangers' stern looks terribly strike me!
Turbid vapours towering vast
Fiery tongues are twining around; they burn
the house!

Zwei Leben
Lachen dir hier:—
Nimm sie, Nothung,
Neidischer Stahl!
Nimm sie mit einem Streich!

BRÜNNHILDE (*im heftigsten Sturme des Mitgefühls*).
Halt' ein Walsung!
Höre mein Wort!
Sieglinde lebe—
Und Siegmund lebe mit ihr!
Beschlossen ist's;
Das Schlachtlos wend' ich:
Dir, Siegmund,
Schaff' ich Segen und Sieg!
Du hörst den Ruf?
Nun rüste dich, Held!
Traue dem Schwert
Und schwing' es getrost:
Treu hält dir die Wehr,
Wie die Walküre treu dich schützt!—
Leb' wohl, Siegmund,
Seligster Held!
Auf der Walstatt grüss' ich dich wieder!

(*Sie stürmt fort, und verschwindet mit dem Rosse. SIEGMUND blickt ihr freudig nach. Die Bühne hat sich allmälig verfinstert; schwere Gewitterwolken senken sich auf den Hintergrund herab.—Von allen Seiten lassen sich aus der Ferne Rufe von Heerhörnern vernehmen, die während des Folgenden allmälig näher erschallen.*)

FÜNFTE SCENE

SIEGMUND (*über SIEGLINDE sich beugend*).
Zauberfest
Bezähmt ein Schlaf
Der Holden Schmerz und Harm:
Da die Walküre zu mir trat,
Schuf sie ihr den wonnigen Trost?
Sollte die grimmige Wal
Nicht schrecken ein gramvolles Weib?
Leblos scheint sie,
Die dennoch lebt:
Der Traurigen kos't
Ein lächelnder Traum.—
So schlumm're nun fort,
Bis die Schlacht gekämpft,
Und Friede dich erfreu'!

(*Er eilt dem Hintergrunde zu.*)
nach abermaligen Hornrufen, auf.)
Der dort mich ruft,
Rüste dich nun;
Was ihm gebührt,
Biet' ich ihm:
Nothung zahl' ihm den Zoll!
(*Er eilt dem Hintergrunde zu.*)

SIEGLINDE (*träumend*).
Kehrte der Vater nun heim?
Mit dem Knaben noch weilt er im Forst.
Mutter! Mutter!
Mir bangt der Muth:
Nicht freund und friedlich
Scheinen die Fremden!—
Schwarze Dämpfe—
Schwüles Gedünst—
Feurige Lohe
Leckt schon nach uns—
Es brennt das Haus—

O help me, brother!
Siegmund! Siegmund!
iolent lightning and thunder awakes SIEGLINDA *from
her dreams: she gazes around in increasing terror.
Nearly the whole stage is veiled in black thunder-
clouds.* HUNDING'S *horn-call sounds close.)*
Siegmund! Ha!

*UNDING (whose voice is heard from the mountain
peak).*
Woeful! Woeful!
Stand to the strife!
Say, with my hounds must I hunt thee?

EGMUND (whose voice is heard from off in the ravine).
Where hid'st thou that I behold thee not?
Forth, that I may face thee!

EGLINDA (listening in fearful anxiety).
Hunding! Siegmund!
Could I but see them!

UNDING. Prepare, thou fugitive foeman!
Fricka fates thee my prey!

EGMUND (now likewise on the peak).
Thou weenest me weaponless,
Foolish wight!
Prate not of females,
But fight unsuccoured:
Her minion Fricka forsakes;
For see! From thy house-tree's harbouring stem
I drew undaunted this sword;
Of its sharpness soon shalt thou judge!

*A flash of lightning lights up the rock with dazzling
light.* HUNDING *and* SIEGMUND *are seen in mortal
combat.)*

EGLINDA'S voice.
Stay your hands, ye madmen!
Murder first me!
*She staggers towards the peak; a flash of lightning
breaks over the combatants and suddenly dazzles her
so that she reels back to one side blinded. In the
glare of light* BRÜNNHILDE *appears soaring over* SIEG-
MUND *and protecting him with her sword.)*

RÜNNHILDE. Fell him, Siegmund!
Firm be thy sword!

But just as SIEGMUND *aims a deadly stroke at* HUND-
ING, *a ruddy glow shines out from the clouds, in
which* WOTAN *is seen standing over* HUNDING *and
holding his spear defensively against* SIEGMUND.)*

OTAN.
Recoil from my spear! Be splintered the sword!

BRÜNNHILDE *retreats in terror before* WOTAN. SIEG-
MUND'S *sword snaps on the outstretched spear.* HU D-
ING *buries his spear in the unarmed man's breast.)*

IEGMUND falls dead to the ground.)

Zu Hülfe, Bruder!
Siegmund! Siegmund!
*(Starke Blitze zucken durch das Gewölk auf; ein furcht-
barer Donnerschlag erweckt* SIEGLINDE: *sie springt
jäh auf.)*
Siegmund!—Ha!
*(Sie starrt mit steigender Angst um sich her:—fast die
ganze Bühne ist in schwarze Gewitterwolken verhüllt;
fortwährender Blitz und Donner. Von allen Seiten
dringen immer näher Hornrufe her.)*

HUNDING'S *Stimme (im Hintergrunde vom Bergjoche
her.)*
Wehwalt! Wehwalt!
Steh' mir zum Streit,
Sollen dich Hunde nicht halten!

SIEGMUND'S *Stimme (von weiter hinten her, aus der
Schlucht).*
Wo birgst du dich,
D   i h vorbei dir schoss?
Steh' dort, dass ich dich stelle?

SIEGLINDE *(die in furchtbarer Aufregung lauscht).*
Hunding—Siegmund!
Könnt' ich sie sehen!

HUNDING'S *Stimme.*
Hieher, du frevelnder Freier:
Fricka fälle dich hier!

SIEGMUND'S *Stimme (nun ebenfalls auf dem Bergjoche).*
Noch wähnst du mich waffenlos,
Feiger Wicht?
Drohst du mit Frauen,
So ficht nun selber,
Sonnst lässt dich Fricka im Stich!
Denn sieh': deines Hauses
Heimischem Stamm
Entzog ich zaglos das Schwert;
Seine Schneide schmecke du jetzt!
*(Ein Blitz erhellt für einen Augenblick das Bergjoch,
auf welchem jetzt* HUNDING *und* SIEGMUND *kämpfend
gewahrt werden.)*

SIEGLINDE. Haltet ein, ihr Männer!
Mordet erst mich!

*(Sie stürzt auf das Bergjoch zu: ein von rechts her über
die Kämpfer ausbrechender, heller Schein blendet sie
aber plötzlich so heftig, dass sie wie erblindet zur Seite
schwankt. In dem Lichte erscheint* BRÜNNHILDE *über
SIEGMUND schwebend und diesen mit dem Schilde
deckend.)*

BRÜNNHILDE'S *Stimme.*
Triff' ihn, Siegmund!
Traue dem Siegesschwert!
(Als SIEGMUND *so eben zu einem tödtlichen Streiche
auf* HUNDING *ausholt, bricht von links her ein glühend-
röthlicher Schein durch das Gewölk aus, in welchem
WOTAN erscheint, über* HUNDING *stehend, und seinen
Speer* SIEGMUND *entgegenhaltend.)*

WOTAN'S *Stimme.* Zurück vor dem Speer!
In Stücken das Schwert!

(BRÜNNHILDE ist vor WOTAN *mit dem Schilde erschrocken
zurückgewichen:* SIEGMUND'S *Schwert verspringt an
dem vorgestreckten Speere; dem Unbewehrten stösst
HUNDING sein Schwert in die Brust.)*

(SIEGMUND stürzt zu Boden.)

(SIEGLINDA, *who has heard his death-sigh, sinks down with a cry, as if lifeless. With* SIEGMUND'S *fall the glare of light on both sides has faded; dense gloom reigns in the clouds up to the front, through it* BRÜNNHILDE *is seen indistinctly hurrying swiftly towards* SIEGLINDA.)

BRÜNNHILDE. To horse, that I may help thee!
(*She lifts* SIEGLINDA *quickly with her on to her horse, standing by in the defile, and they disappear. At this moment the clouds divide in the middle, and* HUNDING *is clearly visible, drawing his spear from the breast of* SIEGMUND.)

WOTAN (*surrounded by clouds, stands behind, leaning on his spear and painfully gazing on* SIEGMUND'S *body*).
> Get hence, knave; kneel before Fricka:
> Tell her how Wotan's spear avenged his spouse's
>   slight. Go! Go!

(*Before the contemptuous wave of his hand* HUNDING *falls dead to the ground.*)

WOTAN (*suddenly bursting into terrible wrath*).
> But Brünnhilde!
> Vengeance shall break on her!
> Fell scourging shall follow her crime,
> If my steed may stay her in flight.

(*He disappears amid thunder and lightning.*)
(*The curtain falls.*)

ACT III

SCENE I

(*On the summit of a rocky mountain. At the right the stage is bordered by a pine wood; at the left is the entrance of a cave, over which the rock rises to its highest. At the back the view is quite open; high and low rocks border a precipice. Occasional clouds, driven by the storm, fly past the mountain summit.*)

(GERHILDA, ORTLINDA, VALTRAUTA and SCHWERTLEITA *are ensconced on the peak over the cave; they are all in full armor.*)

GERHILDA (*higher placed than the rest, calls towards the background*).
> Hoyotoho! Hoyotoho! Heiaha! Heiaha!
> Helmwiga, hail! Hie here with thy horse!

HELMWIGA'S *voice* (*through a speaking-trumpet*).
> Hoyotoho! Hoyotoho! Hoyotoho!
> Hoyotoho! Heiaha!
(*A flash of lightning breaks through the cloud; a Valkyrie on horseback is visible in it: over her saddle hangs a slain warrior.*)

(SIEGLINDE, *die seinen Todesseufzer gehört, sinkt mit einem Schrei wie leblos zusammen. Mit* SIEGMUND[S] *Fall ist zugleich von beiden Seiten der glänzen[den] Schein verschwunden; dichte Finsterniss ruht [im] Gewölk bis nach vorn; in ihm wird* BRÜNNHIL[DE] *undeutlich sichtbar, wie sie in jäher Hast* SIEGLIND[E] *sich zugewendet.*)

BRÜNNHILDE. Zu Ross, dass ich dich rette!
(*Sie hebt* SIEGLINDE *schnell zu sich auf ihr, der [der Schlu]chtschlucht nahe stehendes Ross, und verschwin[det] sogleich gänzlich mit ihr. Alsbald vertheilt sich d[as] Gewölk in der Mitte, so dass man deutlich* HUNDI[NG] gewahrt, wie er sein Schwert dem gefallenen SI[EG]MUND aus der Brust zieht.*)
(WOTAN, *von Gewölk umgeben, steht hinter ihm a[uf] einem Felsen, an seinen Speer gelehnt, und schme[rz]lich auf* SIEGMUND'S *Leiche blickend.*)

WOTAN (*Nach einem kleinen Schweigen, zu* HUNDI[NG] *gewandt*).
> Geh' hin, Knecht!
> Kniee vor Fricka:
> Meld' ihr, dass Wotan's Speer
> Gerächt, was Spott ihr schuf.—
> Geh'!—Geh'!—

(*Vor seinem verächtlichen Handwink sinkt* HUNDI[NG] *todt zu Boden.*)

WOTAN (*plötzlich in furchtbarer Wuth auffahrend*).
> Doch Brünnhilde—
> Weh' der Verbrecherin!
> **Furchtbar sei**
> Die Freche gestraft,
> Erreicht mein Ross ihre Flucht!
(*Er verschwindet mit Blitz und Donner.*)
(*Der Vorhang fällt schnell.*)

DRITTE AKT

ERSTE SCENE

(*Rechts begrenzt ein Tannenwald die Scene. Links [der] Eingang einer Felshöhle, die einen natürlichen S[aal] bildet: darüber steigt der Fels zu seiner höchst[en] Spitze auf. Nach hinten ist die Aussicht gänzli[ch] frei; höhere und niedere Felssteine bilden den Ra[nd] vor dem Abhange der—wie anzunehmen ist—na[ch] dem Hintergrunde zu steil hinabführt.— Einzel[ne] Wolkenzüge jagen, vom Sturm getrieben, am F[el]sensaume vorbei.*)
(*Die namen der acht Walküren, welche—ausser* BRÜN[N]-HILDE — *in dieser Scene auftreten, sind:* GERHIL[DE,] ORTLINDE, WALTRAUTE, SCHWERTLEITE, HELMWI[GE,] SIEGRUNE, GRIMGERDE, ROSSWEISSE.)

(GERHILDE, ORTLINDE, WALTRAUTE *und* SCHWERTLE[ITE] *haben sich auf der Felsspitze, an und über der Höh[le] gelagert; sie sind in voller Waffenrüstung.*)

GERHILDE (*zu höchst gelagert und dem Hintergrun[de] zugewendet.*)
> Hojotoho! Hojotoho!
> Heiaha! Heiaha!
> Helmwige, hier!
> Hieher dein Ross!

HELMWIGE'S *Stimme* (*von aussen*).
> Hojotoho! Hojotoho!

(*In einem vorbeiziehenden Gewölk bricht Blitzesgla[nz] aus; eine Walküre zu Ross wird in ihm sichtbar; ü[ber] ihrem Sattel hängt ein erschlagener Krieger.*)

ORTLINDA, WALTRAUTA *and* SCHWERTLEITA (*all three hailing the new comer*).
Heiaha! Heiaha!

he cloud with the apparition has disappeared behind the trees.)

ORTLINDA (*calling towards the wood*).
By Ortlinda's filly fasten thy horse:
Gladly my gray will graze near thy brown.

WALTRAUTA. Who hangs at thy saddle?

HELMWIGA (*entering from the wood*).
Sintold, the Hegeling!

SCHWERTLEITA.
Fasten thy brown far from the gray, then,
Ortlinda's mare carries
Wittig the Irming!

GERHILDA (*who has descended somewhat lower*).
As foes I have seen them, Sintold and Wittig.

ORTLINDA (*springs up and runs into the wood*).
Heiaha! Heiaha! Thy mare is mau'ed by my horse!

GERHILDA, SCHWERTLEITA *and* HELMWIGA (*laughing*).
Ha, ha, ha, ha, ha, ha, ha, ha, ha, ha!

GERHILDA.
The heroes' strife lives still in the horses!

HELMWIGA (*calling back into the wood*).
Hey there, brownie! Break not the concord!

WALTRAUTA (*has taken* GERHILDA'S *place on the cliff*).
Hoyotoho! Hoyotoho!
Siegruna, here!
Where stay'st thou so long?

SIEGRUNA flies past in the air into the pine wood in the same manner as HELMWIGA.)

SIEGRUNA (*voice from the right*).
Occupied! Are the others all here?

The Valkyrs.
Hoyotoho! Hoyotoho!
Heiaha! Heiaha!

GRIMGERDA *and* ROSSVEISSA (*from below*).
Hoyotoho! Hoyotoho!
Heiaha! Heiaha!

WALTRAUTA. Grimgerda and Rossveissa!

GERHILDA. Arriving at once.

In a train of clouds lit by lightning, which passes from left to right, appear ROSSVEISSA *and* GRIMGERDA, *also on horseback, each bearing a dead body over her saddle.*)

ORTLINDA, HELMWIGA *and* SIEGRUNA (*have entered from the wood, and now beckon from the rocky peak towards the new comer*).
We greet ye, riders twain:
Rossveis' and Grimgerda!

ORTLINDE, WALTRAUTE *und* SCHWERTLEITE (*der Ankommenden entgegenrufend*).
Heiaha! Heiaha!

(*Die Wolke mit der Erscheinung ist rechts hinter dem Tann verschwunden.*)

ORTLINDE (*in den Tann hineinrufend*).
Zu Ortlinde's Stute
Stell' deinen Hengst;
Mit meiner Grauen
Gras't gern dein Brauner!

WALTRAUTE. Wer hängt dir im Sattel?

HELMWIGE (*aus dem Tann schreitend*).
Sintold der Hegeling!

SCHWERTLEITE. Führ' deinen Braunen
Fort von der Grauen:
Ortlinde's Mähre
Trägt Wittig, den Irming!

GERHILDE (*ist etwas naher herabgestiegen*).
Als Feinde sah ich nur
Sintold und Wittig.

ORTLINDE (*bricht schnell auf, und läuft in den Tann*)
Heiaha! Die Stute
Stösst mir der Hengst!

GERHILDE, SCHWERTLEITE *und* HELMWIGE (*lachend*).
Ha, ha, ha, ha, ha, ha, ha, ha, ha, ha!

GERHILDE. Die Rosse entzweit noch
Der Recken Zwist!

HELMWIGE (*in den Tann zurückrufend*).
Ruhig dort, Brauner!
Brichst du den Frieden?

WALTRAUTE (*hat für* GERHILDE *die Wacht genommen*).
Hojotoho! Hojotoho!
Heiaha! Heiaha!
Siegrune, hier!
Wo säumst du so lang?

(*Wie zuvor* HELMWIGE, *zieht jetzt* SIEGRUNE *im gleichen Aufzuge vorbei, dem Tann zu.*)

SIEGRUNE's *Stimme* (*von rechts*).
Arbeit gab's!
Sind die And'ren schon da?

Die Walküren.
Hojotoho! Hojotoho!
Heiaha! Heiaha!

GRIMGERDE *und* ROSSWEISSE (*von unten*).
Hojotoho! Hojotoho!
Heiaha! Heiaha!

WALTRAUTE. Grimgerd' und Rossweisse!

GERHILDE. Sie reiten zu zwei.

(*In einem blitz-erglänzenden Wolkenzuge, der von unten heraufsteigt und dann hinter dem Tann verschwindet, erscheinen* GRIMGERDE *und* ROSSWEISSE, *jede einen Erschlagenen im Sattel führend.*)

ORTLINDE *ist mit* HELMWIGE *und der soeben angekommenen* SIEGRUNE *aus dem Tann herausgetreten: zu* **drei winken sie von dem hinteren Felssaume hinab.**)

ORTLINDE, HELMWIGE *und* SIEGRUNE.
Gegrüsst, ihr Reissige!
Rossweiss' und Grimgerde!

No. 2.

HOYO-TO-HO!

Ho-yo - to ho!.... Ho-yo - to-ho!.... Hei-a - ha!...... Hei-a - ha!
Ho-jo - to-ho!... *Ho-jo - to-ho!....* *Hei-a - ha!......* *Hei-a - ha!*

Ho - yo - to-ho!...... Ho - yo - to-ho!.... Hei-a - ha!...... Hei-a - ha!
Ho-jo - to-ho!...... *Ho-jo - to-ho!....* *Hei-a - ha!......* *Hei-a - ha!*

Ho - yo - to-ho!...... Ho - yo - to-ho!...... Ho - yo - to-ho!.....
Ho-jo - to-ho!...... *Ho-jo - to-ho!......* *Ho-jo - to-ho!......*

Ho - yo - to-ho!...... Hei - a - ha!......................
Ho-jo - to-ho!...... *Hei - a - ha!......................*

The Valkyrs.
  Hoyotoho! Hoyotoho!
  Heiaha! Heiaha!
	Die andern Walküren alle.
	  Hojotoho! Hojotoho!
	  Heiaha! Heiaha!

GERHILDA.
  Your steeds in the forest let stand and feed!
	GERHILDE. In Wald mit den Rossen
	  Zu Weid' und Rast!

ORTLINDA (*calling towards the wood*).
  Fasten the mares afar from each other,
  Till all our heroes' hate be allayed!
	ORTLINDE (*in den Tann rufend*).
	  Führt die Mähren
	  Fern von einander,
	  Bis uns'rer Helden
	  Hass sich gelegt!

HELMWIGA (*while all the rest laugh*).
  The gray, in sooth,
  Through their feud has suffered!
	HELMWIGE (*während die Andern lachen*).
	  Der Helden Grimm
	  Schon büsste die Graue!

GRIMGERDA *and* ROSSVEISSA (*entering from the wood*).
  Hoyotoho! Hoyotoho!
	GRIMGERDE *und* ROSSWEISSE (*treten aus dem Tann auf*).
	  Hojotoho! Hojotoho!

The Valkyrs.
  Be welcome! Be welcome!
  Be welcome!
	Die Walküren.
	  Willkommen! Willkommen!

SCHWERTLEITA (*alone*).
  Went ye wanderers paired?
	SCHWERTLEITE (*allein*).
	  War't ihr Kühnen zu zwei?

GRIMGERDA. Alone journeyed we;
  But lately we met.
	GRIMGERDE. Getrennt ritten wir,
	  Trafen uns heut'.

ROSSVEISSA. Stand we fully assembled?
  Then stay no longer:
  To Valhall' wend we our way,
  Victims for Wotan provide.
	ROSSWEISSE. Sind wir alle versammelt,
	  Dann säumt nicht lange:
	  Nach Walhal lbrechen wir auf,
	  Wotan zu bringen die Wal.

HELMWIGA. Are there but eight?
  All are not here.
	HELMWIGE. Acht sind wir erst,
	  Eine noch fehlt.

GERHILDA. By the brawny Volsung
  Valorous Brünnhild'.
	GERHILDE. Bei dem braunen Wälsung
	  Weilt wohl noch Brünnhild'?

WALTRAUTA. For her arrival must we still rest
Wotan would give us greeting full grim,
Should he not see her with us.

SIEGRUNA (at the look-out).
Hoyotoho! Hoyotoho!
Behold! Behold!
In breath-devoid haste flies Brünnhilde here.

The Valkyrs (hastening up to the look-out).
Hoyotoho! Hoyotoho!
Brünnhilde, ho! Heiaha!

WALTRAUTA.
To the wood guides she her wavering horse.

GRIMGERDA. How snorts Grani from swift career.

ROSSVEISSA. I saw never thus Valkyrie speeding!

ORTLINDA. What mounts she in saddle?

HELMWIGA. That is no man!

SIEGRUNA. 'Tis a maid, merely.

GERHILDA. Where met she that maid?

SCHWERKLEITA. Without a hail hies she toward us.

WALTRAUTA.
Heiaha! Brünnhilda! Hearest thou not?

ORTLINDA. Help our sister to earth in safety!

The Valkyrs (running toward the wood).
Hoyotoho! Hoyotoho!
Hciaha! Heiaha!

WALTRAUTA. To ground hath sunk
Grani the stalwart!

GRIMGERDA. From the saddle lifts she
Lightly the maid!

The Valkyrs (all run towards the wood).
Sister! Sister! What is thy strait?

(All the Valkyries return to the stage; with them comes
BRÜNNHILDA, supporting and leading in SIEGLINDA.)

BRÜNNHILDA. Shield me! O help in hardest need!

The Valkyrs. Why fliest thou in all haste?
Art thou in fear! So flee but culprits who fear!

BRÜNNHILDA.
I am for the first time pursued in flight;
Host-father hunts me down!

The Valkyrs. Wander thy senses? Speak to us!
What! Fleest thou from him?
Ha! Speak! Doth follow Host-father? O say!

BRÜNNHILDA.
O sisters, scale ye the mountain's summit!
Spy to northward if Wotan draws nigh!

ORTLINDA and WALTRAUTA spring up to the heights.)
Speak! Shows he in sight?

WALTRAUTE. Auf sie noch harren
Müssen wir hier:
Walvater gäb' uns
Grimmigen Gruss,
Säh' ohne sie er uns nah'n.

SIEGRUNE (auf der Felsspitze, von wo sie hinausspäht).
Ho otoho! Hojotoho!
Hieher! Hieher!
In brünstigem Ritt
Jagt Brünnhilde her.

Die Walküren (nach der Felspitze eilend).
Ho otoho! Hojotoho!
Brünnhilde, ho! Heiaha!

WALTRAUTE. Nach dem Tann lenkt sie
Das taumelnde Ross.

GRIMGERDE. Wie schnaubt Grane
Vom schnellen Ritt!

ROSSWEISSE. So jach sah ich nie
Walküren jagen!

ORTLINDE. Was hält sie im Sattel?

HELMWIGE. Das ist kein Held!

SIEGRUNE. Eine Frau führt sie.

GERHILDE. Wie fand sie die Frau?

SCHWERTLEITE. Mit keinem Gruss
Grüsst sie die Schwestern?

WALTRAUTE. Heiaha! Brünnhilde!
Hörst du uns nicht?

ORTLINDE. Helft der Schwester
Vom Ross sich schwingen!

Die Walküren (beide nach dem Tann laufend).
Hojotoho! Hojotoho!
Heiaha! Heiaha!

WALTRAUTE. Zu Grunde stürzt
Grane der starke!

GRIMGERDE. Aus dem Sattel hebt sie
Hastig das Weib.

Die übrigen Walküren (dem Tann zueilend).
Schwester! Schwester!
Was ist gescheh'n?

(Alle Walküren kehren auf die Bühne zurück; mit ihnen
kommt BRÜNNHILDE, SIEGLINDE unterstützend und her-
eingeleitend.)

BRÜNNHILDE (athemlos).
Schützt mich und helft
In höchster Noth!

Die Walküren. Wo rittest du her
In rasender Hast?
So fliegt nur, wer auf der Flucht!

BRÜNNHILDE. Zum erstenmal flieh' ich
Und bin verfolgt!
Heervater hetzt mir nach!

Die Walküren. Bist du von Sinnen?
Sprich! Sage uns!
Verfolgt dich Heervater?
Fliehst du vor ihm?

BRÜNNHILDE. O Schwestern, späht
Von des Felsens Spitze!
Schaut nach Norden,
Ob Walvater naht!

(ORTLINDE und WALTRAUTE springen hinauf.)
Schnell! seht ihr ihn schon?

ORTLINDA. A thunder gale nears from northward.

WALTRAUTA. Gathering thick groweth the cloud.

The Valkyrs.
  Host-father strideth his heavenly steed!
BRÜNNHILDA. The savage hunter, pursuing in haste,
  He nears, he nears from northward!
  Shield me, sisters! Watch o'er this wife!

The Valkyrs. Who is she, this woman?
BRÜNNHILDA. Brief be my answer: Sieglinda is she,
  Siegmund's sister and bride!
  Wotan with virulence vows the Volsungs to
    waste:
  The brother should by Brünnhilda's help to-day
    have been slain!
  I sheltered Siegmund, though, with my shield,
  Slighting the god, who slew him himself with
    his spear.
  Siegmund fell, and I fled far with his friend;
  To preserve her, hither I hied to beseech your
    help
  In staving off the blow from us both!

The Valkyrs.
  Unworthy sister! What words are these?
  Woe's me! Brünnhilda, woe's thee!
  Brok'st thou with daring, Brünnhilda,
  Host-father's holiest ban?

WALTRAUTA (from the height).
  Nears the tempest like night from the north.

ORTLINDA. Raging storm-clouds hitherward stride.

The Valkyrs. Howls herald Host-father's steed!
  Shrilly snorting it flies.

BRÜNNNHILDA.
  Woe to the victim, if Wotan should strike!
  To wailing and death devotes he the Volsungs
  Who'll lend me a horse, the lightest of foot,
  To whirl this woman away?

SIEGRUNA. Shall we likewise learn to defy?

BRÜNNHILDA.
  Rossveissa, sister, lend me but thy racer!

ROSSVEISSA. He never yet fled our father in fear.

BRÜNNHILDA. Helmwiga, hear me!

HELMWIGA. Our father I hold to.

BRÜNNHILDA.
  Grimgerda! Gerhilda! Grant me a horse!
  Schwertleita! Siegruna! See my distress!
  Be still my friends! O fall not away!
  Save this unfortunate wife!

ORTLINDE. Gewittersturm
  Naht von Norden.
WALTRAUTE. Starkes Gewölk
  Staut sich dort auf,
Die Walküren. Heervater reitet
  Sein heiliges Ross!
BRÜNNHILDE. Der wilde Jäger,
  Der wüthend mich jagt,
  Er naht, er naht von Nord!
  Schützt mich, Schwestern!
  Wahret dies Weib!

Die Walküren. Was ist mit dem Weibe?
BRÜNNHILDE. Hört mich in Eile!
  Sieglinde ist es,
  Siegmund's Schwester und Braut:
  Gegen die Wälsungen
  Wüthet Wotan in Grimm:—
  Dem Bruder sollte
  Brünnhilde heut'
  Entziehen den Sieg.
  Doch Siegmund schützt' ich
  Mit meinem Schild,
  Trotzend dem Gott:—
  Der traf ihn da selbst mit dem Speer.
  Siegmund fiel:
  Doch ich floh
  Fern mit der Frau:
  Sie zu retten
  Eilt' ich zu euch,
  Ob mich bange auch
  Ihr berget vor dem strafende!
Die Walküren. Bethörte Schwester!
  Was thatest du?
  Wehe! Wehe!
  Brünnhilde, wehe!
  Ungehorsam
  Brach Brünnhilde
  Heervaters heilig Gebot?
WALTRAUTE (Von der Höhe).
  Nächtig ziehet es
  Von Norden heran.
ORTLINDE. Wüthend steuert
  Hierher der Sturm.
Die Walküren. Wild wiehert
  Walvaters Ross,
  Schrecklich schnaubt es daher!

BRÜNNHILDE. Wehe der Armen
  Wenn Wotan sie trifft,
  Den Wälsungen allen
  Droht er Verderben!—
  Wer leih't mir von euch
  Das leichteste Ross,
  Das flink' die Frau ihm entführ'?

SIEGRUNE. Auch uns räth'st du
  Rasenden Trotz?

BRÜNNHILDE. Rossweisse. Schwester!
  Leih' mir deinen Renner!

ROSSWEISSE. Vor Walvater floh
  Der fliegende nie.

BRÜNNHILDE. Helmwige, höre!

HELMWIGE. Dem Vater gehorch ich.

BRÜNNHILDE. Grimgerde! Gerhilde!
  Gönnt mir eu'r Ross!
  Schwertleite! Siegrune!
  Seht meine Angst!
  O seid mir treu,
  Wie traut ich euch:
  Rettet dies traurige Weib!

SIEGLINDA (*who till now has gazed gloomily and coldly before her, starts with a repellent gesture, as* BRÜNNHILDA *clasps her quickly as if for protection*).
Oh. suffer no sorrow for me!
Ah! how dear now were death!
Who bade thee, maid, to bear me from peril?
A stroke I might in the strife have found
From the self-same weapon that Siegmund
    felled;
Then had I fallen and hied with him!
Far from Siegmund—Siegmund—from thee!
O'er master, O death, my remembrance!
If thou wouldst court not, maiden, my curses,
Then one pray'r in pity accord me;
Strike with thy sword to my heart!

BRÜNNHILDA.
Live still, O wife! for the love that waits thee!
Rescue the pledge that with thee he hath placed:
A very Volsung thou bearest!

SIEGLINDA *first is violently startled, then her face lights up with intense joy.*)
SIEGLINDA. Rescue me, brave one!
Rescue my babe!
Shelter me, maidens, with mightiest shield!

A fearful storm arises on the distant horizon. Increasing thunder-clouds mount in the background.)

WALTRAUTA. The storm gathers fast!

ORTLINDA. Fly, all who fear it!

The Valkyrs. Hence with the woman!
Wrath threatens her.
The Valkyries may not venture to aid!

SIEGLINDA (*on her knees before* BRÜNNHILDA).
Save me, O maid! spurn not a mother!

BRÜNNHILDA (*with sudden resolution raises* SIEGLINDA *up*).
Then fly with all swiftness, and fly by thyself!
I'll stay where I am: strike on me Wotan's
    anger!
While I hinder him here in his wrath,
Thou by flight shalt escape from his curse!

SIEGLINDA. Where may I safely wander?

BRÜNNHILDA.
Which of ye, sisters, sped to the eastward?

SIEGRUNA. To east a tangled forest extends;
The Nibelung's hoard has Fafnir
Fled there to hide.

SCHWERTLEITA.
Changed to a dread dragon the churl is,
And in a hole he harbours with Alberic's ring!

GRIMGERDA. 'Tis no haven there for a helpless wife.

SIEGLINDE (*Die bisher finster und kalt vor sich hinge-starrt, fährt uf, als* BRÜNNHILDE *sie lebhaft—wie zum Schutze—umfasst*).
Nicht sehre dich Sorge um mich:
Einzig taugt mir der Tod!
Wer hiess dich Maid
    Dem Harst mich entführen?
Im Sturm dort hätt' ich
    Den Streich empfah'n
Von derselben Waffe,
    Der Siegmund fiel:
Das Ende fand ich
    Vereint mit ihm!
Fern von Siegmund—
    Siegmund von dir!
O deckte mich Tod,
    Dass ich's nicht denke!—
Soll um die Flucht
    Dir Maid ich nicht fluchen,
So erhöre heilig mein Fleh'n—
Stosse dein Schwert mir in's Herz!

BRÜNNHILDE. Lebe, o Weib,
    Um der Liebe willen!
Rette das Pfand,
    Das von ihm du empfingst:
Ein Wälsung wächst dir im Schoosse.

SIEGLINDE (*Ist heftig erschrocken; plötzlich strahlt dann ihr Gesicht in erhabener Freude auf*).
Rete mich, Kühne!
Rette mein Kind!
Schirmt mich, ihr Mädchen,
Mit mächtigstem Schutz!

(*Furchtbares Gewitter steigt im Hintergrunde auf: nahender Donner.*)

WALTRAUTE. Der Sturm kommt heran!

ORTLINDE. Flieh', wer ihn fürchtet!

Die Walküren. Fort mit dem Weibe!
Droht ihm Gefahr:
Der Walküren keine
Wag' ihren Schutz!

SIEGLINDE (*Auf den Knieen vor* BRÜNNHILDE).
Rette mich Maid!
Rette die Mutter!

BRÜNNHILDE (*Mit schnellem Entschluss*).
So fliehe denn eilig—
    Und fliehe allein!
Ich—bleibe zurück,
Biete mich Wotan's Rache:
    An mir zögr' ich
    Den Zürnenden hier,
Während du seinem Rasen entrinnst.

SIEGLINDE. Wohin soll ich mich wenden?

BRÜNNHILDE. Wer von euch Schwestern
Schweifte nach Osten?

SIEGRUNE. Nach Osten weithin
Dehnt sich ein Wald:
    Der Nibelungen Hort
Entführte Fatner dorthin.

SCHWERTLEITE. Wurmes-Gestalt
Schuf sich der Wilde:
    In einer Höhle
Hütet er Alberich's Reif.

GRIMGERDE. Nicht geheu'r ist's dort
Für ein hilflos Weib.

BRÜNNHILDA. And yet from Wotan's wrath,
    Shelter sure were this wood!
    'Tis shunned by him: he abhorreth the spot.

WALTRAUTA (*from the heights*).
    Raging rides the god to our rock!

The Valkyrs.
    Brünnhilda, hark to the gathering bruit!

BRÜNNHILDA.
    Fly then swiftly, and speed to the east!
    Bravely determine all trials to bear.
    Hunger and thirst, thorns and hard ways,
    Smile through all pain while suffering pangs!
    This only heed and hold it ever:
    The highest hero of worlds hidest thou, O wife,
    In sheltering shrine!

(*She produces the pieces of* SIEGMUND's *sword from under her breastplate and hands them to* SIEGLINDA).
    For him keep these shreds of shattered sword-blade;
    From his father's death-field by fortune I saved them:
    Anon renewed this sword shall he swing;
    And now his name I declare—Siegfried, of vict'ry the son!

SIEGLINDA. O marvellous sayings! maiden divine!
    What comfort o'er my mind thou hast cast!
    For his sake I live and save this belov'd one!
    May my blessing frame future reward!
    Fare thee well! Be Sieglinda's sorrow thy weal!

(*She hastens away. The rocky peak is enveloped in black thunder-clouds; a fearful tempest roars up from the back; between the peals of thunder* WOTAN's *voice is heard.*)

WOTAN's *voice.* Stay! Brünnhilda!

The Valkyrs.
    Now steed and rider reach the rocks here:
    Woe, Brünnhilda! Wrath doth he bring!

BRÜNNHILDA. Ah, sisters, help! I sink at heart!
    His ire will crush me,
    If from my aid ye recoil.

The Valkyrs.
    Then here, thou lost one. lest thou be seen!
    Shelter in our midst! Be silent when called!

(*They conceal* BRÜNNHILDA *in their midst and look anxiously towards the wood, which is now lit up by a vivid glare, whilst the background has become quite dark.*)
    Woe! Wildly springeth Wotan from horse:
    Hither hurls in haste for revenge.

BRÜNNHILDE. Und doch vor Wotan's Wuth
    Schützt sie sicher der Wald:
    Ihn scheut der Mächt'ge
    Und meidet den Ort.

WALTRAUTE (*Von der Höhe*).
    Furchtbar fährt
    Dort Wotan zum Fels.

Die Walküren. Brünnhilde, hör'
    Seines Nahen's Gebraus'!

BRÜNNHILDE. Fort denn, eile
    Nach Osten gewandt!
    Muthigen Trotzes
    Ertrag alle Mühn—
    Hunger und Durst,
    Dorn und Gestein;
    Lache, ob Noth
    Und Leiden dich nagt!
    Denn eines wisse
    Und wahr' es immer:
    Den hehrsten Helden der Welt
    Hegst du, o Weib,
    Im schirmenden Schooss!—

(*Sie reicht ihr die Stücken von* SIEGMUND's *zerbroche nem Schwert.*)
    Werwahr' ihm die starken
    Schwertes-Stücken;
    Seines Vaters Walstatt
    Entführt' ich sie glücklich:
    Der neu gefügt
    Das Schwert einst schwingt,
    Den Namen nehm' er von mir—
    "Siegfried" freu' sich des Sieg's!

SIEGLINDE. Du hehrstes Wunder!
    Herrliche Maid!
    Dir, Treuen, dank' ich
    Heiligen Trost!
    Für ihn, den wir liebten,
    Rett' ich das Liebste:
    Meines Dankes Lohn
    Lache dir einst!
    Lebe wohl!
    Dich segnet Sieglinde's Weh'!

(*Sie eilt rechts im Vordergrunde ab.—Die Felsenhöh ist von schwarzen Gewitterwolken umlagert; furch barer Sturm braust aus dem Hintergrunde daher: e feuriger Schein erhellt den Tannenwald zur Seite.*)

WOTAN's *Stimme.* Steh'! Brünnhilde!

Die Walküren. Den Fels erreichten
    Ross und Reiter:
    Weh' dir, Brünnhilde!
    Rache entbrennt!

BRÜNNHILDE. Ach, Schwestern, helft!
    Mir schwankt das Herz!
    Sein Zorn zerschellt mich,
    Wenn eu'r Schutz ihn nicht zähmt.

Die Walküren. Hieher, Verlor'ne!
    Lass' dich nicht seh'n!
    Schmiege dich an uns,
    Und schweige dem Ruf!

(*Sie ziehen sich alle die Felsspitze hinauf, indem s ... unter sich verbergen.*)
    Wehe! Wehe!
    Wüthend schwingt sich
    Wotan vom Ross—
    Hieher ras't
    Sein rächender Schritt!

WOTAN *enters from the wood in the most angry pertur-*
bation and advances before the group of Valkyries
on the height, in search of BRÜNNHILDA.)

WOTAN.

Where is Brünnhilda? where the rebellious one?
Dare ye to veil her from Wotan's vengeance?

The Valkyrs. Fearful and dread thy dictate!
What did, O father, thy daughters,
That such a storm they have stirred in thy
breast?

WOTAN. Would ye defy me?
Foolish ones, tremble!
I know! Brünnhilda hides here from me!
Hence from her aid! the outcast from heaven
Who all things high has spurned from her!

The Valkyrs. To us sped the pursued one,
For our aid seeking with pray'rs.
She sees thy rage in silence and ruth:
Father, hear us; pray
Soften thine anger to her: 'bate thy fury's burst.

WOTAN. Weak-spirited, womanly brood!
Such melting moods ye won not from me!
I tempered your frames for fighting and toil,
Steeled, too, your bosoms to bear distress;
And your minions now moan and groan,
When I grimly chastise breach of faith!
Now wot, ye waverers, what she hath wrought,
For whom your tremulous tear-drops arise!
No one like she knew what my bosom en-
shrouded!
No one like she spied to the depths of my spirit!
'Twas she worked what my will had shaped and
designed;
And now is broken our notable bond, when,
faith annulling,
My will she defied.
My sacred command openly scorned,
Against me attempting to turn e'en the tools
By me bestowed! Hear'st thou, Brünnhilda?
Thou on whom byrnie, helm and glaive,
Glory and hope, honour and strength I be-
stowed?
How to my chiding canst hearken, and fail to
face
The chider, in hope from thy doom to hide?

BRÜNNHILDA *emerges from the midst of the Valkyries,*
walks humbly, but with firm tread, down from the
rock, and thus approaches to within a short distance
of WOTAN.)
Here stand I, father, to suffer my sentence!

(WOTAN *schreitet in furchtbar zürnender Aufregung*
aus dem Tann heraus, und hält vor dem Haufen der
Walküren an, welche BRÜNNHILDE *schützen.)*

WOTAN. Wo ist Brünnhilde?
Wo die Verbrecherin?
Wagt ihr, die Böse
Vor mir zu bergen?

Die Walküren. Schrecklich ertos't dein Toben:—
Was thaten, Vater, die Töchter,
Dass sie dich reizten
Zu rasender Wuth?

WOTAN. Wollt ihr mich höhnen?
Hütet euch, Freche!
Ich weiss: Brünnhilde
Bergt ihr vor mir.
Weichet von ihr,
Der ewig Verworf'nen,
Wie ihren Werth
Von sich sie warf!

Die Walküren. Zu uns floh die Verfolgte,
Uns'ren Schutz flehte sie an!
Mit Furcht und Zagen
Fasst sie dein Zorn.
Für die bange Schwester
Bitten wir nun,
Dass den ersten Zorn du bezähm'st.

WOTAN. Weichherziges
Weibergezücht!
So matten Muth
Gewannt ihr von mir?
Erzog ich euch kühn
Zu Kämpfen zu zieh'n,
Schuf ich die Herzen
Euch hart und scharf,
Dass ihr Wilden nun weint und greint,
Wenn mein Grimme eine Treulose straft?
So wisst den, Winselnde,
Was die verbrach,
Um die euch Zagen
Die Zähre entbrennt!
Keine wie sie
Kannte mein innerstes Sinnen!
Keine wie sie
Wusste den Quell meines Willens;
Sie selbst war
Meines Wunsches schaffender Schooss:
Und so nun brach sie
Den seligen Bund
Dass treulos sie
Meinem Willen getrotzt,
Mein herrschend Gebot
Offen verhöhnt
Gegen mich selbst die Waffe gewandt,
Die allein mein Wunsch ihr schuf!
Hörst du's Brünnhilde?
Du, der ich Brünne,
Helm und Wehr,
Wonne und Huld,
Namen und Leben verlieh?
Hörst du's, Brünnhilde?
Und birgst dich bang dem Kläger,
Dass feig' du der Straf' entflöh'st?

BRÜNNHILDE (*tritt aus der Schaar der Walküren her-*
vor, schreitet demüthigen, doch festen Schrittes, von
der Felsenspitze herab, und tritt so in geringer Ferne
vor WOTAN).
Hier bin ich, Vater:
Gebiete die Strafe!

WOTAN.
I sentence thee not; thou hast shaped the
    stroke for thyself.
Thy father's will awoke thee to life:
Yet against that will hast thou warred;
Acting my orders was only thy part,
Yet against me all hast thou ordered.
Wish-maid wert to me,
Yet against me now hast thou wished;
Shield-maid wert to me,
Yet against me turnest thy shield;
Lot-chooser thou wert to me,
Yet against me lot hast thou chosen;
Hero-stirrer thou wert to me,
Yet against me stirrest thou heroes.
What wert thou erst, Wotan hath uttered;
What now thou art, that say for thyself!
Wish-maid art thou no more.
One time a Valkyrie wert thou,
Remain henceforth but merely thyself!

BRÜNNHILDA (*violently startled*).
Thou disownest me? Thine aim I divine!

WOTAN. From Valhall ne'er more will I send thee:
I'll cause thee no more warriors to call;
No more bring'st thou heroes to fill my hall;
At the Æsir's festal meeting
The flagon no more thou'llt fill me with mead.
Ne'er shall I kiss more thy sweet child-like
    mouth;
From heavenly clans art thou excluded,
Bann'd, degraded from thy blessed degree:
For broken now is our bond; exiled for aye
Art thou banished from bliss.

The Valkyrs. Horror! Woe! Sister! O sister!

BRÜNNHILDA.
All thou hast given, again wouldst take?

WOTAN. To thy lord all must thou lose!
And here where we stand strikes thee my curse:
In powerless sleep shalt thou be cast;
That man shall seize on the maid,
In whose way she is seen and awaked.

The Valkyrs. Oh, halt! O father, recall thy curse!
O father! shall the maiden wither and waste by
    a man?
O stay! hark to our prayers! deal not to her
    this grievous disgrace!
Grim-hearted god: as her sisters we too share
    her shame!

WOTAN. Did ye not hear what I ordained?
From your resort must the treacherous sister be
    severed:

WOTAN. Nicht—straf' ich dich erst:
Deine Strafe schufst du dir selbst.
Durch meinen Willen
Warst du allein:
Gegen ihn doch hast du gewollt;
Meinen Befehl nur
Führtest du aus:
Gegen ihn doch hast du befohlen;
Wunsch-Maid
War'st du mir:
Gegen mich doch hast du gewünscht;
Schild-Maid
War'st du mir:
Gegen mich doch hob'st du den Schild;
Loos-Kieserin
War'st du mir:
Gegen mich doch kies'test du Loose;
Helden-Reizerin
War'st du mir:
Gegen mich doch reiztest du Helden.
Was sonst du war'st,
Das sagte dir Wotan:
Was jetzt du bist.
Das sage dir selbst!
Wunschmaid bist du nicht mehr;
Walküre bist du gewesen:—
Nun sei fortan,
Was so du noch bist!

BRÜNNHILDE (*Heftig erschrocken*).
Du verstössest mich?
Versteh' ich den Sinn?

WOTAN. Nicht send' ich dich mehr aus Walhall,
Nicht weis' ich dir mehr
Helden zur Wal;
Nicht führ'st du mehr Sieger
In meinen Saal;
Bei der Götter traulichem Mahle
Das Trinkhorn reichst du
Mir traut nicht mehr;
Nicht kos' ich dir mehr
Den kindischen Mund.
Von göttlicher Schaar
Bist du geschieden,
Ausgestossen
Aus der Ewigen Stamm;
Gebrochen ist unser Bund;
Aus meinem Angesicht bist du verbannt.

Die Walküren. Wehe! Wehe!
Schwester! O schwester!

BRÜNNHILDE. Nimmst du mir alles,
Was einst du gab'st?

WOTAN. Der dich zwingt,
Wird dir's entzieh'n!
Hieher auf den Berg
Banne ich dich;
In wehrlosen Schlaf
Schliesse ich dich;
Der Mann dann fange die Maid,
Der am Wege sie findet und weckt.

Die Walküren. Halt' ein, Vater!
Halt' ein mit dem Fluch!
Soll die Maid verblüh'n
Und verbleichen dem Mann?
Du Schrecklicher, wende
Die schreiende Schmach:
Wie die Schwester träf' uns ihr Schimpf!

WOTAN. Hörtet ihr nicht,
Was ich verhängt?
Aus eurer Schaar
Ist die treulose Schwester geschieden:

No more a-horse with your troop will she hurl
  through the tempest;
A consort will claim her in conjugal clasp;
She'll follow her master henceforth at his beck;
By the fire to sit and to spin, to free spirits a
  mock and sport!

Mit euch zu Ross
Durch die Lüfte sie reitet nicht länger;
Die magdliche Blume
Verblüht der Maid:
Ein Gatte gewinnt
Ihre weibliche Gunst:
Dem herrischen Manne
Gehorcht sie fortan,
Am Herde sitzt sie und spinnt,
Aller Spottenden Ziel und Spiel.

ÜNNHILDA sinks to the ground with a cry; the Val-
kyries recoil in terror and draw back with a sudden
movement.)
  Fear ye her doom? Then fly the condemned
    one!
  Draw from her side and hold ye afar!
  Dares one undutiful near her to dally?
  Dares one defy me and furnish her help?
  That fool shall find a like fate! So, bold ones,
    I bid ye heed!
  Make no more halt! seek not this mountain!
  Hence I warn ye to hasten, lest I hurl woe on
    your heads!
e Valkyries separate with wild cries of woe and rush
to the wood in hasty flight. Black clouds settle
quickly on the cliffs; a wild, rushing sound is heard
the wood. A vivid lightning-flash breaks through
e clouds; in it the Valkyries are seen with loose
bridle crowding together in a troop, and rushing wildly
way. The storm quickly subsides; the thunder-clouds
gradually disperse. During the following scene evening
twilight falls with the returning fine weather, followed
the close by night.)

(BRÜNNHILDE *sinkt schreiend vor seinen Füssen zu*
Boden; die Walküren machen eine Bewegung des
Entsetzens.)
  Schreckt euch ihr Loos!
  So flieht die Verlor'ne!
  Weichet von ihr
  Und haltet euch fern!
  Wer von euch wagte
  Bei ihr zu weilen,
  Wer mir zum Trotz
  Zu der Traurigen hielt',
  Die Thörin theilte ihr Loos:
  Das künd' ich der Kühnen an!—
    Fort jetzt von hier!
    Meidet den Felsen!
  Hurtig jagt mir von dannen,
  Sonst erharrt Jammer euch hier!
(*Die Walküren fahren mit wildem Wehschrei auseinan-*
der und stürzen in hastiger Flucht in den Tann: bald
hört man sie wie mit Sturm auf ihren Rossen davon-
jagend.—Nach und nach legt sich während des Folgen-
den das Gewitter; die Wolken verziehen sich: Abend-
dämmerung, und endlich Nacht, sinken bei ruhigem
Wetter herein.)

SCENE III

OTAN and BRÜNNHILDA, *she lying still prostrate at*
s feet, remain alone. Long silence; unaltered posi-
ns. She begins slowly to raise her head a little;
e gradually rises to a kneeling position.)

NNHILDA.
  Was it so shameful, what I have done,
  That for my deed I so shamefully am scourged?
  Was it so base to warp thy command, that thou
  For me such debasement must shape?
  Was't such dishonour what I have wrought
  That it should rob me of honour for aye?
  O speak, father! see me before thee: soften thy
    wrath;
  Wreak not thine ire, but make to me clear the
    mortal
  Guilt that with cruel firmness compels thee to
  Cast off thy favorite child!

DRITTE SCENE

(WOTAN *und* BRÜNNHILDE, *sind allein zurückgeblieben.*
Langes, feierliches Schweigen. Endlich das Haupt
langsam erhebend, sucht WOTAN's *noch abgewandten*
Blick, und richtet sich während des Folgenden allmälig
ganz auf.)

BRÜNNHILDE. War es so schmählich,
    Was ich verbrach,
  Dass mein Verbrechen so schmählich du
    bestraf'st?
    War es so niedrig,
    Was ich dir that,
  Dass du so tief mir Erniedrigung schaff'st?
    War es so ehrlos,
    Was ich beging,
  Dass mein Vergeh'n nun die Ehre mir raubt?
    O sag', Vater!
  Sieh' mir in's Auge:
  Schweige den Zorn,
  Zähme die Wuth!
  Deute mir hell
  Die dunkle Schuld,
  Die mit starrem Trotze dich zwingt,
  Zu verstossen dein trautestes Kind!

AN (*gloomily*).
  Ask of thy deed, 'twill surely show thee thy
    guilt!

WOTAN (*finster*).
    Frag' deine That—
  Sie deutet dir deine Schuld!

NNHILDA. But thy decree I carried out.

BRÜNNHILDE. Deinen Befehl
  Führte ich aus.

AN. Decreed I then care of Volsung in combat?

WOTAN. Befahl ich dir
  Für den Wälsung zu fechten?

NNHILDA.
  Thou toldest me so to turn the event!

BRÜNNHILDE. So hiessest du mich
  Als Herrscher der Wal.

WOTAN. But I revoked my unavailing behest!

BRÜNNHILDA.
When Fricka thine own intending did frustrate
When her intending was followed,
To thyself wert thou false.

WOTAN (*softly and bitterly*).
I knew thou understood'st my meaning,
And scourge now thy mutinous act;
Though weak and dull dost thou think me,
But what I must trample on treason,
Thou wert truly beneath my wrath!

BRÜNNHILDA.
My wisdom's scanty; I wist though of one thing,
That thou well lov'dst the Volsung.
I wist of thy struggle, thy constraint to hide
That love in oblivion.
Thou only held'st that other decree though the
Shameful hap shadowed thy heart
That Siegmund should not be shielded.

WOTAN.
And deeming it so, thou dared to lend him thy
shield.

BRÜNNHILDA.
'Twas because I held in my heart thy true
wish,
Which by covenants hampered, fatally clogged
Now thou renouncest so weakly.
I who follow Wotan and fare in his wake,
Have seen a thing once by thee unseen.
Siegmund straight I sought,
I hied to him with his fate;
I looked on his features, heard him at large,
I was stirred by the hero's holy distress;
Widely resounded the warrior's sorrow,
Free was his passion, fearful his pain,
Mournfullest courage, confident might;
And my ear did list.
My eyes did look on what bade in fulness
My heart with holy fervour to beat;
Shy, astonished, stood I ashamed,
I could consider but how to serve him:
Safety or shame, with Siegmund to share them—
This was the fiat I fain had decreed!
Thou who this love within my heart had hid,
Whose purposes had placed me at his side, firm.
Faithful to thee, thwarted I thy command.

WOTAN.
Thou didst for me what I wished so dearly to
work,
But was forced to leave, by fate doubly induced.

WOTAN. Doch meine Weisung
Nahm ich wieder zurück.

BRÜNNHILDE. Als Fricka den eig'nen
Sinn dir entfremdet:
Da ihrem Sinn du dich fügtest,
Warst du selber dir Feind.

WOTAN (*leise und bitter*).
Dass du mich verstanden, wähnt' ich,
Und strafe den wissenden Trotz;
Doch feig und dumm
Dachtest du mich:
So hätt' ich Verrath nicht zu rächen,
Zu gering wärest du meinem Grimm!

BRÜNNHILDE. Nicht weise bin ich;
Doch wusst' ich das Eine—
Dass den Wälsung du liebtest:
Ich wusste den Zwiespalt,
Der dich zwang,
Dies Eine ganz zu vergessen.
Das Andere musstest
Einzig du seh'n,
Was zu schauen so herb
Schmerzte dein Herz—
Dass Schutz du Siegmund versagtest.

WOTAN. Du wusstest es so,
Und wagtest dennoch den Schutz?

BRÜNNHILDE. Weil für dich im Auge
Das eine ich hielt,
Dem, im Zwange des Andren
Schmerzlich entzweit.
Rathlos den Rücken du wandtest.
Die im Kampfe Wotan
Den Rücken bewacht,
Die sah nun das nur,
Was du nicht sah'st:—
Siegmund musste ich seh'n.
Tod kündend
Trat ich vor ihn.
Gewahrte sein Auge,
Hörte sein Wort;
Ich vernahm des Helden
Heilige Noth;
Tönend erklang mir
Des Tapfersten Klage—
Freiester Liebe
Furchtbares Leid,
Traurigsten Muthes
Mächtigster Trotz:
Meinem Ohr erscholl,
Mein Aug' erschaute,
Was tief im Busen das Herz
Zu heil'gem Beben mir traf.—
Scheu und staunend
Stand ich in Scham:
Ihm nur zu dienen
Konnt ich noch denken:
Sieg oder Tod
Mit Siegmund zu theilen—
Dies nur erkannt' ich
Zu kiesen als Loos!
Der mir in's Herz
Diese Liebe gehaucht,
Dem Willen, der mich
Dem Wälsung gesellt,
Ihm innig vertraut—
Trotzt' ich deinem Gebot.

WOTAN. So thatest du,
Was so gern zu thun ich begehrt—
Doch was nicht zu thun
Die Noth zwiefach mich zwang?

With ease ween'st thou to win then the heart's
    fondest wishes?
When burning woe in my heart I bore,
When rankling distress my rage awoke,
That while deeply loving, my love untold
In my tortured heart must be hidden:
When 'gainst my own self,
I in suff'ring contended, and from my spleen
Of spirit in wrath sprang, wasted with longings,
Languished with woe, the furious wish did I
    form
In the wreck of my tott'ring world, these
Eternal wrestlings to termine:
Yet lapp'd wert thou in thralling delights,
Blissful emotions, unrestrained might,
Thou drankest lightly the lovely draught,
While I, god though I be, bitterest gall-cup must
    drain!
Thy so light-turned soul let henceforth lead
    thee;
From me see thyself released!
Thus shall I shun thee, nor share more with
    thee
My thoughts and wishes whispered; apart,
Ne'er more in company work we; so, while
Life days shall last, may the god not give thee
    his greeting!

BRÜNNHILDA.
    Unfit for thee was the foolish maid, who,
Stunned by thy counsel, naught understood,
While her own conviction but one thing advised,
To love all that thou didst love.
If we must sever and part forever, if thou tear-
    est what once was intact,
The one half putting far from thy presence, that
    once was girt to thy service,
Thou god, forget not this! Thine own estate
    thou dar'st not dishonour;
Seek not so deeply to shame thyself;
Thyself would then be sullied, seeing me scoffed
    at and scorned!

WOTAN.
    Thou fain hast followed the might of love:
Follow now him thou needs must love!

BRÜNNHILDA. Shall I from Valhall sever,
    No more to thy service be vassal?
My life to a mortal belong from henceforth?
To boasting poltroon give not the prize!
By a worthless churl let me not be won!

WOTAN. From Fate-father hast thou turned; thy fate
    No more may he move.

BRÜNNHILDA. Once mad'st thou a glorious breed:
    No mean one shall ever debase it!
One valiant o'er all, I vouch it,
Shall spring from Volsung's line.

WOTAN. Peace, with thy Volsung's line!
    As thou'rt relinquished, lost, too, is that:
'Twas wrecked by me in my wrath.

So leicht wähntest du
Wonne der Liebe erworben,
    Wo brennend Weh'
    In das Herz mir brach,
    Wo grässliche Noth
    Den Grimm mir schuf,
    Einer Welt zu Liebe
    Der Liebe Quell
Im gequälten Herzen su hemmen?
    Da labte süss
    Dich, selige Lust;
    Wonniger Rührung
    Ueppigen Rausch
    Enttrankst du lachend
    Der Liebe Trank—
Als mir göttlicher Noth
Nagende Galle gemischt?
    Deinen leichten Sinn
    Lass' dich denn leiten:
    Du sagtest von mir dich los!
    Dich muss ich meiden,
    Gemeinsam mit dir
Nicht darf ich Rath mehr raunen;
    Getrennt nicht dürfen
    Traut wir mehr schaffen;
So weit Leben und Luft,
Darf der Gott dir nicht mehr begegnen!

BRÜNNHILDE. Wohl taugte dir nicht
    Die thör'ge Maid,
    Die staunend im Rathe
    Nicht dich verstand,
    Wie Mein eig'ner Rath
    Nur das Eine mir rieth—
    Zu lieben was du geliebt.—
    Muss ich denn scheiden
    Und scheu dich meiden,
    Musst du spalten
    Was einst sich umspannt,
    Die eig'ne Hälfte
    Fern von dir halten—
Dass sonst sie ganz dir gehörte,
Du, Gott, vergiss das nicht!
    Dein ewig Theil
    Nicht wirst du entehren,
    Schande nicht wollen,
    Die dich beschimpft;
Dich selbst liessest du sinken,
Säh'st du dem Spott mich zum Spiel!

WOTAN. Du folgest selig
    Der Liebe Macht:
    Folge nun dem
    Den du lieben musst!

BRÜNNHILDE. Soll ich aus Walhall scheiden,
    Mit dir nicht mehr schaffen und walten:
    Soll ich gehorchen
    Dem herrschenden Mann—
    Dem feigen Prahler
    Gieb mich nicht Preis!
    Nicht werthlos sei er,
    Der mich gewinnt.

WOTAN. Von Walvater schiedest du—
    Nicht wählen darf er für dich.

BRÜNNHILDE. Du zeugtest ein edles Geschlecht;
    Kein Zager kann ihm entschlagen:
    Der weihlichste Held—ich weiss es—
    Entblüht dem Wälsungenstamm.

WOTAN. Schweig' von dem Wälsungenstamm!
    Von dir geschieden
    Schied ich von ihm:
    Vernichten musst' ihn der Neid.

BRÜNNHILDA.
  I, who crossed thee so, saved it from doom!

WOTAN. Ne'er seek at my hand safety to find,
  Even for her sire-less fruit!

BRÜNNHILDA.
  She guardeth the sword thou had'st shaped for
    Siegmund.
WOTAN. And which I into splinters struck!
  Seek not, O maid, for means to unnerve me!
  Bemoan not thy fate, move as it may;
  I cannot cast thee the lot.
  But hence must I fare, hasten away;
  Too long I'm wavering here.
  Now I turn from thee as thou didst from me;
  I would have naught of what thou dost wish:
  Thy punishment I must promptly deal!

BRÜNNHILDA.
  What hast thou designed that I must suffer?

WOTAN. Unbreaking sleep shall seal thy sense;
  What man the wardless maid wakes,
  Shall win her to wife!

BRÜNNHILDA (*falls on her knees*).
  Shall fetters of sleep firmly bind me,
  To fall a booty to any braggart?
  This one thing thou must allow me;
  Forlorn, I urge thee to hear:
  My helpless form hedge round with hindering
    horrors,
  That but by a free man, fearless of heart,
  Here on the fell I may be found!

WOTAN.
  Too much thou beggest, the boon's too great!
BRÜNNHILDA (*clasping his knees*).
  This one thing must thou concede me:
  Oh, chasten thy child who enchains thy knees!
  Downtread the true heart, destroy thou thy
    maid:
  Let her vital spark be sped by thy spear;
  But cast, cruel one, ne'er a crushing disgrace
    like this!

          (*Wildly*)
  At thy command let magical fire-flame
  Spring forth and enfold me, lambent and fierce.
  To lick with its tongue, to rend with its teeth
    the trembler
  Who rashly dareth to ravish the rock of its
    prize!

BRÜNNHILDE. Die von dir sich riss—
  Ich rettete ihn:
  Sieglinde hegt
  Die heiligste Frucht;
  In Schmerz und Leid,
  Wie kein Weib sie litt,
  Wird sie gebären
  Was bang sie birgt.
WOTAN. Nie suche bei mir
  Schutz für die Frau,
  Noch für ihres Schoosses Frucht!
BRÜNNHILDE. Sie bewahrt das Schwert,
  Das du Siegmund schuf'st.—

WOTAN. Und das ich in Stücken ihm schlug.
  Nicht streb', o Maid,
  Den Muth mir zu stören!
  Erwarte dein Loos.
  Wie ist's dir wirft:
  Nicht kiesen kann ich es dir!—
  Doch fort muss ich jetzt,
  Fern von dir zieh'n:
  Zuviel schon zögert' ich hier.
  Von der Abwendigen
  Wend' ich mich ab;
  Nicht wissen darf ich
  Was sie sich wünscht:
  Die Strafe nur
  Muss vollstreckt ich seh'n.

BRÜNNHILDE. Was hast du erdacht
  Dass ich erdulde?

WOTAN. In festen Schlaf
  Verschliess' ich dich:
  Wer so die Wehrlose weckt,
  Dem ward, erwacht, sie zum Weib.

BRÜNNHILDE (*Stürzt auf ihre Kniee*).
  Soll fesselnder Schlaf
  Fest mich binden,
  Dem feigsten Manne
  Zur leichten Beute:
  Dies Eine musst du erhören,
  Was heil'ge Angst zu dir fleht:
  Die Schlafende schütze
  Mit scheuchenden Schrecken,
  Dass nur ein furchtlos
  Freiester Held
  Hier auf dem Felsen
  Einst mich fänd'!

WOTAN. Zu viel begehrst du—
  Der Gunst zu viel!

BRÜNNHILDE (*Seine Kniee umfassend*).
  Dies Eine musst—
  Musst du erhören!
  Zerknicke dein Kind,
  Das dein Knie umfasst;
  Zertritt die Traute,
  Zertrümm're die Maid;
  Ihres Leibes Spur
  Zerstöre dein Speer:
  Doch gieb, Grausamer, nicht
  Der grässlichsten Schmach sie preis!
        (*Mit Wildheit.*)
  Auf dein Gebot
  Entbrenne ein Feuer;
  Den Fels umglühe
  Lodernde Gluth:
  Es leck' ihre Zunge
  Und fresse ihr Zahn
  Den Zagen, der frech es wagte
  Dem freislichen Felsen zu nah'n!

WOTAN (*overpowered and deeply moved, turns eagerly towards* BRÜNNHILDA, *raises her to her feet and gazes with emotion in her eyes*).

Farewell, my brave and beautiful child!
Thou once the life and light of my heart!
Farewell! Farewell! Farewell!
Loth I must leave thee; no more in love
May I grant thee my greeting:
Henceforth my maid ne'er more with me rideth.
Nor waiteth wine to reach me!
When I relinquish thee, my beloved one,
Thou laughing delight of my eyes,
Thy bed shall be lit by torches more brilliant
Than ever for bridal have burned!
Fiery gleams shall girdle the fell,
With terrible scorchings scaring the timid,
Who, cowed, may cross not Brünnhilda's couch
For one alone freeth the bride;
One freer than I, the God!

BRÜNNHILDA *sinks, rapt and transfigured, on* WOTAN'S *breast; he holds her in a long embrace. She throws her head back again and gazes, still embracing him, with solemn emotion into* WOTAN'S *eyes.*)

WOTAN (*Blickt ihr ergriffen in's Auge und hebt sie auf*).
Leb' wohl, du kühnes
Herrliches Kind!
Du meines Herzens
Heiliger Stolz,
Leb' wohl! leb' wohl! leb' wohl!
Muss ich dich meiden,
Und darf minnig
Mein Gruss nimmer dich grüssen;
Sollst du nicht mehr
Neben mir reiten,
Noch Meth beim Mahl mir reichen;
Muss ich verlieren
Dich, die ich liebte,
Du lachende Lust meines Auges:—
Ein bräutliches Feuer
Soll dir nun brennen,
Wie nie einer Braut es gebrannt!
Flammende Gluth
Umglühe den Fels!
Mit zehrenden Schrecken
Scheuch's es den Zagen,
Der Feige fliehe
Brünnhilde's Fels:—
Denn Einer nur freie die Braut,
Der freier als ich, der Gott!

(BRÜNNHILDE *wirft sich ihm gerührt und entzückt in die Arme.*)

No 3   THOSE EYES SO LUSTROUS AND CLEAR.

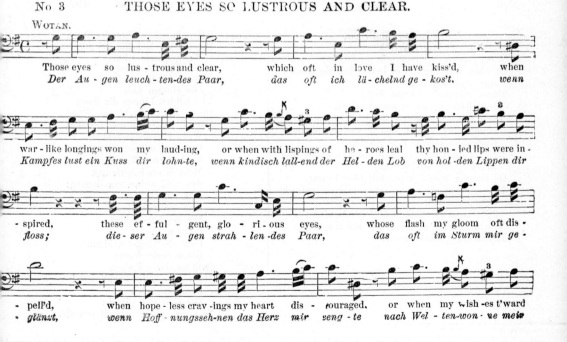

WOTAN.

Those eyes so lus-trous and clear, which oft in love I have kiss'd, when
Der Au-gen leuch-ten-des Paar, das oft ich lä-chelnd ge-kos't, wenn

war-like longings won my laud-ing, or when with lispings of he-roes leal thy hon-ied lips were in-
Kampfes lust ein Kuss dir lohn-te, wenn kindisch lall-end der Hel-den Lob von hol-den Lippen dir

-spired, these ef-ful-gent, glo-ri-ous eyes, whose flash my gloom oft dis-
floss; die-ser Au-gen strah-len-des Paar, das oft im Sturm mir ge-

-pell'd, when hope-less crav-ings my heart dis-couraged, or when my wish-es t'ward
-glänzt, wenn Hoff-nungsseh-nen das Herz mir seng-te nach Wel-ten-won-ne meir

world-ly pleasure from wild warfare were turn-ing, their lus - trous gaz lights on me now, as my
Wunsch ver-langte, aus wild we-bendem Bangen; zum letz - ten Mal letz' es mich heut' mit de

lips im - print this last farewell! On hap - pi - er mor - tal here shall they
Le - be - woh - les letz - tem Kuss! Dem glück - licher'n Man - ne glän - ze sein

beam; the grief - suf - fer - ing god may nev - er hence - forth be
Stern: dem un - se - li - gen Ew' - gen muss es schei - dend ??h

- hold them! Now, heart - torn, he gives thee his
schlies - sen. Denn so kehrt der Gott sich dir

kiss and tak - eth thy god - hood a - way!
ab, so küsst er die Gott - heit von dir!

WOTAN. Those eyes so lustrous and clear,
  Which oft in love I have kissed,
  When warlike longings won my lauding,
  Or when with lispings of heroes leal thy honied
    lips were inspired:
  These effulgent, glorious eyes,
  Whose flash my gloom oft dispelled,
  When hopeless cravings my heart discouraged,
  Or when my wishes t'ward worldly pleasure
    from wild warfare were turning—
  Their lustrous gaze lights on me now as my lips
    imprint this last farewell!
  On happier mortal here shall they beam;
  The grief-suffering god may never henceforth
    behold them!
    (*He clasps her head in both his hands.*)
  Now, heart-torn, he gives thee his kiss, and
  Taketh thy godhood away!

WOTAN. Der Augen leuchtendes **Paar**,
  Das oft ich lächelnd gekos't,
    Wenn Kampfes-Lust
    Ein Kuss dir lohnte,
    Wenn kindisch lallend
    Der Helden Lob
  Von holden Lippen dir floss;
  Dieser Augen strahlendes Paar,
  Das oft im Sturm mir geglänzt,
    Wenn Hoffnungs-Sehnen
    Das Herz mir sengte,
    Nach Welten-Wonne
    Mein Wunsch verlangte
    Aus wild webendem Bangen:
    Zum letzten Mal
    Letz' ich mich heut'
    Mit des Lebewohles
    Letztem Kuss!
    Dem glücklicher'n Manne
    Glänze sein Stern;
  Dem unseligen Ew'gen
  Muss es scheidend schliessen!
    Denn so—kehrt
    Der Gott sich dir ab:
  So küsst er die Gottheit von dir.

(*He imprints a long kiss on her eyes; she sinks back in his arms with closed eyes, her powers gently depart-ing. He tenderly helps her to lie upon a low mossy mound which is overshadowed by a wide-spreading fir-tree. He looks upon her and closes her helmet; his eyes then rest upon the form of the sleeper which he then completely covers with the great steel shield of the Valkyrie. He slowly moves away, then again*

(*Er küsst sie auf beide Augen, die ihr sogleich versch sen bleiben: sie sinkt sanft ermattend in seinen Arr zurück. Er geleitet sie zart auf einen niedrigen M hügel zu liegen, über den sich eine breitästige Ta ausstreckt. Noch einmal betrachtet er ihre Züge u schliesst ihr dann den Helm fest zu; dann veru sein Blick nochmals schmerzlich auf ihrer Gestalt. er endlich mit dem langen Stahlschilde der Walk*

turns round with a painful glance. He stalks with solemn decision to the centre of the stage and directs the point of his spear towards a huge stone.)

Loki, hear! Listen and heed!
As I found thee at first, a fiery glow,
As thou fleddest me headlong,
A hovering glimmer, as then I bound thee,
Bound be thou now!
Appear, wavering spirit, and spread me thy
   Fire round this fell!
Loki! Loki! Appear!

A stream of fire issues from the stone, which swells to an ever-brightening glow of flame. Thereupon a stream of fire flashes forth; bright flames surround WOTAN, *leaping wildly. He directs commandingly with his spear the fiery flood to encircle the rocks, then it spreads to the background, where it flickers permanently round the precipice.)*

WOTAN. He who my spear in spirit feareth,
Ne'er springs through this fiery bar!

He stretches out the spear in a spell. He looks painfully at BRÜNNHILDA *and disappears through the fire.)*
(The curtain falls.)

zudeckt. — Dann schreitet er mit feierlichem Entschlusse in die Mitte der Bühne und kehrt die Spitze seines Speeres gegen einen mächtigen Felsstein.)

Loge hör'!
Lausche hieher!
Wie zuerst ich dich fand
Als feurige Gluth,
Wie dann einst du mir schwandest
Als schweifende Lohe:
Wie ich dich band,
Bann' ich dich heut'!
Herauf, wabernde Lohe,
Umlod're mir feurig den Fels!
Loge! Loge! Hieher!

(Bei der letzten Anrufung schlägt er mit der Spitze des Speeres dreimal auf den Stein, worauf diesem ein Feuerstrahl entfährt, der schnell zu einem Flammenmeere anschwillt, dem Wotan mit einem Winke seiner Speerspitze den Umkreis des Felsens als Strömung zuweist.)

Wer meines Speeres
Spitze fürchtet,
Durchschreite das Feuer nie!
(Er verschwindet in der Gluth nach dem Hintergrunde zu.)
(Der Vorhang fällt.)

THE END.

SIEGFRIED

CHARACTERS.

EGFRIED.
IME.
HE WANDERER (WOTAN).
LBERICH.

FAFNER.
ERDA.
BRÜNNHILDE.

THE ARGUMENT.

ACT I. Mime, the Niblung, and brother of Alberich, has found Sieglinda in the forest and has brough
the child which she died in giving birth to, knowing that he is destined to slay Fafner and gain the ring
he young Siegfried, dissatisfied with all swords made for him, melts up the fragments of his father's blade
Needful' and forges it afresh, to Mime's great awe.

ACT II. Mime induces Siegfried — under pretext of teaching him how to fear, an art which the youth
curious to learn — to accompany him to a distant part of the forest where Fafner in the shape of a huge
ragon, guards the Nibelung treasures, including the ring. Siegfried kills the dragon, but on accidentally
sting its blood, is enabled to understand the speech of birds. They tell him how Mime means to poison him
obtain the treasure; accordingly he kills the traitor. The bird further tells him of a fair sleeping bride
rrounded by fire, and flies before him to show the way to her resting place.

ACT III. Wotan uneasily wandering over the world conscious of impending doom, vainly seeks counse
Erda. Meeting Siegfried, he opposes his path, but the sword Needful hews his spear asunder, and, his
ower destroyed, he retreats to Valhalla to await the Dusk of the gods.
Siegfried, meanwhile, plunges through the fire, finds the Valkyrie, wakes her, woos her and wins ner

SIEGFRIED.

FIRST ACT.

A FOREST.

The foreground represents a portion of a rocky cave which extends inwards on the left, but occupies only three-fourths of the stage on the right. Two natural entrances open on to the wood; one, half-way up the stage, forms the back, the other, R, is wider and slanting at the side. On the left, against the wall stands a large smith's forge, naturally formed of stones, the bellows alone being artificial. The rough chimney — also natural — leads up through the top of the cave. A very large anvil and other smith's appliances.

MIME *(when, after a short orchestral prelude, the curtain rises is discovered sitting at the anvil, and hammering, with increasing discouragement, at a sword. At last he ceases work in despair).*

Forced undertaking!
Toil without fruit!
The stoutest sword
  that ever I shaped;
in a giant's fingers
  firm it were found;
but he whom 'tis forged **for,**
  the fiery stripling,
will strain and twist it in two
  as 'twere a straw or a toy.

(He throws the sword pettishly on the anvil, sets his arms a-kimbo, and gazes thoughtfully on the ground.)

There *is* a blade
  that were not so brittle:
"Needful's" fragments
  he'd fracture me ne'er;
could I but mend
  the mighty metal;
but all my craft
  cannot compass that.
Could I with cunning weld it
I should well be paid for my pains.

(He sinks more back and shakes his head thoughtfully.)

Fafner, the wicked worm,
  rests here in forest wilds;
with his frame of terrific weight
  o'er the Nibelung's gold
  guard doth he hold.
Siegfried's prowess unproved
may master e'en Fafner's might:
  the Nibelung Ring
  would rest then to me.
For this may serve but one sword;
now nought but "Needful" I need,
by Siegfried searchingly swung:—
  and I cannot shape me
  "Needful" the sword!—

(He recommences hammering, much discouraged.)

Forced undertaking!
Toil without fruit!

WALD.

Den Vordergrund bildet ein Theil einer Felsenhöhle die sich links tiefer nach innen zieht, nach rechts aber gegen drei Viertheile der Bühne einnimmt. Zwei natürlich gebildete Eingänge stehen dem Walde zu offen: der eine nach rechts, unmittelbar im Hintergrunde, der andere, breitere, ebenda seitwärts. An der Hinterwand, nach links zu, steht ein grosser Schmiedeherd, aus Felsstücken natürlich geformt; künstlich ist nur der grosse Blasebalg: die rohe Esse geht—ebenfalls natürlich—durch das Felsdach hinauf. Ein sehr grosser Ambos und andre Schmiedegeräthschaften.—

MIME *(sitzt, als der Vorhang nach einem kurzen Orchester-Vorspiel aufgeht, am Ambos, und hämmert mit wachsender Unruhe an einem Schwerte: endlich hält er unmuthig ein).*

Zwangvolle Plage!
Müh' ohne Zweck!
Das beste Schwert,
  das je ich geschweisst,
in der Riesen Fäusten
  hielte es fest:
doch dem ich's geschmiedet,
  der schmähliche Knabe,
er knickt und kneisst es entzwei,
  als schüf' ich Kindergeschmeid!—

(Er wirft das Schwert unmuthig auf den Ambos, stemmt die Arme ein und blickt sinnend zu Boden.)

Es giebt ein Schwert,
  das er nicht zerschwänge:
Nothung's Trümmer
  zertrotzt' er mir nicht,
könnt' ich die starken
  Stücken schweissen,
die meine Kunst
  nicht zu kitten weiss.
Könnt' ich's dem Kühnen schmieden,
meiner Schmach erlangt' ich da Lohn!—

(Er sinkt tiefer zurück, und neigt sinnend das Haupt.)

Fafner, der wilde Wurm,
  lagert im finst'ren Wald;
mit des furchtbaren Leibes Wucht
  der Niblungen Hort
  hütet er dort.
Siegfried's kindischer Kraft
erläge wohl Fafner's Leib:
  des Niblungen Ring
  erränge ich mir.
Ein Schwert nur taugt zu der That.
nur Nothung nützt meinem Neid,
wenn Siegfried sehrend ihn schwingt:
  und nicht kann ich's schweissen.
  Nothung das Schwert!—

(Er fährt in höchstem Unmuth wieder fort zu hämmern.)

Zwangvolle Plage!
Müh' ohne Zweck!

The stoutest sword
that ever I shaped
will ne'er be drawn
in the cause that I need.
I knock and I hammer
but at the boy's behest:
he'll bend and snap it in two,
yet scold me, should I not forge.

Das beste Schwert,
das je ich geschweisst,
nie taugt es je
zu der einz'gen That!
Ich tapp'r' und hämm're nur,
weil der Knab' es heischt:
er knickt und schmeisst es entzwei,
und schmählt doch, schmied' ich ihm nicht?

SIEGFRIED in a wild forest dress, with a silver horn ung by a chain, bursts impetuously from the wood. e has bridled a great bear with a bast rope, and ges it with merry roughness towards MIME, who drops e sword in terror, and flies behind the forge. SIEG-KIED drives the bear everywhere after him.

SIEGFRIED, in wilder Waldkleidung, mit einem silbernen Horn an einer Kette; kommt mit jähem Ungestüm aus dem Walde herein; er hat einen grossen Bären mit einem Bastseile gezäumt, und treibt diesen mit lustigem Uebermuthe gegen MIME an. MIME'N entsinkt vor Schreck das Schwert; er flüchtet hinter den Herd; SIEGFRIED treibt ihm den Bären überall nach.

MOTIVE OF SIEGFRIED, THE FEARLESS.

SIEGFRIED. Oho! Oho!
Come on! come on!
Tear him! tear him!
The trump'ry smith!
(*He shouts with laughter.*)

SIEGFRIED. Hoiho! Hoiho!
Hau' ein! Hau' ein!
Friss' ihn! Friss' ihn,
den Fratzenschmied!
(*Er lacht unbändig.*)

MIME. Take him away!
I want not the bear!

MIME. Fort mit dem Thier!
Was taugt mir der Bär!

SIEGFRIED. We come double
the better to cow you.
Bruin, ask for the sword

SIEGFRIED. Zu zwei komm' ich,
dich besser zu zwicken:
Brauner, frag' nach dem Schwert!

MIME. Ho! keep away!
I've cast the weapon
Fit and fairly to-day.

MIME. He! lass' das Wild!
Dort liegt die Waffe:
fertig fegt' ich sie heut'.

SIEGFRIED. So far you've saved then your skin.
He looses the bear from the rope and gives him a blow on the back with it.)
Run, Bruin;
your business is done!
(*The bear trots back into the wood.*)

SIEGFRIED. So fährst du heute noch heil!
(*Er löst dem Bären den Zaum, und giebt ihm damu einen Schlag auf den Rücken.*)
Lauf', Brauner:
dich brauch' ich nicht mehr!
(*Der Bär läuft in den Wald zurück.*)

MIME (*coming out trembling from behind the forge*).
I like it when
thou slayest bears;
why bringest living
that brute to me?

MIME (*zitternd hinter dem Herde vorkommend.*)
Wohl leid' ich's gern,
erleg'st du Bären:
was bringst du lebend
die braunen heim?

SIEGFRIED (*sitting down to recover from his laughter*).
For better companions pining
than the one at home appears,
to leafy woodland I hied,
while my horn I wound right loudly;
for I fain had discovered
a welcome friend; —
rang forth my notes with that aim.
From the bushes came a bear
who listened with brutish growl,
and I liked him better than you,
though better luck I'd have yet.
With a bast rope strong
I bridled him straight
to seek for my sword from this rascal.
(*He jumps up and goes towards the sword.*)

SIEGFRIED (*setzt sich, um sich vom Lachen zu erholen*)
Nach bess'rem Gesellen sucht' ich,
als daheim mir einer sitzt;
im tiefen Walde mein Horn
liess ich da hallend tönen:
ob sich froh mir gesellte
ein guter Freund?
das frug' ich mit dem Getön'.
Aus dem Busche kam ein Bär,
der hörte mir brummend zu;
er gefiel mir besser als du,
doch bess're wohl fänd' ich noch:
mit dem zähen Baste
zäumt' ich ihn da,
dich, Schelm, nach dem Schwerte zu fragen,
(*Er springt auf und geht nach dem Schwerte.*)

MIME (*taking up the sword to hand it to* SIEGFRIED).
I've shaped the weapon sharp;
With its sheen thou wilt be well pleased.

SIEGFRIED (*taking the sword*).
What purpose would have its shining
were the steel not hard of proof?
(*Tries it in his hand.*)
Hey! what an idle
toy is this!
This silly switch
call you a sword?
! *He beats it on the anvil till the pieces fly around.*
MIME *retreats in terror.*)

MIME (*erfasst das Schwert, es Siegfried zu reichen*).
Ich schuf die Waffe scharf,
ihrer Schneide wirst du dich freu n.

SIEGFRIED (*nimmt das Schwert*).
Was frommt seine helle Schneide
ist der Stahl nicht hart und fest?
(*Er prüft es mit der Hand.*)
Hei! was ist das
für müss'ger Tand!
Den schwachen Stift
nennst du ein Schwert?
(*Er zerschlägt es auf dem Ambos, dass die Stücke
ringsum fliegen:* MIME *weicht erschrocken aus.*)

MOTIVE OF SIEGFRIED THE IMPETUOUS.

Then there are the splinters,
scandalous sloven;
would I had smashed it
over your skull now!—
Shall such a liar
longer delude me?
Prating of giants,
of jousts and battles,
of bravest deeds
and of daring in war;
while weapons he smithies,
swords he shapes me,
praising his art
as if 'twere approved?
Yet when I handle
what he has hammered,
a single stroke
destroys all the trash!
Were he not, sure,
too scurvy a wight,
I would smithy and smite
the smith with his stuff,—
the ancient, imbecile imp!
My anger might then be allayed.
(*He throws himself raging on a stone-seat, R.*)

Da hast du die Stücken,
schändlicher Stümper:
hätt' ich am Schädel
dir sie zerschlagen!
Soll mich der Prahler
länger noch prellen?
Schwatzt mir von Riesen
und rüstigen Kämpfen,
von kühnen Thaten
und tüchtiger Wehr;
will Waffen mir schmieden,
Schwerte schaffen;
rühmt seine Kunst,
als könnt' er was Rechtes:
nehm' ich zur Hand nun
was er gehämmert,
mit einem Griff
zergreif' ich den Quark!—
Wär' mir nicht schier
zu schäbig der Wicht,
ich zerschmiedet' ihn selbst
mit seinem Geschmeid,
den alten albernen Alp!
Des Aergers dann hätt' ich ein End'
(*Er wirft sich wüthend auf eine Steinbank, zur Sei
rechts.*)

MIME (*who has cautiously kept his distance*).
Now ravest thou in a rage!
What gross ingratitude!
This over-bearing boy
if he gets not *all* the best,
the good things I have giv'n
are each and all forgot.
Wilt thou then never think of
what I have said on thanking?
Thou should'st delight to obey him
who's shewn thee love for so long.

MIME (*der ihn immer vorsichtig ausgewichen*).
Nun tob'st du wieder wie toll:
dein Undank, traun! ist arg.
Mach' ich dem bösen Buben
nicht alles gleich zu best,
was ich Gutes ihm schuf,
vergisst er gar zu schnell!
Willst du denn nie gedenken
was ich dich lehrt' vom Danke?
Dem sollst du willig gehorchen,
der je sich wohl dir erwies.

SIEGFRIED *sulkily turns his back on him and remains
with his face to the wall.*)
Thou'rt loth to listen to my blaming!
But spurn not food at least.
Yon spit shall render its roast meat;
or say, would'st thou like the soup?
For thee it simmers long.
Brings food to SIEGFRIED, *who, without turning,
strikes pot and meat out of his hand.*)

(SIEGFRIED *wendet sich unmuthig um, mit dem Gesic
nach der Wand, so dass er ihm den Rücken kehrt.*)
Das willst du wieder nicht hören!—
Doch speisen magst du wohl?
Vom Spiesse bring' ich den Braten:
versuchtest du gern den Sud?
Für dich sott ich ihn gar.
(*Er bietet* SIEGFRIED *Speise hin. Dieser, ohne s
umzuwenden, schmeisst ihm Topf und Braten aus
Hand.*)

SIEGFRIED. Meals I make for myself:
    you can swill your slop alone !

MIME (*appearing much hurt*).
    This is my affection's
    foul reward !
    This my toil's
    disgraceful return!
    A querulous brat
    kindly I reared,
    wrapped in warm linen
    the little wretch:
    water and food
    for thee I found,
    looked upon thee
    as my very life.
    And when thou didst wax
    I waited on thee;
    in care for thy slumber
    a couch made soft.
    I shaped for thee toys,
    and a tuneful horn;
    e'er at thy whim
    willingly worked:
    with cunning redes
    I read thee all craft,
    with subtle wisdom
    sharpened thy wits.
    Moping at home
    I toil and moil,
    while heedless from me
    thou dost hie.
    For thee do I plague me,
    take pains but for thee;
    so dwindle my powers
    —a poor old dwarf ! —
    For all my worry
    is this my reward,
    from the hot-headed boy
    but abuse and hate!
    (*He bursts into a fit of sobbing.*)

SIEGFRIED (*who has again turned round and gazed
    steadily in* MIME'S *face*).
    Much you've taught to me, Mime,
    and many tales have you told;
    but what you would like best to teach me
    were lesson I'd lief let be:—
    how not to loathe your sight.
    Bread do you bring,
    refreshment withal,
    disgust I feed on alone.
    Spread you my couch
    with comforts for sleep —
    then slumber wends from my side:
    when all my wits
    you work to instruct
    I would be deaf and dumb.
    Soon as I open
    my eyes on you
    but evil I see there
    whatever you do.
    Seeing you stand
    shambling and shaking,
    shrinking and slinking,
    with your eyelids blinking, —
    by the neck I'd take
    and shake and wake you,
    your idiot antics
    to end forever!—
    Such feelings, Mime, I foster.
    If you have wisdom

SIEGFRIED. Braten briet ich mir selbst:
    deinen Sudel sauf' allein!

MIME (*stellt sich empfindlich*).
    Das ist nun der Liebe
    schlimmer Lohn!
    Das der Sorgen
    schmählicher Sold!—
    Als zullendes Kind
    zog ich dich auf,
    wärmte mit Kleiden
    den kleinen Wurm:
    Speise und Trank
    trug ich dir zu,
    hütete dich
    wie die eig'ne Haut.
    Und wie du erwuchsest,
    wartet' ich dein;
    dein Lager schuf ich,
    dass leicht du schlief'st.
    Dir schmiedet' ich **Tand**
    und ein tönend Horn;
    dich zu erfreu'n
    müht' ich mich froh:
    mit klugem Rathe
    rieth ich dir klug,
    mit lichtem Wissen
    lehrt' ich dich Witz.
    Sitz' ich daheim
    in Fleiss und Schweiss,
    nach Herzenslust
    schweif'st du umher:
    für dich nur in Plage,
    in Pein nur für dich
    verzehr' ich mich alter
    armer Zwerg!
    Und aller Lasten
    ist das nun der Lohn,
    dass der hastige Knabe
    mich quält und hasst!
    (*Er geräth in Schluchzen.*)

SIEGFRIED (*der sich wieder umgewendet, und in* MIME'S
    Blick ruhig geforscht hat).
    Vieles lehrtest du, Mime,
    und manches lernt' ich von dir;
    doch was du am liebsten mich lehrtest
    zu lernen gelang mir nie:—
    wie ich dich leiden könnt'.—
    Träg'st du mir Speise
    und Trank herbei —
    der Ekel speis't mich allein;
    schaff'st du ein leichtes
    Lager zum Schlaf—
    der Schlummer wird mir da schwer.
    willst du mich weisen
    witzig zu sein—
    gern bleib' ich taub und dumm.
    Seh' ich dir erst
    mit den Augen zu,
    zu übel erkenn' ich
    was alles du thu'st:
    seh' ich dich steh'n,
    gangeln und geh'n,
    knicken und nicken,
    mit den Augen zwicken:
    beim Genick' möcht' ich
    den Nicker packen,
    den Garaus geben
    dem garst'gen Zwicker!—
    So lernt' ich, Mime, dich leiden.
    Bist du nun weise,

then rede me wisely
a thing I have pored upon. —
When I scour forests
seeking to fly you,
what motive makes me return?
Not a beast but I love
better than you;
bird in forest,
or fish in the brook,
dearer than you
I deem all of these:—
what motive then makes me return?
If you've mind, then tell it me.

MIME (*sits affectionately a little way from* SIEGFRIED).
My son, this clearly shews thee
how closely thy heart to me clings.

SIEGFRIED (*laughing*). But I cannot endure you, —
forget not that indeed.

MIME.   This is but thy wilful way,
which were quickly quelled at will.
Young ones are ever yearning,
needing the parent nest;
Love's the name of this longing:
such leaning thou hast to me,
this love thou dost feel for thy Mime.
Thou *must* surely love him!
What the father is to the fledgling
which in the nest it nursed
ere in flight it could flutter,
such to thee, foolish child,
is faithful, cherishing Mime.
Thou must be his charge.

SIEGFRIED.   Hey, Mime, since you're so clever,
explain me this also clearly. —

so hilf mir wissen,
worüber umsonst ich sann:—
in den Wald lauf' ich,
dich zu verlassen,—
wie kommt das, kehr' ich zurück?
Alle Thiere sind
mir theurer als du:
Baum und Vogel,
die Fische im Bach,
lieber mag ich sie
leiden als dich:—
wie kommt das nun, kehr' ich zurück?
Bist du klug, so thu' mir's kund.

MIME (*setzt sich in einiger Entfernung ihm traulich gegenüber*).
Mein Kind, das lehrt dich kennen,
wie lieb ich am Herzen dir lieg'.

SIEGFRIED (*lacht*).
Ich kann dich ja nicht leiden, —
vergiss das nicht so leicht!

MIME.   Dess' ist deine Wildheit schuld,
die du Böser bändigen sollst. —
Jammernd verlangen Junge
nach ihrer Alten Nest;
Liebe ist das Verlangen:
so lechzest du auch nach mir,
so lieb'st du auch deinen Mime—
so musst du ihn lieben!
Was dem Vögelein ist der Vogel,
wenn er im Nest es nährt,
eh' das flügge mag fliegen:
das ist dir kindischem Spross
der kundig sorgende Mime —
das muss er dir sein.

SIEGFRIED.   Ei, Mime bist du so witzig,
so lass' mich eines noch wissen!—

THE MOTIVE OF LOVE LIFE.

The birds in the spring-time
so bravely did sing,
the one beseeching the other:
you said yourself,
when I asked of it,
these warblers husband and wife were.
They kissed with such pleasure
and parted them ne'er,
they built them a nest

Es sangen die Vöglein
so selig im Lenz,
das eine lockte das and're·
du sagtest selbst—
da ich's wissen wollt'—
das wären Männchen und Weibchen.
Sie kos'ten so lieblich,
und liessen sich nicht;
sie bauten ein Nest

and brooded therein;
then fluttered anon
the young fledglings out,
and both took care of the brood.
So duly reposed
the deer which had paired,
e'en wolves and foxes the wildest:
food the male
for the family furnished,
the cubs were nursed by his consort.
I learnt from this
what love must be;
the whelps I ne'er moved
from the mother's side. —
Where have you, Mime,
your minikin consort
that I may call her mother?

MIME (*angrily*).   Art thou a fool?
What is't to thee?
Art thou either fowl or fox?

SIEGFRIED.   A querulous brat
kindly you reared,
wrapped in warm linen
the little wretch: —
how came you, then,
by this clamouring wretch?
D'ye mean that I was
without mother made?

MIME (*much embarrassed*).   Only trust
Whatever I tell thee;
I am thy father
and mother in one.

SIEGFRIED.   You lie! perfidious fool! —
That the young one is like the parent
long since have I proved for myself.
I came to the crystal brook
and could trace bird and beast
within its mirror;
mist and sunlight,
seen as they are,
the faithful reflex of their form.
My own pictured image
I also saw;
unlike yourself
surely I seemed;
as 'twere to compare
with a toad a bright fish;
a fish ne'er had toad for a father.

MIME (*much vexed*).   Terrible stuff
thou tattlest still.

SIEGFRIED (*with increasing animation*).
See now, I vow
myself I've found
what in vain I so long have sought:
when from you I fly
to roam in the forest
how it haps home I return.
(*He springs up.*)
It is to make you inform me
what father and mother are mine.

MIME (*retreating from him*).
What father? What mother?
Meaningless fancies!

SIEGFRIED (*seizing him by the throat*).
Then must I enforce you
some truth to tell me:
good temper
will further me nought.

und brüteten drin:
da flatterte junges
Geflügel auf,
und beide pflegten der Brut.
So ruhten im Busch
auch Rehe gepaart,
selbst wilde Füchse und Wölfe:
Nahrung brachte
zum Nest das Männchen,
das Weibchen säugte die Welpen.
Da lernt' ich wohl
was Liebe sei;
der Mutter entwandt' ich
die Welpen nie.—
Wo hast du nun, Mime,
dein minniges Weibchen,
dass ich es Mutter nenne?

MIME (*verdriesslich*).
Was ist dir, Thor?
Ach, bist du dumm!
Bist doch weder Vogel noch Fuchs?

SIEGFRIED.   Das zullende Kind
zogest du auf,
wärmtest mit Kleiden
den kleinen Wurm:—
wie kam dir aber
der kindishce Wurm?
Du machtest wohl gar
ohne Mutter mich?

MIME (*in grosser Verlegenheit*).
Glauben sollst du,
was ich dir sage:
ich bin dir Vater
und Mutter zugleich.

SIEGFRIED.   Da lügst du, garstiger Gauch!
Wie die Jungen den Alten gleichen,
das hab' ich mir glücklich erseh'n.
Nun kam ich zum klaren Bach:
da erspäht' ich die Bäum'
und Thier' im Spiegel;
Sonn' und Wolken,
wie sie nur sind,
im Glitzer erschienen sie gleich.
Da sah' ich denn auch
mein eigen Bild;
ganz anders als du
dünkt' ich mir da:
so glich wohl der Kröte
ein glänzender Fisch;
doch kroch nie ein Fisch aus der Kröte.

MIME (*höchst ärgerlich*).
Gräulichen Unsinn
kram'st du da aus!

SIEGFRIED (*immer lebendiger*).
Sieh'st du, nun fällt
auch selbst mir ein,
was zuvor ich umsonst besann:
wenn zum Wald ich laufe,
dich zu verlassen,
wie das kommt, kehr' ich doch hein,
(*Er springt auf.*)
Von dir noch muss ich erfahren,
wer Vater und Mutter mir sei!

MIME (*weicht ihm aus*).
Was Vater! was Mutter!
Müssige Frage!

SIEGFRIED (*packt ihn bei der Kehle*).
So muss ich dich fassen
um 'was zu wissen:
gutwillig
erfahr' ich doch nichts!

I must by force
fulfil my wishes:
scarcely language
should I have learned
if not wrested from you,
wretch, by main strength !
So tell me now, rascally knave,
who are my father and mother ?

MIME (*who has signed with his head and hands for*
SIEGFRIED *to release him*).
My life thou nearly hast crushed! —
Let loose! what thou wishest to know
I'll tell thee, now — without wile. —
O thankless
and unthinking boy !
Now hear for what thou dost hate me!
I am no father
nor flesh of thine;
yet owest thou all to my aid.
No kin art of mine
who yet am so kind;
out of goodness have I
guarded thy life.
My love is preciously paid!
Did I look for tender return ?
A poor woman lay wailing
once in yon woodland wild:
I helped her home to this hole,
and gave my hearth for a haven.
Of child proved she in labour;
pining she bore it here;
deep anguish harried her,
I helped her as best I could.
Baleful her lot, — she died,
but Siegfried saw the light.

SIEGFRIED (*who has seated himself*).
So died then my mother of me ?

MIME.
To my charge she confided thee:
I cherished fain the babe.
What work for Mime thou mad'st!
What woes the poor wight has endured!
A querulous brat
kindly I reared ...

SIEGFRIED. Me-seems you have said that before.
Now say, who did name me Siegfried ?

MIME. Anon said thy mother
must I so name thee:
as Siegfried thou didst grow
staunch and strong. —
I wrapped in warm linen
the little wretch ...

SIEGFRIED.
Now, Mime, what name bore my mother ?

MIME. In sooth I scarcely know. —
Water and food
for thee I found ...

SIEGFRIED. Her title instantly tell me!

MIME. 'Tis haply forgot! — Yet hold!
Sieglinde certainly hight she
who gave thee sadly to me. —
I looked upon thee
as my very life ...

SIEGFRIED. Now tell me my father's title.

MIME (*harshly*). His face I never saw.

SIEGFRIED.
But his name my mother has mentioned ?

So musst' ich **Alles**
ab dir trotzen:
kaum das Reden
hätt' ich errathen,
entwand ich's nicht
mit Gewalt dem **Schuft!**
Heraus damit,
räudiger Kerl!
Wer ist mir Vater und Mutter?

MIME (*nachdem er mit dem Kopfe genickt und mit den
Händen gewinkt, ist von* SIEGFRIED *losgelassen worden*).
An's Leben geh'st du mir schier!—
Nun lass'! was zu wissen dich geizt,
erfahr' es, ganz wie ich's weiss. —
O undankbares,
arges Kind!
jetzt hör', wofür du mich hassest!
Nicht bin ich Vater
noch Vetter dir. —
und dennoch verdankst du mir **dich!**
Ganz fremd bist du mir,
deinem einz'gen Freund;
aus Erbarmen allein
barg ich dich hier:
nun hab' ich lieblichen Lohn!
Was verhofft' ich Thor mir auch **Dank?**
Einst lag wimmernd ein Weib
da draussen im wilden Wald:
zur Höhle half ich ihr her,
am warmen Herd sie zu hüten.
Ein Kind trug sie im Schoss;
traurig gebar sie's hier;
sie wand sich hin und her,
ich half so gut ich konnt':
stark war die Noth, sie starb —
doch Siegfried, der genas.

SIEGFRIED (*hat sich gesetzt*).
So starb meine Mutter an mir?

MIME.
Meinem Schutz übergab sie dich:
ich schenkt' ihn gern dem Kind.
Was hat sich Mime gemüht!
was gab sich der Gute für Noth!
Als zullendes Kind
zog ich dich auf . . .

SIEGFRIED. Mich dünkt, dess' gedachtest du schon.
Jetzt sag:' woher heiss' ich Siegfried?

MIME. So hiess mich die Mutter
möcht' ich dich heissen:
als Siegfried würdest
du stark und schön.—
Ich wärmte mit Kleiden
den kleinen Wurm . . .

SIEGFRIED. Nun melde, wie hiess meine **Mutter?**

MIME. Das weiss ich wahrlich kaum!—
Speise und Trank
trug ich dir zu . . .

SIEGFRIED. Den Namen sollst du mir nennen!

MIME. Entfiel er mir wohl? doch halt!
Sieglinde mochte sie heissen,
die dich in Sorge mir gab.—
Ich hütete dich
wie die eig'ne Haut . . .

SIEGFRIED. Dann frag' ich, wie hiess mein **Vater?**

MIME (*barsch*).
Den hab' ich nie geseh'n.

SIEGFRIED. Doch die Mutter nannte den Namen?

MIME. That some one slew him, she said, and no more; thee, fatherless, she confided to me. — And when thou didst wax I waited on thee, in care for thy slumber thy couch made soft...	**MIME.** Erschlagen sei er, das sagte sie nur; dich Vaterlosen befahl sie mir da:— und wie du erwuchsest, wartet' ich dein' dein Lager schuf ich, dass leicht du schlief'st . . .
SIEGFRIED. Stint with that endless starling note! — Shall I believe your tidings, and think you not a liar, then let me see a sign.	**SIEGFRIED.** Still mit dem alten Staarenlied!— Soll ich der Kunde glauben, hast du mir nichts gelogen, so lass mich nun Zeichen seh'n!
MIME. How shall I then assure thee?	**MIME.** Was soll dir's noch bezeugen?
SIEGFRIED. I trust you not with my ears, I trust in nought but my eyes: what witness will you bring?	**SIEGFRIED.** Dir glaub' ich nicht mit dem Ohr, dir glaub' ich nur mit dem Aug': welch' Zeichen zeugt für dich?
MIME (*after some hesitation, brings forward the two pieces of a broken sword*). This had I of thy mother; for menage, toil and trouble, was it my scant reward. See here, but a broken sword! She said thy father had swung it at the fight in which he was felled.	**MIME** (*holt nach einigem Besinnen die zwei Stücke eines zerschlagenen Schwertes herbei*). Das gab mir deine Mutter: für Mühe, Kost und Pflege liess sie's als schwachen Lohn. Sieh' her, ein zerbroch'nes Schwert! Dein Vater, sagte sie, führt' es, als im letzten Kampf er erlag.
SIEGFRIED. And you shall forge now for me the fragments; I'll find so my right defence! Up! arm yourself, Mime! Move and be brisk! Can you be brave? Then show me your craft! Playthings no more on me impose: these pieces alone promise to serve. If you should fail, forge it amiss, find I a flaw in the faultless steel, — you, fumbler, finely I'll beat; — you'll feel the burnish yourself! This day will I surely wield my own sword; I'll win me this weapon at once.	**SIEGFRIEE.** Und diese Stücken sollst du mir schmieden: dann schwing' ich mein rechtes Schwert. Eile dich, Mime, mühe dich rasch; kannst du 'was Recht's. nun zieg' deine Kunst! Täusche mich nicht mit schlechtem Tand: den Trümmern allein tau' ich 'was zu. Find' ich dich faul, füg'st du sie schlecht, flick'st du mit Flausen den festen Stahl,— dir Feigem fahr' ich zu Leib, das Fegen lernst du von mir! Denn heute noch, schwör' ich will ich das Schwert; die Waffe gewinn' ieh noch heut'.
MIME (*frightened*). What would'st thou to-day with the sword?	**MIME** (*erschrocken*). Was willst du noch heut' mit dem Schwer'
SIEGFRIED. In the wide world I will wander, never more to return. What a full joy to have freedom! nothing anchors me here. My father art thou not; I shall find another home! thy hearth is not my house, ne'er I'll rest beneath thy roof. As the fish fain through the flood shoots, as the finch flies to a free shore; far hence I flee, flow like a stream; with the wind o'er the woods wafting away, — then, Mime, ne'er will I return. (*He rushes away into the woods.*)	**SIEGFRIED.** Aus dem Wald fort in die Welt zieh'n: nimmer kehr' ich zurück. Wie ich froh bin, dass ich frei ward, nichts mich bindet und zwingt! Mein Vater bist du nicht; in der Ferne bin ich heim; dein Herd ist nicht mein Haus, meine Decke nicht dein Dach. Wie der Fisch froh in der Fluth schwimmt, wie der Fink frei sich davon schwingt: flieg' ich von hier, fluthe davon, wie der Wind über'n Wald weh' ich dahin— dich, Mime, nie wieder zu seh'n! (*Er stürmt in den Wald fort.*)
MIME (*in great alarm*). Halt there! halt there! what ho!	**MIME** (*in höchster Angst*). Halte! halte! wohin?

(He calls with his utmost strength toward the wood.

Ho! Siegfried!
Siegfried! Ho!
He hurls away,
and here I sit. —
To old distress
comes added trouble;
entangled wholly am I! —
What help can I find
Howhandle him best?
How force him to hasten
to Fafner's nest?
How forge me these stivers
of stubbornest steel?
For no furnace heat
helps me to fuse them,
no kobold's hammer
conquers their hardness,
By Niblung's annoy,
need and sweat,
"Needful" can ne'er be knit;
Mime cannot mend the sword.
*(He crouches down despairingly on his stool behind
the anvil.)*

(Er ruft mit der grössten Anstrengung in den Wald.

Ho! Siegfried!
Siegfried! He! —
Da stürmt er hin! —
Nun sitz' ich da: —
zur alten Noth
hab' ich die neue!
vernagelt bin ich nun ganz! —
Wie helf' ich mir jetzt?
Wie halt' ich ihn fest?
Wie führ' ich den Huien
zu Fafner's Nest?
Wie füg' ich die Stücken
des tückischen Stahl's?
Keines Ofens Gluth
glüht mir die ächten!
keines Zwergen Hammer
zwingt mir die harten;
des Niblungen Neid,
Noth und Schweiss
nietet mir Nothung nicht,
schweisst mir das Schwert nicht zu ganz! —
*(Er knickt verzweifelnd auf dem Schemel hinter dem
Ambos zusammen.)*

MOTIVE REPRESENTING WOTAN AS THE WANDERER.

The WANDERER (WOTAN) *advances from the wood
to the back entrance of the cave. He wears a long,
dark blue cloak, and bears a spear as a staff. On his
head is a large hat with a broad, round brim hanging
low over his missing eye.*

WANDERER.   Hail thee, wisest smith!
     To way-wearied guest
       grant as host
       thy house and hearth.

MIME (*starting up in terror*).
     By whom in this woodland
       wild am I sought?
   Who has tracked me to this retreat?

WANDERER.   "Wanderer" calls me the world:
     wide wanderings I've made;
       all the earth around
       I roam at my will.

MIME.   Then roam on thy way
       and rest thee not here,
   or no Wanderer thou wert.

WANDERER.   Good men render me a greeting,
   gifts they grant to me withal;
       for ever misers
       have evil ends.

MIME.   Evil weighs
       for ever on me;
   would'st to my anguish augment it?

Der WANDERER (WOTAN) *tritt aus dem Wald an
das hintere Thor der Höhle heran.— Er trägt einen
dunkelblauen langen Mantel; einen Speer führt er als
Stab. Auf dem Haupte hat er einen grossen Hut mit
breiter runder Krämpe, die über das fehlende eine
Auge tief hereinhängt.*

WANDERER.   Heil dir, weiser Schmied!
     Dem wegmüden Gast
       gönne hold
       des Hauses Herd!

MIME (*ist erschrocken aufgefahren*).
     Wer ist's, der im wilden
       Wald mich sucht?
   Wer verfolgt mich im öden Forst?

WANDERER.   Wand'rer heisst mich die Welt
     weit wandert' ich schon,
       auf der Erde Rücken
       rührt' ich mich viel.

MIME.   So rühre dich fort
       und raste nicht hier,
   heisst dich Wand'rer die Welt.

WANDERER.   Gastlich ruht' ich bei Guten,
     Gaben gönnten mir viele:
       denn Unheil fürchtet,
       wer unhold ist.

MIME.   Unheil wohnte
       immer bei mir:
   willst du dem Armen es mehren?

WANDERER (*advancing closer*).
Much I've mastered
and treasured much;
wondrous tales
to men I've told,
from many warded
what dismayed them, —
torturing heart's distress.

MIME.
Spyest thou well,
and spae-est thou truth,
I want ne'er a spy nor a spae-wright.
Solitary
I seek to bide,
loungers I leave to their list.

WANDERER (*again approaching a few steps nearer*).
Men have weened
their wisdom was great,
but what should boot them
wist not their brains.
What was goodly
straightway I gave them;
spake, and strengthened their minds.

MIME (*terrified at the approach of the* WANDERER).
Useless matters
many yearn for;
for me my craft doth suffice.
I've sufficient wit,
I want no more;
so, wise one, wend on thy way.

WANDERER (*seating himself at the hearth*).
Here gaining thy hearth,
I gage thee my head
as stake in struggle of wits.
My head is thine,
'twill fall to thy hand
if vainly thou ask
my advice, —
should I not save it by wit.

MIME (*aside, frightened and perplexed*).
How shall I be rid of this rogue?
In trial must I entrap him. —
(*Aloud.*)
Thy head staking
'gainst my hearth,
with care and cunning redeem it.
Three the questions
that I require.

WANDERER. Three times I must answer.

MIME (*after some reflection*).
Thy rovings have led thee
to earth's far regions,
thou hast wandered widely o'er worlds :—
now, rede me aright,
what is the race
born in the earth's deep bowels?

WANDERER. In the earth's deep bowels
burrow the Nibelungs:
Nibelheim is their land.
Black elves are they all;
Black Alberich
guarded and governed them once.
By the mighty spell
of a magical ring
he moved the industrious dwarfs.
Endless riches,
rarest of hoards
he made them heap   [him.
therewith all the world should be won
Propose, dwarf, thy second point.

WANDERER (*weiter hereintretend*.
Viel erforscht' ich,
erkannte viel:
Wichtiges konnt' ich
manchem künden,
manchem wehren
was ihn mühte,
nagende Herzens-Noth.

MIME.
Spürtest du klug
und erspähtest viel,
hier brauch' ich nicht Spürer noch Späher,
Einsam will ich
und einzeln sein,
Lungerern lass' ich den Lauf.

WANDERER (*wieder einige Schritte näher schreitend*)
Mancher wähnte
weise zu sein,
nur was ihm noth that
wusst' er nicht;
was ihm frommte,
liess ich erfragen:
lohnend lehrt' ihn mein Wort.

MIME (*immer ängstlicher, da der* WANDERER *sich nähert*).
Müss'ges Wissen
wahren manche:
ich weiss mir grade genug;
mir genügt mein Witz,
ich will nicht mehr:
dir Weisem weis' ich den Weg!

WANDERER (*setzt sich am Herde nieder*).
Hier sitz' ich am Herd,
und setze mein Haupt
der Wissens-Wette zum Pfand:
mein Kopf ist dein,
du hast ihn erkies't,
erfrägst du dir nicht
was dir frommt,
lös' ich's mit Lehren nicht ein.

MIME (*erschrocken und befangen, für sich*).
Wie werd' ich den Lauernden los?
Verfänglich muss ich ihn fragen.—
(*Laut.*)
Dein Haupt pfänd' ich
für den Herd:
nun sorg', es sinnig zu lösen!
Drei der Fragen
stell' ich mir frei.

WANDERER. Dreimal muss ich's treffen.
MIME (*nach einigem Nachsinnen*).
Du rührtest dich viel
auf der Erde Rücken,
die Welt durchwandert'st du weit;
nun sage mir schlau,
welches Geschlecht
tagt in der Erde Tiefe?

WANDERER. In der Erde Tiefe
tagen die Nibelungen:
Nibelheim ist ihr Land.
Schwarzalben sind sie;
Schwarz-Alberich
hütet' als Herrscher sie einst:
eines Zauberringes
zwingende Kraft
zähmt' ihm das fleissige Volk.
Reicher Schätze
schimmernden Hort
häuften sie ihm:
der sollte die Welt ihm gewinnen. —
Zum zweiten was frägst du Zwerg?

MIME (*in a brown study*).
Much, Wanderer,
wottest thou
of the earth's most central cells —
Now say to me sooth,
what is the stock
which on its back sojourneth?

WANDERER. On its back the giants
live, an ungentle stock;
Giantdom is their land.
Fasolt and Fafner,
the jealous feoffers,
envied Alberich's might,
and his wonderful hoard
they won for themselves,
and ravished also the ring.
Between the brothers
then broke out strife,
and, Fasolt fall'n,
as dragon dread
holdeth now Fafner the hoard.—
Thy third enquiry now threats.

MIME (*who is quite absorbed in thought*).
Much, Wanderer,
wottest thou
of the earth's far stretching surface.
Now rede me as well
what is the race
wards the welkin above?

WANDERER. The welkin above
ward well the Æsir;
where they dwell is Valhall'.
Light elves of heaven,
Light Alberich,
Wotan, wardeth their host.
From the World's ash-tree's
worshipful arm
he shaped himself once a shaft:
true that spear,
though the tree may be spoiled,
with such a sceptre
Wotan sways the world.
Holiest treaties'
truthful runes
he wrote all around the shaft.
The head of worlds
he, by whose hand
is the spear gripped,
that Wotan's grasp now spans.
There kneels to him
The Niblung host;
the giants must bow,
by him enjoined:
all must allegiance owe him,
the spear's resistless lord.
(*He rests his spear, as if accidentally, on the ground; a slight peal of thunder is heard.   MIME terrified.*)
Now tell me, sapient dwarf,
spaed I the answers true?
My head do I hold my own?

MIME (*who has recovered from his dreamy brooding, now shows renewed fear and dares not look at the Wanderer*).
Questions and head
hast thou redeemed:—
now, Wanderer, go thy way.

WANDERER. What thy welfare concerns
thou should'st have sought for
holding in pledge thus my head.

MIME (*in tieferer Sinnen gerathend*)
Viel, Wanderer,
weisst du mir
aus der Erde Nabelnest:—
nun sage mir schlicht,
·   welches Geschlecht
ruht auf der Erde Rücken?

WANDERER. Auf der Erde Rücken
wuchtet der Riesen Geschiecht:
Riesenheim ist ihr Land.
Fasolt und Fafner,
der rauhen Fürsten,
neideten Nibelung's Macht;
den gewaltigen Hort
gewannen sie sich,
errangen mir ihm den Ring:
um den entbrannte
den Brüdern Streit;
der Fasolt fällte,
als wilder Wurm
hütet nun Fafner den Hort.—
Die dritte Frage nun droht.

MIME (*der ganz in Träumerei entrückt ist*).
Viel, Wand'rer,
weisst du mir
von der Erde rauhem Rücken:—
nun sage mir wahr,
welches Geschlecht
wohnt auf wolkigen Höh'n?

WANDERER. Auf wolkigen Höh'n
wohnen die Götter:
Walhall heisst ihr Saal.
Lichtalben sind sie;
Licht-Alberich,
Wotan, waltet der Schaar.
Aus der Welt-Esche
weihlichstem Aste
schuf er sich einen Schaft:
dorrt der Stamm,
nie verdirbt doch der Speer;
mit seiner Spitze
sperrt Wotan die Welt.
Heil'ger Verträge
Treue-Runen
schnitt in den Schaft er ein.
Den Haft der Welt
hält in der Hand,
wer den Speer führt,
den Wotan's Faust umspannt
Ihm neigte sich
der Niblungen Heer;
der Riesen Gezücht
zähmte sein Rath:
ewig gehorchen sie alle
des Speeres starkem Herrn.
(*Er stösst wie unwillkürlich mit dem Speer auf den Boden ; ein leiser Donner lässt sich vernehmen, wovon MIME heftig erschrickt.*)
Nun rede, weiser Zwerg:
wusst' ich der Fragen Rath?
behalte mein Haupt ich frei?

MIME (*is aus seiner träumerischen Versunkenheit aufgefahren, und gebärdet sich nun ängstlich, indem er den Wanderer nicht anzublicken wagt*).
Fragen und Haupt
hast du gelös't:
nun, Wand'rer, geh' deines Weg's?

WANDERER. Was zu wissen dir frommt
solltest du fragen;
Kunde verbürgte mein Kopf.—

Since thou hast **not weened** what is good, **we'll** gamble with thy head as gage. Greeting thou grudgedst thy guest; my head I gave into thy hands. **that** of thy hearth I might be free; so now in pledge placed is thine own, can'st thou not thrice my riddles declare. Make resolute, Mime, thy mind.	dass du nun **nicht weisst** was dir nützt, dess' fass' ich jetzt deines als **Pfand.** Gastlich nicht galt mir dein Gruss: mein Haupt gab ich in deine Hand, um mich des Herdes zu freu'n. Nach Wettens Pflicht pfänd' ich nun dich, lösest du drei der Fragen nicht leicht: drum frische dir, Mime, den Muth.

THE MOTIVE OF MIME COWED AND SUBMISSIVE.

ME (*shyly, and with cowed submission*). Long I've quitted my native land, long I've issued from my mother earth, the eye-glance of Wotan cows me, he peereth into my cave; his gaze melts all my mother wit. But quick must my wisdom be **now.** — Wanderer, question away! Belike may I redeem me, deliver the dwarf's poor head.	MIME (*schüchtern und in furchtsamer Ergebung*). Lang' schon mied ich mein Heimathland, lang' schon schied ich aus der Mutter Schoss; mir leuchtete Wotan's Auge, zur Höhle lugt' es herein: vor ihm magert mein Mutterwitz. Doch frommt mir's nun weise zu **sein** Wand'rer, frage denn zu! Vielleicht glückt' mir's gezwungen zu lösen des Zwergen Haupt.
ANDERER. Now, amiable dwarf, first let me ask you: what is that noble race that Wotan ruthlessly dealt with, and which yet he deemeth most dear ?	WANDERER. Nun, ehrlicher Zwerg, sag, mir zum ersten: welches ist das Geschlecht, dem Wotan schlimm sich zeigt, und das doch das liebste ihm **lebt?**
ME. Of your heroes I hear but little; yet certainly this I can solve. The Volsungs are they, the valued race that Wotan fathered and fondly loved, **though** favour he did withdraw. Siegmund and Sieglind' sprang from the Volsung, a very turbulent twin-born pair; Siegfried too is their son, the stoutest Volsung e'er shaped. My head then, Wanderer, this time do I hold ?	MIME. Wenig hört' ich von Heldensippen: der Frage doch mach' ich mich **frei.** Die Wälsungen sind das Wunschgeschlecht, das Wotan zeugte und zärtlich liebt, zeigt er auch Ungunst ihm. Siegmund und Sieglind' stammten von Wälse, ein wild-verzweifeltes Zwillingspaar: Siegfried zeugten sie selbst. den stärksten Wälsungenspross. Behalt' ich, Wanderer, zum ersten mein Haupt?
ANDERER. Aye, thou hast rightly declared me the race: clearly proved is thy prowess ! The primal question hast thou quit; so, secondly hear and say. — A wily Niblung wardeth Siegfried, — fated slayer of Fafner, that the ring he may ravish and hold the hoard for himself. But what sword must Siegfried then strike with dealing Fafner death ?	WANDERER. Wie doch genau das Geschlecht du mir nennst: schlau eracht' ich dich Argen! Der ersten Frage ward'st du frei: zum zweiten nun sag' mir, Zwerg:— Ein weiser Niblung wahret Siegfried: Fafner'n soll er ihm fällen, dass er den Ring erränge, des Hortes Herrscher zu sein. Welches Schwert muss nun Siegfried schwingen, taug' es zu Fafner's Tod?

MIME (*forgetting his present position in his eager interest in the subject*).
  " Needful " is
the name of the sword;
'twas in an ash-tree's stem
  struck by Wotan:
he solely might own it
whose hand could snatch it out.
  By strongest heroes
  was it not stirred;
  Siegmund, the warlike:
  won the prize:
well he wore it in strife,
till by Wotan's spear it was split.
  Now, a subtle smith
  doth preserve the shreds,
  for he wots with no other
than Wotan's sword
that bold and foolish boy,
Siegfried, will slay the worm.
  (*Quite pleased.*)
  Thus have I saved
  a scond time my head !

WANDERER. The wittiest, surely,
  art thou of wise ones;
whose cunning can come near thine ?
  But since thou hast sought
  this simpleton hero
for Niblung's need to make use of,
  now my third inquiry
  threatens thee.—
  Say then, thou wisest
  weapon-smith,
who will from the stubborn splinters
" Needful," the sword, re-establish ?

MIME (*starts up in the greatest terror*).
  The splinters ! the sword !
  Alas ! it 'scapes me !—
  What can I say ?
  What course pursue ?
  The cursed steel,
  would I ne'er had stol'n it !
To be thus entangled
  in fatal toils !
'Tis far too hard
  to yield to my hammer;
  flux and solder
  serve not to smelt.
  The artfullest smith
  is at a loss !
  Who shapeth the sword
  since I cannot ?
How may I master this marvel ?

WANDERER (*who has risen from the hearth*).
  Three times asked were thy questions,
  three times I was acquit;
  but foreign quite
  thy queries were,
for what was near to thy heart
and thy needs, didst thou not ask.
  Now I have found it,
  wondrous thy fright:
  thy witty pate
  have I won as a prize.
Hear, Fafner's would-be undoer,
heed, thou fated dwarf:—
  none but who fear
  hath never felt
maketh " Needful " new

MIME (*seine gegenwärtige Lage immer mehr verg send, und von dem Gegenstande lebhaft angezogen*)
Nothung heisst
ein neidliches Schwert;
in einer Esche Stamm
  stiess es Wotan:
dem sollt' es geziemen,
der aus dem Stamm' es zög'.
  Der stärksten Helden
  keiner bestand's:
  Siegmund, der Kühne.
  konnt's allein;
fechtend führt' er's im Streit,
bis an Wotan's Speer es zersprang.
  Nun verwahrt die Stücken
  ein weiser Schmied;
  denn er weiss, dass allein
  mit dem Wotansschwert
ein kühnes dummes Kind,
Siegfried, den Wurm versehrt.
  (*Ganz vergnügt.*)
  Behalt' ich Zwerg
  auch zweitens mein Haupt?

WANDERER. Der witzigste bist du
  unter den Weisen:
wer käm' dir an Klugheit gleich?
  Doch bist du so klug,
  den kindischen Helden
für Zwergen-Zwecke zu nützen:
  mit der dritten Frage
  droh' ich nun !—
  sag' mir, du weiser
  Waffenschmied,
wer wird aus den starken Stücken
Nothung, das Schwert, wohl schweisse

MIME (*fährt im höchsten Schrecken auf*).
  Die Stücken ! Schwert !
  O weh ! mir schwindelt !—
  Was fang' ich an ?
  Was fällt mir ein ?
  Verfluchter Stahl,
  dass ich dich gestohlen !
Er hat mich vernagelt
  in Pein und Noth;
mir bleibt er hart,
  ich kann ihn nicht hämmern:
  Niet' und Löthe
  lässt mich im Stich !
  Der weiseste Schmied
  weiss sich nicht Rath:
  wer schweisst nun das Schwert,
  schaff' ich es nicht?
Das Wunder, wie soll ich's wissen?

WANDERER (*ist vom Herd aufgestanden*).
  Dreimal solltest du fragen,
  dreimal stand ich dir frei:
  nach eitlen Fernen
  forschtest du;
doch was zunächst sich dir fand,
was dir nützt, fiel dir nicht ein.
  Nun ich's errathe,
  wirst du verrückt:
  gewonnen hab' ich
  das witzige Haupt.—
Jetzt, Fafner's kühner Bezwinger
hör' verfallener Zwerg:—
  nur wer das Fürchten
  nie erfuhr,
schmiedet Nothung neu.

(MIME stares wildly at him as he turns to depart.)

Thy head so wise
henceforth guard well!
I leave it forfeit to him
who has learnt not yet to rear.

(He turns away, laughing, and disappears in the forest.)

MIME (paralyzed with terror, sinks back on his stool behind the anvil. He stares for a while before him at the sunlit forest. After a long silence he begins to tremble violently).

Accursed light!
how creep'st thou aloft!
What quivers and shivers?
what quickens and sways,
what swirls and enflames
and flickers around?
All glitters and gleams
in the sunlight's glint.
What hisses and hums
and holds my gaze?
It roars and rolls
and rumbles toward;—
it rends through the wood,—
where shall I flee?
Before me a monstrous
maw I behold!—
The dragon has found me!
Fafner! Fafner!

He shrieks aloud and cowers down behind the great anvil.)

SIEGFRIED (breaks from the thicket and calls, still from without).

Ho! lazy fellow!
Hav'n't you finished?
Say now, how goes the sword?
(Enters and pauses in surprise.)
Where hides the smith?
Has he decamped?
Ho, ho! Mime, you moon-calf!
D'ye hear me? where have you hid?

MIME (with feeble voice, from behind the anvil).

Is't thou, boy?
Art thou alone?

SIEGFRIED. Under the anvil!
Say, what seek you down there?
Sharpened yet is my sword?

MIME. The sword? The sword?
How can I shape it?—
(Half aside.)
"None but who Fear
hath never felt
maketh 'Needful' new."
Too wise my wits are
for such a work.

SIEGFRIED. Will you not tell me?
Or must I teach you?

MIME (as before). Where shall I hope for help?
My wily head
I held in wager;
I've lost it, 'tis forfeit to him
"who has learnt not yet to fear."

SIEGFRIED (violently). Still do you flout me?
Would you then fly?

(MIME starrt ihn gross an: er wendet sich zum Fortgange),

Dein weises Haupt
wahre von heut':
verfallen—lass' ich's dem,
der das Fürchten nicht gelernt.
(Er lacht und geht in den Wald.)

MIME (ist, wie vernichtet, auf den Schemel hinter den Ambos zurückgesunken: er stiert, grad' vor sich aus, in den sonnig beleuchteten Wald hinein. — Nach längerem Schweigen geräth er in heftiges Zittern).

Verfluchtes Licht!
Was flammt dort die Luft?
Was flackert und lackert,
was flimmert und schwirrt,
was schwebt dort und webt
und wabert umher?
Da glimmert's und glitzt's
in der Sonne Gluth:
was säuselt und summ't
und saus't nun gar?
Es brummt und braus't
und prasselt hierher!
Dort bricht's durch den Wald,
will auf mich zu!
Ein grässlicher Rachen
reisst sich mir auf!—
Der Wurm will mich fangen!
Fafner! Fafner!

(Er schreit laut auf und knickt hinter dem breiten Ambos zusammen.)

SIEGFRIED (bricht aus dem Waldgesträuch hervor, und ruft noch von aussen).

Heda! Fauler!
bist du nun fertig?
Schnell! wie steht's mit dem Schwert?
(Er ist eingetreten und hält verwundert an.)
Wo steckt der Schmied?
Stahl er sich fort?
Hehe! Mime! du Memme!
Wo bist du? wo birg'st du dich?

MIME (mit schwacher Stimme hinter dem Ambos).

Bist du es, Kind?
Kommst du allein?

SIEGFRIED. Hinter dem Ambos?—
Sag', was schufest du dort?
schärftest du mir das Schwert?

MIME (höchst verstört und zerstreut).

Das Schwert? das Schwert?
wie möcht' ich's schweissen?—
(Halb für sich.)
" Nur wer das Fürchten
nicht erfuhr,
schmiedet Nothung neu."—
Zu weise ward ich
für solches Werk!

SIEGFRIED. Wirst du mir reden?
Soll ich dir rathen?

MIME (wie zuvor).

Wo nehm' ich redlichen Rath?—
Mein weises Haupt
hab' ich verwettet:
verfallen, verlor ich's an den,
" der das Fürchten nicht gelernt."

SIEGFRIED (heftig). Sind mir das Flausen?
Willst du mir flieh'n?

MIME (*gradually recovering himself*).
 I'd fly from him
 who fear had known: —
but that truly I never have taught him.
 I, fool-like, forgot
 the one thing good:
 love towards me
 was my lesson; —
but, alas! I lost my work.
What force can awake in him fear?

SIEGFRIED (*seizing him*). Ho! must I help you?
 What whim's in your head?

MIME. Alone for thy sake
 I sank in absorption.
Would I could weightily warn thee!

SIEGFRIED (*laughing*). Nay, under the seat
 well were you sinking;
what weighty affairs took you there?

MIME (*with still more self-possession*).
 With fear I trembled for thee,
that I the thing might teach thee.

SIEGFRIED. What mean you by fearing?

MIME. Thou feltest it ne'er,
 yet wilt from this wood
 go forth to the world?
How fruitless the firmest of swords
if from thee fear is far!

SIEGFRIED (*impatiently*). Foolish talk
 you're feeding me with.

MIME 'Tis thy mother's rede
 read thee by me:
 to what she left me
 must I be loyal; —
 to the lures of the world
 I never should leave thee
till duly to fear thou had'st learnt.

SIEGFRIED. If 'tis an art
 why am I untaught?
Arede! what is it, this fearing?

MIME (*with increasing animation*).
 Feltest thou ne'er
 in forest dark,
 at gloaming hour
 in gloomy spots,
 when with a rustle,
 rush and roar
 fearful hurtling
 toward thee howls,
 dazzling flickers
 round thee flutter,
 swelling surges
 toward thee swoop, —
feltest thou then, no grisly
gruesomeness grow o'er thy fancy?
 Balefullest shudders
 shake thy whole body,
 all thy senses
 sink and forsake thee,
in thy breast bursting and big
beat thy hammering heart? —
 Feltest thou nought of this,
then fear thou hast not yet found.

MIME (*allmälig sich etwas fassend*).
 Wohl flöh' ich dem,
 der's Fürchten kennt: —
doch das liess ich dem Kinde zu lehren!
 Ich Dummer vergass
 was einzig gut:
 Liebe zu mir
 sollt' er lernen; —
das gelang nun leider faul!
Wie bring' ich das Fürchten ihm bei?

SIEGFRIED (*packt ihn*).
 He! Muss ich helfen?
 Was fegtest du heut'?

MIME. Für dich nur besorgt,
 versank ich in Sinnen,
wie ich dich Wichtiges wiese.

SIEGFRIED (*lachend*).
 Bis unter den Sitz
 warst du versunken:
was Wichtiges fandest du da?

MIME (*sich immer mehr erholend*).
 Das Fürchten lernt' ich für dich,
dass ich's dich Dummen lehre.

SIEGFRIED. Was ist's mit dem Fürchten?

MIME. Erfuhr'st du's noch nie,
 und willst aus dem Wald
 fort in die Welt?
Was frommte das festeste Schwert,
blieb dir das Fürchten fern?

SIEGFRIED (*ungeduldig*). Faulen Rath
 erfindest du wohl?

MIME. Deiner Mutter Rath
 redet aus mir:
 was ich gelobt'
 muss ich nun lösen,
 in die listige Welt
 dich nicht zu lassen,
el.' du nicht das Fürchten gelernt.

SIEGFRIED. Ist's eine Kunst,
 was kenn' ich sie nicht? —
Heraus! Was ist's mit dem Fürchten?

MIME (*immer belebter*).
 Fühltest du nie
 im finstern Wald,
 bei Dämmerschein
 am dunklen Ort,
 wenn fern es säuselt,
 summs't und saus't,
 wildes Brummen
 näher braus't,
 wirres Flackern
 um dich flimmert,
 schwellend Schwirren
 zu Leib' dir schwebt, —
fühltest du dann nicht grieselnd
Grausen die Glieder dir fah'n?
 Glühender Schauer
 schüttelt die Glieder
 wirr verschwimmend
 schwinden die Sinne,
in der Brust bebend und bang
berstet hämmernd das Herz? —
 Fühltest du das noch nicht,
das Fürchten blieb dir dann fremd.

EGFRIED.	Strange and right singular that must seem! Hard and firm feel the strings of my heart. This grimness and growling, this glowing and shaking, this burning and shiv'ring, beating and quaking, — well I wish to acquire them, how for such pastimes I pant! But how bring it, Mime, about? What means could make you my master?	SIEGFRIED.	Sonderlich seltsam muss das sein! Hart und fest, fühl' ich, steht mir das Herz. Das Grieseln und Grausen, Glühen und Schauern, Hitzen und Schwindeln, Hämmern und Beben — gern begehr' ich das Bangen, sehnend verlangt mich's der Lust.— Doch wie bringst du, Mime mir's bei? Wie wär'st du Memme mir Meister?
ME.	Follow me well, I'll find thee a way; thinking, fell I upon't. I wot of a monstrous Worm, who's wasted many folk; fear thou'lt learn from Fafner, follow me but to his hole.	MIME.	Folge mir nur, ich führe dich wohl; sinnend fand ich's aus. Ich weiss einen schlimmen Wurm, der würgt' und schland schon viel. Fafner lehrt dich das Fürchten, folgst du mir zu seinem Nest.
EGFRIED.	Where lieth his hole?	SIEGFRIED.	Wo liegt er im Nest?
ME.	Hate-cavern well is it hight; to east, at end of the wood.	MIME.	Neid-Höhle wird es genannt: im Ost, am Ende des Wald's.
EGFRIED.	And would the world be that way?	SIEGFRIED.	Dann wär's nicht weit von der Welt?
ME.	To Hate-cavern it lies close at hand.	MIME.	Bei Neidhöhl' liegt sie ganz nah'?
EGFIRED..	Toward it then, let me follow, learn about fearing, and forth to the world! Then swift! shape me the sword! In the world would I assay it.	SIEGFRIED.	Dahin denn sollst du mich führen. lernt' ich das Fürchten, dann fort in die Welt! Drum schnell schaffe das Schwert, in der Welt will ich es schwingen.
ME.	The sword? alack!	MIME.	Das Schwert? O Noth!
EGFRIED.	Quick to your smithy! What can you shew?	SIEGFRIED.	Rasch in die Schmiede! Weis' was du schuf'st.
ME.	Accursed steel! I cannot restore it again! Such mighty magic's too much for poor Mime's force. One who knoweth not fear the knack might quickly find.	MIME.	Verfluchter Stahl: Zu flicken versteh' ich ihn nicht! Den zähen Zauber bezwingt keines Zwergen Kraft. Wer das Fürchten nicht kennt, der fänd' wohl eher die Kunst.
EGFRIED.	Famous falsehoods, sluggard, you're framing: that you're a muddler must you admit, not seek to dissemble with lies. — Bring me the bits here! Fly, you old bungler! My father's blade fails not with me: I'll soon shape it myself! (*He quickly prepares for work.*)	SIEGFRIED.	Feine Finten weiss mir der Faule; dass er ein Stümper sollt' er gesteh'n: nun lügt er sich listig heraus.— Her mit den Stücken! Fort mit dem Stümper! Des Vaters Stahl fügt sich wohl mir: ich selbst schweisse das Schwert! (*Er macht sich rasch an die Arbeit.*)
ME.	Had'st thou been careful to master the craft, now might thy work be of use: too lazy wert thou ever to learn; how wilt thou best set about it?	MIME.	Hättest du fleissig die Kunst gepflegt, jetzt käm' dir's wahrlich zu gut; doch lässig warst du stets in der Lehre: was willst du nun Rechtes rüsten?
GFRIED.	Where the master was balked, what more could the boy do, who to his counsel gave heed? — So move afar, meddle not here, for fear you be made to fuel!	SIEGFRIED.	Was der Meister nicht kann, vermöcht' es der Knabe, hätt' er ihm immer gehorcht?— Jetzt mach' dich fort, misch' dich nicht d'rein: sonst fällst du mir mit in's Feuer!

He has heaped a mass of coal on the fire and blown it well up; now, fixing the sword-pieces in a vice, he commences to file them to powder.

MIME (*looking on at his proceedings*).
   What art thou about?
   Take but the solder;
 the flux fused for thee, see!

SIEGFRIED. Out on your flux!
   'twill fit me nought:
 such filth will forge me no sword!

MIME.   But the file is failing,
   the rasp is ruined:
 why dost thou destroy thy steel so?

SIEGFRIED. In shreds each fibre
   and splinter I'd see:
 what is marred were mended but so.

MIME (*while* SIEGFRIED *diligently files away*).
   Here helps no cunning,
   to me 'tis clear:
   here speeds the dullard
   by dulness alone!
   Look how he works
   with mighty will!
   The steel is dissolved,
   yet is he not strained. —
   Though old as this cave
   or wood am I,
 such wondrous sight ne'er I've seen!
   He'll achieve the work,
   I wot full well:
   fearless, fashion the sword,
 as well the Wanderer saw. —
   Where shall I hide
   my shrinking head?
 For by this boy it must fall,
 learns he of Fafner no fear. —
   But woe's me, hapless!
   Who'll waste me the worm
 if terror it teaches to him?
 And the ring how shall I reach?
   Accurs'd dilemma!
   It locks me close,
 comes there no light to me
 how to cozen this bold-hearted boy!

SIEGFRIED (*has reduced the sword to powder and put it in a crucible which he now places in the forge. During the following he blows up the fire with the bellows*).
   Hey! Mime! Now say,
   how hight the sword
 that I have filed into fibres?

MIME (*starting out of a reverie*).
   "Needful" named
   is the notable sword;
 so thy mother stated to me

SIEGFRIED (*over his work*).
   Needful! Needful!
   Notable sword!
 Why wert thou thus dissevered?
   To shreds I've shattered
   thy shining blade,
 the pot shall melt now the shivers!
   Oho! Oho!
   Aha! Aha!

Er hat eine grosse Menge Kohlen auf dem He gehäuft, und unterhält in einem fort die Glu während er die Schwertstücke in den Schraubsto einspannt und sie zu Spähnen zerfeilt.

MIME (*indem er ihm zusieht*).
   Was machst du da?
   Nimm doch die Löthe:
 den Brei brau' ich schon längst.

SIEGFRIED. Fort mit dem Brei!
   ich brauch' ihn nicht:
 mit Bappe back' ich kein Schwert!

MIME.   Du zerfeil'st die Feile,
   zerreib'st die Raspel:
 wie willst du den Stahl zerstampfen?

SIEGFREID. Zersponnen muss ich
   in Spähne ihn seh'n:
 was entzwei ist, zwing' ich mir so.

MIME (*während* SIEGFRIED *eifrig fortfeilt*).
   Hier hilft kein Kluger,
   das seh' ich klar:
   hier hilft dem Dummen
   die Dummheit selbst!
   Wie er sich müht
   und mächtig regt:
   ihm schwindet der Stahl,
   doch wird ihm nicht schwül:—
   Nun ward ich so alt
   wie Höhl' und Wald,
 und hab' nicht so 'was geseh'n!
   Mit dem Schwert gelingt's,
   das lern' ich wohl:
   furchtlos fegt er's zu ganz,—
   der Wand'rer wusst' es gut!—
   Wie berg' ich nun
   mein banges Haupt?
 Dem kühnen Knaben verfiel's,
 lehrt' ihn nicht Fafner die Furcht.—
   Doch weh' mir Armen!
   Wie würgt' er den Wurm,
 erführ' er das Fürchten von ihm?
 Wie erräng' er mir den Ring?
   Verfluchte Klemme!
   Da klebt' ich fest,
 fänd' ich nicht klugen Rath,
 wie den Furchtlosen selbst ich bezwäng

SIEGFRIED (*hat nun die Stücken zerfeilt und in ei Schmelztigel gefangen, den er jetzt in die Herdg stellt: unter dem Folgenden nährt er die Gluth mit Blasebalg*).
   He, Mime, geschwind:
   wie heisst das Schwert,
 das ich in Spähne zersponnen?

MIME (*aus seinen Gedanken auffahrend*).
   Nothung nennt sich
   das neidliche Schwert:
 deine Mutter gab mir die Märe.

SIEGFRIED (*zu der Arbeit*).
   Nothung! Nothung!
   neidliches Schwert!
 was musstest du zerspringen?
   Zu Spreu nun schuf ich
   die scharfe Pracht,
 im Tigel brat' ich die Spähne!
   Hoho! hoho!
   hahei! hahei!

Bellows blow!
brighten the glow!—
Wild in woodlands
waved a tree,
which I in the forest felled:
the brown-hued ash
I baked into coal,
on the hearth it lies now in heaps.

Oho! Oho!
Aha! Aha!
Bellows blow!
brighten the glow!—
The branches' fragments,
how bravely they flame!
their glow how fierce and fair!
They spring in the air
with scattering sparks
and smelt me the steely shreds.

Oho! Oho!
Aha! Aha!
Bellows blow!
brighten the glow!—
Needful! Needful!
notable sword!
I've smelted thy steely shreds.
In thine own sweat
thou swimmest now;—
I soon shall call thee my sword!

MIME (during the last verse of SIEGFRIED's song continues his own reflections aside).
He'll smithy the sword
and fell me Fafner;
I see 'tis as settled as fate.
Store and ring
he'll wrest in the strife:—
in what way the prize can I win?
By wit and craft
I'll win it surely,
and save perhaps my head.
Wearied in fight with the worm,
in his faintness fain he will drink
From potent simples
by me assorted
I will a draught prepare:
but one drop
need he drink of,
senseless, he'll sink to sleep.
With the very weapon
he valiantly welds there
he shall be razed from my way;
the ring and the hoard I'll have.
Hey! wisest Wanderer,
dull was I deemed?
How doth like thee now
my lusty wit?
Lacks me still
a rightful rede?

(he springs up in glee, fetches vessels and pours decoctions from them into a pot.)

SIEGFRIED (has poured the molten steel into a mould and plunged this into water, whereupon the loud hiss of its cooling is heard).
To the water flowed
a fiery flood:
anger and hate
hissed from the depths,
cowed was its head by the cold.
Though scorching it struck
in the watery stream:
it stirs no more:

Blase, Balg!
blase die Gluth!—
Wild im Walde
wuchs ein Baum,
den hab' ich im Forst gefällt:
die braune Esche
brannt' ich zu Kohl',
auf dem Herd nun liegt sie gehäuft.

Hoho! hoho!
hahei! hahei!
Blase, Balg!
blase die Gluth!—
Des Baumes Kohle,
wie brennt sie kühn,
wie glüht sie hell und hehr!
In springenden Funken
sprüht sie auf,
schmilzt mir des Stahles Spreu.

Hoho! hoho!
hahei! hahei!
Blase, Balg!
blase die Gluth!—
Nothung! Nothung!
neidliches Schwert!
schon schmilzt deines Stahles Spreu:
im eig'nen Schweisse
schwimmst du nun—
bald schwing' ich dich als mein Schwert!

MIME (während der Absätze von SIEGFRIED's Lied immer für sich, entfernt sitzend).
Er schmiedet das Schwert,
und Fafner fällt er:
das seh' ich nun sicher voraus;
Hort und Ring
erringt er im Harst:—
wie erwerb' ich mir den Gewinn?
Mit Witz und List
erlang' ich Beides,
und berge heil mein Haupt.
Rang er sich müd' mit dem Wurm,
von der Müh' erlab' ihn ein Trank;
aus würz'gen Säften,
die ich gesammelt,
brau' ich den Trank für ihn;
wenig Tropfen nur
braucht er zu trinken,
sinnlos sinkt er in Schlaf:
mit der eig'nen Waffe,
die er sich gewonnen,
räum' ich ihn leicht aus dem Weg,
erlange mir Ring und Hort.
Hei! Weiser Wand'rer,
dünkt' ich dich dumm,
wie gefällt dir nun
mein feiner Witz?
Fand ich mir wohl
Rath und Ruh'?

(Er springt vergnügt auf, holt Gefässe herbei und schüttet aus ihnen Gewürz in einen Topf.)

SIEGFRIED (hat den geschmolzenen Stahl in einer Stangenform gegossen, und diese in das Wasser gesteckt: man hört jetzt das laute Gezisch der Kühlung)
In das Wasser floss
ein Feuerfluss:
grimmiger Zorn
zischt' ihm da auf;
frierend zähmt' ihm der Frost.
Wie sehrend er floss,
in des Wassers Fluth
fliesst er nicht mehr:

stiff lies it and stark,
haughty and hard the steel.
Haply in blood
it soon will bathe!—

Now sweat once again,
that so I may shape thee,
Needful, notable sword!

(*He thrusts the sword into the coals and heats it. Then he turns to* MIME, *who at the other end of the hearth has carefully put his pipkin on the fire.*)

What is that patch
about with his pot?
While I burn steel
would you brew sauces?

MIME.   The smith has come to shame,
the pupil his conqueror proves;
all the craftman's art for aye is o'er,
thy cook he hath become.
Burn then thy iron to broth,
while I will brew
my eggs into soup.
(*Goes on cooking.*

SIEGFRIED (*still over his work*).
Mime the craftsman
now learns cooking;
the smithy serves him no more;
all the swords he made
I shattered and shivered;
what he cooks I care not to taste.

To fear he will teach me
if I but follow;
afar there dwelleth a tutor.
But the best he can do
will bring 't not about;
a fool have I found him in all things.

(*He has taken out the red-hot steel and proceeds to hammer it on the anvil with a great smith's hammer, during the following song.*)

Oho! Oho! Oho!
Shape me, my hammer,
a hardy sword!
Oho! Aha!
Aha! Oho!
Aha! Oho! Aha!

Thy steely blue
once streamed with blood;
its ruddy ripples
reddened thy sides;
cold laughter was thine,
the warm stream licking to cool!
Heiha! Heiha!
Heiha! Ha! Ha!
Oho! Oho! Oho!
Now in the glow
thou redly gleam'st;
thy weakness heedeth
my hammer's weight:
testy sparks dost thou scatter,
that I thy spirit have tamed!
Heiho! Heiho!
Heiho! Ho! Ho!
Oho! Oho! Aha!

Oho! Aha! Oho!
Shape me, my hammer,
a hardy sword!

---

starr ward er und steif,
herrisch der harte Stahl:
heisses Blut doch
fliesst ihm bald!—

Nun schwitze noch einmal,
dass ich dich schweisse,
Nothung, neidliches Schwert!

(*Er stösst den Stahl in die Kohlen und glüht ihn. Dann wendet er sich zu* MIME, *der vom anderen Ende des Herdes her einen Topf an den Rand der Gluth setzt.*)

Was schafft der Tölpel
dort mit dem Topf?
Brenn' ich hier Stahl,
brau'st du dort Sudel?

MIME.   Zu Schanden kam ein Schmied,
den Lehrer sein Knabe lehrt;
mit der Kunst ist's beim Alten aus,
als Koch dient er dem Kinde:
brennt es das Eisen zu Brei,
aus Eiern brau't
der Alte ihm Sud.
(*Er fährt fort zu kochen.*)

SIEGFRIED (*immer während der Arbeit*).
Mime, der Künstler,
lernt nun Kochen;
das Schmieden schmeckt ihm nicht mehr,
seine Schwerter alle
hab' ich zerschmissen;
was er kocht, ich kost' es ihm nicht.

Das Fürchten zu lernen
will er mich führen;
ein Ferner soll es mich lehren:
was am besten er kann,
mir bringt er's nicht bei;
als Stümper besteht er in allem!

(*Er hat den rothglühenden Stahl hervorgezogen, und hämmert ihn nun, während des folgenden Liedes, mit dem grossen Schmiedehammer auf dem Ambos.*)

Hoho! hahei! hoho!
Schmiede, mein Hammer
ein hartes Schwert!
Hoho! hahei!
hahei! hoho!
Hahei! hoho! hahei!

Einst färbte Blut
dein falbes Blau;
sein rothes Rieseln
röthete dich:
kalt lachtest du da,
das warme lecktest du kühl!
Hahahei! hahahei!
hahahei! hei! hei!
Hoho! hoho! hoho!
Nun hat die Gluth
dich roth geglüht;
deine weiche Härte
dem Hammer weicht:
zornig sprüh'st du mir Funken,
dass ich dich Spröden gezähmt!
Heiaho! heiaho!
heiaho! ho! ho!
Hoho! hoho! hahei!

Hoho! hahei! hoho!
Schmiede, mein Hammer,
ein hartes Schwert!

Oho! Aha!
Aha! Oho!
Aha! Oho! Aha!

These springing sparks
what a sport to see!
In rage the brave
are arrayed the best;
io! thou laughest on me.
yet can'st be grisly and grim
Heiha! Heiha!
Heiha! Ha! Ha!
Oho! Oho! Oho!
Both fire and hammer
failed me not!
With stalwart strokes
I stretched thee out;
let sink now thy blush of shame.
be as cold and hard as thou can'st.
Heiho! Heiho!
Heiho! Ho! Ho!
Aha! Oho! Aha!

*With the last words, he plunges the sword into the
water, laughing at the hiss it makes.*)

*IME while SIEGFRIED is fastening the forged sword-
ade into a handle, — again coming to the front*).

He shapes him a sword so sharp,
Fafner it felleth,
the Nibiung's foe.
A draught of might I've made,
Siegfried to finish
when Fafner falls.
This treach'ry *must* I contrive.
triumph *must* I attain.
What my brother shaped,
the shimmering ring,
endowed with enchantments
charms and control —
the peerless gold
which all power gives, —
I plainly have gained it!
I govern it! —
Alberic e'en,
whom once I served,
as bondsman will I
bind me anon.
As Nibelheim's lord
let me be known there,
I'll humble to me
all their host! —
The poor vilified dwarf
how will they revere!
To the gold will go thronging
men and gods;
before my bidding
bows all the world,
before my anger
awed are they all!
In toil then moveth
Mime no more;
his wealth unending
shall others work.
Mime the mighty,
Mime is monarch;
prince of earth-gnomes,
ruler of all!
Hey, Mime! how glad wert thou then!
Who would believe this of thee?

Hoho! hahei!
hahei! hoho!
Hahei! hoho! hahei!

Der frohen Funken,
wie freu' ich mich!
Es ziert den Kühnen
des Zornes Kraft:
lustig lach'st du mich an,
stellst du auch grimm dich und gram
Hahahei! hahahei!
hahahei! hei! hei!
Hoho! hoho! hoho!
Durch Gluth und Hammer
glückt' es mir!
Mit starken Schlägen
streckt' ich dich:
nun schwinde die rothe Scham;
werde kalt und hart wie du kannst.
Heiaho! heiaho!
heiaho! ho! ho!
Hahei! hoho! hahei!

*Er taucht mit dem letzten den Stahl in das Wasser
und lacht bei dem starken Gezisch.*)

MIME (*während SIEGFRIED die geschmiedete Schwert
klinge in dem Griffhefte befestigt,—wieder im Vorder
grunde*).

Er schafft sich ein scharfes Schwert,
Fafner zu fällen,
der Zwerge Feind:
ich brau' ein Trug-Getränk,
Siegfried zu fällen,
dem Fafner fiel.
Gelingen muss mir die List;
lachen muss mir der Lohn!
Den der Bruder schuf,
den schimmernden Reif,
in den er gezaubert
zwingende Kraft,
das helle Gold,
das zum Herrscher macht—
ich hab' ihn gewonnen!
ich walte sein'! —
Alberich selbst,
der einst mich band,
zu Zwergenfrohne
zwing' ich ihn nun:
als Niblungenfürst
fahr' ich danieder;
gehorchen soll mir
alles Heer! —
Der verachtete Zwerg,
was wird er geehrt!
Zu dem Hort hin drängt sich
Gott und Held:
vor meinem Nicken
neigt sich die Welt,
vor meinem Zorne
zittert sie hin! —
Dann wahrlich müht sich
Mime nicht mehr:
ihm schaffen And're
den ew'gen Schatz.
Mime, der kühne,
Mime ist König,
Fürst der Alben,
Walter des All's!
Hei, Mime! wie glückte mir das
wer glaubte wohl das von dir!

SIEGFRIED (*during the last part of* MIME'S *song has been filing and sharpening the sword and hammering it with a small hammer*).

Needful! Needful!
notable sword!
in handle once more thou art held.
When thou wert wrecked
I wrought thee anew;
no stroke shall again destroy thee.
Thy steel flew in twain
from the stricken sire;
the life-glowing son
shapes it anew;
now laughs upon him its sheen,
and its sharpness surely cuts home.

Needful! Needful!
notable sword!
Thy life again have I given.
Dead lay'st thou
once desolate,
now leapest up dauntless and bright.
Out then, and shew
the cowards thy sheen!
Shatter the false ones,
fall on the sly!—
See! and Mime, thou smith;
so serveth Siegfried's sword!

(*During the second verse he brandishes the sword and now smites it on the anvil which splits in half from top to bottom, falling asunder with a loud noise.* MIME, *in extreme terror, falls flat on the ground.* SIEGFRIED, *shouting with glee, waves his sword in the air. The curtain falls quickly.*)

SIEGFRIED (*während der Absätze von* MIME'S *Li das Schwert feilend, schleifend und mit dem klein Hammer hämmernd*).

Nothung! Nothung!
neidliches Schwert!
jetzt haftest du wieder im Heft.
Warst du entzwei,
ich zwang dich ganz,
kein Schlag soll nun dich zerschlagen.
Dem sterbenden Vater
zersprang der Stahl,
der lebende Sohn
schuf ihn neu:
nun lacht ihm sein heller Schein,
seine Schärfe schneidet ihm hart.

Nothung! Nothung!
neu und verjüngt!
zum Leben weckt' ich dich wieder.
Todt lag'st du
in Trümmern dort,
jetzt leuchtest du trotzig und hehr.
Zeige den Schächern
nun deinen Schein!
schlage den Falschen,
fälle den Schelm!—
Schau, Mime, du Schmied:
so schneidet Siegfried's Schwert!

(*Er hat während des zweiten Verses das Schwe geschwungen, und schlägt nun damit auf den Ambo dieser zerspaltet in zwei Stücken, von oben bis unte so dass er unter grossem Gepolter auseinander fäl MIME, — in höchster Verzückung — fällt vor Schre sitzlings zu Boden.* SIEGFRIED *hält jauchzend d Schwert in die Höhe.—Der Vorhang fällt schnell.*)

SECOND ACT.

A DEEP FOREST.

At the extreme back the opening of a cave. The ground rises in the middle of the stage, forming a little knoll; it sinks again towards the cave at back, so that the upper part of the cavern's mouth alone is visible. L. is to be seen through the trees a rocky cliff rent with fissures. — Gloomy night, darkest at back, where at first the eye of the audience can discern nothing distinctly.

ALBERICH (*leaning against the rocky wall at side, in gloomy reflection*).

In woodland haunt
by Hate-cave I keep watch.
I prick my ear,
keenly peers mine eye.—
Anxious day!
art thou arrived?
Throwest thou there
through the thicket light?

(*A gust of storm passes R. from the wood.*)

But what gleam glances from thence?
Nearer glimmers
a brilliant glow,

TIEFER WALD.

Ganz im Hintergrunde die Oeffnung einer Höh Der Boden hebt sich bis zur Mitte der Bühne, wo eine kleine Hochebene bildet; von da senkt er sich na hinten, der Höhle zu, wieder abwärts, so dass v dieser nur der obere Theil der Oeffnung dem Zuschau sichtbar ist. Links gewahrt man durch Waldbäu eine zerklüftete Felsenwand.—Finstere Nacht, a dichtesten über dem Hintergrunde, wo anfänglich d Blick des Zuschauers gar nichts zu unterscheid vermag.

ALBERICH (*an der Felsenwand zur Seite gelagert, düsterem Brüten*).

In Wald und Nacht
vor Neidhöhl' halt' ich Wacht:
er lauscht mein Ohr,
mühvoll lugt mein Aug'.—
Banger Tag,
beb'st du schon auf?
dämmerst du dort
durch das Dunkel her?

(*Sturmwind erhebt sich rechts aus dem Walde.*)

Welcher Glanz glitzert dort auf?
Näher schimmert
ein heller Schein:

and strides, as of fiery steed,
    course through the wood,
    crashing this way.
Nearer the dragon's death-man?
Is't now that Fafner falls?
(*The wind subsides again and the glow fades.*)
    The light allays —
the glow sinks from my sight:
    night falls once more.—
Who neareth, shining through shadow?

THE WANDERER (*enters from the wood and pauses
    opposite* ALBERICH.)
    To Hate-cave
by night have I hied:
who confronts me in darkness dim?
*As from a suddenly parted cloud, the moonlight breaks
forth and illumines the* WANDERER'*s figure.*)

ALBERICH (*recognizes the* WANDERER *and recoils in
    dread*).
    Thyself is it I see?
    (*Bursting into wrath.*)
    What wouldst thou here?
    Hence, from my way!
Aroint, thou shameless rogue!

WANDERER. Black Alberich,
    bidest thou here?
hast thou kept Fafner's house?

ALBERICH. Comest thou new
    annoy to inflict?
    Tarry not here,
    take thy way homeward!
    This place has sorely
suffered from thee and thy plots.
    Therefore, villain,
    quickly avaunt!

WANDERER. I came as witness,
    not as worker:
who'll bar the Wanderer's way?

ALBERICH (*laughing spitefully*).
    Thou spell-working conspirer!
    Were I dull as once
    in past days thou deemedst,
when I was bound through blindness,
    how soon by ruse
were the ring again from me ravished!
    Beware! all thy wiles
    well do I know;
    also thy weak point
plainly am I aware of.
    With all my wealth
    thy debts hast thou wiped out;
    my gem dowered
    the giants' toil,
what time they built thee thy burg.
    What was agreed upon
    with those grim ones
in runes is writ this day
on thy spear's all-dominant shaft.
    Nor dost dare
    what as price thou hast paid
to juggle back from the giants.
    Thy spear thou speedily
    wouldst spoil thyself:
    in thine own hand
    the heavenly staff,
the strong one, would split like a straw.

---

es rennt wie ein leuchtendes Ross
    bricht durch den Wald
    brausend daher.
Naht schon des Wurmes Würger?
ist's schon, der Fafner fällt?
(*Der Sturmwind legt sich wieder; der Glanz verlischt.*)
    Das Licht erlischt—
der Glanz barg sich dem Blick:
    Nacht ist's wieder.—
Wer naht dort schimmernd im Schatten?

DER WANDERER (*tritt aus Wald auf, und hält
    * ALBERICH *gegenüber an*).
    Zur Neidhöhle
fuhr ich bei Nacht:
wen gewahr' ich im Dunkel dort?
(*Wie aus einem plötzlich zerreissenden Gewölk bricht
Mondschein herein, und beleuchtet des* WANDERER'*s
    Gestalt.*)

ALBERICH (*erkennt den* WANDERER, *und fährt er-
    schrocken zurück*).
    Du selbst lässt dich hier seh'n?
    (*Er bricht in Wuth aus.*)
    Was willst du hier?
    Fort, aus dem Weg!
von dannen, schamloser Dieb!

WANDERER. Schwarz-Alberich,
    schweif'st du hier?
hütest du Fafner's Haus?

ALBERICH. Jag'st du auf neue
    Neidthat umher?
    Weile nicht hier!
    weiche von hinnen!
    Genug deines Truges
tränkte die Stätte mit Noth.
    Drum, du Frecher,
    lass' sie jetzt frei!

WANDERER. Zu schauen kam ich,
    nicht zu schaffen:
wer wehrte mir Wand'rers Fahrt?

ALBERICH (*lacht tückisch auf*).
    Du Rath wüthender Ränke!
    wär' ich dir zu lieb
    doch noch dumm wie damals,
als du mich Blöden bandest!
    Wie leicht gerieth es
den Ring mir nochmals zu rauben!
    Hab' Acht: deine Kunst
    kenne ich wohl;
    doch wo du schwach bist,
bleib mir auch nicht verschwiegen.
    Mit meinen Schätzen
    zahltest du Schulden;
    mein Ring lohnte
    der Riesen Müh',
die deine Burg dir gebaut
    was mit den trotzigen
    einst du vertragen,
dess' Runen wahrt noch heut'
deines Speeres herrischer Schaft.
    Nicht du darfst,
    was als Zoll du gezahlt,
den Riesen wieder entreissen.
    du selbst zerspelltest
    deines Speeres Schaft:
    in deiner Hand
    der herrische Stab,
der starke zerstiebte wie Sprer

WANDERER. Through no runes of righteous compact
bound wert thou,
base one, by it:
it bowed thee down but by its strength:
for strife I ward it then well.

ALBERICH. How proud thy threats
of menacing power,
and yet how thy spirit doth sink!
Decreed unto death
through my curse
is Fanfer, the store's possessor:—
who'll hold it hereafter?
Will the notable hoard
a Nibelung once more inherit?
This tears thee with endless trouble!
For, passes the ring
once more to my palm,
elseways than foolish giants
I'll use the jewel's pow'r.
Then tremble, thou high
protector of heroes,
for Valhalla
I'll sieze on with Hella's host;
the world will then be mine!

WANDERER. Thy intent I know well;
it troubles me nought:
the ring's but wielded
when it is won.

ALBERICH. How darkly thou say'st
what I doubtless know well!
In heroes' offspring
hast thou then trust,
who truly have leapt from thy loins?
Hast thou not fostered a stripling
who straight the fruit should reach thee,
that thou dare'st not to thieve?

WANDERER. Mind me not—
wrangle with Mime:
thy brother brings thee a foe;
for the boy who follows him here
shall fell for him Fafner soon.
Nought knows he of me;
the Nibelung's need he should serve.
And so, my friend, I say,
thou canst work as thou wilt.
Give thou good heed,
be on thy guard;
he nothing knows of the ring:
but Mime needs must disclose.
                                    [hoard?

ALBERICH. And thy hand hold'st thou from the

WANDERER. My belov'd one
I leave to act unmanaged;
he stands or he falls,
unhelped by me;
heroes' aid only I've faith in.

ALBERICH. With Mime wrestle
but I for the ring?

WANDERER. Only he would gather
also the gold.

ALBERICH. Yet I ne'er may win it anew?

WANDERER. A hero nears
the hoard to set free;
two Niblungs are greedy for gold;
Fafner falls,
who dost guard the wealth;

WANDERER. Durch Vertrages Treue-Runen
band er dich
Bösen mir nicht:
dich beugt er mir durch seine Kraft;
zum Krieg drum wahr' ich ihn wohl

ALBERICH. Wie stolz du dräu'st
in trotziger Stärke,
und wie dir's im Busen doch bangt'
Verfallen dem Tod
durch meinen Fluch
ist Fafner, des Hortes Hüter:—
wird ihn beerben?
wird der neidliche Hort
dem Niblung wieder gehören?
Das sehrt dich mit ew'ger Sorge
Denn fass' ich ihn wieder
einst in der Faust,
anders als dumme Riesen
üb' ich des Ringes Kraft:
dann zitt're der Helden
heiliger Hüter!
Walhall's Höhen
stürm' ich mit Hella's Heer:
der Welt walte dann ich!

WANDERER. Deinen Sinn kenn' ich;
doch sorgt er mich nicht:
des Ringes waltet
wer ihn gewinnt.

ALBERICH. Wie dunkel sprichst du,
was ich deutlich doch weiss!
An Heldensöhne
hält sich dein Trotz,
die traut deinem Blute entblüht
Pflegtest du wohl eines Knaben
der klug die Frucht dir pflücke
die du—nicht brechen darf'st?

WANDERER. Mit mir—nicht,
had're mit Mime:
dein Bruder bringt dir Gefahr;
einen Knaben führt er daher,
der Fafner ihm fällen soll.
Nichts weiss der von mir;
der Niblung nützt ihn für sich.
Drum sag' ich dir, Gesell:
thue frei wie's dir frommt!
Höre mich wohl,
sei auf der Hut:
nicht kennt der Knabe den Ring,
doch Mime kundet' ihn aus.

ALBERICH. Deine Hand hieltest du vom Hort

WANDERER. Wen ich liebe
lass' ich für sich gewähren:
er steh' oder fall',
sein Herr ist er:
Helden nur können mir frommen.

ALBERICH. Mit Mime räng' ich
allein um den Ring?

WANDERER. Ausser dir begehrt er
einzig das Gut.

ALBERICH. Und doch gewänn' ich ihn nicht?

WANDERER. Ein Helde naht
den Hort zu befrei'n;
zwei Niblungen geizen das Gold;
Fafner fällt,
der den Ring bewacht:—

when 'tis gained, luck to the winner! —
Would'st thou know more ?
There lies the worm:
warn him then of his risk,
well he will leave thee the ring —
Myself I'll wake him for thee. —
(*He turns towards the back.*)
Fafner, Fafner!
Awaken, worm!

ALBERICH (*aside, in expectancy and wonder*).
Does he mean to tell me
mine is the treasure?
(*From the gloomy depth at back is heard* FAFNER'S *voice*).

FAFNER.   Who stirs me from sleep ?

WANDERER. Here waiteth a friend
to warn thee of danger:
thy life he will allow thee,
light'st thou his life for him
with the treasure that thou tendest.

FAFNER.   What would he ?

ALBERICH.   Waken, Fafner!
Waken, thou worm!
A stalwart hero nears,
thy head to humble in strife.

FAFNER.   For him I starve !

WANDERER. Brave is the boy and bold,
sharply shears his sword.

ALBERICH.   The circlet rare
he seeks alone:
let me the ring but lift,
I'll ward thee from harm;
then watch thou the hoard
and rest in length of life!

FAFNER (*yawning*). I lie in possession: —
let me slumber!

WANDERER (*laughing loudly*).
Now, Alberich, that stroke fails!
But stay thy anger's storm!
One thing I read thee,
think on it well:
all things in their nature act,
nor aught may'st thou alter.
I leave thee thy station:
stand to thy guard!
Encounter Mime, thy brother;
his nature o'ercomest thou better.
What further falls
thou quickly shalt find!
He disappears in the wood. A storm-gust rises and quickly subsides again).

ALBERICH (*after watching his retreat a while in wrath*).

There storms he away
on lightning steed,
and leaves me in scoff and scorn:
Aye, laugh away!
ye light-spirited,
lust-gluttonous,
godly enlightener;
'll see ye yet

---

wer ihn rafft, hat ihn gewonnen.—
Willst du noch mehr?
Dort liegt der Wurm:
warn'st du ihn vor dem Tod,
willig wohl liess' er den Tand.—
Ich selber weck' ihn dir auf.—
(*Er wendet sich nach hinten.*)
Fafner! Fafner!
erwache, Wurm!

ALBERICH (*in gespanntem Erstaunen, für sich*).
Was beginnt der Wilde?
gönnt er mir's wirklich?
(*Aus der finstern Tiefe des Hintergrundes hört man*)

FAFNER'S (*Stimme*).   Wer stört mir den Schlaf ?

WANDERER. Gekommen ist einer,
Noth dir zu künden:
er lohnt dir's mit dem Leben,
lohnst du das Leben ihm
mit dem Horte, den du hütest.

FAFNER.   Was will er ?

ALBERICH.   Wache, Fafner!
wache, du Wurm!
Ein starker Helde naht,
dich Heil'gen will er besteh'n.

FAFNER.   Mich hungert sein'.

WANDERER. Kühn ist des Kindes Kraft
scharf schneidet sein Schwert.

ALBERICH.   Den gold'nen Ring
geizt er allein:
lass' mir den Ring zum Lohn,
so wend' ich den Streit;
du wahrest den Hort,
und ruhig leb'st du lang'!

FAFNER (*gähnt*). Ich lieg' und besitze:—
lasst mich schlafen!

WANDERER (*lacht laut*).
Nun, Alberich, das schlug fehl!
Doch schilt mich nicht mehr Schelm!
Diess Eine, rath' ich,
achte noch wohl:
Alles ist nach seiner Art:
an ihr wirst du nichts ändern.
Ich lass' dir die Stätte:
stelle dich fest!
versuch's mit Mime, dem Bruder:
der Art ja versiehst du dich besser.
Was anders ist,
das lerne nun auch!
(*Er verschwindet im Walde. Sturmwind erhebt sich und verliert sich schnell wieder.*)

ALBERICH (*nachdem er ihm lange grimmig nachgesehen*).
Da reitet er hin
auf lichtem Ross:
mir lässt er Sorg' und Spott!
Doch lacht nur zu,
ihr leichtsinniges,
lustgieriges
Göttergelichter:
euch seh' ich

all in your graves!
So long as the gold
in light shall gleam
I hold warily watch!—
Envy works out its end!—
Morning dawns. ALBERIC hides in a cleft of
the rock at side).

noch alle vergeh'n.'
So lang das Gold
am Lichte glänzt,
hält ein Wissender Wacht!—
trügen wird euch sein Trotz.
(*Morgendämmerung. ALBERICH verbirgt sich* z
Seite im Geklüft).

(As the daybreaks MIME and SIEGFRIED enter. The
latter wears the sword in his girdle. MIME narrowly
reconnoitres the place and at last seeks towards the
background, which remains still in shadow, while the
higher ground in the middle is more and more brightened
by the sun; he then draws SIEGFRIED's attention.)

(MIME *und* SIEGFRIED *treten bei anbrechendem Ta*
auf. SIEGFRIED *trägt das Schwert an einem Gehenk*
MIME *erspäht genau die Stätte, forscht endlich die*
Hintergrunde zu, der—während die Anhöhe im mit
lern Vordergrunde später immer heller von der Son
beleuchtet wird—in finstern Schatten gehüllt bleib
und bedeutet dann SIEGFRIED.

MIME.   The spot thou seest!
         here we stop.

MIME.   Zur Stelle sind wir!
         bleib' hier steh'n!

SIEGFRIED (*seating himself under a great lime-tree*).
         Here shall I in fear take lesson?—
         Far distant you have led me;
         since the fall of night through woodlands.
         we two have wended our way.
         Now shall you, Mime,
         henceforth move from me!
         Find I not here
         what I fain would learn,
         afar then will I wander;
         from thee I want to be free!

SIEGFRIED (*setzt sich unter eine grosse Linde*).
         Hier soll ich das Fürchten lernen?—
         Fern hast du mich geleitet;
         eine volle Nacht im Walde
         selbander wanderten wir:
         nun sollst du, Mime,
         fortan mich meiden!
         Lern' ich hier nicht
         was ich lernen muss,
         allein zieh' ich dann weiter:
         dich werd' ich endlich da los!

MIME (*seats himself opposite, so as to keep the cave in*
         sight still).
         Trust me, dearie!
         Dost thou not here
         in haste discover fear,
         in other hours,
         and other ways
         scarce were it ever learnt. —
         Seest thou yonder
         yawning cavern's shade?
         Therein dwells
         a gruesome dragon dread.
         Awfully grisly
         is he, and great;
         a savage and monstrous
         maw doth he ope;
         both skin and scalp,
         at single snap
         the beast will bolt thee belike.

MIME (*setzt sich ihm gegenüber, so dass er die Höl*
         immer noch im Auge behält).
         Glaub' mir, Lieber!
         lernst du heute
         hier das Fürchten nicht:
         an andrem Ort
         zu and'rer Zeit
         schwerlich erfährst du's je.—
         Siehst du dort
         den dunklen Höhlenschlund?
         Darin wohnt
         ein gräulich wilder Wurm:
         unmassen grimmig
         ist er und gross:
         ein schrecklicher Rachen
         reisst sich ihm auf;
         mit Haut und Haar
         auf einen Happ
         verschlingt der Schlimme dich wohl.

SIEGFRIED.   'Twere well to baffle his biting:
             I'll thrust myself not in his throat.

SIEGFRIED.   Gut ist's, den Schlund ihm zu schliesse
             drum biet' ich mich nicht dem Gebiss.

MIME.   Potent poison
         he pours with his breath;
         he whom his spittle's
         spume doth besplash
         must shrivel up, body and bones.

MIME.   Giftig giesst sich
         ein Geifer ihm aus:
         wen mit des Speichels
         Schweiss er bespei't,
         dem schwinden Fleisch und Gebein.

SIEGFRIED.   That his venom vile may not sear me
             lightly aside will I leap,

SIEGFRIED.   Dass des Geifers Gift mich nicht sehr
             weich' ich zur Seite dem Wurm.

MIME.   A twisting tail
         he turns about;
         if ta'en in its toils
         and firmly twined,
         thy limbs will be ground up like glass.

MIME.   Ein Schlangenschweif
         schlägt sich ihm auf:
         wen er damit umschlingt
         und fest umschliesst,
         dem brechen die Glieder wie Glas

SIEGFRIED. From his tail s entangle to keep I'll have an eye on his acts. — But hark to me now: has this worm a heart?	SIEGFRIED. Vor des Schweifes Schwang mich wahre: halt' ich den Argen im Aug'.—[wahre: Doch heisse mich das: hat der Wurm ein Herz?
MIME. A cruel and hardened heart!	MIME. Ein grimmiges, hartes Herz!
SIEGFRIED. He bears it, sure, where in all it beats, both in man and in beast?	SIEGFRIED. Das sitzt ihm doch wo es jedem schlägt, trag' es Mann oder Thier?
MIME. No doubt, youngster, it lies there indeed. Not yet hast thou learnt what is fear?	MIME. Gewiss, Knabe, da führt's auch der Wurm; nun kommt dir das Fürchten wohl an!
SIEGFRIED. Needful straightway I'll strike to his heart: will that be like fearing, haply? Hey, my ancient, is this only what all your lore can lesson me? Forth on your way then wander, for fearing I learn not here.	SIEGFRIED. Nothung stoss' ich dem Stolzen in's Herz: soll das etwa Fürchten heissen? He, du Alter! ist das alles, was deine List mich lehren kann? Fahr' deines Wegs dann weiter; das Fürchten lern' ich hier nicht.
MIME. Wait but awhile! What I have spoken thinkest thou empty sound: himself must meet thy hearing and sight, thy senses will leave thee then straight! When thy glances swim, the ground 'neath thee sinks, and grimly griped, thy heart doth gasp, then thank thou him who has led thee, and think of Mime's great love.	MIME. Wart' es nur ab! Was ich dir sagte, dünke dich tauber Schall: ihn selber musst du hören und seh'n, die Sinne vergeh'n dir dann schon! Wenn dein Blick verschwimmt, der Boden dir schwankt, im Busen bang dein Herz erbebt:— dann dankst du mir, der dich führte, gedenkst wie Mime dich liebt.
SIEGFRIED (springing up crossly). You shall no more love me! Said I not so? Forth from the sight of me — leave me alone! this nuisance no longer I'll stand. Prate you of loving me still? This idiot shrinking and eyelid winking— whenever shall I lose the sight? when will this old object be gone?	SIEGFRIED (springt unwillig auf). Du sollst mich nicht lieben! sagt' ich dir's nicht? Fort aus den Augen mir; lass' mich allein: sonst halt' ich's hier länger nicht aus, fängst du von Liebe gar an! Das eklige Nicken und Augenzwicken, wann endlich soll ich's nicht mehr seh'n? wann werd' ich den Albernen los?
MIME. I leave thee now; I'll linger nigh the spring. Stay thou but here, soon when the sun is on high look for the worm; from his cave he'll warily come: close this way will he pass to water at the fountain.	MIME. Ich lasse dich schon: am Quell dort lagr' ich mich. Steh' du nur hier; steigt die Sonne zur Höh', merk' auf den Wurm, aus der Höhle wälzt er sich her: hier vorbei biegt er dann, am Brunnen sich zu tränken.
SIEGFRIED (laughing). Mime, wait at the stream and there I'll let the worm proceed. Needful first in his vitals shall nestle when all your joints he has well digested! So now heed what I tell — tarry not by the spring: take yourself off to other tracks; return no more to me!	SIEGFRIED (lachend). Mime, weilst du am Quell dahin lass' ich den Wurm wohl geh'n: Nothung stoss' ich ihm erst in die Nieren, wenn er dich selbst dort mit 'weg gesoffen! Darum, hör' meinen Rath, raste nicht dort am Quell: kehre dich 'weg, so weit du kannst, und komm' nie mehr zu mir!

MIME.   When faint with the strife
               thou wouldst refresh thee,
            would I not win a welcome?
               Call on me then,
               shouldst thou need counsel—
            or if pleasure in fearing thou find.

(SIEGFRIED *bids him begone with a violent gesture.*)

MIME (*aside—going*). Fafner and Siegfried—
               Siegfried and Fafner—
            Would each the other might kill!
               (*He retreats into the wood.*)

———

SIEGFRIED (*alone. He seats himself under the great
            lime again*).
            That he's no father of mine
            how full is the joy I feel!
               Now truly fragrant
               the forest seems;
               now how glad is
               the glorious day!
            since that miscreant wretch has gone,
            never more to confront my gaze!
               (*Thoughtful silence.*)
            My sire—what semblance was his?—
            Ha!—no doubt like myself;
            for, were there of Mime a son,
               must he not look
               Mime's likeness?
               growing as gruesome,
               grizzled and grey,
               cramped and crooked,
               halting and humpbacked,
               with hanging ears stretching,
               bleary eyes staring——
               Out on the sight!
            I'll look on it no more.
[*He leans back and looks up through the branches
of the tree. Long silence. Forest murmur*).
               Surely—my mother,
               what semblance had she?
               I—cannot
               imagine it ever!—
            Like soft fallow doe's
               deeply would shine
            her soft languishing eyes,—
               only more lovely!——

            When balefully she bore me
            why must she have died withal?
            Die thus all mortal mothers,
               leaving their dear ones
               lonely behind?
            Sad were such a fate, sure!——
               Ah! might these looks
               but light on my mother!——
               My own—mother!—
               a mortal's mate!—
(*He sighs and reclines still lower. Long silence.*)

MIME.   Nach freislichem Streit
               dich zu erfrischen,
            wirst du mir wohl nicht wehren?
               Rufe mich auch,
               darbst du des Rathes—
            oder wenn dir das Fürchten gefällt.

(SIEGFRIED *weis't ihn mit einer heftigen Geberde fort*)

MIME (*im Abgehen, für sich*). Fafner und Siegfried—
               Siegfried und Fafner—
            o brächten beide sich um!
               (*Er geht in den Wald zurück.*)

———

SIEGFRIED (*allein*).
            (*Er setzt sich wieder unter die grosse Linde.*)
            Dass der mein Vater nicht ist,
            wie fühl' ich mich drob so froh!
               Nun erst gefällt mir
               der frische Wald;
               nun erst lacht mir
               der lustige Tag,
            da der Garstige von mir schied,
            und ich gar nicht ihn wiederseh'!
               (*Sinnendes Schweigen.*)
            Wie sah wohl mein Vater aus?—
            Ha!—gewiss wie ich selbst:
            denn wär' wo von Mime ein Sohn,
               müsst' er nicht ganz
               Mime gleichen?
               G'rade so garstig,
               griesig und grau,
               klein und krumm
               höckrig und hinkend,
               mit hängenden Ohren,
               triefigen Augen——
               fort mit dem Alp!
            ich mag ihn nicht mehr seh'n.
(*Er lehnt sich zurück und blickt durch den Baumwipfel
auf. Langez Schweigen.—Waldweben.*)
               Aber—wie sah
               meine Mutter wohl aus?
               Das—kann ich
               nun gar nicht mir denken!—
            Der Rehhindin gleich
               glänzten gewiss
            ihr hell schimmernde Augen,—
               nur noch viel schöner!——

            Da bang sie mich geboren,
            warum aber starb sie da?
            Sterben die Menschenmütter
               an ihren Söhnen
               alle dahin?
            Traurig wäre das, traun!——
               Ach! möcht' ich Sohn
               meine Mutter seh'n!——
               meine—Mutter!—
               ein Menschenweib!
(*Er seufzt und streckt sich tiefer zurück. Lang
               Schweigen.—*)

(*Increased rustling of the trees.* SIEGFRIED's *attention is at last riveted by the songs of forest birds.*
(*Wachsendes Waldwehen.* SIEGFRIED's *aufmerksamkeit wird endlich durch den Gesang der Waldvögel
gefesselt.*)

pp

(SIEGFRIED *listens with interest to a bird in the branches above him.*)
(SIEGERIED *lauscht mit wachsender Theilname einem Waldvogel in den Zweigen über ihm.*)

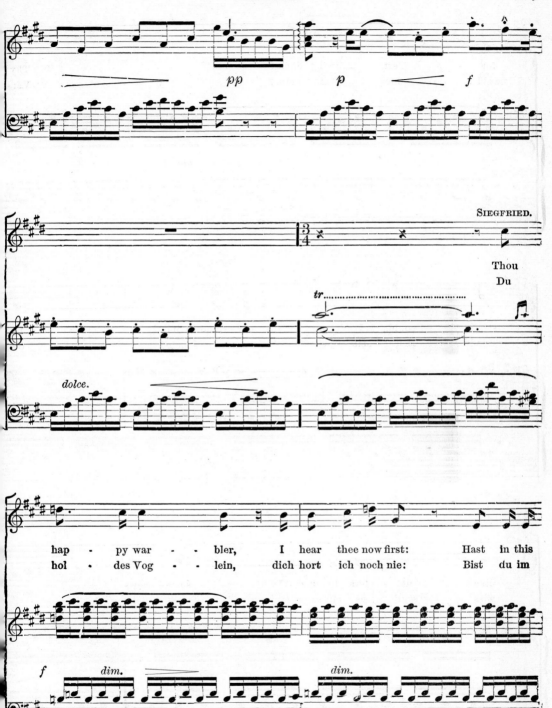

SIEGFRIED.

Thou
Du

dolce.

hap - py war - - bler,   I hear thee now first: Hast in this
hol - des Vog - - lein,   dich hort ich noch nie: Bist du im

f   dim.   dim.

for . . . est thy home?
wald hier da - heim?
Thy Ver-

piu p

strain, could I un - - der-stand it!
stünd' ich sein süs - - ses stam - meln!
Be-
Ge-

like ut - ters to me some news
wiss sagt' es mir' was reil licht,

of my lov - - ing moth - - er!

Von der lie - - ben mut - - ter!

That drivelling dwarf
told me one day
the meaning bound
in language of birds
one could truly attain to: —
would I could learn the way!
(*He reflects. His eyes fall on a clump of reeds, not
far from the lime-tree*).
Ha! I'll essay;
sing with him
on a reed similar sounding;
unrecking the meaning,
seize but the music.
So his speech, if I sing it,
my senses perchance will espy.
(*He cuts himself a reed with his sword and fashions a
pipe out of it.*)
He stops to list:—
I'll stammer along!
(*He tries to imitate the note of the bird on his pipe:
he is unsuccessful, and after repeated trials, shaking
his head in vexation he desists.*)
That sounds not right;
on the reed I see
the melody may not be waked. —
Birdie, I deem
myself but dull:
my deed spans not thy speech.
Now shamed am I quite
by the shrewd little piper:
he peeps to know why I'm pausing. —
Ho there! then hearken
now to my horn;
with the stupid reed
I can render nought.—
To a wild wood-note,
which I can sound,
the lustiest, shalt thou now listen.
A loving companion
lately I called;
nought better came yet
than wolf and bear.
So let me see
whom now it will lure
to make me a loving consort ?
(*He has thrown away the reed and now blows a
merry call on his little silver horn.*)

———

(*There is a stir in the background.* FAFNER, *in the
form of a huge lizard-like dragon, rises from his lair in
the cave; he breaks through the underwood and crawls
from the dell up to the higher ground till his forelegs
rest quite on the knoll. He then utters a loud yawning
growl.*)

SIEGFRIED (*turns round, perceives* FAFNER, *looks at
him in surprise and then laughs*).
At last has my lay
something lovely attracted!
I've waked up a fair-favored friend!

FAFNER (*who has paused, on sight of* SIEGFRIED).
What is that?

SIEGFRIED. Hey! are you a beast
that of speech can boast ?
You surely might teach me something.
Here comes one
who ne'er learnt to fear:
could he by you effect it ?

Ein zankender Zwerg
hat mir erzählt,
der Vöglein Stammeln
gut zu versteh'n,
dazu könnte man kommen:
wie das wohl möglich wär'?
(*Er sinnt nach. Sein Blick fällt auf ein Rohrgebüs
unweit der Linde.*)
Hei! ich versuch's,
sing' ihm nach:
auf dem Rohr tön' ich ihm ähnlich!
Entrath' ich der Worte,
achte der Weise,
sing' ich so seine Sprache,
versteh' ich wohl auch was er spricht.
(*Er hat sich mit dem Schwerte ein Rohr abgeschnitte
und schnitzt sich eine Pfeife draus.*)
Es schweigt und lauscht:—
so schwatz' ich denn los!
(*Er versucht auf der Pfeife die Weise der Voge
nachzuah men es glückt ihm nicht, verdriesslich schi
telt er oft den Kopf: endlich setzt er ganz ab.*)
Das tönt nicht recht:
auf dem Rohre taugt
die wonnige Weise nicht.—
Vöglein, mich dünkt,
ich bleibe dumm:
von dir lernt sich's nicht leicht!
Nun schäm' ich mich gar
vor dem schelmischen Lauscher:
er lugt, und kann nichts erlauschen. —
Heida! so höre
nun auf mein Horn;
auf dem dummen Rohre
geräth mir nichts. —
Einer Waldweise,
wie ich sie kann,
der lustigen sollst du lauschen.
Nach liebem Gesellen
lockt' ich mit ihr:
nichts Bess'res kam noch
als Wolf und Bär.
Nun will ich seh'n,
wen jetzt sie mir lockt:
ob das mir ein lieber Gesell ?
(*Er hat die Pfeife fortgeworfen, und bläst nun a
seinem kleinen silbernen Horne eine lustige Weise.*)

———

(*Im Hintergrunde regt es sich.* FAFNER, *in der G
stalt eines ungeheuren eidechsenartigen Schlange
wurmes, hat sich in der Höhle von seinem Lager erhobe
er bricht durch das Gesträuch, und wälzt sich aus d
Tiefe nach der höheren Stelle vor, so dass er mit de
Vorderleibe bereits auf ihr angelangt ist. Er stös
jetzt einen starken gähnenden Laut aus.*)

SIEGFRIED (*wendet sich um, gewahrt* FAFNER, *blick
ihn verwundert an, und lacht*).
Da hätte mein Lied
mir 'was Liebes erblasen!
du wär'st mir ein saub'rer Gesell!

FAFNER (*hat bei* SIEGFRIED'S *Anblick angehalten*).
Was ist da ?

SIEGFRIED. Ei, bist du ein Thier,
das zum Sprechen taugt,
wohl liess' sich von dir 'was lernen ?
Hier kennt einer
das Fürchten nicht:
kann er's von dir erfahren ?

AFNER.   Art not over-bold?

EGFRIED.   Bold or over-bold —
what wist I?
but you finely I'll tackle,
teach you not fearing to me.

AFNER (*laughs*).   Drink I came for,
now drops to me food!
(*He opens his jaws and shews his teeth.*)

EGFRIED.   An extravagant frontage
you turn on me:
dazzling with teeth
is that dainty maw!
Well were it to close up the cavern:
your gullet gapes far too wide.

AFNER.   For senseless gabble
serves it ill:
rather to eat thee
doth it ope.
(*He lashes his tail menacingly.*)

EGFRIED.   Oho! you gruesome,
grim-looking knave!
To stay your stomach
suits me little:
meetest and wisest were it
to remove you hence, and at once.

AFNER (*roaring*).   Bah! come,
boast-making cub!

EGFRIED (*drawing his sword*).
Look out, growler!
the boaster comes.

(*He confronts* FAFNER: *the latter creeps more over
the knoll and spits from his nostrils at him.* SIEGFRIED
springs aside. FAFNER *curls his tail forwards to reach*
EGFRIED, *but he avoids it and springs over the back
of the dragon with a bound; as the tail follows him and
almost reaches him, he wounds it with his sword.*
AFNER *hastily draws back his tail, roars, and raises
the fore-part of his body, in order to throw his full
weight sideways upon* SIEGFRIED, *thus exposing his
breast to him.* SIEGFRIED *quickly espies the position
of his heart and plunges his sword there up to the very
hilt.* FAFNER *rears still higher in pain and sinks down
upon the wound, while* SIEGFRIED *lets go the sword
and springs aside.*)

EGFRIED.   There lie, noisomest rogue!
Needful sticks in your gizzard.

AFNER (*with weaker voice*).
Who art thou, stalwart stripling,
that hath struck my heart?
Who wakened and stirred thy mind
to this murderous deed?
Thine own brain ne'er, I trow,
brought it about.

EGFRIED.   Much I do not know,
not even who I am:
yourself only did urge me
unto this murderous end.

AFNER.   Thou bright, eager-eyed stripling,
e'en strange to thyself:
whom thou hast murdered
must thou hear.

FAFNER.   Hast du Uebermuth?

SIEGFRIED.   Muth und Uebermuth —
was weiss ich!
Doch dir fahr' ich zu Leibe,
lehrst du das Fürchten mich **nicht!**

FAFNER (*lacht*).   Trinken wollt' ich:
nun treff' ich auch Frass!
(*Er öffnet seinen Rachen und zeigt die Zähne.*)

SIEGFRIED.   Eine zierliche Fresse
zeig'st du mir da:
lachende Zähne
im Leckermaul!
Gut wär's den Schlund dir zu schliessen:
dein Rachen reckt sich zu weit!

FAFNER.   Zu tauben Reden
taugt er schlecht:
dich zu verschlingen
frommt der Schlund.
(*Er droht mit dem Schweife.*)

SIEGFRIED.   Hoho! du grausam
grimmiger Kerl,
von dir verdaut sein
dünkt mich übel:
räthlich und fromm doch **scheint's**
du verreckst hier ohne Frist.

FAFNER (*brüllt*).   Pruh! komm'!
prahlendes Kind.

SIEGFRIED (*fasst das Schwert*).
Sieh' dich vor, Brüller:
der Prahler kommt!
(*Er stellt sich* FAFNER *entgegen: dieser hebt sich
weiter vor auf die Bodenerhöhung, und sprüht aus seinen
Nüstern nach ihm.* SIEGFRIED *springt zur Seite.*
FAFNER *schwingt den Schweif nach vorn, um* SIEG-
FRIED *zu fassen: dieser weicht ihm aus, indem er mit
einem Satze über den Rücken des Wurmes hinweg-
springt; als der Schweif sich auch hierhin ihm schnell
nachwendet, und ihn fast schon packt, verwundet* SIEG-
FRIED *diesen mit dem Schwerte.* FAFNER *zieht den
Schweif hastig zurück, brüllt, und bäumt seinen Vorder-
leib, um mit dessen voller Wucht zur Seite sich auf*
SIEGFRIED *zu werfen: so bietet er diesem die Brust;*
SIEGFRIED *erspäht schnell die Stelle des Herzens, und
stösst sein Schwert bis an das Heft hinein.* FAFNER
bäumt sich von Schwert noch höher, und sinkt, als
SIEGFRIED *das Schwert losgelassen und zur Seite gesprungen ist, auf die Wunde zusammen.*)

SIEGFRIED.   Da lieg', neidischer Kerl!
Nothung trägst du im **Herzen.**

FAFNER (*mit schwächerer Stimme*).
Wer bist du, kühner Knabe,
der das Herz mir traf?
Wer reizte des Kindes Muth
zu der mordlichen That?
Dein Hirn brütete nicht,
was du vollbracht.

SIEGRIED.   Viel weiss ich noch nicht,
noch nicht auch wer ich bin:
mit dir mordlich zu ringen
reiztest du selbst meinen **Muth.**

FAFNER.   Du helläugiger Knabe,
unkund deiner selbst:
wen du gemordet
meld' ich dir.

The giants' generous race
which ruled the world at one time —
    Fasolt and Fafner,
the brothers, fallen now both lie.
    For the fatal gold
    we gained from the gods
death to Fasolt I dealt.
    Now I, as Worm
    the hoard o'erwatching,
Fafner, the last of giants,
fall by a juvenile hand. —
    Bear thou good heed,
    blossoming hero:
    'mid treason treads
    he who holds the hoard:
one who blindly shewed thee this deed
doth shape for thee, boy, surely death.
        (*Dying.*)
    Weigh what happens: —
    heed my words!

SIEGFRIED.   What were my parents
    rede to me yet!
    wise thou appearest,
    wild one, expiring;
rede it too from my title:
Siegfried is it, I trow.

FAFNER.   Siegfried . . .!
    (*He sighs, raises himself up and dies.*)

SIEGFRIED.   The dead can tell no tidings.
    So lead me henceforth
    my life-keeping sword.
(FAFNER *has rolled over on his side in dying. SIEG-
FRIED draws the sword from his breast : in doing so his
hand becomes smeared with blood : he draws it hastily
away.*)
    Like fire burns the blood!
(*He instinctively puts his finger to his mouth to suck
the blood off it. As he gazes thoughtfully before him
his attention is arrested all at once by the song of the
birds. He listens with bated breath.*)
    Would it not seem
yon songster were speaking to me? —
    well the words I distinguish!
    Was it the blood
    that worked this magic?
That stranger bird I hear —
hark! what sings he now?

            VOICE OF A WOOD-BIRD
                (*in the lime-tree*).
Hey! Siegfried doth hold
now the Nibelung's hoard:
O he'll find the hoard
    in the hole anon!
Were he the Tarnhelm to win,
it would tide him through wonderful tasks;
but were he the ring too to ravish
'twould give him the ward of the world!

SIEGFRIED.   Thanks, pretty warbler,
    for thy advice:
    I'll follow thy voice.
(He *goes up and descends into the cavern, where he
    disappears from view.*)

Die einst der Welt gewaltet,
der Riesen ragend Geschlecht,
    Fasolt und Fafner,
die Brüder, fielen nun beide.
    Um verfluchtes Gold,
    von Göttern vergabt,
traf ich Fasolt zu todt:
    der nun als Wurm
    den Hort bewachte,
Fafner, den letzten Riesen,
fällte ein rosiger Held. —
    Blick nun hell,
    blühender Knabe;
    des Hortes Herrn
    umringt Verrath:
der dich Blinden reizte zur That,
beräth nun des Blühenden Tod
        (*Ersterbend.*)
    Merk' wie's endet: —
    acht' auf mich!

SIEGFRIED.   Woher ich stamme,
    rathe mir noch;
    weise ja scheinst du
    Wilder im Sterben;
rath' es nach meinem Namen:
Siegfried bin ich genannt.

FAFNER.   Siegfried . . . ?
    (*Er seufzt, hebt sich und stirbt.*)

SIEGFRIED.   Zur Kunde taugt kein Todter. —
    So leite mich denn
    mein lebendes Schwert!
(FAFNER *hat sich im Sterben zur Seite gewälzt. SIE-
FRIED zieht das Schwert aus seiner Brust: dabei wird
seine Hand vom Blute benetzt; er fährt heftig mit der
Hand auf.*)
    Wie Feuer brennt das Blut!
(*Er führt unwillkürlich die Finger zum Munde, um
das Blut von ihnen abzusaugen. Wie er sinnend vor
sich hinblickt, wird plötzlich seine Aufmerksamkeit von
dem Gesange der Waldvögel angezogen. Er lauscht
mit verhaltenem Athem.*) —
    Ist mir doch fast —
    als sprächen die Vöglein zu mir:
    deutlich dünken mich's Worte!
    Nützte mir das
    des Blutes Genuss? —
Das selt'ne Vöglein hier —
horch! was singt es mir?

            STIMME EINES WALDVOGEL'S
                (*in der Linde*).
Hei! Siegfried gehört
nun der Niblungen Hort:
o fänd' in der Höhle
    den Hort er jetzt!
Wollt' er den Tarnhelm gewinnen,
der taugt' ihm zu wonniger That:
doch möcht' er den Ring sich errathen,
der macht' ihn zum Walter der Welt!

SIEGFRIED.   Dank, liebes Vöglein,
    für deinen Rath:
    gern folg' ich dem Ruf.
(*Er geht und steigt in die Höhle hinab, wo er alsbald
    gänzlich verschwindet.*)

(MIME *sinks on, looking about timidly, to assure imself of* FAFNER'S *death.—At the same time ALBERICH comes out from his cleft at the opposite side; he atches* MIME *narrowly. As the latter, not finding IEGFRIED, carefully steals towards the cave, ALBERICH darts upon him and bars his way.*)

LBERICH.　Whither slinkest thou,
　　　　　　hasty and sly,
　　　　　　slippery scamp?

IME.　　　Accursed brother,
　　　　　　what brings thee here?
　　　　　　I bid thee hence.

LBERICH.　Graspest thou, rogue,
　　　　　　towards my gold?
　　　　　　Dost lust for my goods?

IME.　　　Yield the position!
　　　　　　This station is mine.
　　　　　　What stirrest thou here?

LBERICH.　Startled art thou
　　　　　　from stealthy concerns,
　　　　　　that I've disturbed?

IME.　　　What I have shaped
　　　　　　with shrewdest toil
　　　　　　shall not be shaken.

LBERICH,　Was't thou that robbed
　　　　　　the golden ring from the Rhine?
　　　　　　or charged it with great
　　　　　　and choice enchantment around?

IME.　　　Who formed the Tarnhelm,
　　　　　　which to all forms can turn?
　　　　　　By thee 'twas wanted;
　　　　　　its worker wert thou too?

LBERICH.　What couldst thou e'er, fool,
　　　　　　by thyself have fancied and fashioned?
　　　　　　The magic ring
　　　　　　made the dwarf meet for the task.

IME.　　　Where now is thy ring?
　　　　　　The giants have robbed thee, thou recreant!
　　　　　　What thou hast lost,
　　　　　　by my lore, belike, I will gain.

LBERICH.　By the boy's exploit
　　　　　　shalt thou, booby, be bettered?
　　　　　　Thou shalt have it not,
　　　　　　for its holder in truth is he.

IME.　　　I nourished him,
　　　　　　and his nurse now shall he pay:
　　　　　　for toil and woe
　　　　　　long while have I waited reward.

LBERICH.　For a bantling's keep
　　　　　　would this beggarly
　　　　　　niggardly boor,
　　　　　　bold and blustering,
　　　　　　be well nigh as a king?
　　　　　　To rankest of dogs
　　　　　　booteth the ring
　　　　　　far rather than thee:
　　　　　　never, thou rogue,
　　　　　　shall reach thee the magic round!

IME.　　　Then hold it still
　　　　　　and heed it well,
　　　　　　thy hoarded ring.

(MIME *schleicht heran, scheu umherblickend, um sich von* FAFNER'S *Tod zu überzeugen. — Gleichzeitig kommt von der anderen Seite* ALBERICH *aus dem Geklüft hervor; er beobachtet* MIME *genau. Als dieser* SIEGFRIED *nicht mehr gewahrt, und vorsichtig sich nach hinten der Höhle zuwendet, stürzt* ALBERICH *auf ihn zu, und vertritt ihm den Weg.*)

ALBERICH.　Wohin schleich'st du
　　　　　　eilig und schlau,
　　　　　　schlimmer Gesell?

MIME.　　　Verfluchter Bruder,
　　　　　　dich braucht' ich hier!
　　　　　　Was bringt dich her?

ALBERICH.　Geizt es dich Schelm
　　　　　　nach meinem Gold?
　　　　　　Verlang'st du mein Gut?

MIME.　　　Fort von der Stelle!
　　　　　　Die Stätte ish mein:
　　　　　　was stöberst du hier?

ALBERICH.　Stör' ich dich wohl
　　　　　　im stillen Geschäft,
　　　　　　wenn du hier stiehl'st?

MIME.　　　Was ich erschwang
　　　　　　mit schwerer Müh',
　　　　　　soll mir nicht schwinden.

ALBERICH.　Hast du dem Rhein
　　　　　　das Gold zum Ringe geraubt?
　　　　　　Erzeugtest du gar
　　　　　　den zähen Zauber im Reif?

MIME.　　　Wer schuf den Tarnhelm,
　　　　　　der die Gestalten tauscht?
　　　　　　Der sein' bedurfte,
　　　　　　erdachtest du ihn wohl?

ALBERICH.　Was hättest du Stümper
　　　　　　je wohl zu stampfen verstanden?
　　　　　　Der Zauberring
　　　　　　zwang mir zur Kunst erst den Zwerg?

MIME.　　　Wo hast du den Ring?
　　　　　　Dir Zagem entrissen ihn Riesen!
　　　　　　Was du verlor'st,
　　　　　　meine List erlangt' es für mich.

ALBERICH.　Mit des Knaben That
　　　　　　will der Knicker nun knausern?
　　　　　　Dir gehört sie gar nicht,
　　　　　　der Helle ist selbst ihr Herr!

MIME.　　　Ich zog ihn auf;
　　　　　　für die Zucht zahlt er mir nun:
　　　　　　für Müh' und Last
　　　　　　erlauert' ich lang' meinen Lohn!

ALBERICH.　Für des Knaben Zucht
　　　　　　will der knick'rige
　　　　　　schäbige Knecht
　　　　　　keck und kühn
　　　　　　gar wohl König nun sein?
　　　　　　Dem räudigsten Hund
　　　　　　wäre der Ring
　　　　　　gerath'ner als dir:
　　　　　　nimmer erring'st
　　　　　　du Rüpel den Herrscherreif!

MIME.　　　Behalt' ihn denn:
　　　　　　hüte ihn wohl
　　　　　　den hellen Reif!

Be thou head,
but yet hail me as brother!
For my own Tarnhelm,
excellent toy,
I'll tender it thee!
'twill boot us twain,
twin we the booty like this.

ALBERICH (*laughing scornfully*).
Twin it with thee?
and the Tarnhelm too?
How sly thou art!
Safe I'd sleep then
never from thy ensnarings.

MIME (*beside himself*).   Wilt not bargain?
Wilt not barter?
Bare must I go,
gaining no boon?
Giv'st thou to me no booty?

ALBERICH.   Not an atom,
not e'en a nail's worth:
all I deny thee.

MIME (*furiously*).   In the ring and Tarnhelm
ne'er shalt thou triumph!
Nought talk we of shares!
Unto thee I'll call for
Siegfried to come;
with his carving sword
the caustic boy
shall crush thee, brother of mine!

ALBERICH.   Turn thy head round; —
from the cavern t'wards us he comes. —

MIME.   Trivial toys
have tempted him there. —

ALBERICH.   The Tarnhelm he holds! —

MIME.   Aye, and the ring! —

ALBERICH.   A curse! — the ring! —

MIME (*with an evil laugh*).
Let him the ring to thee render! —
I ween full soon I shall win it.
(*He slips back into the wood.*)

ALBERICH.   And yet to its lord
shall it alone be delivered!
(*He disappears in the cleft.*)

(SIEGFRIED, *with Tarnhelm and ring, has stepped
out, during the last words, from the cave, slowly and
thoughtfully: he inspects his prizes reflectively, and
again pauses on the knoll by the tree.— Deep silence.*)

SIEGFRIED.   How ye may serve
I hardly see;
I snatched ye, though,
from the hoard of heaped-up gold,
as guiding voice did advise.
Let serve then your wealth
as this struggle's witness;
these baubles shall show
that in fight I Fafner laid low
but of fearing no whit I learnt.

Sei du Herr:
doch mich heisse auch Bruder
Um meines Tarnhelm's
lustigen Tand
tausch' ich ihn dir:
uns beiden taugt's,
theilen die Beute wir so.

ALBERICH (*höhnisch lachend*).
Theilen mit dir?
und den Tarnhelm gar?
Wie schlau du bist!
Sicher schlief' ich
niemals vor deinen Schlingen!

MIME (*ausser sich*).   Selbst nicht tauschen?
Auch nicht theilen?
Leer soll ich geh'n,
ganz ohne Lohn?
Gar nichts willst du mir lassen?

ALBERICH.   Nichts von allem,
nicht einen Nagel
sollst du dir nehmen!

MIME (*wüthend*).   Weder Ring noch Tarnhelm
soll dir denn taugen!
nicht theil' ich nun mehr.
Gegen dich ruf' ich
Siegfried zu Rath
und des Recken Schwert:
der rasche Held,
der richte, Brüderchen, dich!

ALBERICH.   Kehre dich um: —
aus der Höhle kommt er schon her. —

MIME.   Kindischen Tand
erkor er gewiss. —

ALBERICH.   Den Tarnhelm hat er! —

MIME.   Doch auch den Ring! —

ALBERICH.   Verflucht! — den Ring! —

MIME (*lacht hämisch*).
Lass' ihn den Ring dir doch geben!
Ich will ihn mir schon gewinnen. —
(*Er schlüpft in den Wald zurück.*)

ALBERICH.   Und von seinem Herrn
soll er allein noch gehören!
(*Er verschwindet im Geklüft.*)

(SIEGFRIED *ist, mit Tarnhelm und Ring, während de
Letzten langsam und sinnend aus der Höhle vorge
schritten: er betrachtet gedankenvoll seine Beute, un
hält, nahe dem Baume, auf der Höhe wieder an. —
Grosse Stille.*)

SIEGFRIED.   Was ihr mir nützet
weiss ich nicht:
doch nahm ich euch
aus des Horts gehäuftem Gold,
weil guter Rath mir es rieth.
So taug' eu're Zier
als des Tages Zeuge:
mich mahne der Tand
dass ich kämpfend Fafner erregt,
doch das Fürchten noch nicht gelernt!

(He sticks the Tarnhelm in his girdle and puts the ring on his finger. — Perfect stillness, Increased rustling of the woods. — SIEGFRIED mechanically looks for the bird and listens to it with bated breath.)

VOICE OF THE WOOD-BIRD
(in the lime-tree).
Hey! Siegfried doth hold
now the helm and the ring!
O trust not in Mime,
the treacherous elf!
Heareth Siegfried but sharply
the shifty hypocrite's words:
what at heart he means
shall by Mime be shewn;
so booteth the taste of the blood.

(SIEGFRIED's expression and gestures shew that he as understood all. He perceives MIME's approach nd remains without moving, leaning on his sword, bserving and self-repressed, in his station on the nound till the end of the following speech.)

MIME *(slowly entering).*
He broods as he weighs
the booty's worth. —
Walked there with him
a wily Wanderer,
foraging here,
informing the boy
with cunning runes and redes?
Doubly sly
shall be my deeds;
my artfullest springes
all shall be set,
that I with true-seeming
traitorous talk
may entrap the truculent boy!
(He advances nearer to SIEGFRIED.)
I hail thee, Siegfried!
Say, my hero,
hast thou then fearing attained?

SIEGFRIED. The teacher I found not here.

MIME. But the serpent-worm,
then hast thou destroyed him?
He, sure, was a foul sort of friend.

SIEGFRIED. Though grim and dreadful he was,
his death grieves me, in sooth,
while far eviller scoundrels
undestroyed are yet living!
Who made me murder him,
I hate him more than the worm.

MIME. Now softly! thou wilt not
see me much more:
an endless sleep
soon upon thine eyes shall weigh!
For all that I wanted
hast thou well worked;
I'll try now from thee
to win me the golden treasure.—
Methinks I'll safely effect it:
thou wert ever easy to fool!

SIEGFRIED. You're seeking to work my death then?

MIME. What? did I say that?—
Siegfried, hear me, my sonny!
Thee and all thy kind
have I constantly hated;
from fondness, thou burden,

(Er steckt den Tarnhelm sich in den Gürtel, und den Reif an den Finger. — Stillschweigen. Wachsendes Waldweben. — SIEGFRIED achtet unwillkürlich wieder des Vogel's, und lauscht ihm mit verhaltenem Athem)

STIMME DES WALDVOGEL'S
(in der Linde).
Hei! Siegfried gehört
nun der Helm und Ring!
O traut' er Mime
dem Treulosen nicht!
Hörte Siegfried nur scharf
auf des Schelmen Heuchlergered':
wie sien Herz es meint
kann er Mime versteh'n;
so nützt' ihm des Blutes Genuss.

(SIEGFRIED's Miene und Geberde drücken aus, dass er alles wohl vernommen. Er sieht MIME sich nähern, und bleibt, ohne sich zu rühren, auf sein Schwert gestützt, beobachtend und in sich geschlossen, in seiner Stellung auf der Anhöhe bis zum Schlusse des folgenden Auftrittes.)

MIME *(langsam auftretend).*
Er sinnt und erwägt
der Beute Werth: —
weilte wohl hier
ein weiser Wand'rer,
schweifte umher,
beschwatzte das Kind
mit listiger Runen Rath?
Zwiefach schlau
sei nun der Zwerg:
die listigste Schlinge
leg' ich jetzt aus,
dass ich mit traulichem
Trug-Gerede
bethöre das trotzige Kind!
(Er tritt näher an SIEGFRIED heran.)
Willkommen, Siegfried!
Sag', du Kühner,
hast du das Fürchten gelernt?

SIEGFRIED. Den Lehrer fand ich noch nicht.

MIME. Doch den Schlangenwurm,
du hast ihn erschlagen:
das war doch ein schlimmer Gesell?

SIEGFRIED. So grimm und tückisch er war,
sein Tod grämt mich doch schier,
da viel üblere Schächer
unerschlagen noch leben!
Der mich ihn morden hiess,
den hass' ich mehr als den Wurm.

MIME. Nur sacht'! nicht lange
sieh'st du mich mehr:
zu ew'gem Schlaf
schliess' ich die Augen dir bald!
Wozu ich dich brauchte,
das hast du vollbracht;
jetzt will ich nur noch
die Beute dir abgewinnen: —
mich dünkt, das soll mir gelingen;
zu bethören bist du ja leicht!

SIEGFRIED. So sinnst du auf meinen Schaden?

MIME. Wie sagt' ich das?—
Siegfried, hör' doch, mein Sohn!
Dich und deine Art
hasst' ich immer von Herzen;
aus Liebe erzog ich

I fostered thee not:
the hoard under Fafner's hold
alone I labored to win.
If thou'llt not give up
that with good will —
Siegfried, my son,
thou see'st thyself —
thy life thou must really relinquish!

SIEGFRIED.   That you should hate me
hurts me not:
but must my life to you be delivered?

MIME.   I said nought of that!
Thou mistakest me quite.
(*Giving himself the most elaborate pains to disguise his meaning.*)
See, thou art tired
with mighty toil;
burneth thy body with heat.
So, to restore thee
with stirring drink,
swiftly I speed to thee.
While thy sword thou didst beat out,
I brewed this stuff:
take but a sip,
I win me thy trusty sword,
and with it hoard and helm.
(*He chuckles.*)

SIEGFRIED.   So, both of my sword
and what I have seized on,
Ring and booty, you'd rob me?

MIME.   How thou dost falsely distort!
Stammers — falters my speech?
The greatest trouble
I give myself
my secret designing
safely to bury,
and thou, stupid boy,
constru'st all opposite-wise!
Open thine ears then
and awake thy wits:
hearken what Mime means!
Here, take! and drink for refreshment!
my draughts freshened thee oft:
deep though thine anger,
sullen thine ire,
yet all I brought
abusing, — tookest thou ever.

SIEGFRIED (*without stirring in the least*).
Of a goodly draught
were I glad:
of what compounded you this?

MIME.   Hey! just try it:
trust to my skill!
In deathly darkness
soon shall thy senses be laid:
without mind or motion
straight stretched will thy limbs be.
Lying then so,
light were it
the prize to take and deposit:
didst thou wake though again,
never were I
safe from thy reach,
did I seize e'en the ring.
So with the sword
thou hast shaped so sharp
truly I'll hew
thy head right off:
then I shall have rest and the ring!
(*He chuckles again.*)

---

dich Lästigen nicht:
dem Horte in Fafners Hut,
dem Golde galt meine Müh'.
Giebst du mir das
nun gutwillig nicht, —
Siegfried, mein Sohn,
das siehst du wohl selbst —
dein Leben musst du mir lassen!

SIEGFRIED.   Dass du mich hassest,
hör' ich gern:
doch mein Leben auch muss ich dir lasse(

MIME.   Das sag' ich doch nicht?
du verstehst mich falsch!
(*Er giebt sich die ersichtlichste Mühe zur Verstellun*
Sieh', du bist müde
von harter Müh';
brünstig brennt dir der Leib:
dich zu erquicken
mit queckem Trank
säum' ich Sorgender nicht.
Als dein Schwert du dir branntest,
braut' ich den Sud:
trinkst du nun den,
gewinn' ich dein trautes Schwert,
und mit ihm Helm und Hort.
(*Er kichert dazu.*)

SIEGFRIED.   So willst du mein Schwert
und was ich erschwungen,
Ring und Beute mir rauben?

MIME.   Was du doch falsch mich versteh'st!
Stamml' ich und fas'le wohl gar?
Die grösste Mühe
geb' ich mir:
mein heimliches Sinnen
heuchelnd zu bergen,
und du dummer Bube
deutest alles doch falsch!
Oeff'ne die Ohren,
und vernimm genau:
höre, was Mime meint! —
Hier nimm! trinke dir Labung!
mein Trank labte dich oft:
that'st du wohl unwirsch,
stelltest dich arg:
was ich dir bot —
erbos't auch — nahmst du's doch immer

SIEGFRIED. (*ohne eine Miene zu verzieh'n.*)
Einen guten Trank
hätt'ich gern:
wie hast du diesen gebrau't?

MIME.   Hei! so trink' nur:
trau' meiner Kunst!
In Nacht und Nebel
sinken die Sinne dir bald:
ohne Wach' und Wissen,
stracks streck'st du die Glieder.
Lieg'st du nun da,
leicht könnt' ich
die Beute nehmen und bergen:
doch erwachtest du je,
nirgends wär' ich
sicher vor dir,
hätt' ich selbst auch den Ring.
D'rum mit dem Schwert,
das so scharf du schuf'st,
hau' ich dem Kind
den Kopf erst ab:
dann hab' ich mir Ruh' und den Ring!
(*Er kichert wieder.*)

SIEGFRIED. In slumber must I be murdered?

MIME. What mean'st thou? did I say that
I will but chop
from the child his head!
For, had I not hated
thee so sore,
and had not thy scoffs
and my shameful endurance
so loudly called for payment,
I must without pausing
fling thee from my pathway;
how else should I earn me the treasure
which Alberich aims at as well? — —
Now, my Volsung,
vulpine cub!
taste and vanish in death:
no drink thou more wilt try.

He has come close up to SIEGFRIED *and now hands in with offensive importunity a drinking-horn into which he has previously poured the draught from his task.* SIEGFRIED *has already grasped his sword, and now, as if with an impulse of sudden disgust, lays* MIME *dead to the ground with one stroke. — From the cleft* ALBERICH *is heard to send forth a peal of mocking laughter.*

SIEGFRIED. Taste thou my sword,
infamous serpent!
"Needful" pays
pests nimbly;
for this I forged the weapon.

(*He seizes the body of* MIME, *drags it to the cave's mouth and throws it inside.*)
In the hollow here
lie with the hoard!
With stubborn lures
thou strovest for it,
so now with its wealth I reward thee! —
And a goodly watch-dog
I give to thee,
that so no thieves may threaten.

(*He drags the carcass of the dragon to the cave's mouth so as to stop it up with it completely.*)
There lie thou too,
twining worm,
the glittering hoard
helping to guard,
with yon booty-ravishing fool!
So find ye both at last your rest!

(*He returns from his task. — It is mid-day.*)
Hot am I
with my heavy load! —
Brawling speeds
my boiling blood;
my hand burns on my head. — —
High stands the sun now!
in heaven's blue
beams his eye,
from the distance darting to me. —
Languid coolness
shall court me under the lime-tree!

He again stretches himself under the lime-tree. — Perfect stillness. Forest murmurs. After a long pause):
Now once more, lovely warbler,
as we have lacked
long a discourse,
I'd list gladly to thy song:
on the twig I see thee
restfully rocking:
twitt'ring soar around
brothers and sisters,
encircling thee, lightsome and loved.

SIEGFRIED. Im Schlafe willst du mich morden?

MIME. Was möcht' ich? sagt' ich denn das? —
Ich will dir Kind
nur den Kopf abhau'n!
Denn hasste ich dich
auch nicht so hell,
und hätt' ich des Schimpf's
und der schändlichen Müh'
auch nicht so viel zu rächen:
aus dem Weg dich zu räumen
darf ich nicht rasten,
wie käm' ich sonst anders zur Beute,
da Alberich auch nach ihr lugt? — —
Nun, mein Wälsung!
Wolfssohn du!
Sauf' und würg' dich zu Tod:
nie thu'st du mehr einen Schluck!

(*Er hat sich nahe an* SIEGFRIED *herangemacht, und reicht ihm jetzt mit widerlicher Zudringlichkeit ein Trinkhorn, in das er zuvor aus einem Gefässe das Getränk gegossen.* SIEGFRIED *hat bereits das Schwert gefasst, und streckt jetzt, wie in einer Anwandlung heftigen Ekel's,* MIME *mit einem Streiche todt zu Boden. — Man hört* ALBERICH *aus dem Geklüft heraus ein höhnisches Gelächter aufschlagen.*)

SIEGFRIED. Schmeck' du mein Schwert,
ekliger Schwätzer!
Neides-Zoll
zahlt Nothung:
dazu durft' ich ihn schmieden.

(*Er packt* MIME'S *Leichnam auf, schleppt ihn nach der Höhle, und wirft ihn dort hinein.*)
In der Höhle hier
lieg' auf dem Hort!
Mit zäher List
erzieltest du ihn:
jetzt magst du des Wonnigen walten! —
Einen guten Wächter
geb' ich dir auch,
dass er vor Dieben dich deckt.

(*Er wälzt die Leiche des Wurmes vor den Eingang der Höhle, so dass er diesen ganz damit verstopft.*)
Da lieg' auch du,
dunkler Wurm!
Den gleissenden Hort
hüte zugleich
mit dem beuterührigen Feind:
so fandet ihr beide nun Ruh'!

Er kommt nach der Arbeit wieder vor. — Es ist Mittag.)
Heiss ward mir
von der harten Last! —
Brausend jagt mein
brünstiges Blut;
die Hand brennt mir am Haupt. —
Hoch steht schon die Sonne:
aus lichtem Blau
blickt ihr Aug'
auf den Scheitel steil mir herab. —
Linde Kühlung
erkies' ich mir unter der Linde!

(*Er streckt sich wieder unter der Linde aus. — Grosse Stille Waldweben. Nach einem längeren Schweigen.*)
Noch einmal, liebes Vöglein,
da wir so lang'
lästig gestört, —
lausch' ich gern deinem Sang:
auf dem Zweige seh' ich
wohlig dich wiegen;
zwitschernd umschwirren
dich Brüder und Schwestern,
umschweben dich lustig und lieb!

But I — am all alone,
have no brother nor sister:
   my mother sped,
   my father fall'n;—
their son ne'er they saw!—
   I did but consort
   with a cankerous dwarf,
   kindness drew us
   not together;
   guilefullest toils
   the traitor contrived:—
to death was I forced to treat him!—

   Friendliest warbler,
   I fain would demand,
   grant unto me
   a gracious friend.
Wilt thou thereto rightly rede me?
   I've called one so oft
   and he comes to me ne'er:
   thou, my fav'rite;
   farest, sure, better!
Already rightly thou'st spaed;
now sing! I list to thy song.
     (Silence; then):

   VOICE OF THE WOOD-BIRD.

   Hey! Siegfried has slain
   now the sinister dwarf!
   I wot for him now
   a glorious wife.
In guarded fastness she sleeps,
fire doth emborder the spot:
   o'erstepped he the blaze,
   waked he the bride,
Brünnhilde then would be his!

SIEGFRIED (*starting impetuously to his feet*).
   O lovely song!
   Sweetest delight!
   How burns its sense
   my suffering breast!
   How flies it headlong,
   firing my heart!
   What swiftly o'ersways
   my heart and senses?
Say to me, dearest friend!

THE WOOD-BIRD. Lightly, though lorn,
   I sing of loving;
   winsome in woe
   weaving my lay:
warm hearts can alone comprehend!

SIEGFRIED.   Forth I hasten
   henceward exulting;
forth from the wood to the fell!–
   But once more say to me,
   lovely singer,—
may I the furnace then break through?
waken the marvellous bride?

THE WOOD-BIRD.   The bride is won,
   Brünnhilde awaked
   by faint-heart ne'er:
but by him who knows not fear.

SIEGFRIED (*laughing with delight*).
   The stupid lad,
   who to fear has not learnt,
dear flutt'rer, that is myself!
   To-day I put me
   to profitless toil
this fearing from Fafner to gather.

Doch ich — bin so allein,
hab' nicht Bruder noch Schwester,
   meine Mutter schwand,
   meine Vater fiel:
nie sah sie der Sohn! —
   Mein einz'ger Gesell
   war ein garst'ger Zwerg;
   Güte zwang
   nie uns zu Liebe;
   listige Schlingen
   warf mir der Schlaue:—

nun musst' ich ihn gar erschlagen!—
   Freundliches Vöglein,
   dich frag' ich nun:
   gönntest du mir
   wohl ein gutes Gesell?
willst du das Rechte mir rathen?
   Ich lockte so oft,
   und erloos't es nicht:
   du, mein Trauter,
   träf'st es wohl besser!
So recht ja riethest du schon:
nun sing'! ich lausche dem Sang.
     (*Schweigen; dann:*)

STIMME DES WALDVOGEL'S.

   Hei! Siegfried erschlug
   nun den schlimmen Zwerg!
   Jetzt wüsst' ich ihm noch
   das herrlichste Weib.
Auf hohem Felsen sie schläft,
ein Feuer umbrennt ihren Saal:
   durchschritt' er die Brunst,
   erweckt' er die Braut,
Brünnhilde wäre dann sein!

SIEGFRIED (*fährt mit jäher Heftigkeit vom Sitze auf*)
   O holder Song!
   süssester Hauch!
   Wie brennt sein Sinn
   mir sehrend die Brust!
   Wie zückt er heftig
   zündend mein Herz!
   Was jagt mir so jach
   durch Herz und Sinne?
Sing' es mir, süsser Freund!

DER WALDVOGEL. Lustig im Leid
   sing' ich von Liebe;
   wonnig und weh'
   web' ich mein Lied:
nur Sehnende kennen den Sinn!

SIEGFRIED.   Fort jagt mich's
   jauchzend von hinnen,
fort aus dem Wald auf den Fels!
   Noch einmal sage mir,
   holder Sänger:
werd' ich das Feuer durchbrechen?
kann ich erwecken die Braut?

DER WALDVOGEL.   Die Braut gewinnt,
   Brünnhild' erweckt
   ein Feiger nie:
nur wer das Fürchten nicht kennt!

SIEGFRIED (*lacht auf vor Entzücken*).
   Der dumme Knab',
   der das Fürchten nicht kennt!
mein Vöglein, das bin ja ich!
   Noch heut' gab ich
   vergebens mir Müh',
das Fürchten von Fafner zu lernen.

I burn now to gain it
from Brünnhilde's reding:
who'll point me the path to her rock?
{ *The bird flutters forth, hovers over* SIEGFRIED *and
flies away.*}

SIEGFRIED (*shouting with joy*).
The road then direct me rightly:
whither thou fliest
follows my foot!
{ *He hastens after the bird. — The curtain falls.*}

Nun brennt mich die Lust,
es von Brünnhild' zu wissen:
wie find' ich zum Felsen den Weg?
(*Der Vogel flattert auf, schwebt über* SIEGFRIED, *und
fliegt davon.*)

SIEGFRIED (*jauchzend*).
So wird mir der Weg gewiesen:
wohin du flatterst
folg' ich dem Flug!
(*Er eilt dem Vogel nach. — Der Vorhang fällt.*)

THIRD ACT.

A WILD REGION

t the foot of a rocky mountain, which rises steeply L.
*wards the back.— Night, storm, thunder, and light-
in7.*
Before a vault-!ike hollow in the rocks stands the

WANDERER. Waken, witch-wife!
Witch-wife, awaken!
Let lengthy sleep
wend from thy slumbering eyes.
I summon thee forth:
arise! arise!
from nebulous depths,
from night and darkness arise!
Erda! Erda!
undying witch!
From hidden abysses
bear thee on high!
Thy reveille I sing,
let it arouse thee;
from sentient slumber
shalt thou arise.
All-wotter of
all world-wisdom!
Erda! Erda!
Undying witch!
Waken, thou witch-wife! awaken!
{ *The hollow has begun to glow with light.* ERDA
*ises from below in a bluish halo. She seems as if
overed with hoar-frost; her hair and garments gleam
ith iridescent light.*}

ERDA. Great might hath song!
strongly moves th' enchantment.
I am awakened
from witful repose:
who drives my sleep away?

WANDERER. Thy summoner am I,
and songs I utter
to stir the senses
in bonds of slumber sealed.
The world I roved through,
wandering far
tidings to win me,
all-wisdom well to be 'ware of.
Counsellors none
can cope with thy lore;

WILDE GEGEND

*am Fusse eines Felsenberges, der links nach hinten
steil aufsteigt. — Nacht, Sturm und Wetter. Blitz und
Donner.
Vor einem gruftähnlichen Höhlenthore im Felsen steht
der*

WANDERER. Wache! Wache!
Wala, erwache!
Aus langem Schlafe
weck' ich dich Schlummernde wach.
Ich rufe dich auf:
herauf! herauf!
Aus nebliger Gruft,
aus nächt'gem Grunde herauf.
Erda! Erda!
Ewiges Weib!
Aus heimischer Tiefe
tauche zur Höh'!
Dein Wecklied sing' ich,
dass du erwach'st;
aus sinnendem Schlafe
sing' ich dich auf.
Allwissende!
Urweltweise!
Erda! Erda!
Ewiges Weib!
Wache, du Wala! erwache!
(*Die Höhlengruft hat zu erdämmern begonnen: in
bläulichem Lichtscheine steigt* ERDA *aus der Tiefe.
Sie erscheint wie von Reif bedeckt; Haar und Gewand
werfen einen glitzernden Schimmer von sich.*)

ERDA. Stark ruft das Lied;
kräftig reizt der Zauber;
ich bin erwacht
aus wissendem Schlaf:
wer scheucht den Schlummer mir?

WANDERER. Der Weckrufer bin ich,
und Weisen üb' ich,
dass weithin wache
was fester Schlaf umschliesst.
Die Welt durchzog ich.
wanderte viel,
Kunde zu werben,
urweisen Rath zu gewinnen.
Kundiger giebt es
keine als dich:

thou canst declare
what the deep doth hold,
what hill and dale,
wind and tide do contain.
Where waketh life
walketh thy spirit,
where brains are searching
broodeth thy soul;
all things they say
straight thou canst tell.
That thou mayst surrender tidings
I arouse thee from thy sleep.

ERDA.   My sleep is dreaming,
my dream is searching,
my search for weapons of wisdom.
But while I slumber
wake the Nornen:
they weave at their rope
and rightly spin what I wis.—
Why seek'st thou not the Nornen?

WANDERER. Controlled by the world
weave on the Nornen,
and they can nought weaken nor ward off.
Yet would I thank
thy wisdom to tell me
how a wheel in its roll to arrest?

ERDA   Mortal workings
bewilder much my mind:
a warder of heaven
subdued my will to him once
I bore to Wotan
a wish-maiden,
who by her will
bands of heroes assembled.
Staunch is she
and wise withal:
why wake then me,
nor question challenge
with Erda's and Wotan's child?

WANDERER. The Valkyrie, mean'st thou?
Brünnhilde, my maid?
She disobeyed the tempest-subduer,
when in truth he himself had subdued:
what the fight-controller
had fain accomplished,
but what he stifled
in spite of himself,
Brünnhilde free
sought then defiantly
to accomplish unbidden,
boldly in battle's assault.
Sternly
descended his wrath;
on her eyes he laid magic sleep:
on the fell she slumbers fast.
Awakened will
the war-maiden be,
but to mate with a man as his wife.
Can I then question with her?

ERDA (*has become absorbed in thought, and replies after a considerable silence*).
Weak I wax
since I awoke;
wild and strange
seems the world!
The war-maiden —
the witch's child,
pines in penance of sleep
which her wisdomful mother shares?

bekannt ist dir
was die Tiefe birgt,
was Berg und Thal,
Luft und Wasser durchwebt.
Wo Wesen sind
weht dein Athem:
wo Hirne sinnen
haftet dein Sinn:
alles, sagt man,
sei dir bekannt.
Dass ich nun Kunde gewänne,
weckt' ich dich aus dem Schlaf.

ERDA.   Mein Schlaf ist Träumen,
mein Träumen Sinnen,
mein Sinnen Walten des Wissens.
Doch wenn ich schlafe,
wachen Nornen:
sie weben das Seil,
und spinnen fromm was ich weiss:—
was fräg'st du nicht die Nornen?

WANDERER. Im Zwange der Welt
weben die Nornen:
sie können nichts wenden noch wandeln
doch deiner Weisheit
dankt' ich den Rath wohl,
wie zu hemmen ein rollendes Rad?

ERDA.   Männerthaten
umdämmern mir den Muth:
mich Wissende selbst
bezwang ein Waltender einst.
Ein Wunschmädchen
gebar ich Wotan:
der Helden Wal
heiss er für ihn sie küren.
Kühn ist sie
und weise auch:
was weck'st du mich,
und fräg'st um Kunde
nicht Erda's und Wotan's Kind?

WANDERER. Die Walküre mein'st du,
Brünnhild', die Maid?
Sie trotzte dem Stürmebezwinger:
wo am stärksten er selbst sich bezwang
was den Lenker der Schlacht
zu thun verlangte,
doch dem er wehrte
— zuwider sich selbst —
allzu vertraut
wagte die Trotzige
das für sich zu vollbringen,
Brünnhild' in brennender Schlacht.
Streitvater
strafte die Maid;
in ihr Auge drückt' er Schlaf;
auf dem Felsen schläft sie fest:
erwachen wird
die Weihliche nur
um einen Mann zu minnen als Weib.
Frommten mir Fragen an sie?

ERDA (*ist in Sinnen versunken, und beginnt erst nac längerem Schweigen*).
Wirr wird mir's
seit ich erwacht:
wild und kraus
kreis't die Welt!
Die Walküre,
der Wala Kind,
büsst' in Banden des Schlaf's,
als die wissende Mutter schlief?

Doth then pride's teacher
punish pride?
Is the plan's arranger
wroth with the plan?
Doth the right's defence—
doth the truth's upholder
fetter the right—
harbor untruth?
Let me quickly depart:
sleep my senses shall quiet!

ANDERER. Thou, mother, shalt not depart
while the power of magic I wield. —
All-witting
struckest thou once
the sting of sorrow
in Wotan's warrior heart:
with fear of shameful,
fatal extinction
thy wisdom filled him:
his courage was cowed by dismay.
Art thou the world's
wisest of women,
give me then rede
how the god may grapple with care.

RDA. Thou art—scarce
what thou dost seem!
Why com'st thou, stubborn and wild one,
to startle the witch from sleep?
Restless one,
let me rest!
Loose thy constraining spell!

ANDERER. Thou art—not
what thou dost ween!
All-mother's wit
draws near its ending:
thy wisdom doth wane
before my wishes.
Wist thou what Wotan—wills?
Thou unwise,
I cry in thine ear,
that thou so unanxious mayst sleep. —

For the Æsir's ending
I feel no anguish,
since it works my will.
What in pain of wild dissension
despairing once I resolved,
fain and fearless
I fitly finish here.
Once though I wished in my anger
the Niblung might net him the world,
now, Volsung most winsome,
willed is its heirdom to thee!
One by me denoted,
but to me unknown,
a notable novice,
all undirected,
has reached the Nibelung's ring.
Lacking in malice,
large of love,
he'll lightly disarm
Alberich's curse;
for far bides he from fear.
She whom thou hast borne,
Brünnhilde,
will this hero hail.
When she wakes
thy child will work
a deed for the world's release.
Then slumber again,
seal up thine eyelids,

Der den Trotz lehrte
straft den Trotz?
Der die That entzündet
zürnt um die That?
Der das Recht wahrt,
der die Eide hütet—
wehret dem Recht?
herrscht durch Meineid?—
Lass' mich wieder hinab:
Schlaf verschliesse mein Wissen!

WANDERER. Dich Mutter lass' ich nicht zieh'n
da des Zaubers ich mächtig bin. —
Urwissend
stachest du einst
der Sorge Stachel
in Wotan's wagendes Herz:
mit Furcht vor schmachvoll
feindlichem Ende,
füllt' ihn dein Wissen,
dass Bangen band seinen Muth.
Bist du der Welt
weisestes Weib,
sage mir nun:
wie besiegt die Sorge der Gott?

ERDA. Du bist—nicht
was du nich nenn'st!
Was kam'st du störrischer Wilder
zu stören der Wala Schlaf?
Friedloser,
lass' mich frei!
Löse des Zaubers Zwang!

WANDERER. Du bist—nicht
was du dich wähn'st!
Urmütter-Weisheit
geht zu Ende:
dein Wissen verweht
vor meinem Willen.
Weisst du, was Wotan—will?
Dir Unweisen
ruf' ich's in's Ohr,
dass du sorglos ewig nun schläf'st. —

Um der Götter Ende
gräm't mich die Angst nicht,
seit mein Wunsch es—will!
Was in Zwiespalt's wildem Schmerze
verzweifelnd einst ich beschloss,
froh und freudig
führ' ich frei es nun aus:
weiht' ich in wüthendem Ekel
des Niblungen Neid schon die Welt
dem wonnigsten Wälsung
weis' ich mein Erbe nun an.
Der von mir erkoren,
doch nie mich gekannt,
ein kühnster Knabe,
meines Rathes bar,
errang des Niblungen Ring:
ledig des Neides,
liebesfroh,
eriahmt an dem Edlen
Alberich's Fluch;
denn fremd bleibt ihm die Furcht.
Die du mir gebar'st,
Brünnhilde,
sie weckt hold sich der Held:
wachend wirkt
dein wissendes Kind
erlösende Weltenthat. —
D'rum schlaf nun du,
schliesse dein Auge;

dream, and foresee my ending.　　　　　　　träumend erschau' mein Ende!
Whatever may happen　　　　　　　　　　Was jene auch wirken —
the god will always　　　　　　　　　　　dem ewig Jungen
hail the heaven of love.　　　　　　　　　weicht in Wonne der Gott. —
Away then, Erda!　　　　　　　　　　　Hinab denn, Erda!
All-mother-fear —　　　　　　　　　　　Urmütter-Furcht!
All-sorrow —　　　　　　　　　　　　　Ur-Sorge!
To endless sleep　　　　　　　　　　　Zu ewigem Schlaf
away! away!　　　　　　　　　　　　　hinab! hinab!
I see that Sigfried comes. —　　　　　　Dort seh' ich Siegfried nah'n. —
(ERDA *vanishes. The hollow again becomes quite* (ERDA *versinkt. Die Höhle ist wieder ganz finster*
dark. THE WANDERER *leans against the rocks and* *geworden: an dem Gestein derselben lehnt sich de*
awaits SIEGFRIED.)—　　　　　　　　　WANDERER *an, und erwartet so* SIEGFRIED. —)
(*Moon-rise slightly illumines the stage. The storm* (*Monddämmerung erhellt die Bühne etwas. Da*
has quite subsided.)　　　　　　　　　*Sturmwetter hört ganz auf.*)

SIEGFRIED (*entering R. in the foreground*).　SIEGFRIED (*von rechts im Vordergrunde auftretend*).
My fav'rite soars not before.—　　　　　　Mein Vöglein schwebte mir fort;—
With fluttering flight　　　　　　　　　　mit flatterndem Flug
and sweetest song　　　　　　　　　　　und süssem Sang
plainly it pointed the path:　　　　　　　wies es mir wonnig den Weg:
now seems it far to have flown.　　　　　　nun schwand es fern mir davon.
'Twere right to find　　　　　　　　　　Am besten find' ich
the rock for myself:　　　　　　　　　　selbst nun den Berg:
the way my feathered friend went　　　　　wohin mein Führer mich wies,
thither will I now fare.　　　　　　　　　dahin wandr' ich jetzt fort.
(*He goes further towards the back.*)　　　　(*Er schreitet weiter nach hinten.*)

WANDERER (*remaining in his station by the cave*).　WANDERER (*in seiner Stellung an der Höhle verblei-*
Say, boy, whither　　　　　　　　　　　*bend*).
bend'st thou thy way?　　　　　　　　　Wohin, Knabe,
　　　　　　　　　　　　　　　　　　heisst dich dein Weg?

SIEGFRIED.　I hear a voice:　　　　　　SIEGFRIED.　Da redet's ja:
will *he* tell me the way?　　　　　　　wohl räth das mir den Weg. —
For a rock I'm seeking　　　　　　　　Einen Felsen such' ich,
around which fire doth wander:　　　　　von Feuer ist der umwabert:
there sleeps a woman　　　　　　　　　dort schläft ein Weib
whom I would awake.　　　　　　　　　das ich wecken will.

WANDERER.　Who stirr'd thy mind　　　WANDERER.　Wer sagt' es dir
the mount to seek for,　　　　　　　　den Fels zu suchen,
and for the maiden to struggle?　　　　　wer nach der Frau dich zu sehnen?

SIEGFRIED.　It was a singing　　　　　SIEGFRIED.　Mich wies es ein singend
wood-minstrel　　　　　　　　　　　Waldvöglein:
who gave the goodly tidings.　　　　　　das gab mir gute Kunde.

WANDERER.　A bird doth sing much nonsense; WANDERER.　Ein Vöglein schwatzt wohl manches,
but none may understand.　　　　　　　kein Mensch doch kann's versteh'n:
How knewest thou so　　　　　　　　　wie mochtest du Sinn
the song's importing?　　　　　　　　　dem Sange entnehmen?

SIEGFRIED.　It was by the blood　　　SIEGFRIED.　Das wirkte das Blut
of a wicked worm,　　　　　　　　　　eines wilden Wurm's,
whom I at Hate-cavern butchered:　　　　der mir vor Neidhöhl' erblasste:
scarce had it tingled　　　　　　　　　kaum netzt' es zündend
the tongue of me　　　　　　　　　　　die Zunge mir,
when I straightway the bird understood.　　da verstand ich der Vöglein Gestimm.

WANDERER.　Thou slewest the giant?　WANDERER.　Erschlugst du den Riesen,
How germed in thee　　　　　　　　　wer reizte dich,
the scheme to fight with the serpent?　　den starken Wurm zu besteh'n?

SIEGFRIED.　I followed Mime,　　　　SIEGFRIED.　Mich führte Mime,
a faithless dwarf,　　　　　　　　　　ein falscher Zwerg;
who wanted to teach me fearing.　　　　das Fürchten wollt' er mich lehren
The sword-stroke, truly,　　　　　　　zum Schwertschlag aber,
'neath which he sank　　　　　　　　　der ihn erschlug,
mainly the worm did seek;　　　　　　reizte der Wurm mich selbst:
with his maw he menaced my life.　　　　seinen Rachen riss er mir auf.

ANDERER. Who shaped the sword
    so sharp and hard
    that so strong a foe it felled?

EGFRIED. I shaped it myself,
    as the smith was helpless;
    swordless else should I be still.

ANDERER. But who shaped
    the sturdy splinters
    from which thou'st smelted the sword?

EGFRIED. What thought I of that?
    But this I knew -
    for no work were fit those fragments
    were they not welded afresh.

ANDERER. (*breaking into a peal of good-humored
    laughter*).
    That well I admit!

EGFRIED. Why laugh you at me?
    Old enquirer,
    hark once for all;—
    lead me no longer to chatter!
    Can you direct
    the road to me, do so;
    and can you not
    then keep your mouth closed!

ANDERER. But soft, my youngster!
    Since I am old
    thou shouldst some honor accord me.

EGFRIED. That is a good one!
    So long as I've lived
    e'er in my way
    an old one waited,
    whom now I have swept aside.
    Stay you here longer
    stiff planted before me,
    it seems fit, see now,
    that you like Mime should fare.
    (*He approaches nearer to the* WANDERER.)
    What do you look like?
    Why have you on
    such an ample hat?
    Wherefore hangs it so far o'er your face?

ANDERER. Such is the wont of Wand'rer,
    when he goes against the wind.

EGFRIED. But below an eyeball is lacking!
    No doubt you lost it
    to one of late,
    when you too boldly
    did bar his way.
    Take yourself off,
    or, may be, I'll quench
    the other one too, and quickly.

ANDERER. I see, my son,
    where thou nought wottest,
    thou well contrivest to help thee.
    With an eye, too,
    like the one that I lack
    thyself dost look on the other
    that yet is left me for sight.

EGFRIED (*laughing*).
    Your language moves me to laughter!
    But come! I'll quibble no longer.
    Be quick! tell me the way;
    then, I warn you, turn on your own!

WANDERER. Wer schuf das Schwert
    so scharf und hart,
    dass der stärkste Feind ihm fiel?

SIEGFRIED. Das schweisst' ich mir selbst,
    da's der Schmied nicht konnte:
    schwertlos noch wär' ich wohl sonst.

WANDERER. Doch wer schuf
    die starken Stücken,
    daraus das Schwert du geschweisst?

SIEGFRIED. Was weiss ich davon!
    Ich weiss allein,
    dass die Stücken nichts mir nützten.
    schuf ich das Schwert mir nicht neu.

WANDERER (*bricht in ein freudig gemüthliches Lachen
    aus*).
    Das — mein' ich wohl auch!

SIEGFRIED. Was lach'st du mich aus?
    Alter Frager,
    hör' einmal auf;
    lass' mich nicht lange mehr schwatzen!
    Kannst du den Weg
    mir weisen, so rede:
    vermag'st du's nicht,
    so halte dein Maul!

WANDERER. Geduld, du Knabe!
    Dünk' ich dich alt,
    so sollst du mir Achtung bieten.

SIEGFRIED. Das wär' nicht übel!
    So lang' ich lebe
    stand mir ein Alter
    stets im Wege:
    den hab' ich nun fort gefegt.
    Stemm'st du dort länger —
    dich steif mir entgegen —
    sieh' dich vor, mein' ich,
    dass du wie Mime nicht fähr'st!
    (*Er tritt näher an den* WANDERER *heran.*)
    Wie sieh'st du denn aus?
    Was hast du gar
    für 'nen grossen Hut?
    Warum hängt der dir so in's Gesicht?

WANDERER. Das ist so Wand'rers Weise,
    wenn dem Wind entgegen er geht.

SIEGFRIED. Doch darunter fehlt dir ein Auge!
    Das schlug dir einer
    gewiss schon aus,
    dem du zu trotzig
    den Weg vertrat'st?
    Mach' dich jetzt fort!
    sonst möchtest du leicht
    das and're auch noch verlieren.

WANDERER. Ich seh', mein Sohn,
    wo nichts du weisst,
    da weisst du dir leicht zu helfen.
    Mit dem Auge,
    das als and'res mir fehlt,
    erblick'st du selber das eine,
    das mir zum Sehen verblieb.

SIEGFRIED (*lacht*).
    Zum Lachen bist du mir lustig! —
    Doch hör', nun schwatz' ich nicht länger
    geschwind zeig' mir den Weg,
    deines Weges ziehe dann du!

In nought else
your aid do I need;
so speak, or I'll spurn you aside!

WANDERER. Didst thou know me,
daring son,
of scoffs sparing wert thou!
Fiercely thy taunts
tear the heart that enfolds thee.
Love though I bear
to thy lineage bright,
fear too I've wrought
by my wrath when it fell.
Thou whom I cherish —
youth enchanting —
chafe not my spirit now
to annihilate thee and me!

SIEGFRIED. Dumb are you still,
stubborn old wight?
Wend from your station!
For I know that way
brings to the slumbering bride.
So warned me the flutterer
that here has fled from me first.
(*It gradually becomes quite dark again.*)

WANDERER (*breaking out into wrath.*)
It fled thee to save its life.
The lord of ravens
its road did let:
woe to it, light they on it! —
The way that it pointed
shalt thou not pass.

SIEGFRIED. Oho! my withholder!
And who are you
that thus arrest my road?

WANDERER. Mock not the mountain's guardian!
A spell engirds
by my might the slumbering maid.
One who can wake her, —
one who can win her,
makes me mightless for ever!

A fiery main
flows round her form,
glittering lightnings
o'erlick the fell:
he who'd find the bride
will feel the brunt of the fire.
(*He points with his spear.*)
Turn t'ward the hill!
Dost look on the light?
Yon waxing sheen,
yon swelling glare —
smothering vapors,
varying lightnings,
vacillate burning
and crackling anigh.
A light-flood
illumines thy head:
the furnace soon
will seize and enfold thee. —
Away then, foolhardy boy!

SIEGFRIED. Away, old boaster, yourself!
Straight where the blaze is burning
to Brünnhilde's side will I haste.
(*He advances on him.*)

WANDERER (*stretching out his spear*).
Hast thou no heed of the fire?
My spear then shall spare thee no path!

zu nichts and'rem
acht' ich dich nütz':
d'rum sprich, sonst spreng' ich dich fort!

WANDERER. Kenntest du mich,
kühner Spross,
den Schimpf — spartest du mir!
Dir so vertraut,
trifft mich schmerzlich dein Dräu'n
Liebt' ich von je
deine lichte Art, —
Grauen auch zeugt' ihr
mein zürnender Grimm:
dem ich so hold bin,
allzu hehrer,
heut' nicht wecke mir Neid,
er vernichtete dich und mich!

SIEGFRIED. Bleib'st du mir stumm,
störrischer Wicht?
Weich' von der Stelle!
Denn dorthin, ich weiss,
führt es zur schlafenden Frau:
so wies es mich Vöglein,
das hier erst flüchtig entfloh.
(*Es wird allmälig wieder ganz finster.*)

WANDERER (*in Zorn ausbrechend*).
Es floh dir zu seinem Heil;
den Herrn der Raben
errieth es hier:
weh' ihm, holen sie's ein! —
Den Weg, den es zeigte,
sollst du nicht zieh'n!

SIEGFRIED. Hoho! du Verbieter!
Wer bist du denn,
dass du mir wehren willst?

WANDERER. Fürchte des Felsens Hüter!
Verschlossen hält
meine Macht die schlafende Maid:
wer sie erweckte,
wer sie gewänne,
machtlos macht' er mich ewig! —

Ein Feuermeer
umfluthet die Frau,
glühende Lohe
umleckt den Fels:
wer die Braut begehrt,
dem brennt entgegen die Brunst.
(*Er winkt mit dem Speere.*)
Blick' nach der Höh'!
erlug'st du das Licht? —
Es wächst der Schein,
es schwillt die Gluth;
sengende Wolken,
wabernde Lohe,
wälzen sich brennend
und prasselnd herab.
Ein Licht-Meer
umleuchtet dein Haupt:
bald frisst und zehrt dich
zündendes Feuer: —
zurück denn, rasendes Kind!

SIEGFRIED. Zurück, du Prahler, mit dir!
Dort, wo die Brünste brennen,
zu Brünnhilde muss ich jetzt hin.
(*Er schreitet darauf zu.*)

WANDERER (*den Speer vorhaltend*).
Fürchtest das Feuer du nicht,
so sperre mein Speer dir den Weg!

Still holdeth my hand
the hallow'd haft;
the sword that thou sway'st
was shivered on this shaft:
so too again
'twill snap on the eternal spear

SIEGFRIED (*drawing his sword*).
Then my father's foe
faces me here?
How that will serve me
for sweet revenge!
Stretch out your spear:
my sword shall strike it to shreds.
He attacks the WANDERER *and hews his spear in
pieces. Terrific clap of thunder.*)

WANDERER (*recoiling*).
Advance! I cannot prevent thee!
(*He disappears.*)

SIEGFRIED.   With defeated weapon
flieth my foeman?
*Fiery clouds have descended from the heights at back
with increasing brightness: the entire stage becomes filled
with a rolling sea of fire.*)

SIEGFRIED.   Ha! heavenly glow!
brightning glare!
roads are now opening
radiantly round me.
In fire will I bathe,
through fire will I fare to my bride!
Oho! Oho!
Aha! Aha!
Gaily! gaily!
Soon greets me a glorious friend!
*He winds his horn and plunges into the fire, blowing
gaily. — The fire now flows over the whole foreground.
SIEGFRIED'S horn is heard, first near, then more distant.
The fiery clouds continue to pour from the back towards
the front, so that* SIEGFRIED, *whose horn is now again
heard nearer, appears to be ascending the mountain.*)

*At last the glow begins to fade and sinks to a fine
transparent veil, which also clears off and reveals the
most lovely blue sky and bright weather.
The scene, from which all the vapors have fled, represents
the summit of a rocky mountain-peak (as in the third Act
of the* "VALKYRIE"): L. *the entrance to a natural rocky
cell; R. spreading fir-trees; the background quite open. —
In the foreground beneath the shade of a spreading fir-
tree lies* BRÜNNHILDE *in deep sleep: she is in a complete
suit of gleaming plate-armor, with helmet on her head and
a shield over her body.
SIEGFRIED has now reached the rocky heights in the
background. (His horn has sounded more and more
distant till it ceased altogether.) He looks around in
astonishment.*)

SIEGFRIED.   Sweet is this haven
on sun-illumed heights!—
(*Looking into the wood.*)
What calmly slumbers

Noch hält meine Hand
der Herrschaft Haft;
das Schwert, das du schwing'st,
zerschlug einst dieser Schaft:
noch einmal denn
zerspring' es am ewigen Speer!

SIEGFRIED (*das Schwert ziehend*).
Meines Vaters Feind!
Find' ich dich hier?
Herrlich zur Rache
gerieth mir das!
Schwing' deinen Speer:
in Stücken spalt' ihn mein Schwert!
(*Er ficht mit dem* WANDERER *und haut ihm den Speer
in Stücken. Furchtbarer Donnerschlag.*)

WANDERER (*zurückweichend*).
Zieh' hin! ich kann dich nicht halten.
(*Er verschwindet.*)

SIEGFRIED.   Mit zerfocht'ner Waffe
wich mir der Feige?
(*Mit wachsender Helle haben sich Feuerwolken aus
der Höhe des Hintergrundes herabgesenkt: die ganze
Bühne erfüllt sich wie von einem wogenden Flammenmeere.*)

SIEGFRIED.   Ha, wonnige Gluth!
leuchtender Glanz!
Strahlend offen
steht mir die Strasse. —
Im Feuer mich baden!
Im Feuer zu finden die Braut!
Hoho! hoho!
hahei! hahei!
Lustig! lustig!
Jetzt lock' ich ein liebes Gesell!
(*Er setzt sein Horn an, und stürzt sich, seine lock-
weise blasend, in das Feuer. — Die Lohe ergiesst sich
nun auch über den ganzen Vordergrund. Man hört
Siegfried's Horn erst näher, dann ferner. — Die Feuer-
wolken ziehen immer von hinten nach vorn, so dass
SIEGFRIED, dessen Horn man wieder näher hört, sich
nach hinten zu, die Höhe hinauf, zu wenden scheint.*)

(*Endlich beginnt die Gluth zu erbleichen; sie löst
sich wie in einen feinen, durchsichtigen Schleier auf, der
nun ganz sich auch klärt und den heitersten blauen
Himmelsäther, im hellsten Tagesscheine, hervortreten
lässt.
Die Scene, von der das Gewölk gänzlich gewichen ist,
stellt die Höhe eines Felsengipfels (wie im dritten
Aufzuge der* "WALKÜRE") *dar: links der Eingang
eines natürlichen Felsengemaches; rechts breite Tan-
nen; der Hintergrund ganz frei. — Im Vordergrunde,
unter dem Schatten einer breitästigen Tanne, liegt
BRÜNNHILDE, in tiefem Schlafe: sie ist in vollständi-
ger, glänzender Panzerrüstung, mit dem Helm auf dem
Haupte, den langen Schild über sich gedeckt.
SIEGFRIED ist so eben im Hintergrunde, am felsigen
Saume der Höhe, angelangt. (Sein Horn hatte zuletzt
wieder ferner geklungen, bis es ganz schwieg.) — Er
blickt staunend um sich.*)

SIEGFRIED.   Selige Oede
auf sonniger Höh'! —
(*In den Tann hinein sehend.*)
Was ruht dort schlummernd

'neath shadowy trees?
A war-horse,
waiting in tranquil sleep!
(*He surmounts the height completely and advances slowly; on seeing* BRÜNNHILDE *at a little distance he pauses in surprise.*)
What strikes me with its gleaming?
What glittering suit of steel!
Blind are my eyes
as yet with the blaze?
(*He comes nearer.*)
Shining weapons!—
Shall I uplift?
[*He raises the shield and discovers* BRÜNNHILDE'S *face, which the helmet still in a great measure conceals.*]
Ha! a warrior, sure!
I scan with wonder his form!—
His haughty head
is press'd by the helm;
lighter would he
lie were it loosed.
(*He carefully unfastens the helmet and removes it from the sleeper; long, curling hair breaks forth.—* SIEGFRIED *starts.*)
Ah!—how fair!
(*He remains absorbed in contemplation.*)
Fleecy as cloudlets
fringing the clearness
of azure æther seas:
laughing, the sun's
enlightening face
shines through the cluster of cloud.
(*He listens for the sleeper's breath.*)
But heavily breathing
heaveth his breast:
better to open his byrnie?
(*He tries very cautiously, but in vain.*)
Come, my sword,
cut through the iron!

(*With tender care he cuts through the rings of mail on each side, and lifts off the corslet and greaves, so that* BRÜNNHILDE *then lies before him in a soft, female garb. —Surprised and astonished, he starts back.*)
This is no man!
Burning enchantment
charges my heart;
fiery awe
falls on my eyesight;
my senses stagger and sway.
O whom shall I hail
that he may help me?
Mother! Mother!
look down on me!—

(*He sinks with his head on* BRÜNNHILDE'S *bosom.— Long silence.—Then he starts up suddenly.*)
O what shall I do
that she her eyelids may open?—
Her eyes to me open!
Blind then were mine with their blaze.
How could I dare
endure such a light?
All sways and swims
and staggers around;
scorching desires
entangle my senses,
and trembles my heart
at touch of my hand!
What is this feeling?
Can it be fearing?
O mother! mother!

---

im schattigen Tann—
Ein Ross ist's,
rastend in tiefem Schlaf!
(*Er betritt vollends die Höhe, und schreitet langsa weiter vor; als er* BRÜNNHILDE *noch aus einiger En fernung gewahrt, hält er verwundert an.*)
Was strahlt mir dort entgegen?—
Welch' glänzendes Stahlgeschmeide!]
Blendet mir noch
die Lohe den Blick?—
(*Er tritt näher hinzu.*)
Helle Waffen!—
Heb' ich sie auf?
(*Er hebt den Schild ab, und erblickt* BRÜNNHILDE'S *Gesicht, das jedoch der Helm noch zum grossen Thei verdeckt.*)
Ha! in Waffen ein Mann:—
wie mahnt mich wonnig sein Bild!
Das hehre Haupt
drückt wohl der Helm?
leichter würd' ihm,
löst' ich den Schmuck.
(*Vorsichtig löst er den Helm und hebt ihn d Schlafenden vom Haupte ab: langes, lockiges Ha bricht hervor.—* SIEGFRIED *erschrickt.*)
Ach!—wie schön!—
(*Er bleibt in den Anblick versunken.*)
Schimmernde Wolken
säumen in Wellen
den hellen Himmelssee:
leuchtender Sonne
lachendes Bild
strahlt durch das Wogengewölk!
(*Er lauscht dem Athem.*)
Von schwellendem Athem
schwingt sich die Brust:—
brech' ich die engende Brünne?
(*Er versucht es mit grosser Behutsamkeit—aber verg bens.*)
Komm', mein Schwert,
schneide das Eisen!

(*Er durchschneidet mit zarter Vorsicht die Panze ringe zu beiden Seiten der ganzen Rüstung, und he dann die Brünne und die Schienen ab, so dass n* BRÜNNHILDE *in einem weichen weiblichen Gewan vor ihm liegt.—Ueberrascht und staunend fährt er auf*)
Das ist kein Mann!—
Brennender Zauber
zückt mir in's Herz;
feurige Angst
fasst mein Augen:
mir schwankt und schwindelt der Sinn!
Wen ruf' ich zum Heil,
dass er mir helfe?—
Mutter! Mutter!
Gedenke mein'!—

(*Er sinkt mit der Stirn an* BRÜNNHILDE'S *Busen.— Langes Schweigen—Dann fährt er seufzend auf.*)
Wie weck' ich die Maid,
dass sie die Augen mir öff'ne?—
Das Auge mir öff'nen?
blende mich auch noch der Blick
Wagt' es mein Trotz?
ertrüg' ich das Licht?—
Mir schwebt und schwankt
und schwirrt es umher;
sehrendes Sengen
zehrt meine Sinne:
am zagenden Herzen
zittert die Hand!—
Wie ist mir Feigem?—
Ist es das Fürchten?—
O Mutter! Mutter!

how mighty thy son!
A woman folded in sleep
at last has enslaved him with fear!

How can I be calm —
recall my mind?
Ere I quell this weakness
must the maid be awakened?

Sweetly beckons
her blossoming mouth:
what mild alarms in me
lightly it stirs! —
Ah! and the ardent
winsome warmth of her breath!

Awaken! awaken!
maiden bewitched! — —
She hears me not. —
Then life I will drain me
from lips the most dainty,
did they e'en doom me to death!

*He imprints a long and ardent kiss upon her lips. —
He starts back in surprise; BRÜNNHILDE has opened
her eyes. He gazes on her in astonishment. Both remain for some time wrapt in mutual contemplation.)*

BRÜNNHILDE (*slowly and solemnly rising to a sitting
position*).
Hail, thou sunshine!
Hail, thou light!
Hail, thou loveliest day!
Long was my rest;
I rise from sleep.
say, who is he
that wakes my sense?

SIEGFRIED (*awe-struck by her appearance and voice*).
Through the fire I thrust
that burns round the fell,
and I broke thy defending helm.
Siegfried I,
by whom thou art waked.

BRÜNNHILDE (*sitting erect.*)
Hail, ye gods all!
Hail, thou world!
Hail, ye glories of nature!
Unknit is now my sleep;
I stand awake;
Siegfried 'tis
who unwinds the spell!

---

dein muthiges Kind!
Im Schlafe liegt eine Frau: —
die hat ihn das Fürchten gelehrt! —

Wie end' ich die Furcht?
wie fass' ich Muth? —
Dass ich selbst erwache,
muss die Maid ich erwecken! — —

Süss erbebt mir
ihr blühender Mund:
wie mild erzitternd
mich Zagen er reizt! —
Ach, dieses Athem's
wonnig warmes Gedüft! —

Erwache, erwache!
heiliges Weib!
Sie hört-mich nicht. —
So saug' ich mir Leben
aus süssesten Lippen —
sollt' ich auch sterbend vergeh'n!

(*Er küsst sie lange und inbrünstig. — Erschreckt
fährt er dann in die Höhe: — BRÜNNHILDE hat die
Augen aufgeschlagen. — Staunend blickt er sie an.
Beide verweilen eine Zeit lang in ihren gegenseitigen
Anblick versunken.*)

BRÜNNHILDE (*langsam und feierlich sich zum Sitze
aufrichtend*).
Heil dir, Sonne!
Heil dir, Licht!
Heil dir, leuchtender Tag!
Lang war mein Schlaf;
ich bin erwacht:
wer ist der Held,
der mich erweckt'?

SIEGFRIED (*von ihrem Blicke und ihrer Stimme feierlich ergriffen*).
Durch das Feuer drang ich,
das den Fels umbrann;
ich erbrach dir den festen Helm:
Siegfried heiss' ich,
der dich erweckt'.

BRÜNNHILDE (*hoch aufgerichtet sitzend*).
Heil euch, Götter!
Heil dir, Welt!
Heil dir, prangende Erde!
Zu End' ist nun mein Schlaf;
erwacht seh' ich:
Siegfried ist es
der mich erweckt!

MOTIVE OF LOVE'S GREETING.

SIEGFRIED (*in exalted rapture*).
O hail to her
who gave me to life!
Hail to earth,
my fostering nurse!
that I should e'er have seen
the sight that smiles on me here!

SIEGFRIED (*in erhabenster Entzückung*).
O Heil der Mutter,
die mich gebar;
Heil der Erde,
die mich genährt:
dass ich das Auge erschaut,
das jetzt mir Seligem strahlt!

MOTIVE OF LOVE'S PASSION.

BRÜNNHILDE (*deeply stirred*).	**BRÜNNHILDE** (*mit grösster Bewegtheit*).

BRÜNNHILDE (*deeply stirred*).
O hail to her
who gave thee to life!
Hail to earth,
thy fostering nurse!
But one glance was to behold me:
for thee I was to awake.

O Siegfried! Siegfried!
sanctified hero!
thou wakener of life,
thou sovereign light!
O wist thou, lord of worlds,
what time thou'st had my love!
Thou wert my object,
my aim wert thou!
I fostered thee
before thou wert formed;
before thou wert born
I brought thee my shield:
so long I've loved thee, Siegfried.

SIEGFRIED (*gently and bashfully*).
My mother did not die then?
she merely drooped in sleep?

BRÜNNHILDE (*smiling*).
Thou innocent child,
thou wilt ne'er be charmed by her image.
Thyself am I,
if thy pure spirit can love.
What thou dost want
well can I teach:
but wisdom only
grew — when that I loved thee.

O Siegfried! Siegfried!
sovereign light!
I loved thee always,
for I alone
distinguished Wotan's intention.
The intention that I
ne'er named nor told of,
that I ne'er tested —
I only felt it: —
for which I fought,
struggled and strove,
for which I flouted
him who framed it,
for which I suffered
in penance of sleep,
having never thought it,
but known it still!
Truly, that intention —
'tis for thy solving —
was but that my love should be thine!

SIEGFRIED. With winsome tones
what wonders thou sing'st!
but bound abideth their sense.
By thine eyes' fair light
I stand illumed,
by thy ardent breath
my breast is warmed,
by thy singing sweet
my ears are soothed;
but what thou sayest in song
strangely doth strike my mind.
Now nought can I fathom
subtle and far off,
for ev'ry sense
on thee is centred and fastened.
With timid fear
thou fillest me:

BRÜNNHILDE (*mit grösster Bewegtheit*).
O Heil der Mutter,
die dich gebar;
Heil der Erde,
die dich genährt:
nur dein Blick durfte mich schau n
erwachen durft' ich nur dir! —

O Siegfried! Siegfried!
seliger Held!
Du Wecker des Lebens,
siegendes Licht!
O wüsstest du, Lust der Welt,
wie ich dich je geliebt!
Du war'st mein Sinnen
mein Sorgen du!
Dich Zarten nährt' ich
noch eh' du gezeugt;
noch eh' du geboren
barg dich mein Schild:
so lang' lieb' ich dich, Siegfried!

SIEGFRIED (*leise und schüchtern*).
So starb nicht meine Mutter?
schlief die Minnige nur?

BRÜNNHILDE (*lächelnd*). Du wonniges Kind,
deine Mutter kehrt dir nicht wieder
Du selbst bin ich,
wenn du mich Selige lieb'st.
Was du nicht weisst,
weiss ich für dich:
doch wissend bin ich
nur — weil ich dich liebe. —

O Siegfried! Siegfried!
siegendes Licht!
dich liebt' ich immer;
denn mir allein
erdünkte Wotan's Gedanke.
Der Gedanke, den nie
ich nennen durfte;
den ich nicht dachte,
sondern nur fühlte;
für den ich focht,
kämpfte und stritt;
für den ich trotzte
dem, der ihn dachte;
für den ich büsste,
Strafe mich band,
weil ich nicht ihn dachte
und nur empfand!
Denn der Gedanke —
dürftest du's lösen! —
mir war er nur Liebe zu dir!

SIEGFRIED. Wie Wunder tönt
was wonnig du sing'st;
doch dunkel dünkt mich der Sinn.
Deines Auges Leuchten
seh' ich licht;
deines Athem's Wehen
fühl' ich warm;
deiner Stimme Singen
hör' ich süss:
doch was du singend mir sag'st
staunend versteh' ich's nicht.
Nicht kann ich das Ferne
sinnig erfassen,
da all' meine Sinne
dich nur sehen und fühlen.
Mit banger Furcht
fesselst du mich.

thou only hast
in me awesomeness waked.
Thou who hast bound me
with manacles breakless,
bring back my manhood once more!

BRÜNNHILDE (*gently repulses him and turns her eyes
towards the wood*).
There feedeth Grani,
my faithful steed:
how briskly he wanders
who with me slept!
He too was by Siegfried awaked.

SIEGFRIED. On glorious lips
my glances are feasting;
with feverish thirst
I feel my own burning,
till the eyes' refreshment they taste of.

BRÜNNHILDE (*pointing with her hand*).
I see there the shield
that sheltered heroes;
I see there the helm
that did ward my head;
they'll shield—they'll ward me no more!

SIEGFRIED. As a woman divine
thou woundest my heart;
mortal the hurt
so shaped by a maid:—
I came without shield or helm.

BRÜNNHILDE (*with growing melancholy*).
I see there the byrnie's
glittering steel;
a sturdy sword
split it apart
and the maiden's protection
tore from her form:
without either guard or glaive
but a weakly woman I feel!

SIEGFRIED. Through billows of fire
I fared to thy side;
nor byrnie nor shield
my body defends.
Now burst the flames
unchecked in my breast;
now bounds my blood
in blissfullest blaze;
a rapturous fire
within me is raging:
the flames that round
Brünnhilde once roared
now rend me with fearful wrath.
O maid, extinguish the rays!
still this disturbance in me!

*He seizes her impetuously; she springs up, repulses
him with the utmost strength of terror and flies to the
opposite side.*)

BRÜNNHILDE. No god e'en has touched me!
as a maiden ever
heroes revered me:
virgin I hied from Valhalla!—
Woe's me! woe's me!
Woe for the shame,
the shunless disgrace!
My wak'ning hero
deals me this wound!
He has burst my byrnie and helm:
Brünnhilde am I no more!

du Einz'ge hast
ihre Angst mich gelehrt.
Den du gebunden
in mächt'gen Banden,
birg' meinen Muth mir nicht mehr!

BRÜNNHILDE (*wehrt ihn sanft ab, und wendet ihren
Blick nach dem Tann*).
—Dort seh' ich Grane,
mein selig Ross:
wie weidet er munter,
der mit mir schlief!
Mit mir hat ihn Siegfried erweckt.

SIEGFRIED. Auf wonnigem Munde
weidet mein Auge:
in brünstigem Durst
doch brennen die Lippen,
dass der Augen Weide sie labe!

BRÜNNHILDE (*ihn mit der Hand bedeutend*).
Dort seh' ich den Schild,
der Helden schirmte;
dort seh' ich den Helm,
der das Haupt mir barg:
er schirmt, er birgt mich nicht mehr!

SIEGFRIED. Eine selige Maid
versehrte mein Herz;
Wunden dem Haupte
schlug mir ein Weib:—
ich kam ohne Schild und Helm!

BRÜNNHILDE (*mit gesteigerter Wehmuth*).
Ich sehe der Brünne
prangenden Stahl:
ein scharfes Schwert
schnitt sie entzwei;
von dem maidlichen Leibe
löst' es die Wehr:—
ich bin ohne Schutz und Schirm,
ohne Trutz ein trauriges Weib!

SIEGFRIED. Durch brennendes Feuer
fuhr ich zu dir;
nicht Brünne noch Panzer
barg meinen Leib:
mir in die Brust
brach nun die Lohe,
es braus't mein Blut
in blühender Brunst;
ein zehrendes Feuer
ist mir entzündet:
die Gluth, die Brünnhild's
Felsen umbrann,
die brennt mir nun in der Brust!—
Du Weib, jetzt lösche den Brand!
schweige die schäumende Gluth!
(*Er umfasst sie heftig; sie springt auf, wehrt ihm mit
der höchsten Kraft der Angst, und entflieht nach der
andern Seite.*)

BRÜNNHILDE. Kein Gott nahte mir je:
der Jungfrau neigten
scheu sich die Helden:
heilig schied sie aus Walhall! —
Wehe! Wehe!
Wehe der Schmach,
der schmählichen Noth!
Verwundet hat mich,
der mich erweckt!
Er erbrach mir Brünne und Helm:
Brünnhilde bin ich nicht mehr!

SIEGFRIED. Still thou'rt to me
the slumbering maid:
Brünnhilde's sleep
bindeth her yet.
Awaken! be but my wife!

BRÜNNHILDE. My senses are swaying,
my wit forsakes:
shall all my wisdom 'scape me?

SIEGFRIED. Said'st thou not
that thy wisdom shewed
the lighting of love unto me?

BRÜNNHILDE. Dismallest blackness
dazes my sight;
my eyes are blinded,
their light is lost:
night veileth me.
In vaporous mists
foully upforces
a grisly fear:
horrors haunt me
and compass me round.
(*She clasps her hands over her eyes hastily.*)

SIEGFRIED (*gently drawing her hands from her face*).
Darkness frightens
closed eyelids;
set them free, and fled
is the fearsome spell.
Draw from the shadow and see:—
sun-illumed smileth the day.

BRÜNNHILDE (*in extreme agitation.*)
Sun-illumed
smileth this day on my shame!—
O Siegfried! Siegfried!
See how I dread!—

SIEGFRIED. Noch bist du mir
die träumende Maid:
Brünnhilde's Schlaf
brach ich noch nicht.
Erwache! sei mir ein Weib!

BRÜNNHILDE. Mir schwirren die Sinne!
Mein Wissen schweigt:
soll mir die Weisheit schwinden?

SIEGFRIED. Sang'st du mir nicht,
dein Wissen sei
das Leuchten der Liebe zu mir?

BRÜNNHILDE. Trauriges Dunkel
trübt mir den Blick;
mein Auge dämmert,
das Licht verlischt:
Nacht wird's um mich:
aus Nebel und Grau'n
windet sich wüthend
ein Angstgewirr:
Schrecken schreitet
und bäumt sich empor!
(*Sie birgt heftig die Augen mit den Händen.*)

SIEGFRIED (*lös't ihr sanft die Hände vom Blicke*)
Nacht umbangt
gebundene Augen;
mit den Fesseln schwindet
das finst're Grau'n:
tauch' aus dem Dunkel und sieh—
sonnenhell leuchtet der Tag!

BRÜNNHILDE (*in höchster Ergriffenheit*).
Sonnenhell
leuchtet der Tag meiner Noth!—
O Siegfried! Siegfried!
Sieh' meine Angst!

MOTIVE OF LOVE'S PEACE.

Deathless was I,
deathless am I,
deathless to sweet
sway of affection—
but deathless for thy good hap!

O Siegfried! happiest
hope of the world!
Life of the universe!
Lordliest hero!
List! ah list!
Leave me in peace!
Press not upon me
thy ardent approaches!
Master me not
with thy conquering might!
Thy servant, O sully her not!—

Saw'st e'er thy face
in crystal floods?
Did it not gladden thy glance?
When into wavelets
the water was roused,
the brook's glassy surface
broken and flawed,
thy face saw'st thou no more:
nought but ripples swirling around.

Ewig war ich,
ewig bin ich,
ewig in süss
sehnender Wonne—
doch ewig zu deinem Heil!

O Siegfried! Herrlicher!
Hort der Welt!
Leben der Erde!
Lachender Held!
Lass', ach lass'!
lasse von mir!
Nahe mir nicht
mit der wüthenden Nähe!
Zwinge mich nicht
mit dem brechenden Zwang!
Zertrümm're die Traute dir nicht!—

Sah'st du dein Bild
im klaren Bach?
Hat es dich Frohen erfreut?
Rührtest zur Woge
das Wasser du auf;
zerflösse die klare
Fläche des Bach's:
dein Bild säh'st du nicht mehr,
nur der Welle schwankend Gewog'

so disturb me no more,
trouble me not:
ever then
thou wilt shine
in me an image reflected,
fair and lovely, my lord!—
O Siegfried! Siegfried!
light of my soul!
Love — thyself
and leave me in peace:
destroy not thy faithful slave!

SIEGFRIED. I love — thee:
O lovest thou me?
I have no more self:
O had I but thee!—
The grandest of floods
before me rolls,
and all my senses
seize on the sight,
these billows beauteous and buoyant.
Likeness — be lost!
I long now myself
straightway my fire
in the flood to slacken;
at once I would spring
into the stream:
O would that its waters
in bliss might embrace me,
and 'bate my blaze with its wave!—
Awake, Brünnhilde!
waken, thou maid!
Laugh that thou livest,
sweetest delight!
Be mine! be mine! be mine!

BRÜNNHILDE. O Siegfried! thine
ever I've been!

SIEGFRIED. Ever thou'st been?
Then so abide.

BRÜNNHILDE. Thine ever
will I be.

SIEGFRIED. What thou then wilt,
be to me now.
Fast in my arms,
enwrapped in their fold,
resting thy breast
beating 'gainst mine,
while glances and breath
are glowing with eagerness,
eye to eye,
and lip to lip —
as, saidst thou, thou wast and wilt be
How briskly were banished thy fears
if indeed Brünnhilde were mine!
(*He has clasped her with his arms.*)

BRÜNNHILDE. *If* I am thine!

Godlike repose
is plunged into tempest,
once tranquil radiance
rises to frenzy,
heavenly teachings
from me are hid,
wildness of passion
whirls it away!

If I am thine!—
O Siegfried! Siegfried!
Seest thou me not?
When mine eyes devour thine,

So berühre mich nicht,
trübe mich nicht:
ewig licht
lachst du aus mir
dann selig selbst dir entgegen,
froh und heiter ein Held!—
O Siegfried! Siegfried!
leuchtender Spross!
Liebe — dich,
und lasse von mir:
vernichte dein Eigen nicht!

SIEGFRIED. Dich — lieb' ich:
o liebtest mich du!
Nicht hab' ich mehr mich
o hätte ich dich!—
Ein herrlich Gewässer
wogt vor mir;
mit allen Sinnen
seh' ich nur sie,
die wonnig wogende Welle:
brach sie mein Bild,
so brenn' ich nun selbst,
sengende Gluth
in der Fluth zu kühlen;
ich selbst, wie ich bin,
spring' in den Bach:—
o dass seine Wogen
mich selig verschlängen,
mein Sehnen schwänd' in der Fluth!—
Erwache, Brünnhilde!
Wache, du Maid!
Lebe und lache,
süsseste Lust!
Sei mein! sei mein! sei mein.

BRÜNNHILDE. O Siegfried! dein —
war ich von je!

SIEGFRIED War'st du's von je,
so sei es jetzt!

BRÜNNHILDE. Dein werde ich
ewig sein!

SIEGFRIED. Was du sein wirst,
sei es mir heut'!
Fasst dich mein Arm,
umschling' ich dich fest;
schlägt meine Brust
brünstig die deine;
zünden die Blicke,
zehren die Athem sich;
Aug' in Auge,
Mund an Mund:
dann bist du mir,
was bang du mir war'st und wirst!
Dann brach sich die brennende Sorge,
ob jetzt Brünnhilde mein?
(*Er hat sie umfasst.*)

BRÜNNHILDE. Ob jetzt ich dein? —

Göttliche Ruhe
ras't mir in Wogen;
keusches Licht
lodert in Gluthen;
himmlisches Wissen
stürmt mir dahin,
Jauchzen der Liebe
jagt es davon!

Ob jetzt ich dein?—
O Siegfried! Siegfried!
siehst du mich nicht?
Wie mein Blick dich verzehrt,

then art thou not blind?
by my arm embraced
then burnest thou not?
and when seething my blood
against thee doth surge,
its fiery fury
feelest thou not?
Fearest thou, Siegfried—
fearest thou not
the mad, mutinous maid?

erblindest du nicht?
Wie mein Arm dich presst
entbrennst du nicht?
Wie in Strömen mein Blut
entgegen dir stürmt,
das wilde Feuer
fühlst du es nicht?
Fürchtest du, Siegfried
fürchtest du nicht
das wild wüthende Weib

SIEGFRIED. Ha!   ing!
How the glowing bloodstreams are bound-
How the glances brightly are burning!
How our arms are gladly entwining!
Cometh now back
my courage bold,
and this fearing, ah!
that to me was strange—
this fear, that scarce
e'en thou could'st bestow—
this fearing — I feel
that fool-like, again 'tis forgot.
(With the last words he has unconsciously released
BRÜNNHILDE.)

SIEGFRIED.   Ha! —
Wie des Blutes Ströme sich zünden
wie der Blicke Strahlen sich zehren
wie die Arme brünstig sich pressen
kehrt mir zurück
mein kühner Muth,
und das Fürchten, ach
das nie ich gelernt
das Fürchten, das du
kaum mich gelehrt:
das Fürchten — mich dünkt
ich Dummer, vergass es schon wieder
(Er lässt bei den letzten Worten BRÜNNHILDE un
kürlich los.)

BRÜNNHILDE (laughing in wild transport of passion).
O high-minded boy!
O blossoming hero!
Thou babe of prowess
past all that breathe!
Gladly love do I glow with,
gladly yield to thee blindly,
gladly glide to destruction,
gladly go down to death!

BRÜNNHILDE (im höchsten Liebesjube
end).
O kindischer Held!
O herrlicher Knabe!
Du hehrster Thaten
thöriger Hort!
Lachend muss ich dich lieben
lachend will ich erblinden;
lachend lass' uns verderben —
lachend zu Grunde geh'n!

Far hence, Valhall'
lofty and vast,
let fall thy structure
of stately tow'rs;
farewell, grandeur
and pride of gods!
End in rapture
ye Æsir, your reign!
Go rend, ye Nornen,
your rope of runes!
Round us darken,
Dusk of the gods!
Night of annulment
now on us gain!
here still is streaming
Siegfried, my star.
He is for ever,
is for aye
my own, my only
and my all.—
Love that illumines,
laughing at death.

Fahr' hin, Walhall's
leuchtende Welt!
Zerfall' in Staub
deine stolze Burg!
Leb' wohl, prangende
Götter-Pracht!
Ende in Wonne,
du ewig Geschlecht!
Zerreisst, ihr Nornen,
das Runenseil!
Götter-Dämm'rung,
dunkle herauf!
Nacht der Vernichtung.
neble herein! —
Mir strahlt zur Stunde
Siegfried's Stern:
er ist mir ewig,
er ist mir immer,
Erb' und Eigen,
ein' und all':
leuchtende Liebe,
lachender Tod!

SIEGFRIED (with BRÜNNHILDE).
Gladly, bewitcher,
wak'st thou to me.
Brünnhilde lives,
Brünnhilde laughs!—
Hail the heavens,
smiling in lightness!
Hail the sun
which down on us shines!
Hail the light
that from night hath burst!
Hail the world
where Brünnhilde lives.

SIEGFRIED (mit Brünnhilde zugleich).
Lachend erwachst
du Wonnige mir:
Brünnhilde lebt!
Brünnhilde lacht! —
Heil der Sonne,
die uns bescheint!
Heil dem Tage
der uns umleuchtet!
Heil dem Licht,
das der Nacht enttaucht!
Heil der Welt,
der Brünnhild' erwacht!

She wakes, she lives!
she laughs as she greets me:
proudly streams down
Brünnhilde, my star.
She is for ever,
is for aye
my own, my only
and my all.
Love that illumines
laughing at death.

(BRÜNNHILDE *throws herself into* SIEGFRIED's *arms.*)

The Curtain falls.

Sie wacht! sie lebt!
sie lacht mir entgegen!
Prangend strahlt
mir Brünnhilde's Stern!
Sie ist mir ewig,
sie ist mir immer,
Erb' und Eigen,
ein' und all':
leuchtende Liebe,
lachender Tod!

(BRÜNNHILDE *stürzt sich in* SIEGFRIED's *Arme.*

Der Vorhang fällt.

CHARACTERS

SIEGFRIED	. . . .	TENO
GUNTHER	. . . .	BAS
HAGEN	. . . .	BAS
BRÜNNHILDE	. . . .	SOPRAN
GUTRUNE	. . . .	SOPRAN
WALTRAUTE	. . . .	SOPRAN
WOGLINDA,		SOPRAN
WELLGUNDA, } RHINE-NYMPHS {	. . . . .	SOPRAN
FLOSSHILDE,	. . . . .	ALT

MEN AND WOMEN

The Argument

PRELUDE. On the Valkyrie's rock, by night, sit the *Nornir* (Fates) weaving the rope of runes. It breaks and they disappear, knowing that the End of the gods is at han At day-dawn Siegfried rises to part from his beloved Brünnhilde and go to fresh exploit At parting he gives her his famous Ring and she gives him her horse in return.

ACT I. He comes to the Hall of the Gibichungs on the Rhine, where live the Kin Gunther, his sister Gutrune and their half-brother Hagen, the son of Alberic. These, fo their own purposes, give Siegfried a magic draught of forgetfulness. He swears brothe hood to Gunther, forgets Brünnhilde, falls in love with Gutrune and, in return for he hand, consents to go through the fire and fetch Brünnhilde as a wife for Gunther, wł cannot perform the feat himself.

Brünnhilde, awaiting, Siegfried's return, is visited by her sister Waltraute, who ir plores her to restore the fatal Ring to the Rhine, as the only means of saving the god who are now expecting their doom; but Brünnhilde, being an outcast from Valhalla, r gards her love-pledge as of more value than all the gods, and refuses: Waltraute fli away in despair, Siegfried, taking Gunther"s shape, by virtue of the Tarnhelm, appea to the horror-stricken Brünnhilde and demands a husband's rights. She resists fiercel but is conquered by his tearing from her finger the Ring which gave her supernatur strength. Siegfried weds her, but lays his sword between them, as his oath to Gunthe demands.

ACT II. Alberic visits his son Hagen in a dream and bids him strive to kill Sie fried and obtain the Ring. Siegfried, followed later by Gunther and Brünnhilde, r turns to the Gibichung's Hall and all the vassals are summoned to rejoice at the doub wedding. Brünnhilde, being brought face to face with Siegfried in his own shape, pe ceives the Ring upon his finger and proclaims to all that she has been betrayed. Explan tions, purposely confused by Hagen, only make it appear that Siegfried has failed in h oath to Gunther, whereupon Hagen persuades Brünnhilde and Gunther to consent to h murder.

ACT III. Siegfried, hunting near the Rhine, is accosted by the Rhine-nymphs, wł strive to coax the Ring from him; failing, they tell him how it will cause his death. I derides their warning, but Hagen, Gunther and the rest of the hunting party join hiɪ and while they are carousing and Siegfried is telling the story of his life, Hagen spea him in the back and kills him.

The body is brought to the Hall and Hagen kills Gunther in a struggle for the Rir The despairing Brünnhilde silences the clamor and orders a funeral pile to be built by t Rhine. This she mounts with the dead Siegfried and both are consumed, when the riv rises and the Nymphs regain at last their Ring from the ashes, Hagen being drowned attempting to seize it. Now a ruddy glare is seen in the sky: the Dusk of the Gods h come, and Valhalla is seen burning with all its array of heroes and gods.

THE DUSK OF THE GODS
(GOETTERDAEMMERUNG)

### PROLOGUE	### VORSPIEL

Scene — On the Valkyries' Rock.

The same as at the end of "Siegfried." It is night and from below, at back, gleams the fire.

The three Norns,

all females in sombre and flowing drapery, are discovered. The first (and oldest) crouches in the foreground R, under the spreading fir-tree; the second (younger) is stretched on a rock before the cave; the third (and youngest) sits in the middle back on a rock below the peak. For a while gloomy silence reigns.

The first Norn
(without moving).

What light lurketh there?

The second.

Think you the day is nigh?

The third.

Loki's flame
leapeth round about the rock.
Night is new:
why should we not spin and sing now?

The second
(to the first).

While we are spinning and singing
on what stretch we the string?

The first Norn
rises and fastens one end of a golden cord to a branch of the fir-tree during her song).

For weal to serve and woe,
setting the string I sing thus:—
At the world's ash-tree
once I wove,
when fast and strong,
the stem with wondrous
verdure was overwhelmed.
In pleasant shade
a fountain purled;
wisdom floated
forth on its wave;
I sang there a mystic song.

Auf dem Walkürenfelsen.

Die Scene ist dieselbe wie am Schlusse des zweiten Tages.—Nacht. Aus der Tiefe des Hintergrundes leuchtet Feuerschein auf.

Die drei Nornen,

hohe Frauengestalten in langen, dunklen und schlei-erartigen Faltengewändern. Die erste (älteste) lagert im Vordergrunde rechts unter der breitästi-gen Tanne; die zweite (jüngere) ist an einer Stein-bank vor dem Felsengemache hingestreckt; die dritte (jüngste) sitzt in der Mitte des Hinter-grundes auf einem Felssteine des Höhensaumes.— Eine Zeit lang herrscht düsteres Schweigen.

Die erste Norn
(ohne sich zu bewegen).

Welch' Licht leuchtet dort?

Die zweite

Dämmert der Tag schon auf?

Die dritte

Loge's Heer
lodert feurig um den Fels.
Noch ist's Nacht:
was spinnen und singen wir nicht?

Die zweite
(zu der ersten).

Wollen wir singen und spinnen,
woran spann'st du das Seil?

Die erste Norn
(erhebt sich, und knüpft während ihres Gesanges ein goldenes Seil mit dem einen Ende an einen Ast der Tanne).

So gut und schlimm es geh',
schling' ich das Seil, und singe.—
An der Welt-Esche
wob ich einst,
da gross und stark
dem Stamm entgrünte
weihlicher Aeste Wald;
im kühlen Schatten
rausch' ein Quell,
Weisheit raunend
rann sein Gewell':
da sang ich heiligen Sinn.—

A fearless god
sought to sip at the fount,
    giving up one eye
to buy the ineffable boon.
    From the world's ash-tree
Wotan wrested off an arm:
    and with sturdy strokes
he shaped the shaft of a spear.
In tardy course of time
cankered the wound in the wood;
the leaves life could retain not;
waned—withered the tree.
    Drooping, the stream
of the fountain dried;
    dark with sorrow
waxed then my song.
    I weave again
at the world's ash-tree no more,
    so must the fir-tree
find me support for the string.
    Sing, O Sister!
    Thou weave it now!—
ween'st thou why this was?

The second Norn
(winding the cord, which the other throws to her,
round a projecting rock at the cave's mouth).

    Truthful runes
    to make treaties rigid
    set Wotan
    on the shaft of his spear:
this served him to sway the world.
    One bold and strong
destroyed in battle that spear.
    The binding witness
of bonds was shivered to shreds.
    Then straight Wotan
    warriors summoned,
    the world's ash-tree's
    withered arms
with its stem to splinter and sunder.
    The ash destroyed,
For ever the spring must go dry.
    Now round the keen-edged
stone I knot the string:
    Sing, O sister!
    Thou weave it now—
ween'st thou why this was?

The third Norn
(catching the rope and throwing the end behind
her).

    A gemmed abode
    by giants was built:
with the Æsir and heroes'

Ein kühner Gott
trat zum Trunk an den Quell;
    seiner Augen eines
zahlt' er als ewigen Zoll:
    von der Welt-Esche
brach da Wotan einen Ast:
    eines Speeres Schaft
entschnitt der Starke dem Stamm.
In langer Zeiten Lauf
zehrte die Wunde den Wald·
    falb fielen die Blätter,
    dürr darbte der Baum:
    traurig versiegte
    des Quelles Trank;
    trüben Sinnes
    ward mein Gesang.
    Doch web' ich heut'
an der Welt-Esche nicht mehr,
    muss mir die Tanne
taugen zu fesseln das Seil:
    singe, Schwester,
    —dir werf' ich's zu—
weisst du wie das ward?

Die zweite Norn
(während sie das zugeworfene Seil um einen he
vorspringenden Felsstein am Eingange des G
maches windet).

    Treu berath'ner
    Verträge Runen
    schnitt Wotan
    in des Speeres Schaft:
den hielt er als Haft der Welt.
    Ein kühner Held
zerhieb im Kampfe den Speer;
    in Trümmern sprang
der Verträge heiliger Haft.—
    Da hiess Wotan
    Walhall's Helden
    der Welt-Esche
    welkes Geäst
mit dem Stamm in Stücke zu fällen
    die Esche sank;
ewig versiegte der Quell!—
    Fess'le ich heut'
an dem scharfen Fels das Seil:
    singe, Schwester,
    —dir werf' ich's zu—
weisst du wie das wird?

Die dritte Norn
(das seil auffangend, und dessen Ende hinter s
werfend).

    Es ragt die Burg,
    von Riesen gebaut:
    mit der Götter und Helden

holy assembly
sitteth Wotan in state.
   And heaps of faggots
   huge are formed,
   ranged on high
   round all Valhalla:
the world's ash-tree were they once.
   When the brand
   brightly, wildly doth burn,
   when the fire
wasteth the fair-fashioned walls,
the deathless immortals draw
towards the dusk of their day.
   This knowest thou?
The thread then be knotted again.
   Anew I throw it thee
   from the north.
Spin, O sister, and sing thou!

he throws the cord to the second Norn, who throws it to the first.)

e first Norn
ties the cord from the branch and fastens it to another branch during the following song).

   Dawneth the daylight,
   or flickers the fire?
My sight sorrow hath dimmed.
   Scarce bides my memory
   of bygone marvels,
   when Loki moved
in burning and lambent flame:
wist thou what was his work?

e second Norn
ain taking the rope and winding it round the stone).

   By the spear's firm yoke
   he yielded to Wotan;
aid he offered the god:
   but in struggle e'er
   his bonds to throw off
he gnashed and tore with his teeth,
   till Wotan's spear's point
   tightly constrained him
   broadly to girdle
Brynhildr's rock with his brightness:
wist thou what was his work?

e third Norn
tching the rope again and throwing it behind her).

   Then the sturdy spear
   that split into splinters
   Wotan dips
in the burning one's wavering breast.
   Quickly the brand

---

heiliger Sippe
Sitzt dort der Wotan im Saal.
   Gehau'ner Scheite
   hohe Schicht
   ragt zu Hauf
   rings um die Halle:
die Welt-Esche war dies einst!
   Brennt das Holz
   heilig brünstig und hell,
   senkt die Gluth
sehrend den glänzenden Saal:
der ewigen Götter Ende
dämmert ewig da auf.—
   Wisset ihr noch?
so windet von neuem das Seil;
   von Norden wieder
   werf' ich's dir nach:
spinne, Schwester, und singe!

(Sie hat das Seil der zweiten, diese es wieder der ersten Norn zugeworfen.)

Die erste Norn
(lös't das Seil vom Zweige, und knüpft es während des folgenden Gesanges wieder an einen andern Ast).

   Dämmert der Tag?
   oder leuchtet die Lohe?
Getrübt trügt sich mein Blick;
   nicht hell eracht' ich
   das heilig Alte,
   da Loge einst
entbrannte in lichter Gluth:—
weisst du was aus ihm ward?

Die zweite Norn
(das zugeworfene Seil wieder um den Stein windend).

   Durch des Speeres Zauber
   zähmte ihn Wotan;
Räthe raunt' er dem Gott:
   an des Schaftes Runen,
   frei sich zu rathen,
nagte zehrend sein Zahn.
   Da mit des Speeres
   zwingender Spitze
   bannte ihn Wotan,
Brünnhilde's Fels zu umbrennen:—
weisst du was aus ihm wird?

Die dritte Norn
(das zugeschwungene Seil wieder hinter sich werfend).

   Des zerschlag'nen Speeres
   stechende Splitter
   taucht' einst Wotan
dem Brünstigen tief in die Brust:
   zehrender Brand

kindles thereat;
this Wotan throws
where the world's ash-tree
is heaped, a forest of faggots.
When this will be
would ye ween?
stretch then, sisters, the string!
(She throws the rope back to the second who
throws it to the first).

The first Norn
(again knotting the cord).
The night wanes;
nought more I wot of;
I cannot find
the fibre again;
it falls entangled and frayed.
The woefullest sight
whirls and weakens my sense:—
The Rhinegold
robbed by Alberic once:
wist thou what was its work?

The second Norn
(with careful haste winding the rope round the
stone).
The crag with keen edge
cutteth the cord;
the threads cling not,
and thin is the clue;
awry hath it been wrought.
From ire and ill
rears to me Alberic's ring:—
a ravaging curse
gnaweth my cord to the core:—
wist thou what it will work?

The third Norn
(hastily catching the rope thrown to her).
The rope is too slack,
I reach it not;
should it anew
to northward be thrown,
yet straighter must it be stretched!
(she pulls the cord forcibly: it breaks in the
middle.)

The second.
It breaks!

The third.
It breaks!

The first.
It breaks!
(The three Norns start up in alarm and advance to
the centre of the stage: they take the broken pieces
of the cord and tie their bodies one to another with
them.)

zündet da auf;
den wirft der Gott
in der Welt-Esche
zu Hauf geschichtete Scheite.—
Wollt ihr wissen
wann das wird,
schwingt mir, Schwestern, das Seil
(Sie wirft das Seil der zweiten, diese es wieder
ersten zu.)

Die erste Norn
(das Seil von neuem anknüpfend).
Die Nacht weicht;
nichts mehr gewahr' ich:
des Seiles Fäden
find' ich nicht mehr;
verflochten ist das Geflecht.
Ein wüstes Gesicht
wirrt mir wüthend den Sinn:—
das Rheingold
raubte Alberich einst:—
weisst du, was aus ihm ward?

Die zweite Norn
(mit mühevoller Hast das Seil um den Stein wi
end).
Des Steines Schärfe
schnitt in das Seil;
nicht fest spannt mehr
der Fäden Gespinnst:
verwirrt ist das Geweb'.
Aus Noth und Neid
nagt mir des Niblungen Ring:—
ein rächender Fluch
nagt meiner Fäden Geflecht:—
weisst du was daraus wird?

Die dritte Norn
(das zugeworfene Seil hastig fassend).
Zu locker das Seil!
mir langt es nicht:
soll ich nach Norden
neigen das Ende,
straffer sei es gestreckt!
(Sie zieht gewaltsam das Seil an: dieses reisst
der Mitte.)

Die zweite.
Es riss!

Die dritte.
Es riss!

Die erste
Es riss!
(Erschreckt sind die drei Nornen aufgefahren
nach der Mitte der Bühne zusammengetreten;
fassen die Stücke des zerrissenen Seiles und bin
damit ihre Leiber an einander.)

The three Norns.

Here ends all of our wisdom!
The world marks
our wise words no more.—
Away! To mother! Away!

(They disappear.)

(The day, which has been slowly breaking, now
dawns brightly and conceals the distant fire-glow
in the valley.)

Siegfried and Brünnhilde

(enter from the cave. Siegfried is in full armor;
Brünnhilde leads her horse by the bridle).

Die drei Nornen.

Zu End' ewiges Wissen!
Der Welt melden
Weise nichts mehr:—
hinab zur Mutter, hinab!

(Sie verschwinden.)

Der Tag, der zuletzt immer heller gedämmert, bricht
vollends ganz an, und dämpft den Feuerschein in
der Tiefe.

Siegfried und Brünnhilde

(treten aus dem Steingemache auf: Siegfried ist in
vollen Waffen. Brünnhilde führt ihr Ross beim
Zaume).

DID I NOT SEND THEE?

BRÜNNHILDE

Zu neu-en Tha-ten, theu-rer Hel-de, wie liebt' ich dich
Did I not send thee, sweet-est he-ro, to fresh ex-ploits,

liess' ich dich nicht Ein ein-zig Sor-gen lässt mich säu-men;
frail were my love. But one mis-giv-ing fights a-gainst it;—

dass dir zu we-nig mein Werth ge-wann. Was
for fear not whol-ly thy heart I hold. I

Göt-ter mich wie-sen, gab ich dir: hei-li-ger Ru-nen
gave to thee all that gods had taught; heav-en-ly runes, the

rei-chen Hort, doch mei-ner Stär-ke magd-li-chen Stamm
rich-est hoard, but my re-store-less maid-en-hood's strength

nahm mir der Held, dem ich nun mich nei-ge. Des Wis-sens
snatch'd thou from me, who but seek to serve thee. My wis-dom

bar,   doch des Wun-sches voll: an Lie - be reich, doch
fails.   *but good will re - mains,*   *so full____ of love, but*

le - dig der Kraft,   mögst du die Ar- me nicht ver - ach-ten,
fail- ing in strength,   *thou wilt de - spise per-chance the poor one,*

die dir .nur gön - nen, nicht ge - ben_ mehr kann.
who hav- ing giv'n____ all, can grant____ thee- ro more.

Siegfried. More hast thou shewn to me than yet my sense can seize: so chide not if unlearned despite thy lessons I'm left. But one thing I wot full well— for me Brünnhilde lives; 'twas a lesson light to learn Brünnhilde aye to worship!	*Siegfried.* Mehr gabst du, Wunderfrau, als ich zu wahren weiss: nicht zürne, wenn dein Lehren mich unbelehret liess! Ein Wissen doch wahr' ich wohl dass mir Brünnhilde lebt; eine Lehre leint' ich leicht: Brünnhilde's zu gedenken!
Brünnhilde. If thou wouldst wake my fondness, recall thy course to mind; recall thy courage dauntless, recall the raging furnace that, fearless, thou didst pass through, when it fanned the rocky brow.	*Brünnhilde.* Willst du mir Minne schenken, gedenke deiner nur, gedenke deiner Thaten! Gedenke des wilden Feuers, das furchtlos du durchschrittest, da den Fels es rings umbrann—
Siegfried. Brünnhilde to attain to!	*Siegfried.* Brünnhilde zu gewinnen!
Brünnhilde. Recall, too the shield-covered maid thou did'st find in sleep of magic, and whose mail and helm thou didst break.	*Brünnhilde.* Gedenk' d e r beschildeten Frau, die in tiefem Schlaf du fandest, der den festen Helm du erbrach'st—
Siegfried. Brünnhilde to awaken!	*Siegfried.* Brünnhilde zu erwecken!
Brünnhilde. Recall the pledges we have plighted; recall our troth,— ne'er was there truer: recall th' affection which enfolds us;	*Brünnhilde.* Gedenk' der Eide, die uns einen; gedenk' der Treue, die wir tragen; gedenk' der Liebe, der wir leben:

Brünnhilde thy bride then e'er
will hold her place in thy breast.

iegfried.   Love, ere leaving thy form
in the leal defence of the fire,
for all thy runes and teachings
take this ring in return.
All my valiant deeds of strength
their virtue sprang from this.
I destroyed an unwieldly worm,
who long had over it watched:
now well preserve thou the charm
as wedding gift to my bride.

rünnhilde
(rapturously donning the ring.)
Aye, gladly my all here I guard,
and instead thou shalt own my
steed:
he could lift me once
athwart the air lightly;
with me
he lost all his magic powers:
over thronging clouds,
through lightning and thunder,
no more
boldly his way he will thread.
But wher-e'er thou shalt force,
were it through fire e'en,
Grani will follow gaily:
He'll serve my hero
trustily henceforth.
Then hold him well,
he'll heed thy word:
O give Grani many
fond greetings from me!

iegfried.   Then through thy virtues alone
am I to vanquish my dangers?
Thou dost choose thy champion's fights;
thou dost turn the chance of
the fray;
thy noble steed bestriding,
and with thy shelt'ring shield
now Siegfried am I no more:
I'm but as Brünnhilde's arm!

rünnhilde.   O were but Brünnhilde thy
spirit!

iegfried.   She spurs my bravery alone.

rünnhilde.   So art thou Siegfried and
Brünnhilde?

Brünnhilde brennt dann ewig
heilig dir in der Brust!—

Siegfried.   Lass' ich, Liebste, dich hier
in der Lohe heiliger Hut,
zum Tausche deiner Runen
reich' ich dir diesen Ring,
Was der Thaten je ich schuf,
dess' Tugend schliesst er ein;
ich erschlug einen wilden Wurm,
der grimmig lang' ihn bewacht.
Nun wahre du seine Kraft
als Weihe-Gruss meiner Treu'!

Brünnhilde
(voll Entzücken den Ring sich ansteckend.)
Ihn geiz' ich als einziges Gut:
für den Ring nun nimm' auch
mein Ross!
Ging sein Lauf mit mir
einst kühn durch die Lüfte—
mit mir
verlor es die mächt'ge Art;
über Wolken hin
auf blitzenden Wettern
nicht mehr
schwingt es sich muthig des
Weg's.
Doch wohin du ihn führst
—sei es durch's Feuer—
grauenlos folgt dir Grane;
denn dir, o Helde,
soll er gehorchen!
Du hüt' ihn wohl;
er hört dein Wort:—
o bringe Grane
oft Brünnhilde's Gruss!

Siegfried.   Durch deine Tugend allein
soll so ich Thaten noch wirken?
Meine Kämpfe kiesest du,
meine Siege kehren zu dir?
Auf deines Rosses Rücken,
in deines Schildes Schirm,
nicht Siegfried acht' ich mich
mehr,
ich bin nur Brünnhilde's Arm!

Brünnhilde.   O wäre Brünnhild' deine
Seele!

Siegfried.   Durch sie entbrennt mir der
Muth.

Brünnhilde.   So wär'st du Siegfried und
Brünnhild'?

Siegfried.   Our hearts both beat in one
bosom.

Brünnhilde.   Is my rock-home deserted
then?

Siegfried.   Both rest still in its bounds.

Brünnhilde
(in exalted rapture.)
O heavenly powers,
holy protectors!
View with delight
our devotion of love!
Apart—who can divide us?
Divided—still we are one!

Siegfried.   Hail, O Brünnhilde,
brightest of stars!
Hail, stream of our love-light!

Brünnhilde.   Hail, O Siegfried,
sovereign light!
Hail, stream of our living!

Both.   Hail! Hail!

(Siegfried leads the horse down the rocks; Brünnhilde gazes after him from the height for a long
while. From the valley, the merry sound of Siegfried's horn is heard. The curtain falls.)
(The orchestra takes up the melody of the horn
and works it up into an animated movement.
Thereupon follows the First Act.)

ACT ONE

Scene One

THE HALL OF THE GIEBICHUNGS ON THE RHINE.

The back is quite open, showing a flat shore down
to the river-stream; rocky heights border the stage.

GUNTHER, HAGEN AND GUTRUNE

Gunther and Gutrune are on the throne, before
which is a table with drinking vessels. Hagen sitting before it.

Gunther.   Now hark, Hagen!
answer me, here:
is my hold of the Rhine
glory for Gibich's race?

Hagen.   Thy wondrous actions
waken my envy;
and much thy mother and mine,
dame Grimhild,' lauded thy greatness.

Siegfried.   Wo ich bin, bergen sich beid

Brünnhilde.   So verödet mein Felsenaa

Siegfried.   Vereint fasst er uns zwei.

Brünnhilde
(in grosser Ergriffenheit.)
O heilige Götter,
hehre Geschlechter!
weidet eur' Aug'
an dem weihvollen Paar
Getrennt—wer will uns scheiden
Geschieden—trennt es sich nie!

Siegfried.   Heil dir, Brünnhilde,
prangender Stern!
Heil, strahlende Liebe!

Brünnhilde.   Heil dir, Siegfried!
siegendes Licht!
Heil, strahlendes Leben!

Beide.   Heil! Heil!

(Siegfried leitet das Ross den Felsen hin
Brünnhilde blickt ihm vom Höhensaume lan
entzückt nach. Aus der Tiefe hört man Siegfrie
Horn munter ertönen. Der Vorhang fällt.

Das Orchester nimmt die Weise des Hornes au
und führt sie in einem kräftigen Satze durch. D
rauf beginnt sogleich der erste Aufzug.)

ERSTER AUFZUG

Erste Scene

DIE HALLE DER GIBICHUNGEN AM RHE

Sie ist dem Hintergrunde zu ganz offen; dies
nimmt ein freier Uferraum, in bis zum Flusse h
ein; felsige Anhöhen umgränzen den Raum.

GUNTHER, HAGEN, UND GUTRUNE

(Gunther und Gutrune auf dem Hochsitze, v
dem ein Tisch mit Trinkgeräth steht; Hagen sit
davor.)

Gunther.   Nun hör', Hagen!
sage mir, Held:
sitz' ich herrlich am Rhein,
Gunther zu Gibich's Ruhm?

Hagen.   Dich ächt genannten
acht' ich zu neiden:
die beid' uns Brüder gebar,
Frau Grimhild' liess mich's begreife

Gunther. Thou envy not;
I am envious of thee.
If I am heir to all,
wisdom was left to thee.
Half-brother's strife
were stifled ne'er better;
and thy wisdom well I praise
when I ask thee of my weal.

Hagen. To blame is my wit
that bad is thy weal;
for rarer goods I wot of
than a Gibichung yet ever won.

Gunther. Then tell them, or
I too shall blame.

Hagen. In radiance of summer ripeness
rises Gibich's race;
but Gunther fails to wed
and Gutrune finds no mate.

Gunther. Whom wouldst thou I should
wed,
that we may win more worth?

Hagen. A wife waits thee,
the rarest in the world:
a far off rock's her home,
a fire-flame embraces her hall:
but he who can brave that fire
may fitly woo Brünnhilde.

Gunther. And may not my might so far
stretch?

Hagen. For a stronger one it is reserved.

Gunther. Who is this most stalwart of
men?

Hagen. Siegfried of Volsung descent:
his is the strongest hand.
A twinborn pair
in loving entwinement——
Siegmund and Sieglind'—
between them begat such a son.
He in woods has mightily waxed,
and well with Gutrune might
mate.

Gutrune. Hath he done marvellous deeds,
that he is called of a courage
so high?

Hagen. At Hate-cavern
the hoard long accursed
was watched by a horrible worm.

Gunther. Dich neide ich:
nicht neide mich du!
Erbt' ich Erstlingsart,
Weisheit ward dir allein:
Halbbrüder-Zwist
bezwang sich nie besser;
deinem Rath nur red' ich Lob,
Frag' ich dich nach meinem
Ruhm.

Hagen. So schelt' ich den Rath,
da schlecht noch dein Ruhm:
denn hohe Güter weiss ich,
die der Gibichung noch nicht gewann.

Gunther. Verschwiegst du sie,
so schelt' auch ich.

Hagen. In sommerlich reifer Stärke
seh ich Gibich's Stamm,
dich, Gunther, unbeweibt,
dich, Gutrun', ohne Mann.

Gunther. Wen räth'st du nun zu frei'n,
Dass uns'rem Ruhm es fromm'?

Hagen. Ein Weib weiss ich,
das herrlichste der Welt:—
auf Felsen hoch ihr Sitz;
ein Feuer entbrennt ihren Saal:
nur wer durch das Feuer bricht,
darf Brünnhilde's Freier sein.

Gunther. Vermag das mein Muth zu
besteh'n?

Hagen. Einem Stärk'ren noch ist's nur
bestimmt.

Gunther. Wer ist der streitlichste Mann?

Hagen. Siegfried, der Wälsungen Spross:
der ist der stärkste Held.
Ein Zwillingspaar,
von Liebe bezwungen,
Siegmund und Sieglinde
zeugten den ächtesten Sohn:
der im Walde mächtig erwuchs,
den wünsch' ich Gutrun' zum Mann.

Gutrune. Welche That schuf er so tapfer,
dass als herrlichster Held er
genannt!

Hagen. Vor Neidhöhle,
den Niblungenhort
bewachte ein riesiger Wurm:

Siegfried shut up
his maw for him straight
and slew him with sovereign sword.
So this unheard-of feat
has founded the hero's fame.

Gunther.   The Nibelungs' hoard I know
of;
it holds most notable wealth.

Hagen.   The one who best knows its worth
annexes the world to his will.

Gunther.   And Siegfried gained it in
strife?

Hagen.   Slaves are the Niblungs to him.

Gunther.   And Brünnhilde were won by
none else?

Hagen.   To no other waneth the blaze.

Gunther
(rising from his seat in displeasure.)
Why wake this discord and
doubt?
Wouldst thou induce in me
desire for a treasure
I may not touch?

Hagen.   Brought this Siegfried
the bride to thee,
would not then Brünnhilde be thine?

Gunther
(pacing up and down the hall in agitation.)
What power could bind the
man
to win the bride for me?

Hagen.   Thy pray'r could work thy wishes,
wove first Gutrune a spell.

Gutrune.   Thou scoffest, wicked Hagen!
What spells then should I
weave him?
And if so wondrous
a warrior he,
the earth's most winsome of women
will he have won ere this.

Hagen.   Recall the drink in yon shrine,
and doubt not him who gained
the charm.
The hero for whom thou burn'st
fondly 'twill bind to thy heart.
Did now but Siegfried come

Siegfried schloss ihm
den freislichen Schlund,
erschlug ihn mit siegendem Schwer
Solch' ungeheurer That
enttagte des Helden Ruhm.

Gunther.   Vom Niblungenhort vernahm
ich.
er birgt den neidlichsten
Schatz?

Hagen.   Wer wohl ihn zu nützen wüsst
dem neigte sich wahrlich di
Welt.

Gunther.   Und Siegfried hat ihn erkämpft

Hagen.   Knecht sind die Niblungen ihm

Gunther.   Und Brünnhild' gewänne nur er

Hagen.   Keinem And'ren wiche die Bruns

Gunther
(unwillig sich vom Sitze erhebend.)
Was weck'st du Zweifel und Zwist!
Was ich nicht zwingen soll,
danach zu verlangen
mach'st du mir Lust?

Hagen.   Brächte Siegfried
die Braut dir heim,
wär' dann Brünnhild' nicht dein?

Gunther
(bewegt in der Halle auf und ab schreitend.)
Was zwänge den frohen Mann
dir mich die Braut zu frei'n?

Hagen.   Ihn zwänge bald deine Bitte,
bänd' ihn Gutrun' zuvor.

Gutrune.   Du Spötter, böser Hagen!
Wie sollt' ich Siegfried binden
Ist er der herrlichste
Held der Welt,
der Erde holdeste Frauen
friedeten längst ihn schon.

Hagen.   Gedenk' des Trankes im Schrein
vertraue mir, der ihn gewann:
den Helden, dess' du verlangs
bindet er liebend an dich.
Träte nun Siegfried ein,

and taste of the wonderful
            draught,
that he'd seen a woman ere
            thee—
or e'er a woman had neared,
would wholly pass from his head.
Reply then,
how like ye Hagen's plan?

Gunther
(who has again approached the table and listened
attentively, leaning on it.)
All praise be to Grimhild'
who such a brother gave!

Gutrune. If but Siegfried I could see!

Gunther. How shall we find him first?

Hagen. When he doth spur
on courses of fame,
the world too strait
can but become;
be sure in his roamings he'll scour
to the Gibich's strand on the Rhine.

Gunther. Welcome I'll heartily give.
(Siegfried's horn is heard in the distance;—they
listen.)
I mark on the Rhine a horn.

Hagen
(goes to the bank, looks down the river and calls
back.)
Within a vessel horse and man!
He blows right gaily the horn.
With a labourless stroke
as if lazy his hand,
he drives the boat,
stemming the stream.
So active a hand
at the oar-blade's sweep
owneth but he
who the dragon slew.
Siegfried is it; surely no other!

Gunther. Doth he proceed?

Hagen
(putting his hands to his mouth and shouting.)
Hoiho! Where hiest,
hero hale?

Siegfried's
(voice in the distance on the river.)
To Gibich's stalwart scion.

Hagen. Behold his hall here! I bid thee
to it.

genöss' er des würzigen Trank's,
dass vor dir ein Weib er ersah,
dass je ein Weib ihm genaht—
vergessen müsst er dess' ganz.—
Nun redet:—
wie dünkt euch Hagen's Rath?

Gunther
(der wieder an den Tisch getreten, und auf ihn gelehnt aufmerksam zugehört hat.)
Gepriesen sei Grimhild,'
die uns den Bruder gab!

Gutrune. Möcht' ich Siegfried je erseh'n!

Gunther. Wie fänden wir ihn auf?

Hagen. Jagt er auf Thaten
wonnig umher,
zum engen Tann
wird ihm die Welt:
wohl stürmt er in rastloser Jagd
auch zu Gibich's Strand an den Rhein.

Gunther. Willkommen hiess' ich ihn gern.
(Siegfried's Horn lässt sich von Ferne verneh-
men.—Sie lauschen.)
Vom Rhein her tönt das Horn.

Hagen
(ist an das Ufer gegangen, späht den Fluss hinab
und ruft zurück:)
In einem Nachen Held und Ross:
der bläst so munter das Horn.—
Ein gemächlicher Schlag
wie von müssiger Hand
treibt jach den Kahn
wider den Strom;
so rüstiger Kraft
in des Ruder's Schwung
rühmt sich nur der,
der den Wurm erschlug:—
Siegfried ist es, sicher kein And'rer!

Gutrune. Jagt er vorbei?

Hagen
(durch die hohlen Hände nach dem Flusse zu rufend:)
Hoiho! wohin,
du heit'rer Held?

Siegfried's
(Stimme, aus der Ferne, vom Flusse her.)
Zu Gibich's starkem Sohne.

Hagen. Zu seiner Halle entbiet' ich dich:

Hither! here lay thee to!
Hail, Siegfried, bravest heart!

Scene Two

(Siegfried lays to).

(Gunther has joined Hagen on the bank. Gutrune looks at Siegfried from the throne, fixing her gaze for some time on him in joyous surprise, and as the men come down into the hall she withdraws, in visible confusion, through a door leading to her chamber L.)

Siegfried

(who has landed his horse and now stands quietly leaning on him).

Which is Gibich's son?

Gunther. Gunther—I—whom thou seek'st.

Siegfried. Thy fame has reached
beyond the Rhine:
now fight with me,
or else be my friend!

Gunther. Nought of war;
thou art welcome!

Siegfried. Where stables my horse?

Hagen. I'll see to him.

Siegfried. Thou hail'st me "Siegfried;"
sure we are strange?

Hagen. Thy strength unapproached
declared thee straight.

Siegfried. Tend heedfully Grani!
thou heldest ne'er
in bridle a horse
of higher degree.

(Hagen leads the horse away, R, behind the hall and returns immediately. Gunther advances into the hall with Siegfried.)

Gunther. Now, hero, freely hail
the homestead of thy fathers.
The hall thou stand'st in,
whate'er thou see'st,
I bid thee hold thy booty.
Thine is my birthright,
soil and serfs:
hear me swear by my body!
Gunther to thee is given.

Siegfried. Nor soil nor serfs I offer thee,
nor father's house and hall:
all I'm heir to,
my able limbs,
life is holding in use.
I've a sword merely,

Hieher! hier lege an!
Heil, Siegfried! theurer Held!

Zweite Scene

(Siegfried legt an.)

(Gunther ist zu Hagen an das Ufer getreten. G trune erblickt Siegfried vom Hochsitze aus, heft eine Zeit lang in freudiger Ueberraschung den Bli auf ihn, und als die Männer dann näher zur Ha schreiten, entfernt sie sich in sichtbarer Verwi rung, nach links durch eine Thüre in ihr Gemach

Siegfried

(der seine Ross an das Land geführt, und jet ruhig an ihm lehnt.)

Wer ist Gibich's Sohn?

Gunther. Gunther, ich, den du such'st

Siegfried. Dich hört' ich rühmen
weit am Rhein:
nun ficht mit mir,
oder sei mein Freund!

Gunther. Lass den Kampf,
sei willkommen!

Siegfried. Wo berg' ich mein Ross?

Hagen. Ich biet' ihm Rast.

Siegfried. Du rief'st mich Siegfried:
sah'st du mich schon?

Hagen. Ich kannte dich nur
an deiner Kraft.

Siegfried. Wohl hüte mir Grane!
Du hieltest nie
von edlerer Zucht
am Zaume ein Ross.

(Hagen führt das Ross rechts hinter die Halle und kehrt bald darauf wieder zurück. Gunth schreitet mit Siegfried in die Halle vor.)

Gunther. Begrüsse froh, o Held,
die Halle meines Vaters;
wohin du schreitest,
was du ersieh'st,
das achte nun dein Eigen:
dein ist mein Erbe,
Land und Leut':
hilf, mein Leib, meinem Eide!
Mich selbst geb' ich zum Mann.

Siegfried. Nicht Land noch Leute biete ic
noch Vater's Haus und Hof:
einzig erbt' ich
den eig'nen Leib;
lebend zehr' ich den auf.
Nur ein Schwert hab' ich,

self-constructed:
hear me swear by my weapon;
with it I'll strengthen our oath.

Hagen

(standing behind them),

But we learn thou art hailed
as lord of Nibelheim's hoard?

Siegfried. That wealth I forgot, well-nigh,
so worthless I deem the gold!
Within a cavern lone I left it,
where a worm did guard it once.

Hagen. Nought hast thou had of it?

Siegfried

pointing to the steel net-work, that hangs in his
girdle.)

But this work, which I cannot use.

Hagen. The Tarnhelm is it,
the Nibelungs' artfullest work:
its trick when set on thy head
is to turn thee to any shape;
or long'st thou for far-off lands,
in a flash, flight canst thou wing.
Hast moved no more of the
wealth?

Siegfried. But a ring.

Hagen. Thou wearest it still?

Siegfried. 'Tis worn by a woman sweet.

Hagen

(aside.)

Brünnhilde!

Gunther. Nought, Siegfried, shalt to me
tender
Toys wouldst for thy treasures get,
taking my wealth in exchange:
without wage I'll serve thee well.

(Hagen has gone to Gutrune's door, and now
opens it. Gutrune enters, and approaches Siegfried
with a filled drinking horn.)

Gutrune. Welcome, O guest,
to Gibich's house!
From its daughter take thou the drink.

Siegfried

(bows friendly, and takes the horn; he holds it
thoughtfully before him, and says softly):

Though gifts thou gav'st
should all be forgot.
I'll grasp alone
one lesson for aye:

selbst geschmiedet—
hilf, mein Schwert, meinem Eide!
das biet' ich mit mir zum Bund.

Hagen

(hinter ihnen stehend.)

Doch des Niblungen-Hortes
nennt die Märe dich Herrn?

Siegfried. Des Schatzes vergass ich fast:
so schätz' ich sein müss'ges Gut!
In einer Höhle liess ich's liegen,
wo ein Wurm es einst bewacht.

Hagen. Und nichts entnahm'st du ihm?

Siegfried

(auf das stählerne Netzgewirk deutend, das er im
Gürtel hängen hat.)

Diess Gewirk, unkund seiner Kraft.

Hagen. Den Tarnhelm kenn' ich,
der Niblungen künstliches Werk:
er taugt, bedeckt er dein Haupt,
dir zu tauschen jede Gestalt;
verlangt dich's an fernsten Ort,
er entführt flugs dich dahin.—
Sonst nichts entnahmst du dem Hort?

Siegfried. Einen Ring.

Hagen. Den hütest du wohl?

Siegfried. Den hütet ein hehres Weib.

Hagen

(für sich.)

Brünnhilde! . .

Gunther. Nicht, Siegfried, sollst du mir
tauschen:
Tand gäb' ich für das Geschmeid,
nähmst all mein Gut du dafür!
Ohn' Entgelt dien' ich dir gern.

(Hagen ist zu Gutrune's Thür gegangen, und öffnet sie jetzt. Gutrune tritt heraus, sie trägt ein
gefülltes Trinkhorn, und naht damit Siegfried.)

Gutrune. Willkommen, Gast,
in Gibich's Haus!
Seine Tochter reicht dir den Trank.

Siegfried

(neigt sich ihr freundlich, und ergreift das Horn;
er hält es gedankenvoll vor sich hin und sagt leise:)

Vergäss' ich alles
was du mir gab'st
von einer Lehre
lass' ich doch nie:—

this goblet's quaffed
with quenchless passion,
Brünnhilde, my bride, to thee!

(He drinks, and hands back the horn to Gutrune,
who, abashed, cast down her eyes before his.)

Siegfried

(gazing on her with swiftly kindling passion.)

Thou fair one, whose beams
my breast have enflamed,
why fall thus thine eyes before mine?

(Gutrune looks up at him, blushing.)

Siegfried. Ha! sweetest maid!
Screen those bright beams,
the heart in my breast
burns with their strength;
in fiery streams I feel
how my blood doth boil in my veins!

(With trembling voice.)

Gunther, what name hath thy sister?

Gunther. Gutrune.

Siegfried. Are good the runes
that now in her eyes I am reading?

(He seizes Gutrune with impatient ardor by the
hand.)

When I sought to serve thy brother
brave
his pride repelled my aid.
Wouldst thou be e'en as arrogant
said I to thee the same?

(Gutrune humbly droops her head, and then, with
an expressive gesture, as if she felt her unworthiness, leaves the hall again with trembling steps.)

Siegfried

(closely observed by Hagen and Gunther, gazes
after her, as if spellbound; then, without turning,
he asks)

Hast thou, Gunther, a wife?

Gunther. I've wooed ne'er yet;
besides, a wife
seems me I scarce can win:
on one my soul I have set,
but no help can gain my wish.

Siegfried

(turning quickly to him.)

What would be gainsaid,
stood I thy friend?

Gunther. A far-off rock's her home,
a fire doth breast her hall.

den ersten Trunk
zu treuer Minne,
Brünnhilde, bring' ich dir!

(Er trinkt und reicht das Horn Gutrune zurüc[k]
welche, verschämt und verwirrt, ihre Augen v[or]
ihm niederschlägt.)

Siegfried

(mit schnell entbrannter Leidenschaft den Blic[k]
auf sie heftend.)

Die so mit dem Blitz
den Blick du mir seng'st,
was senk'st du dein Auge vor mir?

(Gutrune schlägt, erröthend, das Auge zu ihm auf.)

Siegfried. Ha, schönstes Weib!
Schliesse den Blick!
das Herz in der Brust
brennt mir sein Strahl:
zu feurigen Strömen fühl' ich
zehrend ihn zünden mein Blut!—

(Mit bebender Stimme.)

Gunther—wie heisst deine
Schwester?

Gunther. Gutrune.

Siegfried. Sind's gute Runen,
die ihrem Aug' ich entrathe?

(Er fasst Gutrune mit feurigem Ungestüm bei de[r]
Hand.)

Deinem Bruder bot ich mich zu[m]
Mann;
der Stolze schlug mich aus:—
trägst du, wie er, mir Ueber[-]
muth,
böt' ich mich dir zum Bund[?]

(Gutrune neigt demüthig das Haupt, und mit eine[r]
Gebärde, als fühle sie sich seiner nicht werth, ver[-]
lässt sie wankenden Schrittes wieder die Halle.)

Siegfried

(blickt ihr, wie fest gezaubert, nach, von Hage[n]
und Gunther aufmerksam beobachtet; dann, ohn[e]
sich umzuwenden, frägt er:)

Hast du, Gunther, ein Weib?

Gunther. Nicht freit' ich noch,
und einer Frau
soll' ich mich schwerlich freu'n!
Auf eine setzt' ich den Sinn,
die kein Rath je mir gewinnt.

Siegfried

(lebhaft sich zu ihm wendend.)

Was wär' dir versagt,
steh' ich zu dir?

Gunther. Auf Felsen hoch ihr Sitz;
ein Feuer umbrennt den Saal—

egfried
(repeats softly, in wonder, and as if striving to
  remember something long forgotten.)
  "A far-off rock's her home;
  a fire doth breast her hall". . . ?

unther. But he who that fire can brave—

egfried
(hastily chiming in and immediately ceasing.)
  "But he who that fire can brave". . . ?

unther.—is Brünnhilde's fitting mate.
(Siegfried shows, by a silent gesture, that at the
  ntion of Brünnhilde's name the remembrance has
  ite faded.)

unther. That mountain my feet may ap-
            proach not,
  the fire ne'er will pale for me,

egfried
        (with a sudden start.)
  I—fear not the fire,
  and thy bride fain will I fetch;
  for thy own am I
  and my arm is thine:
  if Gutrune for wife I may gain.

unther. Gutrune I'll give to thee gladly.

egfried. Brünnhilde I'll bring thee!

unther. How can she mistake us?

egfried. Through the Tarnhelm's trick,
  turning me into thy shape.

unther. Propose an oath for us pair.

egfried. Blood-brotherhood
  hallowed by oath.
(Hagen fills a horn with fresh wine; Gunther and
  gfried scratch their arms with their sword-
  ints, and hold the wound a moment over the
  ne.)

egfried and Gunther.
  Blossoming life's stream,
  liberal blood
  droppeth into the drink.
  Bravely brewed
  by fiery friends,
  blazes the draught with our blood.
  Truth I drink to my friend:
  fair and free
  be born from our bond
  blood-brotherhood here.
  Breaks a brother the bond,
  fails in faith to his friend,
  What in drops we here

Siegfried
(verwundert, und wie um eines längst Vergesse-
  nen sich zu entsinnen, wiederholt leise:)
  "Auf Felsen hoch ihr Sitz;
  ein Feuer umbrennt den Saal" . . ?

Gunther. Nur wer durch das Feuer bricht,

Siegfried
(hastig einfallend und schnell nachlassend.)
  "Nur wer durch das Feuer bricht" . . ?

Gunther. —darf Brünnhilde's Freier sein.
(Siegfried drückt durch seine schweigende Gebärde
  aus, dass bei Nennung von Brünnhilde's Namen die
  Erinnerung ihm vollends ganz schwindet.)

Gunther. Nun darf ich den Fels nicht er-
            klimmen;
  das Feuer verglimmt mir nie!

Siegfried.
        (Heftig auffahrend.)
  Ich—fürchte kein Feuer:
  für dich frei' ich die Frau;
  denn dein Mann bin ich,
  und mein Muth ist dein—
  erwerb' ich Gutrun' zum Weib.

Gunther. Gutrune gönn' ich dir gern.

Siegfried. Brünnhilde bringe ich dir.

Gunther. Wie willst du sie täuschen?

Siegfried. Durch des Tarnhelm's Trug
  tausch' ich mir deine Gestalt.

Gunther. So stelle Eide zum Schwur

Siegfried. Blut-Brüderschaft
  schwöre ein Eid!
(Hagen füllt ein Trinkhorn mit frischem Wein;
  Siegfried und Gunther ritzen sich mit ihren Schwer-
  tern die Arme und halten diese einen Augenblick
  über das Trinkhorn.)

Siegfried und Gunther.
  Blühenden Lebens
  labendes Blut
  traüfelt' ich in den Trank:
  bruder-brünstig
  muthig gemischt,
  blüh' im Trank unser Blut.
  Treue trink' ich dem Freund,
  froh und frei
  entblühe dem Bund
  Blut-Brüderschaft heut'!
  Bricht ein Bruder den Bund,
  trügt den Treuen der Freund:
  was in Tropfen hold

haste to drink of
in streams be strained from his heart,
forfeit stern to his friend.
Thus compact I claim!
Thus duty I drink.

(They each in turn drink half the contents of the horn, which Hagen, who has stood apart during the oath, then breaks in half with his sword. Gunther and Siegfried clasp hands.)

Siegfried
(to Hagen.)
Why hast thou not joined in the
bond?

Hagen.　Your drink were spoiled by my
blood!
It flows by no means
nobly enough;
stubborn and cold,
scarce it stirs;
my cheek 'tis chary to redden.
I leave perforce the fiery league

Gunther.　Have no heed for the churl.

Siegfried.　Forth let me fare!
There lies my skiff;
swiftly float to the fastness.
At the bank for one night
wait with the boat thou;
the bride bear then away.

Gunther.　Takest thou first no rest?

Siegfried.　I'll return here in a trice.
(Goes to the shore.)

Gunther.　Thou, Hagen, have ward of the
homestead.
(He follows Siegfried.)
(Gutrune appears at the door of her room.)

Gutrune.　O where haste they so swiftly?

Hagen.　They sail, Brünnhilde to find.

Gutrune.　Siegfried?

Hagen.　See what he does
for wife striving to win thee.
(He seats himself before the hall with spear and shield. Siegfried and Gunther float away.)

Gutrune.　Siegfried—mine!
(Goes back to her room in great agitation.)

Hagen
(after a long silence.)
Here I sit to wait,
watching the hall,
warding the house from all foes.

heute wir tranken,
in Strahlen ström' es dahin,
fromme Sühne dem Freund!
So—biet' ich den Bund:
so trink' ich dir Treu!

(Sie trinken nacheinander, jeder zur Hälfte; dann zerschlägt Hagen, der während des Schwures zur Seite gelehnt, mit seinem Schwerte das Horn. Siegfried und Gunther reichen sich die Hände.)

Siegfried
(zu Hagen.)
Was nahmst du am Eide nicht Theil

Hagen.　Mein Blut verdärb' euch den
Trank!
Nicht fliesst mir's ächt
und edel wie euch;
störrisch und kalt
stockt's in mir;
nicht will's die Wange mir röthen.
D'rum bleib' ich fern
vom feurigen Bund.

Gunther.　Lass' den unfrohen Mann!

Siegfried.　Frisch auf die Fahrt!
Dort liegt mein Schiff;
schnell führt es zum Felsen:
eine Nacht am Ufer
harrs't du im Nachen;
die Frau führst du dann heim.

Gunther.　Rastest du nicht zuvor?

Siegfried.　Um die Rückkehr ist's mir jach
(Er geht zum Ufer.)

Gunther.　Du Hagen, bewache die Halle
(Er folgt Siegfried.)
(Gutrune erscheint an der Thüre ihres Gemaches.)

Gutrune.　Wohin eilen die Schnellen?

Hagen.　Zu Schiff', Brünnhild' zu frei'n.

Gutrune.　Siegfried?

Hagen.　Sieh', wie's ihn treibt
zum Weib dich zu gewinnen!
(Er setzt sich mit Speer und Schild vor der Halle nieder. Siegfried und Gunther fahren ab.)

Gutrune.　Siegfried—mein!
(Sie geht, lebhaft erregt, in ihr Gemach zurück.)

Hagen
(nach längerem Stillschweigen.)
Hier sitz' ich zur Wacht,
wahre den Hof,
wehre die Halle dem Feind:—

Gibich's son
is wafted by winds;
a-wooing forth is he gone.
And fleetly steereth
a stalwart man,
whose force all peril can stem.
His own the bride
he brings down the Rhine;
but he will bring *me* the Ring.
Ye gallant partners,
gleeful companions,
push ye then merrily hence!
Slight though your natures,
ye still may serve
the Nibelung's son.

(A curtain closes in from each side and hides the
stage. After a short orchestral interlude, during
which the scene is changed, the curtain, which before closed in all the front of the hall, is completely
withdrawn.)

Scene Three
The Valkyries' rock, as in the Prelude.

Brünnhilde

sits at the entrance of the cave in silent thought,
gazing on Siegfried's ring; overcome by tender rem-
iniscences, she covers it with kisses, when suddenly she hears a distant noise: she listens and
looks off at back.

Old well-recognized sounds
strike on my ear from distance;
a wind-horse hither
wingeth its course,
in the clouds it rumbles
close to the rock.
Who rides my stillness to stir?

Waltrauta's
(voice from the distance).
Brünnhilde—sister!
sleep'st thou or wakest?

Brünnhilde
(starting to her feet).
Welcome that cry,
it wafts from Valtrauta!
Truest sister!
seek'st thou trace of me here?
(Calling towards the back.)
In yon wood,
As thou wert wont,
Straightway descend
and safely stable thy steed.
Com'st thou to me?
bold and uncowed,
dar'st thou again then
banished Brünnhild' to greet?

Gibich's Sohne
wehet der Wind;
auf Werben fährt er dahin.
Ihm führt der Steuer
ein starker Held,
Gefahr ihm will er besteh'n:
die eig'ne Braut
ihm bringt er zum Rhein;
mir aber bringt er— den Ring.—
Ihr freien Söhne,
frohe Gesellen,
segelt nur lustig dahin!
Dünkt er euch niedrig,
ihr dient ihm doch—
des Niblungen Sohn.

(Ein Teppich schlägt vor der Scene zusammen,
und verschliesst die Bühne. Nachdem, während
eines kurzen Orchester-Zwischenspieles, der Schau-
platz verwandelt ist, wird der Teppich, der zuvor den
Vordergrund der Halle einfasste, gänzlich aufgezogen.)

Dritte Scene
Die Felsenhöhe, wie im Vorspiel.

Brünnhilde.

(Sitzt am Eingange des Steingemaches, und betrachtet in stummen Sinnen Siegfried's Ring; von
wonniger Erinnerung überwättigt, bedeckt sie ihn
dann mit Küssen,—als sie plötzlich ein fernes Geräusch vernimmt: sie lauscht und späht zur Seite in
den Hintergrund.)

Altgewohntes Geräusch
raunt meinem Ohr die Ferne:—
ein Luftross jagt
im Laufe daher;
auf der Wolke fährt es
wetternd zum Fels!—
Wer fand mich Einsame auf?

Waltraute's
(Stimme aus der Ferne).
Brünnhilde! Schwester!
schläf'st oder wach'st du?

Brünnhilde
(fährt vom Sitze auf).
Waltraute's Ruf,
so wonnig mir kund!—
Komm'st du, Schwester,
schwing'st du kühn dich zu mir?
(in die Scene rufend.)
Dort im Tann
—dir noch vertraut—
steige vom Ross
und stell' den Renner zu Rast!
Kommst du zu mir?
Bist du so kühn?
mag'st ohne Grauen
Brünnhild' bieten den Gruss?

(Valtrauta has entered hastily from the wood; Brünnhilde rushes to meet her; in her joy she does not perceive Valtrauta's anxious timidity.)

Valtrauta.
'Tis for thee
my gallop is taken.

Brünnhilde.
O was it for Brünnhilde's sake
War-father's ban thou'st broken?
Or for what? O say!
Will Wotan's heart
once more softly wax?
When against the god once
Siegmund I sheltered—
wrongly, I wot well—
I wrought the thing that he wished.
That his anger was ended
well I knew;
for though sealed he mine eyes in
               sleep,
rivetting me to this rock,
destining me to the man
who this way should roam and awake
               me,
yet the boon I begged for
denied he not:
a terrible fire
he knit round the fell,
all tremblers to ward from the way.
So sweet solace
was shaped by my sentence:
the highest of heroes
won me for wife.
Filled with his love
in light and laughter I live.
Lured thee, O sister, my lot?
Dost thou then pine
for part in my pleasures,
seek my pure bliss to share?

Valtrauta.
Share the insaneness
that hath seized on thy soul?
More matter hath worked on my mind
the ban of Wotan to break.

Brünnhilde.
Fear and dread
drive o'er thy features!
Doth our father pardon withhold?
Thou fearest his punishment's force?

Valtrauta.
Did I but fear him

(Waltraute ist aus dem Tann hastig aufgetret[e] Brünnhilde ist ihr stürmisch entgegengeeilt: di[e] beachtet in der Freude nicht die ängstliche Sch[eu] Waltraute's.)

Waltraute.
Einzig dir nur
galt meine Eile.

Brünnhilde
    (in höchster freudiger Aufgeregtheit).
So wagtest du, Brünnhild' zu lieb,
Walvater's Bann zu brechen?
Oder wie? o sag'!
wär' wider mich
Wotan's Sinn erweicht?
Als dem Gott entgegen
Siegmund ich schützte,
fehlend—ich weiss es—
erfüllt' ich doch seinen Wunsch:
dass sein Zorn sich verzogen,
weiss ich auch;
denn verschloss er mich gleich in
               Schlaf,
fesselt' er mich auf den Fels,
wies er dem Mann' mich zur Magd,
der am Weg' mich fänd und er-
               weckt'—
meiner bangen Bitte
doch gab er Gunst:
mit zehrendem Feuer
umgab er den Fels,
dem Zagen zu wehren den Weg.
So zur seligsten
schuf mich die Strafe:
der herrlichste Held
gewann mich zum Weib;
in seiner Liebe
leucht' und lach' ich heut' auf.—
Lockte dich, Schwester, mein Loos?
An meiner Wonne
willst du dich weiden?
theilen, was mich betraf?

Waltraute.
Theilen den Taumel,
der dich Thörin erfasst?—
Ein And'res bewog mich in Angst
zu brechen Wotan's Gebot.

Brünnhilde.
Angst und Furcht
fesselt dich Arme?
So verzieh der Strenge noch nicht?
du zag'st vor des Strafenden Zorn?

Waltraute.
Dürft' ich ihn fürchten,

this alarm fast were allayed.

Brünnhilde.
Scared, I can scarce understand.

Valtrauta.
Mask thy emotion:
wisely hark to my words.
Again the grief
doth hurry me back
which did goad me here from Valhalla.

Brünnhilde
(alarmed).
What ails with the Æsir eternal?

Valtrauta.
Heed with thy soul what I recite
thee.
Since he from thee was severed
our sire no more
sent us to warfare;
undirected
rode we, an awe-stricken host;
Valhall's high-hearted heroes
he viewed no more.
Lonely a-horse,
without halt or home,
through the world as a Wanderer he
went.
He lately came home,
in his hand holding fast
his spear in splinters:
'twas hacked by a hero asunder.
With signs for words
waved he all
the warriors in haste
the world's ash-tree to hew down.
The stem in sticks
he bade them to stack,
and arrange in a bulk
round the Æsir's sanctified seat.
The gods he called
unto the council;
his proud sacred
place then he took:
to his side
appointed the tremblers to assemble.
In rank and ring
the warriors crowded Valhalla.
So sits he,
speaking no word,
in high position,
still and grave,
the splintered spear

meiner Angst fänd' ich ein End'!

Brünnhilde.
Staunend versteh' ich dich nicht!

Waltraute.
Wehr' deiner Wallung:
achtsam höre mich an!
Nach Walhall wieder
treibt mich die Angst,
die von Walhall hieher mich trieb.

Brünnhilde
(erschrocken).
Was ist's mit den ewigen Göttern?

Waltraute.
Höre mit Sinn was ich sage!—
Seit er von dir geschieden,
zur Schlacht nicht mehr
schickte uns Wotan;
irr und rathlos
ritten wir ängstlich zu Heer.
Walhall's muthige Helden
mied Walvater:
einsam zu Ross
ohne Ruh' und Rast
durchstreift' er als Wand'rer die Welt
Jüngst kehrte er heim;
in der Hand hielt er
seines Speeres Splitter:
die hatte ein Held ihm geschlagen.
Mit stummen Wink
Walhall's Edle
wies er zum Forst,
die Welt-Esche zu fällen;
des Stammes Scheite
hiess er sie schichten
zum ragenden Hauf
rings um der Seligen Saal.
Der Götter Rath
liess er berufen;
den Hochsitz nahm
heilig er ein:
ihm zu Seiten
hiess er die Bangen sich setzen,
in Ring und Reih'
die Hall' erfüllen die Helden.
So—sitzt er,
sagt kein Wort,
auf hehrem Sitze
stumm und ernst,
des Speeres Splitter

held fast in his fist.
Hulda's apples
doth he not eat.
Gloomy and awe-struck
all the gods seem frozen.
But he turned his ravens
both out to travel;
when they with goodly
tidings wing their return,
once again then for evermore
over the god breaks a smile.
Round his knees in vigil
twine all we Valkyries;
blind bides he
to eyes that are begging,
and all of us stay,
struck with an ominous awe.
Unto his breast
weeping I press'd me:
his brooding then broke;
and his thoughts turned, Brünnhilde,
to thee!
Deep sighs he uttered,
closed his eyelids,
as were he dreaming,
and reded these words:
"The day the Rhine's three daughters
gain by surrender from her the Ring
from the curse's load
released are gods and men!"
I thought upon't;
and then I threaded
'mid throngs dumb-stricken
thence from his side;
in haste on my horse
I threw me astride,
and straightway thrust towards thee.
Then, my sister,
I supplicate:
do what thou may'st
if but thou hast mind:
ward off the woe of the gods.
(Throws herself at Brünnhilde's feet.)

Brünnhilde.

What dreamy tales of myst'ry
mournfully tell'st thou to me!
From cloudy homes
where the holy gods sit
am I, poor fool, expelled;
no sense conveys thy recital.
Void and vain
seemeth thy speech.
Within thine eyes

fest in der Faust;
Holda's Aepfel
rührt er nicht an:
Staunen und Bangen
binden starr die Götter.—
Seiner Raben beide
sandt' er auf Reise:
kehrten die einst
mit guter Kunde zurück,
dann noch einmal
—zum letzten Mal—
lächelte ewig der Gott.
Seine Knie' umwindend
liegen wir Walküren:
blind bleibt er
den flehenden Blicken;
uns alle verzehrt
Zagen und endlose Angst.
An seine Brust
presst' ich mich weinend:
da brach sich sein Blick—
er gedachte, Brünnhilde, dein!
Tief seufzte er auf,
schloss das Auge,
und wie im Traume
raunt' er das Wort:—
„Des tiefen Rheines Töchtern
gäbe den Ring sie wieder zurück,
von des Fluches Last
erlös't wär' Gott und Welt!"—
Da sann ich nach:
von seiner Seite
durch stumme Reihen
stahl ich mich fort;
in heimlicher Hast
bestieg ich mein Ross,
und ritt im Sturme zu dir.
Dich, o Schwester,
beschwör' ich nun:
was du vermagst,
vollend' es dein Muth!
Ende der Ewigen Qual!

Brünnhilde.

Welch' banger Träume Mären
meldest du Traurige mir!
Der Götter heiligem
Himmels-Nebel
bin ich Thörin enttaucht:
nicht fass' ich, was ich erfahre.
Wirr und wüst
scheint mir dein Sinn;
in deinem Aug'

so over-wearied
gleams fitfully glow.
Thou piteous woman
with pallid features,
what would thy wildness of me?

Waltrauta
(with gloomy haste).
There on thy hand—the ring
'tis that—hark to my rede!
For Wotan wilt thou resign it?

Brünnhilde.
The ring! resign it?

Waltrauta.
Surrender it back to the Rhine!

Brünnhilde.
Surrender it—I—the ring?
Siegfried's bridal gift?
Wander thy senses?

Waltrauta.
Hear me! heed my distress!
The world's trouble
hangs upon it, I trow.
Whirl it from thee
far in the water,
woe from Valhall' averting;
cast the foul thing away in the flood!

Brünnhilde.
Ah! wist thou what 'tis to me?
Thou can'st not fathom,
feelingless maid!
More than Æsir's honor,
More than Valhall's bright realm
I hold this ring.
One look at its beauteous gold,
one light from its brilliant gleam
glads me more
than unending good
to all the mass of the gods.
I see in its beams
lambent how Siegfried loves me.
Siegfried loves me!
How little thou wott'st of this sweet-
ness!
Stays with me the ring.
Get hence to the gods
in holy array,
and of my ring
arede them this:
I'll loose not love from my heart;
no hest shall hinder my loving,

—so übermüde—
glänzt flackernde Gluth:
mit blasser Wange
du bleiche Schwester,
was willst du Wilde von mir?

Waltraute
(mit unheimlicher Hast.)
An deiner Hand der Ring—
er ist's: hör' meinen Rath:
für Wotan wirf ihn von dir!

Brünnhilde.
Den Ring—von mir?

Waltraute.
Den Rheintöchtern gieb ihn zurück!

Brünnhilde.
Den Rheintöchtern—ich—den Ring?
Siegfried's Liebespfand?
Bist du von Sinnen?

Waltraute.
Hör' mich! hör' meine Angst?
Der Welt Unheil
haftet sicher an ihm:—
wirf ihn von dir
fort in die Welle
Walhall's Elend zu enden,
den verfluchten wirf in die Fluth!

Brünnhilde.
Ha! weisst du, was er mir ist?
Wie kannst du's fassen,
fühllose Maid!—
Mehr als Walhall's Wonne,
mehr als der Ewigen Ruhm
ist mir der Ring:
ein Blick auf sein helles Gold,
ein Blitz aus dem hehren Glanz
gilt mir werther
als aller Götter
ewig währendes Glück!
Denn selig aus ihm
leuchtet mir Siegfried's Liebe:
Siegfried's Liebe!
O liess' sich die Wonne dir sagen!
Sie wahrt mir der Reif.
Geh' hin zu der Götter
heiligem Rath;
von meinem Ringe
raun' ihnen zu:
die Liebe liesse ich nie,
mir nehmen nie sie die Liebe,

Sooner to ruins
Valhall's splendor shall crash.

Valtrauta.

This is thy truth then?
So in trouble
thou leavest thy sister all loveless?

Brünnhilde.

Swiftly go forth,
far hence to ride:
the ring thou'lt force not from me.

Valtrauta.

Woe's me, woe's me!
Woe's thee, sister!
Woe to Valhall'—woe!

(She rushes away and is heard without—as if on
horse—galloping away from the wood.)

Brünnhilde

(gazes after a brightly lighted storm-cloud as it
sails away and is quickly lost in the distance).

Black thunder-cloud
that cleav'st the heavens,
stride quickly hence:
no more be steered to me here.

(It is now evening. From the valley glimmers the
firelight, gradually waxing.)

Eve's dusky shadows
shroud the heavens:
Why glare so wildly
the glittering waves o'er the wall?
The raging fire
its way o'er the rock-point would
force.

(Siegfried's horn is heard below in the valley.
Brünnhilde listens, and then starts up enraptured.)

Siegfried!
Siegfried is here!
Sure his horn sounded that call.
Up! up! and be gathered
into my god's strong arm.

(She hurries towards the back in the highest
transport. Flames dart up over the cliff; out of
them springs Siegfried up on to a jutting rock,
whereupon the flames fall back again and gradually
retire to the valley. Siegfried appears in Gunther's
form, wearing the Tarnhelm, the visor of which
covers half his face, leaving only the eyes free.)

Brünnhilde

(retreating in horror.)

Betrayed! What man art thou?

(She flies to the front, and from thence, in
speechless amazement, turns her looks upon Siegfried.)

Siegfried

(remaining at back on the stone, leans on his
shield and gazes at her a long while; then he speaks

---

stürzt auch in Trümmern
Walhall's strahlende Pracht!

Waltraute.

Diess deine Treue?
So in Trauer
entlässest du lieblos die Schwester?

Brünnhilde.

Schwinge dich fort;
fliege zu Ross:
den Ring entführst du mir nicht!

Waltraute.

Wehe! Wehe!
Weh' dir Schwester!
Walhall's Göttern Weh!

(Sie stürzt fort; man hört sie schnell—wie zu Ross
vom Tann aus fortbrausen.)

Brünnhilde

(blickt einer davonjagenden, hellerleuchteten Ge
witterwolke nach, die sich bald gänzlich in de
Ferne verliert).

Blitz und Gewölk,
vom Wind geblasen,
stürme dahin:
zu mir nie steure mehr her!—

(Es ist Abend geworden: aus der Tiefe leuchtet de
Feuerschein stärker auf.)

Abendlich Dämmern
deckt den Himmel:
Was leckt so wüthend
die lodernde Welle zum Wall?
Zur Felsenspitze
wälzt sich der feurige Schwall.

(Man hört aus der Tiefe Siegfried's Hornruf na
hen. Brünnhilde lauscht, und fährt dann entzück
auf.)

Siegfried!
Siegfried zurück?
seinen Ruf sendet er her!
Auf!—Auf, ihm entgegen!
in meines Gottes Arm!

(Sie stürzt in höchstem Entzücken dem Hinter
grunde Feuerflammen schlagen über den Höhensaur
auf: aus ihnen springt Siegfried auf einen hoch ra
genden Felsstein empor, worauf die Flammen wie
der zurückweichen, und abermals nur aus der Tief
des Hintergrundes heraufleuchten.—Siegfried, au
dem Haupte den Tarnhelm, der ihm bis zur Hälft
das Gesicht verdeckt und nur die Augen frei läss
erscheint in Gunther's Gestalt.)

Brünnhilde

(voll Entsetzen zurückweichend.)

Verrath!—Wer drang zu mir?

(Sie flieht bis in den Hintergrund, und heftet vo
da aus in sprachlosem Erstaunen ihren Blick au
Siegfried.)

Siegfried.

(Im Hintergrunde auf dem Steine verweilend, be
trachtet sie lange, auf seinen Schild gelehnt; dan

to her with altered—deeper—voice.)
Brünnhilde! A lover comes,
and alarms him nought thy fire.
I woo thee for my wife;
so bend thy will to me!

Brünnhilde
        (trembling violently.)
Who is the man
has wrought the marvel
that but one alone may work?

Siegfried
      (still standing on the rock at back.)
A hero thou'llt obey
if but by force thou'rt ruled.

Brünnhilde
       (filled with terror.)
A demon stands
upon yon stone!
an eagle has flown here
who would my flesh rend!
Who art thou, awful one?
      (Siegfried is silent.)
Art thou a mortal?
Com'st thou of Hella's
night-dwelling host?

Siegfried
      (after a long silence.)
A Gibichung am I,
and Gunther he is hight
who, maid, will mate with thee.

Brünnhilde
    (in a despairing outburst.)
Wotan! Resentful,
Stern-hearted sire!
Woe! now I fathom
thy fiat fell!
My shame and wailing
well hast thou shaped!

Siegfried
(leaping from the rock and approaching.)
The night doth fall,
thy room I demand;
mine be thou made by marriage.

Brünnhilde
threateningly stretching out her finger on which
      is Siegfried's ring.)
Stand back! bow to this token!
No shame can touch me from thee
while yet this ring is my shield.

redet er sie mit verstellter—tieferer—Stimme an.)
Brünnhild'! ein Freier kam,
den dein Feuer nicht geschreckt.
Dich werb' ich nun zum Weib;
du folge willig mir!

Brünnhilde
       (heftig zitternd).
Wer ist der Mann,
der das vermochte,
was dem Stärksten nur bestimmt?

Siegfried
  (immer noch auf dem Steine im Hintergrunde).
Ein Helde, der dich zähmt
bezwingt Gewalt dich nur.

Brünnhilde
      (von Grausen erfasst).
Ein Unhold schwang sich
auf jenen Stein;
ein Aar kam geflogen
mich zu zerfleischen!
Wer bist du, Schrecklicher?
      (Siegfried—schweigt.)
Stamm'st du von Menschen?
komm'st du von Hella's
nächtlichem Heer?

Siegfried
      (nach längerem Schweigen).
Ein Gibichung bin ich,
und Gunther heisst der Held,
dem, Frau, du folgen soll'st.

Brünnhilde
    (in Verzweiflung ausbrechend.)
Wotan! ergrimmter,
grausamer Gott!
Weh'! nun erseh' ich
der Strafe Sinn:
zu Hohn und Jammer
jag'st du mich hin!

Siegfried
  (springt vom Stein herab und tritt näher.)
Die Nacht bricht an:
in deinem Gemach
musst du dich mit mir vermählen.

Brünnhilde
(den Finger, an dem sie Siegfried's Ring trägt, dro-
      hend emporstreckend.)
Bleib' fern! fürchte dies Zeichen!
Zur Schande zwingst du mich nicht,
so lang' der Ring mich schützt.

Siegfried. Husband's right it gains for
Gunther:
with that ring be wed to him.

Brünnhilde. Aroint, thou robber!
Villainous thief!
Nor venture thyself near my side.
Stronger than steel
makes me the ring;
None rends it from me.

Siegfried. From thee will I take it,
Taught by thy words.

(He presses towards her; they wrestle. Brünnhilde slips herself loose and flies. Siegfried pursues
her. Again they struggle; he seizes her, and plucks
the ring from her finger. She utters a loud scream
and sinks exhausted on the rocky seat in front of
the cave.)

Siegfried. Now be thou mine!
Brünnhilde, Gunther's bride:
go to thy chamber with me.

Brünnhilde

(almost fainting.)

How, woman too hapless,
canst thou find help?

(Siegfried drives her in with a commanding gesture. She goes into the cave trembling, and with
tottering steps.)

Siegfried
(drawing his sword and speaking with his natural
voice.)

Now, Needful, witness thou
that chaste my wooing is.
To seal my oath to my brother,
separate me from his bride.

(He follows Brünnhilde.)
The curtain falls.

ACT TWO

Scene One

River bank before the hall of the Gibichungs: the
banks of the river L., entrance to the hall R. From
the river bank rises diagonally towards the back
a rocky slope divided by sundry mountain paths.
There stands an altar stone, dedicated to Fricka, a
larger one, higher up, for Wotan, and another
towards the side for Donner. It is night.

Hagen, with spear in hand and shield at side, sits
sleeping against the hall. The moon suddenly
throws a keen light on him and his surroundings;
Alberic is seen crouching in front of him, leaning
his arms on Hagen's knees.

Siegfried. Mannesrecht gebe er Gunther
durch den Ring sei ihm ver
mählt!

Brünnhilde. Zurück, Räuber!
frevelnder Dieb!
Erfreche dich nicht zu nah'n.
Stärker als Stahl
macht mich der Ring:
nie raubst du ihn mir!

Siegfried. Von dir ihn zu lösen
lehrst du mich nun.

(Er dringt auf sie ein; sie ringen. Brünnhild
windet sich los und flieht. Siegfried setzt ih
nach. Sie ringen von neuem; er erfasst sie, un
entzieht ihrem Finger den Ring. Sie schreit lau
auf und sinkt, wie zerbrochen, auf der Steinban
vor dem Gemach zusammen.)

Siegfried. Jetzt bist du mein!
Brünnhilde, Gunther's Braut—
gönne mir nun dein Gemach!

Brünnhilde

(fast ohnmächtig.)

Was könntest du wehren,
elendes Weib?

(Siegfried treibt sie mit einer geb:etenden Bewe
gung an: zitternd und wankenden Schrittes geht s
in das Gemach.)

Siegfried
(das Schwert ziehend, mit seiner natürlichen
Stimme.)

Nun, Nothung, zeuge du,
dass ich in Züchten warb:
die Treue wahrend dem Bruder,
trenne mich von seiner Braut!

(Er folgt Brünnhilde nach.)
Der Vorhang fällt.

ZWEITER AUFZUG

Erste Scene

Uferraum vor der Halle der Gibichungen: rech
der offene Eingang zur Halle; links das Rheinufe
von diesem aus erhebt sich eine durch verschieder
Bergpfade gespaltene, felsige Anhöhe, quer über d
Bühne, nach rechts dem Hintergrunde zu aufste
gend. Dort sieht man einen der Fricka errichtete
Weichstein, welchem, höher hinauf, ein grösser
für Wotan, sowie seitwärts ein gleicher für Donne
geweihter entspricht. Es ist Nacht.

Hagen, den Speer im Arm, den Schild zur Seit
sitzt schlafend an der Halle. Der Mond wir
plötzlich ein grelles Licht auf ihn und seine nächs
Umgebung: man gewahrt Alberich vor Hage
kauernd, die Arme auf dessen Knie gelehnt.

Alberic. Sleepest thou, Hagen, my son?
  Thou sleep'st and hear'st not him
  whom rest and sleep have ruined.

Hagen
(softly and without moving, so that he appears still
  to sleep, though his eyes are open.)
  I hear thee well, son of darkness:
  what hast thou to instruct my
      slumber?

Alberic. Remind thee what might
      thy spirit owneth;
    i' 'tis as manly
  as thy mother did make it erst.

Hagen. Though mighty she made me,
  I may na'theless not thank her
  that to thy craft she succumbed.
    Wizened, wan and pale,
      I hate the happy,
      hope for no joy.

Alberic. Hagen, my son!
    hate thou the happy!
    Thy so hapless sire,
    by sorrow besieged,
  then lacks not thy love.
    If thou art fearless,
    fierce and false,
      those whom we fight
      with a nocturnal feud
  shall surely be harmed by our hate.
  He who once wrested my ring,
  Wotan, the worst of all robbers,
    at last is disabled
    by his own offspring:
    all his late power
    through the Volsung is lost.
  All the gods together with him
  in awe are waiting their ending.
  No more him I fear:
  he must fall now among them.
  Sleep'st thou, Hagen, my son?

Hagen
    (remaining motionless as before.)
    The might of the gods,
    whose meed is it?

Alberic.
    Mine and thine!
  We'll master the world;
    if I may reckon
    on thy aid—
  shar'st thou in my wrongs and wrath.
    Wotan's spear

Alberich. Schläfst du, Hagen, mem
          Sohn?
  Du schläfst, und hörst mich nicht,
  den Ruh' und Schlaf verrieth?

Hagen
    (leise und ohne sich zu rühren, so dass er immer
  fort zu schlafen scheint, obwohl er die Augen offen
          hat.)
    Ich höre dich, schlimmer Albe:
  was hast du meinem Schlaf zu sagen?

Alberich. Gemahnt sei der Macht,
    der du gebietest,
    bist du so muthig,
  wie die Mutter dich mir gebar.

Hagen. Gab die Mutter mir Muth,
  nicht doch mag ich ihr danken,
  dass deiner List sie erlag:
    frühalt, fahl und bleich,
    hass' ich die Frohen,
    freue mich nie!

Alberich. Hagen, mein Sohn!
    Hasse die Frohen!
    Mich Lust-freien,
    Leid-belasteten,
  liebst du so wie du sollst!
    Bist du kräftig,
    kühn und klug:
    die wir bekämpfen
    mit nächtigem Krieg,
  schon giebt ihnen Noth unser Neid
  Der einst den Ring mir entriss,
  Wotan, der wüthende Räuber,
    vom eig'nen Geschlechte
    ward er geschlagen:
    an den Wälsung verlor er
    Macht und Gewalt;
  mit der Götter ganzer Sippe
  in Angst ersieht er sein End'.
  Nicht ihn fürcht' ich mehr:
  fallen muss er mit Allen!
  Schläf'st du, Hagen, mein Sohn?

Hagen
    (bleibt unverändert wie zuvor).
    Der Ewigen Macht,
    wer erbte sie?

Alberich.
    Ich—und du:
    wir erben die Welt,
    trüg' ich mich nicht
    in deiner Treu',
  theil'st du meinen Gram und Grimm.
    Wotan's Speer

was spoiled by the Volsung,
  who fiercely did vanquish
  Fafnir in fight,
the fair ring to take as a toy.
  Now he is prince
  of every power,
Valhall' and Nibelheim
  know him their lord.
  On this fear-lacking hero
  my curse cannot fall;
  for, the ring's might
  he uses not:
  he knows nought
  of its notable worth.
Laughter, and love with its glow
glad his life-days alone.
  Only his ruin
  must we now aim at.....
Sleep'st thou, Hagen, my son?

Hagen.

  I help him already
  ruin to seek.

Alberic. The golden round—
  the ring—we must arrive at.
  A woman wise
  loves him well as her life.
  Rendered he e'er
  the river maidens
  —by whose wiles amid
  the waves I was mocked—
the ring, obeying her rede,
for ever gone were the gold,
and no art could earn it again.
  Then, without staying,
  strive for the ring.
  Thou stubborn
  and sturdy wert made,
  that thou shouldst help
  my hate against heroes.
  Strength want'st thou indeed
  to vanquish the worm:
that alone the Volsung might work.
  Yet potent hatred
  I planted, Hagen,
in thee, my avenger:—
  to win me the ring,
thou'lt vanquish Volsung and Wotan.
Swear to me, Hagen, my son?

(From this point an increasing gloom hides
Hagen and Alberic. At the same time day begins
to dawn on the Rhine.)

zerspellte der Wälsung,
  der Fafner, den Wurm,
  im Kampfe gefällt,
und kindisch den Reif sich errang:
  jede Gewalt
  hat er gewonnen;
Walhall und Nibelheim
  neigen sich ihm;
  an dem furchtlosen Helden
  erlahmt selbst mein Fluch:
  denn nicht kennt er
  des Ringes Werth,
  zu nichts nützt er
  die neidlichste Macht;
lachend in liebender Brunst
brennt er lebend dahin.
  Ihn zu verderben
  taugt uns nun einzig . . .
Hörst du, Hagen, mein Sohn?

Hagen.

  Zu seinem Verderben
  dient er mir schon.

Alberich. Den gold'nen Ring,
  den Reif gilt's zu erringen!
  Ein weises Weib
  lebt dem Wälsung zu Lieb':
  rieth' sie ihm je
  des Rheines Töchtern
  —die in Wassers Tiefen
  einst mich bethört!—
zurück zu geben den Ring:
verloren ging' mir das Gold,
keine List erlangte es je.
  Drum ohne Zögern
  ziel' auf den Reif:
  Dich Zaglosen
  zeugt' ich mich ja,
  dass wider Helden
  hart du mich hieltest.
  Zwar stark nicht genug
  den Wurm zu besteh'n,
was allein dem Wälsung bestimmt,
  zu zähem Hass
  erzog ich doch Hagen:
der soll mich nun rächen,
  den Ring zu gewinnen,
dem Wälsung und Wotan zum
            Hohn!
Schwör'st du mir's, Hagen, mein
            Sohn?

(Ein immer finsterer Schatten bedeckt wieder
Hagen und Alberich: vom Rhein her dämmert
der Tag.)

Hagen. The ring I'll lay hands on:
    happily rest.

Alberic. Swear to me, Hagen, my hope.

Hagen. My soul swears it:
    cease from thy sorrow.

Alberic
(as he gradually disappears from view, his voice becoming fainter and fainter.)
    Be true, Hagen, my son.
    Trusty hero, be true.
    Be true!—true!

(He vanishes completely. Hagen, who has persistently remained in his place, gazes motionless and with fixed eyes upon the Rhine.)
(The sun rises and is mirrored in the waters.)
(Siegfried suddenly comes forward from behind a bush on the river bank. He is in his own semblance, but still wears the Tarnhelm; this he now doffs and hangs in his belt.)

Siegfried. Hoiho! Hagen!
    sleepy soul!
    See who is coming!

Hagen
(indolently rising.)
    Hey, Siegfried!
    Thou speedy hero!
    Whence brawlest thou here?

Siegfried. From Brünnhilde's rock.
    'Twas there I imbibed the breath
    with which I waked thee:
    so rapid was my flight.
    Slower will follow the pair;
    by boat they slip up here.

Hagen. Has mastered Brünnhilde?

Siegfried. Wakes Gutrune yet?

Hagen. Hoiho! Gutrune!
    Come without!
    Siegfried is here:
    why stay in house?

Siegfried
(turning to the hall.)
    I took Brünnhilde,
    and how—I'll tell you twain.
(Gutrune enters from the hall and meets him.)

Siegfried.
    Now welcome make me,
    Gibich-maid!
    A goodly herald hast in me.

Hagen. Den Ring soll ich haben:
    harre in Ruh'!

Alberich. Schwör'st du mir's, Hagen,
      mein Held?

Hagen. Mir selbst schwör' ich's:
    schweige die Sorge!

Alberich
(wie er allmälig immer mehr dem Blicke entschwindet, wird auch seine Stimme immer unvernehmbarer.)
    Sei treu, Hagen, mein Sohn!
    Trauter Helde, sei treu!
    Sei treu!—treu!

(Alberich ist gänzlich verschwunden. Hagen, der unverrückt in seiner Stellung verblieben, blickt regungslos und starren Auges nach dem Rheine hin. Die Sonne geht auf und spiegelt sich in der Fluth.
Siegfried tritt plötzlich, dicht am Ufer, hinter einem Busche hervor. Er ist in seiner eigenen Gestalt; nur den Tarnhelm hat er noch auf dem Haupte: er zieht ihn ab, und hängt ihn in den Gürtel.)

Siegfried. Hoiho! Hagen!
    Müder Mann!
    Siehst du mich kommen?

Hagen
(gemächlich sich erhebend.)
    Heil! Siegfried!
    Geschwinder Helde!
    Wo brausest du her?

Siegfried. Von Brünnhildenstein;
    dort zog ich den Athem ein,
    mit dem ich jetzt dich rief:
    so schnell war meine Fahrt!
    Langsamer folgt mir ein Paar:
    Zu Schiff gelangt das her.

Hagen. So zwangst du Brünnhild'!

Siegfried. Wacht Gutrune?

Hagen. Hoiho! Gutrune!
    Komm heraus!
    Siegfried ist da:
    Was säum'st du d'rin?

Siegfried
(zur Halle sich wendend.)
    Euch beiden meld' ich,
    wie ich Brünnhild' band.
(Gutrune tritt ihnen unter der Halle entgegen.)

Siegfried.
    Heiss' mich willkommen,
    Gibichskind!
    Ein guter Bote bin ich dir.

Gutrune.
> Freia give thee joy,
> by ev'ry fair one honored.

Siegfried.
> Freely deign
> to show me favor:
> As wife I've won thee to-day.

Gutrune.
> Doth fare Brünnhilde with my brother?

Siegfried.
> Light was his wooing, I ween.

Gutrune.
> Has he no wound from the fire?

Siegfried.
> It would not e'en have burned him,
> but I in his stead went o'er.
> that I might gain my Gutrune.

Gutrune.
> Then thou hast not been touched?

Siegfried.
> I gleefully trampled the blaze.

Gutrune.
> Did Brünnhilde deem thee Gunther?

Siegfried.
> We differed not a hair.
> The Tarnhelm worked all that,
> as Hagen told me it would.

Hagen.
> I gave thee goodly rede.

Gutrune.
> Didst conquer the maid so fierce?

Siegfried.
> She felt—Gunther's might.

Gutrune.
> Was she married then to thee?

Siegfried.
> To her mate submitted Brünnhilde
> all the night of bridal till morn.

Gutrune.
> And to *thee* she gave herself?

Siegfried.
> For Gutrune waited Siegfried.

Gutrune.
> By his side, though, was Brünnhilde?

Gutrune.
> Freia grüsse dich
> zu aller Frauen Ehre!

Siegfried.
> Frei und hold
> sei nur mir Frohen:
> zum Weib gewann ich dich heut'.

Gutrune.
> So folgt Brünnhild' meinem Bruder?

Siegfried.
> Leicht ward die Frau ihm gefreit.

Gutrune.
> Sengte das Feuer ihn nicht?

Siegfried.
> Ihn hätt' es auch nicht versehrt;
> doch ich durchschritt es für ihn,
> da dich ich wollt' erwerben.

Gutrune.
> Doch dich hat es verschont?

Siegfried.
> Mich freute die schwebende Brunst

Gutrune.
> Hielt Brünnhild' dich für Gunther?

Siegfried.
> Ihm glich ich auf ein Haar:
> der Tarnhelm wirkte das,
> wie Hagen tüchtig es wies.

Hagen.
> Dir gab ich guten Rath.

Gutrune.
> So zwang'st du das kühne Weib?

Siegfried.
> Sie wich Gunther's Kraft.

Gutrune.
> Und vermählte sie sich dir?

Siegfried.
> Ihrem Mann gehorchte Brünnhild'
> eine volle bräutliche Nacht.

Gutrune.
> Als ihr Mann doch galtest du?

Siegfried.
> Bei Gutrune weilte Siegfried.

Gutrune.
> Doch zur Seite war ihm Brünnhild'?

Siegfried
(pointing to his sword.)
'Twixt the East and West lies North:
so near was Brünnhilde to me.

Gutrune.
How then made Gunther the bride his
own?

Siegfried.
In the fiery surges consuming
at first dawn she set foot
and followed me t'ward the vale.
When shore was near,
flash!—in shape
reversed were Gunther and I.
Then by the helmet's virtue,
wishing, I hither flew.
By hast'ning wind impelled,
the pair up the river come.
Make ready then to receive.

Gutrune.
Siegfried. marvellous man!
What fear I feel of thee!

Hagen
looking down on the river from the heights at
back.)
From afar approaches a pinnace.

Siegfried.
Then praise its herald here.

Gutrune.
Let us give her hearty welcome,
that haply she may bide here gladly.
Thou Hagen, please
to summon the people
to Gibich's walls for wedding.
Mirthful maids
shall be brought by me;
my merriment meetly they'll join.
(Going towards the hall, to Siegfried.)
Wouldst thou sleep, naughty guest?

Siegfried.
Rest it gives me helping thee.
(He follows her. Exeunt both into the hall.)

Hagen
(standing on the height, turns landwards and
blows with all his strength a great cattle-horn.)
Hoiho! Hoiho! Hoiho!
Ye men of Gibich
gather yourselves!
Waken! waken!

Siegfried
(auf sein Schwert deutend).
Zwischen Ost und West der Nord:
so nah war Brünnhild' ihm fern.

Gutrune.
Wie empfing sie nun Gunther von
dir?

Siegfried.
Durch des Feuers verlöschende Lohe
im Frühnebel vom Felsen
folgte sie mir zu Thal;
dem Strande nah,
flugs die Stelle
tauschte Gunther mit mir:
durch des Geschmeides Tugend
wünscht' ich mich schnell hieher.
Ein starker Wind nun treibt
die Trauten den Rhein herauf:
d'rum rüstet jetzt den Empfang!

Gutrune.
Siegfried, mächtigster Mann:
wie fasst mich Furcht vor dir!

Hagen
(von der Höhe im Hintergrunde den Fluss hinab
spähend).
In der Ferne seh' ich ein Segel.

Siegfried.
So sagt dem Boten Dank!

Gutrune.
Lasst sie uns hold empfangen,
dass heiter sie und gern hier weile!
Du Hagen! minnig
rufe die Mannen
nach Gibich's Hof zur Hochzeit!
Frohe Frauen
ruf' ich zum Fest:
der Freudigen folgen sie gern.
(Nach der Halle schreitend, zu Siegfried.)
Rastest du, schlimmer Held?

Siegfried.
Dir zu helfen ruh' ich aus.
(Er folgt ihr. Beide gehen in die Halle ab.)

Hagen
(auf der Anhöhe stehend, stösst, der Landseite
zugewendet, mit aller Kraft in ein grosses Stier-
horn.)
Hoiho! Hoiho! Hoiho!
Ihr Gibichs Mannen,
machet euch auf!
Wehe! Wehe!

Weapons! weapons!
weapons are out!
Goodly weapons,
sturdy weapons,
sharp for strife.
Woe! woe is here!
Woe! Waken! Waken!
Hoiho! Hoiho! Hoiho!

(He continues to blow his cattle-horn. Other horns answer it from different directions in the land. From the heights and valleys armed men rush hastily on.)

The Vassals

(first a few at a time, then more together.)

Why brays the horn?
What summons the hosts?
We come with all ward—
we come with all weapons—
Hagen! Hagen!
Hoiho! Hoiho!
What's the peril here?
Will the foe appear?
Who gives us fight?
Is Gunther in need?

Hagen

(from the heights.)

Trim yourselves up
and tarry not;
greet your chief to the full;
a wife Gunther has found.

The Vassals. What is his need?
where is his foe?

Hagen. A fiery wife
fares at his heels.

The Vassals. By furious mass
of foes is menaced?

Hagen. No one follows:
lone he fares.

The Vassals. Has he triumphed o'er ill?
Has he triumphed in war?

Hagen. The Worm-killer
was his defence!
Siegfried the hero
his safety held.

The Vassals.
Then how should our host further
help him?

Hagen. Bulls full sturdy
shall ye slaughter,

Waffen! Waffen!
Waffen durch's Land!
gute Waffen!
Starke Waffen,
scharf zum Streit,
Noth! Noth ist da!
Noth! Wehe! Wehe!
Hoiho! Hoiho! Hoiho!

(Er bläst abermals. Aus verschiedenen Gegenden vom Lande her antworten Heerhörner. Von den Höhen und aus dem Thale stürmen in Hast und Eile gewaffnete Mannen herbei.)

Die Mannen

(erst einzelne, dann immer mehr zusammen.)

Was tos't das Horn?
was ruft es zu Heer?
Wir kommen mit Wehr,
wir kommen mit Waffen;
mit starken Waffen,
mit scharfer Wehr!
Hoiho! Hoiho!
Hagen! Hagen!
Welche Noth ist da?
Welcher Feind ist nah'?
Wer giebt uns Streit?
Ist Gunther in Noth?

Hagen

(von der Anhöhe herab.)

Rüstet euch wohl
und rastet nicht;
Gunther sollt ihr empfah'n:
ein Weib hat der gefreit.

Die Mannen. Drohet ihm Noth?
drängt ihn der Feind?

Hagen. Ein freisliches Weib
führt er heim!

Die Mannen. Ihm folgen der Magen
feindliche Mannen?

Hagen. Einsam fährt er:
keiner folgt.

Die Mannen. So bestand er die Noth,
bestand den Kampf?

Hagen. Der Wurmtödter
wehrte der Noth:
Siegfried, der Held,
der schur' ihm Heil.

Die Mannen. Was soll ihm das Heer nun
noch helfen?

Hagen. Starke Stiere
sollt ihr schlachten:

and wash the altar
of Wotan in blood.

he Vassals. Why, Hagen, what biddest
thou us then?

Iagen. Be a boar then further
struck down for Froh,
and a stalwart he-goat
smitten for Donner;
sheep, moreover,
slaughter for Fricka,
that well she may aid in the wedding.

he Vassals
(with continually increasing mirth.)
When we have done it,
then what is there else?

Iagen. The drink-horn take
from damsels fair,
with wine and mead
mirthfully filled.

he Vassals. The drink-horn in hand,
what have we then to do?

Iagen. Revel away
till you wreck your wits:
All for goodwill of the Æsir,
to win their aid for the wedding.

he Vassals
(bursting out into a ringing peal of laughter.)
Good gain and hap
lights on the Rhine,
if Hagen the grim one
to laughter incline.
The Hardy Thorn
pricks now no more;
to help at weddings
henceforth is his part.

Iagen
(who has remained quite serious.)
Now leave off laughter,
valiant vassals.
Receive Gunther's bride:
Brünnhilde approaches with him.
(He has descended and joined the vassals.)
Love well your lady;
lend her your aid:
if she have wrong
quickly requite it.

(Gunther and Brünnhilde arrive in the boat.
ome of the men spring into the water and drag
e boat ashore. While Gunther conducts Brünn-
ilde ashore the vassals shout and clash their
eapons. Hagen stands aside at back.)

am Weihstein fliesse
Wotan ihr Blut.

Die Mannen. Was, Hagen, was heisst du
uns dann?

Hagen. Einen Eber fällen
sollt ihr für Froh;
einen stämmigen Bock
stechen für Donner;
Schafe aber
schlachtet für Fricka,
Dass gute Ehe sie gebe!

Die Mannen
(mit immer mehr ausbrechender Heiterkeit.)
Schlugen wir Thiere,
was schaffen wir dann?

Hagen. Das Trinkhorn nehm't
von trauten Frau'n,
mit Meth und Wein
wonnig gefüllt.

Die Mannen. Das Horn in der Hand,
Wie halten wir es dann?

Hagen. Rüstig gezecht
bis der Rausch euch zähmt
alles den Göttern zu Ehren,
dass gute Ehe sie geben!

Die Mannen
(in ein schallendes Gelächter ausbrechend.)
Gross Glück und Heil
lacht nun dem Rhein,
da der grimme Hagen
so lustig mag sein!
Der Hage-Dorn
sticht nun nicht mehr:
zum Hochzeitrufer
ward er bestellt.

Hagen
(der immer sehr ernst geblieben.)
Nun lasst das Lachen,
müth'ge Mannen!
Empfangt Gunther's Braut:
Brünnhilde naht dort mit ihm.
(Er ist herabgestiegen und unter die Mannen
getreten.)
Hold seid der Herrin,
helfet ihr treu:
traf sie ein Leid,
rasch seid zur Rache!

(Gunther und Brünnhilde sind im Nachen angekommen Einige der Mannen springen in den Fluss,
und ziehen den Kahn an das Land. Während Gunther Brünnhilde an das Ufer geleitet, schlagen die
Mannen jauchzend an die Waffen. Hagen steht
zur Seite im Hintergrunde.)

The Vassals. Hail! hail!
            Welcome! welcome!
            Hail, O Gunther!
            Hail to thy bride!

Gunther
(leading Brünnhilde by the hand from the boat.)
            Brünnhilde, the rarest dame
            borne by the Rhine to you.
            There never was won
            a nobler woman.
            The Gibichungs as a race
            gained often goods from the gods;
            to high renown
            now will they rise.

The Vassals
            (clashing their weapons.)
            Hail to thee,
            glorious Gibichung!

(Brünnhilde, pale and with eyes fixed on the
ground, follows Gunther, who leads her towards
the hall, from which issue forth Siegfried and
Gutrune attended by a train of women.)

Gunther
(pausing with Brünnhilde before the hall.)
            All hail, my hero bold!
            All hail, beauteous sister!
            I see thee gladly beside him
            by whom as wife thou'rt won.
            Two happy couples
            here have encountered;
            Brünnhilde and Gunther,
            Gutrune and Siegfried!

(Brünnhilde, startled, raises her eyes and perceives Siegfried; she drops Gunther's hand, advances one step towards Siegfried, then recoils in
horror and fixes her eyes glarily upon him.—All
the others are wonderstruck.)

Men and Women. What ails her? Is she
                distraught?

Siegfried
(goes a few steps nearer to Brünnhilde.)
            What clouds Brünnhilde's brow?

Brünnhilde
            (almost fainting.)
            Siegfried ... here? ... Gutrune! ...

Siegfried. Gunther's mild-eyed sister,
            mate to me
            as thou to him.

Brünnhilde. I? ... Gunther? ... you lie!
            I see not the light..
(She is about to fall: Siegfried, who is nearest,
supports her.)

Die Mannen.
            Heil! Heil!
            Willkommen! Willkommen!
            Heil dir, Gunther!
            Heil deiner Braut!

Gunther
(Brünnhilde an der Hand aus dem Kahn geleitend.
            Brünnhilde, die hehrste Frau,
            bring' ich euch her zum Rhein:
            ein edleres Weib
            ward nie gewonnen!
            Der Gibichungen Geschlecht,
            gaben die Götter ihm Gunst,
            zum höchsten Ruhm
            rag' es nun auf!

Die Mannen
            (an die Waffen schlagend.)
            Heil! Heil dir, Gunther!
            Glücklicher Gibichung!

(Brünnhilde bleich, und mit zu Boden gesenkter
Blicke, folgt Gunther, der sie zur Halle führt, au
welcher jetzt Siegfried und Gutrune, von Frauer
begleitet, heraustreten.)

Gunther
(mit Brünnhilde vor der Halle anhaltend.)
            Gegrüsst sei, theurer Held!
            gegrüsst, holde Schwester!
            Dich seh' ich froh zur Seite
            ihm, der zum Weib dich gewann.
            Zwei selige Paare
            seh' ich hier prangen:
            Brünnhilde—und Gunther,
            Gutrune—und Siegfried!

(Brünnhilde erschrickt, schlägt die Augen au
und erblickt Siegfried; sie lässt Gunther's Han
fahren, geht heftig bewegt einen Schritt auf Sieg
fried zu, weicht entsetzt zurück, und heftet star
den Blick auf ihn.—Alle sind sehr betroffen.)

Mannen und Frauen. Was ist ihr?

Siegfried
(geht ruhig einige Schritte auf Brünnhilde zu.)
            Was müh't Brünnhilde's Blick?

Brünnhilde
            (kaum ihrer mächtig).
            Siegfried ... hier ... ! Gutrune ..

Siegfried. Gunther's milde Schwester,
            mir vermählt,
            wie Gunther du.

Brünnhilde. Ich ... Gunther ..? du
                lüg'st!—
            Mir schwindet das Licht ...
(Sie droht umzusinken: Siegfried, ihr zunächs
stüzt sie.)

Brünnhilde
(faintly and softly, in Siegfried's arms.)
Siegfried ... knows me not! ...

Siegfried.   Gunther, see, thy wife is faint-
ing.
(Gunther approaches.)
Awaken, dame!
Here stands thy husband.
(As Siegfried points to Gunther, Brünnhilde per-
ceives the ring on his finger.)

Brünnhilde
(starting with fearful impetuosity..
Ha! That Ring
upon his hand!
His—? Siegfried's—?

Vassals.   What is it?

Hagen
(advancing from the back among the men.)
Now well attend
to the woman's tale.

Brünnhilde
(struggling to command herself and repressing
with great effort her terrific storm of emotion.)
On thy hand there
I beheld the ring:
thou hold'st it wrongly.
It was ravished
(Pointing to Gunther.)
—by this man.
What means didst thou use
the ring thus to gain?

Siegfried
(attentively inspecting the ring on his finger.)
That ring I gained,
but not from him.

Brünnhilde
(to Gunther.)
Torest thou from me the ring
with which thou'st wedded me,
then make him feel thy power:
get back the pledge again.

Gunther
(greatly perplexed.)
The ring?—I gave him nothing:
but—know'st thou this our guest?

Brünnhilde.   Where guardest thou the
ring
that thou didst make me give thee?
(Gunther, much puzzled, remains silent.)

Brünnhilde
(matt und leise in Siegfried's Arme.)
Siegfried ... kennt mich nicht? ..

Siegfried.   Gunther, deinem Weib ist übel!
(Gunther tritt hinzu.)
Erwache, Frau!
hier ist dein Gatte.
(Indem Siegfried auf Gunther mit dem Finger
deutet erkennt an diesem Brünnhilde den Ring.)

Brünnhilde
(mit furchtbarer Heftigkeit aufschreckend.)
Ha!—der Ring ...
an seiner Hand!
Er ... Siegfried?

Mannen und Frauen.   Was ist?

Hagen
(aus dem Hintergrunde unter die Mannen tretend.)
Jetzt merket klug,
was die Frau euch klagt!

Brünnhilde
(sich ermannend, indem sie die schrecklichste
Aufregung gewaltsam zurückhält.)
Einen Ring sah ich
an deiner Hand:—
nicht dir gehört er,
ihn entriss mir
(auf Gunther deutend)
—dieser Mann!
Wie mochtest von ihm
den Ring du empfah'n?

Siegfried
(aufmerksam den Ring an seiner Hand betrach
tend.)
Den Ring empfing ich
nicht von ihm.

Brünnhilde
(zu Gunther.)
Nahm'st du von mir den Ring,
durch den ich dir vermählt;
so melde ihm dein Recht,
ford're zurück das Pfand!

Gunther
(in grosser Verwirrung.)
Den Ring?—ich gab ihm keinen:
doch kennst du ihn auch gut?

Brünnhilde.   Wo bärgest du den Ring,
den du von mir erbeutet?
(Gunther schweigt in höchster Betroffenheit.)

Brünnhilde
    (bursting out frantically.)
    Ha! this one 'twas then
    that from me wrenched the ring
    Siegfried, the treacherous thief.

Siegfried
(who is quite absorbed in contemplating the ring.)
    No girl, I ween,
    gave me that ring;
    Nor woman 'twas
    from whom the prize I won.
    This hoop I bear
    as the battle prize,
    when at Hate Cave once I did strive
    and destroyed the dragon so strong.

Hagen
        (coming between them.)
    Brünnhilde, noble dame,
    know'st thou full well this ring?
    If 'tis that that Gunther gained,
        he owns it still,—
    and Siegfried has won it by trick,
    which the traitor should pay for
                    straight.

Brünnhilde
    (screaming out in the most terrible anguish.)
    By trick! By trick!
    Shamefullest of tricks!
    Deceit! deceit!
    Worse than thought can conceive!

Gutrune.   Deceit!

Vassals.   What was the trick?

Brünnhilde.
        Holy gods!
        Ye heavenly guardians!
        Was this indeed
        your whispered will?
        Grief do ye give
        such as none ever grasped,
        shape me a shame
        no mortal has shared?
        Vouchsafe revenge then
        like none ever viewed,
        rouse me to wrath
        such as none can arrest!
        Here let Brünnhilde's
        heart straight be broken
        if he who wronged her
        may but be wrecked.

Brünnhilde
    (wüthend auffahrend.)
    Ha!—Dieser war es,
    der mir den Ring entriss:
    Siegfried, der trugvolle Dieb!

Siegfried
(der über der Betrachtung des Ringes in ferner
Sinnen entruckt war.)
    Von keinem Weib
    kam mir der Reif;
    noch war's ein Weib,
    dem ich ihn abgewann:
    genau erkenn' ich
    des Kampfes Lohn,
    den vor Neidhöhl' einst ich bestand,
    als den starken Wurm ich erschlug.

Hagen
        (zwischen sie tretend.)
    Brünnhilde, kühne Frau!
    kennst du genau den Ring?
    Ist's der, den du Gunther'n gab'st,
        so ist er sein,—
    und Siegfried gewann ihn durch
                    Trug
    den der Treulose büssen sollt'!

Brünnhilde
    (in furchtbarstem Schmerz aufschreiend.)
    Betrug! Betrug!
    Schändlichster Betrug!
    Verrath! Verrath—
    Wie noch nie er gerächt!

Gutrune.   Betrug?

Mannen und Frauen.   An wem Verrath?

Brünnhilde.
        Heilige Götter!
        himmlische Lenker!
        Rauntet ihr diess
        in eurem Rath?
        Lehrt ihr mich Leiden
        Wie keiner sie litt?
        Schuft ihr mir Schmach
        wie nie sie geschmerzt?
        Rathet nun Rache
        wie nie sie geras't!
        Zündet mir Zorn
        wie nie er gezähmt!
        Heisset Brünnhilde
        ihr Herz zu zerbrechen,
        den zu zertrümmern,
        der sie betrog!

nther. Brünnhilde! my consort,
calm thyself!

nnhilde. Away, thou traitor!
Thou'rt betray'd too.
People all, hearken:
Not—he—
that man yonder
was wed to me.

ssals. Siegfried? Gutrune's mate?

nnhilde. He forced delights
of love from me.

gfried. Art thou so careless
of thine honor?
The lips, then, that revile it
must I convict them of lying?
Hear whether truth I broke!
Blood-brotherhood
I and Gunther have sworn to:
"Needful," my goodly sword,
guarded the oath intact:
its edge did keep me sundered
from this ill-omened bride.

nnhilde. Thou lord of deceit,
see how thou liest!
Little thy sword
will serve as a proof!
Well known to me its sharpness,
but known too its scabbard,
encased in which
reposed on the wall
"Needful," the trusty friend,
when a true love his master did win.

e Vassals
(crowding together in quick anger.)
What! Has he been traitor?
Trifled with Gunther's honor?

ther. Disgrace o'ertakes me,
grossest contempt.
if thou repliest
not to her plea.

rune. Faithless—Siegfried,
say, art thou false?
Attest as untrue
what she hath told.

Vassals. Right thyself straight,
if thou art wronged.
Stay her upbraidings!
Swear us the oath.

Gunther. Brünnhilde, Gemahlin!
Mäss'ge dich!

Brünnhilde. Weich' fern, Verräther!
Selbst-verrath'ner!
Wisset denn Alle!
nicht—ihm—
dem Manne dort
bin ich vermählt.

Mannen und Frauen.
Siegfried? Gutrune's Gemahl?

Brünnhilde. Er zwang mir Lust
und Liebe ab.

Siegfried. Achtest du so
der eig'nen Ehre?
Die Zunge, die sie lästert,
muss ich der Lüge sie zeihen?—
Hört, ob ich Treue brach!
Blutbrüderschaft
hab' ich Gunther geschworen:
Nothung, mein werthes Schwert,
wahrte der Treue Eid;
mich trennte seine Schärfe
von diesem traurigen Weib.

Brünnhilde. Du listiger Held,
sieh' wie du lüg'st!
wie auf dein Schwert
du schlecht dich beruf'st!
Wohl kenn' ich die Schärfe,
doch kenn' auch die Scheide,
darin so wonnig
ruht' an der Wand
Nothung, der treue Freund,
als die Traute sein Herr sich gewann.

Die Mannen
(in lebhafter Entrüstung zusammentretend.)
Wie? brach er die Treue!
trübte er Gunther's Ehre?

Gunther. Geschändet wär' ich,
schmählich bewahrt,
gäb'st du die Rede
nicht ihr zurück!

Gutrune. Treulos, Siegfried,
sannest du Trug?
Bezeuge, dass falsch
Jene dich zeiht!

Die Mannen. Reinige dich,
bist du im Recht:
schweige die Klage,
schwöre den Eid!

Siegfried. Should I refute her,
            Swearing the oath,
            which of ye war-men
            his weapon will lend?

Hagen. My unsullied spear-point
          well will I lend
          to ward in honor the oath.

(The Vassals make a ring around Siegfried and
Hagen. Hagen holds out his spear; Siegfried lays
two fingers of his right hand on its point.)

Siegfried. Schweig' ich die Klage,
            schwör' ich den Eid:
            wer von euch wagt
            seine Waffe daran?

Hagen. Meines Speeres Spitze
          wag' ich daran:
          sie wahr' in Ehren den Eid!

(Die Mannen schliessen einen Ring um Siegfried;
Hagen hält diesem die Spitze seines Speeres hin:
Siegfried legt zwei Finger seiner rechten Hand
darauf.)

THE OATH ON THE SPEAR

tref - fen, tref - fe du mich: klag - te das Weib dort
dealt me deal it to me· if she is real - ly

wahr, brach ich dem Bru - der den Eid!
wrong'd, 'f___ I have in - jured my friend!

BRÜNNHILDE

Hel - le Wehr!___ Hei - li - ge Waf - fe!
Haft of war!___ Hal - low - ed weap - on!

Hilf mei - nem e - wi - gen Ei - de! Bei des
hold thou___ my oath from dis - hon - or! On this

Spee - res Spi - tze sprech ich dem Eid:
spot - less spear - head I___ speak an oath:

Spi - tze___ ach - te des Spruchs! Ich wei -
Spear - point, ___ aid___ thou my speech! I sanc -

- he dei - ne Wucht___ dass sie ihn wer - fe!
- ti - fy thy strength to his de - struc - tion!

Dei - ne Schär - fe seg - ne ich, ___ dass sie ihn
And I bless ___ thy blade with - al ___ that it may

schnei - de! Denn brach ___ sei - ne Ei - de er
blight him! For bro ~ ken are all of his

all, schwur Mein - eid jetzt die - ser Mann.
oaths, and per - jured now doth he - prove.

The Vassals	**Die Mannen**
(in the greatest commotion.)	(im höhsten Aufruhr.)
Help, Donner!	Hilf, Donner!
down with thy tempest,	tose dein Wetter,
to silence this terrible shame.	zu scbweigen die wüthende
	Schmach!
Siegfried. Gunther, look to thy lady,	*Siegfried.* Gunther, wehr' deinem **Weibe,**
who shapes thee shame with her lies.	das schamlos Schande dir lügt!
Give her time and rest,	Gönn't ihr Weil' und Ruh',
the tameless mountain maid,	der wilden Felsen-Frau,
until her mind's disturbance slackens	dass ihre freche Wuth sich lege,
which by some demon's	die eines Unhold's
deadly spite	arge List
has been drawn down on us all.	wider uns Alle erregt!—
Ye vassals, scatter yourselves,	Ihr Mannen, kehret euch ab,
leave the women to scold!	lasst das Weiber-Gekeif'!
As cowards well will we act	Als Zage weichen wir gern,
if 'tis a contest of words.	gilt es mit Zungen dem Streit.
(He goes close up to Gunther.)	(Dicht zu Gunther tretend.)
Troth! it cuts me more than thee,	Glaub,' mehr zürnt es mich als dich,
that ill I did the trick;	Dass schlecht ich sie getäuscht:
the Tarnhelm, I suspect,	der Tarnhelm, dünkt mich fast,
has hid me only half.	hat halb mich nur gehehlt.
But woman's ire	Doch Frauengroll
waneth apace:	friedet sich bald:
that I won her for thee,	dass dir ich es gewann
one day she'll thank thee, methinks.	dankt gewiss noch das Weib.
(Turning again to the men.)	(Er wendet sich wieder zu den **Mannen.**)
Frolic, good fellows!	Munter, ihr Mannen!
move to the feast!	folgt mir zum Mahl!
Make the marriage	Froh zur Hochzeit

merry, ye maidens!
Filled with delight,
laugh as you may.
In fort and field
foremost among you
in the frolic am I.
He whom love hath blest,
let my blythesome laughter
move him to join in my joy.

(In exuberant joy he puts his arm round Gutrune
draws her into the hall with him. The Men
Women follow.)
Brünnhilde, Gunther, and Hagen remain be-
d.—Gunther has seated himself apart, with
ered face in deep shame and depression.)

ünnhilde
(anding in the foreground, gazes vacantly before
)

What infernal craft
can here be hidden?
What magician's rod
raised up this storm?
Where now my wisdom
'gainst this bewitchment?
What can all my runes do
against this riddle?
Ah sorrow! sorrow!
Woe's me! Woe's me!
He has won
all wisdom from me!
I am his maid,
held by his might;
I am his booty,
held in his bondage,
and, languished with shame and woe,
lightly he gives me away.
Whose sword shall I have to beg,
with which I may sever my bonds?

gen
(coming close up to her.)
Have trust in me,
betrayed dame:
and for thy wrongs
I'll wreak revenge.

ünnhilde. On whom?

gen. On Siegfried, who hath betrayed.

ünnhilde. On Siegfried? thou?
(She laughs bitterly.)
One angry glance
of his glittering eyeball—
that, e'en through his fraudulent
                                    shape
fell unshadowed on me,
would subdue thy most

helfet, ihr Frau'n!—
Wonnige Lust
lache nun auf:
in Hof und Hain
heiter vor Allen
sollt ihr heute mich seh'n.
Wen die Minne freut,
meinem frohen Muthe
thu' es der Glückliche gleich!

(Er schlingt in ausgelassenem Uebermuthe seinen
Arm um Gutrune, und zieht sie mit sich in die
Halle; die Mannen und Frauen folgen ihm nach.)
(Brünnhilde, Gunther, und Hagen bleiben zurück.
Gunther hat sich, in tiefer Scham und furchtbarer
Verstimmung, mit verhülltem Gesicht abseits nieder-
gesetzt.)

Brünnhilde
(im Vordergrunde stehend und vor sich hin starrend.)

Welches Unhold's List
liegt hier verhohlen?
Welches Zaubrer's Rath
regte diess auf?
Wo ist nun mein Wissen
gegen dieses Wirrsal?
Wo sind meine Runen?
gegen diess Räthsel?
Ach Jammer! Jammer!
Weh'! ach Weh'!
All mein Wissen
wies ich ihm zu:
In seiner Macht
hält er die Magd;
in seiner Banden
hält er die Beute,
die, jammernd ob ihrer Schmach,
jauchzend der Reiche verschenkt!—
Wer bietet mir nun das Schwert,
mit dem ich die Bande zerschnitt'?

Hagen
(dicht an sie herantretend.)
Vertraue mir,
betrog'ne Frau.
Wer dich verrieth,
das räche ich.

Brünnhilde. An wem?

Hagen. An Siegfried, der dich betrog.

Brünnhilde. An Siegfried? . . du?
(Sie lacht bitter)
Ein einz'ger Blick
seines blitzenden Auges
—das selbst durch die Lügengestalt
leuchtend strahlte zu mir—
deinen besten Muth

mettlesome daring!

Hagen. His falsehood speeds
my spear to his felling.

Brünnhilde. Oath and falsehood,
futile to aid!
Find stronger spells
to inspire thy weapon,
when it would strike at such
strength!

Hagen. I mind well Siegfried's
sovereign might,
he scarce were mastered in battle;
but whisper to me
some cunning way
to make him weak in my hands.

Brünnhilde. O thankless! shameful
return!
Each single art
that once I owned
did I lend, his life to protect.
Unwitting, magical
means I used,
which safely ward him now from
wounds.

Hagen. No blade borne in war can harm
him?

Brünnhilde. In battle, none—yet—
if at his back thou strike:—
Never, I well knew
would he retreat
and, flying, turn it to the foeman;
and so no spell did I set there.

Hagen. And there he shall be speared!
(He turns quickly from Brünnhilde to Gunther.)
Up, Gunther,
honored Gibichung!
Here stands thy stalwart wife:
why hangs thy head in grief!

Gunther
(rising sorrowfully.)
O shame!
O sorrow!
Woe to me,
the most distrest of mortals!

Hagen. That shame o'erwhelms thee
well I grant.

Brünnhilde. O timid spouse!

machte erbangen!

Hagen. Doch meinem Speere
spart' ihn sein Meineid?

Brünnhilde. Eid und Meineid—
müss'ge Acht!
Nach Stärk'rem späh',
deinen Speer zu waffnen,
willst du den Stärksten besteh'n!

Hagen. Wohl kenn' ich Siegfried's
siegende Kraft,
wie schwer im Kampf er zu fälle
d'rum raune nun du
mir guten Rath,
wie doch der Recke mir wich'?

Brünnhilde. O Undank; schändlichst
Lohn!
Nicht eine Kunst
war mir bekannt,
die zum Heil nicht half seinem Leib
Unwissend zähmt' ihn
mein Zauberspiel,
das ihn nun vor Wunden gewahrt.

Hagen. So kann keine Wehr ihm sch
den?

Brünnhilde. Im Kampfe nicht:—doch
träf'st du im Rücken ihn.
Niemals—das wusst' ich—
wich' er dem Feind,
nie reicht' er ihm fliehend den Rü
ken
an ihm d'rum spart' ich den Sege

Hagen. Und dort trifft ihn mein Speer!
(Er wendet sich rasch zu Gunther um.)
Auf, Gunther!
edler Gibichung!
Hier steht dein starkes Weib:
was häng'st du dort in Harm?

Gunther
(leidenschaftlich auffahrend.)
O Schmach!
O Schande!
Wehe mir
dem jammervollsten Manne!

Hagen. In Schande liegst du—
läugn' ich das?

Brünnhilde. O feiger Mann!

treacherous friend!
Hidden behind
the hero wert thou,
that valour's reward
his courage should win thee!
Low had sunk
thy lordliest race
when such a faint-heart was formed.

unther

(bursting out into rage.)

Betrayed am I—the betrayer!
Deceived am I—the deceiver!
It cuts to my core!
It harrows my heart!
Help, Hagen!
Help for my honor!
help for my mother,
who thee also did bear.

agen.   No head can help,
no hand can help:—
nought helps but—Siegfried's death!

unther.   Siegfried's death!—

agen.
Nought else saves thee from shame!

unther

(staring before him horror-struck.)

Blood-brotherhood
surely we swore!.

agen.

The broken bond
calls for his blood!

unther.

Broke he the bond?

agen.

When thou wert betrayed!

unther.

Was I betrayed?

ünnhilde.
He betrayed thee;
and I'm betrayed too on all sides!
Barely, in truth,
could a world of blood
wipe from my mind your offence.
But the death of one
well will condone all.
Siegfried falleth
for sins of himself and thee.

falscher Genoss!
Hinter dem Helden
hehltest du dich,
dass Preise des Ruhmes
er dir erränge!
Tief wohl sank
das theure Geschlecht,
das solche Zagen erzeugt!

Gunther

(ausser sich.)

Betrüger ich—und betrogen!
Verräther ich—und verrathen!—
Zermalmt mir das Mark,
zerbrecht mir die Brust!
Hilf, Hagen!
hilf meiner Ehr'!
hilf deiner Mutter,
die dich auch ja gebar!

Hagen.   Dir hilft kein Hirn,
dir hilft keine Hand:
dir hilft nur—Siegfried's Tod!

Gunther.   Siegfried's Tod!

Hagen.
Nur der sühnt deine Schmach.

Gunther

(von Grausen gepackt, vor sich hin starrend).

Blutbrüderschaft
schwuren wir uns!

Hagen.

Des Bundes Bruch
sühne nun Blut!

Gunther.

Brach er den Bund?

Hagen.

Da er dich verrieth!

Gunther.

Verrieth er mich?

Brünnhilde.
Dich verrieth er,
und mich verriethet ihr Alle!
Wär' ich gerecht,
alles Blut der Welt
büsste mir nicht eure Schuld!
Doch des Einen Tod
taugt mir für Alle:
Siegfried falle—
zur Sühne für sich und euch!

Hagen
    (turning close to Gunther.)
His falling brings thee gain!
Might gigantic would be thine
by merely getting his Ring
which but death can make him
    surrender.

Gunther.
    Brünnhilde's Ring?

Hagen.
    By Nibelungs 'twas wrought.

Gunther
    (sighing deeply.)
Shall this be Siegfried's end then?

Hagen.   Aye, all demands his death.

Gunther.   But Gutrune, alas!—
    unto him given!—
Slew we her glorious spouse,
could we stand before her face?

Brünnhilde
    (furiously.)
What gain was my wisdom?
What were my runes good for?
Now hapless and anguished
    all I behold!
Gutrune doth hold the charm
that has beguiled from me my lord
Ill light on her!

Hagen
    (to Gunther.)
Lest his death grieve her deeply
we'll hide from her the deed.
    We hie tomorrow
    merrily hunting:
he'll boldly stray from our band—
and be brought home struck by a
    boar.

Brünnhilde and Gunther.
    It shall be so!
    Siegfried falleth!
    Soothed be the shame
    which he hath shaped!
    The oath of brotherhood
    hath he broken:
    so let his blood
    blot out guilt.
    All-guiding
    god of revenge!
    Thou witness

Hagen
    (nahe zu Gunther gewendet).
Er falle—dir zum Heile!
Ungeheure Macht wird dir,
gewinn'st du von ihm den Ring,
den der Tod ihm nur entreisst.

Gunther.
    Brünnhilde's Ring?

Hagen.
    Des Niblungen Reif.

Gunther
    (schwer seufzend).
So wär' es Siegfried's Ende!

Hagen.   Uns allen frommt sein Tod.

Gunther.   Doch Gutrune, ach!
    der ich ihn gönnte:
straften den Gatten wir so,
wie bestünden wir vor ihr?

Brünnhilde
    (wild auffahrend.)
Was rieth mir mein Wissen?
was wiesen mich Runen?
Im hiflosen Elend
    ahnet mir's hell:
Gutrune heisst der Zauber,
der mir den Gatten entzückt!
Angst treffe sie!

Hagen
    (zu Gunther)
Muss sein Tod sie betrüben,
verhehlt sei ihr die That.
    Auf munt'res Jagen
    ziehen wir morgen:
der Edle braus't uns voran—
ein Eber bracht' ihn da um.

Gunther und Brünnhilde.
    So soll es sein!
    Siegfried falle:
    sühn' er die Schmach
    die er mir schuf!
    Eid-Treue
    hat er getrogen:
    mit seinem Blute
    büss' er die Schuld!
    Allrauner!
    rächender Gott!
    Schwurwissender

and lord of oaths!	Eideshort!
Wotan! Wotan!	Wotan! Wotan!
wilt thou give ear?	wende dich her!
Waft now thy awful	weise dich schrecklich
hosts unto us,	heilige Schaar,
here let them hark	hieher zu horchen
to our vengeful oath!	dem Racheschwur!

Hagen.	Thus it shall be!	*Hagen.*	So soll es sein!
	Siegfried must die:		Siegfried falle:
	so perish he		sterb' er dahin,
	the spirit so high!		der strahlende Held!
	Mine is the hoard,		Mein ist der Hort,
	my might shall soon hold it:		mir muss er gehören:
	so of the ring		entrissen d'rum
	must we rob him.		sei ihm der Ring!
	Elfin parent,		Alben-Vater!
	thou prince deposed!		gefallener Fürst!
	Night-keeper		Nacht-Hüter!
	Nibelung king,		Niblungen-Herr!
	Alberic! Alberic!		Alberich! Alberich!
	Up to my aid!		achte auf mich!
	Warn all the Nib'lungs		Weise von neuem
	anew of the might:		der Niblungen Schaar,
	thou art their leader,		dir zu gehorchen,
	the Ring's true lord.		des Ringes Herrn!

(Gunther and Brünnhilde turn hastily towards the hall. Siegfried and Gutrune (Siegfried wearing a wreath of oak leaves, Gutrune crowned with flowers) meet them at the entrance with their followers. Gunther grasps Brünnhilde by the hand and follows with her. Hagen alone remains behind.)

(The curtain falls.)

(Gunther und Brünnhilde wenden sich heftig zur Halle Siegfried und Gutrune (Siegfried mit einen Eichenkranz, Gutrune bunte Blumen auf dem Haupte) treten ihnen, zur Nachfolge auffordernd, am Eingange entgegen. Gunther fasst Brünnhilde bei der Hand, und folgt mit ihr schnell. Hagen bleibt allein zurück.)

(Der Vorhang fällt.)

ACT THREE

Scene One

DRITTER AUFZUG

Erste Scene

TRIO OF THE RHINEDAUGHTERS

WOGLINDA, WELLGUNDA and FLOSSHILDE

Frau Son - ne sen - det lich - te Strah - len, Nacht liegt
The sun - god send - eth rays of splen - dor; *Night reigns*

— in der Tie - fe. Einst war sie hell da heil und
— in the wa - ters. Once did they beam when brave and

hehr des Va-ters, Gold noch in ihr glänz-te Rhein-gold,
bright our fa-ther's gold yet in them glit - ter'd. Rhine-gold,

kla - res Gold! wie hell__ du ein-stens strahl -
clear - est gold! how bright-ly once thou stream -

kla - res Gold!__ wie hell__ du ein-stens strahl - test,
clear - est gold!__ how bright-ly once thou stream - edst,

- test, heh-rer Stern der Tie - fe!
.- edst, beau-teous star of wa - ters!

(Sie schliessen wieder den Schwimmreigen)
(They again form their circling dance)

heh - rer__ Stern__ der Tie - fe! Wei-a-la - la
beau - teous__ star__ of wa - ters! Wei-a-la - la

wei - a - la - la, lei - a - lei - a, wal - la la, ____ la
wei - a - la - la, lei - a - lei - a, wal - la la, ____ la

lei - la la la lei__ la la la la____ la
lei - la la la lei la la la la.____ la

lei,__ la la la lei la la ia la ____ lei - la
lei__ la la la lei la lu lu la ____ lei la

la - - lei, wal-la la la la wei - a la wal-la la
la - - lei, wal-la la la la wei - a la wal-la la

wei - a - la___ la la wal - la - la___ la la lei - a lei - a lei - a
wei - a - la___ la la wal - la - la___ la la lei - a lei - a lei - a

lei - la la - la la
lei - la la - la la

lei la la _____
lei la la _____

Echo (Sie schlagen jauchzend das Wasser)
(They joyously splash the water)

Frau Son - ne,
Fair sun - god,

sen - de uns den Hel - den, der das Gold uns___ wie - der gä - be!
send to us the he - ro, who a - gain our___ gold will give us!

Liess' er___ es uns___ dein lich - tes Au - ge nei - de - ten
If it___ were ours,___ thine ar - dent eye___ no more should we

dann wir nicht län - ger! Rhein - gold! Kla - res Gold, wie
look on with en - vy! Rhine - gold! Clear - est gold, how

froh du dann strahl - - test, frei - er Stern der Tie - fe!
glad - ly wouldst stream _____ then, glo - rious star of wa - ters!

froh___ du dann strahl - test, frei - er Stern___ der Tie - fe!
glad - ly wouldst stream then, glo - rious star___ of wa - ters!

(Siegfried's horn is heard on the heights)

Woglinda.   I hear his horn!

Wellgunda.   The hero comes.

Flosshilde.   Let us take counsel.
(They all dive quickly down. Siegfried appears on the cliff in full armor.)

Siegfried.   Some imp has tempted me on
    until the track I have lost.—
    Hey, rogue! what gulf in hillside
    hast thou then rent for my game?

The three Rhine-Nymphs
      (rising again.)
    Siegfried!

Flosshilde.   Why scold you so at the
           ground?

Wellgunda.   With what imp are you ag-
           grieved?

Woglinda.   Are you annoyed by a gnome?

The Three.   Speak then, Siegfried; speak
           to us!

Siegfried
    (looking smilingly at them.)
    My friend with hairy hide
    has fled, perchance enticed
    away by your tricks?
    If he's your lover
    I'll willingly leave him,
    wenches, with you.
    (The Nymphs laugh loudly.)

Woglinda.
    Siegfried, what boon wilt grant
    if we give up the booty?

Siegfried.
    Still I have empty hands.
    What is it then you would beg?

Wellgunda.   A golden ring
    gleams on your finger.

The three Nymphs
      (together.)
    Give us that.

Siegfried.   A terrific worm
    I slew to gain that ring;
    and shall it slip my palm to buy
    the paws of a sorry bear?

Woglinda.   Are you so mean?

(Man hört Siegfried's Horn von der Höhe her.)

Woglinda.   Ich höre sein Horn.

Wellgunda.   Der Helde naht.

Flosshilde.   Lasst uns berathen!
(Sie tauchen schnell in die Fluth.)
(Siegfried erscheint auf dem Abhange in voller Waffen.)

Siegfried.   Ein Albe führte mich irr',
    dass ich die Fährte verlor:—
    He, Schelm! in welchem Berg
    barg'st du so schnell das Wild?

Die drei Rheintöchter
      (wieder auftauchend.)
    Siegfried!

Flosshilde.   Was schilt'st du in den Grund?

Wellgunda.   Welchem Alben bist du gram?

Woglinda.   Hat dich ein Nicker geneckt?

Alle Drei.   Sag'es uns, Siegfried! sag' es
           uns!

Siegfried
    (sie lächelnd betrachtend.)
    Entzücktet ihr zu euch
    den zottigen Gesellen,
    der mir verschwand?
    Ist's euer Friedel,
    euch lustigen Frauen
    lass' ich ihn gern.
    (Die Mädchen lachen laut auf.)

Woglinda.   Siegfried, was giebst du uns,
    wenn wir das Wild dir gönnen?

Siegfried.   Noch bin ich beutelos:
    d'rum bittet, was ihr begehrt.

Wellgunda.   Ein gold'ner Ring
    ragt dir am Finger—

Die drei Mädchen
      (zusammen.)
    den gieb uns!

Siegfried.   Einen Riesenwurm
    erschlug' ich um den Ring.
    für des schlechten Bären Tatzen
    böt' ich ihn nun zum Tausch?

Woglinda.   Bist du so karg?

Wellgunda. So higgling a man?

Flosshilde. Free-handed
mortals fare best with maids.

Siegfried. For wasting my goods on you
my wife would be rightly wroth.

Flosshilde. Is she so strict?

Wellgunda. She strikes you perhaps?

Woglinda. He has felt already her fist!
(They laugh.)

Siegfried. Well, make your merry jest!
in grief must you be left:
fair Nymphs, the yearned for Ring
I'll yield up never to you!

Flosshilde. So fair!

Wellgunda. So fierce!

Woglinda. So meet for love!

The Three
(together.)
Unfortunate he's miserly!
(They laugh and dive down.)

Siegfried
(descending more towards the ground.)
Is't meet to bear
their idle mocks?
Must I thus be shamed?
If they would show
near the shore again
the Ring I would relinquish.
Hey, hey, ye merry
water-maidens:
Arise! I'll give ye the Ring!

The three Rhine-Nymphs
(diving up again now solemn and grave.)
Preserve it still
and ward it well
until the illhap is read
that in thy Ring lies hid;
full fain then thou'lt be
if from the ban thou art freed.

Siegfried
(quietly replacing the ring on his finger.)
Then sing me what ye wis.

Wellgunda. So geizig beim Kauf?

Flosshilde. Freigebig
solltest Frauen du sein.

Siegfried. Verzehrt' ich an euch mein
Gut,
des' zürnte mir wohl mein Weib.

Flosshilde. Sie ist wohl schlimm?

Wellgunda. Sie schlägt dich wohl?

Woglinda. Ihre Hand fühlt schon der
Held!
(Sie lachen.)

Siegfried. Nun lacht nur lustig zu!
in Harm lass' ich euch doch:
denn giert ihr nach dem Ring
euch Neckern geb' ich ihn nie.

Flosshilde. So schön!

Wellgunda. So stark!

Woglinda. So gehrenswerth!

Die Drei
(zusammen.)
Wie Schade, dass er geizig ist!
(Sie lachen und tauchen unter.)

Siegfried
(tiefer in den Grund hinabsteigend.)
Was leid' ich doch
das karge Lob?
Lass' ich so mich schmäh'n?—
Kämen sie wieder
zum Wasserrand,
den Ring könnten sie haben.—
He he! ihr munt'ren
Wasserminnen!
kommt rasch: ich schenk' euch den
Ring!

Die drei Rheintöchter
(tauchen wieder auf, und zeigen sich ernst und
feierlich.)
Behalt' ihn, Held,
und wahr' ihn wohl,
bis du das Unheil räth'st,
das in dem Ring du heg'st.
Froh fühl'st du dich dann,
befrei'n wir dich von dem Fluch.

Siegfried
(gelassen den Ring wieder ansteckend.)
Nun singet was ihr wisst!

The Rhine-Nymphs
(severally and together.)

Siegfried! Siegfried! Siegfried!
Sorrow waits thee we know.
    To nought but ill
    thou wardest the Ring.
    It was wrought from gold
    that in Rhine once glowed:
    he who shaped it with labor
    and lost it in shame,
    laid a curse on it,
    to cause that to
    all time its possesser
    should be slain.
    As the Worm has fallen,
    thou'llt fall thyself,
    this very day
    —we vouch it to thee—
if thou refuse us the Ring
that in the flood we may hide it.
    Nought but this stream
    breaketh the spell!

Siegfried.   Untrustworthy sisters,
    talk no more!
Scarce I trust your allurements;
and your threats still less can disturb
        me.

The Rhine-Nymphs. Siegfried! Siegfried!
    'Tis truth that we tell—
Turn thee! turn from the ban!
    The braiding Nornir
    wove it by night-time
    in their endless rope
    of wonderful runes.

Siegfried.   My sword once splintered a
        spear:
    this woven rope
    of wonderful runes,
    if they have bound
    within it a curse,
"Needful" shall cut for the Nornir!
    The Worm of this danger
    did tell me once,
but he taught me not how to fear.
    The world's wealth
    should be won me by a ring:
    for a gaze of love
    gladly I'd leave it,
I'd let you have't lightly for love.

Die Rheintöchter
(einzeln und zusammen.)

Siegfried! Siegfried! Siegfried!
Schlimmes wissen wir dir.
    Zu deinem Unheil
    wahr'st du den Ring!
    Aus des Rheines Gold
    ist der Ring geglüht:
    der ihn listig geschmiedet
    und schmählich verlor,
    der verfluchte ihn,
    in fernster Zeit
    zu zeugen den Tod
    dem, der ihn trüg'.
    Wie den Wurm du fälltest,
    so fällst auch du,
    und heute noch
    so heissen wir dir's;
tauschest den Ring du uns nicht,
im tiefen Rhein inn zu bergen.
    Nur seine Fluth
    sühnet den Fluch!

Siegfried.   Ihr listigen Frauen
    lass't das sein!
Traut' ich kaum eurem Schmeichel
euer Schrecken trügt mich noch
        minder

Die Rheintöchter. Siegfried! Siegfred!
    Wir weisen dich wahr:
weiche! weiche dem Fluch!
    Ihn flochten nächtlich
    webende Nornen
    in des Urgesetzes
    ewiges Seil.

Siegfried.   Mein Schwert zerschwang eine
        Speer:
    des Urgesetzes
    ewiges Seil,
    flochten sie wilde
    Flüche hinein,
Nothung zerhaut es den Nornen!
    Wohl warnte mich einst
    vor dem Fluch ein Wurm,
doch das Fürchten lehrt' er mich
        nicht!—
    der Welt Erbe
    gewann mir ein Ring:
    für der Minne Gunst
    miss' ich ihn gern—
ich geb' ihn euch, gönnt ihr mir
        Gunst,

If you threaten my limbs, though,
and life,
hardly you'll win
from my hand the ring,
e'en were it worth not a rush.
For limbs and life
—should without love
they be fettered
in fear's strong bonds,
My limbs and my life
see!—so
freely I'd fling away!

(He has picked up a clod of earth, which he holds
up and with the last words, flings behind him.)

The Rhine-Nymphs. Come, sisters,
speed from this dullard!
He fancies himself
as fearless and wise
as he truly is trammelled and blind.
He has sworn oaths
and heeded them not;
Runes, he knows well
and reads them not.
A noble gift
once did he gain,
that it is wasted
wots he not.
But the ring, which will deal him
death,
that ring he wishes to ward still.
Farewell, Siegfried!
A stately woman
to-day your hoop will inherit.
Our bidding better she'll do:
to her! to her! to her!

(They swim away singing.)

Siegfried
(looks after them smiling.)
Alike on land and water,
women's ways I've learnt to know.
The man who resists their smiles
they seek by threats to frighten.
And when these both are scorned
they bait him with bitter words.
And yet—
were Gutrune not my wife,
I must have promptly captured
one of those pretty maids.

(Calls of hunting horns approaching are heard
in the hills. Siegfried answers gaily on his own
horn.)
(Gunther, Hagen and Vassels come down the
hills during the following.)

Hagen
(still on the heights.)
Hoiho!

Doch bedroh't ihr mir Leben und
Leib:
fasste er nicht
eines Finger's Werth—
den Reif entringt ihr mir nicht!
Denn Leben und Leib
—sollt' ohne Lieb'
in der Furcht Bande
bang ich sie fesseln—
Leben und Lieb'—
seht!—so
werf' ich sie weit von mir!

(Er hat eine Erdscholle vom Boden aufgehoben
und mit den letzten Worten sie über sein Haupt
hinter sich geworfen.)

Die Rheintöchter. Kommt, Schwestern!
schwindet dem Thoren!
So stark und weise
wähnt er sich,
als gebunden und blind er ist.
Eide schwur er—
und achtet sie nicht;
Runen weiss er—
und räth sie nicht;
ein hehrstes Gut
ward ihm gegönnt—
dass er's verworfen
weiss er nicht:
nur den Ring, der zum Tod ihm
taugt—
den Reif nur will er sich wahren!
Leb' wohl, Siegfried!
Ein stolzes Weib
wird heut' noch dich Argen beerben:
sie beut uns bess'res Gehör
Zu ihr! Zu ihr! Zu ihr!

(Sie schwimmen singend davon.)

Siegfried
(sieht ihnen lächelnd nach.)
Im Wasser wie am Lande
lernt' ich nun Weiberart:
wer nicht ihrem Schmeicheln traut,
den schrecken sie mit Drohen;
wer dem nun kühnlich trotzt,
dem kommt dann ihr Keifen d'ran.
Und doch—
trüg' ich nicht Gutrun' Treu',
der zieren Frauen eine
hätt' ich mir frisch gezähmt!

(Jagdhornrufe kommen von der Höhe näher:
Siegfried antwortet lustig auf seinem Horne.)
(Gunther, Hagen und Mannen kommen wäh-
rend des Folgenden von der Höhe herab.)

Hagen
(noch auf der Höhe.)
Hoiho!

Siegfried.   Hoiho!

The Vassals.   Hoiho! Hoiho!

Hagen.   Have we at last then
            found where thou hidest?

Siegfried.   Come below! Here 'tis fresh
                  and cool.

Hagen.   'Twill do to rest
            and dress us a meal.
            Lay down your booty
            and bring out the wine-skins.

(Game is stacked, skins of wine and drinking
horns are produced. All encamp themselves.)

Hagen.   You drove away our quarry,
            let's see the wondrous prize then
            that Siegfried seized upon.

Siegfried
            (laughing.)
            Ill is it with my meal;
            I fain must beg
            your bags to furnish me.

Hagen.   Thou bootyless?

Siegfried.   To wood-hunt I went forth,
            but water-fowl only could find:
            had I only reckoned rightly,
            three wild young water-maids
            I well might have won this morning,
            who sang in the Rhine their warning,
            ere wane of day I should die.

Gunther
            (starts and looks gloomily at Hagen.)

Hagen.   A dismal chase were that,
            if the hunter, luckless still,
            by lurking beasts were laid low.

Siegfried.   I'm thirsty.
(He has seated himself between Hagen and Gunther. Filled drinking-horns are handed to them.)

Hagen.   I've heard asserted, Siegfried,
            that what the song-birds speak of
                  thou straightly canst tell.
                  Is truth in the tale?

Siegfried.   Their prattle long
            I have put from my mind.
(He drinks and then offers his horn to Gunther.)
                  Drink, Gunther, drink:
                  thy brother brings it thee.

Siegfried.   Hoiho!

Die Mannen.   Hoiho! Hoiho!

Hagen.   Finden wir endlich
            wohin du flog'st?

Siegfried.   Kommt herab! hier ist's frisc
                  und kühl.

Hagen.   Hier rasten wir
            und rüsten das Mahl.
            Lasst ruh'n die Beute
            und bietet die Schläuche!

(Jagdbeute wird zu Hauf gelegt; Trinkhörner u
Schläuche werden hervorgeholt. Dann lagert si
alles.)

Hagen.   Der uns das Wild verscheucht,
            nun sollt' ihr Wunder hören
            was Siegfried sich erjagt.

Siegfried
            (lachend.)
            Schlimm steht's um mein Mahl:
                  von eurer Beute
                  bitt' ich für mich.

Hagen.   Du beutelos?

Siegfried.   Auf Waldjagd zog ich aus,
            doch Wasserwild zeigte sich nur;
            war ich dazu recht berathen,
            drei wilde Wasservögel,
            hätt' ich euch gefangen,
            die dort auf dem Rhein mir sanger
            erschlagen würd' ich noch heut'.

Gunther
            (erschrickt und blickt düster auf Hagen.)

Hagen.   Das wäre böse Jagd,
            wenn den Beutelosen selbst
            ein lauernd Wild erlegte!

Siegfried.   Mich dürstet!
(Er hat sich zwischen Hagen und Gunther gela
gert; gefüllte Trinkhörner werden ihnen gereicht.

Hagen.   Ich hörte sagen, Siegfried,
            der Vögel Sanges-Sprache
                  verstündest du wohl:
                  so wär' das wahr?

Siegfried.   Seit lange acht' ich
                  des Lallens nicht mehr.
(Er trinkt und reicht dann sein Horn Gunther.)
                  Trink', Gunther! trink'!
                  dein Bruder bringt es dir.

Gunther
(gazing thoughtfully and gloomily into the horn.)

The wine is weak and blanched:
Thy blood alone is here!

Siegfried
(laughing.)

Let mingle mine with thine then.
(He pours out of Gunther's horn into his own,
so that it overflows.)

Now flows the mixture over:
to mother Earth
let it be an offering!

Gunther
(sighing.)

Thou over-joyous heart!

Siegfried
(softly to Hagen.)

He feels Brünnhilde's frown.

Hagen.   His spouse he scarce can read
as thou the wood-bird's song.

Siegfried.
Since hearing the songs of women
I heed not the birds o'erhead.

Hagen.   They once were known to thee?

Siegfried.   Hey, Gunther,
gloom-ridden man!
If 'twill amuse
I'll song thee some marvellous
matters of my boyhood.

Gunther.   With all my heart.

Hagen.   So sing to us!
(All ensconce themselves on the ground about
Siegfried who alone sits upright while the others
recline more.)

Siegfried.   Mimi hight
a mannikin grim,
who in nought but greed
granted me care,
to count on me,
when manful I'd wax'd,
in the wood to slay a worm,
which long had hidden there a hoard.
He trained me to smith's work
and metal smelting;
but what the teacher
could not attempt
the pupil did
by daring and patience,

Gunther
(gedankenvoll und schwermüthig in das Horn blickend.)

Du mischtest matt und bleich:—
dein Blut allein darin!

Siegfried
(lachend.)

So misch' es mit dem deinen!
(Er giesst aus Gunther's Horn in das seine, so
dass es überläuft.)

Nun floss gemischtes über:
der Mutter Erde
lass' das ein Labsal sein!

Gunther
(seufzend.)

Du überfroher Held!

Siegfried
(leise zu Hagen.)

Ihm macht Brünnhilde Müh?

Hagen.   Verstünd' er sie so gut,
wie du der Vögel Sang!

Siegfried.   Seit Frauen ich singen hörte,
vergass ich der Vöglein ganz.

Hagen.   Doch einst vernahmst du sie?

Siegfried.   Hei! Gunther!
grämlicher Mann!
Dank'st du es mir,
so sing' ich dir Mären
aus meinen jungen Tagen.

Gunther.   Die hör' ich gern.

Hagen.   So singe, Held!
(Alle lagern sich nahe um Siegfried, welcher allein auf recht sitzt, während die andern tiefer gestreckt liegen.)

Siegfried.   Mime hiess
ein mürrischer Zwerg;
in des Neides Zwang
zog er mich auf,
dass einst das Kind,
wann kühn es erwuchs,
einen Wurm ihm fällt im Wald,
der lang' schon hütet' einen Hort.
Er lehrte mich schmieden
und Erze schmelzen:
doch was der Künstler
selbst nicht konnte,
des Lehrling's Muthe
musst' es gelingen—

so that from shattered steely splinters
whole I smithied a sword.
My father's blade
freshly I knit.
Now a fair
weapon was "Needful!"
meet 'twas for fight,
Mimi declared,
and fared with me t'ward the wood;
I felled there Fafnir, the Worm.
Pray now attend
well to my tale;
wonders truly I tell of.
When his welling blood
did blister my finger;
the flesh I cooled in my mouth:
scarce touched the wet
to the tip of my tongue
when what the birds were singing
at once my brain perceived.
On a branch one settled and sang:
"Hey! Siegfried shall hold now
the Nibelung's hoard;
he'll find in the hollow
the hoard anon!
Were he the Tarnhelm to win,
it would tide him through the wonderful tasks;
but were he the Ring too to ravish
'twould give him the ward of the
world."

Hagen.   Ring and Tarnhelm
took'st thou away!

One Vassal.   And what else did the bird
sing thee?

Siegfried.   Ring and Tarnhelm
holding in reach,
I once more harked
to the heavenly warbler,
who sat on high there and sang:
"Hey! Siegfried doth hold now
the helm and the ring:
O trust not in Mimi,
the treacherous elf!
Himself would have handled the
hoard,
so below there he lieth in wait;
for thy life he's trying, O Siegfried—
then trust not, Siegfried, in Mimi!"

Hagen.   Admonished it well?

eines zerschlag'nen Stahles Stücken
neu zu schweissen zum Schwert.
Des Vater's Wehr
fügt' ich mir neu;
nagelfest
schuf ich mir Nothung,
tüchtig zum Kampf
dünkt' er dem Zwerg:
der führte mich nun zum Wald;
dort fäll't ich Fafner, den Wurm.
Jetzt aber merkt
wohl auf die Mär':
Wunder muss ich euch melden.
Von des Wurmes Blut
mir brannten die Finger;
sie führt' ich kühlend zum Mund:
kaum netzt' ein wenig
die Zunge das Nass,
was da die Vöglein sangen
das konnt' ich flugs versteh'n:
Auf Aesten sass es und sang—
„Hei, Siegfried gehört nun
der Niblungen Hort:
o fänd' in der Höhle
den Hort er jetzt!
Wollt' er den Tarnhelm gewinnen,
der taugt' ihm zu wonniger That:
doch möcht' er den Ring sich errathen.
der macht' ihn zum Walter der Welt."

Hagen.   Ring und Tarnhelm
trug'st du nun fort?

Die Mannen.   Das Vöglein hörtest du
wieder?

Siegfried.   Ring und Helm
hatt' ich gerafft;
da lausch't' ich wieder
dem wonnigen Laller;
der sass im Wipfel und sang:
„Hei, Siegfried gehört nun
der Niblungen Hort:
o traute er Mime,
dem treulosen, nicht!
Ihm sollt' er den Hort nur erheben;
nun lauert er listig am Weg:
nach dem Leben trachtet er Siegfried:
o traute Siegfried nicht Mime!"

Hagen.   Es mahnte dich gut?

The Vassals.　And what didst to Mimi?

Siegfried.　With death-dealing drink
　　he drew to my side,
　　pale and stamm'ring,
　　he showed his vile purpose:
　"Needful" settled the scamp.

Hagen
　　　　(laughing.)
　　The blade he could forge not
　　fell upon Mimi!

The Vassals.　And told the birds other
　　　　　　　tidings?

Hagen
(who has squeezed the juice of an herb into the
horn.)
　　Drink first, hero,
　　from my horn:
　I mingled a herb with the draught
　to awaken and hold thy remem-
　　　　　　　brance,
　that past things may be apparent!

Siegfried
　　　　(after he has drunk.)
　　In grief through the boughs
　　I gazed up aloft,
　where still he sat and sang;
　　"Hey! Siegfried has slain now
　　the sinister dwarf!
　　I wot he may gain
　　the loveliest wife;
　in loftly fastness she sleeps,
　fire doth emborder the spot;
　　o'erstepped he the blaze—
　　wakened the bride—
　Brünnhilde were then his own!"

Hagen.　Obeyedst thou
　　the bird's instruction?

Siegfried.　Straight without pause
　　I passed on my way,
　and I fared to the fire-girt rock.
　　The furnace was stepped
　　　　　　　through,
　　the prize was found:
　sleeping, a marvellous maid
　in suit of mirror-like mail.
　　The helm soon
　　from her head I unloosed,
　she quickly waked to my kiss;
　O then how glowingly embraced me
　Brünnhilde's glorious arm!

Die Mannen.　Vergaltest du Mime?

Siegfried.　Mit tödtlichem Tranke
　　trat er zu mir;
　　bang und stotternd
　　gestand er mir Böses:
　Nothung streckte den Strolch.

Hagen
　　　　(lachend.)
　　Was nicht er geschmiedet
　　schmeckte doch Mime!

Die Mannen.
　　Was wies das Vöglein dich wieder?

Hagen
(nachdem er den Saft eines Krautes in das Trinkhorn ausgedruckt.)
　　Trink' erst, Held,
　　aus meinem Horn:
　ich würzte dir holden Trank.
　die Erinnerung hell dir zu wecken,
　dass Fernes nicht dir entfalle!

Siegfried
　　　　(nachdem er getrunken.)
　　In Lied zum Wipfel
　　lauscht' ich hinauf;
　da sass es noch und sang:
　　„Hei, Siegfried erschlug nun
　　den schlimmen Zwerg!
　　Jetzt wüsst' ich ihm noch
　　das herrlichste Weib:—
　auf hohem Felsen sie schläft,
　ein Feuer umbrennt ihren Saal;
　　durchschritt' er die Brunst,
　　erweckt' er die Braut,
　Brünnhilde wäre dann sein!"
(Gunther hört mit wachsendem Erstaunen zu.)

Hagen.　Und folgtest du
　　des Vögleins Rath?

Siegfried.　Rasch ohne Zögern
　　zog ich da aus,
　bis den feurigen Fels ich traf;
　　die Lohe durchschritt ich,
　　und fand zum Lohn—
　schlafend ein wonniges Weib
　in lichter Waffen Gewand.
　　Den Helm löst' ich
　　der herrlichen Maid;
　mein Kuss erwachte sie kühn!—
　o wie mich brunstig da umschlang
　der schönen Brünnhilde Arm!

Gunther. What say'st thou?

(Two ravens fly from a bush, circle over Siegfried and fly away over the Rhine).

Hagen. Canst read the speech
of those ravens aright?

(Siegfried starts up quickly and looks after the ravens, turning his back towards Hagen.)

Hagen. Revenge they rouse in me!

(He thrusts his spear into Siegfried's back, Gunther catches his arm, too late)

Gunther and the Men. Hagen what deed
is this?

(Siegfried swings his shield aloft with both hands to crush Hagen with it; his strength leaves him; the shield falls back and he himself falls upon it).

Hagen

(pointing at the prostrate figure.)

Retribution!

(He turns coolly away and gradually disappears over the hills where his retreating form is for some time visible. Gunther, siezed with anguish, bends down by Siegfried's side. The Men gather in sympathy round the dying man.

Dusk commences to fall with the apparition of the ravens.)

Siegfried

(once more opens his glaring eyes and begins with solemn voice.)

Brünnhilde!
Heavenly bride!
Look up! Open thine eyelids!
What hath sunk thee
once more in sleep?
Who drowns thee in slumber so
drear?
The wak'ner came,
his kiss awoke;
again now the bride's
bonds he has broken;
enchant him Brünnhilde's charms!
Ah! now for ever
open her eyelids!
Ah! and what od'rous
breeze is her breath!
Thrice blessed ending—
thrill that dismays not!
Brünnhilde beckons to me!

(He dies.)

(The Vassals raise Siegfried's body on his shield and bear it away over the height in mournful procession. Gunther follows at a little distance.)

(The moon breaks through the clouds and illuminates with increasing brightness the distant train. —Mists rise up from the Rhine and gradually fill the whole stage up to the front. When after a while they again disperse, the scene is changed.)

Gunther. Was hör' ich!

(Zwei Raben fliegen aus einem Busche auf, kreisen über Siegfried, und fliegen davon.)

Hagen. Erräth'st du auch
dieser Raben Geraun'?

(Siegfried fährt heftig auf, und blickt, Hagen den Rücken wendend, den Raben nach.)

Hagen. Rache riethen sie mir!

(Er stösst seinen Speer in Siegfried's Rücken: Gunther fällt ihm—zu spät—in den Arm.)

Gunther und die Mannen.
Hagen! was thu'st du?

(Siegfried schwingt mit beiden Händen seinen Schild hoch empor, Hagen damit zu zerschmettern: die Kraft verlässt ihn, der Schild entsinkt seiner Hand; er selbst stürzt krachend über ihm zusammen.)

Hagen

(auf den zu Boden gestreckten deutend.)

Meineid räch' ich!

(Er wendet sich ruhig zur Seite ab, und verliert sich dann einsam uber die Höhe, wo man ihn langsam von dannen schreiten sieht.—Gunther beugt sich schmerzergriffen zu Siegfried's Seite nieder. Die Mannen umstehen theilnahmvoll den Sterbenden. Lange Stille der tiefsten Erschütterung.)

(Dämmerung ist bereits mit der Erscheinung der Raben eingebrochen.)

Siegfried

(noch einmal die Augen glanzvoll aufschlagend, mit feierlicher Stimme beginnend.)

Brünnhilde!
heilige Braut!
wach' auf! öffne dein Auge!
Wer verschloss dich
wieder in Schlaf?
wer band dich in Schlummer so
bang?
Der Wecker kam;
er küsst dich wach,
und aber der Braut
bricht er die Bande:—
da lacht ihm Brünnhilde's Lust!—
Ach, dieses Auge,
ewig nun offen!
ach, dieses Athems
wonniges Wehen!
Süsses Vergehen—
seliges Grauen!
Brünnhild' bietet mir Gruss!

(Er stirbt.)

(Die Mannen erheben die Leiche auf den Schild, und geleiten sie in feierlichem Zuge über die Felsenhöhe langsam von dannen. Günther folgt der Leiche zunächst.—)

(Der Mond bricht durch die Wolken hervor, und beleuchtet auf der Höhe den Trauerzug.—Dann steigen Nebel aus dem Rheine auf, und erfüllt allmälig die ganze Bühne bis nach vornen.—Sobald sich dann die Nebel wieder zertheilen, ist die Scene verwandelt).

Third Scene

(The Hall of the Gibichungs with the river bank, s in the first Act.—Night. Moonlight glittering n the Rhine.)

(Gutrune enters the Hall from her chamber.)

Gutrune.

Was that his horn?
(Listens.)
No!—not
yet is he home.—
Sombre visions
startled me from sleep.
His horse
I heard wildly neigh:
Brünnhilde's laughter
awakened my sense.
What woman was't
I saw descend the bank but now?
I fear this Brünnhilde!
Is she still here?

(Listens at the door at right and calls softly.)

Brünnhilde! Brünnhilde!
art thou awake?

(Opens the door tremblingly and looks in.)

Bare is the room.
It was then she
that to the Rhine I saw descend?

(She starts and listens to a distant sound.)

Was that his horn?
Nay!
Nought neareth!—
If he only would come!

(She is about to return to her room, but hears Hagen's voice, pauses, and remains awhile motionless, transfixed by fear.)

Hagen's

(voice without approaching).
Hoiho! Hoiho!
Wake up! wake up!
Torches! torches!
Lighted brands here!
Fair booty
bring we along.
Hoiho! Hoiho!

(Lights and increasing glow of fires without.)

Hagen

(entering the hall.)
Up! Gutrune,
and greet your Siegfried!
the stalwart hero
is coming home.

(Men and Women with lights and firebrands conduct, in great confusion, the train with Siefgried's body. Gunther is among them.)

Dritte Scene

(Die Halle der Gibichungen mit dem Uferraume, wie im ersten Aufzuge.—Nacht. Mondschein spiegelt sich im Rhein.)

(Gutrune tritt aus ihrem Gemach in die Halle heraus.)

Gutrune. War das sein Horn?
(Sie lauscht.)
Nein!—noch
kehrt er nicht heim.—
Schlimme Träume
störten mir den Schlaf!—
Wild hört ich
wiehern sein Ross:—
Lachen Brünnhilde's
weckte mich auf.— —
Wer war das Weib,
das zum Rhein ich schreiten sah?—
Ich fürchte Brünnhild'!—
ist sie daheim?

(Sie lauscht an einer Thüre rechts, und ruft dann leise.)

Brünnhild'! Brünnhild'!
bist du wach?—

(Sie öffnet schüchtern und blickt hinein.)

Leer das Gemach!
so war es sie,
die zum Rhein ich schreiten sah?

(Sie erschrickt und lauscht nach der Ferne.)

Hört' ich sein Horn?
Nein!—
Oede alles!—
Säh' ich Siegfried nur bald!

(Sie will sich wieder ihrem Gemache zuwenden, als sie jedoch Hagen's Stimme vernimmt, hält sie an, und bleibt, von Furcht gefesselt, eine Zeit lang unbeweglich stehen.)

Hagen's

(Stimme von aussen sich nähernd.)
Hoiho! Hoiho!
Wacht auf! wacht auf!
Lichte! Lichte!
helle Brände!
Jagdbeute
bringen wir heim.
Hoiho! Hoiho!

(Licht und wachsender Feuerschein von aussen.)

Hagen

(in die Halle tretend.)
Auf! Gutrun'!
begrüsse Siegfried!
Der starke Held,
er kehret heim.

(Mannen und Frauen begleiten, mit Lichtern und Feuerbränden, in grosser Verwirrung den Zug der mit Siegfried's Leiche Heimkehrenden, unter denen Gunther.)

Gutrune

(in great terror.)

What is this, Hagen?
I heard not his horn!

Hagen.

The bloodless hero
blows it no more;
he'll bound to the chase
or battle no more,
nor fight for the fairest of women!

Gutrune

(with increasing dread.)

What do they bring?

Hagen.

A wild boar's ill-fated victim:
Siegfried—'tis thy husband's corpse.

(Gutrune starts up and precipitates herself upon
the body which has been set down in the middle of
the hall. General emotion and grief.)

Gunther

(bending over her senseless form and striving to
raise her).

Gutrune! lovely sister!
lift up thine eyes—
speak unto me!

Gutrune

(reviving.)

Siegfried!—Siegfried is slaughtered!

(Thrusts Gunther away)

Hence, treacherous brother!
Assassin of my Siegfried!
O help me! help me!
Horror! Horror!
My husband's murdered among ye!

Gunther.   Give no reproach to me!
reproach thou rather Hagen.
He is the wild boar so hateful
by whom our hero has bled.

Hagen.   Art thou then wroth with me?

Gunther.   Ill and anguish
rend thee forever!

Hagen

(stepping forward in terrible defiance.)

Well then! — 'tis I that have slain
him!
I—Hagen—
smote him to death!
He was spoil unto my spear,
on which false oath he spake.
Holiest booty right
here to me should be rendered:
I claim to have then this Ring.

Gutrune

(in grosser Angst.)

Was geschah', Hagen?
nicht hört' ich sein Horn!

Hagen.   Der bleiche Held,
nicht bläs't er's mehr;
nicht stürmt er zum Jagen,
zum Streit nicht mehr,
noch wirbt er um wonnige Frauen!

Gutrune

(mit wachsendem Entsetzen).

Was bringen die?

Hagen.   Eines wilden Ebers Beute:
Siegfried: deinen todten Mann!

(Gutrune schreit auf, und stürtz über die Leiche
hin, welche in der Mitte der Halle niedergesetzt ist
—Allgemeine Erschütterung und Trauer.)

Gunther

(indem er die Ohnmächtige aufzurichten sucht.)

Gutrune! holde Schwester!
Hebe dein Aug'!
schweige mir nicht!

Gutrune

(weider zu sich kommend.)

Siegfried!—Siegfried erschlagen!

(Sie stösst Gunther heftig zurück.)

Fort! treuloser Bruder!
du Mörder meines Mannes!
O Hilfe! Hilfe!
Wehe! Wehe!
Sie haben Siegfried erschlagen!

Gunther.   Nicht klage wider mich!
dort klage wider Hagen:
er ist der verfluchte Eber,
der diesen Edlen zerfleischt.

Hagen.   Bist du mir gram darum?

Gunther.   Angst und Unheil
greife dich immer!

Hagen

(mit furchtbarem Trotze herantretend.)

Ja denn! ich hab' ihn erschlagen
ich—Hagen—
schlug ihn zu todt!
Meinem Speer war er gespart,
bei dem er Meineid sprach.
Heiliges Beute-Recht
hab' ich mir nun errungen:
d'rum fordr' ich hier diesen Ring.

Gunther.   Aroint! thou ne'er shalt clutch
   what I for mine declare.

Hagen.   Ye vassals, speak on my side!

Gunther.   Seek'st thou for Gutrune's
                        dowry,
      spawn of the dwarfish stock?

Hagen
            (drawing his sword.)
      The dwarf's own dower
   thus—his son assumes

(He rushes on Gunther who defends himself:
they fight. The Men throw themselves between.
Gunther falls dead by a stroke of Hagen.)

Hagen.   Now the ring!
(He snatches at Siegfried's hand. It raises it-
self threateningly. General terror. Gutrune and
Women shriek aloud.)
(From the back appears Brünnhilde, who ad-
vances with firm and solemn tread to the front.)

Brünnhilde
            (still at the back.)
   Peace with your surge
      of sorrow that peals.
      Ye betrayed his wife vilely:
   for revenge now hath she come.
            (She quietly advances.)
      Children I heard
      crying to their mother,
   to say that milk has been spilled:
      but nought I marked
      a fitting lament
   for the highest hero's fate.

Gutrune
            (raising herself suddenly.)
   Brünnhilde, hurt by baseness,
   thou broughtest on us this harm:
   'tis thou didst stir the men to kill him.
   Woe the day thou camest hither!

Brünnhilde.
   Nay, poor soul, peace!
   Thou never wert wife of his:
         thou ownedst him
         only in name.
   'Tis I was his honored spouse.
   The oath of our union was sworn,
   ere Siegfried thy face had seen!

Gutrune
            (in an outburst of poignant despair.)
      Accursed Hagen!
   Woe's me! woe's me!
   Thou gav'st the hateful philtre
   to make her husband play false!
      O sorrow! sorrow!
      I see it all now!

Gunther.   Zurück! was mir verfiel
   sollst du nimmer empfah'n.

Hagen.   Ihr Mannen, richtet mein Recht!

Gunther.   Rühr'st du an Gutrun's Erbe,
   schamloser Albensohn?

Hagen
            (sein Schwert ziehend.)
      Des Alben Erbe
   fordert so sein Sohn!
(Er dringt auf Gunther ein; dieser wehrt sich:
sie fechten. Die Mannen werfen sich dazwischen.
Gunther fällt von einen Streiche Hagen's todt darnieder.)

Hagen.   Her den Ring!
(Er greift nach Siegfried's Hand; diese hebt sich
drohend empor. Allgemeines Entsetzen. Gutrune
und die Frauen schreien laut auf.)
(Vom Hintergrunde her schreitet Brünnhilde fest
und feierlich dem Vordergrunde zu)

Brünnhilde
            (noch im Hintergrunde.)
      Schweigt eures Jammers
      jauchzenden Schwall!
      Das ihr alle verriethet,
   zur Rache schreitet sein Weib.
            (Sie schreitet ruhig weiter vor.)
      Kinder hört' ich
      greinen nach der Mutter,
   da süsse Milch sie verschüttet:
      doch nicht erklang mir
      würdige Klage,
   des höchsten Helden werth.

Gutrune.
   Brünnhilde! Neid-erbos'te!
   du brachtest uns diese Noth!
   Die du ihm die Männer verhetztest,
   weh', dass dem Haus du genah't!

Brünnhilde.
   Armselige, schweig'!
   Sein Eheweib warst du nie:
         als Buhlerin nur
         bandest du ihn.
   Sein Mannes-Gemahl bin ich,
   der er ewige Eide schwur,
   eh' Siegfried je dich ersah.

Gutrune
            (in heftigster Verzweiflung.)
      Verfluchter Hagen!
   Weh! ach weh!
   dass du das Gift mir riethest,
   das ihr den Gatten entrückt!
      O Jammer! Jammer!
      wie jäh nun weiss ich,

Brünnhilde was his true-love,
whom he betrayed by that draught:

(Filled with shame, she turns from the body
Siegfried and bends almost dying over Gunther's
body; she remains thus motionless to the end. Long
silence.)

(Hagen stands leaning defiantly on his spear and
shield, sunk in gloomy meditation, at the extreme
opposite side.)

Brünnhilde

(alone in the centre: after remaining long
absorbed in the contemplation of Siegfried, first
convulsed with horror, then overpowered by grief,
she turns with solemn exultation to the people.)

Friends, let fitting
funeral pyre
be reared by the river here.
Hot and high
kindle the flames,
to consume the corse
of him who was hero o'er all!—
His steed bring to me here;
to its master straight it shall bear
me:
for my body burneth
to share in the honor
that here we show unto him.
Obey Brünnhilde's will.

(The young men erect, during the following, a
huge funeral pyre before the Hall on the bank of
the Rhine; women adorn it with drapery, on which
they strewn flowers and herbs.)

Brünnhilde

(again becoming absorbed in gazing on Siegfried's dead face.)

What sunny light
outstreams from his look!
The truest was he,
yet could betray!
His wife deluding
—leal to friendship—
from his own true lady,
—only belov'd—
he shut himself with his sword.—
Nobler than he
swore fealty never;
prouder than he
held no man a promise;
love pure as his
lived not in hero;
and yet ev'ry oath made,
ev'ry assurance,
the sheerest affection,—
sure none broke like he!—
Ween ye why that was!
Ye gods who guard
our gages for ever,
turn not away

dass Brünnhild' die Traute war,
die durch den Trank er vergass!

(Sie wendet sich voll Scheu von Siegfried ab, und
beugt sich in Schmerz aufgelös't über Gunther's
Leiche: so verbleibt sie regungslos bis an das Ende.
—Langes Schweigen.)

(Hagen steht, auf Speer und Schild gelehnt, in
finsteres Sinnen versunken, trotzig auf der äussersten anderen Seite.)

Brünnhilde

(allein in der Mitte: nachdem sie lange, zuerst
mit tiefer Erschütterung, dann mit fast überwälti-
gender Wehmuth das Angesicht Siegfried's betrachtet, wendet sie sich mit feierlicher Erhebung an
die Männer und Frauen.)

Starke Scheite
schichtet mir dort
am Rande des Rhein's zu Hauf:
hoch und hell
lod're die Gluth,
die den edlen Leib
des hehrsten Helden verzehrt!—
Sein Ross führet daher,
dass mit mir dem Recken es folge:
denn des Helden heiligste
Ehre zu theilen
verlangt mein eig'ner Leib.—
Vollbringt Brünnhilde's Wort!

(Die jüngeren Männer errichten während des
Folgenden vor der Halle nahe am Rheinufer, einen
mächtigen Scheithaufen. Frauen schmücken ihn
mit Decken; auf die sie Kräuter und Blumen
streuen.)

Brünnhilde

(von neuem in den Anblick der Leich eversunken.)

Wie Sonne lauter
strahlt mir sein Licht;
der Reinste war er,
der mich verrieth!
Die Gattin trügend
—treu dem Freunde—
von der eig'nen Trauten
—einzig ihm theuer—
schied er sich durch sein Schwert.—
Aechter als er
schwur keiner Eide;
treuer als er
hielt keiner Verträge:
laut'rer als er
liebte kein And'rer:
und doch alle Eide,
alle Verträge,
die treueste Liebe—
trog keiner wie er!—
Wisst ihr wie das ward!
O ihr, der Eide
ewige Hüter!
lenkt eu'ren Blick

from my waxing distress,
but gaze on our endless disgrace!
Hear my wild lament,
thou mightiest god!
Because he dared a great deed,
which was dear to thy hopes,
how couldst thou thus
throw upon him
'he curse to which thou succumbest?
Ought I
to be harmed by my hero,
that wise a woman should wax?—
Ween I now what thou wouldst?—
All things, all things,
all I wot now:
all at once is made clear!
Even thy ravens
I hear rustling:
to tell the longed-for tidings,
let them return to their home.
Rest thee! Rest thee, O God!

(She signs to the men to take up Siegfried's body and place it on the funeral pyre; then she takes from his finger the Ring.)

Redeemed, my hand
holdeth my dower.
Thou fatal round!
fearfullest Ring!
my hand folds thee
to hurl thee afar.
Ye water-dwelling
wary sisters,
the Rhine's fair sinuous daughters,
my thanks ye reap for your rede.
What ye would gain
I give to you;
out from my ashes
take it for ever!
The red flame that burneth me
cleanses the Ring from its curse:
ye in the Rhine
melt it away
and merely preserve
the metal bright,
whose theft has thrown you in grief.

(She turns to the back, where Siegfried's body lies already on the pyre, and takes a huge firebrand from a man.)

Fly home, ye ravens!
rede it in Vallhalla
what here on the Rhine ye have
                    heard!
To Brünnhilde's rock
go round about,
Yet Loki burns there:

auf mein blühendes Leid:
erschaut eu're ewige Schuld!
Meine Klage hör',
du hehrster Gott!
Durch seine tapferste That,
dir so tauglich erwünscht,
weihtest du den,
der sie gewirkt,
dem Fluche, dem du verfielest,
mich musste
der Reinste verrathen,
dass wissend würde ein Weib!—
Weiss ich nun was dir frommt?—
Alles! Alles!
Alles weiss ich:
alles ward mir nun frei!
Auch deine Raben
hör' ich rauschen:
mit bang ersehnter Botschaft
send' ich die beiden nun heim.
Ruhe! Ruhe, du Gott!

(Sie winkt den Mannen, Siegfried's Leiche aufzuheben, und auf das Scheitgerüste zu tragen; zugleich zieht sie von Siegfried's Finger den Ring).

Mein Erbe nun
nehm' ich zu eigen.
Verfluchter Reif!
furchtbarer Ring!
dein Gold fass' ich,
und geb' es nun fort.
Der Wassertiefe
weise Schwestern,
des Rheines schwimmende Töchter,
euch dank' ich redlichen Rath!
Was ihr begehrt,
geb' ich euch:
aus meiner Asche
nehmt es zu eigen!
Das Feuer, das mich verbrennt,
rein'ge den Ring vom Fluch:
ihr in der Fluth
löset ihn auf,
und lauter bewahrt
das lichte Gold,
den strahlenden Stern des Rhein's,
der zum Unheil euch geraubt.

(Sie wendet sich nach hinten, wo Siegfried's Leiche bereits auf dem Gerüste ausgestreckt liegt, und entreiss einem Manne den mächtigen Feuerbrand.)

Fliegt heim, ihr Raben!
raun't es eurem Herrn.
was hier am Rhein ihr gehört!
An Brünnhild's Felsen
fahret vorbei:
der dort noch lodert,

Vallhall' bid him revisit!
    Draweth near in gloom
    the Dusk of the gods.
Thus, casting my torch,
I kindle Vallhalla's tow'rs.

(She thrusts the torch into the pile, which rapidly kindles. Two ravens fly up from the rocks on the bank and disappear at the back.)

(Two young men bring in the horse; Brünnhilde takes it and quickly unbridles it.)

    Grani, my horse,
    greet thee again!
Wouldst thou know, dear friend,
what journey we follow?
    By flame illumined
    lies there thy lord,
Siegfried, the star of my life.
To meet with thy master
neighest thou merrily?
Lo! how the flame
doth leap and allure thee!
Feel how my breast too
hotly doth burn;
sparkling fireflame
my spirit enfolds.
O, but to clasp him—
recline in his arms!
in madd'ning emotion
once more to be his!
Heiajaho! Grani!
Greet we our hero!
Siegfried! Siegfried! see!
sweetly greets thee thy wife!

(She leaps wildly on to the horse and takes it with one bound into the burning pyre. The flames instantly blaze up and fill the entire space before the hall, seeming even to seize on the building. In terror the women cower towards the front. Suddenly the fire falls together, leaving only a mass of smoke which collects at back and forms a cloud bank on the horizon. The Rhine swells up mightily and sweeps over the fire. On the surface appear the three Rhine-daughters, swimming close to the fire-embers. Hagen who has watched Brünnhilde's proceedings with increasing anxiety, is much alarmed on the appearance of the Rhine-daugh ers. He flings away hastily his spear, shield and helmet, and madly plunges into the flood crying:

The ring's my right!

(Woglinda and Wellgunda twine their arms round his neck and draw him thus down below. Flosshilde swimming before the others to the back, holds the recovered ring joyously up.)

(Through the cloud-bank on the horizon breaks an increasing red glow. In its light the Rhine is seen to have returned to its bed and the nymphs are circling and playing with the ring on the calm waters.)

(From the ruins of the half-burnt hall the men and women perceive with awe the light in the sky, in which now appears the hall of Vallhalla, where the gods and heroes are seen sitting together, as described by Valtrauta in the first Act. Bright flames seize on the abode of the gods; and when this is completely enveloped by them, the curtain falls.)

weiset Loge nach Walhall!
    Denn der Götter Ende
    dämmert nun auf;
so werf' ich den Brand
in Walhall's prangende Burg.

(Sie schleudert den Brand in den Holzstoss, der sich schnell hell entzündet. Zwei Raben sind von Ufer aufgeflogen, und verschwinden nach dem Hintergrunde zu.)

(Zwei junge Männer führen das Ross herein; Brünnhilde fasst es, und entzäumt es schnell.)

    Grane, mein Ross,
    sei mir gegrüsst!
Weisst du, Freund,
wohin ich dich führe?
    Im Feuer, leuchtend,
    liegt dort dein Herr,
Siegfried, mein seliger Held.
    dem Freunde zu folgen
    wieherst du freudig?
Lockt dich zu ihm
die lachende Lohe?
Fühl' meine Brust auch,
wie sie entbrennt:
helles Feuer
das Herz mir erfasst,
ihn zu umschlingen,
umschlossen von ihm,
in mächtigster Minne
vermählt ihm zu sein!—
Heiajaho! Grane!
grüsse deinen Herrn!
Siegfried! Siegfried! Sieh!
Selig grüsst dich dein Weib!

(Sie hat sich stürmisch auf das Ross geschwungen, und sprengt es mit einem Satze in den brennenden Scheithaufen. Sogleich steigt prasselnd der Brand hoch auf so dass das Feuer den ganzen Raum vor der Halle erfüllt, und diese selbst schon zu ergreifen scheint. Entsetzt drängen sich die Frauen nach dem Vordergrunde. Plötzlich bricht das Feuer zusammen, so dass nur noch eine düstere Gluthwolke über der Stätte schwebt; diese steigt auf und zertheilt sich ganz, der Rhein ist vom Ufer her mächtig angeschwollen, und wälzt seine Fluth über die Brandstätte bis an die Schwelle der Halle. Auf den Wogen sind die drei Rheintöchter herbeigeschwommen.—Hagen, der seit dem Vorgange mit dem Ringe in wachsender Angst Brünnhilden's Benehmen beobachet hat, geräth beim Anblicke der Rheintöchter in höchsten Schreck; er wirft hastig Speer, Schild und Helm von sich ab, und stürzt wie wahnsinnig mit dem Rufe:

Zurück vom Ringe!

sich in die Fluth. Woglinda und Wellgunda umschlingen mit ihren Armen seinen Nacken, und ziehen ihn so zurückschwimmend mit sich in die Tiefe; Flosshilde, ihnen voran, hält jubelnd den gewonnenen Ring in die Höhe.—Am Himmel bricht zugleich von fern her eine, dem Nordlicht ähnliche röthliche Gluth aus, die sich immer weiter und stärker verbreitet. Die Männer und Frauen schauen in sprachloser Erschütterung dem Vorgange und der Erscheinung zu.)

(Der Vorhang fällt.)

TRISTAN AND ISOLDE

TRISTAN AND ISOLDE

ACT I

Tristan, a valiant Cornish knight, is bringing Isolda, princess of Ireland, over as a bride for his uncle, King Mark. He is himself in love with her, but owing to a blood feud between them, forces himself to conceal his passion. Isolda, in anger at his seeming unkindness, attempts to poison herself and him, but her attendant, Brangæna, changes the draft for a love potion, which enflames their passion beyond power of restraint.

ACT II

Isolda has been wedded to King Mark, but holds stolen interviews with Tristan, during one of which they are surprised, for Tristan has been betrayed by a jealous friend, Melot. Touched by King Mark's bitter reproaches, Tristan provokes Melot to fight and suffers himself to be mortally wounded.

ACT III

Tristan's faithful servant, Kurvenal, has carried his wounded master to his native home in Brittany, where he is carefully tended. Isolda has also been sent for, as being skilled above all others in the healing art. The excitement of her approach only hastens Tristan's death, and he breathes his last sigh in her arms. Mark has followed Isolda: he has had matters explained, and is prepared to reunite the lovers, but it is too late. Isolda utters her lament over the body of her lover, and her heart breaks: in death alone are they united.

TRISTAN AND ISOLDE

ACT I	ERSTE AKT
[*A pavilion erected on the deck of a ship, richly hung with tapestry, quite closed in at back at first. A narrow hatchway at one side leads below into the cabin.*]	[*Zeltartiges Gemach auf dem Vorderdeck eines See-schiffes, reich mit Teppichen behangen, beim Begin nach dem Hintergrunde zu gänzlich geschlossen; zu Seite führt eine schmale Treppe in den Schiffsraun hinab.*]
## SCENE I	## ERSTE SCENE
[ISOLDA *on a couch, her face buried in the cushions.* —BRANGÆNA *holding open a curtain, looks over the side of the vessel.*] THE VOICE OF A YOUNG SAILOR (*from above as if at the mast-head*).	[ISOLDE *auf einem Ruhebett, das Gesicht in die Kisse gedrückt.* — BRANGÆNA, *einen Teppich zurückge schlagen haltend, blickt zur Seite über Bord.*] STIMME EINES JUNGEN SEEMANNES (*aus der Höhe wi vom Maste her, vernehmbar*).

West - ward sur - ges slip, East - ward speeds the ship. The wind so wild blows
West - wärts schweift der Blick, Ost - wärts streicht das Schiff. Frisch weht der Wind der

home-ward now; my I - rish child, where wait - est thou? Say, must our sails be
Hei - math zu: — mein I - rische Kind, wo wei - lest du? Sind's dei - ner Seuf - zer

weight-ed, Fill'd by thy sighs un - bat - ed? Waft us, wind strong and wild! Woe, ah,
We - hen, die mir die Se - gel - blä - hen? We - he, we - he, du Wind! Weh, ach,

woe for my child! .. O I - rish maid! .. my win-some, mar - vel-lous maid
we - he, mein Kind! I - rische Maid .. du wil - de, mi - ni - ge Maid

ISOLDA (*starting up suddenly*). What wight dares insult me? (*She looks round in agitation.*) Brangæna, ho! Say, where sail we?	ISOLDE (*jäh auffahrend*). Wer wagt mich zu höhnen?— (*Sie blickt verstört um sich*). Brangäne, du?— Sag', wo sind wir?
BRANGÆNA (*at the opening*). Bluish stripes are stretching along the west; swiftly sails the ship to shore; if restful the sea by eve we shall readily set foot on land	BRANGÆNE (*an der Oeffnung*). Blaue Streifen stiegen im Westen auf; sanft und schnell segelt das Schiff; auf ruhiger See vor Abend erreichen wir sicher das Land.
ISOLDA. What land?	ISOLDE. Welches Land?
BRANGÆNA. Cornwall's verdant strand.	BRANGÆNE. Kornwall's grünen Strand.

ISOLDA. Never more!
　　To-day nor to-morrow!
BRANGÆNA. What mean you, mistress? say!
　　(*She lets the curtain fall and hastens to* ISOLDA.)

ISOLDA (*with wild gaze*).
　　A fainthearted child,
　　false to thy fathers!
　　Ah, where, mother,
　　hast given thy might
　　that commands the wave and the tempest?
　　O subtle art
　　of sorcery,
　　for mere leech-craft followed too long!
　　Awake in me once more,
　　power of will!
　　Arise from thy hiding
　　within my breast!
　　Hark to my bidding,
　　fluttering breezes!
　　Arise and storm
　　in boisterous strife!
　　With furious rage
　　and hurricane's hurdle
　　waken the sea
　　from slumbering calm;
　　rouse up the deep
　　to its devilish deeds!
　　Shew it the prey
　　which gladly I proffer!
　　Let it shatter this too daring ship
　　and enshrine in ocean each shred!
　　And woe to the lives!
　　Their wavering death-sighs
　　I leave to ye, winds, as your lot.

BRANGÆNA (*in extreme alarm and concern for* ISOLDA).
　　Out, alas!
　　Ah, woe!
　　I've ever dreaded some ill!—
　　Isolda! mistress!
　　Heart of mine!
　　What secret dost thou hide?
　　Without a tear
　　thou'st quitted thy father and mother,
　　and scarce a word
　　of farewell to friends thou gavest;
　　leaving home thou stood'st,
　　how cold and still!
　　pale and speechless
　　on the way,
　　food rejecting,
　　reft of sleep,
　　stern and wretched,
　　wild, disturbed;
　　how it pains me
　　so to see thee!
　　Friends no more we seem,
　　being thus estranged.
　　Make me partner
　　in thy pain!
　　Tell me freely
　　all thy fears!
　　Lady. thou hearest,
　　sweetest and dearest;
　　if for true friend you take me,
　　your confidant O make me!

ISOLDA. Air! air!
　　or my heart will choke!
　　Open! open there wide!

(BRANGÆNA *hastily draws the centre curtains apart.*)

ISOLDE. Nimmermehr!
　　Nicht heut', nicht morgen!
BRANGÆNE. Was hör' ich? Herrin! Ha!
　　(*Lässt den Vorhang zufallen, und eilt bestürzt zu* ISOLDE.)

ISOLDE (*wild vor sich hin*).
　　Entartet' Geschlecht,
　　unwerth der Ahnen!
　　Wohin, Mutter,
　　vergab'st du die Macht,
　　über Meer und Sturm zu gebieten?
　　O zahme Kunst
　　der Zauberin,
　　die nur Balsamtränke noch brau't!
　　Erwache mir wieder,
　　kühne Gewalt,
　　herauf aus dem Busen,
　　wo du dich barg'st!
　　Hört meinen Willen,
　　zagende Winde!
　　Heran zu Kampf
　　und Wettergetös',
　　zu tobender Stürme
　　wüthendem Wirbel!
　　Treibt aus dem Schlaf
　　dies träumende Meer,
　　weckt aus dem Grund
　　seine grollende Gier;
　　zeigt ihm die Beute,
　　die ich ihm biete;
　　zerschlag' es, dies trotzige Schiff,
　　des zerschellten Trümmer verschling's!
　　Und was auf ihm lebt,
　　den wehenden Athem,
　　den lass' ich euch Winden zum Lohn!

BRANGÆNE (*im äussersten Schreck, um* ISOLDE *sich bemühend*).
　　Weh'! O weh'!
　　Ach! Ach!
　　Des Übels, das ich geahnt!—
　　Isolde! Herrin!
　　Theures Herz!
　　Was barg'st du mir so lang'?
　　Nicht eine Thräne
　　weintest du Vater und Mutter;
　　kaum einen Gruss
　　den Bleibenden botest du:
　　von der Heimath scheidend
　　kalt und stumm,
　　bleich und schweigend
　　auf der Fahrt,
　　ohne Nahrung,
　　ohne Schlaf,
　　wild verstört,
　　starr und elend,—
　　wie ertrugs ich's
　　so dich sehend,
　　nichts dir mehr zu sein,
　　fremd vor dir zu steh'n?
　　O, nun melde
　　was dich müh't!
　　Sage, künde
　　was dich quält.
　　Herrin Isolde,
　　trauteste Holde!
　　soll sie werth sich dir wähnen,
　　vertraue nun Brangänen!

ISOLDE. Luft! Luft!
　　Mir erstickt das Herz.
　　Öffne! Öffne dort weit!

(BRANGÆNE *zieht eilig die Vorhänge in der Mitte auseinander.*)

SCENE II

[*The whole length of the ship is now seen, down to the
stern, with the sea and horizon beyond. Round the
mainmast sailors are ensconced, busied with ropes;
beyond them in the stern are groups of knights and
attendants, also seated; a little apart stands* TRISTAN
*folding his arms and thoughtfully gazing out to sea;
at his feet* KURVENAL *reclines carelessly. From the
mast-head above is once more heard the voice of the*
YOUNG SAILOR.]

THE YOUNG SAILOR (*at the mast-head invisible*).
    The wind so wild
    blows homewards now;
    my Irish child,
    where waitest thou?
    Say, must our sails be weighted,
    filled by thy sighs unbated?
    Waft us, wind strong and wild!
    Woe, ah woe for my child!

ISOLDA (*whose eyes have at once sought* TRISTAN *and
fixed stonily on him—gloomily*).
    Once beloved—
    now removed—
    brave and bright,
    coward knight!
    Death-devoted head!
    Death-devoted heart!—
        (*laughing unnaturally*).
    Think'st highly of yon minion?

BRANGÆNA (*following her glance*).
    Whom mean'st thou?

ISOLDA. There, that hero
    who from mine eyes
    averts his own:
    in shrinking shame
    my gaze he shuns—
    Say, how hold you him?

BRANGÆNA. Mean you Sir Tristan,
    lady mine?
    Extolled by ev'ry nation,
    his happy country's pride,
    The hero of creation,—
    whose fame's so high and wide?

ISOLDA (*jeeringly*).
    In shrinking trepidation
    his shame he seeks to hide,
    While to the king, his relation,
    he brings the corpse-like bride!—
    Seems it so senseless
    what I say?
    Go ask himself,
    our gracious host,
    dare he approach my side?
    No courteous heed
    or loyal care
    this hero t'wards
    his lady turns;
    but to meet her his heart is daunted,
    this knight so highly vaunted!
    Oh! he wots
    well the cause!
    To the traitor go,
    bearing his lady's will!
    As my servant bound,
    straightway should he approach.

ZWEITE SCENE

[*Man blickt dem Schiff entlang bis zum Steuerbord, über
dem Bord hinaus auf das Meer und den Horizont. Um
den Hauptmast in der Mitte ist Seevolk, mit Tauen
beschäftigt, gelagert; über sie hinaus gewahrt man
am Steuerbord Ritter und Knappen, ebenfalls gelagert; von ihnen etwas entfernt* TRISTAN, *mit versch-
ränkten Armen stehend, und sinnend in das Meer
blickend; zu Füssen ihm, nachlässig ausgestreckt,*
KURWENAL.—*Vom Maste her, aus der Höhe, vernimmt
man wieder den Gesang des* JUNGEN SEEMANNS.]

DER JUNGE SEEMAN (*Auf dem Maste, unsichtbar*).
    Frisch weht der Wind
    der Heimath zu:—
    mein irisch Kind,
    wo weilest du?
    Sind's deiner Seufzer Wehen,
    die mir die Segel blähen?—
    Wehe! Wehe, du Wind
    Weh'! Ach wehe, mein Kind!

ISOLDE (*deren Blick sogleich* TRISTAN *fand, und starr
auf ihm geheftet bleibt, dumpf für sich*).
    Mir erkoren,—
    mir verloren,—
    heer und heil
    kühn und feig—;
    Tod geweihtes Haupt!
    Tod geweihtes Herz!—
        (*unheimlich lachend*)
    Was hällst von dem Knechte?

BRANGÆNE (*ihrem Blicke folgend*).
    Wen meinst du?

ISOLDE. Dort den Helden,
    Der meinem Blick
    den seinen birgt,
    in Scham und Scheue
    abwärts schaut:—
    sag', wie dünkt er dich!

BRANGÆNE. Frägst du nach Tristan,
    theure Frau,
    dem Wunder aller Reiche,
    dem hochgepries'nen Mann,
    dem Helden ohne Gleiche,
    des Ruhmes Hort und Bann?

ISOLDE (*sie verhöhnend*).
    Der zagend vor dem Streiche
    sich flüchtet wo er kann,
    weil eine Braut er als Leiche
    für seinen Herrn gewann!—
    Dünkst es dich dunkel,
    mein Gedicht?
    Frag' ihn denn selbst,
    den freien Mann,
    ob mir zu nah'n er wagt?
    Der Ehren Gruss
    und zücht'ge Acht
    vergisst der Herrin
    der zage Held,
    dass ihr Blick ihn nur nicht erreiche—
    den Kühnen ohne Gleiche!
    O, er weiss
    wohl warum!—
    Zu dem Stolzen geh',
    meld' ihm der Herrin Wort:
    meinem Dienst bereit
    schleunig soll er mir nah'n.

RANGÆNA. Shall I beseech him
    to attend thee?

OLDA. Nay, order him:
    pray, understand it:—
    I, Isolda
    do command it!

At an imperious sign from ISOLDA BRANGÆNA *withdraws and timidly walks along the deck towards the stern, past the working sailors.* ISOLDA, *following her with fixed gaze, sinks back on the couch, where she remains seated during the following, her eyes still turned sternward.*]

URVENAL (*observing* BRANGÆNE's *approach, plucks* TRISTAN *by the robe without rising*).
    Beware, Tristan!
    Message from Isolda!

RISTAN (*starting*). What is't?—Isolda?—

He quickly regains his composure as BRANGÆNA *approaches and curtsies to him.*)
    What would my lady?
    I her liegeman,
    fain will listen
    while her loyal
    woman tells her will.

RANGÆNA. My lord, Sir Tristan,
    Dame Isolda
    would have speech
    with you at once.

RISTAN. Is she with travel worn?
    The end is near:
    nay, ere the set of sun
    sight we the land.
    All that your mistress commands me,
    trust me, I shall mind.

RANGÆNA. That you, Sir Tristan,
    go to her,—
    this is my lady's wish.

RISTAN. Where yonder verdant meadows
    in distance dim are mounting,
    wait my sov'reign
    for his mate:
    to lead her to his presence
    I'll wait upon the princess:
    'tis an honor
    all my own.

RANGÆNA. My lord, Sir Tristan,
    list to me:
    this one thing
    my lady wills,
    that thou at once attend her,
    there where she waits for thee.

RISTAN. In any station
    where I stand
    I truly serve but her,
    the pearl of womanhood.
    If I unheeding
    left the helm,
    how might I pilot her ship
    in surety to King Mark?

RANGÆNA. Tristan, my master,
    why mock me thus?
    Seemeth my saying
    obscure to you?
    list to my lady's words:
    thus, look you, she hath spoken:
    "Go order him,
    and understand it,
    I—Isolda—
    do command it.

BRANGÆNE. Soll ich ihn bitten,
    dich zu grüssen?

ISOLDE. Befehlen liess'
    dem Eigenholde
    Furcht der Herrin
    ich, Isolde.

[*Auf* ISOLDE's *gebieterischen Wink entfernt sich* BRANGÆNE, *und schreitet das Deck entlang dem Steuerbord zu, an den arbeitenden Seeleuten vorbei.* ISOLDE, *mit starrem Blicke ihr folgend, zieht sich rücklings nach dem Ruhebett zurück, wo sie während des Folgenden bleibt, das Auge unabgewandt nach dem Steuerbord gerichtet.*]

KURWENAL (*der* BRANGÆNE *kommen sieht, zupft, ohne sich zu erheben,* TRISTAN *am Gewande*).
    Hab' Acht, Tristan!
    Botschaft von Isolde.

TRISTAN (*auffahrend*). Was ist?—Isolde?—

(*Er fasst sich schnell, als* BRANGÆNE *vor ihm anlangt und sich verneigt.*)
    Von meiner Herrin?—
    Ihr gehorsam
    was zu hören
    meldet höfisch
    mir die traute Magd?

BRANGÆNE. Mein Herre Tristan,
    dich zu sehen
    wünscht Isolde,
    meine Frau.

TRISTAN. Grämt sie die lange Fahrt,
    die geht zu End';
    eh' noch die Sonne sinkt,
    sind wir am Land:
    was meine Frau mir befehle,
    treulich sei's erfüllt.

BRANGÆNE. So mög' Herr Tristan
    zu ihr gehn:
    das ist der Herrin Will'.

TRISTAN. Wo dort die grünen Fluren
    dem Blick noch blau sich färben,
    harrt mein König
    meiner Frau:
    zu ihm sie zu geleiten
    bald nah' ich mich der Lichten;
    Keinem gönnt' ich
    diese Gunst.

BRANGÆNE. Mein Herre Tristan,
    höre wohl:
    deine Dienste
    will die Frau,
    dass du zur Stell' ihr nahtest,
    dort wo sie deiner harrt.

TRISTAN. Auf jeder Stelle
    wo ich steh',
    getreulich dien' ich ihr,
    der Frauen höchster Ehr'.
    Liess' ich das Steuer
    jetzt zur Stund',
    wie lenkt' ich sicher den Kiel
    zu König Marke's Land?

BRANGÆNE. Tristan, mein Herre,
    was höhnst du mich?
    Dünkt dich nicht deutlich
    die thör'ge Magd,
    hör' meiner Herrin Wort!
    So, hiess sie, sollt' ich sagen:—
    befehlen liess'
    dem Eigenholde
    Furcht der Herrin
    sie, Isolde.

KURVENAL (*springing up*). May I an answer make her?

TRISTAN. What wouldst thou wish to reply?

KURVENAL. This should she say
    to Dame Isold':
    "Though Cornwall's crown
    and England's isle
    for Ireland's child he chose,
    his own by choice
    she may not be;
    he brings the king his bride.
    A hero-knight
    Tristan is hight!
    I've said, nor care to measure
    your lady's high displeasure."

[*While* TRISTAN *seeks to stop him, and the offended* BRANGÆNA *turns to depart,* KURVENAL *sings after her at the top of his voice, as she lingeringly withdraws.*]

    "Sir Morold toiled
    o'er mighty wave
    the Cornish tax to levy;
    In desert isle
    was dug his grave,
    he died of wounds so heavy.
    His head now hangs
    in Irish lands,
    Sole were-gild won
    at English hands.
    Bravo, our brave Tristan!
    Let his tax take who can!"

[KURVENAL, *driven away by* TRISTAN's *chidings, descends into the cabin.* BRANGÆNA *returns in discomposure to* ISOLDA, *closing the curtains behind her, while all the men take up the chorus and are heard without.*]

KNIGHTS AND ATTENDANTS. "His head now hangs
    in Irish lands,
    sole were-gild won
    at English hands.
    Bravo, our brave Tristan!
    Let his tax take who can!"

SCENE III

[ISOLDA *and* BRANGÆNA *alone, the curtain being again completely closed.* ISOLDA *rises with a gesture of despair and wrath.* BRANGÆNA *falls at her feet.*]

BRANGÆNA. Ah! an answer
    so insulting!

ISOLDA (*checking herself on the brink of a fearful outburst*). How now? of Tristan?
    I'd know if he denies me.

BRANGÆNA. Ah! question not!

ISOLDA. Quick, say without fear!

BRANGÆNA. With courteous phrase
    he foiled my will.

ISOLDA. But when you bade him hither?

BRANGÆNA. When I had straightway
    bid him come,
    wher'eer he stood,
    he said to me,
    he truly served but thee,
    the pearl of womanhood;
    if he unheeded
    left the helm
    how could he pilot the ship
    in surety to King Mark?

KURWENAL (*aufspr*). Darf ich die Antwort sag
    ingend?

TRISTAN. Was wohl erwiedertest du?

KURWENAL. Das sage sie
    Der Frau Isold'.—
    Wer Kornwall's Kron'
    und England's Erb'
    an Irland's Maid vermacht,
    der kann der Magd
    nicht eigen sein,
    die selbst dem Ohm er schenkt.
    Ein Herr der Welt
    Tristan der Held!
    Ich ruf's: du sag's, und grollten
    mir tausend Frau Isolden.

[*Da* TRISTAN *durch Gebärden ihm zu wehren sucht, u* BRANGÆNE *entrüstet sich zum Weggehen wend singt* KURWENAL *der zögernd sich Entfernenden* r *höchster Stärke nach.*]

    "Herr Morold zog
    zu Meere her,
    in Kornwall Zins zu haben;
    ein Eiland schwimmt
    auf ödem Meer,
    da liegt er nun begraben!
    Sein Haupt doch hängt
    im Iren-Land,
    als Zins gezahlt
    von Engeland.
    Hei! unser Held Tristan!
    Wie der Zins zahlen kann!"

[KURWENAL, *von* TRISTAN *fortgescholten, ist ir d Schiffsraum des Vorderdecks hinabgestiegen.* BRA GÆNE, *in Bestürzung zu* ISOLDE *zurückgekehrt, schlie hinter sich die Vorhänge, während die ganze Mar schaft aussen sich hören lässt.*]

ALLE MÆNNER. "Sein Haupt doch hängt
    im Iren-Land,
    als Zins gezahlt
    von Engeland.
    Hei! unser Held Tristan!
    Wie der Zins zahlen kann!"

DRITTE SCENE

[ISOLDE *und* BRANGÆNE *allein, bei vollkommen wie geschlossenen Vorhängen.* ISOLDE *erhebt sich* r *verzweiflungsvoller Wuthgebärde.* BRANGÆNE *ihr Füssen stürzend.*]

BRANGÆNE. Weh'! Ach, wehe!
    dies zu dulden!

ISOLDE (*dem furchtbarsten Ausbruche nahe, schnell s fassend*). Doch nun von Tristan:
    genau will ich's vernehmen.

BRANGÆNE. Ach, frage nicht!

ISOLDE. Frei sag's ohne Furcht.

BRANGÆNE. Mit höf'schen Worten
    wich er aus.

ISOLDE. Doch als du deutlich mahntest?

BRANGÆNE. Da ich zur Stell'
    ihn zu dir rief:
    wo er auch steh',
    so sagte er,
    getreulich dien' er ihr,
    der Frauen höchster Ehr',
    liess' er das Steuer
    jetzt zur Stund',
    wie lenkt' er sicher den Kiel
    zu König Marke's Land?

ISOLDA (*bitterly*). "How could he pilot the ship

    in surety to King Mark!"
And wait on him with were-gild
from Ireland's island won!

BRANGÆNA. As I gave out the message
and in thy very words,
thus spoke his henchman Kurvenal—

ISOLDA. Heard I not ev'ry sentence?
it all has reached my ear.
If thou hast learnt my disgrace
now hear too whence it has grown.
    How scoffingly
    they sing about me!
Quickly could I requite them!
    What of the boat
    so bare and frail,
that floated by our shore?
    What of the broken
    stricken man,
feebly extended there?
    Isolda's art
    he gladly owned;
    with herbs, simples
    and healing salves
the wounds from which he suffered
she nursed in skilful wise.
    Though "Tantris"
The name that he took unto him,
    as "Tristan"
anon Isolda knew him,
when in the sick man's keen blade
she perceived a notch had been made,
    wherein did fit
    a splinter broken
in Morold's head,
the mangled token
sent home in hatred rare:
this hand did find it there.
I heard a voice
from distance dim;
with the sword in hand
I came to him.
Full well I willed to slay him,
for Morold's death to pay him.
But from his sick bed
he looked up
not at the sword,
not at my arm—
his eyes on mine were fastened,
and his feebleness
softened my heart:
the sword—dropped from my fingers.
Though Morold's steel had maimed him
to health again I reclaimed him!
when he hath homeward wended
my emotion then might be ended.

BRANGÆNA. O wondrous! Why could I not see this?
The guest I sometime
helped to nurse—?

ISOLDA. His praise briskly they sing now:—
"Bravo, our brave Tristan!"—
he was that distressful man.
A thousand protestations
of truth and love he prated.
Hear how a knight
fealty knows!—
When as Tantris
unforbidden he'd left me,
as Tristan

ISOLDE (*schmerzlich bitter*). "Wie lenkt' er sicher den Kiel
zu König Marke's Land"—
den Zins ihm auszuzahlen,
den er aus Irland zog!

BRANGÆNE. Auf deine eig'nen Worte,
als ich ihm die entbot
liess seinen Treuen Kurwenal—

ISOLDE. Den hab' ich wohl vernommen,
kein Wort das mir entging.
Erfuhrst du meine Schmach,
nun höre, was sie mir schuf.—
Wie lachend sie
mir Lieder singen,
wohl könnt' auch ich erwiedern:
von einem Kahn,
der klein und arm
an Irland's Küste schwamm;
darinnen krank
ein siecher Mann
elend im Sterben lag.
Isolde's Kunst
ward ihm bekannt;
mit Heil-Salben
und Balsamsaft
der Wunde, die ihn plagte,
getreulich pflag sie da.
Der "Tantris"
mit sorgender List sich nannte,
als "Tristan"
Isold' ihn bald erkannte,
da in des Müss'gen Schwerte
eine Scharte sie gewahrte,
darin genau
sich fügt' ein Splitter,
den einst im Haupt
des Iren-Ritter,
zum Hohn ihr heimgesandt,
mit kund'ger Hand sie fand.—
Da schrie's mir auf
aus tiefstem Grund;
mit dem hellen Schwert
ich vor ihm stund,
an ihm, dem Ueber-Frechen,
Herrn Morold's Tod zu rächen.
Von seinem Bette
blickt' er her,—
nicht auf das Schwert,
nicht auf die Hand,—
er sah' mir in die Augen.
Seines Elendes
jammerte mich;
das Schwert—das liess ich fallen:
die Morold schlug, die Wunde,
sie heilt' ich, dass er gesunde,
und heim nach Hause kehre,—
mit dem Blick mich nicht mehr beschwere!

BRANGÆNE. O Wunder! Wo hatt' ich die Augen?
Der Gast, den einst
ich pflegen half—?

ISOLDE. Sein Lob hörtest du eben:—
"Hei! Unser Held Tristan!"—
Der war jener traur'ge Mann!—
Er schwur mit tausend Eiden
mir ew'gen Dank und Treue
Nun hör' wie ein Held
Eide hält!—
Den als Tantris
unerkannt ich entlassen,
als Tristan

boldly back he came,
in stately ship
from which in pride
Ireland's heiress
in marriage he asked
for Mark, the Cornish monarch,
his kinsman worn and old.
In Morold's lifetime
dared any have dreamed
to offer us such an insult?
For the tax-paying
Cornish prince
to presume to court Ireland's princess!
Ah, woe is me!
I it was
who for myself
did shape this shame!
with death-dealing sword
should I have stabbed him;
weakly it escaped me:—
now serfdom I have shaped me.
Curse him, the villain!
Curse on his head!
Vengeance! Death!
Death for me too!

BRANGÆNA (*throwing herself upon* ISOLDA *with impetuous tenderness*). Isolda! lady!
    loved one! fairest!
    sweet perfection!
    mistress rarest!
    Hear me! come now,
    sit thee here.—

    (*Gradually draws* ISOLDA *to the couch.*)
    What a whim!
    what causeless railing!
    How came you so wrong-minded
    and by mere fancy blinded?
    Sir Tristan gives thee
    Cornwall's kingdom;
    then, were he erst thy debtor,
    how could he reward thee better?
    His noble uncle
    serves he so:
    think too what a gift
    on thee he'd bestow!
    With honor unequalled
    all he's heir to
    at thy feet he seeks to shower,
    to make thee a queenly dower.
        (ISOLDA *turns away.*)
    If wife he'd make thee
    unto King Mark
    why wert thou in this wise complaining?
    Is he not worth thy gaining?
    Of royal race
    and mild of mood,
    who passes King Mark
    in might and power?
    If a noble knight
    like Tristan serves him,
    who would not but feel elated,
    so fairly to be mated.

ISOLDA (*gazing vacantly before her*).
    Glorious knight!
    And I must near him
    loveless ever languish!
    How can I support such anguish?

BRANGÆNA. What's this, my lady?
    loveless thou?

---

kehrt' er kühn zurück
auf stolzem Schiff
von hohem Bord,
Irland's Erbin
begehrt er zur Eh'
für Kornwall's müden König,
für Marke, seinen Ohm.
Da Morold lebte,
wer hätt' es gewagt,
uns je solche Schmach zu bieten?
Für der zinspflichtigen
Kornen Fürsten
um Irland's Krone zu werben?
O wehe mir!
Ich ja war's,
die heimlich selbst
die Schmach sich schuf!
Das rächende Schwert,
statt es zu schwingen,
machtlos liess ich's fallen:—
nun dien' ich dem Vasallen.
Fluch dir, Verruchter!
Fluch deinem Haupt!
Rache, Tod!
Tod uns Beiden!

BRANGÆNE (*mit ungestümer Zärtlichkeit sich auf* ISOLD *stürzend*). O Süsse! Traute!
    Theure! Holde!
    Gold'ne Herrin!
    Lieb' Isolde!
    Hör' mich! Komme!
    Setz' dich her!—

    (*Sie zieht* ISOLDE *allmählich nach dem Ruhebett.*)
    Welcher Wahn!
    Welch eitles Zürnen?
    Wie magst du dich bethören,
    nicht hell zu sehn noch hören!
    Was je Herr Tristan
    dir verdankte,
    sag', konnt' er's höher lohnen,
    als mit der herrlichsten der Kronen?
    So dient' er treu
    dem edlen Ohm,
    dir gab er der Welt
    begehrlichsten Lohn
    dem eig'nen Erbe,
    echt und edel,
    entsagt' er zu deinen Füssen,
    als Königin dich zu grüssen.
        (ISOLDE *wendet sich ab.*)
    und mildem Muth,
    dir zum Gemahl,
    wie wolltest du die Wahl doch schelten,
    muss er nicht werth dir gelten?
    Von edler Art
    Und mildem Muth,
    wer gliche dem Mann
    an Macht und Glanz?
    Dem ein hehrster Held
    so treulich dient,
    wer möchte sein Glück nicht theilen,
    als Gattin bei ihm weilen?

ISOLDE (*starr vor sich hinblickend*).
    Ungeminnt
    den hehrsten Mann
    stets mir nah' zu sehen,—
    wie könnt' ich die Qual bestehen!

BRANGÆNE. Was wähnst du Arge?
    Ungeminnt?—

(*Approaching coaxingly and kissing* ISOLDA.)
Where lives there a man
would not love thee?
Who could see Isolda
And not sink
at once into bondage blest?
And if e'en it could be
any were cold,
did any magic
draw him from thee,
I'd bring the false one
back to bondage,
And bind him in links of love.—

(*Secretiy and confidentially, close to* ISOLDA.)

Mindest thou not
thy mother's arts?
Think you that she
who'd mastered those
would have sent me o'er the sea,
without assistance for thee?

ISOLDA (*darkly*). My mother's rede
I mind aright,
and highly her magic
arts I hold:—
Vengeance they wreak for wrongs,
rest give to wounded spirits.—
Yon casket hither bear.

BRANGÆNA. It holds a balm for thee.—

(*She brings forward a small golden coffer, opens it, and
points to its contents.*)
Thy mother place inside it
her subtle magic potions.
There's salve for sickness
or for wounds,
and antidotes
for deadly drugs.—
(*She takes a bottle.*)
The helpfullest draught
I hold in here

ISOLDA. Not so, I know a better.
I make a mark
to know it again—
This draught 'tis I would drain.
(*Seizes flask and shows it.*)

BRANGÆNA (*recoiling in horror*).
The draught of death!

(ISOLDA *has risen from the sofa and now hears with increasing dread the cries of the sailors.*)

VOICES OF THE CREW (*without*).
"Ho! heave ho! hey!
Reduce the sail!
The mainsail in!
Ho! heave ho! hey!"

ISOLDA. Our journey has been swift.
Woe's me! Near to the land!

SCENE IV

KURVENAL *boisterously enters through the curtains.*)

KURVENAL. Up, up, ye ladies!
Look alert!
Straight bestir you!
Loiter not—here is the land!—
To dame Isolda

(*Sie nähert sich* ISOLDEN *schmeichelnd und kosend.*)
Wo lebte der Mann,
der dich nicht liebte?
Der Isolde säh',
und in Isolden
selig nicht ganz verging'?
Doch, der dir erkoren,
wär' er so kalt,
zög' ihn von dir
ein Zauber ab,
den bösen wüsst' ich
bald zu binden;
ihn bannte der Minne Macht.—

(*Mit geheimnissvoller Zutraulichkeit ganz nah zu*
ISOLDEN.)
Kennst du der Mutter
Künste nicht?
Wahnst du, die Alles
klug erwägt,
ohne Rath in fremdes Land
hätt' sie mit dir mich entsandt?

ISOLDE (*düster*). Der Mutter Rath
gemahnt mich recht;
willkommen preis' ich
ihre Kunst:—
Rache für den Verrath,—
Ruh' in der Noth dem Herzen!—
Den Schrein dort bring' mir her.

BRANGÆNE. Er birgt, was Heil dir frommt.

(*Sie holt eine kleine goldne Truhe herbei, öffnet sie, und
deutet auf ihren Inhalt.*)
So reihte sie die Mutter,
die mächt'gen Zaubertränke.
Für Weh' und Wunden
Balsam hier;
für böse Gifte
Gegen-Gift:—
(*Sie zieht ein Fläschchen hervor.*)
den hehrsten Trank,
ich halt' ihn hier.

ISOLDE. Du irr'st, ich kenn' ihn besser;
ein starkes Zeichen
schnitt ich ein:—
der Trank ist's, der mir frommt.
(*Sie ergreift ein Fläschchen und zeigt es.*)

BRANGÆNE (*entsetzt zurückweichend*).
Der Todestrank!

(ISOLDE *hat sich vom Ruhebett erhoben, und vernimmt
jetzt mit wachsendem Schrecken den Ruf des Schiffsvolkes:*)

RUF DES SCHIFFSVOLKES (*von aussen*).
"He! ha! ho! he!
Am Untermast
die Segel ein!
He! ha! ho! he!"

ISOLDE. Das deutet schnelle Fahrt.
Weh' mir! Nahe das Land!

VIERTE SCENE

[*Durch die Vorhänge tritt mit Ungestüm* KURWENAL
herein.]

KURWENAL. Auf, auf! Ihr Frauen!
Frisch und froh!
Rasch gerüstet!
Fertig, hurtig und flink!—
Und Frau Isolden

says the servant
of Tristan,
our hero true:—
Behold our flag is flying!
it waveth landwards aloft:
in Mark's ancestral castle
may our approach be seen.
So, dame Isolda,
he prays to hasten,
for land straight to prepare her,
that thither he may bear her.

ISOLDA (*who has at first cowered and shuddered on hearing the message, now speaks calmly and with dignity*).
My greeting take
unto your lord
and tell him what I say now:
Should he assist to land me
and to King Mark would he hand me,
unmeet and unseemly
were his act,
the while my pardon
was not won
for trespass black and base:
So bid him seek my grace.

    (KURVENAL *makes a gesture of defiance.*)
Now mark me well
This message take:—
Nought will I yet prepare me,
that he to land may bear me;
I will not by him be landed,
nor unto King Mark be handed
ere granting forgiveness
and forgetfulness,
which 'tis seemly
he should seek:—
for all his trespass base
I tender him my grace.

KURVENAL. Be assured,
I'll bear your words:
we'll see what he will say!
               (*He retires quickly.*)

SCENE V

ISOLDA (*hurries to* BRANGÆNA *and embraces her vehemently*). Now farewell, Brangæna!
Greet ev'ry one,
Greet my father and mother!

BRANGÆNA. What now? what mean'st thou?
Wouldst thou flee?
And where must I then follow?

ISOLDA (*checking herself suddenly*). Here I remain:
heard you not?
Tristan will I await.—
I trust in thee
to aid in this:
prepare the true
cup of peace:
thou mindest how it is made.

BRANGÆNA. What meanest thou?

ISOLDA (*taking a bottle from the coffer*). That it is!
From the flask go pour
this philtre out;
yon golden goblet 'twill fill.

BRANGÆNA (*filled with terror receiving the flask*).
Trust I my wits?

ISOLDA. Wilt thou be true?

BRANGÆNA. The draught—for whom?

sollt' ich sagen
von Held Tristan,
meinem Herrn:—
vom Mast der Freude Flagge
sie wehe lustig in's Land;
in Marke's Königschlosse
mach' sie ihr Nahen bekannt.
Drum Frau Isolde
bät' er eilen,
für's Land sich zu bereiten,
dass er sie könnt' geleiten.

ISOLDE (*nachdem sie zuerst bei der Meldung in Schaue zusammengefahren, gefasst und mit Würde*).
Herrn Tristan bringe
meinen Gruss,
und meld' ihm was ich sage.—
Sollt' ich zur Seit' ihm gehen,
vor König Marke zu stehen,
nicht möcht' es nach Zucht
und Fug gescheh'n,
empfing' ich Sühne
nicht zuvor
für ungesühnte Schuld:
drum such' er meine Huld.—

    (KURWENAL *macht eine trotzige Gebärde.*)
Du merke wohl
und meld' es gut!—
Nicht wollt' ich mich bereiten,
an's Land ihn zu begleiten;
nicht werd' ich zur Seit' ihm gehen,
vor König Marke zu stehen,
begehrte Vergessen
und Vergeben
nach Zucht und Fug
er nicht zuvor
für ungebüsste Schuld:—
die böt' ihm meine Huld.

KURWENAL. Sicher wisst,
das sag' ich ihm:
nun harrt, wie er mich hört!
               (*Er geht schnell zurück.*)

FÜNFTE SCENE

ISOLDE (*eilt auf* BRANGÆNE *zu und umarmt sie heftig*).
Nun leb' wohl, Brangäne!
Grüss' mir die Welt,
grüsse mir Vater und Mutter!

BRANGÆNE. Was ist's! Was sinnst du?
Wolltest du fliehen?
Wohin sollt' ich dir folgen?

ISOLDE (*schnell gefasst*). Hörtest du nicht?
Hier bleib' ich;
Tristan will ich erwarten.—
Treu befolg',
was ich befehl',
den Sühne-Trank
rüste schnell,—
du weisst, den ich dir wies.

BRANGÆNE. Und welchen Trank?

ISOLDE (*entnimmt dem Schreine das Fläschchen*).
Diesen Trank!
In die gold'ne Schale
giess' ihn aus;
gefüllt fasst sie ihn ganz.

BRANGÆNE (*voll Grausen das Fläschchen empfangend*
Trau' ich dem Sinn?

ISOLDE. Sei du mir treu!

BRANGÆNE. Der Trank—für wen?

ISOLDA. Him who betrayed!

BRANGÆNA. Tristan!

ISOLDA. Truce he'll drink with me.

BRANGÆNA (*throwing herself at* ISOLDA'S *feet*).
    O horror! Pity thy handmaid!

ISOLDA. Pity thou me,
    false-hearted maid!
    Mindest thou not
    my mother's arts?
    Think you that she
    who'd mastered those
    would have sent thee o'er the sea
    without assistance for me?
    A salve for sickness
    doth she offer
    and antidotes
    for deadly drugs:
    for deepest grief
    and woe supreme
    gave she the draught of death.
    Let Death now give her thanks!

BRANGÆNA (*scarcely able to control herself*). O deep-
    est grief!

ISOLDA. Now, wilt thou obey?

BRANGÆNA. O woe supreme!

ISOLDA. Wilt thou be true?

BRANGÆNA. The draught?

KURVENAL (*entering*). Sir Tristan!

BRANGÆNA *rises, terrified and confused.* ISOLDA *strives
    with immense effort to control herself.*)

ISOLDA (*to Kurvenal*). Sir Tristan may approach!

SCENE VI

KURVENAL *retires again.* BRANGÆNA, *almost beside
herself, turns up the stage.* ISOLDA, *mustering all
her powers of resolution, walks slowly and with dignity towards the sofa, by the head of which she supports herself, turning her eyes firmly towards the
entrance.*]

(TRISTAN *enters, and pauses respectfully at the entrance.*)

ISOLDE. Wer mich betrog,

BRANGÆNE. Tristan?

ISOLDE. Trinke mir Sühne.

BRANGÆNE (*zu* ISOLDE'S *Füssen stürzend*).
    Entsetzen! Schone mich Arme!

ISOLDE (*heftig*). Schone du mich,
    untreue Magd!
    Kennst du der Mutter
    Künste nicht?
    Wähn'st du, die Alles
    klug erwägt,
    ohne Rath in fremdes Land
    hätt' sie mit Dir mich entsandt?
    Für Weh' und Wunden
    gab sie Balsam;
    für böse Gifte
    Gegen-Gift;
    für tiefstes Weh',
    für höchstes Leid—
    gab sie den Todes-Trank.
    Der Tod nun sag' ihr Dank!

BRANGÆNE (*kaum ihrer mächtig*). O tiefstes Weh'!

ISOLDE. Gehorchst du mir nun?

BRANGÆNE. O höchstes Leid!

ISOLDE. Bist du mir treu?

BRANGÆNE. Der Trank?

KURWENAL (*eintretend*). Herr Tristan

(BRANGÆNE *erhebt sich erschrocken und verwirrt;* ISOLDE
    sucht mit furchtbarer Anstrengung sich zu fassen.)

ISOLDE (*zu Kurwenal*). Herr Tristan trete nah.

SECHSTE SCENE

[KURWENAL *geht wieder zurück.* BRANGÆNE, *kaum ihrer
mächtig, wendet sich in den Hintergrund.* ISOLDE
ihr ganzes Gefühl zur Entscheidung zusammenfassena,
schreitet langsam, mit grosser Haltung, dem Ruhebett
zu, auf dessen Kopfende sich stützend sie den Blick
fest dem Eingange zuwendet.*]

(TRISTAN *tritt ein, und bleibt ehrerbietig am Eingange
stehen.*)

TRISTAN. Demand, lady,
     what you will.

ISOLDA. While knowing not
     what my demand is,
     wert thou afraid
     still to fulfil it,
     fleeing my presence thus?

TRISTAN. Honor
     Held me in awe.

ISOLDA. Scant honor hast thou
     shown unto me;
     for, unabashed,
     withheldest thou
     obedience unto my call.

TRISTAN. Obedience 'twas
     forbade me to come.

ISOLDA. But little I owe
     thy lord, methinks,
     if he allows
     ill manners
     unto his own promised bride.

TRISTAN. Begehrt, Herrin,
     was Ihr wünscht.

ISOLDE. Wüsstest du nicht
     was ich begehre,
     da doch die Furcht,
     mir's zu erfüllen,
     fern meinem Blick dich hielt?

TRISTAN. Ehr-Furcht
     hielt mich in Acht.

ISOLDE. Der Ehre wenig
     botest du mir:
     mit off'nem Hohn
     verwehrtest du
     Gehorsam meinem Gebot.

TRISTAN. Gehorsam einzig
     hielt mich in Bann.

ISOLDE. So dankt' ich Geringes
     deinem Herrn,
     rieth dir sein Dienst
     Un-Sitte
     gegen sein eigen Gemahl?

TRISTAN. In our land
    it is the law
    that he who fetches
    home the bride
    should stay afar from her.

ISOLDA. On what account?

TRISTAN. 'Tis the custom.

ISOLDA. Being so careful,
    my lord Tristan,
    another custom
    can you not learn?
    Of enemies friends make:
    for evil acts amends make.

TRISTAN. Who is my foe?

ISOLDA. Find in thy fears!
    Blood-guilt
    gets between us.

TRISTAN. That was absolved.

ISOLDA. Not between us.

TRISTAN. In open field,
    'fore all the folk
    our old feud was abandoned.

ISOLDA. 'Twas not there
    I held Tantris hid
    when Tristan was laid low,
    He stood there brawny,
    bright and brave;
    but in his truce
    I took no part:
    my tongue its silence had learnt.
    When in chambered stillness
    sick he lay
    with the sword I stood
    before him, stern;
    silent—my lips,
    motionless—my hand.
    But that which my hand
    and lips had once vowed,
    I swore in stealth to adhere to:
    lo! now my desire I'm near to.

TRISTAN. What hast thou sworn?

ISOLDA (*quickly*). Vengeance for Morold!

TRISTAN (*quietly*). Mindst thou that?

ISOLDA (*animated*). Dare you to flout me?—
    Was he not my betrothed,
    that noble Irish knight?
    For his sword a blessing I sought;
    for me only he fought.
    When he was murdered
    no honor fell.
    In that heartfelt misery
    my vow was framed;
    if no man remained to right it,
    I, a maid, must needs requite it.—
    Weak and maimed,
    when might was mine,
    why at thy death did I pause?
    Thou shalt know the secret cause.—
    Thy hurts I tended
    that, when sickness ended,
    thou shouldst fall by some man,
    as Isolda's revenge should plan.
    But now attempt
    thy fate to foretell me:
    if their friendship all men do sell thee,
    what foe can seek to fell thee?

TRISTAN. Sitte lehrt
    wo ich gelebt:
    zur Brautfahrt
    der Brautwerber
    meide fern die Braut.

ISOLDE. Aus welcher Sorg'?

TRISTAN. Fragt die Sitte!

ISOLDE. Da du so sittsam,
    mein Herr Tristan,
    auch einer Sitte
    sei nun gemahnt:
    den Feind dir zu sühnen,
    soll er als Freund dich rühmen.

TRISTAN. Und welchen Feind?

ISOLDE. Frag' deine Furcht!
    Blut-Schuld
    schwebt zwischen uns.

TRISTAN. Die ward gesühnt.

ISOLDE. Nicht zwischen uns.

TRISTAN. Im off'nen Feld
    vor allem Volk
    ward Ur-Fehde geschworen.

ISOLDE. Nicht da war's
    wo ich Tantris barg,
    wo Tristan mir verfiel.
    Da stand er herrlich,
    hehr und heil;
    doch was er schwur,
    das schwur ich nicht:—
    zu schweigen hatt' ich gelernt.
    Da in stiller Kammer
    krank er lag,
    mit dem Schwerte stumm
    ich vor ihm stund,
    schwieg—da mein Mund,
    bannt'—ich meine Hand,
    doch was einst mit Hand
    und Mund ich gelobt,
    das schwur ich schweigend zu halten.
    Nun will ich des Eides walten.

TRISTAN. Was schwurt Ihr, Frau?

ISOLDE (*schnell*). Rache für Morold.

TRISTAN (*mässig*). Müh't Euch die?

ISOLDE (*lebhaft*). Wag'st du mir Hohn?—
    Angelobt war er mir,
    der hehre Irenheld;
    seine Waffen hatt' ich geweiht,
    für mich zog er in Streit.
    Da er gefallen,
    fiel meine Ehr';
    in des Herzens Schwere
    schwur ich den Eid,
    würd' ein Mann den Mord nicht sühnen,
    wollt' ich Magd mich des' erkühnen.—
    Siech und matt
    in meiner Macht,
    warum ich dich da nicht schlug,
    das sag' dir mit leichtem Fug:—
    ich pflag des Wunden,
    dass den heil Gesunden
    rächend schlüge der Mann,
    der Isolden ihn abgewann.—
    Dein Loos nun selber
    magst du dir sagen:
    da die Männer sich all' ihm vertragen,
    wer muss nun Tristan schlagen?

TRISTAN (*pale and gloomy, offers her his sword*). If
     thou so lovedst this lord,
     then lift once more my sword,
     nor from thy purpose refrain;
     let the weapon not fail again.

ISOLDA. Put up thy sword
     which once I swung,
     when vengeful rancor
     my bosom wrung,
     when thy masterful eyes
     did ask me straight
     whether King Mark
     might seek me for mate.
     The sword harmless descended.—
     Drink, let our strife be ended!

(ISOLDA *beckons* BRANGÆNA. *She trembles and hesitates
to obey.* ISOLDA *commands her with a more imperious gesture.* BRANGÆNA *sets about preparing the
drink.*)

VOICES OF THE CREW (*without*). Ho! heave ho! hey!
     Reduce the sail!
     The foresail in!
     Ho! heave ho! hey!

TRISTAN (*starting from his gloomy brooding*). Where
     are we?

ISOLDA. Near to shore.
     Tristan, is warfare ended?
     Hast not a word to offer?

TRISTAN (*darkly*). Concealment's mistress
     makes me silent:
     I know what she conceals,
     conceal, too, more than she knows.

ISOLDA. Thy silence nought
     but feigning I deem.
     Friendship wilt thou still deny?
                    (*Renewed cries of the Sailors.*)

(*At an impatient sign from* ISOLDA BRANGÆNA *hands
     her the filled cup.*)

ISOLDA (*advancing with the cup to* TRISTAN, *who gazes
     immovably into her eyes*).
     Thou hear'st the cry?
     The shore's in sight:
     we must ere long   (*with slight scorn*)
     stand by King Mark together.

SAILORS (*without*). Haul the warp!
     Anchor down!

TRISTAN (*starting wildly*). Down with the anchor!
     Her stern to the stream!
     The sails a-weather the mast!
                    (*He takes the cup from* ISOLDA.)
     I know the Queen
     of Ireland well,
     unquestioned are
     her magic arts:
     the balsam cured me
     which she brought;
     now bid me quaff the cup,
     that I may quite recover.
     Heed to my all-
     atoning oath,
     which in return I tended
     Tristan's honor—
     highest truth!
     Tristan's anguish—
     brave distress!
     Traitor spirit,

TRISTAN (*bleich und düster, reicht ihr sein Schwert hin*).
     War Morold dir so werth,
     nun wieder nimm das Schwert,
     und führ' es sicher und fest,
     dass du nicht dir's entfalten lässt.

ISOLDE. Wahre dein Schwert!
     Da einst ich's schwang,
     als mir die Rache
     im Busen rang,
     als dein messender Blick
     mein Bild sich stahl,
     ob ich Herrn Marke
     taug' als Gemahl:
     das Schwert—da liess ich's sinken.
     Nun lass' uns Sühne trinken!—

(*Sie winkt* BRANGÆNE. *Diese schaudert zusammen,
schwankt und zögert in ihrer Bewegung.* ISOLDE *treibt
sie durch gesteigerte Gebärde an. Als* BRANGÆNE *zur
Bereitung des Tranks sich anlässt, vernimmt man den
Ruf des Schiffsvolkes.*)

SCHIFFSVOLK (*von aussen*). Ho! he! ha! he!
     Am Obermast
     die Segel ein!
     Ho! he! ha! he!

TRISTAN (*aus finst'rem Brüten auffahrend*).
     Wo sind wir?

ISOLDE. Hart am Ziel.
     Tristan, gewinn' ich Sühne?
     Was hast du mir zu sagen?

TRISTAN (*düster*). Des Schweigens Herrin
     heisst mich schweigen:
     fass' ich, was sie verschwieg,
     verschweig' ich, was sie nicht fasst.

ISOLDE. Dein Schweigen fass' ich,
     weichst du mir aus.
     Weigerst du Sühne mir?

(*Neue Schiffsrufe. Auf* ISOLDE's *ungeduldigen Wink
reicht* BRANGÆNE *ihr die gefüllte Trinkschale.*)

ISOLDE (*mit dem Becher zu* TRISTAN *tretend, der ihr
     starr in die Augen blickt*).
     Du hörst den Ruf?
     Wir sind am Ziel:
     in kurzer Frist
     stehn wir—   (*mit leisem Hohne.*)
     vor König Marke.

SCHIFFSRUF (*aussen*). Auf das Tau!
     Anker ab!

TRISTAN (*wild auffahrend*). Los den Anker!
     Das Steuer dem Strom!
     Den Winden Segel und Mast!
     (*Er entreisst* ISOLDEN *ungestüm die Trinkschale.*)
     Wohl kenn' ich Irlands
     Königin,
     und ihrer Künste
     Wunderkraft:
     den Balsam nützt' ich,
     den sie bot;
     den Becher nehm' ich nun,
     dass ganz ich heut' genese!
     Und achte auch
     des 'Sühne-Eid's,
     den ich zum Dank dir sage.—
     Tristan's Ehre—
     höchste Treu':
     Tristan's Elend—
     kühnster Trotz.
     Trug des Herzens;

dawn-illumined!
Endless trouble's
only truce!
Oblivion's kindly draught,
with rapture thou art quaff'd!
(*He lifts the cup and drinks.*)

ISOLDA. Betrayed e'en here?
I must halve it!—
(*She wrests the cup from his hand.*)
Betrayer, I drink to thee!

[*She drinks, and then throws away the cup. Both, seized
with shuddering, gaze with deepest emotion, but im-
movable demeanor, into one another's eyes, in which
the expression of defiance to death fades and melts
into the glow of passion. Trembling seizes them, they
convulsively clutch their hearts and pass their hands
over their brows. Their glances again seek to meet,
sink in confusion, and once more turn with growing
longing upon one another.*]

ISOLDA (*with trembling voice*). Tristan!

TRISTAN (*overpowered*). Isolda!

ISOLDA (*sinking upon his breast*). Traitor beloved!

TRISTAN. Woman divine!
(*He embraces her with ardor. They remain in a silent
embrace.*)

ALL THE MEN (*without*). Hail! Hail!
Hail our monarch!
Hail to Mark, the king!

BRANGÆNA (*who, filled with confusion and horror, has
leaned over the side with averted face, now turns to
behold the pair locked in their close embrace, and
rushes to the front, wringing her hands in despair*).

Woe's me! Woe's me!
Endless mis'ry
I have wrought
instead of death!
Dire the deed
of my dull fond heart:
it cries aloud to heav'n!
(*They start from their embrace.*)

TRISTAN (*bewildered*). What troubled dream
of Tristan's honor?

ISOLDA. What troubled dream
Of Isolda's shame?

TRISTAN. Have I then lost thee?

ISOLDA. Have I repulsed thee?

TRISTAN. Fraudulent magic,
framing deceit!

BOTH. Languishing passion,
longing and growing,
love ever yearning,
loftiest glowing!
Rapture confess'd
rides in each breast!
Isolda! Tristan!
Tristan! Isolda!
World, I can shun thee
my love is won me!
Thou'rt my thought, all above:
highest delight of love!

Traum der Ahnung:
ew'ger Trauer
einz'ger Trost,
Vergessens güt'ger Trank!
Dich trink' ich sonder Wank.
(*Er setzt an und trinkt.*)

ISOLDE. Betrug auch hier?
Mein die Hälfte!—
(*Sie entwindet ihm den Becher.*)
Verräther, ich trink' sie dir!

[*Sie trinkt. Dann wirft sie die Schale fort.—Beide,
von Schauer erfasst, blicken sich mit höchster Aufregung, doch mit starrer Haltung, unverwandt in die
Augen, in deren Ausdruck der Todestrotz bald der
Liebesgluth weicht.—Zittern ergreift sie. Sie fassen
sich krampfhaft an das Herz,—und führen die Hand
weiter an die Stirn.—Dann suchen sie sich wieder
mit dem Blicke, senken ihn verwirrt, und heften ihn
von Neuem mit steigender Sehnsucht auf einander.*]

ISOLDE (*mit bebender Stimme*). Tristan!

TRISTAN (*überströmend*). Isolde!

ISOLDE (*an seine Brust sinkend*). Treuloser Holder!

TRISTAN. Seligste Frau!—
(*Er umfasst sie mit Gluth. Sie verbleiben in stummer
Umarmung.*)

ALLE MÆNNER (*aussen*). Heil! Heil!
König Marke!
König Marke, Heil!

BRANGÆNE (*die, mit abgewandtem Gesicht, voll Verwirrung und Schauder sich über Bord gelehnt hatte,
wendet sich jetzt dem Anblick des in Liebesumar-
mung versunkenen Paares zu, und stürzt hände-
ringend, voll Verzweiflung, in den Vordergrund*).
Wehe! Wehe!
Unabwendbar
ewige Noth
für kurzen Tod!
Thör'ger Treue
trugvolles Werk
blüht nun jammernd empor!
(*Sie fahren verwirrt aus der Umarmung auf.*)

TRISTAN (*verwirrt*). Was träumte mir
von Tristan's Ehre?

ISOLDE. Was träumte mir
von Isolde's Schmach?

TRISTAN. Du mir verloren?

ISOLDE. Du mich verstossen?

TRISTAN. Trügenden Zaubers
tückische List!

BEIDE. Sehnender Minne
schwellendes Blühen,
schmachtender Liebe
seliges Glühen!
Jach in der Brust
jauchzende Lust!
Isolde! Tristan!
Tristan! Isolde!
Welten-entronnen
du mir gewonnen!
Du mir einzig bewusst,
höchste Liebes-Lust!

SCENE VII

[*The curtains are now drawn wide apart; the whole ship is covered with knights and sailors, who, with shouts of joy, make signs over towards the shore which is now seen to be quite near, with castle-crowned cliffs. TRISTAN and ISOLDA remain absorbed in mutual contemplation, perceiving nothing that is passing.*]

BRANGÆNA (*to the women, who at her bidding ascend from below*). Quick—the mantle!
the royal robe!—

(*Rushing between* TRISTAN *and* ISOLDA.)
Up, hapless ones!
See where we are!
(*She places the royal mantle on* ISOLDA, *who notices nothing.*)

ALL THE MEN. Hail! Hail!
Hail our monarch!
Hail to Mark the king!

KURVENAL (*advancing gaily*). Hail, Tristan,
knight of good hap!
Behold King Mark approaching,
in a bark
with brave attendance.
Gladly he stems the tide,
coming to seek his bride.

TRISTAN (*looking up in bewilderment*). Who comes?

KURVENAL. The king 'tis.

TRISTAN. What king mean you?

(KURVENAL *points over the side.* TRISTAN *gazes stupefied at the shore.*)

ALL THE MEN (*waving their hats*). Hail to King Mark!
All hail!

ISOLDA (*bewildered*). What is't, Brangæna?
What are those cries?

BRANGÆNA. Isolda—mistress!
Compose thyself!

ISOLDA. Where am I! living?
What was that draught?

BRANGÆNA (*despairingly*). The love-potion!

ISOLDA (*staring with horror at* TRISTAN). Tristan!

TRISTAN. Isolda!

ISOLDA. Must I live, then?
(*Falls fainting upon his breast.*)

BRANGÆNA (*to the women*). Look to your lady!

TRISTAN. O rapture fraught with cunning!
O fraud with bliss o'er-running!

ALL THE MEN (*in a general burst of acclamation*).
Hail to King Mark!
Cornwall, hail!

[*People have clambered over the ship's side, others have extended a bridge, and the aspect of all indicates the immediate arrival of the expected ones, as the curtain falls.*]

SIEBENTE SCENE

[*Die Vorhänge werden weit auseinander gerissen. Das ganze Schiff ist von Rittern und Schiffsleuten erfüllt, die jubelnd über Bord winken, dem Ufer zu, das man, mit einer hohen Felsenburg gekrönt, nahe erblickt. TRISTAN und ISOLDE bleiben, in ihrem gegenseitigen Anblick verloren, ohne Wahrnehmung des um sie Vorgehenden.*]

BRANGÆNE (*zu den Frauen, die auf ihren Wink aus dem Schiffsraum heraufsteigen*).
Schnell den Mantel,
den Königsschmuck!
(*Zwischen* TRISTAN *und* ISOLDE *stürzend.*)
Unsel'ge! Auf!
Hört wo wir sind.
(*Sie legt* ISOLDEN, *die es nicht gewahrt, den Mantel um.*)

ALLE MÆNNER. Heil! Heil!
König Marke!
König Marke, Heil!

KURWENAL (*lebhaft herantretend*). Heil Tristan!
Glücklicher Held!—
Mit reichem Hofgesinde
dort auf Nachen
naht Herr Marke.
Hei! wie die Fahrt ihn freut,
dass er die Braut sich freit!

TRISTAN (*in Verwirrung aufblickend*). Wer naht?

KURWENAL. Der König?

TRISTAN. Welcher König?

(KURWENAL *deutet über Bord.* TRISTAN *starrt wie sinnlos nach dem Lande.*)

ALLE MÆNNER (*die Hüte schwenkend*).
Heil! König Marke!

ISOLDE (*in Verwirrung, zu* BRANGÆNE).
Was ist's? Brangäne!
Ha! welcher Ruf?

BRANGÆNE. Isolde! Herrin!
Fassung nur heut'!

ISOLDE. Wo bin ich? Leb' ich?
Ha, welcher Trank?

BRANGÆNE (*verzweiflungsvoll*). Der Liebestrank!

ISOLDE (*starrt entsetzt auf* TRISTAN). Tristan!

TRISTAN. Isolde!

ISOLDE. Muss ich leben?
(*Sie stürzt ohnmächtig an seine Brust.*)

BRANGÆNE (*zu den Frauen*). Helft der Herrin!

TRISTAN. O Wonne voller Tücke!
O Trug geweihtes Glücke!

ALLE MÆNNER (*Ausbruch allgemeinen Jauchzens*).
Heil dem König!
Kornwall, Heil!

[*Leute sind über Bord gestiegen, andere haben eine Brücke ausgelegt, und die Haltung Aller deutet auf die soeben bevorstehende Ankunft der Erwarteten, als der Vorhang schnell fällt.*]

ACT II

—

A Garden before ISOLDA'S *Chamber which lies at one side and is approached by steps. Bright and pleasant summer night. At the open door a burning torch is fixed. Sounds of hunting heard.*]

SCENE I

[BRANGÆNA, *on the steps leading to the chamber, is watching the retreat of the still audible hunters. She looks anxiously back into the chamber as* ISOLDA *emerges thence in ardent animation.*]

ISOLDA. Yet do you hear?
    I lost the sound some time.

BRANGÆNA (*listening*) Still do they stay:
    clearly ring the horns.

ISOLDA (*listening*). Fear but deludes
    thy anxious ear;
    by sounds of rustling
    leaves thou'rt deceived,
    aroused by laughter of winds.

BRANGÆNA. Deceived by wild
    desire art thou,
    and but hear'st as would thy will:—
    I still hear the sound of horns.

ISOLDA (*listens*). No sound of horns
    'were so sweet:
    yon fountain's soft
    murmuring current
    moves so quietly hence.
    If horns yet brayed,
    how could I hear that?
    In still night alone
    it laughs on mine ear.
    My lov'd one hides
    in darkness unseen:
    wouldst thou hold from my side my dearest?
    deeming that horns thou hearest?

BRANGÆNA. Thy lov'd one hid—
    oh heed my warning!—
    for him a spy waits by night.
    Listening oft
    I light upon him:
    he lays a secret snare.
    Of Melot oh beware!

ISOLDA. Mean you Sir Melot?
    O, how you mistake!
    Is he not Tristan's
    trustiest friend?
    May my true love not meet me,
    with none but Melot he stays.

BRANGÆNA. What moves me to fear him
    makes thee his friend then?
    Through Tristan to Mark's side
    is Melot's way:
    he sows suspicion's seed.
    And those who have
    to-day on a night-hunt
    so suddenly decided,
    a far nobler game
    than is guessed by thee
    taxes their hunting skill.

II AKT

—

[*Garten mit hohen Bäumen vor dem Gemache* ISOLDE'S, *zu welchem, seitwärts gelegen, Stufen hinaufführen. Helle, anmuthige Sommernacht. An der geöffneten Thüre ist eine brennende Fackel aufgesteckt. Jagdgetön.*]

ERSTE SCENE

[BRANGÆNE, *auf den Stufen am Gemach, späht dem immer entfernter vernehmbaren Jagdtrosse nach. Zu ihr tritt aus dem Gemach, feurig bewegt,* ISOLDE.]

ISOLDE. Hörst du sie noch?
    Mir schwand schon fern der Klang.

BRANGÆNE (*lauschend*). Noch sind sie nah':
    deutlich tönt's daher.

ISOLDE (*lauschend*). Sorgende Furcht
    beirrt dein Ohr;
    dich täuscht des Laubes
    säuselnd Getön',
    das lachend schüttelt der Wind.

BRANGÆNE. Dich täuscht deines Wunsches
    Ungestüm,
    zu vernehmen was du wähnst:—
    ich höre der Hörner Schall.

ISOLDE (*lauschend*). Nicht Hörnerschall
    tönt so hold;
    des Quelles sanft
    rieselnde Welle
    rauscht so wonnig daher;
    wie hört' ich sie,
    tos'ten noch Hörner?
    Im Schweigen der Nacht
    nur lacht mir der Quell:
    der meiner harrt
    in schweigender Nacht,
    als ob Hörner noch nah' dir schallten,
    willst du ihn fern mir halten?

BRANGÆNE. Der deiner harrt—
    O hör' mein Warnen!—
    Des' harren Späher zur Nacht.
    Tückisch lauschend
    treff' ich ihn oft:
    der heimlich euch umgarnt,
    vor Melot seid gewarnt.

ISOLDE. Mein'st du Herrn Melot?
    O wie du dich trüg'st!
    Ist er nicht Tristan's
    treuster Freund?
    Muss mein Trauter mich meiden
    dann weilt er bei Melot allein.

BRANGÆNE. Was mir ihn verdächtig,
    macht dir ihn theuer.
    Von Tristan zu Marke
    ist Melot's Weg:
    dort sä't er üble Saat.
    Die heut' im Rath
    dies nächtliche Jagen
    so eilig schnell beschlossen
    einem edlern Wild,
    als dein Wähnen meint,
    gilt ihre Jägers-List.

ISOLDA. For Tristan's sake
contrived was this scheme
by means of
Melot, in truth:
now would you decry his friendship!
He serves Isolda
better than you
his hand gives help
which yours denies:
what need of such delay?
The signal, Brangæna!
O give the signal!
Tread out the torch's
trembling gleam,
that night may envelop
all with her veil.
Already her peace reigns
o'er hill and hall,
her rapturous awe
the heart does enthral;
allow then the light to fall!
Let but its dread lustre die!
let my beloved draw nigh!

BRANGÆNA. The light of warning suppress not!
Let it remind thee of peril!—
Ah, woe's me! Woe's me!
Fatal folly!
The fell pow'r of that potion!
That I framed
a fraud for once
thy orders to oppose!
Had I been deaf and blind,
thy work
were then thy death:
but thy distress,
thy distraction of grief,
my work
has contrived them, I own it!

ISOLDA. Thy—act?
O foolish girl!
Love's goddess dost thou not know?
nor all her magic arts?
The queen who grants
unquailing hearts,
the witch whose will
the world obeys,
life and death
she holds in her hands,
which of joy and woe are wove?
she worketh hate into love.
The work of death
I took into my own hands;
Love's goddess saw
and gave her good commands
The death—condemned
she claimed as her prey,
planning our fate
in her own way.
How she may bend it,
how she may end it,
what she may make me
wheresoe'er take me,
still hers am I solely;—
so let me obey her wholly

BRANGÆNA. And if by the artful
love-potion's lures
thy light of reason is ravished,
if thou art reckless
when I would warn thee,
this once, oh, wait

ISOLDE. Dem Freunde zu lieb
erfand diese List
aus Mit-Leid
Melot der Freund:
nun willst du den Treuen schelten?
Besser als du
sorgt er für mich;
ihm öffnet er,
was du mir sperr'st;
o spar' mir des Zögerns Noth!
Das Zeichen, Brangäne!
O gieb das Zeichen!
Lösche des Lichtes
letzten Schein!
Dass ganz sie sich neige,
winke der Nacht!
Schon goss sie ihr Schweigen
durch Hain und Haus;
schon füllt sie das Herz
mit wonnigem Graus:
o lösche das Licht nun aus!
Lösche den scheuchenden Schein!
Lass' meinen Liebsten ein!

BRANGÆNE. O lass' die warnende Zünde!
Die Gefahr lass' sie dir zeigen!—
O wehe! Wehe!
Ach mir Armen!
Des unseligen Tranks!
Dass ich untreu
einmal nur
der Herrin Willen trog!
Gehorcht' ich taub und blind,
dein—Werk
war dann der Tod:
doch deine Schmach,
deine schmählichste Noth,
mein—Werk
muss ich Schuld'ge es wissen!

ISOLDE. Dein—Werk?
O thör'ge Magd!
Frau Minne kenntest du nicht?
Nicht ihrer Wunder Macht?
Des kühnsten Muthes
Königin,
des Welten-Werdens
Walterin,
Leben und Tod
sind ihr unterthan,
die sie webt aus Lust und Leid,
in Liebe wandelnd den Neid.
Des Todes Werk
nahm ich's vermessen zur Hand,
Frau Minne hat
meiner Macht es entwandt:
die Todgeweihte
nahm sie in Pfand,
fasste das Werk
in ihre Hand;
wie sie es wendet
wie sie es endet,
was sie mir küret,
wohin mich führet,
ihr ward ich zu eigen:—
nun lass' mich gehorsam zeigen!

BRANGÆNE. Und musste der Minne
tückischer Trank
des Sinnes Licht dir verlöschen;
darfst du nicht sehen,
wenn ich dich warne:
nur heute hör',

and weigh my pleading!
I implore, leave it alight!—
The torch! the torch!
O put it not out this night!

SOLDA. She who causes thus
my bosom's throes,
whose eager fire
within me glows,
whose light upon
my spirit flows,
Love's goddess needs
that night should close;
that brightly she may reign
and shun the torchlight vain.

(*She goes up to the door and takes down the torch.*)
Go watch without—
keep wary guard!
The signal!—
and were it my spirit's spark,
smiling
I'd destroy it and hail the dark!

*She throws the torch to the ground where it slowly dies
out.* BRANGÆNA *turns away, disturbed, and mounts
an outer flight of steps leading to the roof, where she
slowly disappears.* ISOLDA *listens and peers, at first
shyly, towards an avenue. Urged by rising impa-
tience, she then approaches the avenue and looks more
boldly. She signs with her handkerchief, first slightly,
then more plainly, waving it quicker as her impa-
tience increases. A gesture of sudden delight shows
that she has perceived her lover in the distance. She
stretches herself higher and higher, and then, to look
better over the intervening space, hastens back to the
steps, from the top of which she signals again to the
on-comer. As he enters, she springs to meet him.*]

SCENE II

TRISTAN (*rushing in*). Isolda! Beloved!
SOLDA. Tristan! Beloved one!
*Passionate embrace, with which they come down to the
front.*)

BOTH. Art thou mine?
Do I behold thee?
Do I embrace thee?
Can I believe it?
At last! At last!
Here on my breast!
Do I then clasp thee!
Is it thy own self?
Are these thine eyes?
These thy lips?
Here thy hand?
Here thy heart?
Is't I?—Is't thou,
held in my arms?
Am I not duped?
Is it no dream?
O rapture of spirit!
O sweetest, highest,
fairest, strongest,
holiest bliss!
Endless pleasure!
Boundless treasure!
Ne'er to sever!
Never! Never!
Unconceived,
unbelieved,
overpowering

o hör' mein Flehen!
Der Gefahr leuchtendes Licht—
nur heute! heut'!—
die Fackel dort lösche nicht!

ISOLDE. Die im Busen mir
die Gluth entfacht,
die mir das Herze
brennen macht,
die mir als Tag
der Seele lacht,
Frau Minne will,
es werde Nacht,
dass hell sie dorten leuchte,
wo sie dein Licht verscheuchte.—

(*Sie geht zu der Thür und nimmt die Fackel herab.*)
Zur Warte du!
Dort wache treu.
Die Leuchte—
wär's meines Lebens Licht,—
lachend
sie zu löschen zag' ich nicht.

[*Sie wirft die Fackel zur Erde, wo sie allmälig verlöscht.*
BRANGÆNE *wendet sich bestürz tab, um auf einer
äusseren Treppe die Zinne zu ersteigen, wo sie langsam verschwindet.* ISOLDE *lauscht und späht, zunächst
schüchtern, in einen Baumgang. Von wachsendem
Verlangen bewegt, schreitet sie dem Baumgang näher,
und späht zuversichtlicher. Sie winkt mit einem Tuche,
erst seltener, dann häufiger, und endlich, in leiden-
schaftlicher Ungeduld, immer schneller. Eine Gebärde
des plötzlichen Entzückens sagt, dass sie den Freund
in der Ferne gewahr geworden. Sie streckt sich höher,
und höher, und um besser den Raum zu übersehen,
eilt sie zur Treppe zurück, von deren oberster Stufe
sie dem Herannahenden zuwinkt. Als er eintritt,
springt sie ihm entgegen.*]

ZWEITE SCENE

TRISTAN. Isolde! Geliebte!
ISOLDE. Tristan! Geliebter!
(*Stürmische Umarmungen Beider, unter denen sie in
den Vordergrund gelangen.*)

BEIDE. Bist du mein?
Hab' ich dich wieder?
Darf ich dich fassen?
Kann ich mir trauen?
Endlich! Endlich!
An meiner Brust!
Fühl' ich dich wirklich?
Bist du es selbst?
Dies deine Augen?
Dies dein Mund?
Hier deine Hand?
Hier dein Herz?
Bin ich's? Bist du's?
Halt' ich dich fest?
Ist es kein Trug?
Ist es kein Traum?
O Wonne der Seele!
O süsse, hehrste,
kühnste, schönste,
seligste Lust!
Ohne Gleiche!
Ueberreiche!
Ungeahnte,
Ewig! Ewig!
Ungeahnte,
nie gekannte,
überschwänglich

exaltation!
Joy-proclaiming,
bliss-outpouring,
high in heaven,
earth ignoring!
Tristan mine!
Isolda mine!
Tristan!
Isolda!
Mine alone!
Thine alone!
Ever all my own!

TRISTAN. The light! The light!
    O but this light,
    how long 'twas let to burn!
    The sun had sunk,
    the day had fled;
    but all their spite
    not yet was sped:
    the scaring signal
    they set alight,
    before my belov'd one's dwelling,
    my swift approach repelling.

ISOLDA. Thy belov'd one's hand
    lowered the light,
    for Brangæna's fears
    in me roused no fright:
    while Love's goddess gave me aid,
    sunlight a mock I made.
    But the light its fear
    and defeat repaid;
    with thy misdeeds
    a league it made.
    What thou didst see
    in shadowing night,
    to the shining sun
    of kingly might
    must thou straightway surrender,
    that it should
    exist in bright
    bonds of empty splendor.—
    Could I bear it then?
    Could I bear it now?

TRISTAN. O now were we
    to night devoted,
    the dishonest day
    with envy bloated,
    lying, could not mislead,
    though it might part us indeed.
    Its pretentious glows
    and its glamouring light
    are scouted by those
    who worship night.
    All its flickering gleams
    in flashes out-blazing
    blind us no more
    where we are gazing.
    Those who death's night
    boldly survey,
    those who have studied
    her secret way,
    the daylight's falsehoods—
    rank and fame,
    honor and all
    at which men aim—
    to them are no more matter
    than dust which sunbeams scatter,

hoch erhab'ne!
Freude-Jauchzen!
Lust-Entzücken!
Himmel-höchstes
Welt-Entrücken!
Mein Tristan!
Mein' Isolde!
Tristan!
Isolde!
Mein und dein!
Immer ein!
Ewig, ewig ein!

TRISTAN. Das Licht! Das Licht!
    O dieses Licht!
    Wie lang' verlosch es nicht!
    Die Sonne sank,
    der Tag verging;
    doch seinen Neid
    erstickt' er nicht:
    sein scheuchend Zeichen
    zündet er an,
    und steckt's an der Liebsten Thüre,
    dass ich nicht zu ihr führe.

ISOLDE. Doch der Liebsten Hand
    löschte das Licht.
    Wes' die Magd sich wehrte,
    scheut' ich mich nicht:
    in Frau Minne's Macht und Schutz
    bot ich dem Tage Trutz.
    Doch es rächte sich
    der verscheuchte Tag;
    mit deinen Sünden
    Raths er pflag:
    was dir gezeigt
    die dämmernde Nacht,
    an des Taggestirnes
    Königsmacht
    musstest du's übergeben,
    um einsam
    in oder Pracht
    schimmernd dort zu leben.—
    Wie ertrug ich's nur?
    Wie ertrag' ich's noch?

TRISTAN. O! nun waren wir
    Nacht-geweihte:
    der tückische Tag,
    der Neid-bereite,
    trennen konnt' uns sein Trug,
    doch nicht mehr täuschen sein Lug.
    Seine eitle Pracht,
    seinen prahlenden Schein
    verlacht, wem die Nacht
    den Blick geweih't:
    seines flackernden Lichtes
    flüchtige Blitze
    blenden nicht mehr
    uns're Blicke.
    Wer des Todes Nacht
    liebend erschau't,
    wem sie ihr tief
    Geheimniss vertraut,
    des Tages Lügen,
    Ruhm und Ehr',
    Macht und Gewinn,
    so schimmernd hehr,
    wie eitler Staub der Sonnen
    sind sie vor dem zerronnen.

In the daylight's visions thronging
only abides one longing;
we yearn to hie
to holy night,
where, unending,
only true,
Love extendeth delight!

In des Tages eitlem Wähnen
bleibt ihm ein einzig Sehnen,
das Sehnen hin
zur heil'gen Nacht,
wo ur-ewig,
einzig wahr
Liebeswonne ihm lacht.

TRISTAN *draws* ISOLDA *gently aside to a flowery bank,
sinks on his knee before her and rests his head on
her arm.*)

(TRISTAN *zieht* ISOLDE *sanft zur Seite auf eine Blumenbank nieder, senkt sich vor ihr auf die Knie und
schmiegt sein Haupt in ihren Arm.*)

lie, . . thou'rt . my world, thine am I . .
heut, *selbst . . dann bin ich die Welt .*

un-daunt-ed by falsehoods which we de - fy. Thou'rt my world, thine am I . .
zu täu-schendem Wahn ent - ge - gen - ge - stellt, selbst dann oin ich die Welt

. . Won - drous rap - ture weav - ing cher - ish'd vis - ions a - chiev -
. . Won - ne - hehr - stes We - ben lie be hei - lig - stes Le -

. . ing, Ne'er daunt-ed by day light's beam be our un - dy - ing dream.
. . ben Nie wie - der er - war - chens wahn - los hold be - wuss - ter Wunsch.

(TRISTAN *and* ISOLDA *sink into oblivious ecstasy, reposing on the flowery bank close together.*)	(TRISTAN *und* ISOLDE *versinken wie in gänzliche Entrücktheit, in der sie, Haupt an Haupt auf die Blumenbank zurückgelehnt, verweilen.*)

BRANGÆNA (*from the turret, unseen*). Long I watch
    alone by night:
    ye enwrapt
    in love's delight,
    heed my boding
    voice aright.
    I forewarn you
    woe is near;
    waken to
    my words of fear.
    Have a care!
    Have a care!
    Swiftly night doth wear!

BRANGÆNE (*unsichtbar, von der Höhe der Zinne*).
    Einsam wachend
    in der Nacht,
    wem der Traum
    der Liebe lacht,
    hab' der Einen
    Ruf in Acht,
    die den Schläfern
    Schlimmes ahnt,
    bange zum
    Erwachen mahnt.
    Habet Acht!
    Habet Acht!
    Bald entweicht die Nacht.

ISOLDA. List, belovéd!

ISOLDE. Lausch', Geliebter!

TRISTAN. Let me die thus!

TRISTAN. Lass' mich sterben!

ISOLDA (*slowly raising herself a little*).
    Envious watcher!

ISOLDE (*allmälig sich ein wenig erhebend*).
    Neid'sche Wache!

TRISTAN (*remaining in reclining position*). I'll ne'er
    waken.

TRISTAN (*zurückgelehnt bleibend*). Die erwachen!

ISOLDE. But the Day
    must dawn and rouse thee?

ISOLDE. Doch der Tag
    muss Tristan wecken?

TRISTAN (*raising his head slightly*). Let the Day
    to Death surrender!

TRISTAN (*ein wenig das Haupt erhebend*).
    Lass' den Tag
    dem Tode weichen!

ISOLDA. Day and Death
 will both engender
 feud against
 our passion tender.
TRISTAN (*drawing* ISOLDA *gently towards him with expressive action*). O might we then
 together die,
 each the other's
 own for aye!
 never fearing,
 never waking,
 blest delights
 of love partaking,—
 each to each be given,
 in love alone our heaven!
ISOLDA (*gazing up at him in thoughtful ecstasy*).
 O might we then
 together die!
TRISTAN. Each the other's—
ISOLDA. Own for aye,—
TRISTAN. Never fearing—
ISOLDA. Never waking—
TRISTAN. Blest delights
 of love partaking—
ISOLDA. Each to each be given;
 in love alone our heaven.
(ISOLDA, *as if overcome, droops her head on his breast.*)

BRANRÆNA'S VOICE (*as before*).
 Have a care!
 Have a care!
 Night yields to daylight's glare.
TRISTAN (*bends smilingly to* ISOLDA).
 Shall I listen?
ISOLDA (*looking fondly up at* TRISTAN).
 Let me die thus!
TRISTAN. Must I waken?
ISOLDA. Nought shall wake me!
TRISTAN. Must not daylight
 dawn, and rouse me?
ISOLDA. Let the Day
 to Death surrender!
TRISTAN. May thus the Day's
 evil threats be defied?
ISOLDA (*with growing enthusiasm*).
 From its thraldom let us fly.
TRISTAN. And shall not its dawn
 be dreaded by us?
ISOLDA (*rising with a grand gesture*).
 Night will shield us for aye!
(TRISTAN *follows her; they embrace in fond exaltation.*)

BOTH. O endless Night!
 blissful Night!
 glad and glorious
 lover's Night!
 Those whom thou holdest,
 lapped in delight,
 how could e'en the boldest
 unmoved endure thy flight?
 How to take it,
 how to break it,—
 joy existent,
 sunlight distant.
 Far from mourning,
 sorrow-warning,
 fancies spurning,
 softly yearning,
 fear expiring,
 sweet desiring!
 Anguish flying,

ISOLDE. Tag und Tod
 mit gleichen Streichen
 sollten uns're
 Lieb erreichen?
TRISTAN (*zieht* ISOLDE, *mit bedeutungsvoller Gebärde sanft an sich*). So stürben wir,
 um ungetrennt,
 ewig einig,
 ohne End',
 ohn' Erwachen,
 ohne Bangen,
 namenlos
 in Lieb' umfangen,
 ganz uns selbst gegeben,
 der Liebe nur zu leben.
ISOLDE (*wie in sinnender Entrücktheit zu ihm auf blickend*). So stürben wir,
 um ungetrennt—
TRISTAN. Ewig einig—
ISOLDE. Ohne End'—
TRISTAN. Ohn' Erwachen—
ISOLDE. Ohne Bangen—
TRISTAN. Namenlos
 in Lieb' umfangen—
ISOLDE. Ganz uns selbst gegeben,
 der Liebe nur zu leben!
(ISOLDE *neigt, wie überwältigt, das Haupt an seine Brust.*)

BRANRÆNE (*wie vorher*). Habet Acht!
 Habet Acht!
 Schon weicht dem Tag die Nacht.
TRISTAN (*lächelnd zu* ISOLDE *geneigt*).
 Soll ich lauschen?
ISOLDE. Lass' mich sterben!
TRISTAN. Muss ich wachen?
ISOLDE. Nie erwachen!
TRISTAN. Soll der Tag
 noch Tristan wecken?
ISOLDE. Lass' den Tag
 dem Tode weichen!
TRISTAN. Des Tages Dräuen
 trotzen wir so?
ISOLDE (*mit wachsender Begeisterung*).
 Seinen Trug ewig zu fliehn.
TRISTAN. Sein dämmernder Schein
 verscheuchte uns nie?
ISOLDE (*mit grosser Gebärde ganz sich erhebend*).
 Ewig währ' uns die Nacht!
(TRISTAN *folgt ihr, sie umfangen sich in schwärmerischer Begeisterung.*)

BEIDE. O süsse Nacht!
 Ew'ge Nacht!
 Hehr erhab'ne,
 Liebes-Nacht!
 Wen du umfangen,
 Wem du gelacht,
 wie—wär' ohne Bangen
 aus dir er je erwacht?
 Wie es fassen?
 Wie sie lassen,
 diese Wonne,
 fern der Sonne,
 fern der Tage
 Trennungs-Klage?
 Ohne Wähnen
 sanftes Sehnen,
 ohne Bangen
 süss Verlangen,
 ohne Wehen

gladly dying;
no more pining,
night-enshrining,
ne'er divided
whate'er betided,
side by side
still abide
in realms of space unmeasured,
vision blest and treasured!
Thou Isolda,
Tristan I;
no more Tristan,
no more Isolda.
Never spoken,
never broken,
newly sighted,
newly lighted,
endless ever
all our dream,
in our bosoms gleam
love delights supreme!

hehr Vergehen,
ohne Schmachten
hold Umnachten;
ohne Scheiden,
ohne Meiden,
traut allein,
ewig heim,
in ungemess'nen Räumen,
übersel'ges Träumen.
Du Isolde,
Tristan ich,
nicht mehr Tristan,
nicht Isolde;
ohne Nennen,
ohne Trennen,
neu Erkennen,
neu Entbrennen;
endlos ewig
ein-bewusst:
heiss erglühter Brust
höchste Liebes-Lust!

SCENE III

[BRANGÆNA *utters a piercing cry.* TRISTAN *and* ISOLDA *remain in their absorbed state.* KURVENAL *rushes in with drawn sword.*]

KURVENAL. Save yourself, Tristan!

[*He looks fearfully off behind him.* MARK, MELOT, *and courtiers, in hunting dress, come swiftly up the avenue and pause in the foreground in consternation before the lovers.* BRANGÆNA *at the same time descends from the roof and hastens towards* ISOLDA. *The latter in involuntary shame leans on the flowery bank with averted face.* TRISTAN *with an equally unconscious action stretches his mantle wide out with one arm, so as to conceal* ISOLDA *from the gaze of the new-comers. In this position he remains for some time, turning a changeless look upon the men, who gaze at him in varied emotion. The morning dawns.*]

TRISTAN. The dreary day—
   its last time comes!

MELOT (*to Mark*). Now say to me, my sov'reign,
   was my impeachment just?
   I staked my head thereon:
   now is the pledge redeemed?
   Behold him in
   the very act:
   honor and fame,
   faithfully I
   have saved from shame for thee.

MARK (*deeply moved, with trembling voice*). Hast thou
      preserved them?
   Say'st thou so?—
   See him there,
   the truest of all true hearts!
   Look on him
   the faithfulest of friends,
   His offence
   so black and base
   fills my heart
   with anguish and disgrace
   Tristan traitor,
   what hope stayeth
   that the honor
   he betrayeth
   should by Melot's rede
   rest to me indeed?

DRITTE SCENE

[BRANGÆNE *stösst einen gellenden Schrei aus.* TRISTAN *und* ISOLDE *bleiben in verzückter Stellung.* KURWENAL *stürzt mit entblösstem Schwert herein.*]

KURWENAL. Rette dich, Tristan!

[*Er blickt mit Entsetzen hinter sich in die Scene zurück.* MARKE, MELOT *und Hofleute* (*in Jägertracht*) *kommen aus dem Baumgange lebhaft nach dem Vordergrunde und halten entsetzt der Gruppe der Liebenden gegenüber an.* BRANRÆNE *kommt zugleich von der Zinne herab, und stürzt auf* ISOLDE *zu. Diese, von unwillkürlicher Scham ergriffen, lehnt sich mit abgewandtem Gesichte auf die Blumenbank.* TRISTAN, *in ebenfalls unwillkürlicher Bewegung, streckt mit dem einen Arme den Mantel breit aus, so dass er* ISOLDE *vor den Blicken der Ankommenden verdeckt. In dieser Stellung verbleibt er längere Zeit, unbeweglich den starren Blick auf die Männer gerichtet, die in verschiedener Bewegung die Augen auf ihn heften.—Morgendämmerung.*]

TRISTAN. Der öde Tag—
   zum letzten Mal!

MELOT (*zu Marke*). Das sollst du, Herr, mir sagen,
   ob ich ihn recht verklagt?
   Das dir zum Pfand ich gab,
   ob ich mein Haupt gewahrt?
   Ich zeigt' ihn dir
   in off'ner That:
   Namen und Ehr'
   hab' ich getreu
   vor Schande dir bewahrt.

MARKE (*nach tiefer Erschütterung, mit bebender Stimme*)
      Thatest du's wirklich?
   Wähnst du das?—
   Sieh ihn dort,
   den treu'sten aller Treuen;
   blick' auf ihn,
   den freundlichsten der Freunde;
   seiner Treue
   frei'ste That
   traf mein Herz
   mit feindlichstem Verrath.
   Trog mich Tristan,
   sollt' ich hoffen,
   was sein Trügen
   mir getroffen,
   sei durch Melot's Rath
   redlich mir bewahrt?

TRISTAN (*with convulsive violence*). Daylight phantoms—
  morning visions
  empty and vain—
  Avaunt! Begone!

MARK (*in deep emotion*). This—blow.
  Tristan, to me?
  Where now has truth fled,
  if Tristan can betray?
  Where now are faith
  and friendship fair,
  when from the fount of faith,
  my Tristan, they are gone?
  The buckler Tristan
  once did don,
  where is that shield
  of virtue now?
  when from my friends it flies,
  and Tristan's honor dies?

(TRISTAN *slowly lowers his eyes to the ground. His
features express increasing grief while* MARK *continues.*)
  Why hast thou noble
  service done,
  and honor, fame
  and potent might
  amassed for Mark, thy king?
  Must honor, fame,
  power and might,
  must all thy noble
  service done
  be paid with Mark's dishonor?
  Seemed the reward
  too slight and scant
  that what thou hast won him—
  realms and riches—
  thou art the heir unto, all?
  When childless he lost
  once a wife,
  he loved thee so
  that ne'er again
  did Mark desire to marry.
  When all his subjects,
  high and low,
  demands and pray'rs,
  on him did press
  to choose himself a consort—
  a queen to give the kingdom,
  when thou thyself
  thy uncle urged
  that what the court
  and country pleaded
  well might be conceded,
  opposing high and low,
  opposing e'en thyself,
  with kindly cunning
  still he refused,
  till, Tristan, thou didst threaten
  forever to leave
  both court and land
  if thou receivedst
  not command
  a bride for the king to woo:
  then so he let thee do.—
  This wondrous lovely wife,
  thy might for me did win,
  who could behold her,
  who address her,
  who in pride
  and bliss possess her,
  but would bless his happy fortune?

TRISTAN (*krampfhaft heftig*). Tage-Gespenster!
  Morgen-Träume—
  täuschend und wüst—
  entschwebt, entweicht!

MARKE (*mit tiefer Ergriffenheit*). Mir—dies?
  Dies—, Tristan, mir?—
  Wohin nun Treue,
  da Tristan mich betrog?
  Wohin nun Ehr'
  und echte Art,
  da aller Ehren Hort,
  da Tristan sie verlor?
  Die Tristan sich
  zum Schild erkor,
  wohin ist Tugend
  nun entflohn,
  da meinen Freund sie flieht,
  da Tristan mich verrieth?

(TRISTAN *senkt langsam den Blick zu Boden; in seine
Mienen ist, während* MARKE *fortfährt, zunehmen
Trauer zu lesen.*)
  Wozu die Dienste
  ohne Zahl,
  der Ehren Ruhm,
  der Grösse Macht,
  die Marken du gewannst,
  musst' Ehr' und Ruhm,
  Grösse und Macht,
  musste die Dienste
  ohne Zahl
  der Marke's Schmach bezahlen?
  Dünkte zu wenig
  dich sein Dank,
  dass was du erworben,
  Ruhm und Reich,
  er zu Erb' und Eigen dir gab?
  Dem kinderlos einst
  schwand sein Weib,
  so liebt' er dich,
  dass nie auf's Neu'
  sich Marke wollt' vermählen.
  Da alles Volk
  zu Hof und Land
  mit Bitt' und Dräuen
  in ihn drang,
  die Königin dem Reiche,
  die Gattin sich zu kiesen;
  da selber du
  den Ohm beschwor'st,
  des Hofes Wunsch,
  des Landes Willen
  gütlich zu erfüllen:
  in Wehr gegen Hof und Land,
  in Wehr selbst gegen dich,
  mit Güt' und List
  weigert' er sich,
  bis, Tristan, du ihm drohtest
  für immer zu meiden
  Hof und Land,
  würdest du selber
  nicht entsandt,
  dem König die Braut zu frei'n,
  Da liess er's denn so sein.—
  Dies wunderhehre Weib,
  das mir dein Muth erwarb,
  wer durft' es sehen,
  wer es kennen,
  wer mit Stolze
  sein es nennen,
  ohne selig sich zu preisen?

She whom I have
paid respect to ever
whom I owned,
yet possess'd her never
she, the princess
proud and peerless,
lighting up
my life so cheerless,
'spite foes,—without fear,
the fairest of brides
thou didst bring me here.
Why in hell must I bide,
without hope of a heaven?
Why endure disgrace
unhealed by tears or grief?
The unexplained,
unpenetrated
cause of all these woes,
who will to us disclose?

TRISTAN (*raising his eyes pitifully towards* MARK).
O monarch! I—
may not tell thee, truly;
what thou dost ask
remains for aye unanswered.—

(*He turns to* ISOLDA, *who looks tenderly up at him.*)

Where Tristan now is going,
wilt thou, Isolda, follow?
The land that Tristan means
of sunlight has no gleams;
it is the dark
abode of night,
from whence I first
came forth to light,
and she who bore me
thence in anguish,
gave up her life,
nor long did languish.
She but looked on my face,
then sought this resting-place.
This land where Night doth reign,
where Tristan once hath lain—
now thither offers he
thy faithful guide to be.
So let Isolda
straight declare
if she will meet him there.

ISOLDA.   When to a foreign land
before thou didst invite,
to thee, traitor,
resting true,
did Isolda follow.
Thy kingdom now art showing,
where surely we are going!
why should I shun that land
by which the world is spann'd?
For Tristan's house and home
Isold' will make her own.
The road whereby
we have to go
I pray thee quickly show!—

(TRISTAN bends slowly over her and kisses her softly on
the forehead. MELOT starts furiously forward.)

MELOT (*drawing his sword*).   Thou villain! Ha!
Avenge thee, monarch!
Say, wilt suffer such scorn?

Der mein Wille
nie zu nahen wagte,
der mein Wunsch
Ehrfurcht-scheu entsagte,
die so herrlich
hold erhaben
mir die Seele
musste laben,
trotz—Feind und Gefahr,
die fürstliche Braut
brachtest du mir dar.
Die kein Himmel erlöst,
warum—mir diese Hölle?
Die kein Elend sühnt,
warum—mir diese Schmach?
Den unerforschlich
furchtbar tief
geheimnissvollen Grund,
wer macht der Welt ihn kund?

TRISTAN (*das Auge mitleidig zu* MARKE *erhebend*).
O König, das
kann ich dir nicht sagen;
und was du frägst,
das kannst du nie erfahren.—

(*Er wendet sich seitwärts zu* ISOLDE, *welche die Augen
sehnsüchtig zu ihm aufgeschlagen hat.*)

Wohin nun Tristan scheidet,
willst du, Isold', ihm folgen?
Dem Land, das Tristan meint,
der Sonne Licht nicht scheint;
es ist das dunkel
nächt'ge Land,
daraus die Mutter
einst mich sandt',
als, den im Tode
sie empfangen,
im Tod' sie liess
zum Licht gelangen,
Was, da sie mich gebar,
ihr Liebes-Berge war,
das Wunderreich der Nacht,
aus der ich einst erwacht,—
das bietet dir Tristan,
dahin geht er voran.
Ob sie ihm folge
treu und hold,
das sag' ihm nun Isold'.

ISOLDE.   Da für ein fremdes Land
der Freund sie einstens warb,
dem Un-holden
treu und hold,
musst' Isolde folgen.
Nun führst du in dein Eigen,
dein Erbe mir zu zeigen;
wie flöh' ich wohl das Land,
das alle Welt umspannt?
Wo Tristan's Haus und Heim,
da kehr' Isolde ein:
auf dem sie folge
treu und hold,
den Weg nun zeig' Isold'!

(TRISTAN *neigt sich langsam über sie und küsst sie sanft
auf die Stirn.* MELOT *fährt wüthend auf.*)

MELOT (*das Schwert ziehend*).   Verräther! Ha!
Zur Rache, König!
Duldest du diese Schmach?

TRISTAN (*drawing his sword and turning quickly round*).
　　Who's he will set his life against mine?
　　　　　　　(*casting a look at* MELOT).
　　　This was my friend;
　　　he told me he loved me truly:
　　　my fame and honor
　　　he upheld more than all men.
　　　With arrogance
　　　he filled my heart,
　　　and led on those
　　　who prompted me
　　　fame and pow'r to augment me
　　　by wedding thee to our monarch.—
　　　Thy glance, Isolda,
　　　glamoured him thus;
　　　and, jealous, my friend
　　　played me false
　　　to King Mark, whom I betrayed.—
　　　　　　　(*He sets on* MELOT.)
　　　Guard thee, Melot!

[*As* MELOT *presents his sword* TRISTAN *drops his own guard and sinks wounded into the arms of* KURVENAL. ISOLDA *throws herself upon his breast.* MARK *holds* MELOT *back. The curtain falls quickly.*]

TRISTAN Azieht *sein Schwert und wendet sich schne um*).
　　Wer wagt sein Leben an das meine?
　　　　　　　(*Er heftet den Blick auf* MELOT.)
　　Mein Freund war der,
　　er minnte mich hoch und theuer:
　　um Ehr' und Ruhm
　　mir war er besorgt wie Keiner.
　　Zum Uebermuth
　　trieb er mein Herz:
　　die Schaar führt' er,
　　die mich gedrängt,
　　Ehr' und Ruhm mir zu mehren,
　　dem König dich zu vermählen.—
　　Dein Blick, Isolde,
　　blendet' auch ihn:
　　aus Eifer verrieth
　　mich der Freund
　　dem König, den ich verrieth.—
　　　　　　　(*Er dringt auf* MELOT *ein.*)
　　Wehr' dich, Melot!

(*Als* MELOT *ihm das Schwert entgegenstreckt, lässt* TRIS TAN *das seinige fallen und sinkt verwundet in* KUR WENAL'S *Arme.* ISOLDE *stürzt sich an seine Brus* MARKE *hält* MELOT *zurück.—Der Vorhang fäl schnell.*)

ACT III

A Castle-Garden

[*At one side high castellated buildings, on the other a low breastwork interrupted by a watch tower; at back the castle-gate. The situation is supposed to be on rocky cliffs; through openings the view extends over a wide sea horizon. The whole gives an impression of being deserted by the owner, badly kept, and here and there dilapidated and overgrown.*]

SCENE I

[*In the foreground, in the garden, lies* TRISTAN *sleeping on a couch under the shade of a great lime-tree, stretched out as if lifeless. At his head sit* KURVENAL. *bending over him in grief and anxiously listening to his breathing. From without comes the mournful sound of a shepherd's pipe.*

III AKT

Burggarten.

[*Zur einen Seite hohe Burggebäude, zur anderen ein niedrige Mauerbrüstung von einer Warte unter brochen; im Hintergrunde das Burgthor. Die Lag ist auf felsiger Höhe anzunehmen; durch Oeffnunge blickt man auf einen weiten Meereshorizont. Da Ganze macht den Eindruck der Herrenlosigkeit, übe gepflegt, hie und da schadhaft und bewachsen.*]

ERSTE SCENE

[*Im Vordergrunde, an der inneren Seite, liegt* TRISTAN *unter dem Schatten einer grossen Linde, auf einem Ruhebett schlafend, wie leblos ausgestreckt. Zu Häupten ihm sitzt* KURVENAL, *in Schmerz über ihn hingebeugt, und sorgsam seinem Athem lauschend Von der Aussenseite hört man einen Hirtenreigen blasen.*

Presently the shepherd comes and looks in with interest showing the upper half of his body over the wall.]

SHEPHERD. Kurvenal, ho!—
    Say, Kurvenal,—
    tell me, friend!
    Does he still sleep?   ..

KURVENAL (*turning a little towards him and shaking his head sadly*). If he awoke
    it would be
    but for evermore to leave us,
    unless we find
    the lady-leech;
    alone can she give help.—
    See'st thou nought?
    No ship yet on the sea?

SHEPHERD. Quite another ditty
    then would I play
    as merry as ever I may.
    But tell me truly,
    trusty friend,
    why languishes our lord?

KURVENAL. Do not ask me;—
    for I can give no answer.
    Watch the sea,
    if sails come in sight
    a sprightly melody play.

DER HIRT *erscheint mit dem Oberleibe über der Mauerbrüstung und blickt theilnehmend herein.]*

HIRT. Kurwenal! He!—
    Sag', Kurwenal!—
    Hör' dort, Freund!
    Wacht er noch nicht?

KURWENAL (*wendet ein wenig das Haupt nach ihm und schüttelt traurig mit dem Kopf*). Erwachte er,
    wär's doch nur
    um für immer zu verscheiden,
    erschien zuvor
    die Aerztin nicht,
    die einz'ge, die uns hilft?
    Sah'st du noch nichts?
    Kein Schiff noch auf der See?—

HIRT. Eine and're Weise
    hörtest du dann,
    so lustig wie ich sie kann.
    Nun sag' auch ehrlich,
    alter Freund,
    was hat's mit uns'rem Herrn?

KURWENAL. Lass' die Frage;—
    du kannst's doch nie erfahren.—
    Eifrig späh',
    und siehst du das Schiff,
    dann spiele lustig und hell.

SHEPHERD (*turns round and scans the horizon, shading his eyes with his hand*).
    Blank appears the sea!
(*He puts the reed pipe to his mouth and withdraws, playing.*)
	HIRT (*sich wendend, und mit der Hand über'm Auge nach dem Meer ausspähend*).
	    Oed' und leer das Meer!—
	(*Er setzt die Schalmei an den Mund und entfernt sich blasend.*)

TRISTAN (*motionless—faintly*).
    The tune so well known—
    why wake to that?
    (*opens his eyes and slightly turns his head*).
    Where am I?
	TRISTAN (*bewegungslos, dumpf*). Die alte Weise—
	    was weckt sie mich?
	(*Er schlägt die Augen auf und wendet das Haupt ein wenig.*)
	    Wo bin ich?

KURVENAL (*starting in joyous surprise*).
    Ha!—who is speaking?
    It is his voice!—
    Tristan! lov'd one!
    My lord! my Tristan!
	KURWENAL (*freudig erschrocken auffahrend*).
	    Ha!—die Stimme!
	    Seine Stimme!—
	    Tristan! Herr!
	    Mein Held! Mein Tristan!

TRISTAN (*with effort*). Who—calls me?	TRISTAN (*mit Anstrengung*). Wer—ruft mich?

KURVENAL. Life—at last—
    O thanks be to heaven!—
    sweetest life
    unto my Tristan newly given!
	KURWENAL. Endlich! Endlich!
	    Leben! O Leben—
	    süsses Leben—
	    meinem Tristan neu gegeben!

TRISTAN (*faintly*). Kurvenal!—thou?
    Where—was I?—
    Where—am I?
	TRISTAN (*matt*). Kurwenal—du!
	    Wo—war ich?—
	    Wo—bin ich?

KURVENAL. Where art thou?
    In safety, tranquil and sure!
    Kareol 'tis;
    dost thou not know
    thy fathers' halls?
	KURWENAL. Wo du bist?
	    In Frieden, sicher und frei!
	    Kareol, Herr:
	    Kennst du die Burg
	    der Väter nicht?

TRISTAN. This my fathers'?	TRISTAN. Meiner Väter?
KURVENAL. Look but around.	KURWENAL. Schau dich nur um!
TRISTAN. What awoke me?	TRISTAN. Was erklang mir?

KURVENAL. The herdsman's ditty
    hast thou heard, doubtless;
    he heedeth thy herds
    above on the hills there.
	KURWENAL. Des Hirten Weise,
	    die hörtest du wieder;
	    am Hügel ab
	    hütet er deine Heerde.

TRISTAN. Have I herds, then?	TRISTAN. Meine Heerde?

KURVENAL. Sir, I say it!
    Thine are court,
    castle—all.
    To thee yet true,
    thy trusty folk,
    as best they might,
    have held thy home in guard:
    the gift which once
    thy goodness gave
    to thy serfs and vassals here,
    when going far away,
    in foreign lands to dwell.
	KURWENAL. Herr, das mein' ich!
	    Dein das Haus,
	    Hof und Burg.
	    Das Volk, getreu
	    dem trauten Herrn,
	    so gut es konnt',
	    hat's Haus und Heerd gepflegt
	    das einst mein Held
	    zu Erb' und Eigen
	    an Leut' und Volk verschenkt,
	    als Alles er verliess,
	    in ferne Land' zu ziehn.

TRISTAN. What foreign land?	TRISTAN. In welches Land?

KURVENAL. Why! in Cornwall;
    where cool and able,
    all that was brilliant,
    brave and noble,
    Tristan, my lord, lightly took.
	KURWENAL. Hei! nach Kornwall;
	    kühn und wonnig
	    was sich da Glückes,
	    Glanz und Ehren
	    Tristan hehr ertrotzt!

TRISTAN. Am I in Cornwall?	TRISTAN. Bin ich in Kornwall?
KURVENAL. No, no; in Kareol.	KURWENAL. Nicht doch: in Kareol.
TRISTAN. How came I here?	TRISTAN. Wie kam ich her?

KURVENAL. Hey now! how you came?
    No horse hither you rode:
    a vessel bore you across.
    But on my shoulders
    down to the ship
    you had to ride: they are broad,
    they carried you to the shore.
    Now you are at home once more;
    your own the land,
    your native land;
	KURWENAL. Hei nun, wie du kam'st?
	    Zu Ross rittest du nicht;
	    ein Schifflein führte dich her:
	    doch zu dem Schifflein
	    hier auf den Schultern
	    trug ich dich; die sind breit,
	    die brachten dich dort zum Strand.
	    Nun bist du daheim zu Land,
	    im echten Land,
	    im Heimat-Land.

all loved things now are near you,
unchanged the sun doth cheer you.
The wounds from which you languish
here all shall end their anguish.
(*He presses himself to* TRISTAN'S *breast.*)
RISTAN. Think'st thou thus!
I know 'tis not so,
but this I cannot tell thee.
Where I awoke
ne'er I was,
but where I wandered
I can indeed not tell thee.
The sun I could not see,
nor country fair, nor people;
but what I saw
I can indeed not tell thee.
It was—
the land from which I once came
and whither I return:
the endless realm
of earthly night.
One thing only
there possessed me:
blank, unending,
all-oblivion.—
How faded all forebodings?
O wistful goadings!—
Thus I call
the thoughts that all
t'ward light of day have press'd me.
What only yet doth rest me,
the love-pains that possess'd me,
from blissful death's affright
now drive me toward the light,
which, deceitful, bright and golden,
round thee, Isolda, shines.
Accurséd day
with cruel glow!
Must thou ever
wake my woe?
Must thy light
be burning ever,
e'en by night
our hearts to sever?
Ah, my fairest,
sweetest, rarest!
When wilt thou—
when, ah, when—
let the torchlight dwindle,
that so my bliss may kindle?
The light, how long it glows!
When will the house repose?

His voice has grown fainter and he sinks back gently,
exhausted.)

URVENAL (*who has been deeply distressed, now quickly*
rouses himself from his dejection).
I once defied,
through faith in thee,
the one for whom
now with thee I'm yearning.
Trust in my words,
thou soon shalt see her
face to face.
My tongue that comfort giveth,—
if on the earth still she liveth.

RISTAN (*very feebly*). Yet burns the beacon's spark:
yet is the house not dark.
Isolda lives and wakes:
her voice through darkness breaks.
URVENAL. Lives she still,
then let new hope delight thee.
If foolish and dull you hold me,
this day you must not scold me.

auf eig'ner Weid' und Wonne,
im Schein der alten Sonne,
darin von Tod und Wunden
du selig sollst gesunden
(*Er schmiegt sich an* TRISTAN'S *Brust.*)
TRISTAN. Dünkt dich das,—
ich weis es anders,
doch kann ich's dir nicht sagen.
Wo ich erwacht,
weilt' ich nicht;
doch wo ich weilte,
das kann ich dir nicht sagen.
Die Sonne sah' ich nicht,
nicht sah' ich Land noch Leute;
doch was ich sah,
das kann ich dir nicht sagen.
Ich war—
wo ich von je gewesen,
wohin auf je ich gehe:
im weiten Reich
der Welten Nacht.
Nur ein Wissen
dort uns eigen:
göttlich ew' ges
Ur-Vergessen,—
wie schwand mir seine Ahnung!
Sehnsücht'ge Mahnung
nenn' ich dich,
die neu dem Licht
des Tag's mich zugetrieben?
Was einzig mir geblieben?
Ein heiss-inbrünstig Lieben,
aus Todes-Wonne-Grauen
jagt mich's, das Licht zu schauen
das trügend hell und golden
noch dir, Isolden, scheint!
Verfluchter Tag
mit deinem Schein
Wach'st du ewig
meiner Pein?
Brennt sie ewig,
diese Leuchte,
die selbst Nachts
von ihr mich scheuchte?
Ach, Isolde!
Süsse! Holde!
Wann—endlich,
wann, ach wann
löschest du die Zünde,
dass sie mein Glück mir künde?
Das Licht, wann löscht es aus?
Wann wird es Nacht im Haus?

KURWENAL (*nach grosser Erschütterung aus der Nieder-*
geschlagenheit sich aufraffend).
Der einst ich trotzt',
aus Treu' zu dir,
mit dir nach ihr
nun muss ich mich sehnen!
Glaub' meinem Wort,
du sollst sie sehen,
hier—und heut'—
den Trost kann ich dir geben,
ist sie nur selbst noch am Leben.

TRISTAN (*sehr matt*). Noch losch das Licht nicht aus,
noch ward's nicht Nacht im Haus.
Isolde lebt und wacht,
sie rief mich aus der Nacht.
KURWENAL. Lebt sie denn,
so lass' dir Hoffnung lachen.—
Muss Kurwenal dumm dir gelten,
heut' sollst du ihn nicht schelten.

As dead lay'st thou
since the day
when that accurséd Melot
so foully wounded thee.
Thy wound was heavy:
how to heal it?
Thy simple servant
there bethought
that she who once
closed Morold's wound
with ease the hurt could heal thee
that Melot's sword did deal thee.
I found the best
of leeches there,
to Cornwall have I
sent for her:
a trusty serf
sails o'er the sea,
bringing Isold' to thee.

TRISTAN (*transported*). Isolda comes!
Isolda nears!   (*He struggles for words.*)

O friendship! high
and holy friendship!
(*Draws* KURVENAL *to him and embraces him.*)
O Kurvenal,
thou trusty heart,
my truest friend I rank thee!
Howe'er can Tristan thank thee?
My shelter and shield
in fight and strife;
in weal or woe
thou'rt mine for life.
Those whom I hate
thou hatest too;
those whom I love
thou lovest too.
When good King Mark
I followed of old,
thou wert to him truer than gold.
When I was false
to my noble friend,
to betray too thou didst descend.
Thou art selfless,
solely mine;
thou feel'st for me
when I suffer.
But—what I suffer,
thou canst not feel *for* me!
this terrible yearning in my heart,
this feverish burning's
cruel smart,—
did I but show it,
couldst thou but know it,
no time here wouldst thou tarry,
to watch from tow'r thou wouldst hurry;
with all devotion
viewing the ocean,
with eyes impatiently spying,
there, where her ship's sails are flying.
Before the wind she
drives to find me;
on the wings of love she neareth,—
Isolda hither steereth!—
she nears, she nears,
so boldly and fast!
It waves, it waves,
the flag from the mast!
Hurra! Hurra!
she reaches the bar!
Dost thou not see?
Kurvenal, dost thou not see?

Wie todt lag'st du
seit dem Tag,
da Melot, der Verruchte,
dir eine Wunde schlug.
Die böse Wunde,
wie sie heilen?
Mir thör'gem Manne
dünkt' es da,
wer einst dir Morold's
Wunde schloss,
der heilte leicht die Plagen
von Melot's Wehr geschlagen.
Die beste Aerztin
bald ich fand:
nach Kornwall hab' ich
ausgesandt:
ein treuer Mann
wohl über's Meer
bringt dir Isolden her.

TRISTAN (*ausser sich*). Isolde kommt!
Isolde naht!—
            (*Er ringt gleichsam nach Sprache*
O Treue! hehre,
holde Treue!
(*Er zieht* KURVENAL *an sich und umarmt ihn*
Mein Kurwenal,
du trauter Freund,
du Treuer ohne Wanken,
wie soll dir Tristan danken?
Mein Schild, mein Schirm
in Kampf und Streit;
zu Lust und Leid
mir stets bereit:
wen ich gehasst,
den hasstest du;
wen ich geminnt,
den minntest du.
Dem guten Marke,
dient ich ihm hold,
wie warst du ihm treuer als Gold!
Musst' ich verrathen
den edlen Herrn,
wie betrogst du ihn da so gern!
Dir nicht eigen,
einzig mein,
mitleidest du
wenn ich leide:—
nur—was ich leide,
das—kannst du nicht leiden!
Dies furchtbare Sehnen,
das mich zehrt;
dies schmachtende Brennen,
das mich zehrt;
wollt' ich dir's nennen,
könntest du's kennen,—
nicht hier würdest du weilen;
zur Warte müsstest du eilen,
mit allen Sinnen
sehnend von hinnen,
nach dorten trachten und spähen,
wo ihre Segel sich blähen;
wo vor den Winden,
mich zu finden,
von der Liebe Drang befeuert,
Isolde zu mir steuert!—
es naht, es naht
mit muthiger Hast!
Sie weht, sie weht,
die Flagge am Mast
Das Schiff, das Schiff!
Dort streicht es am Riff!
Siehst du es nicht?
Kurwenal, siehst du es nicht?

As KURVENAL *hesitates to leave* TRISTAN, *who is gazing at him in mute expectation, the mournful tune of the shepherd is heard, as before.*)

KURVENAL (*dejectedly*). Still is no ship in sight.

TRISTAN (*has listened with waning excitement and now recommences with growing melancholy*).
Is this the meaning then,
thou old pathetic ditty,
of all thy sighing sound?—
On evening's breeze
it sadly rang
when, as a child,
my father's death-news chill'd me:
through morning's mist
it stole more sadly,
when the son
his mother's fate was taught,
when they who gave me breath
both felt the hand of death
to them came also
through their pain
the ancient ditty's
yearning strain,
which asked me once
and asks me now
which was the fate before me
to which my mother bore me?—
What was the fate?—
The strain so plaintive
now repeats it:—
for yearning—and dying!
(*He falls back senseless.*)

KURVENAL (*who has been vainly striving to calm* TRIS-
TAN *cries out in terror*).
My master! Tristan!—
Frightful enchantment!—
O love's deceit!
O passion's pow'r!
Most sweet dream 'neath the sun,
see the work thou hast done!—
Here lies he now,
the noblest of knights,
with his passion all others above:
behold! what reward
his ardor requites;
the one sure reward of love!
(*with sobbing voice.*)
Art thou then dead?
Liv'st thou not?
Hast to the curse succumbed?—
(*He listens for* TRISTAN'S *breath.*)
O rapture! No!
He still moves! He lives!
and gently his lips are stirr'd.

TRISTAN (*very faintly*). The ship—is't yet in sight?

KURVENAL. The ship? Be sure
t'will come to-day:
it cannot tarry longer.

TRISTAN. On board Isolda,—
see, she smiles—
with the cup
that reconciles.
Dost thou see?
Dost thou see her now!
Full of grace
and loving mildness,
floating o'er
the ocean's wildness?

(*Als* KURWENAL *um* TRISTAN *nicht zu verlassen, zögert, und dieser in schweigender Spannung nach ihm blickt, ertönt, wie zu Anfang, die klagende Weise des Hirten.*)

KURWENAL (*niedergeschlagen*).
Noch ist kein Schiff zu seh'n!

TRISTAN (*hat mit abnehmender Aufregung gelauscht, und beginnt nun mit wachsender Schwermuth*).
Muss ich dich so versteh'n,
du alte, ernste Weise,
mit deiner Klage Klang?—
Durch Abendwehen
drang sie bang,
als einst dem Kind
des Vaters Tod verkündet:
durch Morgengrauen
bang und bänger,
als der Sohn
der Mutter Loos vernahm.
Da er mich zeugt' und starb,
sie sterbend mich gebar,
die alte Weise
sehnsuchts bang
zu ihnen wohl
auch klagend drang,
die einst mich frug,
und jetzt mich frägt,
zu welchem Loos erkoren
ich damals wohl geboren?
Zu welchem Loos?—
Die alte Weise
sagt mir's wieder:
mich sehnen—und sterben.
(*Er sinkt ohnmächtig zurück.*)

KURWENAL (*der vergebens* TRISTAN *zu mässigen suchte, schreit entsetzt auf*).
Mein Herre! Tristan!—
Schrecklicher Zauber!—
O Minne-Trug!—
O Liebes-Zwang!
Der Welt holdester Wahn,
wie ist's um dich gethan!
Hier liegt er nun,
der wonnige Mann,
der wie Keiner geliebt und geminnt:
nun seht, was von ihm
sie Dankes gewann,
was je sich Minne gewinnt!
(*Mit schluchzender Stimme.*)
Bist du nun todt?
Lebst du noch?
Hat dich der Fluch entführt?—
(*Er lauscht seinem Athem.*)
O Wonne! Nein!
Er regt sich! Er lebt!—
Wie sanft er die Lippen rührt!

TRISTAN (*sehr leise beginnend*).
Das Schiff—siehst du's noch nicht?

KURWENAL. Das Schiff? Gewiss,
das naht noch heut';
es kann nicht lang' mehr säumen.

TRISTAN. Und drauf Isolde,
wie sie winkt—
wie sie hold
mir Sühne trinkt?
Siehst du sie?
Siehst du sie noch nicht?
Wie sie selig,
hehr und milde
wandelt durch
des Meer's Gefilde?

By billows of flowers
lightly lifted,
gently toward
the land she's drifted.
Her look brings ease
and sweet repose;
her hand one last
relief bestows.
Isolda! Ah, Isolda!
How fair, how sweet art thou!—
And Kurvenal, why!—
what ails thy sight?
Away, and watch for her,
foolish wight.
what I see so well and plain'y,
let not thine eye seek vainly.
Dost thou not hear?
Away, with speed!
Haste to the watch-tow'r!
Wilt thou not heed?
The ship, the ship!
Isolda's ship!— —
Thou must discern it,
must perceive it!
The ship—dost thou see it?—

(Whilst KURVENAL, *still hesitating, opposes* TRISTAN, *the Shepherd's pipe is heard without, playing a joyous strain.)*

KURVENAL *(springing joyously up).*
O rapture! Transport!
(He rushes to the watch-tower and looks out.)
Ha! the ship!
From northward it is nearing.

TRISTAN. So I knew,
so I said!
Yes, she yet lives,
and life to me gives.
How could Isold'
from this world be free,
which only holds
Isolda for me?

KURVENAL *(shouting).* Ahoy! Ahoy!
See her bravely tacking!
How full the canvas is filled!
How she darts! how she flies!

TRISTAN. The pennon? the pennon?

KURVENAL. A flag is floating at mast-head,
joyous and bright.

TRISTAN. Aha! what joy!
Now through the daylight
comes my Isolda.
Isolda, oh come!
See'st thou herself?

KURVENAL. The ship is shut
from me by rocks.

TRISTAN. Behind the reef?
Is there not risk!
Those dangerous breakers
ships have oft shattered.—
Who steereth the helm?

KURVENAL. The steadiest seaman.

TRISTAN. Betrays he me?
Is he Melot's ally?

KURVENAL. Trust him like me.

Auf wonniger Blumen
sanften Wogen
kommt sie licht
an's Land gezogen:
sie lächelt mir Trost
und süsse Ruh';
sie führt mir letzte
Labung zu.
Isolde! Ach, Isolde!
wie hold, wie schön bist du!—
Und Kurwenal, wie?
Du säh'st sie nicht?
Hinauf zur Warte,
du blöder Wicht,
was so hell und licht ich sehe,
dass das dir nicht entgehe.
Hörst du mich nicht?
Zur Warte schnell!
Eilig zur Warte!
Bist du zur Stell'?
Das Schiff, das Schiff!
Isolden's Schiff—
du musst es sehen,
musst es sehen!
Das Schiff—säh'st du's noch nicht?

(Während KURWENAL *noch zögernd mit* TRISTAN *ring lässt der Hirt von aussen die Schalmei ertönen.)*

KURWENAL *(freudig aufspringend).*
O Wonne! Freude!
(Er stürzt auf die Warte und späht aus.)
Ha! Das Schiff!
Von Norden seh' ich's nah'n.

TRISTAN. Wusst' ich's nicht?
Sagt' ich es nicht?
Dass sie noch lebt,
noch am Leben mir webt.
Die mir Isolde
einzig enthält,
wie wär' Isolde
mir aus der Welt?

KURWENAL *(jauchzend).* Hahei! Hahei!
Wie es muthig steuert!
Wie stark das Segel sich bläht!
Wie es jagt! Wie es fliegt!

TRISTAN. Die Flagge? Die Flagge?

KURWENAL. Der Freude Flagge
am Wimpel lustig und hell.

TRISTAN. Heiaha! Der Freude!
Hell am Tage
zu mir Isolde.
Isolde zu mir!—
Siehst du sie selbst?

KURWENAL. Jetzt schwand das Schiff
hinter dem Fels.

TRISTAN. Hinter dem Riff?
Bringt es Gefahr?
Dort wüthet die Brandung,
scheitern die Schiffe.—
Das Steuer, wer führt's?

KURWENAL. Der sicherste Seemann.

TRISTAN. Verrieth er mich?
Wär' er Melot's Genoss?

KURWENAL. Trau' ihm wie mir!

TRISTAN. A traitor thou, too!—
　　O caitiff!
　　Canst thou not see her?

KURVENAL. Not yet.

TRISTAN. Destruction!

KURVENAL. Aha! Halla-halloa!
　　they clear! they clear!
　　Safely they clear!
　　Inside the surf
　　steers now the ship to the strand.

TRISTAN (shouting in joy). Hallo-ho! Kurvenal!
　　Trustiest friend!
　　All the wealth I own
　　to-day I bequeath thee.

KURVENAL. With speed they approach.

TRISTAN. Now dost thou see her?
　　See'st thou Isolda?

KURVENAL. 'Tis she! she waves!

TRISTAN. O woman divine!

KURVENAL. The ship is a-land!
　　Isolda!—ha!—
　　With but one leap
　　lightly she springs to land!

TRISTAN. Descend from the watch-tow'r,
　　indolent gazer!
　　Away! away
　　to the shore!
　　Help her! help my belov'd!

KURVENAL. In a trice she shall come;
　　Trust in my strong arm!
　　But thou, Tristan,
　　hold thee tranquilly here!
　　　　　　　　(He hastens off.)

TRISTAN (tossing on his couch in feverish excitement.)
　　O sunlight glowing,
　　glorious ray!
　　Ah, joy-bestowing
　　radiant day!
　　Boundeth my blood,
　　boisterous flood!
　　Infinite gladness!
　　Rapturous madness!
　　Can I bear to lie
　　couched here in quiet?
　　Away, let me fly
　　to where hearts run riot!
　　Tristan the brave,
　　exulting in strength,
　　has torn himself
　　from death at length.
　　　　　　　(He raises himself erect.)
　　All wounded and bleeding
　　Sir Morold I defeated;
　　all bleeding and wounded
　　Isolda now shall be greeted.
　　　　　　(He tears the bandage from his wound.)
　　Ha, ha, my blood!
　　Merrily flows it.
　　　　(He springs from his bed and staggers forward.)
　　She who can help
　　my wound and close it,
　　she comes in her pride,
　　she comes to my aid.
　　Be space defied
　　let the universe fade!
　　　　　　(He reels to the centre of the stage.)

TRISTAN. Verräther, auch du!
　　Un-seliger!
　　Siehst du sie wieder?

KURWENAL. Noch nicht.

TRISTAN. Verloren!

KURWENAL. Haha! Heiahaha!
　　Vorbei! Vorbei!
　　Glücklich vorbei!
　　In sich'ren Strom
　　steuert zum Hafen das Schiff.

TRISTIAN (jauchzend). Heiaha! Kurwenal!
　　Truester Freund!
　　All' mein Hab' und Gut
　　vererb' ich noch heut'.

KURWENAL. Sie nahen im Flug.

TRISTAN. Siehst du sie endlich?
　　Siehst du Isolde?

KURWENAL. Sie ist's! Sie winkt.

TRISTAN. O seligstes Weib!

KURWENAL. Im Hafen der Kiel!—
　　Isolde—ha!
　　mit einem Sprung
　　springt sie vom Bord zum Strand.

TRISTAN. Herab von der Warte!
　　Müssiger Gaffer!
　　Hinab! Hinab
　　an den Strand!
　　Hilf ihr! Hilf meiner Frau!

KURWENAL. Sie trag' ich herauf:
　　trau' meinen Armen!
　　Doch du, Tristan,
　　bleib' mir treulich am Bett! (Er eilt fort.)

TRISTAN (in höchster Aufregung auf dem Lager sich
　　mühend). O, diese Sonne!
　　Ha, dieser Tag!
　　Ha, dieser Wonne
　　sonnigster Tag!
　　Jagendes Blut,
　　jauchzender Muth!
　　Lust ohne Maassen,
　　freudiges Rasen:
　　auf des Lagers Bann
　　wie sie ertragen?
　　Wohlauf und daran,
　　wo die Herzen schlagen!
　　Tristan. der Held,
　　in jubelnder Kraft
　　hat sich vom Tod
　　emporgerafft!
　　　　　　　　(Er richtet sich hoch auf.)
　　Mit blutender Wunde
　　bekämpft' ich einst Morolden:
　　mit blutender Wunde
　　erjag' ich mir heut' Isolden.
　　　　　　(Er reisst den Verband der Wunde auf.)
　　Hahei! Mein Blut,
　　lustig nun fliesse!
　(Er springt vom Lager herab und schwankt vorwärts.)
　　Die mir die Wunde
　　auf ewig schliesse,
　　sie naht wie ein Held,
　　sie naht mir zum Heil:
　　vergehe die Welt
　　meiner jauchzenden Eil'!
　　　　　　(Er taumelt nach der Mitte der Bühne.)

Isolda's Voice (*without*).
    Tristan! Tristan! Belovéd!

Tristan (*in frantic excitement*).
    What! hails me the light?
    The torchlight—ha!—
    The torch is extinct!
    I come! I come!

SCENE II

[Isolda *hastens breathlessly in.* Tristan, *delirious with excitement, staggers wildly towards her. They meet in the centre of the stage; she receives him in her arms, where he sinks slowly to the ground.*]

Isolda. Tristan! Ah!

Tristan (*turning his dying eyes on* Isolda). Isolda!—
                        (*He dies.*)

Isolda. 'Tis I, 'tis I—
    dearly belov'd!
    Wake, and once more
    hark to my voice!
    Isolda calls.
    Isolda comes,
    with Tristan true to perish.—
    Speak unto me!
    But for one moment,
    only one moment
    open thine eyes!
    Such weary days
    I waited and longed,
    that one single hour
    I with thee might awaken.
    Betrayed am I then?
    Deprived by Tristan
    of this our solitary,
    swiftly fleeting,
    final earthly joy?—
    His wound, though—where?
    Can I not heal it?
    The rapture of night
    O let us feel it!
    Not of thy wounds,
    not of thy wounds must thou expire!
    Together, at least,
    let fade life's enfeebled fire!—
    How lifeless his look!—
    still his heart!—
    Dared he to deal me
    such a smart?
    Stayed is his breathing's
    gentle tide!
    Must I be wailing
    at his side,
    who, in rapture coming to seek him,
    fearless sailed o'er the sea?
    Too late, too late!
    Desperate man!
    Casting on me
    this cruelest ban!
    Comes no relief
    for my load of grief?
    Silent art keeping
    while I am weeping?
    But once more, ah!
    But once again!— —
    Tristan!—ha!
    he wakens—hark!
    Beloved—
    —dark!
       (*She sinks down senseless upon his body.*)

Isolde (*von aussen*). Tristan! Tristan! Geliebter!

Tristan (*in der furchtbarsten Aufregung*).
    Wie hör' ich das Licht!
    Die Leuchte—ha!
    Die Leuchte verlischt!
    Zu ihr! Zu ihr!

ZWEITE SCENE

[Isolde *eilt athemlos herein.* Tristan, *seiner nicht mächtig, stürzt sich ihr schwankend entgegen. In der Mitte der Bühne begegnen sie sich; sie empfängt ihn in ihren Armen.*]

Isolde. Tristan! Ha!

Tristan. (*sterbend zu* Isolden *aufblickend*). Isolde!—
                        (*Er stirbt.*)

Isolde. Ich bin's, ich bin's—
    süssester Freund!
    Auf! noch einmal!
    Hör' meinen Ruf!
    Achtest du nicht?
    Isolde ruft:
    Isolde kam,
    mit Tristan treu zu sterben.—
    Bleibst du mir stumm!
    Nur eine Stunde,—
    nur eine Stunde
    bleibe mir wach!
    So bange Tage
    wachte sie sehend,
    um eine Stunde
    mit dir noch zu wachen.
    Betrügt Isolden,
    betrügt sie Tristan
    um dieses einz'ge
    ewig-kurze
    letzte Welten-Glück?—
    Die Wunde—wo?
    Lass sie mich heilen,
    dass wonnig und hehr
    die Nacht wir theilen.
    Nicht an der Wunde,
    an der Wunde stirb mir nicht!
    Uns beiden vereint
    erlösche das Lebenslicht!—
    Gebrochen der Blick!
    Still das Herz?
    Treuloser Tristan,
    mir diesen Schmerz?
    Nicht eines Athems
    flücht'ges Weh'n?
    Muss sie nun jammernd
    vor dir steh'n,
    die sich wonnig dir zu vermählen
    muthig kam über Meer?
    Zu spät! Zu spät!
    Trotziger Mann!
    Straf'st du mich so
    mit hartestem Bann?
    Ganz ohne Huld
    meiner Leidens-Schuld?
    Nicht meine Klagen
    darf ich dir sagen?
    Nur einmal, ach!
    Nur einmal noch!—
    Tristan—ha!
    horch'—er wacht!
    Geliebter—
    —Nacht!
  (*Sie sinkt bewusstlos über die Leiche zusammen.*)

SCENE III

RVENAL, *who reëntered close behind* ISOLDA, *has re-*
ained by the entrance speechless and petrified,
azing motionless on TRISTAN. *From below is now*
eard the dull murmur of voices and the clash of
eapons. The SHEPHERD *clambers over the wall.*]

PHERD (*coming hastily and softly to* KURVENAL).
    Kurwenal! Hear!
    Another ship!

RVENAL *starts up in haste and looks over the ram-*
art, whilst the SHEPHERD *stands apart, gazing in con-*
ernation on TRISTAN *and* ISOLDA.)

RVENAL. Fiends and furies!
        (*In a burst of anger.*)
    All are at hand!
    Melot and Mark
    I see on the strand,—
    Weapons and missiles!—
    Guard we the gate!

hastens with the SHEPHERD *to the gate, which they*
oth try quickly to barricade.)

STEERSMAN (*rushing in*).
    Mark and his men
    have set on us:
    defence is vain!
    We're overpowered.

RVENAL. Stand to and help!—
    Whi'e lasts my life
    I'll let no foe enter here!

NGÆNA'S VOICE (*without, calling from below*).
    Isolda! Mistress!

RVENAL. Brangæna's voice! (*Falling down.*)
    What want you here?

NGÆNA. Open, Kurwenal!
    Where is Isolda?

RVENAL. With foes do you come?
    Woe to you, false one!

LOT'S VOICE (*without*). Stand back, thou fool!
    Bar not the way!

RVENAL (*laughing savagely*). Hurrah for the day
    on which I confront thee!

ELOT, *with armed men, appears under the gateway.*
URVENAL falls on him and cuts him down.)

    Die, damnable wretch!

SCENE IV

LOT. Woe's me!—Tristan!   (*He dies.*)

NGÆNA (*still without*). Kurwenal! Madman!
    O hear—thou mistakest!

RVENAL. Treacherous maid!   (*To his men.*)
    Come! Follow me!
    Force them below!   (*They fight.*)

RK (*without*). Hold, thou frantic man!
    Lost are thy senses?

RVENAL. Here ravages Death!
    Nought else, O king,
    is here to be holden!
    If you would earn it, come on!
        (*He sets upon* MARK *and his followers.*)

RK. Away, rash maniac!

NGÆNA (*has climbed over the wall at the side and*
astens to the front).
    Isolda! lady.
    Joy and life!—
    What sight's here—ha!
    Liv'st thou, Isolda! (*She goes to* ISOLDA'S *aid.*)

DRITTE SCENE

[KURWENAL *was sogleich hinter* ISOLDE *zurückgekom-*
men; sprachlos in furchtbarer Erschütterung hat er
dem Auftritte beigewohnt und bewegungslos auf
TRISTAN *hingestarrt. Aus der Tiefe hört man jetzt*
dumpfes Getümmel und Waffengeklirr. Der HIRT
kommt über die Mauer gestiegen.]

HIRT (*hastig und leise sich zu* KURWENAL *wendend*).
    Kurwenal! Hör'!
    Ein zweites Schiff.

(KURWENAL *fährt heftig auf, und blickt über die Brüst-*
ung, während der HIRT *aus der Ferne erschüttert auf*
TRISTAN *und* ISOLDE *sieht.*)

KURWENAL. Tod und Hölle! (*In Wuth ausbrechend.*)

    Alles zur Hand!
    Marke und Melot
    hab' ich erkannt.—
    Waffen und Steine!
    Hilf mir! An's Thor!

(*Er springt mit dem* HIRT *an das Thor, das Beide in*
der Hast zu verrammeln suchen.)

DER STEUERMANN (*stürzt herein*).
    Marke mir nach
    mit Mann und Volk!
    Vergeb'ne Wehr!
    Bewältigt sind wir.

KURWENAL. Stell' dich, und hilf'!—
    So lang' ich lebe,
    lugt mir Keiner herein!

BRANGÆNE'S STIMME (*aussen, von unten her*).
    Isolde, Herrin!

KURWENAL. Brangäne's Ruf? (*Hinabrufend.*)
    Was such'st du hier?

BRANGÆNE. Schliess' nicht, Kurwenal!
    Wo ist Isolde?

KURWENAL. Verräth'rin auch du?
    Weh' dir, Verruchte!

MELOT'S STIMME (*von aussen*). Zurück, du Thor!
    Stemm' dich dort nicht!

KURWENAL (*wüthend auflachend*). Heiaha dem Tag,
    da ich dich treffe!

(MELOT, *mit gewaffneten Männern, erscheint unter dem*
Thor. KURWENAL *stürzt sich auf ihn und streckt ihn*
zu Boden.)
    Stirb, schändlicher Wicht!

VIERTE SCENE

MELOT. Wehe mir!—Tristan!   (*Er Stirbt.*)

BRANGÆNE (*noch ausserhalb*). Kurwenal! Wüthender?
    Hör', du betrügst dich.

KURWENAL. Treulose Magd!—   (*Zu den Seinen.*)
    Drauf! Mir nach!
    Werft sie zurück!   (*Sie kämpfen.*)

MARKE (*ausserhalb*). Halte, Rasender!
    Bist du von Sinnen?

KURWENAL. Hier wüthet der Tod.
    Nichts and'res, König,
    ist hier zu holen!
    willst du ihn kiesen, so komm!
        (*Er dringt auf* MARKE *und dessen Gefolge ein.*)

MARKE. Zurück, Wahnsinniger!

BRANGÆNE (*hat sich seitwärts über die Mauer geschwun-*
gen, und eilt in den Vordergrund).
    Isolde! Herrin!
    Glück und Heil!—
    Was seh' ich, ha!
    Lebst du? Isolde! (*Sie müht sich um* ISOLDE.)

MARK (*who with his followers has driven* KURVENAL *and his men back from the gate and forced his way in*).
　　O wild mistake!
　　Tristan, where art thou?

KURVENAL (*desperately wounded, totters before* MARK *to the front*).
　　He lieth—there—
　　here, where I lie too.—
　　　　　　(*Sinks down at* TRISTAN's *feet.*)

MARK.　Tristan! Tristan!
　　Isolda! Woe!

KURVENAL (*trying to grasp* TRISTAN's *hand*).
　　Tristan! true lord!
　　Chide me not
　　that I try to follow thee!　　(*He dies.*)

MARK.　Dead together!—
　　All are dead!
　　My hero Tristan!
　　truest of friends,
　　must thou again
　　be to thy king a traitor?
　　Now, when he comes
　　another proof of love to give thee!
　　Awaken! awaken!
　　O hear my lamentation,
　　thou faithless, faithful friend!
　　　　(*Kneels down sobbing over the bodies.*)

BRANGÆNA (*who has revived* ISOLDA *in her arms*).

　　She wakes! she lives!
　　Isolda, hear!
　　Hear me, mistress beloved!
　　Tidings of joy
　　I have to tell thee:
　　O list to thy Brangæna!
　　My thoughtless fault I have atoned;
　　after thy flight
　　I forthwith went to the king:
　　the love potion's secret
　　he scarce had learned
　　when with sedulous haste
　　he put to sea,
　　that he might find thee,
　　nobly renounce thee
　　and give thee up to thy love.

MARK.　O why, Isolda,
　　Why this to me?
　　When clearly was disclosed
　　what before I could fathom not,
　　what joy was mine to find
　　my friend was free from fault!
　　In haste to wed
　　thee to my hero
　　with flying sails
　　I followed thy track:
　　but howe'er can
　　happiness
　　o'ertake the swift course of woe?
　　More food for Death did I make:
　　more wrong grew in mistake.

BRANGÆNA.　Dost thou not hear?
　　Isolda! Lady!
　　O try to believe the truth!

MARKE (*mit seinem Gefolge hat* KURWENAL *mit dess Helfern vom Thore zurückgetrieben und drin herein*).
　　O Trug und Wahn!
　　Tristan, wo bist du?

KURWENAL (*schwer verwundet, schwankt vor* MARK *her nach dem Vordergrund*).
　　Da liegt er—da—
　　hier, wo ich liege—!
　　　　　　(*Er sinkt zu* TRISTAN's *Füssen zusammen*)

MARKE.　Tristan! Tristan!
　　Isolde! Weh'!

KURWENAL (*nach* TRISTAN's *Hand fassend*).
　　Tristan! Trauter!
　　Schilt mich nicht,
　　dass der Treue auch mit kommt!　　(*Er stirbt*)

MARKE.　Todt denn Alles!
　　Alles todt?
　　Mein Held! Mein Tristan!
　　Trautester Freund?
　　Auch heute noch
　　musst du den Freund verrathen?
　　Heut', wo er kommt
　　dir höchst Treu' zu bewähren!
　　Erwach'! Erwach'!
　　Erwache meinem Jammer,
　　du treulos treuester Freund!
　　(*Schluchzend über die Leichen sich hera beugend*).

BRANGÆNE (*die in ihren Armen* ISOLDE *wieder zu si gebracht*).
　　Sie wacht! Sie lebt!
　　Isolde, hör'!
　　Hör' mich, süsseste Frau!
　　Glückliche Kunde
　　lass' mich dir melden:
　　vertrautest nicht Brangänen?
　　Ihre blinde Schuld
　　hat sie gesühnt;
　　als du verschwunden,
　　schnell fand sie den König:
　　des Trankes Geheimniss
　　erfuhr er kaum,
　　als mit sorgender Eil'
　　in See er stach,
　　dich zu erreichen,
　　dir zu entsagen,
　　dich zuzuführen dem Freund.

MARKE.　Warum, Isolde,
　　warum, mir das?
　　Da hell mir ward enthüllt,
　　was zuvor ich nicht fassen konnt',
　　wie selig, das ich den Freund
　　frei von schuld da fand!
　　Dem holden Mann
　　dich zu vermählen,
　　mit vollen Segeln
　　flog ich dir nach:
　　doch Unglückes
　　Ungestüm,
　　wie erreicht es, wer Frieden bringt?
　　Die Aernte mehrt' ich dem Tod:
　　der Wahn häufte die Noth!

BRANGÆNE.　Hörst du uns nicht?
　　Isolde! Traute!
　　Vernimmst du die Treue nicht?

ᴵꜱOLDA (*unconscious of all around her, turning her eyes with rising inspiration on* TRISTAN'S *body*).

Mild and softly
he is smiling;
how his eyelids sweetly open!
See, oh comrades,
see you not
how he beameth
ever brighter—
how he rises
ever radiant
steeped in starlight,
borne above?
See you not
how his heart
with lion zest,
calmly happy
beats in his breast?
From his lips
in heavenly rest
sweetest breath
he softly sends.
Harken, friends!
Hear and feel ye not?
Is it I
alone am hearing
strains so tender
and endearing?
Passion swelling,
all things telling,
gently bounding,
from him sounding,
in me pushes,
upward rushes
trumpet tone
that round me gushes.
Brighter growing,
o'er me flowing,
are these breezes
airy pillows?
Are they balmy
beauteous billows?
How they rise
and gleam and glisten!
Shall I breathe them?
Shall I listen?
Shall I sip them,
dive within them,
to my panting
breathing win them?
In the breezes around.
in the harmony sound
in the world's driving
whirlwind be drown'd—
and, sinking,
be drinking—
in a kiss,
highest bliss!

ISOLDE (*die nichts um sich her vernommen, heftet das Auge mit wachsender Begeisterung auf* TRISTAN'S *Leiche*).

Mild und leise
wie er lächelt,
wie das Auge
hold er öffnet:
seht ihr, Freunde,
seh't ihr, Freunde,
Immer lichter
wie er leuchtet,
wie er minnig
immer mächt'ger,
Stern-umstrahlet
hoch sich hebt:
seh't ihr Freunde,
seh't ihr's nicht?
Wie das Herz ihm
muthig schwillt,
voll und hehr
im Busen quillt:
wie den Lippen
wonnig mild,
süsser Athem
sanft entweht:—
Freunde, seh't—
fühlt und seh't ihr's nicht!—
Höre ich nur
diese Weise,
die so wunder-
voll und leise,
Wonne klagend,
Alles sagend,
mild versöhnend
aus ihm tönend,
auf sich schwingt,
in mich dringt,
hold erhallend
um mich klingt?
Hell erschallend,
mich umwallend,
sind es Wellen
sanfter Lüfte?
Sind es Wogen
wonniger Düfte?
Wie sie schwellen,
mich umrauschen,
soll ich athmen,
soll ich lauschen?
soll ich schlürfen,
untertauchen,
süss in Düften
mich verhauchen?
In dem wogenden Schwall,
in dem tönenden Schall,
in des Welt-Athems
wehendem All—
ertrinken—
versinken—
unbewusst—
höchste Lust!

ISOLDA *sinks, as if transfigured, in* BRANGÆNA'S *arms upon* TRISTAN'S *body. Profound emotion and grief of the bystanders.* MARK *invokes a blessing on the dead. Curtain.*)

(ISOLDE *sinkt wie verklärt in* BRANGÆNE'S *Armen sanft auf* TRISTAN'S *Leiche.—Grosse Rührung und Entrückt-heit unter den Umstehenden.* MARKE *segnet die Leihen.—Der Vorhang fällt langsam.*)

THE END

DIE MEISTERSINGER VON NÜRNBERG

PREFACE.

"Die Meistersinger von Nürnberg" is the eighth in der of Wagner's published operas.

Some acquaintance with the history of the Master-singers of Germany, their manners and customs, and their technical phraseology, is indispensable for a due appreciation much which would otherwise appear strange and incomprehensible in the text of this opera. The subject being one which has not been made readily accessible to English readers, it seems imperative that an English version of the work should not go forth to the world unaccompanied by some few elucidatory remarks.

The Master-singers are not to be regarded as mythical personages or as emanations of Wagner's brain, as certain his critics have fondly imagined, but were real flesh and blood. Impossible as it often is to assign a boundary to the different periods of literary history, it is within the mark to assert that Master-singing is most properly to be regarded as the eventual outcome of Minne-singing, and that the culture of poetic art, which in the twelfth and thirteenth centuries belonged exclusively to the Minne-singers, in the fourteenth and four following centuries devolved upon the Master-singers. The Minne-singers, it should be borne in mind, were mostly of noble birth, and lived in kings' houses or wandered about from court to court; the Master-singers, on the other hand, belonged to the burgher and artisan class. Heinrich von Meissen, surnamed Frauenlob, who died in 1318, is generally looked upon as the founder of their schools and guilds. From his time verse-craft became one of the incorporated trades in nearly all German cities, and the burghers obtained the freedom of it as of any other corporation. The aims of the Master-singers' schools and guilds were strictly moral; by the culture and improvement of poetry, and by the discipline which their rules imposed, they sought to raise the mental and moral standard of their youth. But, ascribing an extravagant antiquity to their institutions, placing form above matter, and hedging themselves about with hard and fast rules, the Master-singers arrogated to themselves an undue importance. It is the conceit arising from this, their sacrifice of matter to form, their pendantry and their conventionalism, that Wagner has sought to satirize in this opera.

In Nuremberg the principal meetings of the Master singers were held in the Church of St. Catharine after afternoon service on Sundays and Holydays. For an insight into the constitution of their guilds and schools their rules and regulations, reference is due to the "Schul ordnung" or "Lagerbuch," and to the "Tabulatur. The one regulated the discipline and business of their organization, the other its artistic side. The singing at their sittings was divided into "Freisingen" (free singing) and "Hauptsingen" (principal singing). In the former, any one, even a stranger, might take part; in the latter, which was competitive, the faults against the rules committed by the singer were noted on a slate by a "Merker" (marker) ensconced behind a curtain. Seven faults were allowed, and he who exceeded this number was declared "outsung" and "outdone" ("versungen und verthan"). The candidate for admission into a guild was obliged to find vouchers for his respectability, and had also to undergo the ordeal of singing before the members. If the Marker declared that he had complied with the rules and regulations he was decorated with a silver chain and badge—the latter representing King David playing upon the harp—and was honorably admitted into the guild.

Candidates for admission into a guild, and the younger members thereof, were apprenticed to and instructed free of cost by the elder members, who held the rank of Masters. The members of a guild were thus classified: He who had only partially mastered the "Tabulatur" was called a "Schüler" (scholar); he who had completely familiarized himself with it was a "Schulfreund" (schoolman); he who could sing some half-dozen tunes was a "Singer;" he who could make verses to a given tune was a "Poet"; and he who could invent a new scheme of verse and a new tune was dubbed a "Master."

The "Tabulatur" consisted of rules and prohibitions. The different modes of rhyming were thus defined therein

Monosyllabic rhymes were called "stumpfe;" dissyllabic "klingende." "Waisen" were rhymeless lines; "Körner" were lines rhyming with one in the following stanza. "Pausen" were monosyllabic words constituting an entire line and rhyming with another similarly situated; dissyllables thus positioned were called "Schlagreime." Thirty-three "Feller" (faults) which were to be guarded against were specified: e. g., a single line might not contain more than thirteen syllables, because more could not be sung in a single breath. A singer must be careful to choose a key within the register of his voice. Among the faults were "blinde Meinung" (clouded meaning, i. e., the omission of conjunctions); "falsch Gebänd" (faulty versification); "unredbare Wörter" (unsingable phrases); "Klebsilbe" (word clippings, i. e., the contraction of two syllables into one); "Laster" (vices, i. e., faulty rhymes) "Aequivoca" (words of a double meaning); "Differenz" (the displacement of the letters in a word, etc.).

The poems of the Master-singers were always lyrical, and generally sung to a given tune. The length of the verse, the number of the lines, and the order of the rhymes being variable, their poems were susceptible of a great variety of forms. "Töne" (tones) denoted the scheme of versification; "Weisen" (modes), the melodies to which they were sung. There were some hundreds of these tones and modes, each of which had its particular title. The Masters were bound to know not only their titles, but to be able to sing them. The construction of a Master-song was governed by fixed rules. The scheme on which it was based was called a "Bar" (stave) and was divided into three or more "Gesätze" (stanzas). Each "Gesätz" consisted generally of two "Stollen" (shorter stanzas) in the same metre, and sung to the same tune. The first "Gesätz" was followed by an "Abgesang" (after-song), differing in metre and in length from the preceding stanzas, and sung to a different melody. The "Abgesang" was sometimes supplemented by another "Gesätz" in the same metre as the first. A complete Master-song generally consisted of three such "staves."

Of the circumstances which led to the choice of the Master-singers as the subject for an opera, Wagner has himself told us in a pamphlet entitled "Eine Mittheilung an meine Freunde" (A Communication to my Friends), first published in 1851. As the account he therein gives is both interesting in itself and at the same time furnishes a sketch of the plot of the opera, it seems best to reproduce it here, as far as translation will allow, in his own words. Wagner writes:—

"Immediately after the conclusion of 'Tannhäuser' (in 1845), I was fortunate in being able to visit a Bohemian bathing-place for the benefit of my health. Here, as on all occasions when I have been able to withdraw myself from the air of the 'footlights,' and from my official duties in such an atmosphere, I soon felt myself in a light and joyous mood. For the first time, and with artistic significance, a gaiety peculiar to my character manifested itself within me. Almost without premeditation I had a

short time previously resolved that my next show be a *comic* opera. I recall that this determination resulted principally from the advice of well-meaning friends, who wished me to write an opera in a 'lighter style,' because this, they said, would procure my admission to the German theatres, and thus insure that success for the continued want of which my outward circumstances had been seriously threatened.

"As among the Athenians of old a tragedy was followed by a merry satirical piece, there suddenly appeared to me during this journey for my health the picture of a comic play, which might suitably be made to serve as a satirical supplement for my 'Battle of the Bards at the Wartburg.' This was 'Die Meistersinger von Nürnberg,' with Hans Sachs at their head. I conceived Hans Sachs as the last example of the artistically productive folk's-spirit, and in this relation I opposed him to the narrow-mindedness of Master-singer-like Burgherdom, to the extremely droll and tabulatur-poetical pedantry of which I gave a personal expression in the character of the 'Marker.' This 'Marker' as every one knows, or as perhaps our critic did not know, was the overseer appointed by the Singers' Guild to 'mark' with strokes the faults against the rules committed by the executants, especially if they were candidates for admission to the Guild. Whoever got a certain number of strokes against him had 'versungen,' i. e., had failed in his singing.

"Now the eldest of the Guild offered the hand of his young daughter to the Master who, at an approaching public singing-match, should win the prize. The Marker who has already been paying his addresses to the maiden finds a rival in the person of a young knight, who, inspired by reading the 'Book of Heroes' and the old Minnesingers, has left the poverty-stricken and decaying castle of his ancestors with a view to learning in Nuremberg the art of the Master-singers. He announces his wish to be admitted into the Guild, being prompted thereto by a passion which he has suddenly conceived for the prize-maiden 'whom only a Master of the Guild may win.' On putting himself up for examination he sings an enthusiastic song in praise of women, which so repeatedly arouses the disapprobation of the Marker that, before he has half got through it, he has 'failed in his singing.' Sachs, who is pleased with the young man, frustrates, with a view to his welfare, a desperate attempt to carry off the maiden. In doing this he at the same time finds an opportunity of grievously offending the Marker. The latter, who has already been speaking rudely to Sachs with the view of humbling him about a pair of shoes which he has still left unfinished, stations himself at night under the maiden's window, in order to make trial of the song with which he hopes to win her by singing it to her as a serenade, it being his object to secure her voice in his favor in the adjudication of the prize. Sachs, whose workshop is opposite the house thus besung, begins singing loudly just as the Marker has commenced his serenade, because, as he tells the Marker, who is enraged at his doing so, it is

cessary to keep himself awake when he has to work so te, and that the work is wanted in a hurry nobody knows etter than the Marker, who has pressed him so hardly r it. At last he promises the luckless fellow to give ver singing, but on condiction of his being allowed to ark also in his manner — as a shoemaker — the faults hich, according to his feelings, he may find in the arker's song, viz., by a stroke of his hammer for each ult upon the shoe stretched upon the last. The Marker ngs; Sachs strikes the last again and again. In a passion e Marker jumps up; Sachs coolly asks him if he has nished his song. 'Not nearly' he shouts. Sachs, now ughing, holds up the shoes outside his shop, and declares at they are now quite finished, thanks to the 'Marker's ps.' With the rest of his song, which in despair he reams out without a pause, the Marker makes a miser- ole failure in the presence of the female figure which is en violently shaking her head at the window. Discon- late at this, he begs Sachs the following day to furnish im with a new song for his wooing. Sachs accordingly ves him a poem by the young knight, pretending that he oes not know from whence it has come. He advises him, owever, to make sure of having an appropriate tune to ng it to. The conceited Marker fancies he is all right this respect, and accordingly sings the poem before the ublic assembly of the Masters and people to a tune which thoroughly unsuited to it, and so disfigures it that, once ore, and this time decisively, he fails entirely. Enraged ereat, he accuses Sachs of having played him a' mean ick in thus foisting upon him so ignominious a poem. achs declares that the poem is an exceedingly good one,

only it requires to be sung to an appropriate tune. It is then determined that he who knows the proper tune shall be adjudged the victor. The young knight accomplishes this and wins his bride, but rejects with scorn the offer now made him of admission into the Guild. Sachs humourously stands up in defence of the Master-singers' Guild, and finishes with the rhyme:

"'Though holy Rome herself should pass away,
Our glorious German Art will ne'er decay.'"

The sketch which Wagner at once drew up was not, however, destined to be carried out in the rapid manner in which it was conceived. First, "Lohengrin" engrossed his attention; then the "Death of Siegfried," which event- ually grew into the "Nibelung" tetralogy; and then "Tristan und Isolde." "Die Meistersinger" which must therefore have occupied his thoughts, more or less, for nearly a quarter of a century, was not completed till 1867. It was brought to a public hearing for the first time in the course of the following year, under the direction of Hans von Bulow, at Munich.

As a comical pendant to "Tannhäuser," though not so satirical a one of the Master-singers as Wagner originally intended it to be, "Die Meistersinger" is not without its analogy to this. In "Tannhäuser" it is the victory of vir- tue over vice that is typified; "Die Meistersinger" repre- sents the victory of genius, aided by good sense, over ped- antry and conventionalism. The moral sought to be con- veyed is this: that Art is progressive, and that rules are useful, and are only to be broken by those who have learned to observe them.   C. A. B.

THE MASTER-SINGERS OF NUREMBURG
(DIE MEISTERSINGER VON NÜRNBERG.

<table>
<tr><td>

ACT FIRST.

The scene represents the interior of St. Katherine's church, in oblique section; only the last few rows of pews in the nave — which is supposed to extend out L towards the back — are visible; the foreground is the open space before the choir; this is afterwards shut off by a black curtain from the nave.

As the curtain rises the people are singing, to organ accompaniment, the last verse of a Chorale, which concludes afternoon service on the vigil of the Feast of St. John.

Hymn of the People.
   When to thee our Saviour went
   To receive thy Sacrament,
   Ere His sacrifice divine,
   We were giv'n salvation's sign,
   That through Baptism we might prove
   Worthy of His death and love.
       Interceder,
       Christ's preceder!
       Take us gently o'er
       Unto Jordan's shore.

(During the Chorale and its interludes the following dumb show takes place, accompanied by the orchestra:—

In the last pew are seated Eva and Magdalena; Walter v Stolzing is leaning against a pillar at a little distance, h.s eyes fixed on Eva. Eva turns repeatedly towards the knight and answers his now importunate, now tender glances of entreaty and passion shyly and modestly, but tenderly and encouragingly. Magdalena often breaks off her singing to give Eva a reproving nudge. — When the hymn is ended and while, during a long postlude on the organ, the congregation is gradually leaving by the principal door (supposed to be L at back), Walter advances hastily towards Eva and her companion. who have also risen from their seats and turned to go.)

Walter.
   (Softly but ardently to Eva.)
   Oh stay! — One word, I do entreat!

Eva.
   (Quickly turning to Magdalena.)
   My kerchief! Look! 'T is on the seat!

Magdalena.
   Forgetful child! Now here's a hunt!
       (Goes back to the pew.)
   (6)

</td><td>

ERSTER AUFZUG.

Die Bühne stellt das Innere der Katharinenkirche, schrägem Durchschnitt, dar; von dem Hauptstschiff, we ches links ab dem Hintergrunde zu sich ausdehnend a zunehmen ist, sind nur noch die letzten Reihen der Kirc enstühlbänke sichtbar; den Vordergrund nimmt der fre Raum vor dem Chor ein; dieser wird später durch ein Vorhang gegen das Schiff zu gänzlich abgeschlossen.

Beim Aufzug hört man, unter Orgelbegleitung, von d Gemeinde den letzten Vers eines Chorals, mit welchem d Nachmittagsgottesdienst zur Einleitung des Johannisfest schliesst, singen.

Choral der Gemeinde.
   Da zu dir der Heiland kam,
   Willig deine Taufe nahm,
   Weihte sich dem Opfertod,
   Gab er uns des Heil's Gebot:
   Dass wir durch dein' Tauf' uns weih'n,
   Seines Opfers werth zu sein.
       Edler Täufer,
       Christ's Vorläufer!
   Nimm uns freundlich an,
   Dort am Fluss Jordan.

(Während des Chorales und dessen Zwischenspiele entwickelt sich, vom Orchester begleitet, folgende pa tomimische Scene.

In der letzten Reihe der Kirchenstühle sitzen Eva un Magdalene; Walther v. Stolzing steht, in einiger Entfe nung, zur Seite an eine Säule gelehnt, die Blicke auf Ev heftend. Eva kehrt sich wiederholt seitwärts nach de Ritter um, und erwiedert seine bald dringend, bald zärtlic durch Gebärden sich ausdrückenden Bitten und Betheue ungen schüchtern und verschämt, doch seelenvoll und e muthigend. Magdalene unterbricht sich öfter im Gesang um Eva zu zupfen und zur Vorsicht zu mahnen. — Als de Choral zu Ende ist, und, während eines längeren Orge nachspieles, die Gemeinde dem Hauptausgange, welche links dem Hintergrunde zu anzunehmen ist, sich zuwende um allmählich die Kirche zu verlassen, tritt Walther a die beiden Frauen, welche sich ebenfalls von ihren Sitze erhoben haben, und dem Ausgange sich zuwenden wolle lebhaft heran.)

Walther.
   (Leise, doch feurig zu Eva.)
   Verweilt! — Ein Wort! Ein einzig Wort!

Eva.
   (Sich rasch zu Magdalene wendend.)
   Mein Brusttuch! Schau! Wohl liegt's im Ort?

Magdalene.
   Vergesslich Kind! Nun heisst es: such'!
       (Sie kehrt nach den Sitzen zurück.)

</td></tr>
</table>

Walter. Maiden, forgive if I affront—
One thing to ask you, one to discover,
What rules would I not dare pass over?
Is life for me or death?—Is bliss for me or
  bane?
Thy answer let in one word be clothed:
Fair maiden, say—

Magdalena.
(Returning.)
Here 't is again!

Eva. Alack! my scarf-pin! . . .

Magdalena. Did it fall out?
(She goes back, searching on the ground.)

Walter.
Is 't light and laughter, or gloom and doubt?
Can I attain the aim I approach to,
Or must I hear the syllable loathed—
Fair maiden, say—

Magdalena.
(Returning again.)
I have found the brooch, too!
Come, child, here's pin and 'kerchief, look!
Good lack! if I 've not forgot my book!
(Goes back once more.)

Walter. This single word, you speak it not—
This syllable that casts my lot?
Say Yes or No,—'t is quickly mouthed:
Fair maiden, say, are you betrothed?

Magdalena.
(Who has returned again, curtsies to Walter.)
Sir knight, your servant!
This is a compliment!
Our Eva's escort
Do you then represent?
Pray, Master Pogner is it
Your worship seeks to visit?

Walter.
(Sorrowfully.)
Would I never his house had seen!

Magdalena.
Hey day, sir! why, what do you mean?
When unto Nuremberg first you wended
Was not his friendly hand extended?
The bed and board, the dishes, drinks
He gave deserve some thanks, methinks?

Eva.
Good Lena! Pray! He meant it not so:
He is only eager to know—

Walther.
Fräulein! Verzeih't der Sitte Bruch!
Eines zu wissen, Eines zu fragen,
Was nicht müsst' ich zu brechen wagen!
Ob Leben oder Tod? Ob Segen oder Fluch?
Mit einem Worte sei mir's vertraut:—
Mein Fräulein, sagt—

Magdalene.
(Zurückkommend.)
Hier ist das Tuch.

Eva. O weh! die Spange?

Magdalene. Fiel sie wohl ab?
(Sie geht, am Boden suchend, wieder zurück.)

Walther.
Ob Licht und Lust, oder Nacht und Grab?
Ob ich erfahr', wonach ich verlange,
Ob ich vernehme, wovor mir graut.—
Mein Fräulein, sagt . . .

Magdalene.
(Wieder zurückkommend.)
Da ist auch die Spange.—
Komm' Kind! Nun hast du Spang' und
Tuch.—
O weh! da vergass ich selbst mein Buch!
(Sie kehrt wieder um.)

Walther.
Dies eine Wort, ihr sagt mir's nicht?
Die Sylbe, die mein Urtheil spricht?
Ja, oder: Nein!—ein flücht'ger Laut:
Mein Fräulein, sagt, seid ihr schon Braut?

Magdalene.
(Die bereits zurückgekommen, verneigt sich vor
Walther.)
Sieh da, Herr Ritter?
Wie sind wir hochgeehrt:
Mit Evchen's Schutze
Habt ihr euch gar beschwert?
Darf den Besuch des Helden
Ich Meister Pogner melden?

Walther.
(Leidenschaftlich.)
Betrat ich doch nie sein Haus!

Magdalene.
Ei! Junker! Was sagt ihr da aus!
In Nürnberg eben nur angekommen,
War't ihr nicht freundlich aufgenommen?
Was Küch' und Keller, Schrein und Schrank
Euch bot, verdient' es keinen Dank?

Eva.
Gut' Lenchen! Ach! das meint er ja nicht.
Doch wohl von mir wünscht er Bericht—

How shall I say? — I scarce comprehend —
His words my senses nearly suspend! —
He asks — about my choice!

Magdalena.
(Looking about apprehensively.)
Oh lud! subdue your voice!
Come directly home with me,
Just suppose the folks should see!

Walter. Not yet, till I know my fate!

Eva. They 're gone, there 's no one nigh.

Magdalena. That 's why I 'm in a state!
Sir knight, pray elsewhere try!

(David enters from the sacristy and busies himself with drawing together dark curtains which are so disposed as to close off the foreground of the stage from the nave.)

Walter. Nay! your reply?

Eva.
(Holding Magdalena.)
Reply?

Magdalena.
(Who has turned away, perceives David, pauses and calls tenderly aside.)
David! Why, can it be?

Eva.
(Urgently.)
What answer? Speak for me!

Magdalena.
(Distracted in her attention, looking round repeatedly at David.)
Chevalier, what of this maid you ask
To answer is no easy task:
She is betrothed, you might expect —

Eva.
(Quickly interrupting.)
But none has seen the bridegroom elect.

Magdalena.
The groom, in sooth, will not be known
Until to-morrow by trial snewn,
When a Master-Singer receives the prize —

Eva.
(As before.)
And my own hand his bay-wreath ties.

Walter. A Master-Singer?

Eva.
(Timidly.)
Are you not one?

Wie sag' ich's schnell? — Versteh' ich's aoch
kaum! —
Mir ist, als wär' ich gar wie im Traum! —
Er frägt, — ob ich schon Braut?

Magdalene.
(Sich scheu umsehend.)
Hilf Gott! Sprich nich so laut!
Jetzt lass' uns nach Hause gehn;
Wenn uns die Leut' hier sehn!

Walther. Nicht eher, bis ich Alles weiss!

Eva. 's ist leer, die Leut' sind fort.

Magdalene.
D'rum eben wird mir heiss! —
Herr Ritter, an andrem Ort!

(David tritt aus der Sacristei ein und macht sich darüber her, dunkle Vorhänge, welche so angebracht sind, dass sie den Vordergrund der Bühne nach dem Kirchenschiff zu schräg abschliessen, aneinander zu ziehen.)

Walther. Nein! Erst dies Wort?

Eva.
(Magdalene haltend.)
Dies Wort?

Magdalene.
(Die sich bereits umgewendet, erblickt David, hält an und ruit zärtlich für sich.)
David? Ei! David hier!

Eva.
(Drängend.)
Was sag' ich? Sag' du's mir!

Magdalene.
(Mit Zerstreutheit, öfters nach David sich umsehend.)
Herr Ritter, was ihr die Jungfer fragt,
Das ist so leichtlich nicht gesagt:
Fürwahr ist Evchen Pogner Braut —

Eva.
(Schnell unterbrechend.)
Doch hat noch Keiner den Bräut'gam er-
schaut.

Magdalene.
Den Bräut'gam wohl noch Niemand kennt,
Bis morgen ihn das Gericht ernennt,
Das dem Meistersinger ertheilt den Preis —

Eva.
(Wie zuvor.)
Und selbst die Braut ihm reicht das Reis.

Walther. Dem Meistersinger?

Eva.
(Bang.)
Seid ihr das nicht?

Walter. A trial-song?

Magdalena. 'Fore judges done.

Walter. Who wins the prize?

Magdalena. 'T is for them to shew one.

Walter. The bride will choose—?

Eva.
(Forgetting herself.)
You, or else no one!

(Walter turns aside in great perturbation, pacing up and down.)

Magdalena.
(Greatly shocked.)
Why, Eva! Eva! Are you insane?

Eva. Good Lena! Help me my lover to gain!

Magdalena.
Yesterday first did you see his face.

Eva. Kindled my love at so swift a pace
Having his portrait so oft in sight.
Say, is he not like David quite?

Magdalena. Are you mad? Like David?

Eva. The picture, I mean.

Magdalena. Oh! he with the harp and beard
long flowing,
As on the Masters' escutcheon seen?

Eva.
Nay! he Goliath with pebble o'erthrowing,
With sword at side and sling in hand,
Light locks surrounding his head like rays,
As Master Albrecht Dürer portrays.

Magdalena.
(Sighing loudly.)
Ah! David! David!

David.
(Who has gone out, now returns with a rule stuck in his girdle, and swinging in his hand a large piece of chalk tied to a string.)
Here am I! who calls?

Magdalena.
Ah, David! through thee what ill befalls!
(Aside.)
The darling rogue! he knows it, too!
(Aloud.)
Why, look! he's shut us all up inside here!

David.
(Tenderly to Magdalena.)
But *you* in my heart!

Walther. Ein Werbgesang?

Magdalene. Vor Wettgericht.

Walther. Den Preis gewinnt?

Magdalene. Wen die Meister meinen.

Walther. Die Braut dann wählt?

Eva.
(Sich vergessend.)
Euch, oder Keinen!
(Walther wendet sich, in grosser Aufregung auf und abgehend, zur Seite.)

Magdalene.
(Sehr erschrocken.)
Was? Evchen! Evchen! Bist du von
Sinnen?

Eva.
Gut' Lene! hilf mir den Ritter gewinnen!

Magdalene.
Sah'st ihn doch gestern zum ersten Mal?

Eva. Das eben schuf mir so schnelle Qual,
Dass ich schon längst ihn im Bilde sah;
Sag', trat er nicht ganz wie David nah'?

Magdalene. Bist du toll? Wie David?

Eva. Wie David im Bild.

Magdalene.
Ach! meinst du den König mit der Harfen,
Und langem Bart in der Meister Schild?

Eva.
Nein! der, dess' Kiesel den Goliath warfen,
Das Schwert im Gurt, die Schleuder zur
Hand,
Von lichten Locken das Haupt umstrahlt,
Wie ihn uns Meister Dürer gemalt.

Magdalene.
(Laut seufzend.)
Ach, David! David!

David.
(Der herausgegangen und jetzt wieder zurückkommt,
ein Lineal im Gürtel und ein grosses Stück weisser Kreide
an einer Schnur in der Hand schwenkend.)
Da bin ich! Wer ruft?

Magdalene.
Ach, David! Was ihr für Unglück schuft!
(Für sich.)
Der liebe Schelm! wüsst' er's noch nicht?
(Laut.)
Ei, seht! da hat er uns gar verschlossen?

David.
(Zärtlich zu Magdalene.)
In's Herz euch allein!

Magdalena.
          (Aside.)
              His face is so true!
          (Aloud.)
Come, say! what frolic's to be tried here?

David.   Forefend it! Frolic? A serious thing!
For the Masters I'm preparing the ring.

Magdalena.   What! will there be singing?

David.   A trial mere:
That Prentice wins his enfranchisement
Who ne'er gained for breach of the rules
    chastisement;
He who passes is Master here.

Magdalena.
Then the knight has dropped on the proper
    spot.
Now, Evy, come, we ought to trot.

Walter.
          (Quickly turning to them.)
To Master Pogner let me escort you.

Magdalena.
Await his approach; he'll be here soon.
If to win our Eva sought you,
Both time and place were opportune.
     (Two Prentices enter, bearing benches.)
    Quick! bid us adieu!

Walter.   What must I do?

Magdalena.   Let David supply all
        The facts of the trial.—
David, my dear, just heed what I say!
You must induce Sir Walter to stay.
        The larder I'll sweep,
        The best for you keep;
To-morrow rewards shall fall faster
If this young knight is made Master.
     (She hurries towards the door.)

Eva.
          (To Walter.)
When shall I see you?

Walter.
          (Ardently.)
            This evening, for sure!
What use declaring
How great my daring?
New is my heart, new my mind,
New to my senses is all I find,
      One thing I spring to
      One thing I cling to;

Magdalene.
          (Bei Seite.)
            Das treue Gesicht!—
          (Laut.)
Nein sagt! Was treibt ihr hier für Possen?

David.
Behüt' es! Possen! Gar ernste Ding'?
Für die Meister hier richt' ich den Ring.

Magdalene.   Wie? Gäb' es ein Singen?

David.   Nur Freiung heut'
Der Lehrling wird da losgesprochen,
Der nichts wider die Tabulatur verbrochen:
Meister wird, wen die Prob' nicht reu't.

Magdalene.
Da wär' der Ritter ja am rechten Ort.—
Jetzt, Evchen, komm', wir müssen fort.

Walther.
     (Schnell sich zu den Frauen wendend.)
Zu Meister Pogner lasst mich euch geleiten.

Magdalene.
Erwartet den hier: er ist bald da.
Wollt ihr euch Evchen's Hand erstreiten,
Rückt Ort und Zeit das Glück euch näh'.
     (Zwei Lehrbuben kommen dazu und tragen Bänke.)
    Jetzt eilig von hinnen!

Walther.
          Wass soll ich beginnen?

Magdalene.
        Lasst David euch lehren
        Die Freiung begehren.—
Davidchen! hör', mein lieber Gesell,
Den Ritter bewahr' hier wohl zur Stell'!
        Was Fein's aus der Küch'
        Bewahr' ich für dich:
Und morgen begehr' du noch dreister,
Wird heut' der Junker hier Meister.
     (Sie drängt fort.)

Eva.
          (Zu Walther.)
Seh' ich euch wieder?

Walther.
          (Feurig.)
            Heut' Abend, gewiss!—
Was ich will wagen,
Wie könnt' ich's sagen!
Neu ist mein Herz, neu mein Sinn,
Neu ist mir Alles, was ich beginn'.
      Eines nur weiss ich,
      Eines begrief' ich:

The hope sustaining
Thy hand of gaining !
Though to obtain thee my sword avail not,
As Master-Singer surely I 'll fail not.
For thee gold untold !
For thee
Poet's courage bold !

Eva.

(With great warmth.)
My heart's secret fold
For thee
Loving heed doth hold !

Magdalena   Quick, home, or shall scold !

David.

(Measuring Walter.)
A Master ?   Oho ! you 're bold !

(Magdalena pulls Eva quickly away through the curtains.
Walter, disturbed and brooding, has thrown himself
upon a raised ecclesiastical arm-chair which two Prentices
had just moved away from the wall to the middle of the
stage.
More Prentices enter ; they bring and arrange benches
and prepare everything (during the following dialogue)
for the sitting of the Master-Singers.)

First Prentice.   David, why skulk ?

Second Prentice.   Work apace !

Third Prentice.
The Marker's platform help us place !

David.   My labor and industry shame ye :
Work by yourselves ; my own affairs claim
me !

Second Prentice.   What airs he takes !

Third Prentice.   A model Prentice !

First Prentice.
His time to a shoemaker lent is.

Third Prentice.
His last and pen he holds together.

Second Prentice.
While cobbling he writes his stuff.

First Prentice.
He scribbles verses on scarlet leather.

Third Prentice.
(With expressive gesture.)
We'll soon give him tanning enough !

(They pursue their work, laughing.)

David.
(After observing the meditating knight awhile, calls
loudly):
"Now, begin ! "

Mit allen Sinnen
Euch zu gewinnen !
Ist's mit dem Schwert nicht, mus es gelingen
Gilt es als Meister euch zu ersingen.
Für euch Gut und Blut !
Für euch
Ditchter's heil'ger Muth !

Eva.

(Mit grosser Wärme.)
Mein Herz, sel'ger Gluth,
Für euch
Liebesheil'ge Huld !

Magdalene.
Schnell! heim, sonst geht's nicht gut !

David.
(Walther messend.)
Gleich Meister ? Oho ! viel Muth !

(Magdalene zieht Eva rasch durch die Vorhänge fort
Walther hat sich, aufgeregt und brütend, in einen erhöhten, kathederartigen Lehnstuhl geworfen, welchen zuvor
zwei Lehrbuben, von der Wand ab, mehr nach der Mitte
zu, gerückt hatten.
Noch mehrere Lehrbuben sind eingetreten: sie tragen
und richten Bänke, und bereiten Alles (nach der unter
folgenden Angabe) zur Sitzung der Meistersinger vor.)

Erster Lehrbube.
David ! was stehst ?

Zweiter Lehrbube.   Greif's an's Werk !

Dritter Lehrbube.
Hilf uns richten das Gemerk !

David.
Zu eifrigst war ich vor euch allen :
Nun schafft für euch ; hab' ander Gefal
len !

Zweiter Lehrbube.
Was der sich dünkt ?

Dritter Lehrbube.   Der Lehrling Muster

Erster Lehrbube.
Das macht, weil sein Meister ein Schuster.

Dritter Lehrbube.
Beim Leisten sitzt er mit der Feder.

Zweiter Lehrbube.
Beim Dichten mit Draht und Pfriem'.

Erster Lehrbube.
Sein' Verse schreibt er auf rothes Leder.

Dritter Lehrbube.
(Mit der entsprechenden Gebärde.)
Das, dächt' ich, gerbten wir ihm !

(Sie machen sich lachend an die fernere Herrichtung.)

David.
(Nachdem er den sinnenden Ritter eine Weile be-
trachtet, ruft sehr stark.)
"Fanget an ! "

Walter.
      (Looking up, surprised.)
            What is it ?

David.
      (Still louder.)
" Now, begin ! " — So cries the Marker ;
Then you must sing up ; don't you know that ?

Walter. Who is the Marker ?

David.   Don't you know that ?
Trials of song were you never at ?

Walter.
No, ne'er with for judge a trade-worker.

David. Are you a " Poet ? "

Walter.   May be so !

David. Are you a " Singer ? "

Walter.   I dont know.

David.
But " Schoolman," surely, and " Scholar "
  you 've been ?

Walter.
The terms I 've never heard nor seen.

David.
And yet you would be at once a Master ?

Walter.
Why should that seem to threaten disaster ?

David. O Lena ! Lena !

Walter.   What do you say ?

David. O Magdalena !

Walter.   Shew me the way !

David. The Tones and Modes we render
    Have many a form and name ;
    The harsh ones and the tender :
    Who would try a list to frame ?
A " Singer " and " Poet," both, d' ye see,
Previous to " Master " one must be

Walter. Who *is* a Poet ?

Prentices.
      (At work.)
         David ! ho there !

David. Presently, wait !
      (To Walter.)
         Who 's Poet, sir ?
When you a " Singer " have been created
And the Master-phrases have rightly stated,

Walther.
      (Verwundert aufblickend.)
            Was soll's !

David.
      (Noch stärker.)
  " Fanget an ! " — So ruft der " Merker ; "
  Nun sollt ihr singen : — wisst ihr das nicht ?

Walther.
Wer ist der Merker ?

David.   Wisst ihr das nicht.
War't ihr noch nie bei 'nem Sing-Gericht ?

Walther.
Noch nie, wo die Richter Handwerker.

David.
Seid ihr ein " Dichter ? "

Walther.   Wär' ich's doch !

David.
Waret ihr " Singer ? "

Walther.   Wüsst ich's noch !

David.
Doch " Schulfreund " war't ihr, und " Schüler " zuvor ?

Walther.
Das klingt mir alles fremd vor'm Ohr.

David.
Und so grad'hin wollt ihr Meister werden !

Walther.
Wie machte das so grosse Beschwerden ?

David. O Lene ! O Lene !

Walther.   Wie ihr doch so thut

David. O Magdalene !

Walther.   Rathet mir gut !

David. Der Meister Tön' und Weisen,
    Gar viel an Nam' und Zahl,
    Die starken und die leisen,
    Wer die wüsste allzumal !
Denn " Singer " und " Dichter " müsst ihr
  sein,
Eh' ihr zum " Meister " kehret ein.

Walther. Wer ist nun Dichter ?

Lehrbuben.
      (Während der Arbeit.)
         David ! kommst' her !

David. Warte nur, gleich ! —
      (Zu Walther.)
         Wer Dichter wär' ?
Habt ihr zum " Singer " euch aufgeschwun
  gen
Und der Meister-Töne richtig gesungen,

If by yourself, with rhyme and word,
You can construct and let be heard
Straightway a novel Master-strain,
At once the Poet's prize you'll gain.

Prentices.

Hey, David! shall we report this matter?
Will you never have finished your chatter?

David.

Oh, that's it! When I'm not by,
Of yourselves you place the things awry!

Walter.

Yet, one thing: Who is Master indeed?

David.

Sir knight, that matter is thus decreed:
The Poet who, with brain so witty,
To words and rhymes by himself prepared,
Can shape from the Tones a new Strain or
    Ditty,
He is a "Master-Singer" declared.

Walter
(Quickly.)

I only think of the Master-gain!
    If I sing,
    Vict'ry I wring
Only through verse with the proper strain.

David.
(Turning to the Prentices.)

What are you doing? Because I'm not there,
All wrong you're placing the platform and
    chair!
Is to-day "Song-class?" *You* know how;
Make smaller the stage!   'T is "Trial"
    now.

(The Prentices, who are preparing to erect a large
platform hung with curtains in the middle of the stage,
put this away, by David's direction, and build instead a
smaller platform of boards; on this they place a seat with
little desk before it, near this a large black-board to
which they hang a piece of chalk by a string; round this
erection are hung black curtains, which are drawn round
the back and sides and then over the front.)

Prentices.
(During their work.)

Oh! of course, Master David is clev'rer than
    most!
Doubtless he's hoping to get a high post.
    'T is Trial to-day,
    He'll try away;
That he's quite a "Singer" is now his boast.
The "Whack" rhyme he knows all through
    and through,
The "Sharp-hunger" tune he'll sing you,
    too:

Füget ihr selbst nun Reim und Wort',
Dass sie genau an Stell' und Ort
Passten zu einem Meister-Ton,
Dann trüg't ihr den Dichterpreis davon.

Lehrbuben.

He, David! Soll man's dem Meister klagen!
Wirst dich bald des Schwatzens entschlagen?

David.

Oho! Ja wohl! Denn helf' ich euch nicht,
Ohne mich wird Alles doch falsch gericht'!

Walther.

Nun dies' noch; wer wird "Meister" ge-
    nannt?

David.

Damit, Herr Ritter, ist's so bewandt! —
Der Dichter, der aus eig'nem Fleisse
Zu Wort' und Reimen, die er erfand,
Aus Tönen auch fügt eine neue Weise,
Der wird als "Meistersinger" erkannt.

Walther.
(Rasch.)

So bleibt mir nichts als der Meisterlohn!
    Soll ich hier singen,
    Kann's nur gelingen,
Find' ich zum Vers auch den eig'nen Ton.

David.
(Der sich zu den Lehrbuben gewendet.)

Was macht ihr denn da? — Ja, fehl' ich beim
    Werk,
Verkehrt nur richtet ihr Stuhl und Ge-
    merk! —
Ist denn heut' "Singschul'?" — dass ihr's
    wisst,
Das kleine Gemerk! — nur "Freiung" ist!

(Die Lehrbuben, welche Anstalt getroffen hatten, in der
Mitte der Bühne ein grösseres Gerüste mit Vorhängen
aufzuschlagen, schaffen auf Davids Weisung dies schnell
bei Seite und stellen dafür ebenso eilig ein geringeres
Brettbodengerüste auf; darauf stellen sie einen Stuhl mit
einem kleinen Pult davor, daneben eine grosse schwarze
Tafel, daran die Kreide am Faden aufgehängt wird; um
das Gerüst sind schwarze Vorhänge angebracht, welche
zunächst hinten und an beiden Seiten, dann auch vorn
ganz zusammengezogen werden.)

Die Lehrbuben.
(Während der Herrichtung.)

Aller End' ist doch David der Allerge-
    scheit'st!
Nach hohen Ehren gewiss er geizt:
    's ist Freiung heut';
    Gar sicher er freit,
Als vornehmer "Singer" schon er sich
    spreizt!
Die "Schlag"-Reime fest er inne hat,
"Arm-Hunger"-Weise singt er glatt:

But the "Hearty-kick" strain is what he
　knows best,
His master oft plays it him with zest.

(*They laugh.*)

David.

Aye, jeer away! but not at me;
Another laughing-stock you'll see.
He ne'er was "Scholar," learnt no singing,
But yet o'er "Poets" would be springing;
　　　A noble knight he,
　　　In single fight he
Thinks without any disaster
Here to rise to a "Master."
　　　So settle with care
　　　Both stage and chair!
Come here! Place there the board on wall,
That on it the Marker's fingers may fall!
　　　(*Turning to Walter.*)
Aye, Aye! the "Marker!" Are n't you
　afraid?
With him have many their failures made.
Seven faults you are suffered to make;
They 're marked with his chalk ev 'ry one;
If you commit one further mistake,
You 're "outsung," and declared "outdone."
　　　So have a care!
　　　The Marker's there.
God speed your Master-singing,
May you the chaplet be winning;
The wreath of flowers in silk so bright;
I hope it may fall to your lot, sir knight!

The Prentices.

(Who have closed the Marker's place, take hands and
dance in a ring round it.)

　"The wreath of flowers in silk so bright,
　I hope it may fall to your lot, sir knight."

(The erection is now completed in the following
manner:—at the R side covered benches are placed in
such a way as to curve towards the C. At the end of
these in the middle of the stage is the Marker's place, as
before described. L stands only the elevated seat ("the
Singer's Seat") opposite to the benches. At back, against
the large curtain, is a long, low bench for the Prentices—
Walter, vexed with the gibes of the boys, has seated himself on the front bench.

Pogner and Beckmesser enter from the sacristy, con-
versing; gradually the other masters assemble. The
Prentices, on seeing the Masters, enter, disperse and wait
respectfully by the back bench. Only David stands by
the entrance to the sacristy.)

Die "harte-Tritt"-Weis' doch kennt er am
　best',
Die trat ihm sein Meister hart und fest.
　　　(*Sie lachen.*)

David.

Ja, lacht nur zu! Heut' bin ich's nicht;
Ein Andrer stellt sich zum Gericht:
Der war nicht "Schüler," ist nicht "Sin-
　ger,"
Den "Dichter," sagt er, überspring' er;
　　　Denn er ist Junker,
　　　Und mit einem Sprung er
Denkt ohne weit're Beschwerden
Heut' hier "Meister" zu werden. —
　　　D'rum richtet nur fein
　　　Das Gemerk dem ein!
Dorthin!—Hierher!—Die Tafel an die
　Wand,
So dass sie recht dem Merker zur Hand!
　　　(*Sich zu Walther umwendend*)
Ja, ja!—dem "Merker!"—Wird euch wohl
　bang?
Vor ihm schon mancher Werber vorsang.
Sieben Fehler giebt er euch vor,
　　　Die merkt er mit Kreide dort an;
Wer über sieben Fehler verlor,
　　　Hat versungen und ganz verthan!
　　　Nun nehmet euch in Acht!
　　　Der Merker wacht.
Glück auf zum Meistersingen!
Mög't ihr euch das Kränzlein erschwin-
　gen!
Das Blumenkränzlein aus Seiden fein,
Wird das dem Herrn Ritter beschieden
　sein?

Die Lehrbuben.

(Welche das Gemerk zugleich geschlossen, fassen sich
an und tanzen einen verschlungenen Reihen darum.)

　"Das Blumenkränzlein aus Seiden fein
　　Wird das dem Herrn Ritter beschieden
　sein?

(Die Einrichtung ist nun folgender Massen beendigt:—
Zur Seite rechts sind gepolsterte Bänke in der Weise
aufgestellt, dass sie einen schwachen Halbkreis nach der
Mitte zu bilden. Am Ende der Bänke, in der Mitte der
Scene, befindet sich das "Gemerk" benannte Gerüste,
welches zuvor hergerichtet worden. Zur linken Seite
rechts nur der erhöhte, kathederartige Stuhl ["der Singstuhl"] der Versammlung gegenüber. Im Hintergrunde,
den grossen Vorhang entlang, steht eine lange niedere
Bank für die Lehrlinge. Walther, verdriesslich über das
Gespött der Knaben, hat sich auf die vordere Bank niedergelassen.

Pogner und Beckmesser kommen im Gespräch aus der
Sacristei; allmählich versammeln sich immer mehrere der
Meister. Die Lehrbuben, als sie die Meister eintreten
sahen, sind sogleich zurückgegangen und harren ehr-
bietig an der hinteren Bank. Nur David stellt sich
anfänglich am Eingang bei der Sacristei auf.)

Pogner.

(To Beckmesser.)
Trust me, my friendship is unshaken,
What I intend is for your good,
This trial must be undertaken;
None doubts your Mastership — who could?

Beckmesser.
But won't you in that matter falter,
Which caused in sooth my doubtful mood?
If Eva's whim the whole can alter,
What use is all my Masterhood?

Pogner.
Ah, what! It seems you've mainly rested
On that your hopes equivocal;
But if her heart's not interested,
How come you wooing her at all?

Beckmesser.
Why yes, that's true; therefore I drop a
Request that you will speak for me;
Say that my wooing's fair and proper,
That with Beckmesser you agree.

Pogner. With right good will.

Beckmesser.

(Aside.)
He won't give way!
How shall I disappointment stay?

Walter.
(Who, on perceiving Pogner, has risen and advanced to
meet him, now bows to him.)
Permit me, Master!

Pogner. What! Sir Walter?

(They greet one another.)

Beckmesser.
(Still to himself.)
If women had taste! But rather to palter
Than to hear poetry they prefer.

Walter.
This truly should be my proper groove.
I frankly state that what did move
Me from my land to part
Was solely love of Art.
I had forgotten to announce it,
But now in public I pronounce it:
A Master-Singer I would be.
Ope, Master, pray, the Guild to me.

(Other Masters have entered and advanced.)

Pogner.
(To those near him.)
Kunz Vogelgesang — Friend Nachtigal!

Pogner.

(Zu Beckmesser.)
Seid meiner Treue wohl versehen;
Was ich bestimmt, ist euch zu Nutz.
Im Wettgesang müsst ihr bestehen;
Wer böte euch als Meister Trutz?

Beckmesser.
Doch wollt ihr von dem Punkt nicht
weichen,
Der mich — ich sag's — bedenklich macht:
Kann Evchen's Wunsch den Werber
streichen,
Was nützt mir meine Meister-Pracht?

Pogner.
Ei, sagt! Ich mein', vor allen Dingen
Sollt' euch an dem gelegen sein?
Könnt ihr der Tochter Wunsch nicht
zwingen,
Wie möchtet ihr wohl um sie frei'n?

Beckmesser.
Ei ja! Gar wohl! D'rum eben bitt' ich,
Dass bei dem Kind ihr für mich sprecht,
Wie ich geworben zart und sittig,
Und wie Beckmesser grad' euch recht.

Pogner. Das thu' ich gern.

Beckmesser.
(Bei Seite.)
Er lässt nicht nach!
Wie wehrt' ich da 'nem Ungemach?

Walther.
(Der, als er Pogner gewahrt, aufgestanden und ihm ent-
gegengegangen ist, verneigt sich vor ihm.)
Gestattet, Meister!

Pogner. Wie! mein Junker!
Ihr sucht mich in der Singschul' hie?
(Sie begrüssen sich.)

Beckmesser.
(Immer bei Seite, für sich.)
Verstünden's die Frau'n! Doch schlechtes
Geflunker
Gilt ihnen mehr als all' Poesie.

Walther.
Hie eben bin ich am rechten Ort
Gesteh' ich's frei, vom Lande fort,
Was mich nach Nürnberg trieb,
War nur zur Kunst die Lieb'.
Vergass ich's gestern euch zu sagen,
Heut' muss ich's laut zu künden wagen:
Ein Meistersinger möcht' ich sein.
Schliesst, Meister, in die Zunft mich ein!

(Andere Meister sind gekommen und herangetreten.)

Pogner.
(Zu den nächsten.)
Kunz Vogelgesang! Freund Nachtigall!

Hear what I've got to tell you all!
This noble knight, a friend of mine,
In the Master Art doth seek to shine.

(Greetings and introductions.)

Beckmesser.
(Still aside.)
Once more I'll essay him, but if he'll not waver
I'll strive with my voice to win the maid's favor;
In silent night, heard only by her.
I'll see if my singing her heart can stir.
(Turns.)
What man is that?

Pogner.
(To Walter.)
'Faith, I am glad!
Old times are come again, my lad.

Beckmesser.
(Aside.)
I mislike his looks.
Pogner.
(Continuing.)
In your demand
My influence you may command.

Beckmesser.
(As before.)
What wants he here with his smiling air?

Pogner.
(As before.)
Truly I helped you your lands to sell,
In our Guild I'll enter you now as well.

Beckmesser.
(As before.)
Hallo, Sixtus! Of him beware!

Walter.
(To Pogner.)
Best thanks I proffer
And gratitude offer!
Then have I permission
To seek for admission
As striver for the prize,
And Master-Singer to rise?

Beckmesser.
Oho! that's nice! His ideas are not addled!

Pogner.
Sir Walter, these things with rules are saddled.
To-day is "Trial," I'll state your case;
The Masters will always lend me their face.

(The Master-Singers have now all assembled, Sachs the last)

Sachs. God greet ye, Masters!

Hört doch, welch' ganz besonderer Fall!
Der Ritter hier, mir wohlbekannt,
Hat der Meisterkunst sich zugewandt.

(Begrüssungen.)

Beckmesser.
(Immer noch für sich.)
Noch such' ich's zu wenden: doch sollt' nicht gelingen,
Versuch' ich des Mädchens Herz zu ersinger.
In stiller Nacht, von ihr nun gehört,
Erfahr' ich, ob auf mein Lied sie schwört.
(Er wendet sich.)
Wer ist der Mensch?

Pogner.
(Zu Walther.)
Glaubt, wie mich's freut
Die alte Zeit dünkt mich erneut.

Beckmesser.
(Immer noch für sich.)
Er gefällt mir nicht!

Pogner.
(Fortfahrend.)
Was ihr begehrt.
Soviel an mir, euch sei's gewährt.

Beckmesser.
(Ebenso.)
Was will der hier? — Wie der Blick ihm lacht!

Pogner.
(Ebenso.)
Half ich euch gern zu des Gut's Verkauf.
In die Zunft nun nehm' ich euch gleich gen auf.

Beckmesser.
(Ebenso.)
Holla! Sixtus! Auf den hab' Acht.

Walther.
(Zu Pogner.)
Habt Dank der Güte
Aus tiefstem Gemüthe!
Und darf ich denn hoffen,
Steht heut' mir noch offen
Zu werben um den Preis,
Dass ich Meistersinger heiss'?

Beckmesser.
Oho! Fein sacht! Auf dem Kopf steht kein Kegel!

Pogner.
Herr Ritter, diess geh' nun nach der Rege.
Doch heut' ist Freiung! ich schlag' euch vor
Mir leihen die Meister ein willig Ohr.

(Die Meistersinger sind nun alle angelangt. zuletzt auch Hans Sachs.)

Sachs.
Gott grüss' euch, Meister!

Vogelgesang. Are all arriven?

Beckmesser. Yes, Sachs is here, too.

Nachtigal. Let names be given.

Fritz Kothner.

(Produces a list, stands apart from the rest, and calls.)
To hold a Trial-examination,
Masters, I give ye invitation:
  Of one and all
  The names I call,
And first my own, which though I note ne'er,
I answer to, and am Fritz Kothner.
Are you there, Veit Pogner?

Pogner. Here at hand.
    (Sits.)

Kothner. Kunz Vogelgesang?

Vogelgesang. Yes, here I stand.
    (Sits.)

Kothner. Herman Ortel?

Ortel. Comes when he ought.
    (Sits.)

Kothner. Balthazar Zorn?

Zorn. Ne'er late I'm caught.
    (Sits.)

Kothner. Conrad Nachtigal?

Nachtigal. True as my song.
    (Sits.)

Kothner. Augustin Moser?

Moser Here all along.
    (Sits.)

Kothner. Nicholas Vogel? — No?

A Prentice.
(Jumping up from his seat at back.)
    He's ill.

Kothner. God send him recovery.

All the Masters. Amen.

Prentice. Good will.
    (Sits down again.)

Kothner. Hans Sachs?

David.
(Officiously rising.)
    He's there, sir.

Sachs.
(Threatening David.)
    Tingles thy skin?—
Excuse me, Master! Sachs has come in.
    (Sits.)

Kothner. Sixtus Beckmesser?

Vogelgesang. Sind wir beisammen

Beckmesser.
Der Sachs ist ja da!

Nachtigall. So ruft die Namen

Fritz Kothner.
(Zieht eine Liste hervor, stellt sich zur Seite auf und ruft.)
Zu einer Freiung und Zunftberathung
Ging an die Meister ein' Einladung:
  Bei Nenn' und Nam'
  Ob jeder kam,
Ruf' ich nun auf, als letzt-entbot'ner,
Der ich mich nenn' und bin Fritz Kothner.
Seid ihr da, Veit Pogner?

Pogner. Hier zur Hand
    (Er setzt sich.)

Kothner. Kunz Vogelgesang?

Vogelgesang. Ein sich fand
    (Setzt sich.)

Kothner. Hermann Ortel?

Ortel. Immer am Ort.
    (Setzt sich.)

Kothner. Balthasar Zorn?

Zorn. Bleibt niemals fort
    (Setzt sich.)

Kothner. Konrad Nachtigall?

Nachtigall. Treu seinem Schlag
    (Setzt sich.)

Kothner. Augustin Moser?

Moser. Nie fehlen mag
    (Setzt sich.)

Kothner. Niklaus Vogel? — Schweigt?

Ein Lehrbube.
(Sich schnell von der Bank erhebend.)
    Ist krank

Kothner. Gut' Bess'rung dem Meister!

Alle Meister. Walt's Gott

Der Lehrbube. Schön Dank
    (Setz sich wieder.)

Kothner. Hans Sachs?

David.
(Vorlaut sich erhebend.)
    Da steht er!

Sachs.
(Drohend zu David.)
    Juckt dich das Fell?
Verzeiht, Meister! — Sachs ist zur Stell'
    (Er setz sich.)

Kothner. Sixtus Beckmesser?

Beckmesser.   Always near Sachs,
Then I have a rhyme to "bloom and wax."
(Sits close to Sachs, who laughs.)

Kothner. Ulrich Eisslinger?

Eisslinger.   Here!
(Sits.)

Kothner.   Hans **Foltz**?

Foltz. I'm there.
(Sits.)

Kothner.   Hans Schwarz?

Schwarz.   The list now halts.
(Sits.)

Kothner. The meeting's full; a goodly show.
Shall we make choice of a Marker now?

Vogelgesang. The festival first.

Beckmesser.
(To Kothner.)
       If you are pressed,
My turn I'll yield to you with zest.

Pogner.
Not yet, my Masters! let that alone,
A weighty matter I would make known.
(All the Masters rise and reseat themselves.)

Kothner. With pleasure, Master; tell.

Beckmesser.   Immer bei Sachs
Dass den Reim ich lern' von "blüh' und wachs'."
(Er setzt sich neben Sachs, dieser lacht.)

Kothner. Ulrich Eisslinger?

Eisslinger.   Hier!
(Setzt sich.)

Kothner.   Hans **Foltz**

Foltz. Bin da.
(Setzt sich.)

Kothner. Hans Schwarz?

Schwarz.   Zuletzt: **Gott wollt's**
(Setzt sich.)

Kothner. Zur Sitzung gut und voll die Zahl.
Beliebt's, wir schreiten zur Merkerwahl?

Vogelgesang. Wohl eh'r nach dem Fest.

Beckmesser.
(Zu Kothner.)
       Pressirt's den Herrn
Mein Stell' und Amt lass' ich ihm gern.

Pogner.
Nicht doch, ihr Meister! Lasst das jetzt fort:
Für wicht'gen Antrag bitt' ich um's Wort.
(Alle Meister stehen auf und setzen sich wieder.)

Kothner.
Das habt ihr, Meister! Sprecht!

POGNER'S ADDRESS.

(POGNER'S ANREDE.)

English Version by L. U.

Moderato. POGNER.

> Give heed now to what I say! The feast of John the Bap-tist's
> *Nun hört, und ver-steht mich recht! Das schö-ne Fest, Jo-han-nis-*

> day You know we keep to-mor-row: On mea-dow green, 'mid flow-ers gay, With feast, and
> *tag, ihr wisst begeh'n wir mor-gen· auf grü-ner Au', am Blu-men-hag, bei Spiel und*

> dance, and mer-ry play, The cares the mind be-set-ting With mer-ry heart for-
> *Tanz im Lust-ge-lag, an fro-her Brust ge-bor-gen, ver-ges-sen sei-ner*

> get-ting, Each one re-joic-es as he may. The sing-ing school to great church
> *Sor-gen, ein Je-der freut sich, wie er mag. Die Sing-schul' ernst im Kir-chen-*

Copyright, 1882, by O. Ditson & Co.

choir The mas - ters e'en are chang - ing, With noise and din the gate they gain, Ad - vanc - ing
chor die Meis - ter selbst ver - tau - schen, mit Kling und Klang hi - naus zum Thor, auf off' - ne

o'er the o - pen plain, Where ga - la sounds are ring - ing; As list - 'ners to their
Wie - se zieh'n sie vor, bei hel - len Fes - tes Rau - schen das Volk sie las - sen

sing - ing, Th'un - tu - tored folk they'll not dis - dain. A prize is set, for
lau - schen dem Frei - ge - sang mit Lai - en Ohr. Zu ei - nem Werb - und

which with song Each year have sing - ers striv - en, And both are praised both
Wett - ge - sang ge - stellt sind Sie - ges - prei - se, und bei - de preist man

far and long, The song and what is giv - en. I am, thank God, a prosp'rous
weit und lang, die Ga - be, wie die Wei - se. Nun schuf mich Gott zum rei - chen

man, And since each one gives what he can, What gift I could de -
Mann; und gibt ein Je - der wie er kann, so muss - te ich wohl

cide on, That I could look with pride on, This much my mind has tried. Now
sin - nen was ich gäb zu ge - win - nen, dass ich nicht käm' zu Schand'; so

con molto espress.

hear what I de - cide. It oft has caused me sor - row
hört denn, was ich fand. In deut - schen Lan - den viel ge -

keen, To find throughout the na - tion The burgher nig - gard - ly and mean In each one's es - ti -
reis't, hat oft es mich ver - dros - sen, dass man den Bür - ger we - nig preis't, ihn karg nennt und ver -

un poco animato.

ma - tion. By lof - ty and by low - ly born, The same re - proach is made with
schlossen. An Hö - fen, wie an nied' - rer Statt, des bitt' - ren Ta - dels ward' ich

a tempo.

scorn: "By base de - sire for gold The burgher's mind's con - trolled!" That we, as
satt, dass nur auf Schacher und Geld, sein Merk der Bür - ger stellt! Dass wir im

all . . in Ger - man lands, Give art a - lone de - vo - tion, They seem to have no
wei - - ten deutschen Reich die Kunst ein - zig noch pfle - gen, d'ran dünkt ih - nen we - nig ge

no-tion. Yet how this to our hon-or stands, That no-bly, as man should, We
le-gen. Doch wie uns das zur Eh-re ge-reich', und das mit ho-hem Muth wir

prize the fair and good, That art . . in ev-'ry form we love, 'Twas this to the world I
schä-tzen was schön und gut, was werth die Kunst und was sie gilt, das ward ich der Welt zu

wish'd to prove, And there-fore, mas-ters, know What gift I shall be-stow!
zei-gen ge-willt, d'rum hört, Meis-ter die Gab' die als Preis be-stimmt ich hab'!

The vic - - tor in the art of song, Who wins the prize be-fore the throng,
Dem Sie - - ger der im Kunst-ge-sang vor al-lem Volk den Preis er-rang,

On John the Bap-tist's day, Be he who-e'er he may, Him give I, of art a
am Sanct Jo-han-nis-tag, sei er, wer er auch mag, dem geb ich, ein Kunst-ge-

lov-er, Of Nu-rem-berg, Veit Pog-ner, With gold and
wog-ner, von Nü-ren-berg Veit Pog-ner, mit all' mein-em

lands and all be-side, E-va, my on-ly child, as bride!
Gut, wie's geh' und steh', E-va, mein ein-zig Kind, zur Eh'!

The Masters.
(Animatedly to one another.)
That 's nobly said! Brave words — brave
man!
You see now what a Nuremberger can!
So far and wide we 'll raise always
The worthy burgher Pogner's praise!

Prentices.
(Jumping up merrily.)
All our days raise and blaze
Pogner's praise.

Vogelgesang.
Who would not now unmarried be!

Sachs.
There 's some would give their wives with
glee.

Nachtigal.   Come, single man,
Do all ye can.

Pogner. My meaning you must clearly see;
No lifeless gift I offer you:

Die Meister.
(Sehr lebhaft durcheinander.)
Das nenn' ich ein Wort! Ein Wort, ei
Mann!
Da sieht man, was ein Nürnberger kann!
D'rob preis't man euch noch weit und breit,
Den wack'ren Bürger Pogner Veit!

Die Lehrbuben.
(Lustig aufspringend.)
Alle Zeit, weit und breit,
Pogner Veit!

Vogelgesang.
Wer möchte da nicht ledig' sein!

Sachs.
Sein Weib' gäb' gern wohl mancher d'rei

Nachtigall.
Auf, ledig' Mann!
Jetzt macht euch dran!

Pogner.
Nun hört noch, wie ich's ernstlich mein'
Ein' leblos' Gabe stell' ich nicht:

The maid shall sit in judgment, too.
Our Guild the winner shall declare,
But as to marriage, 'tis but fair
   That, 'spite the Master's choice,
   The bride should have a voice.

Beckmesser.
       (To Kothner.)
Do you like that?

Kothner.
      (Aloud.)
      You mean to say
That we the maiden must obey.

Beckmesser. 'T were dangerous!

Kothner.   I cannot see
How then our judgment would be free.

Beckmesser.
Let her choose as may please her heart,
And leave the Master-Song business apart.

Pogner. Nay, nay! why so? Let me correct!
Any man whom we all elect
   May be by her rejected,
   But never another accepted:
A Master-Singer he must be;
None may she wed uncrowned by ye.

Sachs. But stay!
Perhaps that were too much to say.
The fire that warms a maiden's heart
Is not like flames of Master-Art;
Undisciplined, the female mind
Level with public voice I find.
So, if you hold to public vision
   Your high esteem of Art,
If you desire the girl's decision
   Should not the matter thwart,
Then let the people, too, decide;
With the maiden's voice they'd coincide.
   (The Prentices jump up and rub their hands.)

Beckmesser. Hey! Are not the boys contented!

Sachs.
     (Earnestly continuing.)
   So may it be ne'er repented
That once, on St. John's day, ev'ry year,
Ye do not bring the people here,
But bend your Guild of Masters proud
Right willingly towards the crowd.
   You cater here for the masses;
   I think then 't were but right
   To ask the vote of those classes
   And hear if they find delight.

Ein Mägdlein sitzt mit zu Gericht.
Den Preis erkennt die Meister-Zunft;
Doch gilt's der Eh', so will's Vernunft,
   Dass ob der Meister Rath
   Die Braut den Ausschlag hat.

Beckmesser.
     (Zu Kothner.)
Dünkt euch das klug?

Kothner.
      (Laut.)
      Versteh' ich gut,
Ihr gebt uns in des Mägdlein's Huth?

Beckmesser.
Gefährlich das!

Kothner.   Stimmt es nicht bei.
Wie wäre dann der Meister Urtheil frei?

Beckmesser.
Lasst's gleich wählen nach Herzen's Ziel,
Und lasst den Meistergesang aus dem Spiel.

Pogner.
Nicht so! Wie doch! Versteht mich recht!
Wenn ihr Meister den Preis zusprecht,
   Die Maid kann dem verwehren,
   Doch nie einen Andren begehren:
Ein Meistersinger muss er sein;
Nur wen ihr krönt, den soll sie frei'n.

Sachs. Verzeiht!
Vielleicht schon ginget ihr zu weit.
Ein Mädchenherz und Meisterkunst
Erglüh'n nicht stets von gleicher Brunst;
Der Frauen Sinn, gar unbelehrt,
Dünkt mich dem Sinn des Volks gleich
   werth.
Wollt ihr nun vor dem Volke zeigen,
   Wie hoch die Kunst ihr ehrt;
Und lasst ihr dem Kind die Wahl zu eigen,
   Wollt nicht, dass dem Spruch es
   wehrt':
So lasst das Volk auch Richter sein;
Mit dem Kinde sicher stimmts überein,
   (Die Lehrbuben springen auf und reiben sich die
Hände.)

Beckmesser.
Hei! wie sich die Buben freuen!

Sachs.
     (Eifrig fortfahrend.)
   D'rum möcht's euch nie gereuen,
Dass jährlich am Sankt Johannisfest,
Statt dass das Volk man kommen lässt,
Herab aus hoher Meister-Wolk'
Ihr selbst euch wendet zu dem Volk'.
   Dem Volke wollt ihr behagen;
   Nun dächt' ich, läg es nah',
   Ihr liesset es selbst euch auch sagen,
   Ob das ihm zur Last geschah?

Thus Art and Nation shall bloom and wax
By your good help, say I, Hans Sachs.

Vogelgesang.   That s very right!

Kothner.   And yet all wrong!

Nachtigal.
When riff-raff speak I'll hold my tongue.

Kothner.
Our Art would quickly be disgraced,
If it were swayed by public taste.

Beckmesser.
He's tried for that who talks so loud;
Clap-trap stuff he writes for the crowd.

Pogner.   Friend Sachs, what I propose is new;
Too many novelties won't do! —
I ask, then, if ye Masters will hold
My offer on the terms just told?
          (The Masters rise assentingly.)

Sachs.   I am content the maid should decide.

Beckmesser.
               (Aside.)
That cobbler-man I can't abide!

Kothner.   What candidate comes to me?
          A bachelor he must be.

Beckmesser.
He may be a widower!   How about Sachs?

Sachs.
Nay, nay, good Marker!   Of younger wax
Must be the suitor who comes to woo
Our Eva, than myself or you.

Beckmesser.   Than even I? — Mannerless
          knave!

Kothner.   If suitors offer, their names I crave!
Is any one here who seeks to essay?

Pogner.
Well, Masters, to the work of the day!
          And be it understood
That I, as Masters should,
          To this knight have offered protection,
          Who seeks for our election
To woo, as Master-Singers may.—
Sir Walter von Stolzing step this way!
          (Walter advances and makes obeisance.)
Sir Walter Stolzing, Franconian knight:
My friends his praise both speak and write,
The last survivor of his race,
He lately left his native place

Dass Volk und Kunst gleich blüh' und
          wachs',
Bestellt ihr so, mein' ich Hans Sachs.

Vogelgesang.   Ihr meint s wohl recht!

Kothner.   Doch steht's d'rum faul.

Nachtigall.
Wenn spricht das Volk, halt' ich das Maul.

Kothner.
Der Kunst droht' allweil' Fall und Schmach,
Läuft sie der Gunst des Volkes nach.

Beckmesser.
D'rin bracht' er's weit, der hier so dreist:
Gassenhauer dichtet er meist.

Pogner.
Freund Sachs, was ich mein', ist schon neu:
Zuviel auf einmal brächte Reu'! —
So frag' ich, ob den Meistern gefällt,
Gab' und Regel, wie ich's gestellt?
          (Die Meister erheben sich.)

Sachs.
Mir genügt der Jungfer Ausschlag-Stimm'.

Beckmesser.
               (Für sich.)
Der Schuster weckt doch stets mir Grimm!

Kothner.   Wer schreibt sich als Werber ein?
          Ein Jung-Gesell muss es sein.

Beckmesser.
Vielleicht auch ein Wittwer?   Fragt nur den
          Sachs!

Sachs.
Nicht doch, Merr Merker!   Aus jüng'rem
          Wachs
Als ich und ihr muss der Freier sein,
Soll Evchen ihm den Preis verleih'n.

Beckmesser.
Als wie auch ich? — Grober Gesell!

Kothner.
Begehrt wer Freiung, der komm' zur Stell'!
Ist Jemand gemeld't der Freiung begehrt!

Pogner.
Wohl Meister!   Zur Tagesordnung kehrt!
          Und nehmt von mir Bericht,
          Wie ich auf Meister-Pflicht
          Einen jungen Ritter empfehle,
          Der wünscht, dass man ihn wähle,
Und heut' als Meistersinger frei'. —
Mein Junker von Stolzing, kommt herbei!
          (Walter tritt vor und verneigt sich.)
Von Stolzing Walther aus Frankenland,
Nach Brief' und Urkund mir wohlbekannt.
Als seines Stammes letzter Spross,
Verliess er neulich Hof und Schloss,

To Nuremberg to come
And make this town his home.

Beckmesser.
(To his neighbor.)
Young good-for-nothing! This is nice!

Nachtigal.
(Aloud.)
Friend Pogner's word will quite suffice.

Sachs. We Masters did long since decide
Nor lord nor peasant should be denied.
Art is indeed the sole concern
Of those who Master-Song would learn.

Kothner. First I pray you impart
What Master taught you your Art.

Walter. By silent hearth in winter tide,
When house and hall in snow did hide,
How once the Spring so sweetly smiled
And soon should wake to glory mild,
An ancient book my sire compiled
Set all before me duly
Sir Walter von der Vogelweid'
Has been my master, truly.

Sachs. A goodly master!

Beckmesser. But long since dead!
So what could he of our precepts have read?

Kothner. But in any school or college
Of singing gained you your knowledge?

Walter. Yes, when the fields the frost defied
Beneath returning summer-tide,
What once in dreary winter's night
Within that book I read aright
Now pealed aloud through forest bright:
I heard the music ringing.
The wood before the Vogelweid'—
'T was there I learnt my singing.

Beckmesser. Can any one his meaning trace?

Vogelgesang. Good sooth, he 's bold!

Nachtigal. Peculiar case!

Kothner. Now, Masters, if you will,
The Marker's place we 'll fill.
Sacred theme do you choose, sir knight?

Walter. My sacred trove 's
The banner of love,
Swung and sung to my delight!

Kothner. Secular be it. Now inside.
Marker Beckmesser, please to hide.

Und zog nach Nürnberg her,
Dass er hier Bürger wär'.

Beckmesser.
(Zum Nachbar.)
Neu Junker-Unkraut! Thut nicht gut.

Nachtigall.
(Laut.)
Freund Pogner's Wort Genüge thut.

Sachs.
Wie längst von den Meistern beschlossen ist,
Ob Herr, ob Bauer, hier nichts beschliesst:
Hier fragt sich's nach der Kunst allein,
Wer will ein Meistersinger sein.

Kothner. D'rum nun frag' ich zur Stell':
Welch' Meister's seid ihr Gesell'?

Walther. Am stillen Herd in Winterszeit,
Wenn Burg und Hof mir eingeschnei't,
Wie einst der Lenz so lieblich lacht',
Und wie er bald wohl neu erwacht',
Ein altes Buch, vom Ahn' vermacht'
Gab das mir oft zu lesen:
Herr Walther vor. der Vogelweid',
Der ist mein Meister gewesen.

Sachs. Ein guter Meister!

Beckmesser. Doch lang schon todt
Wie lehrt' ihm der wohl der Regel Gebot?

Kothner. Doch in welcher Schul' das Singen
Mocht' euch zu lernen gelingen?

Walther.
Wann dann die Flur vom Frost befreit,
Und wiederkehrt die Sommerszeit,
Was einst in langer Winternacht
Das alte Buch mir kund gemacht,
Das schallte laut in Waldespracht,
Das hört' ich hell erklingen:
Im Wald dort auf der Vogelweid'
Da lernt' ich auch das Singen.

Beckmesser.
Entnahmt ihr was der Worte Schwall?

Vogelgesang. Ei nun, er wagt's.

Nachtigall. Merkwürd'ger Fall!

Kothner. Nun Meister, wenn's gefällt,
Werd' das Gemerk bestellt.—
Wählt der Herr einen heil'gen Stoff!

Walther. Was heilig mir,
Der Liebe Panier,
Schwing' und sing' ich, mir zu Hoff'.

Kothner.
Das gilt uns weltlich. D'rum allein,
Merker Beckmesser, schliesst euch ein!

370

Beckmesser.

(Rising and going as if reluctantly to the Marker's box.

Unpleasant work, and more so now ;
My chalk will harass you, I trow !
    Sir knight, now hark !
Sixtus Beckmesser goes to mark.
    Here in this cell
He silently does his duty fell.
Seven faults are given you clear ;
    With chalk on a slate they are scored :
But if more mistakes than seven appear,
    Then, sir knight, without hope you are
    floor'd.
    My ears are keen ;
But as, if what I do were seen,
    You might be curbed,
    Be not disturbed ;
I hide myself from view : —
So Heav'n be kind to you.

(He has seated himself in the box and with the last words stretches his head out with a scornfully familiar nod, then pulls to the front curtains, which a Prentice had opened for him, so that he becomes invisible.)

Kothner.

(Taking down the " *Leges Tabulaturae* " which the Prentices had hung upon the wall.)

All that belongs to song mature
Now hear read from the Tabulature.
    (Reads.)
" Each Master-Singer-created Stave
Its regular measurement must have,
By sundry regulations stated
And never violated.
What we call a ' Section' is two Stanzas ;
For each the self-same melody answers .
A Stanza several lines doth blend,
And each line with a rhyme must end.
Then come we to the ' After-Song,'
Which must be also some lines long,
And have its especial melody
Which from the other must diff'rent be.
So Staves and Sections of such measure
A Master-Song may have at pleasure.
He who a new song can outpour,
Which in four syllabes — not more —
Another strain doth plagiarize,
He may obtain the Master-Prize." —
Now sit you on the Singer's stool !

Walter.   Here, on this stool?

Kothner.   It is the rule.

Walter.

(Mounting the stool, with dissatisfaction.)
For thee I'm sitting, love, herein.

Kothner.
          (Loudly.)
The Singer sits !

Beckmesser.

(Aufstehend und dem Gemerk zuschreitend.,

Ein sau'res Amt, und heut' zumal ;
Wohl giebt's mit der Kreide manche Qual
    Herr Ritter wisst :
Sixtus Beckmesser Merker ist ;
    Hier im Gemerk
Verrichtet er sein strenges Werk.
Sieben Fehler giebt er euch vor,
    Die merkt er mit der Kreide dort an .
Wenn er über sieben Fehler verlor,
    Dann versang er Herr Rittersmann.
    Gar fein er hört :
Doch dass er euch den Muth nicht stört,
    Säh't ihr ihm zu,
    So giebt er euch Ruh',
    Und schliesst sich gar hier ein, —
    Lässt Gott euch befohlen sein.

(Er hat sich in das Gemerk gesetzt, streckt mit dem Letzten den Kopf höhnisch freundlich nickend heraus, und zieht den vorderen Vorhang, den zuvor einer der Lehrbuben geöffnet hatte, wieder ganz zusammen, so dass er unsichtbar wird.)

Kothner.

(Hat die von den Lehrbuben aufgehängten " *Leges Tobulaturae* " von der Wand genommen.)

Was euch zum Leide Richt' und Schnur,
Vernehmt nun aus der Tabulatur. —
    (Er liest.)
" Ein jedes Meistersanges Bar
Stell' ordentlich ein Gemässe dar
Aus unterschiedlichen Gesetzen,
Die Keiner soll verletzen.
Ein Gesetz besteht aus zweenen Stollen,
Die gleiche Melodei haben sollen ;
Der Stoll' aus etlicher Vers' Gebänd',
Der Vers hat seinen Reim am End'.
Darauf so folgt der Abgesang,
Der sei auch etlich' Verse lang,
Und hab' sein' besondere Melodei,
Als nicht im Stollen zu finden sei.
Derlei Gemässes mehre Baren
Soll ein jed' Meisterlied bewahren ;
Und wer ein neues Lied gericht',
Das über vier der Sylben nicht
Eingreift in andrer Meister Weis',
Des' Lied erwerb' sich Meister-Preis." —
Nun setzt euch in den Singstuhl !

Walther.
Hier in den Stuhl?

Kothner.   Wie's Brauch der Schul

Walther.
(Besteigt den Stuhl und setzt sich mit Missbehagen.
Für dich, Geliebte, sei's gethan !

Kothner.
          (Sehr laut.)
Der Sänger sitzt.

Beckmesser.

(From his box, very harshly.)
Now begin!

Walter.

(After a short consideration.)
Now begin!—
So cries through woodlands the **Spring**,
And makes them loudly ring:
Then, as to distance urging,
The echoes ripple thence,
From far there comes a surging
That swells with pow'r intense:
   It booms and bounds,
   The forest sounds
With thousand heavenly voices;
   Now loud and clear,
   Approaching near,
   The murmurs steal
   Like bells that peal:
Exultant Nature rejoices!
   This call,
   How all
The wood an answer makes,
As life again awakes,
   Pouring forth
A tender song of Spring!

(During this, repeated groans of discouragement and
scratchings of the chalk are heard from the Marker. Walter hears them also, and after a momentary pause of discomposure continues.)

There, like a hiding craven
With hate and envy torn,
A thorny hedge his haven,
Sits Winter, all forlorn,
In withered leaves array'd
His lurking head is laid;
He seeks the joyous singing
To sorrow to be bringing.
   (Rising from the stool in displeasure.)
   But—"Now begin!"
So cried a voice in my breast
Ere aught of love I had guess'd;
There stirred a deep emotion
And waked me, as I had slept:
My heart with throbbing commotion
My bosom's restraint o'erlept:
   My blood did course
   With giant force.
To novel sensations soaring;
   From warmth of night
   With boundless might
   Sighs hurried me
   Towards the sea.
The pent-up passion outpouring:
   The call
   How all

Beckmesser.

(Im Gemerk, sehr grell.)
Fanget an!

Walther.

(Nach einiger Sammlung.)
Fanget an!
So rief der Lenz in den Wald.
Dass laut es ihn durchhallt:
Und wie in fern'ren Wellen
Der Hall von dannen flieht,
Von weither nah't ein Schwellen
Das mächtig näher zieht;
   Es schwillt und schallt,
   Es tönt der Wald
Von holder Stimmen Gemenge;
   Nun laut und hell
   Schon nah' zur Stell',
   Wie wächst der Schwall!
   Wie Glockenhall
Ertos't des Jubels Gedränge!
   Der Wald,
   Wie bald
Antwortet' er dem Ruf,
Der neu ihm Leben schuf,
   Stimmte an
Das süsse Lenzes-Lied!—

(Man hat aus dem Gemerk wiederholt unmuthige Seufzer des Merkers, und heftiges Anstreichen mit der Kreide
vernommen. Auch Walther hat es bemerkt, und fährt
dadurch für eine kurze Weile gestört, fort.)

In einer Dornenhecken,
Von Neid und Gram verzehrt,
Musst' er sich da verstecken,
Der Winter, Grimm-bewehrt:
Von dürrem Laub umrauscht
Er lauert da und lauscht,
Wie er das frohe Singen
Zu Schaden könnte bringen. —
   (Unmuthig vom Stuhl aufstehend.)
   Doch: fanget an!
So rief es mir in die Brust,
Als ich noch von Liebe nicht wusst'
Da fühlt' ich's tief sich regen,
Als weckt' es mich aus dem Traum
Mein Herz mit bebenden Schlägen
Erfüllte des Busen's Raum:
   Das Blut, es wall't
   Mit Allgewalt,
Geschwellt von neuem Gefühle;
   Aus warmer Nacht
   Mit Uebermacht
   Schwillt mir zum Meer
   Der Seufzer Heer
In wildem Wonne-Gewühle:
   Die Brust
   Mit Lust

My breast an answer makes,
As life anew it takes,
   Pouring forth
A glorious lay of love!

Beckmesser.
(Who has grown still more restive, tears open the cur-
tains.)
   Is 't nearly finished?

Walter   What means this call?

Beckmesser.
(Holding out the slate completely covered with chalk-
marks.)
   I've finished with the slate, that 's all!
      (The Masters cannot restrain their laughter.)

Walter. Yet hear! My lady's praise to ring,
My second verse I ought to sing.

Beckmesser.
               (Leaving his box.)
Sing where you will! Here you 're undone.
My Masters, see the slate, ev'ry one:
The like of this I never knew;
I'd credit no man's work thereto!
      (The Masters are in commotion.)
Walter. D' ye let him, Masters, plague me so!
Shall I be heard by you or no?

Pogner.
One word, friend Marker! You 're somewhat
wroth?

Beckmesser.
Be Marker he who likes henceforth!
But that this man is quite out-sung
You can decide yourselves among.

Sachs.
(Who has listened to Walter from the first with serious
interest.)
Not all have like opinion passed.
   The song you 've so derided
To me is new, but not confused:
   Though not by us 't was guided,
His course was firm, as though well used.
   One way you measure solely
A work that your rules do not fit:
   Resign your own views wholly,
Some other rules apply to it.

Beckmesser.
Aha! That 's fine! Just listen, pray!
Sachs opes a gap for fools that way,
   Where in and out at pleasure
   Their minds a course can measure.
Let in the streets the rabble holloa;
Here must we, at least, some discipline
follow.

Antwortet sie dem Ruf,
Der neu ihr Leben schuf:
   Stimmt nun an
Das hehre Liebes-Lied!

Beckmesser.
(Der immer unruhiger geworden, reisst den Vorhang
auf.)
   Seid ihr nun fertig?

Walther.   Wie fraget ihr?

Beckmesser.
(Die ganz mit Kreidestrichen bedeckte Tafel heraus
haltend.)
   Mit der Tafel ward ich fertig schier.
      (Die Meister müssen lachen.)

Walther.
Hört doch!   Zu meiner Frauen Preis
Gelang' ich jetzt erst mit der Weis'.

Beckmesser.
               (Das Gemerk verlassend.)
Singt, wo ihr wollt! Hier habt ihr ver
   than.—
Ihr Meister, schaut die Tafel euch an:
So lang ich leb', ward's nicht erhört;
Ich glaubt's nicht, wenn ihr's all' auch
   schwört!
      (Die Meister sind im Aufstand durcheinander.)

Walther.
Erlaubt ihr's, Meister, dass er mich stört?
Blieb' ich von Allen ungehört?

Pogner.
Ein Wort, Herr Merker!   Ihr seid gereizt?

Beckmesser.
Sei Merker fortan, wer darnach geizt!
Doch dass der Ritter versungen hat,
Beleg' ich erst noch vor der Meister Rath.

Sachs.
(Der vom Beginn an Walther mit zunehmendem Ernst
zugehört hat.)
Nicht jeder eure Meinung theilt.—
      Des Ritters Lied und Weise,
Sie fand ich neu, doch nicht verwirrt;
      Verliess er uns're G'leise,
Schritt er doch fest und unbeirrt.
      Wollt ihr nach Regeln messen,
Was nicht nach eurer Regeln Lauf,
      Der eig'nen Spur vergessen,
Sucht davon erst die Regeln auf!

Beckmesser.
Aha!   Schon recht!   Nun hört ihr's doch
Den Stümpern öffnet Sachs ein Loch,
      Da aus und ein nach Belieben
      Ihr Wesen leicht sie trieben.
Singet dem Volk auf Markt und Gassen:
Hier wird nach den Regeln nur eingelassen.

Sachs. Friend Marker, why in such a flutter?
 Wherefore so angry, pray?
A riper judgment you might utter,
 If better heed you 'd pay.
And so, to speak my final word,
The young knight to the end must be heard.

Beckmesser.
The Master's Guild, the school and all,
Weighed against Sachs' word must fall.

Sachs. The Lord forbid I should demand
Aught contrary to our law's command:
 But surely there 't is written:
" The Marker shall be chosen so,
 By prejudice unbitten
That nought of bias he may show."
If this one turns his step to wooing
Can he refrain a wrong from doing,
To bring to shame 'fore all the school.
His rival yonder on the stool?
   (Walter flames up.)

Nachtigal. You go too far!

Kothner.   Too free you are!

Pogner.
   (To the Masters.)
I pray you, Masters, cease this jar.

Beckmesser.
Hey! What needs Master Sachs to mention
 Which way my steps may be turned?
With the state of my *sole* his attention
 Better might be concerned!
But since my shoemaker follows the Muse
It fares but ill with my boots and shoes.
 Just look, how they 're split!
 See, here 's a great slit!
All of his verse and rhyme
I would declare sublime;
His dramas, plays, his farces and all,
If with my new pair of shoes he 'd call.

Sachs.
   (Scratching his head.)
I fear you have me there:
 But, Master, if 't is fair
That on the merest boor's shoe-leather
 Some little verse I frame,
I ask you, worthy town-clerk, whether
 You should not have the same?
A motto such as you require,
With all my poor poetic fire,
 Not yet I 've hit upon;
 But I will come anon,
When I have heard the knight's song through:
So let him sing on without ado!
(Walter. much put out, remounts the Singer's Seat.)

The Masters. Enough! Conclude!

Sachs.
Herr Merker, was doch solch ein Eifer?
  Was doch so wenig Ruh'?
Eu'r Urtheil, dünkt mich, wäre reifer,
  Hörtet ihr besser zu.
Darum, so komm ich jetzt zum Schluss,
Dass den Junker zu End' man hören muss

Beckmesser.
Der Meister Zunft, die ganze Schul',
Gegen den Sachs da sind wie Null.

Sachs. Verbüt' es Gott, was ich begehr',
 Dass das nicht nach den Gesetzen wär'!
  Doch da nun steht's geschrieben,
Der Merker werde so bestellt,
  Dass weder Hass noch Lieben
Das Urtheil trüben, das er fällt,
Geht er nun gar auf Freiers-Füssen,
Wie sollt' er da die Lust nicht büssen
Den Nebenbuhler auf dem Stuhl
Zu schmähen vor der ganzen Schul'!
   (Walther flammt auf.)

Nachtigall. Ihr geht zu weit!

Kothner.   Persönlichkeit

Pogner.
   (Zu den Meistern.)
Vermeidet, Meister, Zwist und Streit!

Beckmesser.
Ei, was kümmert's doch Meister Sachsen,
 Auf was für Füssen ich geh'?
Liess' er d'rob lieber Sorge sich wachsen,
 Dass nichts mir drück' die Zeh'!
Doch seit mein Schuster ein grosser Poet,
Gar übel es um mein Schuhwerk steht!
  Da seht, wie es schlappt,
  Und überall klappt!
  All' seine Vers' und Reim'
  Liess' ich ihm gern daheim,
Historien, Spiel' und Schwänke dazu,
Brächt' er mir morgen die neuen Schuh'!

Sachs. Ihr mahnt mich da gar recht:
  Doch schickt sich's, Meister, sprecht,
Dass, find' ich selbst dem Eseltreiber
  Ein Sprüchlein auf die Sohl',
Dem hochgelahrten Herrn Stadtschreiber
  Ich nichts d'rauf schreiben soll?
Das Sprüchlein, das eu'r würdig sei,
Mit all' meiner armen Poeterei
  Fand ich noch nicht zur Stund';
  Doch wird's wohl jetzt mir kund,
Wenn ich des Ritters Lied gehört:—
D'rum sing er nun weiter ungestört!
(Walther, in grosser Aufregung, stellt sich auf den Sing
stuhl.)

Die Meister. Genug! Zum Schluss!

Sachs.

(To Walter.)

Sing, 'spite the Marker's angry mood!

Beckmesser.

(As Walter recommences, fetches out his board from the box and shows it, during the following, first to one and then to another, to convince the Masters, whom he at last gathers into a circle round him while he continues to exhibit his slate.)

What rubbish is this to shock us?
He surely means to mock us!
Every fault, both grave and slight,
I have marked on the board aright.
"Faulty verses," "Unsingable phrases,"
"Word-clippings," and "Vices" grave,
"Equivocal," "Rhymes in wrong places,"
"Reserved," "Displaced" is all the Stave.
A "Patch-work-Song" between the two verses,
"Clouded meaning" in every part,
"Uncertain words," then a "Change," that worse is,
There's "Breath ill-managed," here's "Sudden start,"
"Incomprehensible melody,"
A hotch-potch, made of all tones that be.
If at such toil you do not halt,
Masters, count after me each fault.
Already with the eight he was spent,
But so far as this sure none ever went!
Well over fifty, roughly told.
Say, would you this man a master hold?

The Masters.

(To one another.)

Ah yes, that's true! 't is plain indeed,
That this young knight cannot succeed.
By Sachs he may be a genius thought,
But in our singing-school he is nought.
Who should in justice remain neglected,
If this novice a master were made?
If all the world's to be elected,
What good were the Masters' high grade?
Ha! look how the knight is enraged.
Hans Sachs on his side has engaged.
'T is really too bad! Quick make an end!
Up, Masters, speak and your hands extend!

Pogner.

(Aside.)

Ah yes, I see! 't is sad indeed:
My poor young knight will scarce succeed!
Should I retract my first decree,
I fear me sad results there'd be.
I'd fain see him no more neglected;
My kinship he would not degrade:
And when the victor is elected
Who knows if he will please my maid?
Some trouble I presage,
For Eva can I engage?

Sachs.

(Zu Walther.)

Singt, dem Herrn Merker zum Verdruss!

Beckmesser.

(Holt, während Walther beginnt, aus dem Gemerk die Tafel herbei, und hält sie während des Folgenden, von Einem zum Andern sich wendend, zur Prüfung den Meistern vor, die er schliesslich zu einem Kreis um sich zu vereinigen bemüht ist, welchem er immer die Tafel zur Einsicht vorhält.)

Was sollte man da noch hören?
Wär's nicht nur uns zu bethören?
Jeden der Fehler gross und klein,
Sehr genau auf der Tafel ein. —
"Falsch Gebänd," "unredbare Worte,"
"Kleb Sylben," hier "Laster" gar;
"Aequivoca," "Reim am falschen Orte,"
"Verkehrt," "verstellt" der ganze Bar;
Ein "Flickgesang" hier zwischen den Stollen;
"Blinde Meinung" allüberall;
"Unklare Wort'," "Differenz," hie "Schrollen,"
Da "falscher Athem," hier "Ueberfall."
Ganz unverständliche Melodei!
Aus allen Tönen ein Mischgebräu'!
Scheu'tet ihr nicht das Ungemach,
Meister, zählt mir die Striche nach!
Verloren hätt' er schon mit dem acht',
Doch so weit wie der hat's noch Keiner gebracht:
Wohl über fünfzig, schlecht gezählt!
Sagt, ob ihr euch den zum Meister wählt?

Die Meister.

(Durcheinander.)

Jo wohl, so ist's! Ich seh' es recht!
Mit dem Herrn Ritter steht es schlecht.
Mag Sachs von ihm halten, was er will,
Hier in der Singschul' schweig' er still!
Bleibt einem Jeden doch unbenommen,
Wen er zum Genossen begehrt?
Wär' uns der erste Best' willkommen,
Was blieben die Meister dann werth?
Hei! Wie sich der Ritter da quält!
Der Sachs hat ihn sich erwählt. —
's ist ärgerlich gar! Drum macht ein End'!
Auf Meister, stimmt und erhebt die Händ'!

Pogner.

(Für sich.)

Ja wohl, ich seh's, was mir nicht recht:
Mit meinem Junker steht es schlecht!
Weiche ich hier der Uebermacht,
Mir ahnet, dass mir's Sorge macht.
Wie gern säh' ich ihn angenommen,
Als Eidam wär' er mir gar werth;
Nenn' ich den Sieger nun willkommen,
Wer weiss, ob ihn mein Kind begehrt!
Gesteh' ich's, dass mich das quält,
Ob Eva den Meister wählt!

Walter.

(In wild and desperate euthusiasm, standing erect in the singer's seat and looking down on commotion of the Masters.)

From gloomy thicket breaking
Behold the screech-owl swoop
With circling flight awaking
The ravens' croaking troop!
In sombre ranks they rise
And utter piercing cries;
With voices hoarse and hollow
The daws and magpies follow.
 Up then soars,
By golden pinions stirr'd,
A wondrous lovely bird.
Each brightly glowing feather
Gleams in the glorious day;
It signs me hither — thither,
To float and flee away.
 The swelling heart,
 With pleasing smart,
Sore need with wings supplieth;
 It mounts in flight
 To giddy height,
 From the city's tomb,
 Through heaven's pure dome,
To hills of home it hieth,
Towards the verdant Vogelweid'
Where Master Walter lived and died;
And there I'll rightly raise
In song my lady's praise:
 Up shall soar,
When raven-Masters croak no more,
My noble loving lay.
Farewell, ye Masters, for aye!
(With a gesture of proud contempt he leaves the singer's Seat and quits the building.)

Sachs.

(Following Walter's song.)
Ha! what a flow
Of genius' glow!
My Masters, pray now give o'er!
Listen, when Sachs doth implore!
Friend Marker, there! grant us some peace!
Let others listen! — Why won't you cease?
No use! A vain endeavor!
I can scarcely my own voice hear!
They'll heed the young fellow never:
He's bold indeed to persevere!
His heart must be placed aright:
A true born poet-knight! —
Hans Sachs may make both verse and shoe;
A knight is he and a poet, too.

The Prentices.

(Who have been rubbing their hands in glee and jump-

Walther.

(In übermüthig verzweifelter Begeisterung, hoch auf dem Singstuhl aufgerichtet, und auf die unruhig durchein ander sich bewegenden Meister herabblickend.)

Aus finst'rer Dornenhecken
Die Eule rauscht' hervor,
Thät rings mit Kreischen wecken
Der Raben heis'ren Chor:
In nächt'gem Heer zu Hauf',
Wie krächzen all' da auf,
Mit ihren Stimmen, den hohlen,
Die Elstern, Kräh'n und Dohlen!
 Auf da steigt
Mit gold'nem Flügelpaar,
Ein Vogel wunderbar:
Sein strahlend hell Gefieder
Licht in den Lüften blinkt;
Schwebt selig hin und wieder,
Zu Flug und Flucht mir winkt
 Es schwillt das Herz
 Von süssem Schmerz,
Der Noth entwachsen Flügel;
 Es schwingt sich auf
 Zum kühnen Lauf,
 Zum Flug durch die Luft
 Aus der Städte Gruft,
Dahin zum heim'schen Hügel;
Dahin zur grünen Vogelweid',
Wo Meister Walther einst mich freit';
Da sing' ich hell und hehr
Der liebsten Frauen Ehr':
 Auf da steigt,
Ob Meister-Kräh'n ihm ungeneigt,
Das stolze Minne-Lied. —
Ade! ihr Meister, hienied'!
(Er verlässt mit einer stolz verächtlichen Gebärde den Stuhl und wendet sich zum Fortgehen.)

Sachs.

(Walther's Gesang folgend.)
Ha, welch ein Muth!
Begeistrungs-Gluth! —
Ihr Meister, schweigt doch und hört!
Hört, wenn Sachs euch beschwört!
Herr Merker da! gönnt doch nur Ruh'!
Lasst And're hören! gebt das nur zu! —
Umsonst! All eitel Trachten!
Kaum vernimmt man sein eigen Wort!
Des Junkers will Keiner achten: —
Das heiss' ich Muth, singt der noch fort!
Das Herz auf dem rechten Fleck:
Ein wahrer Dichter-Reck'!
Mach' ich, Hans Sachs, wohl Vers und Schuh',
Ist Ritter der und Poet dazu.

Die Lehrbuben.

(Welche längst sich die Hände rieben und von der Ban-

ing up from their bench, towards the end take hands and
iance in a ring round the Marker's box.)

      God speed your Master-singing,
        And may you the prize soon be winning:
    The wreath of flowers in silk so bright,
    i hope it may fall to your lot, sir knight!

Beckmesser.   Now, Masters, give it tongue!

    (Most of them hold up their hands.)

All the Masters.   Rejected and outsung!

(General confusion, augmented by the Prentices, who
shoulder the benches and Marker's box, causing hindrance
and disorder to the Masters who are crowding to the door.
Sachs remains alone in front, looking pensively at the
empty seat: when the boys remove this too he turns away
with humorous gesture of discouragement, and the curtain
falls.)

aufsprangen, schliessen jetzt gegen das Ende wieder **ihren**
Reihen und tanzen um das Gemerk.)

      Glück auf zum Meistersingen.
      Mög't ihr euch das Kränzlein erschwin-
   gen:
    Das Blumenkränzlein aus Seiden fein,
    Wird das dem Herrn Ritter beschieden sein

Beckmesser.
    Nun, Meister, kündet's an!
      (Die Mehrzahl hebt die Hände **auf.**'

Alle Meister.
    Versungen und verthan!

(Alles geht in Aufregung auseinander, lustiger Tumul
der Lehrbuben, welche sich des Gemerkes und der Me's
terbänke bemächtigen, wodurch Gedränge und Durchein
ander der nach dem Ausgange sich wendenden Meister
ensteht. — Sachs, der allein im Vordergrunde verblieben
blickt noch gedankenvoll nach dem leeren Singstuhl. als
die Lehrbuben auch diesen erfassen, und Sachs darob mi
humoristisch-unmuthiger Gebärde sich abwendet, fällt de
Vorhang.)

SECOND ACT.

The stage represents in front the section of a street running across, intersected in the middle by a narrow alley which winds crookedly towards the back, so that in C are two corner houses, of which one, a handsome one, R, is that of Pogner, the other, simpler, L, is Sachs's shop. — A flight of several steps leads up to Pogner's door: porch sunk in, with stone seats. At side R a lime-tree shades the place before the house; green shrubs at its foot, surrounding a stone seat. — The entrance to Sachs's house is also towards the street; a divided door leads into the cobbler's workshop; close by, an elder-tree spreads its boughs over it. Two windows, one of the workshop, the other of an inner chamber, look on to the alley. (All houses in both street and alley must be practicable.)

Genial summer evening; during the first scene night gradually closes.

David is putting up the shutters outside. Other Prentices are doing the same for other houses.

Prentices

(as they work).

Midsummer day ! Midsummer day !
Flowers and ribbons in goodly display !

David

(aside).

" The wreath of flowers in silk so fine,
Would that to-morrow it might be mine."

Magdalena

coming out of Pogner's house with a basket on her arm and seeking to approach David unperceived).

Hist ! David !

David

(turning toward the alley).

Whom are you calling?
Get along with your foolish squalling !

Prentices.

David, what cheer?
Why so severe?
Turn round your skull,
If you 're not dull !
" Midsummer day ! Midsummer day !"
And he can't see Mistress Lena right in his way !

ZWEITER AUFZUG.

Die Bühne stellt im Vordergrunde eine Strasse im Längendurchschnitte dar, welche in der Mitte von einer schmalen Gasse, nach dem Hintergrunde zu krumm abbiegend, durchschnitten wird, so dass sich in Front zwei Eckhäuser darbieten, von denen das eine, reichere, rechts — das Haus Pogner's, das andere, einfachere — links — das des Hans Sachs ist. — Zu Pogner's Hause führt von der vorderen Strasse aus eine Treppe von mehreren Stufen; vertiefte Thüre, mit Steinsitzen in den Nischen. Zur Seite ist der Raum, ziemlich nah an Pogner's Hause, durch eine dickstämmige Linde abgegränzt; grünes Gesträuch umgibt sie am Fuss, vor welchem auch eine Steinbank angebracht ist. — Der Eingang zu Sachsens Hause ist ebenfalls nach der vorderen Strasse zu gelegen: eine getheilte Ladenthüre führet hier unmittelbar in die Schusterwerkstatt; dicht dabei steht ein Fliederbaum, dessen Zweige bis über den Laden hereinhängen. Nach der Gasse zu hat das Haus noch zwei Fenster, von welchen das eine zur Werkstatt, das andere zu einer dahinterliegenden Kammer gehört. [Alle Häuser, namentlich auch der engeren Gasse, müssen praktikabel sein.]

Heiterer Sommerabend, im Verlaufe der ersten Auftritte allmählich einbrechende Nacht.

David ist darüber her, die Fensterläden nach der Gasse zu von aussen zu schliessen. Andere Lehrbuben thun das Gleiche bei andern Häusern.

Lehrbuben

(während der Arbeit).

Johannistag ! Johannistag !
Blumen und Bänder so viel man mag !

David

(für sich).

" Das Blumenkränzlein von Seiden fein,
Möcht' es mir balde beschieden sein ! "

Magdalene

(ist mit einem Korbe am Arm aus Pogner's Haus gekommen und sucht David unbemerkt sich zu nähern).

Bst ! David !

David

(nach der Gasse zu sich umwendend).

Ruft ihr schon wieder !
Singt allein eure dummen Lieder !

Lehrbuben.

David, was soll's?
Wär'st nicht so stolz,
Schaut'st besser um,
Wär'st nicht so dumm !
"Johannistag ! Johannistag ! "
Wie der nur die Jungfer Lene nicht kennen mag!

Magdalena.

David, listen!   Turn round, my dear!

David.

Ah, Mistress Lena!   You are here?

Magdalena
           (pointing to her basket).

Here 's something nice ; peep in and see 't !
'T is all for my dear lad to eat.
Tell me though first, What of Sir Walter?
You counseled him well?   Has the crown been
                                        won?

David.

Ah, Mistress Lena, how I falter !
He was outsung and declared outdone.

Magdalena.

Rejected !   Outdone !

David.
             What ails you, dear one?

Magdalena
(snatching the basket away from David's outstretched
                    hand).

       Hands off the basket !
       Dare you to ask it !
       Good lack ! Our chevalier outdone !

(she hastens back into the house, wringing her hands in
                    despair.)

     (David looks after her dumfounded)

Prentices

(who have stolen near and overheard, now advance to
        David as if congratulating him).

Hail to the Prentice and his bride !
       How well his wooing speeds !
We all have heard and seen beside :
       She upon whom he feeds
       Within his heart's true casket,
Has gone and refused him the basket !

Davia.
           (flying out).

       Be off with you boys !
       Give over your noise !

Prentices
           (dancing round David).

Midsummer day ! Midsummer day !
All go a-courting as they may.

Magdalene.

David ! hör' doch ! kehr' dich zu **mir** !

David.

Ach, Jungfer Lene ! Ihr seid hier?

Magdalene
           (auf ihren Korb deutend).

Bring' dir was Gut's ! schau nur hinein !
Das soll für mein lieb' Schätzel sein —
Erst aber schnell, wie ging's mit dem Ritter ?
Du riethest ihm gut?   Er gewann den Kranz ?

David.

Ach, Jungfer Lene ! Da steht's bitter ;
Der hat verthan und versungen ganz !

Magdalene.

Versungen? Verthan?

David.
           Was geht's euch nur an?

Magdalene
(den Korb, nach welchem David die Hand ausstreckt, nei
           tig zurückziehend).

       Hand von der Taschen !
       Nichts da zu naschen ! —
Hilf Gott !   Unser Junker verthan !

(Sie geht mit Gebärden der Trostlosigkeit nach dem Haus
                    zurück).

David
           (sieht ihr verblüfft nach).

Die Lehrbuben

(welche unbemerkt näher geschlichen waren, gelausch
hatten und sich jetzt, wie glückwünschend, David präsen
                    tiren).

Heil, Heil zur Eh' dem jungen Mann !
       Wie glücklich hat er gefrei't !
Wir hörten's All', und sahen's an :
       Der er sein Herz geweiht,
       Für die er lässt sein Leben,
Die hat ihm den Korb nicht gegeben.

David
           (auffahrend).

       Was steht ihr hier faul?
       Gleich haltet eu'r Maul !

Die Lehrbuben.
           (David umtanzend).

Johannistag ! Johannistag !
Da frei't ein Jeder wie er mag.

The Masters woo,
And workmen too,
Old folks as well as the babbies!
And graybeards grim
Wed maidens slim,
Young fellows wed ancient tabbies.
Hooray! Hooray! Midsummer day!

(David is about to fly at the boys in his rage, when Sachs, who had come down the alley, steps between them. The Prentices separate.)

Sachs.

What now? Are you again in a fray?

David.

Not I! They sang a mocking stave.

Sachs.

Pay no heed; show how to behave!
Get in! To bed! Shut up and light!

David.

Have I to sing, sir?

Sachs.

Not to-night!
As punishment for to-day's offending,
Put all these shoes on the lasts for mending.

(Both go into the workshop and exeunt through an inner door. The Prentices have also dispersed.)

———

(Pogner and Eva, as if returning from a walk, come silently and thoughtfully down the alley, the daughter leaning on her father's arm.)

Pogner

(still in the alley, peeping through a chink in Sachs' shutter).

Let's see if Sachs is in to-night;
I'd speak with him. Suppose I call!

(David comes out of the inner room with a light and sits down to work at the bench by the window.)

Eva.

He seems at home : I see a light.

Pogner.

Shall I? Why should I after all?
(Turns away.)
If strange things I should venture,
Might I not earn his censure?
(After some reflection.)
Who said that I went too far? 'T was he,
Yet, if our rules I exceeded,
I have but done as he did!
But that might be mere vanity.

(To Eva.)
And you, my child, your thoughts are hid?

Der Meister freit!
Der Bursche freit!
Da gibt's Geschlamb' und Geschlumbfer!
Der Alte freit
Die junge Maid,
Der Bursche die alte Jungfer!—
Juchhei! Juchhei! Johannistag!

David ist im Begriff, wüthend drein zu schlagen, als Sachs, der aus der Gasse hervorgekommen, dazwischen tritt. Die Buben fahren auseinander.

Sachs.

Was gibt's? Treff' ich dich wieder am Schlag?

David.

Nicht ich! Schandlieder singen die.

Sachs.

Hör' nicht drauf! Lern's besser wie sie!
Zur Ruh'! in's Haus! Schliess' und mach Licht!

David.

Hab' ich noch Singstund'?

Sachs.

Nein, singst nicht!
Zur Straf' für dein heutig' frech' Erdreisten. —
Die neuen Schuh' steck' auf die Leisten!

(Sie sind Beide in die Werkstatt eingetreten und gehen durch innere Thüren ab. Die Lehrbuben haben sich ebenfalls zerstreut.)

Pogner und Eva, wie vom Spaziergange heimkehrend, die Tochter leicht am Arme des Vaters eingehenkt, sind beide schweigsam und in Gedanken die Gasse heraufgekommen.

Pogner

(noch auf der Gasse, durch eine Klinze im Fensterladen von Sachsens Werkstatt spähend).

Lass' sehn, ob Nachbar Sachs zu Haus?
Gern spräch' ich ihn. Trät' ich wohl ein?

(David kommt mit Licht aus der Kammer, setzt sich damit an den Werktisch am Fenster und macht sich über die Arbeit her.)

Eva.

Er scheint daheim : kommt Licht heraus.

Pogner.

Thu' ich's? — Zu was doch! — Besser, nein!
(Er wendet sich ab.)
Will Einer Selt'nes wagen,
Was liess' er da sich sagen? — —
(Nach einigem Sinnen.)
War er's nicht, der meint', ich ging zu weit?
Und blieb ich nicht im Geleise.
War's nicht in seiner Weise? —
Doch war's vielleicht auch — Eitelkeit?

(Zu Eva.)
Und du, mein Kind, du sagst mir nichts?

Eva.

Good children only speak when bid.

Pogner.

How sharp ; how good ! Come now, my wench,
And sit beside me on this bench.

(Sits on the stone seat under the linden-tree.)

Eva.

    Too chill to stay ;
    'T was close all day.

Pogner.

    Oh, no ! 't is mild and charming ;
    The evening air is calming.

(Eva sits, nervously.)

A token of a morrow fair
    And brilliant in its weather.
Oh, child, does not thy heart declare
The joys that morrow doth prepare,
When Nuremberg — yes, all the town,
    Both rich and poor together,
The guilds, the burghers of renown,
    Will meet in highest feather,
        To see thee rise
        And give the prize
    To him, the Master's head,
    To whom thou shalt be wed?

Eva.

Dear father, can but a Master win?

Pogner.

Be sure a Master is your fate.

(Magdalena appears at the door and signs to Eva.)

Eva
    (disturbed).

Aye — 't is my fate. — But now come in —
Yes, Lena, yes ! — our suppers wait.

Pogner
    (rising vexedly).

But we have no guest?

Eva
    (as before).

        Not Sir Walter?

Pogner
    (surprised).

           Hey, what?

Eva.

Did you not meet?

Eva.

Ein folgsam Kind, gefragt nur spricht's.

Pogner.

Wie klug ! Wie gut ! — Komm', setz' dich hier
Ein Weil' noch auf die Bank zu mir.

(Er setzt sich auf die Steinbank unter der Linde.)

Eva.

    Wird's nicht zu kühl?
    's war heut' gar schwül.

Pogner.

    Nicht doch, 's ist mild und labend ;
    Gar lieblich lind der Abend.

(Eva setzt sich beklommen.)

Das deutet auf den schönsten Tag,
    Der morgen dir soll scheinen.
O Kind, sagt dir kein Herzensschlag,
Welch' Glück dich morgen treffen mag,
Wenn Nürnberg, die ganze Stadt
    Mit Bürgern und Gemeinen.
Mit Zünften, Volk und hohem Rath,
    Vor dir sich soll vereinen,
        Dass du den Preis,
        Das edle Reis,
    Ertheilest als Gemahl
    Dem Meister deiner Wahl.

Eva.

Lieb' Vater, muss es ein Meister sein?

Pogner.

Hör' wohl : ein Meister deiner Wahl.

(Magdalene erscheint an der Thür und winkt Eva.)

Eva
    (zerstreut).

Ja, — meiner Wahl. — Doch, tritt nun ein —
Gleich, Lene, gleich ! — zum Abendmahl.

Pogner
    (ärgerlich aufstehend).

's giebt doch keinen Gast?

Eva
    (wie oben).

        Wohl den Junker?

Pogner
    (verwundert).

           Wie so

Eva.

Sahst ihn heute nicht?

Pogner

(half to himself).

I want him not.
Why, no !—What now ?—Ah ! dare I guess ?

Eva.

Dear father, come in and change your dress.

Pogner

(going into the house before her).

Hum !—What way does my fancy go ?

(Exit.)

Magdalena

(secretly).

Why do you wait ?

Eva.

(the same).

Be still ! speak low !

Magdalena.

Saw David !—says that he has n't won

Eva.

Sir Walter ?—O heavens ! what 's to be done ?
Ah, Lena, I quake ; who will disclose all ?

Magdalena.

Perhaps Hans Sachs ?

Eva.

Ah, he 's fond of me !
T is well, I will go

Magdalena.

Mind not to expose all !
If you stay longer your father will see.
When we 've supped : another thing I 'll unfold
thee ;
A secret which some one has just now told me.

Eva.

Who was 't ?   Sir Walter ?

Magdalena.

Not he, nay !
Beckmesser.

Eva.

Worth hearing I should say !

(They go into the house.)

Sachs, in light indoor dress, has reëntered the workshop.
He turns to David, who is still at his workbench.)

Pogner

(halb für sich).

Ward sein nicht froh. —
Nicht doch !—Was denn ?—Ei ! werd' ich dumm !

Eva.

Lieb' Väterchen, komn' ! Geh', kleid' dich um !

Pogner

(voran in das Haus gehend).

Hm !—Was geht mir im Kopf doch 'rum ?

(Ab.)

Magdalene

(heimlich).

Hast was heraus ?

Eva

(ebenso).

Blieb still und stumm

Magdalene.

Sprach David : meint', er habe verthan.

Eva.

Der Ritter !—Hilf Gott, was fing' ich an !
Ach, Lene ! die Angst : wo 'was erfahren ?

Magdalene.

Vielleicht vom Sachs !

Eva.

Ach, der hat mich lieb !
Gewiss, ich geh' hin,

Magdalene.

Lass drin nichts gewahren !
Der Vater merkt' es, wenn man jetzt blieb'. —
Nach dem Mahl ; dann hab' ich dir noch 'was zu
sagen.
Was Jemand geheim mir aufgetragen.

Eva.

Wer denn ?   Der Junker ?

Magdalene.

Nichts da !   Nein !
Beckmesser.

Eva.

Das mag 'was Rechtes sein

(Sie gehen in das Haus.)

Sachs ist, in leichter Hauskleidung, in die Werkstat
zurückgegangen. Er wendet sich zu David, der an seinem
Werktisch verblieben ist.

Sachs.

Come here ! — that 's right. — There by the door
Put my stool and workbench before ;
Then get to bed and early rise ;
Sleep off your folly, to-morrow be wise !

David
              (arranging bench and stool).

Are you still working?

Sachs.
                        What 's that to you?

David
              (aside).

What ailed Magdalena? — Would I knew !
And why works my Master by this light?

Sachs.

Why wait you?

David.

          Good-night, Master !

Sachs.
                        Good-night !

(Exit David into the inner room.)

Sachs

(arranges his work, sits on his stool at the door and then,
laying down his tools again, leans back, resting his arm on
          the closed lower half of the door).

The elder's scent is waxing
So mild, so full and strong?
Its charm my limbs relaxing :
Words unto my lips would throng. —
What boot such thoughts as I can span?
I 'm but a poor, plain-minded man !
When work 's despised altogether,
Thou, friend, settest me free ;
But I 'd better stick to my leather
And let all this poetry be ! —

(He tries again to work.   Leaves off and reflects.)

And yet — it haunts me still. —
I feel, but comprehend ill ; —
Cannot forget it, — and yet cannot grasp it. —
I measure it not e'en when I clasp it. —
But how then would I gauge it?
'T was measureless to my mind ;
No rule could fit it or cage it,
Yet there was no fault to find.
It seemed so old, yet new in its chime, —
Like songs of birds in sweet Maytime : —
          He who heard
          And, fancy-stirr'd,
Sought to repeat the strain,
But shame and scorn would gain —

Sachs.

Zeig' her ! — 's ist gut. — Dort an die **Thür'**
Rück' mir Tisch und Schemel herfür ! —
Leg' dich zu Bett !   Wach' auf bei Zeit,
Verschlaf' die Dummheit, sei morgen gescheit !

David
              (richtet Tisch und Schemel).

Schafft ihr noch Arbeit?

Sachs.
                        Kümmert dich das

David
              (für sich).

Was war nur der Lene? — Gott weiss, **was !** —
Warum wohl der Meister heute **wacht !**

Sachs.

Was steh'st noch?

David.

          Schlaft wohl, Meister !

Sachs.
                        Gut Nacht !

(David geht in die Kammer ab.)

Sachs

(legt sich die Arbeit zurecht, setzt sich an der Thüre auf
den Schemel, lässt dann die Arbeit wieder liegen, und lehnt
mit dem Arm auf den geschlossenen Untertheil des Ladens
gestützt, sich zurück).

          Wie duftet doch der Flieder
          So mild, so stark und voll !
          Mir lös't es weich die Glieder,
          Will, das ich was sagen soll. —
Was gilt's, was ich dir sagen kann?
Bin gar ein arm einfältig Mann !
          Soll mir die Arbeit nicht schmecken,
          Gäb'st, Freund, lieber mich frei :
          Thät' besser das Leder zu strecken,
          Und liess' alle Poeterei ! —

(Er versucht wieder zu arbeiten.   Lässt ab und sinnt.)

          Und doch, 's will halt nicht geh'n. —
          Ich fühl's — und kann's nicht versteh'n —
Kann's nicht behalten, — doch auch nicht ver-
                                        gessen ;
Und fass' ich es ganz, — kann ich's nicht messen. —
          Doch wie auch wollt' ich's fassen
          Was unermesslich mir schien ?
          Kein' Regel wollte da passen,
          Und war doch kein Fehler drin. —
Es klang so alt, und war so neu, —
Wie Vogelsang im süssen Mai :
          Wer ihn hört,
          Und wahnbethört
Sänge dem Vogel nach,
Dem brächt' es Spott und Schmach.

Spring's command
  And gentle hand
His soul with this did entrust:
He sang because he must!
His power rose as needed;
  That virtue well I heeded.
  The bird who sang to-day
Has got a throat that rightly waxes;
  Masters may feel dismay,
But well content with him Hans Sachs is.

Eva comes out into the street, peeps shyly towards the workshop and advances unnoticed to the door by SACHS.

Eva.

Good-evening, Master! Still at labor?

Sachs
          (starting up in agreeable surprise).

Ah, child! Sweet Eva! still about?
And yet I guess the cause, fair neighbor:
The new-made shoes?

Eva.
                    How far you 're out!
The shoes I have not even essay'd;
They are so fine, so richly made,
I dare not such gems to my feet confide.

Sachs.

You 'll wear them, though, to-morrow as bride?

Eva
(who has now seated herself on the stone seat by Sachs).

Who is to be the bridegroom, then?

Sachs.
                    Can I tell?
Eva.

How know you I 'm to be bride?

Sachs.
                    Eh, well!
Ev'ry one knows.

Eva.
                Aye, ev'ry one knows.
That 's proof positive, I suppose.
I thought you knew more.

Sachs.
              What should I know?
Eva.

See there! Must I my meaning show?
How dull I must be!

Sachs.
                    I say not so.

Lenzes Gebot,
  Die süsse Noth,
Die legten's ihm in die Brust:
Nun sang er, wie er musst'!
Und wie er musst', so konnt' er's;
  Das merkt' ich ganz besonders:
  Dem Vogel, der heut' sang,
Dem war der Schnabel hold gewachsen;
  Macht' er den Meistern bang,
Gar wohl gefiel er doch Hans Sachsen.

Eva ist auf die Strasse getreten, hat schüchtern spähend sich der Werkstatt genähert, und steht jetzt unvermerkt an der Thüre bei Sachs.

Eva.

Gut'n Abend, Meister! Noch so fleissig?

Sachs
          (ist angenehm überrascht aufgefahren).

Ei, Kind! Lieb' Evchen? Noch so spät?
Und doch, warum so spät noch, weiss ich:
Die neuen Schuh'?

Eva.
                    Wie fehl er räth!
Die Schuh' hab' ich noch gar nicht probirt;
Die sind so schön, so reich geziert,
Dass ich sie noch nicht an die Füss' mir getraut.

Sachs.

Doch sollst sie morgen tragen als Braut?

Eva
(hat sich dicht bei Sachs auf den Steinsitz gesetzt).

Wer wäre denn Bräutigam?

Sachs.
                    Weiss ich das?
Eva.

Wie wisst denn ihr, ob ich Braut?

Sachs.
                    Ei was!
Das weiss die Stadt.

Eva.
                Ja, weiss es die Stadt,
Freund Sachs gute Gewähr dann hat.
Ich dacht', er wüsst' mehr.

Sachs.
              Was sollt' ich wissen?
Eva.

Ei seht doch! Werd' ich's ihm sagen müssen?
Ich bin wohl recht dumm?

Sachs.
                Das sagt' ich nicht.

Eva.

Then you must be bright?

achs.

That I don't know.

Eva.

You know naught! You say naught!
Ah, friend Sachs!
I see now clearly, pitch is not wax.
I really believ'd you were sharper.

Sachs.

My dear!

Both pitch and wax are well known here.
With wax I rubbed the silken stitching
With which I sewed your pretty shoes;
The thread for these coarser ones I'm pitching;
'T is good enough for a man to use.

Eva.

Whom do you mean! Some grandee:

Sachs.

Aye, marry!

A Master proud who boldly woos,
Expecting to-morrow all to carry;
For Master Beckmesser I make these shoes.

Eva.

Then pitch in plenty let there be,
To stick him fast and leave me free.

Sachs.

He hopes by singing to attain thee.

Eva.

Why should he hope?

Sachs.

Why should he not?
Few bachelors are on the spot.

Eva.

Might not a widower hope to gain me?

Sachs.

My child, I am too old for you.

Eva.

Ah, stuff! too old! Art is the thing;
Who masters that is free to woo.

Sachs.

Dear Eva, are you flattering?

Eva.

Dann wär't ihr whol klug?

Sachs.

Das weiss ich nicht

Eva.

Ihr wisst nichts? Ihr sagt nichts?— Ei, Freund
Sachs
Jetzt merk' ich wahrlich, Pech ist kein Wachs.
Ich hätt' euch für feiner gehalten.

Sachs.

Kind

Beid', Wachs und Pech vertraut mir sind.
Mit Wachs strich ich die Seidenfäden,
Damit ich die zieren Schuh' dir gefasst:
Heut' fass ich die Schuh' mit dicht'ren Drähten,
Da gilt's mit Pech für den derben Gast.

Eva.

Wer ist denn der? Wohl 'was Rechts?

Sachs.

Das mein' ich

Ein Meister stolz auf Freiers Fuss,
Denkt morgen zu siegen ganz alleinig:
Herrn Beckmesser's Schuh' ich richten muss.

Eva.

So nehmt nur tüchtig Pech dazu:
Da kleb' er drin, und lass' mir Ruh'!

Sachs.

Er hofft dich sicher zu ersingen.

Eva.

Wie so denn der?

Sachs.

Ein Junggesell:
's gibt deren wenig dort zur Stell'.

Eva.

Könnt's einem Wittwer nicht gelingen?

Sachs.

Mein Kind der wür' zu alt für dich.

Eva.

Ei was, zu alt! Hier gilt's die Kunst:
Wer sie versteht, der werb' um mich!

Sachs.

Lieb' Evchen! Machst mir blauen Dunst?

Eva.

Not I ; 't is you are an impostor !
Admit now, your affections veer ;
Heav'n knows whom now your heart may foster !
I 'd thought it my own this many a year.

Sachs.

Because in my arms I oft carried you?

Eva.

I see.   You had no child of your own.

Sachs.

I once had wife and children too.

Eva.

But they are dead and I am grown.

Sachs.

Grown tall and fair.

Eva.

'T was my idea
That I might fill their places here.

Sachs.

Then I should have child and also wife :
That were indeed a joy in life !
Aye, that was an idea I vow !

Eva.

I think you 're trying to mock me now.
In short, 't would give you little sorrow
If under your nose from all to-morrow,
This Beckmesser sang me away !

Sachs.

If he succeeded what could I say !
'T would rest on what your father said.

Eva.

Where does a Master keep his head?
Were I with you could it be found?

Sachs.

Ah, yes ! you 're right ! all my brain turns round.
've been annoyed and vexed to-day,
And in my mind some traces stay.

Eva.

Aye, in the Song-school?   You met, I see.

Sachs.

Yes, child ; an election has worried me.

Eva.

Nicht ich !   Ihr seid's ; ihr macht mir Flausen !
Gesteht nur, dass ihr wandelbar ;
Gott weiss, wer jetzt euch im Herzen mag hausen !
Glaubt' ich mich doch drin so manches Jahr.

Sachs.

Wohl, da ich dich gern in den Armen trug?

Eva.

Ich seh', 's war nur, weil ihr kinderlos.

Sachs.

Hatt' einst Weib und Kinder genug.

Eva.

Doch starb eure Frau, so wuchs ich gross.

Sachs.

Gar gross und schön !

Eva.

Drum dacht' ich aus
Ihr nähm't mich für Weib und Kind in's Haus.

Sachs.

Da hätt' ich ein Kind und auch ein Weib :
's wär' gar ein lieber Zeitvertreib !
Ja, ja ! das hast du dir schön erdacht.

Eva.

Ich glaub', der Meister mich gar verlacht?
Am End' gar liess' er sich auch gefallen,
Dass unter der Nas' ihm weg von Allen
Der Beckmesser morgen mich ersäng'?

Sachs.

Wie sollt, ich's wehren, wenn's ihm geläng'?—
Dem wüsst' allein dein Vater Rath.

Eva.

Wo so ein Meister den Kopf nur hat !
Käm' ich zu euch wohl, fänd' ich's zu Haus?

Sachs.

Ach, ja ! Hast Recht ! 's ist im Kopf mir kraus :
Hab' heut' manch' Sorg' und Wirr erlebt :
Da mag's dann sein, dass 'was drin klebt.

Eva.

Wohl in der Singschul'? 's war' heut' Gebot

Sachs.

Ja, Kind : eine Freiung machte mir Noth.

Eva.

O Sachs! but you should at once have said so,
Then my tongue would not have plagued your
                                    head so.
Now say, who was it entrance besought?

Sachs.

A knight, my child, and quite untaught.

Eva.

A knight? Dear me! And did he succeed?

Sachs.

Why, no, my child, we disagreed.

Eva.

Dear me! how strange! relate it, pray;
If you are vexed, can I be gay?
Then he was defeated and baffled quite?

Sachs.

Truly hopeless the case of the noble knight.

Magdalena

      (comes to the house-door and calls softly).

Hist! Eva! Hist!

Eva.

             Truly hopeless! And why?
Were there no means to help him by?
Sang he so ill, so faultily
He never a Master can hope to be?

Sachs.

My child, it is a hopeless disaster;
No leader he'll be in any land;
For when one is born to be a Master,
'Mong other Masters he cannot stand.

Magdalena

      (approaching).

Your father awaits.

Eva.

          But tell me the end,
If none of the Masters he won for a friend?

Sachs

That is a good joke! friend could we call
One before whom we all felt so small?
My young lord Haughty, let him toddle,
In the world to cool his noddle.
What we have learnt with toil and care,
Let us digest in peace unhurried!
Here we must by none be worried:
So let his fortune shine elsewhere!

Eva.

Ja, Sachs! Das hättet ihr gleich soll'n sagen;
Plagt' euch dann nicht mit unnützen Fragen. —
Nun sagt, wer war's, der Freiung begehrt?

Sachs.

Ein Junker, Kind, gar unbelehrt.

Eva.

Ein Junker! Mein, sagt! — und ward er gefreit?

Sachs.

Nichts da, mein Kind! 's gab zu viel Streit.

Eva.

So Sagt! Erzählt wie ging es zu?
Macht's euch Sorg', wie liess' mir es Ruh'?
So bestand er übel und hat verthan?

Sachs.

Ohne Gnad' versang der Herr Rittersmann.

Magdalene

      (kommt zum Haus heraus und ruft leise).

Bst! Evchen! Bst!

Eva.

             Ohne Gnade? Wie
Kein Mittel gäb's, das ihm gadieh'?
Sang er so schlecht, so fehlervoll,
Dass nichts mehr zum Meister ihm helfen soll?

Sachs.

Mein Kind, für den ist Alles verloren,
Und Meister wird der in keinem Land;
Denn wer als Meister ward geboren,
Der hat unter Meistern den schlimmsten Stand.

Magdalene

      (näher).

Der vater verlangt.

Eva.

          So sagt mir noch an
Ob keinen der Meister zum Freund er gewann?

Sachs.

Das wär nicht übel! Freund ihm noch sein!
Ihm, vor dem All' sich fühlen so klein!
Den Junker Hochmuth, lasst ihn laufen,
Mag er durch die welt sich raufen:
Was wir erlent mit Noth und Müh',
Dafei lasst uns in Ruh' verschnaufen!
Hier renn' er nichts uns über'n Haufen ·
Sein Glück ihm anderswo erblüh'!

Eva.

(rising hastily).

Yes, elsewhere it will shine, I know,
In spite of what your envious pack says;
Some place where hearts still warmly glow,
With no deceitful Master Sachses! —
Yes, Lena! Yes! I'm coming, dear!—
Nice consolation I get here!
I smell the pitch, Heav'n keep us whole!
Burn it, rather, and warm up your soul.

(She crosses over hastily with Magdalena and remains in
agitation at her own door.)

Sachs

(with a meaning nod of his head).

I thought as much! Now then they 'll prate!

(During the following he closes the upper half of his door
also, so nearly as only to leave a little crack of light, he
himself being quite invisible.)

Magdalena.

Good lack! why have you stayed so late?
Your father called.

Eva.

Go you instead,
And say that I am gone to bed.

Magdalena.

No, no! Hark now! I have news too!
Beckmesser found me; such a to-do!
To-night, if but at the window stay'd you,
He said he would come and serenade you.
The song he intends for your winning he 'll sing,
To try if your approval 't will bring.

Eva.

He need not trouble!—where can he be?

Magdalena.

Has David been here?

Eva.

What 's that to me?

Magdalena

(half to herself).

I was too harsh; he 's vexed, I fear.

Eva.

No one in sight?

Magdalena.

Some one draws near.

Eva.

Is 't he?

Eva

(erhebt sich heftig).

Ja, anderswo soll's ihm erblüh'n,
Als bei euch garst'gen, neid'schen Mannsen:
Wo warm die Herzen noch erglüh'n,
Trotz allen tück'schen Meister Hansen!
Ja, Lene! Gleich! ich komme schon!
Was trüg' ich hier für Trost davon?
Da riecht's nach Pech, dass Gott erbarm'!
Brennt' er's lieber, da würd er doch warm!

Sie geht heftig mit Magdalene hinüber und verweilt sehr
aufgeregt dort unter der Thüre.

Sachs.

(nickt bedeutungsvoll mit dem Kopfe).

Das dacht' ich wohl. Nun heisst's: schaff' Rath!

Er ist während des Folgenden damit beschäftigt, auch die
obere Ladenthüre so weit zu schliessen, dass sie nur ein
wenig Licht noch durchlässt; er selbst verschwindet so fast
ganz.

Magdalene.

Hilf Gott! was bliebst du nur so spat?
Der Vater rief.

Eva

Geh' zu ihm ein:
Ich sei zu Bett im Kämmerlein.

Magdalene.

Nicht doch! Hör' nur! Komm' ich dazu?
Beckmesser fand mich: er lässt nicht Ruh',
Zur nacht sollst du dich an's Fenster neigen,
Er will dir 'was Schönes singen und geigen,
Mit dem er dich hofft zu gewinnen, das Lied,
Ob dir das zu Gefallen gerieth.

Eva.

Das fehlte auch noch!— Käme nur Er!

Magdalene.

Hast' David geseh'n?

Eva

Was soll mir der:

Magdalene

(halb für sich).

Ich war zu streng; er wird sich grämen.

Eva.

Siehst du noch nichts?

Magdalene.

's ist als ob Leut' dort kämen

Eva.

Wär' er's?

Magdalena.

Come; 't is time to depart.

Eva.

Not till I 've seen the man of my heart.

Magdalena.

I made a mistake, it is not he.
Come in, for fear your father should see.

Eva.

What shall I do?

Magdalena.

We 'll hold consultation
As to this Beckmesser's invitation.

Eva.

Stand you at the window for me.

Magdalena.

What, I?
'T would rouse poor David's jealousy.
He sleeps on the street side.   He he! what fun!

Eva.

I hear a footstep!

Magdalena.

Come now, let us run!

Eva.

It nears us!

Magdalena.

You 're wrong, I 'll bet my head.
Do come! You must, till your father 's in bed.

Pogner
(calling within).

Hey! Lena! Eva!

Magdalena.

No more delay!
D' ye hear? Come — your knight 's far away.

Walter has come up the alley and now turns the corner
by Pogner's house. Eva, who is being dragged indoors by
Magdalena, tears herself free with a slight cry and rushes
towards Walter.

Eva.

It is he!

Magdalena.
(going in).

Now all 's up.   Be quick, I say!

(Exit).

Magdalene.

Mach' und komm' jetzt hinan!

Eva.

Nicht eh'r, bis ich sah den theuersten Mann!

Magdalene.

Ich täuschte mich dort: er war es nicht.
Jetzt komm, sonst merkt der Vater die G'schicht'!

Eva.

Ach! meine Angst!

Magdalene.

Auch lass uns berathen,
Wie wir des Beckmesser's uns entladen.

Eva.

Zum Fenster gehst du für mich.

Magdalene.

Wie. ich?
Das machte wohl David eiferlich!
Er schläft nach der Gassen! Hihi! 's wär' fein! —

Eva.

Dort hör' ich Schritte.

Magdalene.

Jetzt komm', es muss sein!

Eva.

Jetzt näher!

Magdalene.

Du irrst! 's ist nichts, ich wett'.
Ei, komm'! Du musst, bis der Vater zu Bett.

Pogner
(von innen rufend).

He! Lene! Eva!

Magdalene

's ist höchste Zeit!
Hörst du's? — Komm'! — der Ritter ist Weit. —

Walther ist die Gasse heraufgekommen; jetzt biegt er um
Pogner's Haus herum; Eva, die bereits von Magdalene am
Arm hineingezogen worden war, reisst sich mit einem leisen
Schrei los und stürzt Walther entgegen.

Eva.

Da ist er!

Magdalene
(hineingehend).

Nun haben wir's!   Jetzt heisst's gescheit!

(Ab.)

Eva

(transported).

'T is my true love !
Yes, my own love !
Naught conceal I,
All is known, love :
All reveal I.
For I know it :
It is you, love,
Hero-Poet
And my only friend !

Walter

(sorrowfully).

Ah, thou 'rt wrong ! I 'm but thy friend ;
Not as Poet
Masters prize me,
For my station
They despise me :
Inspiration
They can brook not,
And — I know it —
I may look not
To my lady's hand !

Eva.

Thou art wrong ! Thy lady's hand
Awards the prize alone.
Thy courage doth my heart command ;
Be then the wreath thine own.

Walter.

Ah, no, thou 'rt wrong ! My lady's hand,
Though no one else should gain it,
Upon the terms thy father plann'd
I never may attain it.
"A Master-Singer he must be :
None may'st thou wed uncrowned by thee."
Thus to the Guild he firmly spake ;
What he hath pledged he may not break.
That spurred my heart's desire,
Though strange to me were place and folk :
I sang, all love and fire,
And strove to make a Master-stroke.

The loud sound of a night-watchman's cowhorn is heard.
Walter clasps his hand to his sword and stares wildly before him.

Ha !

Eva

(taking him soothingly by the hand)

Belovëd, govern thy wrath !
'T is but the watchman goes forth.—
Hide 'neath the lime-tree !
Lose no more time ! See,
The watchman passes this way.

Magdalena

(at the door, softly).

Eva ! 't is late : come in, I say !

Eva

(ausser sich).

Ja, ihr seid es !
Nein, du bist es
Alles sag' ich,
Denn ihr wisst es ;
Alles klag' ich,
Denn ich weiss es ;
Ihr seid Beides,
Held des Preises,
Und mein einz'ger Freund !

Walther

(leidenschaftlich).

Ach, du irrst ! Bin nur dein **Freund,**
Doch des Preises
Noch nicht würdig,
Nicht den Meistern
Ebenbürtig :
Mein Begeistern
Fand Verachten,
Und ich weiss es,
Darf nicht trachten
Nach der Freundin Hand !

Eva.

Wie du irrst ! Der Freundin Hand,
Ertheilt nur sie den Preis.
Wie deinen Muth ihr Herz erfand,
Reicht sie nur dir das Reis.

Walther.

Ach nein, du irrst ! Der Freundin Hand,
Wär Keinem sie erkoren,
Wie sie des Vaters Wille band,
Mir wär' sie doch verloren.
„Ein Meistersinger muss er sein :
Nur wen ihr krönt, den darf sei frei'n ! "
So sprach er festlich zu den Herrn,
Kann nicht zurück, möcht er's auch gern !
Das eben gab mir Muth ;
Wie ungewohnt mir alles schien,
Ich sang mit Lieb' und Gluth,
Dass ich den Meisterschlag verdien'.

Man hört den starken Ruf eines Nachtwächter horne
Walther legt mit emphatischer Gebärde die Hand an se
Schwert, und starrt wild vor sich hin.

Ha ! . . .

Eva

(fasst ihn besänftigend an der Hand).

Geliebter, spare den Zorn !
's war nur des Nachtwächters Horn. —
Unter der Linde
Birg' dich geschwinde.
Hier kommt der Wächter vorbei.

Magdalene

(an der Thüre, leise).

Evchen ! 's ist Zeit, mach' dich frei !

Walter.

You fly?

Eva.

Must I not flee?

Walter.

You fear —?

Eva.

The powers that be !

(She disappears with Magdalena into the house.)

The Watchman

(has meanwhile appeared in the alley. He comes forward singing, turns the corner of Pogner's house and exit L).

" Hark to what I say, good people ;
Striketh ten from every steeple.
Put out your fire and eke your light,
That none may come to harm this night.
     Praise the Lord of Heav'n ! "

(He has by this time gone off, but his horn is still heard).

Sachs

(who has listened to the foregoing from behind his shop-door, now opens it a little wider, having shaded his lamp).

Pretty doings now are in hand !
Here 's an elopement being plann'd.
I 'm awake ! This must not be.

Walter

(behind the lime-tree).

Has she then left me ? Woe is me ! —
Yet no ! who comes here ? — Ah, not she !
T is Magdalena.— Yet surely ! — *Thou!*

Eva

(returns in Magdalena's dress and goes to Walter).

Thy foolish child, she 's all thine now !

(She sinks on his breast.)

Walter.

O heaven ! here before my eyes
I see indeed the Master-prize !

Eva.

Now no more delay !
Let 's hasten away !
Oh, would that we were gone !

Walter.

Here, through this alley : on !
Servants at the gate
With my horses wait.

Walther.

Du fliehst?

Eva.

Muss ich denn nicht?

Walther.

Entweichst?

Eva.

Dem Meistergericht.

(Sie verschwindet mit Magdalene im Hause.)

Der Nachtwächter.

(ist währenddem in der Gasse erschienen, kommt singend nach vorn, biegt um die Ecke von Pogner's Haus, und geht nach links zu weiter ab).

„ Hört ihr Leut' und lasst euch sagen,
Die Glock' hat Zehn geschlagen :
Bewahrt das Feuer und auch das Licht,
Damit Niemand kein Schad' geschicht !
     Lobet Gott den Herrn ! "

(Als er hiermit abgegangen, hört man ihn abermals blasen.)

Sachs

(welcher hinter der Ladenthüre dem Gespräche gelauscht, öffnet jetzt, bei eingezogenem Lampenlicht. ein wenig mehr).

Ueble Dinge, die ich da merk' :
Eine Entführung gar im Werk !
Aufgepasst : das darf nicht sein !

Walther

(hinter der Linde).

Käm' sie nicht wieder ? O der Pein ! —
Doch' ja ! sie kommt dort ! Weh' mir, nein !
Die Alte ist's ! — doch aber — ja !

Eva

(ist in Magdalene's Kleidung wieder zurückgekehrt und geht auf Walther zu).

Das thör'ge Kind : da hast du's ! da !

(Sie sinkt ihm an die Brust.

Walther.

O Himmel ! Ja ! nun wohl ich weiss,
Dass ich gewann den Meisterpreis.

Eva.

Doch nun kein Besinnen !
Von hinnen ! Von hinnen !
O wären wir weit schon fort !

Walther.

Hier durch die Gasse : dort
Finden wir vor dem Thor
Knecht und Rosse vor.

As they turn to dive into the alley Sachs places his lamp behind a water-globe and sends a bright stream of light through the now wide-open door across the street, so that Eva and Walter suddenly find themselves illuminated.

Eva

(hastily pulling Walter back).

Ah me ! the cobbler !   What would he say !
Hide thee ! — keep well out of his way !

Walter.

What other road leads to the gate ?

Eva

(pointing R).

Round by the street here, but 't is not straight ;
I know it not well ; besides, we should meet
With the watchman.

Walter.
          Well, then, through the alley !

Eva.

The cobbler must first leave his windowseat.

Walter.

I 'll force him then.   Here 's for a sally !

Eva.

Shew not yourself : he knows you !

Walter.
                                Who is he ?

Eva.

'T is Sachs !

Walter.

          Hans Sachs ? my friend ?

Eva.
                                Not quite !
With slanders against you he is busy.

Walter.

What Sachs !   He too ? — I 'll put out his light !

Beckmesser comes up the alley slinking at some distance in the rear of the watchman.   He peers up to Pogner's windows and, leaning against Sach's house, seeks out a stone seat on which he places himself, still looking at the upper windows, and now he commences to tune a lute he has brought with him.

Eva

(restraining Walter).

Forbear ! — Now hark !

Walter.

                    A lute I hear.

Als sich Beide wenden, um die Gasse einzubiegen, lässt Sachs, nachdem er die Lampe hinter eine Glasskugel gestellt, einen hellen Lichtschein durch die ganz wieder geöffnete Ladenthüre, quer über die Strasse fallen, so dass Eva und Walther sich plötzlich hell erleuchtet sehen.

Eva

(Walther heftig zurückziehend).

O weh', der Schuster !   Wenn der uns säh' !
Birg' dich ? komm' ihm nicht in die Näh' !

Walther.

Wel 'h' andrer Weg führt uns hinaus ?

Eva

(nach rechts deutend).

Do durch die Strasse : doch der ist kraus,
Ic kenn' ihn nicht gut ; auch stiessen wir dort
A   den Wächter.

Walther.
                    Nur denn : durch die Gasse !

Eva.

Der Schuster muss erst vom Fenster fort.

Walther.

Ich zwing' ihn dass er's verlasse.

Eva.

Zeig dich ihm nicht : er kennt dich !

Walther.
                                Der Schuster ?

Eva.

's ist Sachs.

Walther.

          Hans Sachs, mein Freund ?

Eva.
                                Glaub's nicht !
Von dir zu sagen Uebles nur wusst' er.

Walther.

Wie, Sachs ?   Auch er ? — Ich lösch' ihm das
                                Licht !

Beckmesser ist, dem Nachtwächter in einiger Entfernung nachschleichend die Gasse herauf gekommen, hat nach den Fenstern von Pogner's Hause gespäht, und, an Sachsen's Hause angelehnt, zwischen den beiden Fenstern einen Steinsitz sich ausgesucht, auf welchem er sich, immer nur nach dem gegenüberliegenden Fenster aufmerksam lugend, niedergelassen hat ; jetzt stimmt er eine mitgebrachte Laute

Eva

(Walther zurückhaltend).

Thu's nicht ! — Doch horch !

Walther.

                    Einer Laute Klang !

Eva.

What a mishap!

Walter.

Why need you fear?

The cobbler's light has ceased to glare:
Let 's make the attempt!

Eva.

Ah! see you not there?

Some other comes to spoil our plans.

Walter.

I hear and see: some player man.
What wants he here so late at night?

Eva.

'T is Beckmesser!

Sachs

(on hearing the first sounds of the lute has, as if struck with
a new idea, withdrawn his light, gently opened the lower
half of his shopdoor and placed his workbench on the
threshold. He now hears Eva's exclamation).

Aha! I 'm right!

Walter.

The Marker here? and placed in my pow'r?
Here goes! The fool shall rue this hour!

Eva.

O heav'n! Forbear! Would you wake my father?
He 'll sing his song and quit us then.
Let 's hide behind the foliage rather.
Oh, dear! what trouble you give, you men!

(She draws Walter behind the bushes which surround the
bench under the lime-tree.)

Beckmesser impatiently tinkles on his lute waiting for the
window to open. As he is about to commence his song
Sachs turns his light full on the street again and begins to
hammer loudly on his last, singing lustily the while.

Sachs.

Tooral looral!
Tiddy fol de rol!
Oho! Tralala! Oho!
When Mother Eve from Paradise
Was by the Almighty driven,
Her naked feet, so small and nice,
By stones were sorely riven.
This troubled much the Lord,
Her tootsies he ador'd
An angel he did straightway choose:
" Go make that pretty sinner shoes!
And as poor Adam limps around;
And breaks his toes on stony ground,
That well and wide
His legs may stride,
Measure him for boots beside!"

Eva.

Ach, meine Noth!

Walther.

Wie, wird dir bang?

Der Schuster, sieh, zog ein das Licht:—
So sei's gewagt!

Eva.

Weh'! Hörst du denn nicht
Ein Andrer kam, und nahm dort Stand.

Walther.

Ich hör's und seh's:—ein Musikant.
Was will der hier so spät des Nachts?

Eva.

's ist Beckmesser schon!

Sachs

(als er den ersten Ton der Laute vernommen, hat, von einem
plötzlichen Einfal erfasst, das Licht wieder etwas eingezogen,
leise auch den unteren Theil des Ladens geöffnet, und
seinen Werktisch ganz unter die Thüre gestellt. Jetzt hat er
Eva's Ausruf vernommen).

Aha! ich dacht's!

Walther.

Der Merker? Er? in meiner Gewalt?
D'rauf zu, den Lung'rer mach' ich kalt?

Eva.

Um Gott! So hör'! Willst den Vater wecken?
Er singt ein Lied, dann zieht er ab.
Lass dort uns im Gebüsch verstecken.—
Was mit den Männern ich Müh' doch hab'!

(Sie zieht Walther hinter das Gebüsch auf die Bank unter der
Linde.)

Beckmesser

(klimpert voll Ungeduld heftig auf der Laute, ob sich das
Fenster nicht öffnen wolle. Als er endlich anfangen will zu
singen beginnt Sachs, der soeben das Licht wieder hell auf
die Strasse fallen liess, laut mit dem Hammer auf den
Leisten zu schlagen, und singt sehr kräftig dazu).

Sachs.

Jerum! Jerum!
Halla halla he!
O ho! Trallalei! o he!
Als Eva aus dem Paradies
Von Gott dem Herrn verstossen,
Gar schuf ihr Schmerz der harte Kiess
An ihrem Fuss, dem blossen.
Das jammerte den Herrn,
Ihr Füsschen hat er gern,
Und seinem Engel rief er zu:
„ Da mach' der armen Sünd'rin Schuh'!
Und da der Adam, wie ich seh',
An Steinen dort sich stösst die Zeh,
Dass recht fortan
Er wandeln kann,
So miss' dem auch Stiefel an!"

Beckmesser

(as Sachs begins to sing).

What is it now?
Atrocious row!
The vulgar cobbler 's drunk, I trow!

(Advancing.)

What, Master! Up, so long after dark?

Sachs.

You also out, Master Town-clerk?
The shoes perhaps on your mind are weighing?
You see me at work: I 'm not delaying.

Beckmesser.

Deuce take boot and shoe!
Be quiet do!

Walter

(to Eva).

What is that song? He speaks of thee.

Eva.

I know it well; he means not me.
But hidden malice here I trace.

Walter.

What vile delay! Time flies apace!

Sachs

(working).

Tooral looral!
Tiddy fol de rol!
Oho! Tralala! Oho!
O Eve! Hear how my poor heart aches,
By grief and trouble sodden;
The works of Art a cobbler makes
All under foot are trodden.
Did not an angel bring
For such work comforting,
And call me oft to Heaven's gate,
I 'd quickly leave this trade I hate!
But when he takes me up on high,
The world beneath my feet doth lie:
Then rest doth woo
Hans Sachs, the shoe-
Maker and the Poet too.

Beckmesser

(watching the window which now opens softly).

The window 's unclosed! — O heavens! 't is she!

Eva

(to Walter).

Why does that song dispirit me?
Oh, hence, let us hasten!

Beckmesser

(alsbald nach Beginn des Verses).

Was soll das sein? —
Verdammtes Schrein!
Was fällt dem groben Schuster ein?

(Vortretend.)

Wie, Meister? Auf? So spät zur Nacht?

Sachs.

Herr Stadtschreiber! Was, ihr wacht?
Die Schuh' machen euch grosse Sorgen?
Ihr seht, ich bin dran: ihr habt sie morgen.

Beckmesser.

Hol' der Teufel die Schuh'!
Ich will hier Ruh'!

Walther

(zu Eva).

Wie heisst das Leid? Wie nennt er dich?

Eva.

Ich hört' es schon: 's geht nicht auf mich,
Doch eine Bosheit steckt darin.

Walther.

Welch' Zögerniss! Die Zeit geht hin!

Sachs

(fortarbeitend).

Jerum! Jerum!
Halla halla he!
O ho! Trallalei! O he!
O Eva! Hör' mein Klageruf,
Mein Noth und schwer Verdrüssen!
Die Kunstwerk', die ein Schuster schuf,
Sie tritt die Welt mit Füssen!
Gäb nicht ein Engel Trost,
Der gleiches Werk erlos't,
Und rief mich oft in's Paradies,
Wie machen ich Schuh' und Stiefel liess'!
Doch wenn der mich im Himmel hält,
Dann liegt zu Füssen mir die Welt,
Und bin in Ruh'
Hans Sachs ein Schuh-
macher und Poet dazu.

Beckmesser

(das Fenster gewahrend, welches jetzt sehr leise geöffnet wird).

Das Fenster geht auf: — Herr Gott, 's ist sie!

Eva

(zu Walther).

Mich schmerzt das Lied, ich weiss nicht wie!
O fort, lass uns fliehen!

Walter
             (half-drawing his sword).
                         But one way remains !

Eva.

Oh, no !   Forbear !

Walter.
                         He 's scarce worth the pains !

Eva.

Yes, patience is best.   O dearest love,
That I should such a trouble prove !

Walter.

Who 's at the window?

Eva.
                         'T is Magdalena.

Walter.

That 's real retribution : it sets me grinning.

Eva.

Would we could end, and fly this arena !

Walter.

I only wish he 'd make a beginning.

(They follow the proceedings with increasing interest.)

Beckmesser

(who, while Sachs has continued his song and work, takes
counsel with himself in great perturbation).

Now if he continues I am undone !

(He advances to the shop.)

Friend Sachs ! pray hear a word — just one !
You work there at my shoes so fleetly,
While I 'd forgotten them completely.
The cobbler worshipful I deem ;
The critic, though, I more esteem.
Your taste, I know, is seldom wrong ;
So, please you, hear this little song,
With which I seek to win to-morrow :
Your estimate I fain would borrow.

(With his back turned to the alley he strums on the lute to
attract the attention of Magdalena and keep her at the
window.)

Sachs.

Aha !   A trap your words are holding !
But I 'll not earn another scolding.
Since that your cobbler courts the Muse
It fares but ill with your boots and shoes :
          I see they 're slit :
          And ev'rywhere split ;
So all my verse and rhyme
I 'll lay aside for a time,
My sense, my wit, my knowledge and all ;
Then with your new pair of shoes I 'll call.

Walther
             (das Schwert halb ziehend).
                         Nun denn : mit dem Schwert !

Eva.

Nicht doch !   Ach halt' !

Walther.
                         Kaum wär' er's werth

Eva.

Ja, besser Geduld !   O lieber Mann !
Dass ich so Noth dir machen kann !

Walther.

Wer ist am Fenster?

Eva.
                         's ist Magdalene.

Walther.

Das heiss' ich vergelten : fast muss' ich lachen.

Eva.

Wie ich ein End' und Flucht mir ersehne !

Walther.

Ich wünscht' er möchte den Anfang machen.

(Sie folgen dem Vorgang mit wachsender Theilnahme.)

Beckmesser

(der, während Sachs fortfährt zu arbeiten und zu singen, in
grosser Aufregung mit sich berathen hat).

Jetzt bin ich verloren, singt er noch fort !

(Er tritt an den Laden heran.)

Freund Sachs !   So hört doch nur ein Wort !
Wie seid ihr auf die Schuh' versessen !
Ich hatt' sie wahrlich schon vergessen.
Als Schuster seid ihr mir wohl werth,
Als Kunstfreund doch weit mehr verehrt.
Eu'r Urtheil, glaubt, das halt' ich hoch ;
D'rum bitt' ich, hört das Liedlein doch,
Mit dem ich morgen möcht' gewinnen,
Ob das auch recht nach euren Sinnen.

Er klimpert, mit seinem Rücken der Gasse zugewendet
auf der Laute, um die Aufmerksamkeit der dort am Fenster
sich zeigenden Magdalene zu beschäftigen, und sie dadurch
zurückzuhalten.

Sachs.

O ha !   Wollt mich beim Wahne fassen !
Mag mich nicht wieder schelten lassen.
Seit sich der Schuster dünkt Poet,
Gar übel es um eu'r Schuhwerk steht ;
          Ich seh' wie's schlappt,
          Und überall klappt :
D'rum lass' ich Vers' und Reim'
          Gar billig nun daheim,
Verstand und Kenntniss auch dazu,
Mach' euch für morgen die neuen Schuh'

Beckmesser.

Atrocious malice ! — Zounds ! it grows late !
She 'll go from the window if longer I wait !

(He strums a prelude.)

Sachs

(with a blow of his hammer).

" Now begin " ! Look sharp, or I too shall sing !

Beckmesser.

Aught but that ! Pray hush ! — What a madd'ning
thing !
Would you the post of Marker aspire to,
Then hammer away as you desire to : —
But you must agree to restrain your tool ;
Not strike unless I 'm breaking a rule.

Sachs.

Though a cobbler I 'll keep the rules like you,
If my fingers itch to complete this shoe.

Beckmesser.

Your Master's word ?

Sachs.

And cobbler's truth.

Beckmesser.

If it is faultless, fair, and smooth —

Sachs.

Then you must go unshod, forsooth !
Sit you down here !

Beckmesser

(placing himself at the corner of the house).

I 'd rather leave you.

Sachs.

Why so far off ?

Beckmesser.

Not to perceive you :
The Marker in school hides in his place.

Sachs.

But I shall scarce hear you.

Beckmesser.

My pow'rful bass
Will not then stun you with its din.

Sachs.

That 's good ! — All right then ! — " Now begin " !

Short prelude on the lute by Beckmesser, during which
Magdalena leans out of the window.)

Beckmesser.

Verdammte Bosheit ! — Gott, und 's wird spät :
Am End' mirdie Jungfervom Fenstergeht !

(Er klimpert wie um anzufangen.)

Sachs

(aufschlagend).

Fanget an ! 's pressirt ! Sonst sing' ich für mich !

Beckmesser.

Haltet ein ! Nur das nicht ! — Teufel ; wie ärger-
lich !
Wollt ihr euch denn als Merker erdreisten,
Nun gut, so merkt mit dem Hammer auf dem
Leisten ; —
Nur mit dem Beding, nach den Regeln scharf ;
Aber nichts, was nach den Regeln ich darf.

Sachs.

Nach den Regeln, wie sie der Schuster kennt,
Dem die Arbeit unter den Händen brennt.

Beckmesser.

Auf Meister-Ehr' !

Sachs.

Und Schuster-Muth

Beckmesser.

Nicht einen Fehler : glatt und gut !

Sachs.

Dann ging't ihr morgen unbeschuht. —
Setzt euch denn hier !

Beckmesser

(an die Ecke des Hauses sich stellend).

Lasst hier mich stehen !

Sachs.

Warum so fern ?

Beckmesser.

Euch nicht zu sehen,
Wie's Brauch in der Schul' vor dem Gemerk.

Sachs.

Da hör' ich euch echlecht !

Beckmesser.

Der Stimme Stärk
Ich so gar lieblich dämpfen kann.

Sachs.

Wie fein ! — Nun gut denn ! — Fanget an !

(Kurzes Vorspiel Beckmesser's auf der Laute, wozu Magda
lene sich breit in das Fenster legt.)

Walter

(to Eva).

What crazy sounds !   'T is like a dream :
Still in the Singer's seat I seem.

Eva.

Sleep steals upon me like a spell.
For good or evil, who can tell?

(She sinks, as if stupefied, on Walter's breast.   In this position they remain.)

Beckmesser

(with his lute).

   " I see the dawning daylight,
      With great plea*sure* I do.

(Sachs knocks. — Beckmesser starts but continues.)

      " For now my breast takes *a* right
         Courage both fresh and " —

(Sachs has dealt two blows.   Beckmesser turns round softly
but in anger.)

      Is this a jest?
      What d' ye find bad there?

Sachs.

      Better have had there,
   " For now my breast
Takes a right courage fresh and " —

Beckmesser.

      How would that lay right
      To rhyme with my " daylight " ?

Sachs.

The melody do you think no matter?
Both words and notes should fit in song.

Beckmesser.

Absurd discussion ! — Leave off that clatter !
Or is it a plot?

Sachs.

      Oh, get along !

Beckmesser.

I 'm quite upset !

Sachs.

      Begin it once more,
And three bars rest meanwhile I 'll score.

Beckmesser

(aside).

'T is better that no attention I pay : —
If only she is not scared away !

(He clears his throat and begins again.)

   " I see the dawning daylight,
      With great plea*sure* I do ;

Walther

(zu Eva).

Welch' toller Spuck !   Mich dünkt's ein Traum :
Den Singstuhl, scheint's, verliess ich kaum !

Eva.

Die Schläf' umwebt's mir, wie ein Wahn :
Ob's Heil, ob Unheil, was ich ahn' ?

(Sie sinkt wie betäubt an Walther's Brust : so verbleiben
sie.)

Beckmesser

(zur Laute).

   „ Den Tag seh' ich ercheinen,
      Der mir wohl gefall'n thut. . .

(Sachs schlägt auf.)

(Beckmesser zuckt, fährt aber fort :)

      „ Da fasst mein Herz sich einen
         guten und frischen Muth."

(Sachs hat zweimal aufgeschlagen.   Beckmesser wendet
sich leise doch wüthend um.)

      Treibt ihr hier Scherz?
      Was wär' nicht gelungen?

Sachs.

      Besser gesungen :
      „ Da fasst mein Herz
   sich einen guten und frischen Muth."

Beckmesser.

      Wie sollt' sich das reimen
      Auf „ seh' ich erscheinen? "

Sachs.

Ist euch an der Weise nichts gelegen?
Mich dünkt, 'sollt' passen Ton und Wort.

Beckmesser.

Mit euch hier zu streiten? — Lasst von den Schlä
gen,
Sonst denkt ihr mir d'ran !

Sachs.

      Jetzt fahret fort

Beckmesser.

Bin ganz verwirrt !

Sachs.

      So fangt noch 'mal an
Drei Schläg' ich jetzt pausiren kann.

Beckmesser

(für sich).

Am Besten, wenn ich ihn gar nicht beacht' : —
Wenn's nur die Jungfrau nicht irre macht !

(Er räuspert sich und beginnt wieder.)

   „ Den Tag seh' ich erscheinen,
      Der mir wohl gefall'n thut :

For now my heart takes a right
Cou*rage* both fresh and new.
I do not think of dying,
Rather of trying
A young mai*den* to win.
Oh, wherefore doth the weather
Then *to*-day so excel?
i to all say together
'T is *because* a dam*sel*
By her beloved father,
At *his* wish rather,
To *be* wed *doth* go in.
    The bold man who
    Would come and view,
May see the maiden there so true,
On whom my hopes I firmly glue:
There*fore* is *the* sky *so* bright blue,
As I said to begin."

Beckmesser, keeping his eyes fixed on the window has
perceived with rising chagrin Magdalena's evident signs of
dissatisfaction; he has sung louder and more hurriedly in
order to overpower the continued hammering of Sachs. —
He is about to continue when the latter, knocking the key
of the last out and withdrawing the shoes, rises from his
stool and leans out over the shopdoor.

Sachs.

Have n't you finished?

Beckmesser
    (in great trepidation).
           What means your call?

Sachs
   (triumphantly holding out the shoes from the door).

've finished with the shoes, that's all ! —
I call that a famous Marker's shoe:
Now hear my Marker's maxim too. —
    By long and short strokes dinted
    Here on the sole 'tis printed !
        Behold it here,
        Let it be clear,
    And hold it ever dear. —
        " Good songs must scan."
        On any man,
Ev'n the Town-clerk, who'd transgress it
The cobbler's strap shall impress it. —
    Now run along,
    Your shoes are strong;
Thrust henceforth to your feet:
They 'll keep you on the beat.
        (He laughs loudly.)

Beckmesser

who has retired into the alley again and leaned against the
wall between Sachs's two windows, hastens on with his third
verse, shouting breathlessly with violent efforts to drown
Sachs's voice).

Da fasst mein Herz sich einen
Guten und frischen Muth.
Da denk' ich nicht an Sterben,
    Lieber an Werben
Um jung' Mägdeleins Hand.
Warum wohl aller Tage
Schönster mag dieser sein?
Allen hier ich es sage:
Weil ein schönes Fräulein,
Von ihrem lieb'n Herrn Vater,
Wie gelobt hat er,
Ist bestimmt zum Eh' stand.
    Wer sich getrau',
    Der komm' und schau'
Da steh'n die hold lieblich Jungfrau,
Auf die ich all' mein' Hoffnung bau',
D'rum ist der Tag so schön blau,
Als ich anfänglich fand."

Beckmesser, nur den Blick auf das Fenster heftend, hat mit
wachsender Angst Magdalene's missbehagliche Gebärden
bemerkt; um Sachsen's fortgesetzte Schläge zu übertäuben,
hat er immer stärker und athemloser gesungen. — Er ist im
Begriffe sofort weiter zu singen, als Sachs, der zuletzt die
Keile aus den Leisten schlug, und die Schuhe abgezogen
hat, sich vom Schemel erhebt, und über den Laden sich
herauslehnt.

Sachs.

Seid ihr nun fertig?

Beckmesser
    (in höchster Angst).
           Wie fraget ihr?

Sachs
   (die Schuhe triumphirend aus dem Laden heraushaltend).

Mit den Schuhen ward' ich fertig schier !
Das heiss' ich mir rechte Merkerschuh';
Mein Merkersprüchlein hört dazu !
    Mit lang' und kurzen Hieben,
    Steht's auf der Sohl' geschrieben:
        Da les't es klar
        Und nehmt es wahr,
    Und merkt's euch immerdar. —
        Gut Lied will Takt,
        Wer den verzwackt,
    Dem Schreiber mit der Feder
    Haut ihn der Schuster auf's Leder.
        Nun lauft iu Ruh',
        Habt gute Schuh';
    Der Fuss euch d'rin nicht knackt:
    Ihn hält die Sohl' im Takt !
        (Er lacht laut.)

Beckmesser

(der sich ganz in die Gasse zurückgezogen, und an die
Mauer zwischen den beiden Fenstern von Sachsens Hause
sich anlehnt, singt, um Sachs zu übertäuben, zugleich, mit
grösster Anstrengung, schreiend und athemlos hastig, seinen
dritten Vers).

That I 've a Master's learning
Wil*ling*ly I 'd show her,
To win the *re*ward burning
I 'm *with* thirst *and* hun*ger*.
Now I call *the* nine Muses
　　To witness whose is
The *poetic* gift true.
I lay no faulty stresses,
In *the* rules I 'm no dunce ;
Some little awkwardnesses
May *ex*cused *be* for once,
When *one*'s heart fear is swaying
　　At thus essaying
A fair mai*den* to woo.
　　A bachelor,
　　　I 'd give my gore,
My place, rank, honor, all my store,
If *you* my song would not abhor ;
And *the* mai*den* would me adore
　　If she admires it too."

Neighbors

(first a few, then more, open their windows in the alley dur-
　　ing the song and peep out).

Who 's howling there ?　Who bawls so loud ?
So late at night, is that allowed ?
'T is time for bed !　Be still, I say !
Just listen to that donkey's bray !
You there !　Shut up and beat retreat !
Go halloo in some other street !

David

　　(who has opened his shutter close to Beckmesser).

Whoever 's this, and who 's up there ?
'T is Magdalena, I declare !
'Oddzounds ! that 's it — I clearly see
'T is he she favors more than me !
You 'll catch it !　Just wait !　I 'll tan your skin !
The devil help you when I begin !

(David, arming himself with a cudgel, springs out of the
window, knocks Beckmesser's lute out of his hands and
　　throws himself upon him.)

Magdalena

(who at last, to make the Marker go, has made exaggerated
　　gestures of pleasure at him, now cries aloud).

O heavens !　David !　Lord, how I 'm thrilled !
A rescue ! a rescue ! or both will be killed !

Beckmesser
　　　　　　　　(struggling with David).

Infernal rogue !　Let me alone !

David.

I will when I 've broken every bone.

　　(They continue to struggle and fight.)

„ Darf ich Meister mich nennen,
　Das bewähr' ich heut gern,
　Weil nach dem Preis ich brennen
　Muss dursten und hungern,
　Nun ruf' ich die neun Musen,
　　　Dass an sie blusen
　Mein dichtr'schen Verstand.
　Wohl kenn' ich alle Regeln,
　Halte gut Mass und Zahl ;
　Doch Sprung und Ueberkegeln
　Wohl passirt je einmal,
　Wann der Kopf, ganz voll Zagen,
　　　Zu frei'n will wagen
　Um ein jung' Mägdleins Hand.
　　Ein Junggesell,
　　　Trug ich mein Fell,
Mein Ehr', Amt, Würd' und Brod zur Stell',
Dass euch, mein Gesang wohl gefäll',
Und mich das Jungfräulein erwähl',
　　　Wenn sie mein Lied gut fand."

Nachbarn

(erst einige, dann mehrere, öffnen während des Gesanges in
　der Gasse die Fenster und gucken heraus).

Wer heult denn da !　Wer kreischt mit Macht ?
Ist das erlaubt, so spät zur Nacht ? —
Gebt Ruhe hier !　's ist Schlafenszeit ! —
Nein, hört nur, wie der Esel schreit ! —
Ihr da !　Seid still, und scheert euch fort !
Heult, kreischt und schreit an and'rem Ort !

David

(hat ebenfalls den Fensterladen, dicht bei Beckmesser, ein
　　wenig geöffnet und lugt hervor).

Wer Teufel hier ? — Und drüben gar ?
Die Lene ist's, — ich seh' es klar !
Herr Je ! das war's, den hat sie bestellt ;
Der ist's, der ihr besser als ich gefällt ! —
Nun warte !　du kriegst's !　dir streich' ich das
　　　　　　　　　　　　　　Fell ! —
Zum Teufel mit dir, verdammter Gesell' !

(David ist, mit einem Knüpple bewaffnet, hinter dem Laden
aus dem Fenster hervorgesprungen, zerschlägt Beckmesser's
　　Laute und wirft sich über ihn selbst her.)

Magdalene

(die zuletzt, um den Merker zu entfernen, mit übertriebenen
beifälligen Bewegungen herabgewinkt hat, schreit jetzt laut
　　　　　　　　　auf).

Ach Himmel !　David !　Gott, welche Noth !
Zu Hülfe ! zu Hülfe !　Sie schlagen sich todt !

Beckmesser
　　　　　　　(mit David sich balgend).

Verfluchter Kerl !　Lässt du mich los ?

David.

Gewiss !　Die Glieder brech' ich dir blos !

　　(Sie balgen und prügeln sich in einem fort

Neighbors
                (at the windows).

Look there !   Go to !   They 're hard at it now !

Other Neighbors
                (coming into the alley).

Hallo ?   What 's up ?   See, here 's a row !
You there !   stand back !   Give him fair play !
If you don't part we 'll join the fray.

One Neighbor.

Halloa ?   Have you come ?   Why are you here ?

A Second.

What 's that to you !   Don't interfere !

First Neighbor.

You 're a big rogue !

Second Neighbor.
                                You are no lesser !

First Neighbor.
                Prove it, then !

Second Neighbor
                (hitting out).
                There !

Magdalena
                (screaming down).
                David !   Beckmesser !

Prentices
                (entering).

Hooray ! hooray !   Here 's cudgel play !

Some.

It 's the cobblers !

Others.
                No, it 's the tailors !

The First.

The drunken patches !

The Others.
                The starveling railers !

The Neighbors
                (in the street, to one another).

That pays what I owe you ! —
Coward !   I know you ! —
Take that to requite you ! —
Mind your eye if I smite you ! —
Was your wife's temper high ? —
See how the cudgels fly ! —
Have n't you found your wits ? —
Lay on, then ! — That hits !

Nachbarn
                (an den Fenstern).

Seht nach !   Springt zu !   Da würgen sich zwei !

Andere Nachbarn
                (auf die Gasse heraustretend).

Heda, Herbei !   's gibt Prügelei !
Ihr da !   auseinander !   Gebt freien Lauf !
Lasst ihr nicht los, wir schlagen drauf !

Ein Nachbar.

Ei seht !   Auch ihr da ?   Geht's euch 'was an ?

Ein Zweiter.

Was sucht ihr hier ?   Hat man euch 'was gethan ?

Erster Nachbar.

Euch kennt man gut !

Zweiter Nachbar.
                                Euch noch viel besser !

Erster Nachbar.

Wie so denn ?

Zweiter Nachbar
                (zuschlagend).
                Ei, so !

Magdalene
                (hinabschreiend).
                David !   Beckmesser !

Lehrbuben
                (kommen dazu).

Herbei !   Herbei !   's gibt Keilerei !

Einige.

's sind die Schuster !

Andere.
                Nein, 's sind die Schneider !

Die Ersteren.

Die Trunkenbolde !

Die Anderen.
                Die Hungerleider !

Die Nachbarn.
                (auf der Gasse, durcheinander).

Euch gönnt ich's schon lange ! —
Wird euch wohl bange ?
Das für die Klage ! —
Seht euch vor, wenn ich schlage ! —
Hat euch die Frau gehetzt ? —
Schau' wie es Prügel setzt ! —
Seid ihr noch nicht gewitzt !
So schlagt doch ! — Das sitzt !

Rogue, there 's a thumper !—
You counter-jumper !—
You gutter-sweeper !—
You false-measure-keeper !
Blockhead ! — Looby !—
You great Booby !—
Dolt, I say !
Don't give way !

Prentices

(to one another, with the **neighbors)**.

We know the locksmiths' way :
They surely started this fray !—
I think the smiths began the fight. —
I see the joiners by the light. —
Look where the coopers come along *!*
And now the barbers join the throng. —
There the Guild of grocers comes,
With lollipops and sugarplums,
With pepper, spice, and cinnamon.
How nice they smell !
How nice they smell !
But they don't like the fun,
And wish that it were done.
See that fool there,
With his nose ev'rywhere !
Pray did you allude to me?—
Pray did I allude to thee?
There 's one nose I 've pounded !—
Lord ! how that sounded !—
Hey ! whack ! fire and fury oh !
Where that fell no hair will grow !
Cudgels, whack hard !
Smash the blackguard !
Show yourselves worth freemen's **name :**
To give way would be a shame !
Join the brawl,
Each and all.
We are ready to help the row !

(Gradually the neighbors and Prentices **have come** to a
general fight.)

Journeymen

(arriving from all **quarters).**

Hallo ! Companions, come !
The people here seem quarrelsome.
There 'll surely be some fighting **then :**
Be ready, lusty journeymen.
'T is the weaver and tanners !—
Which well I know !—
'T is like their manners !—
They always do so !—
Klaus the butcher 's there ;
He 's one to beware !—
Guilds ! Guilds !
Guilds ! ev'rywhere !—

Dass dich, Hallunke !—
Hie Färbertunke !—
Wartet, ihr Racker !
Ihr Maassabzwacker !—
Esel ! — Dummrian !—
Du Grobian !—
Lümmel du !—
Drauf und zu !

Lehrbuben

(durcheinander, zugleich mit den **Nachbarn)**.

Kennt man die Schlosser nicht?
Die haben's sicher angericht' !
Ich glaub' die Schmiede werden's sein. —
Die Schreiner seh' ich dort beim Schein.
Hei ! Schau' die Schäffler dort beim **Tanz.**
Dort seh' die Bader ich im Glanz. —
Krämer finden sich zur Hand
Mit Gerstenstang und Zuckerkand ;
Mit Pfeffer, Zimmt, Muscatennuss,
Sie riechen schön,
Sie riechen schön,
Doch haben viel Verdruss,
Und bleiben gern vom Schuss. —
Seht nur, der Hase
Hat üb'rall die Nase !
Meinst du damit etwa mich !—
Mein' ich damit etwa dich?
Da hast's auf die Schnautze !—
Herr, jetzt setzt's Plautze !—
Hei ! Krach ! Hagelwetterschlag !
Wo das sitzt, da wächst nichts nach :
Keilt euch wacker,
Haut die Racker !
Haltet selbst Gesellen Stand ;
Wer da wich', 's wär' wahrlich **Schand' !**
Drauf und dran !
Wie ein Mann
Steh'n wir alle zur Keilerei !

(Bereits prügeln sich Nachbarn und Lehrbuben **fast allge**
mein durcheinander.)

Gesellen

(von allen Seiten dazu **kommend).**

Heda ! Gesellen 'ran !
Dort wird mit Streit und Zank gethan,
Da giebt's gewiss gleich Schlägerei ;
Gesellen, haltet euch dabei !
'Sind die Weber und Gerber !—
Dacht' ich's doch gleich !—
Die Preisverderber !
Spielen immer Streich' !—
Dort den Metzger Klaus,
Den kennt man heraus !—
Zünfte ! Zünfte !
Zünfte heraus !—

Tailors here are hieing !—
See the cudgels flying !
Girdlers !— Pewterers !
Glue-boilers !— Fruiterers !
Clothworkers here !
Linenweavers here !
Come here !   Come here !
More appear !   More appear !
All do your best !   We're going to strike !
Now will the fight be something like !—
Run home ! your wife is after you !
Here you'll get painted black and blue !
    There they go !
    Blow for blow !
    Knock them over !
Guildsmen !   Guildsmen !   come out !

The Masters

    (and old Burghers arriving on all sides).

What is this noise of brawl and fight,
That sounds far through the night?
Leave off and let each go his way,
Or else there'll be the deuce to pay !
Don't crowd up like this in bands,
Or else we too must use our hands.

Women

    (at the windows to one another).

What is this noise of fight and brawl?
It really terrifies us all !
My husband's there, as sure as fate !
Some one will get a broken pate !
    Hey, sirs !   You below there,
    Be reasonable now !
    Are you then all so ready
    To join a vulgar row?
What a confusion and halloa !
Now blows will be certain to follow !
Hark ye ! hark ye !
Are ye insane?
    Are ye still fuddled
    With wine on the brain?
O murder ! murder !
My man's in the fight !
There's father ! there's father !
Look ! what a sight !
Christian !   Peter !
Nicholas !   Hans !
Watch ! be fleeter !—
Don't you hear, Franz?
Lord ! how the hair flies !
See how they go it !
Water here !   Water, quick !
On their heads throw it !

(The row has become general.   Shrieks and blows.)

Schneider mit dem Bügel !
Hei ! hie setzt's Prügel !
Gürtler !— Zinngiesser !—
Leimsieder !— Lichtgiesser !—
Tuchscherer her !
Leinweber her !
Hierher !   Hierher !
Immer mehr !   Immer mehr
Nur tüchtig drauf !   Wir schlagen los
Jetzt wird die Keilerei erst gross !—
Lauft heim, sonst kriegt ihr's von der Frau ;
Hier giebt's nur Prügel-Färberblau !
    Immer 'ran !
    Mann für Mann !
    Schlagt sie nieder !
Zünfte !   Zünfte !   Heraus !—

Die Meister

    (und älteren Bürger von verschiedenen Seiten daer kommend).

Was giebt's denn da für Zank und Streit?
Das tos't ja weit und breit !
Gebt Ruh' und scheer' sich jeder heim !
Sonst schlag' ein Hageldonnerwetter drein !
Stemmt euch hier nicht mehr zu Hauf,
Oder sonst wir schlagen krauf.—

Die Nachbarinnen

    (an den Fenstern, durcheinander).

Was ist denn da für Streit und Zank?
's wird einem wahrlich angst und bang !
Da ist mein Mann gewiss dabei :
Gewiss kommt's noch zur Schlägerei !
    He da !   Ihr dort unten,
    So seid doch nur gescheit !
    Seid ihr zu Streit und Raufen
    Gleich Alle so bereit?
Was für ein Zanken und Toben !
Da werden schon Arme erhoben,
Hört doch !   Hört doch !
Seid ihr denn toll?
    Sind euch die Köpfe
    Vom Weine noch voll?
Zu Hülfe !   Zu Hülfe !
Da schlägt sich mein Mann !
Der Vater !   Der Vater !
Sieht man das an?
Christian !   Peter !
Nikolaus !   Hans !
Auf ! schrei't Zeter !—
Hörst du nicht, Franz?
Gott, wie sie walken !
's wackeln die Zöpfe !
Wasser her !   Wasser her !
Giesst's ihn' auf die Köpfe !

(Die Rauferei ist allgemein.   Schreien und Toben.)

Magdalena

(wringing her hands despairingly at the window).

Oh heaven ! what is to be done !
David, for goodness' sake attend !
Do leave the gentleman alone !

Pogner

(coming to the window in his nightgown, pulls Magdalena in).

Come in, Eva ! Odd so !
I 'll see if all is right below.

The window is shut and Pogner appears below at the door.

Sachs at the commencement of the row has extinguished his light and set his door ajar, so as still to be able to watch the place under the lime-tree.

(Walter and Eva have observed the riot with increasing anxiety. Now Walter seizes Eva in his arms.)

Walter.

Now we may do it —
Cut our way through it !

Brandishing his sword he forces a way to the middle of the stage.—Sachs rushes with one bound out of his shop and grasps Walter's arms.

Pogner

(on the steps).

Ho ! Lena ! where are you?

Sachs

(pushing the half-fainting Eva up the steps).

Go in, Mistress Lena !

Pogner receives her and pulls her within.

Sachs brandishing his knee-strap, with which he has cleared a path to Walter, now catches David one, and kicking him into the shop, drags Walter, whom he still holds, indoors with him, closing and barring the door behind them.

Beckmesser, released from David by Sachs, seeks hasty flight through the crowd.

At the moment Sachs rushes into the street a loud note from the Nightwatchman's horn is heard R. U. E. Prentices, Burghers, and Journeymen, panic-struck, seek flight on all sides, so that the stage is speedily completely cleared : all doors are closed and women gone from windows, which are also shut.—The full moon shines out and brightly illumines the now peaceful alley.

The Watchman

(enters R. U. E., rubs his eyes, stares about him in surprise, shakes his head, and in a somewhat tremulous voice calls out) :

" Hark to what I say, good people !
Eleven strikes from every steeple ;
Defend you all from spectre and sprite,
Let no power of ill your souls affright.
　　　Praise the Lord of Heaven."

He goes slowly up the alley. As the curtain falls his distant horn is still heard.

Magdalene

(am Fenster verzweifelt die Hände ringend).

Ach Himmel ! Meine Noth ist gross ! —
David ! So hör, mich doch nur an !
So lass' doch nur den Herrn los !

Pogner

(ist im Nachtgewand oben an das Fenster getreten und zieht Magdalene herein).

Um Gott ! Eva ! schliess' zu !
Ich seh', ob im Haus unten Ruh' !

Das Fenster wird geschlossen; bald darauf erscheint Pogner an der Hausthüre.

Sachs hat, als der Tumult begann, sein Licht gelöscht und den Laden so weit geschlossen, dass er durch eine kleine Oeffnung stets den Platz unter der Linde beobachten kann.

Walther und Eva haben mit wachsender Sorge dem anschwellenden Tumult zugesehen. Jetzt fasst Walther Eva dicht in den Arm.

Walther.

Jetzt gilt's zu wagen,
Sich durchzuschlagen !

Mit geschwungenem Schwerte dringt er bis in die Mitte der Bühne vor. — Da springt Sachs mit einem Satz aus dem Laden auf die Strasse, und packt Walther beim Arm.

Pogner

(auf der Treppe).

He, Lene, wo bist du?

Sachs

(die halb ohnmächtige Eva auf die Treppe stossend).

In's Haus, Jungfer Lene !

Pogner empfängt sie, und zieht sie beim Arme herein.

Sachs mit dem geschwungenen Knieriemen, mit dem er sich bereits bis zu Walther Platz gemacht hatte, jetzt dem David eines überhauend, und ihn mit einem Fusstritt voran in den Laden stossend, zieht Walther, den er mit der andern Hand gefasst hält, gewaltsam schnell mit sich ebenfalls hinein, und schliesst songleich fest hinter sich zu.

Beckmesser, durch Sachs von David befreit, sucht sich eilig durch die Menge zu flüchten.

Im gleichen Augenblicke, wo Sachs auf die Strasse sprang, hörte man, rechts zur Seite im Vordergrunde, einen besonders starken Hornruf des Nachtwächters. Lehrbuben, Bürger und Gesellen suchten in eiliger Flucht sich nach allen Seiten hin zu entfernen, so dass die Bühne sehr schnell gänzlich geleert ist, alle Hausthüren hastig geschlossen, und auch die Nachbarinnen von den Fenstern, welche sie zugeschlagen, verschwunden sind — Der Vollmond tritt hervor und scheint hell in die Gasse hinein.

Der Nachtwächter

(betritt im Vordergrunde rechts die Bühne, reibt sich die Augen, sieht sich verwundert um, schüttelt den Kopf, und stimmt, mit etwas bebender Stimme, seinen Ruf an) :

Hört ihr Leut', und lasst euch sagen :
Die Glock' hat Eilfe geschlagen,
Bewahrt euch vor Gespenstern und Spuck,
Dass kein böser Geist eur' Seel' beruck' !
　　　Lobet Gott den Herrn !

Er geht währenddem langsam die Gasse hinab. Als der Vorhang fällt, hört man den Hornruf des Nachtwächters wiederholen.

THIRD ACT.

In Sachs's workshop. (Front scene.) At back the half-open shopdoor leads to the street. R. the door of a chamber. L. the window looking into the alley, flowers in pots before it; a workbench beside it. Sachs sits at this window in a great armchair, the bright morning sun streaming in on him; he has a large folio on his lap and is absorbed in reading. — David peeps in at the door from the street; on seeing that Sachs does not notice him he enters with a basket on his arm, which he first hides quickly under the other workbench; then again assured that Sachs does not heed him, he carefully takes it out again and investigates the contents: he lifts out flowers and ribbons and at last finds at the bottom a sausage and a cake; these he is about to devour when Sachs, who is still unconscious of his presence, turns over a leaf of his book with a loud rustle.

David

(starts, hides the eatables, and turns round).

Here, Master! Yes! —
The shoes were taken duly
To clerk Beckmesser's address.
I thought you summoned me, truly.

(Aside.)

He seems to notice me not!
When he is dumb his anger 's hot.

(Gradually approaching humbly.)

Ah, Master! won't you forgive?
Can a Prentice quite faultless live?
If with my eyes Lena you 'd see
You 'd pardon me assuredly.
She is so good, so kind to me,
And eyes me at times so tenderly.
When I 've been thrashed soothing is she
And smiles upon me so prettily!
When on short commons she feedeth me,
And acts in all things right lovingly.
Last night, though, when that knight was discarded,
There was no basket to me awarded:
That worried me, and when I found
At night when some one lurked around,
And sang to her and cried like mad,
I gave him all the stick I had.
What dreadful consequence befell!
But yet for our love it turned out well;
Now Lena 's explained the matter to me,
And sent all these ribbons and flowers you see.

(He bursts out in still greater anxiety.)

O Master! speak one word I pray!

(Aside.)

Would I 'd put the cake and sausage away!

DRITTER AUFZUG.

In Sachsen's Werkstatt. (Kurzer Raum.) Im Hintergrund die halb geöffnete Ladenthüre, nach der Strasse führend. Rechts zur Seite eine Kammerthüre. Links das nach der Gasse gehende Fenster, mit Blumenstöcken davor, zur Seite ein Werktisch. Sachs sitzt auf einem grossen Lehnstuhle an diesem Fenster, durch welches die Morgensonne hell auf ihn hereinscheint; er hat vor sich auf dem Schoose einen grossen Folianten und ist im Lesen vertieft. — David lugt spähend von der Strasse zur Ladenthüre herein: da er sieht, dass Sachs seiner nicht achtet, tritt er herein, mit einem Korbe im Arm, den er zuvörderst schnell und verstohlen unter den andern Werktisch beim Laden stellt; — dann von neuem versichert, dass Sachs ihn nicht bemerkt, nimmt er den Korb vorsichtig herauf, und untersucht den Inhalt; er hebt Blumen und Bänder heraus; endlich findet er auf dem Grunde eine Wurst und einen Kuchen, und lässt sich sogleich an, diese zu verzehren, als Sachs, der ihn fortwährend nicht beachtet, mit starkem Geräusch eines der grossen Blätter des Folianten unwendet.

David

(fährt zusammen, verbirgt das Essen und wendet sich).

Gleich! Meister! Hier! —
Die Schuh' sind abgegeben
In Herrn Beckmesser's Quartier. —
Mir war's, ihr rieft't mich eben?

(Bei Seite.)

Er thut, als säh' er mich nicht?
Da ist er bös', wenn er nicht spricht!

(Sich demüthig sehr allmählich nähernd.)

Ach Meister woll't ihr mir verzeih'n!
Kann ein Lehrbub' vollkommen sein?
Kennet ihr die Lene, wie ich,
Da vergäbt ihr mir sicherlich.
Sie ist so gut, so sanft für mich,
Und blickt mich oft an, so innerlich:
Wenn ihr mich schlagt, streichelt sie mich,
Und lächelt dabei holdseliglich!
Muss ich cariren, füttert sie mich,
Und ist in Allem gar liebelich.
Nur gestern, weil der Junker versungen,
Hab' ich den Korb ihr nicht abgerungen:
Das schmerzte mich; und da ich fand,
Dass Nachts Einer vor dem Fenster stand,
Und sang zu ihr, und schrie wie toll,
Da hieb ich dem den Buckel voll.
Wie käm' nun da 'was Gross' drauf an?
Auch hat's uns'rer Lieb' gar gut gethan:
Die Lene hat eben mir Alles erklärt,
Und zum Fest Blumen und Bänder bescheert.

(Er bricht in immer grössere Angst aus.)

Ach, Meister, sprecht doch nur ein Wort!

(Bei Seite.)

Hätt' ich nur die Wurst und den Kuchen fort.

Sachs

(who has read on undisturbed, claps his book to. At the loud noise David is so startled that he stumbles and falls unintentionally on his knees before Sachs. The latter gazes far away beyond the book which he still holds, beyond David who, from his kneeling posture looks up at him in terror, and his eyes fall on the farther table).

> Yonder are flowers and ribbons gay
> In youthful beauty and bloom:
> How came they into my room?

David

        (astonished at Sachs's friendliness).

Why, Master! to-day's a feast, you know,
And all must smarten to grace the show.

Sachs.

Is 't a marriage feast?

David.

                    Yes, so it would be
If only Lena might marry me.

Sachs.

Your Folly-evening* was last night?

David

        (aside).

Folly-evening? — I 'm all in a fright!

        (Aloud.)

Forgive me, Master! Forget it, pray!
The Feast of St. John we keep to-day.

Sachs.

St. John's day?

David

        (aside).
        Deaf he must be!

Sachs.

Know you your verses? Repeat them me.

David.

My verses? Yes, they 're in my brain. —

        (Aside.)

All right! the master is kind again! —

        (Aloud.)

"St. John stood on the Jordan's strand" —

(In his agitation he sings his lines to the melody of Beckmesser's serenade; he is pulled up by Sachs's movement of astonishment.)

Forgive me, master, and pardon the slip!
That Folly-evening caused me to trip.

* "Polterabend" — the merrymaking on the eve of a German wedding.

Sachs

(der unbeirrt weiter gelesen, schlägt jetzt den Folianten zu Von dem starken Geräusch erschrickt David so, dass er strauchelt und unwillkürlich vor Sachs auf die Knie fällt. Sachs sieht über das Buch, das er noch auf dem Schoosse behält, hinwig, über David, welcher immer auf den Knieen, furchtsam nach ihm hinauf blickt, hin, und heftet seinen Blick unwillkürlich auf den hintern Werktisch).

> Blumen und Bänder seh' ich dort: —
> Schaut hold und jugendlich aus!
> Wie kamen die mir in's Haus?

David

        (verwundert über Sachsens Freundlichkeit).

Ei, Meister? 's is heut' hoch festlicher Tag;
Da putzt sich jeder, so schön er mag.

Sachs.

Wär' Hochzeitsfest?

David.

                   Ja, käm's so weit
Dass David erst die Lene freit!

Sachs.

's war Polterabend dünkt mich doch?

David

        (für sich).

Polterabend? — Da krieg ich's wohl noch! —

        (Laut.)

Verzeiht das, Meister! Ich bitt', vergesst,
Wir feiern ja heut' Johannisfest.

Sachs.

Johannisfest?

David

        (bei Seite).
        Hört er heut' schwer?

Sachs.

Kannst du ein Sprüchlein? Sag' es her!

David.

Mein Sprüchlein? Denk', ich kann es gut.

        (Bei Seite.)

'Setzt nichts! der Meister ist wohlgemuth! —

        (Laut.)

„Am Jordan Sankt Johannes stand" —

(Er hat in der Zerstreuung die Worte mit der Melodie von Beckmesser's Werbelied aus dem vorhergehennden Aufzuge gesungen; Sachs macht eine verwundernde Bewegung, worauf David sich unterbricht.)

Verzeiht, Meister; ich kam in's Gewirr:
Der Polterabend machte mich irr.

(He recommences to the proper tune.)

"St. John stood on the Jordan's strand,
    Where all the world he christened:
A woman came from distant land,
    From Nuremberg she 'd hastened:
Her little son she led in hand,
    Baptized him with a name there,
And then toward home she took her flight;
    But when at last she came there
It soon turned out in German lands,
That he who on the Jordan's sands
    Johannes had been hight,
    On the Pegnitz was called Hans."

(Impetuously.)

ir! Master! 'T is your name-day, sure!
here! Well, my memory must be poor!
ere! all the flowers are for you.
he ribbons — something else there was, too?
es, here! Look. Master! Here 's a fine pasty!
ry, too, this sausage, you 'll find it tasty.

achs

(still dreamily, without moving).

est thanks, my lad! You keep it though!
non to the meadow with me you shall go.
ith ribbons and flowers make yourself gay;
s my herald you are to act to-day.

David.

ould I not be your groomsman more fain?
faster, dear master! you *must* wed again!

achs.

o you wish for a mistress then here?

David.

fethinks more dignified it would appear.

achs.

ho knows? But time will show.

David.

ime 's come.

achs.

Ias it brought knowledge then to some?

David.

ye, sure! I know things have been repeated;
nd Beckmesser's singing you have defeated.
think he will scarce make a stir to-day.

achs.

is likely! That I 'll not gainsay.
ow, go; disturb not Sir Walter's rest!
ome back when you are finely dress'd.

(Er fährt in der richtigen Melodie fort.)

„Am Jordan Sankt Johannes stand,
    All Volk der Welt zu taufen:
Kam auch ein Weib aus fremden Land,
    Von Nürnberg gar gelaufen;
Sein Söhnlein trug's zum Nferrand,
    Empfing da Tauf' und Namen;
Doch als sie dann sich heimgewandt,
    Nach Nürnberg wieder kamen,
Im deutschen Land gar bald sich fand's,
Dass, wer am Ufer des Jordans
    Johannes war genannt,
    An der Pegnitz hiess der Hans."

(Feurig.)

Herr Meister! 's ist eu'r Namenstag!
Nein! Wie man so 'was vergessen mag!
Hier! hier, die Blumen sind für euch,
Die Bänder, — und was nur Alles noch gleich?
Ja hier! schaut, Meister! Herrlicher Kuchen
Möchtet ihr nicht auch die Wurst versuchen?

Sachs

(immer ruhig, ohne seine Stellung zu verändern).

Schön Dank, mein Jung'! behalt's für dich!
Doch heut' auf die Wiese' begleitest du mich:
Mit den Bändern und Blumen putz' dich fein;
Sollst mein stattlicher Herold sein.

David.

Sollt' ich nicht lieber Brautführer sein?
Meister! lieb' Meister! ihr müsst wieder frei'n!

Sachs.

Hätt'st wohl gern eine Meist'rin im Haus?

David.

Ich mein', es säh doch viel stattlicher aus.

Sachs.

Wer weiss! Kommt Zeit, kommt Rath.

David.

's ist Zeit!

Sachs.

Da wär' der Rath wohl auch nicht weit?

David.

Gewiss! geh'n die Reden schon hin und wieder.
Den Beckmesser, denk' ich säng't ihr doch nieder?
Ich mein', dass der heut' sich nicht wenig wichtig
                                                    macht.

Sachs.

Wohl möglich! Hab's mir auch schon bedacht
Jetzt geh'; doch stör' mir den Junker nicht!
Komm wieder, wenn du schön gericht'.

David

moved, kisses Sachs's hand, collects his things and goes into chamber).

He ne'er was like this, though sometimes kind !
Why, the taste of his strap has gone out of my mind !

(Exit.)

Sachs

(still with the book on his knees leans back deep in thought, resting his head on his hand, and after a pause begins).

Mad ! Mad !
All the world 's mad !
Where'er enquiry dives
In town or world's archives
And seeks to learn the reason
Why people strive and fight,
Both in and out of season,
In fruitless rage and spite.
What do they gain
For all their pain ?
Repulsed in fight,
They feign joy in flight ;
Their pain-cries not minding,
They joy pretend
When their own flesh their fingers rend,
And pleasure deem they 're finding.
What tongue the cause can phrase ?
'T is just the same old craze !
Naught haps without it ever,
In spite of all endeavor,
Pause doth it make ;
In sleep it but acquires new force,
Soon it will wake,
Then, lo ! who can control its course ?
Old ways and customs keeping,
How peacefully I see
My dear old Nurnberg sleeping
In midst of Germany !
But on one evening late,
To hinder in some fashion
The follies of youthful passion,
A man worries his pate ;
A shoemaker, all unknowing,
Sets the old madness going :
How soon from highways and alleys
A raging rabble sallies !
Man, woman, youth, and child
Blindly fall to as if gone wild ;
And ere the craze lose power
The cudgel blows must shower ;
They seek with fuss and pother
The fires of wrath to smother.
God knows how this befell !
'T was like some impish spell !
Some glowworm could not find his mate ;
'T was he aroused this wrath and hate.

David

(küsst ihm gerührt die Hand, packt Alles zusammen, und geht in die Kammer).

So war er noch nie, wenn sonst auch gut !
Kann mir gar nicht mehr denken, wie der Knierie-men thut !

(Ab.)

Sachs

(immer noch den Folianten auf dem Schoose, lehnt sich, mit untergestütztem Arme, sinnend darauf und beginnt dann nach einem Sohweigen).

Wahn ! Wahn !
Uberall ! Wahn !
Wohin ich forschend blick',
In Stadt- und Welt-Chronik,
Den Grund mir aufzufinden,
Warum gar bis auf's Blut
Die Leut' sich quälen und schinden
In unnütz toller Wuth !
Hat keiner Lohn
Noch dank davon :
In Flucht geschlagen,
Meint er zu jagen.
Hört nicht sein eigen
Schmerz-Gekreisch,
Wenn er sich wühlt in's eig'ne Fleisch
Wähnt Lust sich zu erzeigen.
Wer giebt den Namen an !
's bleibt halt der alte Wahn,
Ohn' den nichts mag geschehen,
's mag gehen oder stehen !
Steht's wo im Lauf,
Er schläft nur neue Kraft sich an ;
Gleich wacht er auf,
Dann schaut wer ihn bemeistern kann !
Wie friedsam treuer Sitten,
Getrost in That und Werk,
Liegt nicht in Deutschlands Mitten
Mein liebes Nürenberg !
Doch eines Abends spat,
Ein Unglück zu verhüten
Bei jugendheissen Gemüthen,
Ein Mann weiss sich nicht Rath ;
Ein Schuster in seinem Laden
Zieht an des Wahnes Faden :
Wie bald auf Gassen und Strassen
Fängt der da an zu rasen ;
Mann, Weib, Gesell' und Kind,
Fällt sich an wie toll und blind ;
Und will's der Wahn gesegnen,
Nun muss es Prügel regnen,
Mit Hieben, Stöss' und Dreschen
Den Wuthesbrand zu löschen.
Gott weiss, wie das geschah ?
Ein Kobold half wohl da !
Ein Glühwurm fand sein Weichen nicht ;
Der hat den Schaden angericht'.

The elder's charm — Midsummer eve :
But now has dawned Midsummer day.
Let 's see, then, what Hans Sachs can weave
To turn the madness his own way,
    To serve for noble works ;
    For if still here it lurks
    In Nuremberg the same,
    We 'll use it to such aim
As seldom by the mob 's projected,
And never without trick effected.

(*Walter enters from the chamber. He pauses a moment at the door looking at Sachs. The latter turns and allows his book to slip to the ground.*)

Sachs.

Good-day, Sir Walter !   Late is my guest.
You sat up long ; you 've had some rest?

Walter
              (very quietly).

A little, but that rest was sound.

Sachs.

So, then, your courage you have found?

Walter.

I had a wondrous lovely dream.

Sachs.

That augurs well !   Relate it, pray.

Walter.

In words I scarce dare touch its theme,
For fear it should all fade away.

Sachs.

My friend, that is the poet's art,
His dreams to cherish and impart.
Trust me, the best ideas of men
In dreams are opened to their ken :
All book-craft and all poetry
Are naught but dreams made verity.
But did your dream at all advise
How you might win the Master-prize?
But let that go ;
And hark to my counsel short and strong :
Bend your mind to a Master-Song.

Walter.

A Master-Song and one that 's fine :
How shall I make the two combine?

Sachs.

My friend, in youth's delightful days,
    When first in the direction
    Of blissful, true affection
The heart some power turns and sways,

Der Flieder war's : — Johannis-Nacht.—
Nun aber kam Johannis-Tag : —
Jetzt schau'n wir, wie Hans Sachs es macht,
Dass er den Wahn fein lenken mag,
Ein edles Werk zu thun ;
Denn lässt er uns nicht ruh'n,
Selbst hier in Nürenberg,
So sei's um solche Werk',
Die selten vor gemeinen Dingen,
Und nie ohn' ein'gen Wahn gelingen.—

Walther tritt unter der Kammerthüre ein. Er bleibt einen Augenblick dort stehen und blickt auf Sachs. Dieser wendet sich und lässt den Folianten auf den Boden gleiten.

Sachs.

Grüss Gott, mein Junker !   Ruhtet ihr noch?
Ihr wachtet lang' : nun schlieft ihr doch?

Walther
              (sehr ruhig).

Ein wenig, aber fest und gut.

Sachs.

So ist euch nun wohl bass zu Muth?

Walther.

Ich hatt' einen wunderschönen Traum.

Sachs.

Das deutet gut's !   Erzählt mir den.

Walther.

Ihn selbst zu denken wag' ich kaum ;
Ich fürcht' ihn mir vergeh'n zu seh'n.

Sachs.

Mein Freund, das grad' ist Dichter's Werk,
Dass er sein Träumen deut' und merk'.
Glaubt mir, des Merschen wahrster Wahn
Wird ihm im Traume aufgethan :
All' Dichtkunst und Poeterei
Ist nichts als Wahrtraum-Deuterei.
Was gilt's, es gab der Traum euch ein.
Wie heut' ihr sollet Sieger sein?
O, lasst dem Ruh' ;
Und folgt meinem Rathe, kurz und gut,
Fasst zu einem Meisterliede Muth.

Walther.

Ein schönes Lied, ein Meisterlied :
Wie fass' ich da den Unterschied?

Sachs.

Mein Freund ! in holder Jugendzeit,
    Wenn uns von mächtigen Trieben
    Zum sel'gen ersten Lieben
Die Brust sich schwellet hoch und weit,

All can, or else 't were pity,
Compose a loving ditty :
For Spring cries out in ye.
But Summer, Autumn, Winter days
Bring care and sorrow often,
With wedded bliss to soften.
Children and business — frets and frays,
One who, 'spite care and duty,
Yet sings a song of beauty,
A Master he must be.

Walter.

I love a maiden and I pine
In wedlock true to make her mine.

Sachs.

Your dream alone let occupy you ;
With all the rest Hans Sachs will ply you.

Walter
(places himself near Sachs, and after a moment's thought
begins in a very low voice).

" Morning was gleaming with roseate light,
    The air was filled
    With scent distilled,
  Where, beauty beaming
  Past all dreaming,
    A garden did invite
    My raptured sight."
      (He pauses awhile.)

Sachs.

That was a stanza : now then, take heed
That one just similar may succeed.

Walter.

Why similar?

Sachs.

          That folks may know
That coupled you intend to go.

Walter
       (continuing).

" Over the glorious garden, behold !
    With leafy crown
    A tree looked down,
  Majestic bending,
  And extending
    Its weight of fruit untold,
    Like burnished gold."
      (He pauses.)

Sachs.

You close not in the starting key :
  The Masters hate this thing :
Hans Sachs, though, can with you agree ;
  It must be so in the Spring.
Now to an Aftersong proceed.

Ein schönes Lied zu singen
Mocht' vielen da gelingen :
Der Lenz, der sang für sie.
Kam Sommer, Herbst und Winterszeit,
  Viel Noth und Sorg' im Leben,
  Manch ehlich Glück daneben,
Kindtauf', Geschäfte, Zwist und Streit :
  Denen 's dann noch will gelingen,
  Ein schönes Lied zu singen,
  Seht, Meister nennt man die.

Walther.

Ich lieb' ein Weib und will es frei'n
Mein dauernd Ehgemahl zu sein.

Sachs.

Gedenkt des schönen Traum's am Morgen :
Für's Andre lasst Hans Sachs nur sorgen !

Walther
(setzt sich zu Sachs, und beginnt, nach kurzer Sammlung,
sehr leise).

„ Morgenlich leuchtet in rosigem Schein,
    Von Blüth' und Duft
    Geschwellt die Luft,
    Voll aller Wonnen
    Nie ersonnen,
    Ein Garten lud mich ein
    Gast ihm zu sein."
      (Er hält etwas an.)

Sachs.

Das war ein Stollen : nun achtet wohl,
Dass ein ganz gleicher ihm folgen soll.

Walther.

Warum ganz gleich?

Sachs.

          Damit man seh'
Ihr wähltet euch gleich ein Weib zur Eh'.

Walther
       (fährt fort).

„Wonnig entragend dem seligen Raum,
    Bo' gold'ner Frucht
    Heilsaft'ge Wucht
  Mit holdem Prangen
  Dem Verlangen
    An duft'ger Zweige Saum
    Herrlich ein Baum."
      (Er hält inne.)

Sachs.

Ihr schlosset nicht im gleichen Ton :
  Das macht den Meistern Pein :
Doch nimmt Hans Sachs die Lehr' davon,
  Im Lenz wohl müss' es so sein. —
Nun stellt mir einen Abgesang.

alter.

hat is that for?

chs.

If here indeed
A pair you 've coupled truly
The offspring shows us duly.

alter

(in continuation).

" Let me confide
What lovely miracle ensued:
maiden stood before my face,
sweet and fair I ne'er had viewed;
Like to a bride
She took me to her embrace;
With bright eyes glowing,
Her hand was showing,
What stirred my longing profound;
The wond'rous fruit that crowned
The tree of life."

chs

(concealing his emotion).

hat is an Aftersong, I allow!
e, the whole verse is perfect now!
But in the melody
You were a little free;
do not say that that displeases me;
To catch it right though 's perplexing,
A thing to our Masters vexing.
second verse will you please indite,
o set the first in a clearer light?
cannot yet tell — your art 's so supreme —
ow much was poetry, how much dream.

alter

(as before).

" There on the height
babbling stream the silence stirr'd;
s murm'ring tones now louder swelled,
sweet and strong I never heard;
Sparkling and bright
Distinctly the stars I beheld:
In twinkling dances
Among the branches
A golden host did collect:
Not fruit, but stars bedeck'd
The tree of Fame." —

chs

(deeply moved, softly).

riend, your dream was well conceived;
he second verse you have achieved;
ow might you fashion a third verse meetly,
show the vision's meaning completely.

Walther.

Was soll nun der?

Sachs.

Ob euch gelang
Ein rechtes Paar zu finden,
Das zeigt sich jetzt an den Kinden.

Walther

(fortfahrend).

„Sei euch vertraut
Welch' hehres Wunder mir gescheh'n:
An meiner Seite stand ein Weib,
So schön und hold ich nie geseh'n;
Gleich einer Braut
Umfasste sie sanft meinen Leib,
Mit Augen winkend,
Die Hand wies blinkend,
Was ich verlangend begehrt,
Die Frucht so hold und werth
Vom Lebensbaum."

Sachs

(seine Führung verbergend).

Das nenn' ich mir einen Abgesang:
Seht, wie der ganze Bar gelang!
Nur mit der Melodei
Seid ihr ein wenig frei;
Doch sag' ich nicht, dass es ein Fehler sei;
Nur ist's nicht leicht zu behalten,
Und das ärgert unsre Alten! —
Jetzt richtet mir noch einen zweiten Bar,
Damit man merk', welch' der erste war.
Auch weiss ich noch nicht, so gut ihr's gereim',
Was ihr gedichtet, was ihr geträumt.

Walther

(wie vorher).

„Lieblich ein Quell
Auf stiller Höhe dort mir rauscht;
Jetzt schwellt er an sein hold Getön'
So süss und stark ich's nie erlauscht:
Leuchtend und hell
Wie strahlten die Sterne da schön;
Zu Tanz und Reigen
In Laub und Zweigen
Der gold'nen sammeln sich mehr
Statt Frucht ein Sternenheer
Im Lorbeerbaum."

Sachs

(sehr gerührt, sanft).

Freund! eu'r Traumbild wies euch wahr
Gelungen is auch der zweite Bar.
Wollet ihr noch einen dritten dichten,
Des Traumes Deutung wurd' er berichten.

Walter.

How can I now?   Enough of rhyme !

Sachs.
                    (rising).

Then we will rhyme some fitter time !—
Lose not the tune, though, I entreat it ;
'T is fit and fair for poetry :
You shall before the world repeat it.
Hold fast the dream you 've told to me.

Walter.

What 's your intent ?

Sachs.
                                Your servant true,
Bearing your packs, has sought for you.
The garments in the which I guessed
You meant at home to have been married
Unto my house in doubt he carried.
Some bird, sure must have shewn the nest
        Wherein his master lay.
Then follow to the chamber here !
        In costume rich and gay
'T is fitting that we both appear,
When striving for a victory.
So come, if you agree with me.

(He opens the door for Walter and goes in with him.)

Beckmesser

(peeps into the shop; finding it empty he comes in. He is
richly dressed, but in a very deplorable state. He limps,
rubs and stretches himself; then contorts himself; he tries
to sit down on a stool, but jumps quickly up and again
rubs his bruised limbs. In despair he wanders up and
down. Then pausing, he looks through the window at the
house opposite; makes gestures of wrath; strikes his hand
on his forehead. At last his eyes fall on the paper which
Sachs has written and left on the workbench; he takes it
up inquisitively, runs his eyes over it in great agitation,
and finally bursts out wrathfully) :

A Trial-song ! by Sachs ? — is 't so ?
Ha ! — Now then ev'rything I know !

(Hearing the chamber door open he starts and **conceals the**
paper hurriedly in his pocket.)

Sachs
        (in holiday dress, enters and stops short).

You, sir ? So early ? Why this visit ?
No fault of the shoes I sent you, is it ?
Let 's feel ! They fit you well, I 'm sure !

Beckmesser.

Confound you ! So thin ne'er were shoes before :
Through them I feel the smallest stone.

Sachs.

My Marker's motto there is shown :
My Marker's hammer beat it so flat.

Walther.

Wie fänd ich die ?   Genug der Wort' !

Sachs.
                    (aufstehend).

Dann Wort und That am rechten Ort !—
D'rum bitt' ich, merkt mir gut die Weise ;
Gar lieblich d'rin sich's dichten lässt :
Und singt ihr sie in weit'rem Kreise,
Dann haltet mir auch das Traumbild fest.

Walther.

Was habt ihr vor ?

Sachs.
                                Eu'r treuer Knecht
Fand sich mit Sack' und Tasch' zurecht ;
Die Kleider, d'rin am Hochzeitsfest
Daheim bei euch ihr wolltet prangen,
Die lies er her zu mir gelangen ; —
Ein Täubchen zeigt' ihm wohl das Nest,
        Darin sein Junker träumt :
D'rum folgt mir jetzt in's Kämmerlein !
        Mit Kleiden, wohlgesäumt,
Sollen Beide wir gezieret sein,
Wann's Stattliches zu wagen gilt : —
D'rum kommt, seid ihr gleich mir gewillt !

(Er öffnet Walther die Thür, und geht mit ihm hinein.)

Beckmesser.

(lugt zum Laden herein; da er die Werkstatt leer findet
tritt er näher. Er ist reich aufgeputzt, aber in sehr leiden-
dem Zustande. Er hinkt, streicht und reckt sich; zuckt
wieder zusammen; er sucht einen Schemel, setzt sich
springt aber sogleich wieder auf, und streichelt sich
Glieder von Neuem. Verzweiflungsvoll sinnend geht
dann umher. Dann bleibt er stehen, lugt durch das Fenst
nach dem Hause hinüber; macht Gebärden der Wut
schlägt sich wieder vor den Kopf. — Endlich fällt sein Bli
auf das von Sachs zuvor beschriebene Papier auf dem Wer
tische: er nimmt es neugierig auf, überfliegt es mit imm
grösserer Aufregung, und bricht endlich wütnend aus).

Ein Werbelied ! von Sachs ? — ist's wahr ?
Ah ! — Nun wird mir Alles klar !

(Da er die Kammerthüre gehen hört, fährt er zusammen, u
versteckt das Blatteilig in seiner Tasche.)

Sachs
        (im Festgewande, tritt ein, und hält an).

Sieh da ! Herr Schreiber ? Auch am Morgen ?
Euch machen die Schuh' doch nicht mehr Sorgen
Lasst sehen ! Mich dünkt sie sitzen gut ?

Beckmesser.

Den Teufel ! So dünn war ich noch nie beschuht
Fühl' durch die Sohle den feinsten Kies !

Sachs.

Mein Merkersprüchlein wirkte dies :
Trieb sie mit Merkerzeichen so weich.

Beckmesser.

merry jest ! Enough of that !
riend Sachs, I know what you are at !
    Have you forgotten quite
    What happened yesternight?
id you not raise all that uproar, pray,
lerely to get me out of your way?

achs.

'T was Folly-evening : be not affrighted ;
nd your wedding made the people excited.
    The madder that evening's glee,
    The more blest the marriage will be.

Beckmesser
       (bursting out into a rage).

Oh ! cobbler full of cunning,
With vulgar tricks o'er-running !
You always were my foe :
You base designs I 'll show.
You hoary-headed reprobate !
Attempting to appropriate
The maiden who alone
Is destined for my own !
Allured by Pogner's capital
Hans Sachs would like to snap it all ;
So, when the Guild discussed,
He caviled and he fussed.
But you see I got away,
And your ill-turn I 'll pay.
Attend the singing trial,
And see if you outvie all !
    If I 'm attacked
    And badly thwacked,
'll soon expose your wicked act !

achs.

ood friend, your anger makes you mad !
'hink all you will of me that 's bad,
ut prithee calm this jealous ire ;
'or courtship I have no desire.

Beckmesser.

'ack of lies ! I know you 're double !

achs.

Vhy, Master Town-clerk, what 's your trouble?
ly intended plans concern not you ;
ut, sooth, you 're deceived if you think I 'd woo.

Beckmesser.

'ou mean to sing?

achs.

           Not in competing.

Beckmesser.

'o wooing song?

Beckmesser

Schon gut der Witz' ! Und genug der Streich' !
Glaubt mir, Freund Sachs, jetzt kenn' ich euch
    Der spass von dieser Nacht,
    Der wird euch noch gedacht ;
Dass ich euch nur nicht im Wege sei,
Schuft ihr gar Aufruhr und Meuterei !

Sachs.

's war Polterabend, lasst euch bedeuten :
Eure Hochzeit spuckte unter den Leuten ;
    Je toller es da hergeh',
    Je besser bekommt's der Eh'.

Beckmesser
       (ausbrechend).

O Schuster voll von Ränken
Und pöbelhaften Schwänken,
Du warst mein Feind von je :
Nun hör' ob hell ich seh'.
Die ich mir auserkoren,
Die ganz für mich geboren,
Zu aller Wittwer Schmach,
Der Jungfer stellst du nach.
Dass sich Herr Sachs erwerbe
Des Goldschmied's reiches Erbe,
Im Meister-Rath zur Hand
Auf Klauseln er bestand,
Doch kam ich noch so davon,
Dass ich die That euch lohn' !
Zieht heut' nur aus zum Singen,
Merkt auf, wie's mag gelingen ;
    Bin ich gezwackt
    Auch und zerhackt,
Euch bring' ich doch sicher aus dem Takt !

Sachs.

Gut' Freund, ihr seid in argem Wahn !
Glaubt was ihr wollt, dass ich's gethan,
Gebt eure Eifersucht nur hin ;
Zu werben kommt mir nicht in Sinn.

Beckmesser.

Lug und Trug ! Ich weiss es besser.

Sachs.

Was fällt euch nur ein, Meister Beckmesser?
Was ich sonst im Sinn, geht euch nichts an :
Doch glaubt, ob der Werbung, seid ihr im Wahn.

Beckmesser.

Ihr säng't heut' nicht?

Sachs.

           Nicht zur Wette.

Beckmesser.

Kein Werblied?

Sachs.

           Dismiss the fear !

Beckmesser.

But I 've a proof there 's no defeating.

Sachs (looking on the workbench).

Did you take the poem ?   I left it here.

Beckmesser (producing the paper).

Is this not your hand ?

Sachs.

           Well, and what then ?

Beckmesser.

The writing is fresh !

Sachs.

           Still wet from the pen ?

Beckmesser.

Perhaps, then, 't is a biblical song ?

Sachs.

To call it so indeed were wrong.

Beckmesser.

Well, then ?

Sachs.

        What more ?

Beckmesser.

           You ask ?

Sachs.

             For sure !

Beckmesser.

Why, that, in all sincerity,
A most consummate rogue you must be !

Sachs.

May be ! but I was never known
To pocket papers not my own ;
But that you should not be called a thief,
You 're welcome to it — I give you the leaf.

Beckmesser (springing up in joyous surprise).

You do !   What, a song !   A song by Sachs !

(He peers sideways at the paper : suddenly he frowns.)

And yet ! — If this were some villainy ! —
    But yesterday you were my foe :
How, after your behavior to me,
    Such friendship can you show ? —

Sachs.

           Gewisslich, nein !

Beckmesser.

Wenn ich aber drop ein Zeugniss hätte ?

Sachs. (blickt auf den Werktisch).

Das Gedicht ?   Hier liess ich's : — stecktet ihr's ein

Beckmesser (zieht das Blatt hervor).

Ist das eure Hand ?

Sachs.

           Ja, — war es das ?

Beckmesser.

Ganz frisch noch die Schrift ?

Sachs.

           Und die Dinte noch nass

Beckmesser.

's wär wohl gar ein biblisches Lied ?

Sachs.

Der fehlte wohl, wer darauf rieth.

Beckmesser.

Nun denn ?

Sachs.

        Wie doch ?

Beckmesser.

           Ihr fragt ?

Sachs.

            Was noch ?

Beckmesser.

Dass ihr mit aller Biederkeit
Der ärgste aller Spitzbuben seid !

Sachs.

Mag sein !   Doch hab' ich noch nie entwandt,
Was ich auf fremden Tischen fand :
Und dass man von euch auch nicht übels denkt,
Behaltet das Blatt, es sei euch geschenkt.

Beckmesser (in freudigem Schreck aufspringend).

Herr Gott ! . . Ein Gedicht ! . . Ein Gedicht vo
            Sachs ? . .

(Er blickt seitwärts in das Blatt : plötzlich runzelt sich sei
Stirn.)

Und doch !   Wenn's nur eine Falle wär' ! —
    Noch gestern war't ihr mein Feind :
Wie käm's, dass nach so grosser Beschwer
    Ihr's freundlich heut' mit mir meint ?

Sachs.

sat up late to make your shoes :
t is not thus our foes we use.

Beckmesser.

Aye, aye ! that 's true ! — But one thing swear :
That when you hear this, no matter where !
To nobody shall be disclosed
The fact that 't was by you composed.

Sachs.

swear it and I guarantee
That none shall know the song 's by me.

Beckmesser
(very joyous).

What more remains ? I 'm joyful-hearted !
Beckmesser's troubles have departed !
(He rubs his hands with elation.)
Farewell, I 'm away !
Some other day,
When in this latitude,
I 'll pay my gratitude
For your kind attitude ;
Buy all your works, you know ;
You shall as Marker show ; —
Chalk you must mark with, though,
Not with the hammer's blow !
Marker !   Marker !   Marker Hans Sachs !
May he and Nuremberg bloom and wax !
(As if intoxicated he limps, stumbling and blundering,
away.)

Sachs.

I ne'er met with so evil a man :
He 'll come to grief one of these days.
Their reason most men squander who can,
Yet keep some little relays :
But some weak moments all discover ;
Then they are fools and we talk them over. —
That Master Beckmesser wasn't square,
Finely will further my affair. —
(Through his window he sees Eva approaching.)
Ha, Eva !   Here she is, I declare !
(Eva, richly tricked out and in a gleaming white dress,
enters the shop.)

Sachs.

My child, good morning ! Ah ! how pretty
And smart you are to-day !
Both old and young — why, all the city
You 'll win in such array.

Eva.

Master, surely now you flatter !
And if my dress is all right,
Will no one notice what 's the matter?
My shoe is much too tight.

Sachs.

Ich machte euch Schuh' in später Nacht :
Hat man so je einen Feind bedacht?

Beckmesser.

Ja ja ! recht gut ! — doch Eines schwört :
Wo und wie ihr das Lied auch hört,
Dass nie ihr euch beikommen lass't,
Zu sagen, es sei von Euch verfasst.

Sachs.

Das schwör ich und gelob' euch hier,
Nie mich zu rühmen, das Lied sei von mir.

Beckmesser
(sehr glücklich).

Was will ich mehr, ich bin geborgen !
Jetzt hat sich Beckmesser nicht mehr zu sorgen
(Er reibt sich froh die Hände.)
Ade ! ich muss fort !
An and'rem Ort
Dank' ich euch inniglich,
Weil ihr so minniglich ;
Für euch nun stimme ich,
Kauf' eure Werke gleich,
Mache zum Merker euch :
Doch fein mit Kreide weich,
Nicht mit dem Hammerstreich !
Merker !   Merker !   Merker Hans Sachs !
Dass Nürnberg schusterlich blüh' und wachs' !
(Er hinkt, poltert und taumelt wie besessen fort.)

Sachs.

So ganz boshaft doch keinen ich fand,
Er hält's auf die Länge nicht aus :
Vergeudet mancher oft viel Verstand,
Doch hält er auch damit Haus :
Die schwache Stunde kommt für Jeden ;
Da wird er dumm und lässt mit sich reden. —
Dass hier Herr Beckmesser ward zum Dieb,
Ist mir für meinen Plan sehr lieb.
(Er sieht durch das Fenster Eva kommen.)
Sieh, Evchen !   Dacht' ich doch, wo sie blieb' !
(Eva, reich geschmückt und in glänzender weisser Kleidung
tritt zum Laden herein.)

Sachs.

Grüss' Gott, mein Evchen ! Ei, wie herrlich,
Wie stolz du's heute meinst !
Du machst wohl Jung und Alt begehrlich,
Wenn du so schön erscheinst.

Eva.

Meister ! 's ist nicht so gefährlich :
Und ist's dem Schneider geglückt,
Wer sieht dann an wo's mir beschwerlich,
Wo still der Schuh mich drückt?

Sachs.

The naughty shoe !　But 't was your haste ;
You would not try it on, you see.

Eva.

Not so ; too great a trust I placed :
The Master 's disappointed me.

Sachs.

I 'm really griev'd !　Come here, my pet,
And I will help you even yet.

Eva.

If I would stand, it will away ;
Would I begone, it makes me stay.

Sachs.

Upon the stool here place your foot.
A shocking fault !　I 'll look into 't.

　　(She puts her foot upon a stool by the workbench.)

.What is amiss?

Eva.

　　　　　　　Too wide, you see.

Sachs.

Child, that is purely vanity :
The shoe is tight.

Eva.

　　　　　　　I told you so,
And that is why it hurts my toe.

Sachs.

Here — left?

Eva.

　　　　　　　No, right.

Sachs.

　　　　　　What !　On the sole?

Eva.

Here, at the ankle.

Sachs.

　　　　　　　Well !　That 's droll !

Eva.

Nay, Master ! do you know better than I
Where the shoe pinches?

Sachs.

　　　　　　　I wonder why,
If it 's too wide, it pinches you so.

Walter, in glittering knightly apparel, appears at the chamber
door, and stands there spellbound at the sight of Eva. She
utters a slight cry, but remains in her position with one foot
on the stool. Sachs is kneeling before her with his back
towards the door.

Sachs.

Der böse Schuh !　's war deine Laun',
Dass du ihn gestern nicht probirt.

Eva.

Merk' wohl, ich hatt' zu viel Vertrau'n :
Im Meister hab' ich mich geirrt.

Sachs.

Ei, 's thut mir leid !　Zeig' her, mein Kind,
Dass ich dir helfe, gleich geschwind.

Eva.

Sobald ich stehe, will es geh'n :
Doch will ich geh'n, zwingt's mich zu steh'n.

Sachs.

Heir auf den Schemel streck' den Fuss :
Der üblen Noth ich wehren muss.

　　(Sie streckt den Fuss auf den Schemel beim Werktisch.

Was ist's mit dem?

Eva.

　　　　　　　Ihr sekt, zu weit !

Sachs.

Kind, dat ist pure Eitelkeit :
Der Schuh ist knapp.

Eva.

　　　　　　　Das sag' ich ja :
Drum drückt er mir die Zehen da.

Sachs.

Hier links?

Eva.

　　　　　　　Nein, rechts.

Sachs.

　　　　　　Wohl mehr am Spann

Eva.

Mehr hier am Hacken.

Sachs.

　　　　　　　Kommt der auch dran

Eva.

Ach Meister !　Wüsstet ihr besser als ich,
Wo der Schuh mich drückt?

Sachs.

　　　　　　Ei, 's wundert mic
Dass er zu weit, und doch drückt überall?

Walther, in glänzender Rittertracht, tritt unter die Thür
der Kammer, und bleibt beim Anblick Eva's wie festgeban
stehen. Eva stösst einen leisen Schrei aus und blei
ebenfalls unverwandt in ihrer Stellung, mit dem Fusse a
dem Schemel. Sachs, der vor ihr sich gebückt hat, ist m
　　　　dem Rücken der Thüre zugekehrt.

ha! 't is here! Now the reason I know!
hild, you are right: 't is in the *sole!*
ne moment, and I 'll make it whole.
tand so awhile, I 'll fasten your shoe
)n the last a moment, then it will do.

(He has gently drawn off her shoe; while she remains in
e same position he pretends to busy himself with it, and to
e oblivious of all else.)

Sachs
(as he works).

Cobbling always! That is my fate;
keep it up both early and late.
Hark ye, child! I 've given it much thought,
How should my work to an end be brought.
The best way 's to join the contest for you;
should win some fame as a poet too.
Come now, reply! You do not heed!
T was you put that in my head indeed!
All right! You say, "Stick to your shoes!"
Will some one give us a song to amuse?
heard to-day a lovely one;
Let 's see if the third verse can be done!

Walter
(still in the same position opposite Eva).

Lingered the stars in their dance of delight?
They rested there
Upon her hair,
That wondrous maiden
So beauty-laden,
And formed a circlet bright
All star bedight,
Wonder on wonder now waked my surprise;
The light of day
Had twofold ray;
For two transcendent
Suns resplendent
Within her heavenly eyes
I saw arise.
Image so rare,
Which boldly I approached and viewed!
By all this light the crown above
At once was faded and renewed.
Tender and fair
She wove it round the head of her love.
Thus grace-directed,
To fame elected,
She poured the joys of the blest
Into the poet's breast,
In Love's sweet dream."

Sachs
busily at work, brings back the shoe during the last verse
of Walter's song and fits it on Eva's foot again).

Hark, child! that is a Master-song;
You hear such music where I dwell now.
So try if still my shoe is wrong.

Aha! hier sitzt's! Nun begreif' ich den Fall!
Kind, du hast recht: 's stack in der Nath: —
Nun warte, dem Uebel schaff' ich Rath.
Bleib' nur so steh'n; ich nehm' dir den Schuh
Eine Weil' auf den Leisten: dann lässt er dir Ruh'.

(Er hat ihr sanft den Schuh vom Fusse gezogen; während
sie in ihrer Stellung verbleibt, macht er sich mit dem Schuh
zu schaffen, und thut, als beachte er nichts andres.)

Sachs
(bei der Arbeit).

Immer Schustern! das ist nun mein Loos;
Des Nachts, des Tags — komm' nicht davon los! —
Kind, hör' zu! Ich hab's überdacht,
Was meinem Schustern ein Ende macht:
Am Besten, ich werbe doch noch um dich;
Da gewänn' ich doch 'was als Poet für mich! —
Du hörst nicht drauf? — So sprich doch jetzt!
Hast mir's ja selbst in den Kopf gesetzt?
Schon gut! — ich merk'! — Mach deinen Schuh!
Säng' mir nur wenigstens Einer dazu!
Horte heut' gar ein schönes Lied: —
Wem dazu ein dritter Vers gerieth'!

Walther.
(immer Eva gegenüber in der vorigen Stellung)

„Weilten die Sterne im lieblichen Tanz?
So licht und klar
Im Lockenhaar,
Vor allen Frauen
Hehr zu schauen
Lag ihr mit zartem Glanz
Ein Sternenkranz. —
Wunder ob Wunder nun bieten sich dar:
Zwiefachen Tag
Ich grüssen mag;
Denn Gleich zwei'n Sonnen
Reinster Wonnen,
Der hehrsten Augen Paar
Nahm ich nun wahr. —
Huldreichstes Bild,
Dem ich zu nahen mich erkühnt:
Den Kranz, vor zweier Sonnen Strahl
Zugleich verblichen und ergrünt,
Minnig und mild,
Sie flocht ihn um's Haupt dem Gemahl.
Dort Huld-geboren,
Nun Rhum-erkoren,
Giesst paradiesche Lust
Sie in des Dichters Brust —
Im Liebstraum." —

Sachs
(hat, immer mit seiner Arbeit beschäftigt, den Schuh zurück
gebracht, und ist jetzt während der Schlussverse von
Walther's Gesang darüber her, ihn Eva wieder anzuziehen)

Lausch', Kind! das ist ein Meisterlied:
Derlei hörst du jetzt bei mir singen:
Nun schau', ob dabei mein Schuh gerieth?

Was I not right?
And fits it well now?
Let's see! Stand down! Is it still tight?

(Eva, who has stood still as if enchanted, gazing and listening, bursts into a sudden fit of weeping and sinks on Sachs's breast, sobbing and clinging to him. — Walter advances toward them and wrings Sachs's hand in silent ecstasy. — Sachs at last composes himself, tears himself gloomily away and causes Eva to rest unconsciously on Walter's shoulder.)

Eva

(stops Sachs and draws him to her again).

O Sachs! best friend and dearest! Say
How can I e'er my debt repay?
　　Bereft of thy great kindness
　　How helpless should I be!
　　Still wrapped in childish blindness
　　Had it not been for thee.
　　　　Through thee life's treasure
　　　　I control,
　　　　Through thee I measure
　　　　First my soul.
　　　　Through thee I wake;
　　　　My feelings take
　　A higher, nobler tone:
　　I bloom through thee alone! —
Yes, dearest Master, scold you may!

Sachs.

　　My child:
　　Sir Tristan I have read of —
　　Isolde's story dark:
　　Hans Sachs had prudent dread of
　　The fate of poor king Mark. —
'T was time the right man did appear,
Or I should have been caught, I fear! —
Aha! There's Magdalena's found us out.
Come in! — Ho, David! — What's he about?

(Magdalena in holiday attire enters from the street and David at the same time comes out of the chamber, also gayly dressed and very splendid with ribbons and flowers.)

The witnesses wait, the sponsors are found;
So now for a christening gather around!

(All look at him with surprise.)

　　A child here was created;
　　Let its name by you be stated.
Such is the Masters' constant use,
When they a Master-song produce:
They give it a fitly chosen name
That men may know it by the same.
　　So let me tell all you here
　　What 't is we have to do here!
A Master-song has been completed,
By young Sir Walter made and repeated;
The newborn poem's father, delighted,
For sponsors has Eva and me invited:

Mein' endlich doch.
　　Es thät' mir gelingen?
Versuch's! tritt auf! — Sag', drückt er dich noch

(Eva, die wie bezaubert bewegungslos gestanden, geseh
und gehört hat, bricht jetzt in heftiges Weinen aus, sin
Sachs an die Brust und drückt ihn schluchzend an sich.
Walther ist zu ihnen getreten, und druckt Sachs begeiste
die Hand. — Sachs thut sich endlich Gewalt an, reisst si
wie unmuthig los, und lässt dadurch Eva unwillkürlich a
Walther's Schulter sich anlehnen.)

Eva

(hält Sachs, und zieht ihn von Neuem zu sich).

O Sachs! Mein Freund! Du theurer Mann!
Wie ich dir Edlem lohnen kann!
　　Was ohne deine Liebe,
　　Was wär' ich ohne dich,
　　Ob je auch Kind ich bliebe
　　Erwecktest du nicht mich?
　　　　Durch dich gewann ich
　　　　Was man preist.
　　　　Durch dich ersann ich
　　　　Was ein Geist!
　　　　Durch dich erwacht,
　　　　Durch dich nur dacht'
　　Ich edel, frei und kühn:
　　Du liessest mich erblüh'n! —
O lieber Meister! schilt mich nur!

Sachs.

　　Mein Kind:
　　Von Tristan und Isolde
　　Kenn' ich ein traurig Stück:
　　Hans Sachs war klug, und wollte
　　Nichts von Herrn Marke's Gluck. —
's war Zeit, dass ich den Rechten erkannt:
Wär' sonst am End' doch hineingerannt!
Aha! da streicht schon die Lene um's Haus,
Nur herein! — He, David! Kommst nicht heraus

(Magdalene, in festlichem Staate, tritt durch die Ladenthü
herein; aus der Kammer kommt zugleich David, ebenfal
im Festkleid, mit Blumen und Bändern sehr reich un
zierlich ausgeputzt.)

Die Zeugen sind da, Gevatter, zur Hand;
Jetzt schnell zur Taufe; nehmt euren Stand!

(Alle blicken ihn verwundert an.)

　　Ein Kind ward hier geboren;
　　Jetzt sei ihm ein Nam' erkoren!
So ist's nach Meister-Weis' und Art,
Wenn eine Meisterweise geschaffen ward:
Dass die einen guten Namen trag',
Dran Jeder sie erkennen mag. —
　　Vernehmt, respectable Gesellschaft,
　　Was euch hierher zur Stell' schafft!
Eine Meisterweise ist gelungen,
Von Junker Walther gedichtet und gesungen;
Der jungen Weise lebender Vater
Lud mich und die Pognerin zu Gevatter;

As to the song we have been list'ning
We now come hither to its christ'ning.
To see that we act with solemn fitness
Shall David and Lena be called to witness:
But as no Prentice a witness can be,
And as he 's repeated his task to me,
A Journeyman I will make him here.
Kneel, David, and take this box on the ear.

(David kneels and Sachs gives him a smart box on the ear.)

Arise, my man; remember that blow;
'Twill mark this baptism for you, you know.
Lacks aught beside, what blame indeed?
Who knows if private baptism we need?
That the melody lack not anything vital
I now proceed to give it its title.
The glorious morning-dream's true story." —
So be it named, to the Master's glory.
And may it increase in size and strength. —
I bid the young god-mother speak at length.

Eva.

    Dazzling as the dawn
    That smiles upon my glee,
    Rapture-laden morn
    To bliss awakens me.
    Dream of palmy beauty,
    Brilliant morning-glow!
    Hard but sweet the duty
    Thy intent to know.
    That divine and tender strain
    With its tones of gladness
    Has revealed my heart's sweet pain
        And subdued its sadness.
    It is but a morning-dream?
    Scarcely real doth it seem.
        What the ditty,
        Soft and pretty,
        Told to me,
        A quiet theme,
        Loud and free.
    In the Masters' conclave wise
    Shall achieve the highest prize.

Walter.

    'T was thy love — the highest gain —
        Allured me by its gladness,
    To reveal my heart's sweet pain
        And subdue its sadness,
    Is it still my morning-dream?
    Scarcely real doth it seem.
        What the ditty,
        Soft and pretty,
        Told to thee,
        A quiet theme,
        Loud and free
    In the Masters' conclave wise
    Shall achieve the highest prize.

Weil wir die Weise wohl vernommen,
Sind wir zur Taufe hierher gekommen.
Auch dass wir zur Handlung Zeugen haben,
Ruf' ich Jungfer Lene, und meinen Knaben:
Doch da's zum Zeugen kein Lehrbube thut,
Und heut' auch den Spruch er gesungen gut,
So mach' ich den Burschen gleich zum Gesell':
Knie' nieder, David, und nimm diese Schell'!

(David ist niedergekniet: Sachs giebt ihm eine starke
Ohrfeige.)

Steh' auf, Gesell! und denk' an den Streich:
Du merkst dir dabei die Taufe zugleich!
Fehlt sonst noch 'was, uns Keiner drum schilt:
Wer weiss ob's nichr ger eine Nothtaufe gilt.
Dass die Weise Kraft bahalte zum Leben,
Will ich uur gleich den Numen ihr geben: —
„ Die selige Morgentraumdeut-Weise "
Sei sie genannt zu des Meisters Preise.
Nun wachse sie gross, ohn' Schad' und Bruch:
Die jüngste Gevatt'rin spricht den Spruch.

Eva.

    Selig, wie die Sonne
    Meines Glückes lacht,
    Morgen voller Wonne,
    Selig mir erwacht!
    Traum der höchsten Hulden,
    Himmlisch Morgenglüh'n!
    Deutung euch zu schulden,
    Selig süss Bemüh'n'!
    Einer Weise mild und hehr,
        Sollt' es hold gelingen,
    Meines Herzens süss Beschwer
        Deutend zu bezwingen.
    Ob es nur ein Morgentraum?
    Selig' deut' ich mir es kaum.
        Doch die Weise,
        Was sie leise
        Mir vertraut
        Im stillen Raum,
        Hell und laut,
    In der Meister volleim Kreis,
    Deute sie den höchsten Preis!

Walther.

    Deine Liebe, rein und hehr,
        Liess es mir gelingen,
    Meines Herzens süss Beschwer
        Deutend zu bezwingen.
    Ob es noch der Morgentraum?
    Selig deut' ich mir es kaum.
        Doch die Weise,
        Was sie leise
        Dir vertraut
        Im stillen Raum,
        Hell und laut,
    In der Meister vollem Kreis,
    Werbe sie um höchsten Preis!

Sachs.

With the maiden I would fain
    Sing for very gladness ;
But my heart I must restrain,
    Quell my passion's madness.
'T was a tender evening-dream :
Undiscovered let it beam.
    What the ditty,
    Soft and pretty,
    Told to me
    In quiet theme,
    Here I see :
Youth and love that never dies
Flourish through the master-prize.

David.

Am I awake or dreaming still ?
Scarce to explain it have I skill.
Sure 't is but a morning-dream !
All these things unreal seem.
    Can it be, man,
    You 're a freeman ?
    And that she —
    Oh, joy supreme ! —
    My spouse shall be ?
Round and round my headpiece flies
That a Master I now rise !

Magdalena.

Am I awake or dreaming still ?
Scarce to explain it have I skill.
Sure 't is but a morning-dream !
All these things unreal seem.
    Can it be, man,
    You 're a freeman ?
    And that we —
    Oh, joy supreme ! —
    Shall wedded be ?
Yes, what honor near me lies ?
Soon I shall as Madam rise !

(The orchestra goes into a broad march-like theme.— Sachs
    makes the group break up.)

Sachs.

Now let 's be off ! — Your father stays !
Quick, to the fields all go your ways !

Eva tears herself away from Sachs and Walter and leaves
    the house with Magdalena.)

So come, sir knight ! take heart of grace !
David, my man, lock up the place.

  As Sachs and Walter also go into the street, and David is
eft shutting up the shop, curtains descend from each side of
the proscenium so as to cunceal the stage. — When the
music has gradually swelled to the loudest pitch the curtains
are drawn up again and the scene is changed.

Sachs.

Vor dem Kinde lieblich hehr,
    Mocht' ich gern wohl singen ;
Doch des Herzens süss Beschwer
    Galt es zu bezwingen.
's war ein schöner Abendtraum :
Dran zu deuten wag ich kaum.
    Diese Weise,
    Was sie leise,
    Mir vertraut
    Im stillen Raum,
    Sagt mir laut :
Auch der Jugend ew'ges Reis
Grünt nur durch des Dichters Preis.

David.

Wach' oder träum' ich schon so früh'?
Das zu erklären macht mir Müh'.
's ist wohl nur ein Morgentraum?
Was ich seh', begreif' ich kaum.
    Ward zur Stelle
    Gleich Geselle?
    Lene Braut?
    Im Kirchenraum
    Wir getraut?
's geht der Kopf mir, wie im Kreis,
Dass ich bald gar Meister heiss' !

Magdalene.

Wach' oder träum' ich schon so früh?
Das zu erklären macht mir Müh' !
's ist wohl nur ein Morgentraum?
Was ich seh', begreif' ich kaum.
    Er, zur Stelle
    Gleich Geselle?
    Ich die Braut?
    Im Kirchenraum
    Wir getraut?
Ja, wahrhaftig ! 's geht : wer weiss?
Bald ich wohl Frau Meist'rin heiss' !

(Das Orchester geht sehr leise in eine marschmässige, heiter
    Weise über. — Sachs ordnet den Aufbruch an.)

Sachs.

Jetzt All' am Fleck ! Den Vater küss' !
Auf, nach der Wies', schnell auf die Füss'.

(Eva trennt sich von Sachs und Walther und verlässt mi
    Magdalene die Werkstatt.)

Nun, Junker ! Kommt ! Habt frohen Muth !
David' Gesell' ! Schliess den Laden gut !

  Als Sachs und Walther ebenfalls auf die Strasse geher
und David sich über das Schliessen der Ladenthüre her
macht, wird im Proscenium ein Vorhang von beiden Seite
zusammengezogen, so dass er die Scene gänzlich schliesst. —
Als die Musik allmählich zu grösserer Stärke angewachser is
wird der Vorhang nach der Höhe zu aufgezogen. Di
Bühne ist verwandelt.

CHANGE OF SCENE.	VERWANDLUNG.

The stage now represents an open meadow, in the distance at back the town of Nuremberg. The Pegnitz winds across the plain; the narrow river is practicable in the foreground. Boats gaily decorated with flags continually discharge fresh parties of Burghers of the different Guilds with their wives and families, who land on the banks. A raised stand with benches on it is erected R, already adorned with flags of those as yet arrived; as the scene opens, the standard-bearers of freshly arriving Guilds also place their banners against the Singer's stage, so that it is at last quite closed in on three sides by them. Tents with all kinds of refreshments border the sides of the open space in front.

Before the tents is much merry-making: Burghers and their families sit and group round them.—The Prentices of the Master-singers, in holiday attire, finely decked out with ribbons and flowers, and bearing slender wands, also ornamented, fulfil frolicsomely the office of heralds and stewards. They receive the new comers on the bank, arrange them in procession and conduct them to the stand, whence, after the standard-bearer has deposited his banner, the Burghers and Journeymen disperse under the tents.

Among the arriving Guilds the following are prominent.

The Shoemakers.
(As they march past.)
Saint Crispin !
   Honor him !
He was both wise and good,
   Did all a cobbler could.
That was a fine time for the poor !
   He made them all warm shoes ;
When none would lend him leather more,
   To steal he 'd not refuse.
The cobbler has a conscience easy,
   No obstacles to labor sees he ;
When from the tanner 't is sent away
     Then hey ! hey ! hey !
Leather becomes his rightful prey.

(The Town-pipers, Lute- and Toy-instrument-makers, playing on their instruments, follow. These are succeeded by)

The Tailors.
When Nuremberg besieged did stand
   And famine wrought despair,
Undone had been both folk and land
   Had not a tailor been there
   Of craft and courage rare :
Within a goatskin he did hide
And showed upon the wall outside,
   There took to gaily tripping
   And gambolling and skipping.
The foe beheld it with dismay :
"The devil fetch that town away

Die Scene stellt einen freien Wiesenplan dar, im fernen Hintergrunde die Stadt Nürnberg. Die Pegnitz schlängelt sich durch den Plan: der schmale Fluss ist an den nächsten Punkten praktikabel gehalten. Buntbeflaggte Kähne setzen unablässig die noch ankommenden, festlich geschmückten Bürger der Zunfte, mit Frauen und Kindern, an das Ufer der Festwiese über. Eine erhöhte Buhne mit Bänken darauf ist rechts zur Seite aufgeschlagen; bereits ist sie mit den Fahnen der angekommenen Zünfte ausgeschmückt; im Verlaufe stecken die Fahnenträger der noch ankommenden Zünfte ihre Fahnen ebenfalls um die Sängerbühne auf, so dass diese schliesslich nach drei Seiten hin ganz davon eingefasst ist.— Zelte mit Getränken und Erfrischungen aller Art begrenzen im Uebrigen die Seiten des vorderen Hauptraumes.

Vor den Zelten geht es bereits lustig her : Bürger mit Frauen und Kindern sitzen und lagern daselbst.— Die Lehrbuben der Meistersinger festlich gekleidet, mit Blumen und Bändern reich und anmuthig geschmückt, über mit schlanken Stäben, die ebenfalls mit Blumen und Bändern reich geziert sind, in lustiger Weise das Amt von Herolden und Marschällen aus. Sie empfangen die am Ufer Aussteigenden, ordnen die Züge der Zünfte, und geleiten diese nach der Singerbühne, von wo aus, nachdem der Bannerträger die Fahne aufgepflanzt, die Zunftbürger und Gesellen nach Belieben sich unter den Zelten zerstreuen.

Unter den noch anlangenden Zünften werden die folgenden besonders bemerkt.

Die Schuster.
(Indem sie aufziehen.)
Sankt Crispin,
   Lobet ihn !
War gar ein heilig Mann,
   Zeigt was ein Schuster kann.
Die Armen hatten gute Zeit,
   Macht' ihnen warme Schuh' ;
Und wenn ihm Keiner Leder leiht',
   So stahl er sich's dazu.
Der Schuster hat ein weit Gewissen,
Macht Schuhe selbst mit Hindernissen ;
Und ist vom Gerber das Fell erst weg,
   Dann streck' ! streck' ! streck' !
Leder taugt nur am rechten Fleck.

(Die Stadtpfeifer, Lauten- und Kinderinstrumentmacher ziehen, auf ihren Instrumenten spielend, auf Ihnen folgen.)

Die Schneider. Als Nürnberg belagert war,
   Und Hungersnoth sich fand,
Wär' Stadt und Volk verdorben gar,
   War nicht ein Schneider zur Hand.
   Der viel Muth hat und Verstand :
Hat sich in ein Bockfell eingenäht,
Auf dem Stadtwall da springen geht,
   Und macht wohl seine Sprünge
   Gar lustig guter Dinge.
Der Feind, der sieht's und zieht vom Fleck,
Der Teufel hol' die Stadt sich weg,

Where goats yet merrily play, play, play.
Me-ey! me-ey! me-ey!
(Imitating the bleating of a goat.)
Who'd think that a tailor within there lay?

The Bakers.
(Coming close behind the Tailors, so that the two songs
join together.)
Want of bread! Want of bread!
That is a hardship true, sirs!
If you were not by the baker fed
Old Death would feed on you, sirs.
Pray! pray! pray!
Baker every day,
Hunger turn away!

Prentices.
Heyday! Heyday! Maidens from Fürth!
Play up, town-piper, one merry spurt!

(A gaily painted boat, filled with young Girls in fine
peasant-costumes, arrives. The Prentices help the Girls
out and dance with them, while the town-pipers play,
towards the front.— The character of this dance consists
in the Prentices appearing only to wish to bring the Girls
to the open place; the Journeymen endeavor to capture
them and the Prentices move on as if seeking another
place, thus making the tour of the stage and continually
delaying their original purpose in fun and frolic.)

David.
(Advancing from the landing-place.)
You dance! The Masters will rate such folly.
(The boys make faces at him.)
Don't care? Why, then, let me too be jolly!
(He seizes a young and pretty girl and mingles in the
dance with great ardor. The spectators notice him and
laugh.)

Some of the Prentices.
David! there's Lena! There's Lena sees
you!

David.
(Alarmed, hastily releases the maiden, but seeing noth-
ing, quickly regains his courage and resumes his dancing.)
Have done with your silly jokes, my boys, do!

Journeymen.
(At the landing-place.)
The Master-singers! the Master-singers!

David.
Oh. lor'! — Farewell, ye pretty clingers!
(He gives the maiden an ardent kiss and tears himself
away. The Prentices quickly discontinue their dance,
hasten to the bank and arrange themselves to receive the
Master-singers. All stand back, by command of the
Prentices. — The Master-singers arrange their procession
on the bank and then march forwards to take their places
on the stand. First Kothner, as standard-bearer, then
Pogner leading Eva by the hand; she is attended by
richly dressed Maidens among whom is Magdalena. Then
follow the other Master-singers. They are greeted with
cheers and waving of hats. When all have reached the

Hat's drin noch so lustige Meck-meck-meck
Meck! Meck! Meck!
(Das Gemecker der Ziege nachahmend.)
Wer glaubt's, dass ein Schneider im Bock
steck'!

Die Bäcker.
(Ziehen dicht hinter den Schneidern auf, so dass ihr
Lied in das der Schneider hineinklingt.)
Hungersnoth! Hungersnoth!
Das ist ein gräulich Leiden!
Gäb' euch der Bäcker kein täglich Brod,
Müsst' alle Welt verscheiden.
Beck! Beck! Beck!
Täglich auf dem Fleck!
Nimm uns den Hunger weg!

Lehrbuben.
Herr Je! Herr Je! Mädel von Fürth!
Stadtpfeifer spielt! dass 's lustig wird!

(Ein bunter Kahn, mit jungen Mädchen in reicher
bäuerischer Tracht, ist angekommen. Die Lehrbube
heben die Mädchen heraus, und tanzen mit ihnen, währen
die Stadtpfeifer spielen, nach dem Vordergrunde. Das
Charakteristische des Tanzes besteht darin, dass die
Lehrbuben die Mädchen scheinbar nur an den Platz
bringen wollen; sowie die Gesellen zugreifen wollen
ziehen die Buben die Mädchen aber immer wieder zurück
als ob sie sie anderswo unterbringen wollten, wobei sie
meistens den ganzen Kreis, wie wähiend, ausmessen, und
somit die scheinbare Absicht auszuführen, anmuthig und
lustig verzögern.)

David.
(Kommt vom Landungsplatze vor.)
Ihr tanzt? Was werden die Meister sagen?
(Die Buben drehen ihm Nasen.)
Hört nicht? — Lass' ich mir's auch beha
gen!
(Er nimmt sich ein junges, schönes Mädchen, und
geräth im Tanze mit ihr bald in grosses Feuer. Die
Zuschauer freuen sich und lachen.)

Ein paar Lehrbuben.
David! die Lene! die Lene sieht zu!

David.
(Erschrickt, lässt das Mädchen schnell fahren, fasst sich
aber Muth, da er nichts sieht, und tanzt noch feuriger
weiter.)
Ach! lasst mich mit euren Possen in Ruh'!

Gesellen.
(Am Landungsplatz.)
Die Meistersinger! Die Meistersinger!

David.
Herr Gott! — Ade, ihr hübschen Dinger
(Er giebt dem Mädchen einen feurigen Kuss und reisst
sich los. Die Lehrbuben unterbrechen alle schnell den
Tanz, eilen zum Ufer und reihen sich dort zum Empfang
der Meistersinger. Alles macht auf das Geheiss der
Lehrbuben Platz. — Die Meistersinger ordnen sich am
Landungsplatze und ziehen dann festlich auf, um auf
der erhöhten Bühne ihre Plätze einzunehmen. Voran
Kothner als Fahnenträger; dann Pogner, Eva an der
Hand führend; diese ist von festlich geschmückten
und reich gekleideten jungen Mädchen begleitet, denen
sich Magdalene anschliesst. Dann folgen die übrigen

latform, **Eva** has taken the place of honor, with her Maidens round her, and Kothner has placed his banner in he middle of the others, which it overtops; the Prentices olemnly advance in rank and file before the stand, turning o the people.)

Prentices.

Silentium! Silentium!
Make no sound, e'en the merest hum!

(Sachs rises and steps forward. At sight of him all urst out into fresh acclamations and wavings of hats and kerchiefs.)

All the People.

Ha! Sachs! 'T is Sachs!
See! Master Sachs!
Sing all! Sing all! Sing all!
(With solemn delivery.)
" Awake! draws nigh the break of day:
" I hear upon the hawthorn spray
" A bonny little nightingale;
" His voice resounds o'er hill and dale.
" The night descends the western sky
" And from the east the morn draws nigh,
" With ardor red the flusk of day
" Breaks through the cloud-bank dull and
grey."
Hail, Sachs! Hans Sachs!
Hail, Nuremberg's darling Sachs!

(Long silence of deep feeling. Sachs, who, as if wrapt, as stood motionless, gazing far away beyond the multi-ude, at last turns a genial glance on them, bows courte-usly and begins in a voice at first trembling with emotion ut soon gaining firmness.)

Sachs.

Your hearts you ease, mine you oppress,
I feel my own unworthiness.
What I must prize all else above
Is your esteem and honest love.
Already honor I have gained,
To-day as spokesman I'm ordained;
And in the matter of my speech,
You will be honored, all and each.
If Art so much you honor, sirs,
We ought to show you rather
That one who's altogether hers
Esteems her even farther.
A Master, noble, rich, and wise,
Will prove you this with pleasure:
His only child, the highest prize
With all his wealth and treasure,
He offers as inducement strong
To him who in the art of song
Before the people here
As victor shall appear.
So hear my words and follow me:
To poets all this trial's free.
Ye Masters who compete to-day,
To you before all here I say:
Bethink you what a prize this is!
Let each, if he would win it,

Meistersinger. Sie werden mit Hutschwenken und Freudenrufen begrüsst. Als Alle auf der Bühne angelangt sind, Eva, von den Mädchen umgeben, den Ehrenplatz eingenommen, und Kothner die Fahne gerade in der Mitte der übrigen Fahnen, und sie alle überragend, aufgepflanzt hat, treten die Lehrbuben, dem Volke zugewendet, feierlich vor der Bühne in Reih und Glied.

Lehrbuben. Silentium! Silentium!
Lasst all' Reden und Gesumm'!

(Sachs erhebt sich und tritt vor. Bei seinem Anblick stösst sich sofort Alles an und bricht sofort unter Hut- und Tücherschwenken in grossen Jubel aus.)

Alles Volk. Ha! Sachs! 's ist Sachs!
Seht! Meister Sachs!
Stimmt an! Stimmt an! Stimmt an!
(Mit feierlicher Haltung.)
" Wach' auf, es nahet gen den Tag,
" Ich hör' singen im grünen Hag,
" Ein wonnigliche Nachtigall,
" Ihr Stimm' durchklinget Berg und Thal,
" Die Nacht neigt sich zum Occident,
" Der Tag geht auf von Orient,
" Die rothbrünstige Morgenröth'
" Her durch die trüben Wolken geht."
Heil Sachs! Hans Sachs!
Heil Nürnberg's theurem Sachs!

(Längeres Schweigen grosser Ergriffenheit. — Sachs der unbeweglich, wie geistesabwesend, über die Volks menge hinweg geblickt hatte, richtet endlich seine Blick, vertrauter auf sie, verneigt sich freundlich, und beginnt mit ergriffener, schnell aber sich festigender Stimme.)

Sachs.

Euch wird es leicht, mir macht ihr's schwer,
Gebt ihr mir Armen zu viel Ehr':
Such' vor der Ehr' ich zu besteh'n,
Sei's, mich von euch geliebt zu seh'n!
Schon grosse Ehr' ward mir erkannt,
Ward heut' ich zum Spruchsprecher ernannt,
Und was mein Spruch euch künden soll,
Glaubt, das ist hoher Ehre voll!
Wenn ihr die Kunst so hoch schon ehrt,
Da galt es zu beweisen,
Dass, wer ihr selbst gar angehört,
Sie schätzt ob allen Preisen.
Ein Meister reich und hochgemuth,
Der will euch heut' das zeigen:
Sein Töchterlein, sein höchstes Gut,
Mit allem Hab und eigen,
Dem Singer, der im Kunstgesang
Vor allem Volk den Preis errang,
Als höchsten Preises Kron'
Er bietet das zum Lohn.
Darum so hört, und stimmet bei:
Die Werbung steht dem Dichter frei.
Ihr Meister, die ihr's euch getraut,
Euch ruf' ich's vor dem Volke laut:
Erwägt der Werbung selt'nen Preis,
Und wem sie soll gelingen,

Be sure a guileless heart is his ;
　　Pure love and music in it.
　　This crown 's of worth infinite,
And ne'er, in recent days or olden,
By any hand so highly holden.
　　As by this maiden tender :
　　Good fortune may it lend her !
Thus Nuremberg gives honor due
To Art and all her Masters too.

(Great stir among all present. — Sachs goes up to Pogner, who presses his hand, deeply moved.)

Pogner.
　O Sachs ! my friend ! what thanks I owe !
　How well my heart's distress you know !

Sachs.
　There 's much at stake ! 　But care dispel !

(The Prentices have hastily heaped up before the platform of the Master-singers a little mound of turf, beaten it solid, and bestrewn it with flowers.)

Sachs. 　Now then, my Masters, if you're agreed,
　We will to our Trial-songs proceed.

Kothner.
　　　　　(Advancing.)
　Unmarried Masters, forward to win !
　Let him commence who 's most mature. —
　Friend Beckmesser, it is time ! 　Begin !

Beckmesser.
(Quits the stand ; the Prentices conduct him to the mound ; he stumbles up to it, treads uncertainly, and totters.)
　The devil ! 　How rickety ! Make that secure !

(The boys snigger, and beat the turf lustily.)

The People.
　(Severally, whilst Beckmesser is settling himself.)
　What ! he to woo ! 　Is n't he a fat one ?
　In the lady's place, I'd not have that one !
　　　He cannot keep his feet :
　　　How will the man compete ?
　Be still ! 　He 's quite a great professor :
　That is the Town-clerk, Master Beckmesser.
　　　He 'll tumble soon,
　　　Old pantaloon !
　Hush ! leave off your jokes and prate ;
　He is a learned magistrate.

The Prentices.
　　　　　(Drawn up in order.)
　Silentium ! 　Silentium !
　Make no sound — e'en the merest hum !

(Beckmesser, anxiously scanning all faces, makes a grand bow to Eva.)

Kothner. 　Now begin !

Dass er sich rein und edel weiss,
　　Im Werben, wie im Singen,
　　Will er das Reis erringen,
Dass nie bei neuen noch bei Alten
Ward je so herrlich hoch gehalten,
　　Als von der lieblich Reinen,
　　Die niemals soll beweinen,
Dass Nürnberg mit höchstem Werth
Die Kunst und ihre Meister ehrt.

(Grosse Bewegung unter Allen. — Sachs geht auf Pogner zu, der ihm gerührt die Hand drückt.)

Pogner.
　O 　Sachs ! 　Mein Freund ! 　Wie dankens werth !
　Wie wisst ihr, was mein Herz beschwert !

Sachs.
　's war viel gewagt ! Jetzt habt nur Muth !

(Die Lehrbuben haben vor der Meistersinger-Bühne schnell von Rasenstücken einen kleinen Hugel aufgeworfen, fest gerammelt, und reich mit Blumen überdeckt.)

Sachs.
　Nun denn, wenn's Meistern und Volk beliebt,
　Zum Wettgesang man den Anfang giebt.

Kothner.
　　　　　(Tritt vor.)
　Ihr ledig' Meister, macht euch bereit !
　Der Aeltest' sich zuerst anlässt : —
　Herr Beckmesser, ihr fangt an, 's ist Zeit !

Beckmesser.
　(Verlässt die Singerbühne ; die Lehrbuben führen ihn zu dem Blumenhügel : er strauchelt darauf, tritt unsicher und schwankt.)
　Zum Teufel ! 　Wie wackelig ! 　Macht das hübsch fest !
(Die 　Buben lachen unter sich und stopfen an dem Rasen.)

Das Volk.
　(Unterschiedlich, während Beckmesser sich zurecht macht.)
　Wie, der ? Der wirbt ? Scheint mir nicht der Rechte !
　An der Tochter Stell' ich den nicht möchte.
　　　Er kann nicht 'mal stehn :
　　　Wie wird's mit dem geh'n ?
　Seid still ! 's ist gar ein tücht'ger Meister !
　Stadtschreiber ist er : Beckmesser heisst er.
　　　Gott ist der dumm !
　　　Er fällt fast um ! —
　Still ! macht keinen Witz ;
　Der hat im Rathe Stimm' und Sitz.

Die Lehrbuben.
　　　　　(In Aufstellung.)
　Silentium ! 　Silentium !
　Lasst all das Reden und Gesumm' !
(Beckmesser macht, ängstlich in ihren Blicken forschend eine gezierte Verbeugung gegen Eva.)

Kothner. 　　　　　Fanget an !

Beckmesser.

(Sings to his old melody, a vain attempt at Walter's song; his ornamental phrases being spoiled by continual failure of memory and increasing confusion.)

" Yawning and steaming with roseate light,
　　My hair was filled
　　With scent distilled,
　　My boots were beaming
　　With no meaning,
　The guard I did invite
　　To strap me tight."

(After having settled his feet more securely, and taken a peep at the manuscript :)

" Oh for the claws of the guard for my hold !
　　A flea looked down
　　Upon my crown,
　　My chest intending
　　I suspending
　My weight from roots unrolled
　　That furnished hold."

(He again tries to steady himself, and to correct himself by the manuscript.)

The Masters. What is the matter? Is he insane?
　His song's sheer nonsense, that is plain !

The People.
　　　(Louder.)
Charming wooer ! He'll soon get his due :
Suspend on the gallows—that's what he'll do !

Beckmesser.
　　(More and more confused.)
　　　" Get me a bride !
A lovely merry girl I sued —
Afraid, she could not score my face —
As sweet and fair as she was rude.
　　Like to have died,
She shook me from her embrace ;
　　With white eyes glowing,
　　Her hound was going
To stir my long legs as I found.
Such thunderous brutes surround
　　The tree of tripe ! "

(Here all burst into a peal of loud laughter.)

Beckmesser.
　(Descends the mound and hastens to Sachs.)
Accursed cobbler ! This is through you !
That song is not my own, 't is true ;
'T was Sachs, the idol of your throng,
Hans Sachs himself gave me the song !
The wretch, on purpose to abash,
Has palmed on me this sorry trash.

(He rushes away furiously, and disappears in the crowd. Great confusion.)

People.
Why ! How can that be ? 'T is still more
　surprising !
That song by Sachs ? Our wonder is rising !

Beckmesser.

(Singt mit seiner Melodie, verkehrter Prosodie und mit süsslich verzierten Absätzen, öfters durch mangelhaftes Memoriren gänzlich behindert, und mit immer mehr wachsender ängstlicher Verwirrung.)

" Morgen ich leuchte in rosigem Schein
　　Voll Blut und Duft
　　Geht schnell die Luft ; —
　　Wohl bald gewonnen,
　　Wie zerronnen, —
　Im Garten lud ich ein —
　　Garstig und fein."

(Nachdem er sich mit den Füssen wieder gerichtet, und im Manuscript heimlich nachgelesen.)

　Wohn' ich erträglich im selbigen Raum,
　　Hol' Gold und Frucht —
　　Bleisaft und Wucht:
　　Mich holt am Pranger —
　　Der Verlanger, —
　Auf luft'ger Steige kaum —
　　Häng' ich am Baum."

(Er sucht sich wieder zurecht zu stellen und im Manuscript zurecht zu finden.)

Die Meister.
　Was soll das heissen? Ist er nun toll?
　Sein Lied ist ganz von Unsinn voll !

Das Volk.
　　　(Immer lauter.)
　Schöner Werber ! Der find't seinen Lohn :
　Bald hängt er am Galgen ; man sieht ihn
　schon.

Beckmesser.
　　　(Immer verwirrter.)
　　　" Heimlich mir graut —
　Weil hier es munter will hergeh'n : —
　An meiner Leiter stand ein Wieb,
　Sie schämt' und wollt mich nicht beseh'n.
　　Bleich wie ein Kraut —
　Umfasert mir Hanf meinen Leib ; —
　　Die Augen zwinkend —
　　Der Hund blies winkend —
　Was ich vor langem verzehrt, —
　Wie Frucht, so Holz und Pferd —
　　Vom Leberbaum." —

(Hier bricht Alles in schallendes Gelächter aus.)

Beckmesser.
　(Verlässt wüthend den Hügel und eilt auf Sachs zu.)
　Verdammter Schuster ! Das dank' ich dir !
　Das Lied, es ist gar nicht von mir :
　Von Sachs, der hier so hoch verehrt,
　Von eu'rem Sachs ward mir's bescheert '
　Mich hat der Schändliche bedrängt,
　Sein schlechtes Lied mir aufgehängt.

(Er stürzt wüthend fort und verliert sich unter dem Volke. Grosser Aufstand.)

Volk.
　Mein ! Was soll das ? Jetzt wird's immer
　　bunter !
　Von Sachs das Lied ? Das nähm' uns doch
　　Wunder !

Master-Singers.
  Explain this, Sachs!   What a disgrace!
  Is that song yours?   Most novel case!

Sachs.
  (Who has quietly picked up the paper which Beckmes-
ser threw away.)
  That song, indeed, is not by me:
  Friend Beckmesser's wrong as he can be.
  I tell you, sirs, the work is fine;
  But it is easy to divine
  That Beckmesser has sung it wrong.
  I am accused and must defend:
  A witness let me bid attend!—
  Is there one here who knows I'm right,
  Let him appear before our sight!
  (Walter advances from out the crowd.—General stir.)
  Bear witness the song is not by me,
  And prove to all that, in the plea
    I have advanced for it,
    I said but what was fit.

The Masters.
  Ah, Sachs!   You're very sly indeed!—
  But you may for this once proceed.

Sachs.
  It shews our rules are of excellence rare
  If now and then exceptions they'll bear.

People.   A noble witness, proud and bold!
  Methinks he should some good unfold.

Sachs.   Masters and people all agree
  To give my witness liberty.
  Sir Walter von Stolzing, sing the song!
  You, Masters, see if he goes wrong.
  (He gives the Masters the paper to follow with.)

Prentices.   All are intent, hushed is the hum;
  So we need not call out Silentium!

Die Meistersinger.
  Erkiärt doch, Sachs! Welch ein Skandal!
  Von euch das Lied? Welch eigner Fall!

Sachs.
  (Der ruhig das Blatt, welches ihm Beckmesser hinge
worfen, aufgehoben hat.)
  Das Lied, fürwahr, ist nicht von mir:
  Herr Beckmesser irrt, wie dort, so hier!
  Ich sag' euch Herr'n, das Lied ist schön:
  Nur ist's auf den ersten Blick zu erseh'n,
  Dass Freund Beckmesser es entstellt.
  Ich bin verklagt, und muss besteh'n:
  Drum lasst meinen Zeugen mich auser
    seh'n!—
  Ist Jemand hier, der Recht mir weiss,
  Der tret' als Zeug' in diesen Kreis!
  (Walther tritt aus dem Volke hervor.   Allgemeine Be
wegung.)
  So zeuget, das Lied sei nicht von mir;
  Und zeuget auch, dass, was ich hier
    Hab' von dem Lied gesagt,
    Zuviel nicht sei gewagt.

Die Meister.
  Ei, Sachs! Gesteht, ihr seid gar fein!—
  So mag's denn heut' geschehen sein.

Sachs.   Der Regel Güte daraus man erwägt,
  Dass sie auch 'mal 'ne Ausnahm' verträgt.

Das Volk.   Ein guter Zeuge, schön und kühn
  Mich dünkt, dem kann 'was Gut's erblüh'n!

Sachs.   Meister und Volk sind gewillt
  Zu vernehmen, was mein Zeuge gilt.
  Herr Walther von Stolzing, singt das Lied!
  Ihr Meister, les't, ob's ihm gerieth.
  (Er giebt den Meistern das Blatt zum Nachlesen.)

Die Lehrbuben.
  Alles gespannt, 's gibt kein Gesumm',
  Da rufen wir auch nicht Silentium!

PRIZE SONG.

English Version by L. U.

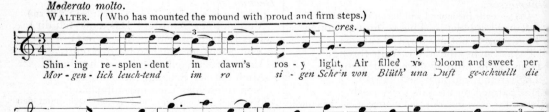

Moderato molto.
WALTER. (Who has mounted the mound with proud and firm steps.)

Shin - ing re - splen - dent in dawn's ros - y light, Air filled with bloom and sweet per
Mor - gen - lich leuch-tend im ro si - gen Schein von Blüth' una Duft ge-schwellt die

fume, Where joys out - meas - ure Dreamed of pleas - ure, A gar - den doth in
Luft, voll al - ler Won - nen, nie er - son - nen, ein Gar - ten lud mich

un poco rit. con estasia.

vite. And there be-neath a mag-ic tree, Of fruits hung rich with treas-ure, In
ein, dort ur-ter ei-nem Wun-der-baum, von Früch-ten reich be-han-gen, zu

bless-ed dream of love I see What ar-dent thirst for pleas-ure With prom-ise doth en
schau'n in sel'-gem Lie-bes-traum, was höchs-tem Lust-ver-lan-gen Er-fül-lung kühn ver

dolce.

tice, The fair-est maid:.. E - va in Pa-ra-dise!
hiess, das schön-ste Weib:.. E - va im Pa-ra-dies!

Closed round by shad-ows, sur-round-ed by night, By path-way steep I reach a
A - bend-lich däm-mernd um-schloss mich die Nacht, auf stei-lem Pfad war ich ge-

dim.

deep And no-ble foun-tain on a moun-tain Whose waves smile on .... me
naht zu ei-ner Quel-le rei-ner Wel-le, die lo-ckend mir ... ge-

p ritard.

bright. And there be-neath a lau-rel tree Through which the stars are gleam-ing, The
lacht: dort un-ter ei-nem Lor-beer-baum, von Ster-nen hell durch-schie-nen, ich

no-blest wom-an's form I see In wak-ing po-et dream-ing, While
schaut' im wa-chen Dich-ter-traum von hei-lig hol-den Mie-nen, mich

she with ho-ly, gra-cious mien My brow be-dews. Par-nas - sus' sa-cred
net-zend mit dem e-dlen Nass, das hehr-ste Weib, die Mu - se des Par-

con molto fuoco.

muse! Most bless-ed day When I from po-et's dream a-
nass! Huld-reich-ster Tag dem ich aus Dichter's Traum er-

wake! Now what I dreamed of Pa-ra-dise, Di-vine in fresh-er glo-ry, lies
wacht! das ich er-träumt, das Pa-ra-dies, in himmlisch neu ver-klär-ter Pracht,

Be-fore my eyes, While smil - ing still the foun-tain shows the way, The
hell vor mir lag, da-hin la-chend nun der Quell den Pfad mir wies, die

maid E - lys - ian I saw in vis - ion, She whom my heart doth
dort ge - bo - ren, mein Herz er - ko - ren, der Er - de lieb - lich - stes

choose, Earth's fair - est, and my muse, So ho - - ly, grave, and good, By
Bild, als Mu - se mir ge - weiht, so hei - - lig ernst als mild, ward

me is bold - ly wooed, Here by the day's bright sun, By
kühn von mir ge - freit; am lich - ten Tag der Son - nen, durch

power of song is won Par - nas - sus and Pa - ra - dise!"
San - ges Sieg ge - won - nen Par - nass und Pa - ra - dies!"

People.　Give him the prize! Maiden, rise! No one could woo in nobler wise!	**Volk.**　Reich' ihm das Reis! Sein der Preis! Keiner wie er zu werben weiss!
Masters.　Yes, glorious singer!　Victor, rise! Your song has won the Master-prize!	**Die Meister.** Ja, holder Sänger!　Nimm das Reis! Dein Sang erwarb dir Meisterpreis!
Pogner.　O Sachs!　All this I owe to you: My happiness revives anew.	**Pogner.** O Sachs! Dir dank' ich Glück und Ehr', Vorüber nun all' Herzbeschwer!
(Eva, who from the commencement of the scene has preserved a calm composure, and has seemed wrapt from all that passed around, has listened to Walter immovably; but now, when at the conclusion both Masters and people express their involuntary admiration, she rises, advances to the edge of the platform and places on the brow of Walter, who kneels on the steps, a wreath of myrtle and laurel, whereupon he rises and she leads him to her father, before whom they both kneel. Pogner extends his hands in benediction over them.)	(Eva, die von Anfang des Auftrittes her in sicherer, ruhiger Haltung verblieben, und bei allen Vorgängen wie in seliger Geistesentrücktheit sich erhalten, hat Walther unverwandt zugehört; jetzt, während am Schlusse des Gesanges Volk und Meister, gerührt und ergriffen, unwillkürlich ihre Zustimmung ausdrücken, erhebt sie sich, schreitet an den Rand der Singerbühne, und drückt auf die Stirn Walthers, welcher zu den Stufen herangetreten ist und vor ihr sich niedergelassen hat, einen aus Lorbeer und Myrthen geflochtenen Kranz, worauf dieser sich erhebt und von ihr zu ihrem Vater geleitet wird, vor welchem Beide niederknieen; Pogner streckt segnend seine Hände über sie aus.)
Sachs. (Pointing to the group.) My witness answered not amiss! Do you find fault with me for this?	**Sachs.** (Deutet dem Volke mit der Hand auf die Gruppe.) Den Zeugen, denk' es, wählt' ich gut; Tragt ihr Hans Sachs drum üblen Muth?
People. (Jubilantly.) Hans Sachs!　No!　It was well devised! Your tact you 've once more exercised!	**Volk.** (Jubelnd.) Hans Sachs! Nein! Das war schön erdacht! Das habt ihr einmal wieder gut gemacht!
Several Master-Singers. Now, Master Pogner!　As you should, Give him the honor of Masterhood!	**Mehrere Meistersinger.** Auf, Meister Pogner! Euch zum Ruhm, Meldet dem Junker sein Meisterthum.
Pogner. (Bringing forward a gold chain with three medallions.) Receive kind David's likeness true: The Master's Guild is free to you.	**Pogner.** (Eine goldene Kette mit drei Denkmünzen tragend.) Geschmuckt mit König David's Bild, Nehm' ich euch auf in der Meister Gild'.

Walter.

(Shrinking back involuntarily.)
A Master! Nay!
I 'll find reward some other way!

(The Masters look disconcertedly towards Sachs.)

Sachs.

(Grasping Walter by the hand.)
Disparage not the Master's ways,
But show respect to Art!
So heed my words:—
Honor your German Masters
If you would stay disasters!
For while they dwell in every heart,
Though should depart
The pride of holy Rome,
Still thrives at home
Our sacred German Art!

(All join enthusiastically in the last verse.— Eva takes
the crown from Walter's head and places it on Sachs's; he
takes the chain from Pogner's hand and puts it round
Walter's neck.— Walter and Eva lean against Sachs, one
on each side: Pogner sinks on his knee before him as if
in homage. The Master-singers point to Sachs, with outstretched hands, as to their chief. While the Prentices
clap hands and shout and dance, the people wave hats and
'kerchiefs in enthusiasm.)

All. Hail Sachs! Hans Sachs!
Hail Nuremberg's darling Sachs!

(The Curtains falls.)

Walther.

(Zuckt unwillkürlich heftig zurück.)
Nicht Meister! Nein!
Will ohne Meister selig sein!
(Die Meister blicken in grosser Betretenheit auf Sachs.)

Sachs.

(Walther fest bei der Hand fassend.)
Verachtet mir die Meister nicht,
Und ehrt mir ihre Kunst!
Drum sag' ich Euch:
Ehrt eure deutschen Meister,
Dann bannt ihr gute Geister!
Und gebt ihr ihrem Wirken Gunst,
Zerging' in Dunst
Das heil'ge röm'sche Reich
Uns bliebe gleich
Die heil'ge deutsche Kunst!

(Alle fallen begeistert in den Schlussvers ein. Eva
nimmt den Kranz von Walther's Stirn und drückt ihn
Sachs auf; dieser nimmt die Kette aus Pogner's Hand,
und hängt sie Walther um, Walther und Eva lehnen sich
zu beiden Seiten an Sachsen's Schultern; Pogner lässt
sich, wie huldigend, auf ein Knie vor Sachs nieder. Die
Meistersinger deuten mit erhobenen Händen auf Sachs, als
auf ihr Haupt. Während die Lehrbuben jauchzend in die
Hände schlagen und tanzen, schwenkt das Volk begeistert
Hüte und Tücher.)

Volk.

Heil Sachs! Hans Sachs!
Heil Nürnberg's theurem Sachs!

(Der Vorhang fällt.)

PARSIFAL

For the basis of his last music-drama, "Parsifal," Wagner selected from the host of mediæval legends surrounding the Grail the version found in the poems of the old German Minnesinger, Wolfram von Eschenbach, modifying the details and enriching the meaning to suit his dramatic purposes. The idea of the Grail dates from the earliest times, and during the Middle Ages became a most poetic conception, representing the *Ideal* of the pious devotions of chivalry. It was the sacred chalice, of wonderful spiritual power, from which Christ drank at the Last Supper, and in which were caught the last drops of His blood as He hung on the cross. According to Wagner, both the Grail, and the Sacred Spear, with which Longinus pierced the side of Christ, were brought down from heaven by an angel host and given into the keeping of Titurel, who built for them a temple in the mountains of northern Spain (Monsalvat), and founded an order of knighthood to watch and protect the sacred relics. None but the pure in heart could find the magic temple; none but the noblest and bravest could remain in its service.

Titurel was succeeded by Amfortas, who fell a victim to the wiles of a witchwoman Kundry,[1] and was wounded in conflict with her master, the magician Klingsor, who wrested from Amfortas the Sacred Spear, with which he administered a wound which would not heal, though the unfortunate knight remained in life, through the sustaining power of the Grail. It was prophesied, however, that there should one day come to Monsalvat a youth (Parsifal), pure and unsophisticated, who should become wise through compassion (*durch Mitleid wissend*) and who, after having himself withstood temptation and evil, should regain the Spear, and by its aid heal Amfortas' wound. It is with the coming of Parsifal that the action commences.

[1] Kundry in the legend was the female prototype of the Wandering Jew; having mocked at Christ on the Cross, she was condemned to perpetual laughter. Wagner makes her a dual personality, who seeks expiation in zealous service to the Grail, and yet is condemned to lapse periodically into a magic sleep, during which she is bound to the powers of evil.

THE STORY OF THE DRAMA.

Act I. A wood near the Grail Mountain, where Gurnemanz and some young esquires are at their morning devotions. They are interrupted by the wild arrival of Kundry, who staggers in exhausted, bearing an ointment for Amfortas' wound. The latter then enters on his way to the bath, borne in a litter and attended by a train of knights. Though despairing of help, he takes the ointment and is carried to the lake. While Gurnemanz is relating the incidents which led to Amfortas' undoing, a wild swan, wounded to the death, flutters to the ground. In horror the esquires hasten to seize its slayer, and bring forward Parsifal, bow in hand, and unaware of the enormity of his deed. His replies to Gurnemanz' questions betray deep ignorance of himself and of the world; but Kundry relates what she knows of his birth and parentage, and Gurnemanz, in the hope that this is the "pure fool" (*der reine Thor*) promised in the prophecy, leads him toward the Temple of the Grail. Kundry has meanwhile crawled into the thicket and fallen into a deep sleep.

The scene changes gradually until the stage represents the interior of a vast hall, furnished with long tables, and Amfortas, in spite of the agony it causes him, uncovers the Grail; this becomes illumined, and the knights partake of the Lord's Supper. When the rite is finished, Parsifal, who has been an interested spectator of the scene, still shows no comprehension of its meaning; and Gurnemanz, in ill-humor, pushes him out of the hall.

ACT II. Klingsor's castle. Klingsor with sorcerer's arts, calls Kundry from her magic sleep, and bids her seduce Parsifal. While she pleads with him, Parsifal is heard mounting the ramparts and driving Klingsor's knights in headlong flight. The castle sinks with the sorcerer, and the scene changes to a luxuriant garden, where Parsifal enters, and is surrounded by flower girls, seeking to entice him. Finally Kundry, bound to Klingsor's service, appears in the guise of a beautiful woman, disperses the flower girls, and with devilish ingenuity attempts Parsifal's seduction. But at her first kiss, the knowledge of Amfortas' temptation and agony comes to him in a flood of compassion, and he casts her off. Enraged, she calls to her aid Klingsor, who hurls at Parsifal the Sacred Spear. It remains poised above the youth's head; he seizes it, and makes the sign of the cross, whereat the castle falls in ruins.

ACT III. A flowery meadow near the Grail Mountain. It is Good Friday. Gurnemanz, grown very old, discovers Kundry asleep in the thicket. He wakes her, and she sets at once to her menial tasks. Parsifal, in heavy armor, returns after years of wandering, bearing the Sacred Spear. Before leading him to Amfortas, Gurnemanz, overjoyed, removes his armor and sprinkles his head with water; while Kundry anoints his feet from a golden flask, and dries them with her hair. Bells are heard; the scene changes until the great hall is reached, as in Act I. The knights enter in solemn procession, bearing the wounded Amfortas. With the Spear, Parsifal touches his wound, which is healed. Kundry, redeemed, sinks back dead. Now the Grail glows with light, and a white dove descends to Parsifal, in heavenly benediction.

PUBLISHERS' NOTE.

In Parsifal, the last of his completed works, Wagner's theories of dramatic composition reach their logical conclusion. Set musical forms are abolished; in their stead is reared a wonderful and colossal tone structure, developed almost entirely from a number of essential themes or motives — short musical sentences which characterize and are definitely associated with the personages and incidents of the drama, or with the ethical and spiritual ideas which underlie and govern the action. An acquaintance with at least the most important of these "leading motives"

(*Leitmotiven*), will greatly aid the hearer to an intelligent appreciation of the musical side of the drama, its significance, and faithfulness to the poem. The publishers have therefore deemed it advisable to give the following list of themes, in the belief that it will prove of real use to opera-goers, where excerpts from the score would be highly unsatisfactory. The themes are numbered for convenience; corresponding reference numerals are placed in the margin of the poem opposite the place or line, where each one occurs for the first time.

LEADING MOTIVES (LEITMOTIVEN) OF THE DRAMA.

No. 1.   MOTIVE OF THE LAST SUPPER (DER LIEBESMAHL–SPRUCH).

No. 2.   MOTIVE OF THE GRAIL (GRALMOTIV).

No. 3.   FAITH MOTIVE (GLAUBENMOTIV).

No. 4.   THE SAVIOUR'S CRY OF ANGUISH (SCHMERZENFIGUR). (See No 1 *a*.)

No. 5.   SACRED SPEAR MOTIVE (DAS SPEERMOTIV). (See No. 1 *b*.)

No. 6.   MOTIVE OF THE ORDER OF THE GRAIL (DAS MOTIV DER GRALSRITTER).

No. 7.   MOTIVE OF AMFORTAS' SUFFERING (AMFORTAS' LEIDENSMOTIV).

No. 8.   PROMISE OF REDEMPTION MOTIVE (DER VERHEISSUNGSSPRUCH).

By pi - ty 'lighten'd, the guile - less Fool, wait for him, my cho-sen tool.

Wait . . . . . for him.

No. 9.   KUNDRY MOTIVE (DAS KUNDRYMOTIV).

No. 10.   SORCERY MOTIVE (DAS ZAUBERMOTIV).

No. 11.   KLINGSOR MOTIVE (DAS KLINGSORMOTIV).

No. 12. PARSIFAL MOTIVE (DAS PARSIFALMOTIV).

No. 13. HERZELEIDE MOTIVE (DAS HERZELEIDEMOTIV).

No. 14. THE BELL THEME (DAS GLOCKENTHEMA).

No. 15 THE SAVIOUR'S LAMENT (DIE HEILANDSKLAGE).

No. 16. MELODY OF THE FLOWER GIRLS (KOSEMELODIE).

Come, come, hand - some strip - ling, Come, etc.

No. 17 THEME OF KUNDRY'S NARRATIVE (KUNDRY'S ERZÄHLUNGSTHEMA).

No. 18. SECOND HERZELEIDE MOTIVE (DAS ZWEITE HERZELEIDEMOTIV).

No. 19. GOOD FRIDAY MOTIVE (DAS CHARFREITAGMOTIV).

No. 20. WILDERNESS MOTIVE (DAS THEMA DER ÖDE).

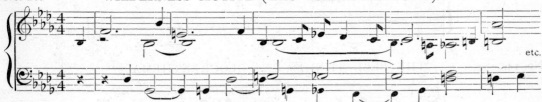

No. 21. BAPTISM SCENE (DER SEGENSPRUCH).

No. 22. GOOD FRIDAY SPELL (CHARFREITAGS ZAUBER).

PARSIFAL.

ACT I.	ERSTER AUFZUG.
PRELUDE.	**VORSPIEL.**

ACT I.
PRELUDE.

A Forest shadowy and impressive, but not gloomy. Rock-strewn ground. A glade in the middle. L. rises the way to the Grail's castle. The ground sinks in the middle at back to a low-lying forest lake. — Day dawn. — GURNEMANZ (an old but vigorous man) and two ESQUIRES (tender youths) are ensconced asleep under a tree. From L. as if from the castle, rises the solemn morning reveille of trombones.

Gurnemanz

(waking, and shaking the ESQUIRES).

Hey! Ho! Wood-keepers twain!
Sleep-keepers I deem ye!
At least be moving with morning!

(The two ESQUIRES spring up, and then immediately sink on their knees again, ashamed.)

Hear ye the call? Now thank the Lord
That ye are called in time to hear it.

(He also falls on his knees with them; they offer up a silent morning prayer together; when the trombones have ceased, they rise again.)

Now up, young vassals; see to the bath;
'Tis time to wait there for our monarch:
Already I behold approach
Runners before his litter bed.

(Two KNIGHTS enter from the castle.)

Hail, both! How goes Amfortas' health?
He craves to-day his bath right early:
    The simple that Gawaine
With bravest craft did win for him,
I'm hopeful it hath brought relief?

First Knight. Thou knowest all and still canst hope!
    With keener smart than before
    Full soon his pain returned:
Sleepless from strong oppression,
His bath he bade us to prepare.

Gurnemanz

(drooping his head sorrowfully).

Fools are we, alleviation seeking,
    When but one salve relieves him!
For ev'ry simple, ev'ry herb we search
    And hunt wide through the world,
        When helps but one thing —
        And but one man.

First Knight. Expound us that!

ERSTER AUFZUG.
VORSPIEL.

Wald, schattig und ernst, doch nicht düster.

Felsiger Boden. Eine Lichtung in der Mitte. Links aufsteigend wird der Weg zur Gralsburg angenommen. Der Mitte des Hintergrundes zu senkt sich der Boden zu einem tiefer gelegenen Waldsee hinab. — Tagesanbruch. — GURNEMANZ (rüstig greisenhaft) und zwei KNAPPEN (von zartem Jünglingsalter) sind schlafend unter einem Baume gelagert. — Von der linken Seite, wie von der Gralsburg her, ertönt der feierliche Morgenweckruf der Posaunen.

Gurnemanz

(erwachend und die KNAPPEN rüttend).

He! Ho! Waldhüter ihr!
Schlafhüter mitsammen!
So wacht doch mindest am Morgen!

(Die beiden KNAPPEN springen auf, und senken sich, beschämt, sogleich wieder auf die Knie.)

Hört ihr den Ruf? Nun danket Gott,
dass ihr berufen ihn zu hören!

(Er senkt sich zu ihnen ebenfalls nieder; gemeinschaftlich verrichten sie stumm ihr Morgengebet; sobald die Posaunen schweigen erheben sie sich dann.)

Jetzt auf, ihr Knaben; seht nach dem Bad,
Zeit ist's, des Königs dort zu harren:
dem Siechbett, das ihn trägt, voraus
seh' ich die Boten vor uns nah'n.

(Zwei RITTER treten, von der Burg her, auf.)

Heil euch! Wie geht's Amfortas heut'?
Wohl früh verlangt er nach dem Bade:
    das Heilkraut, das Gawan
    mit List und Kühnheit ihm gewann,
ich wähne, dass es Lind'rung schuf?

Der erste Ritter. Das wähn'st du, der doch
        Alles weiss?
    Ihm kehrten sehrender nur
    die Schmerzen bald zurück:
    schlaflos von starkem Bresten
    befahl er eifrig uns das Bad.

Gurnemanz

(das Haupt traurig senkend).

Thoren wir, auf Lind'rung da zu hoffen,
    wo einzig Heilung lindert!
Nach allen Kräutern, allen Tränken forsch
    und jagt weit durch die Welt:
        ihm hilft nur Eines —
        nur der Eine.

Erster Ritter. So nenn' uns den!

Column markers: 1, 2, 3, 4, 5 / 2 / 3 / 6 / 7 / 8

Gurnemanz

(evasively).

See to the bath !

First Esquire

(as he turns away towards the back with the second ESQUIRE looking off R.).

Behold yon frenzied horsewoman !

Second Esquire. Hey !
  The mane of the devil's mare flyeth madly !

First Knight. Aye ! Kundry 'tis.

Second Knight. With news she surely cometh ?

First Esquire. The mare is tottering.

Second Esquire. Did she fly through air ?

First Esquire. Now lowly she grovels.

Second Esquire. Mark her mane that brushes the moss.

First Knight. The wild witch has swung herself off.

KUNDRY rushes in hastily, almost reeling. Wild garb fastened up high ; girdle of snakeskin hanging long, black hair flowing in loose locks ; dark brownish red complexion, piercing black eyes, sometimes wild and blazing, but usually fixed and glassy. — She hurries to GURNEMANZ and presses upon him a small crystal flask.

Kundry. Here, take it ! — Balsam !

Gurnemanz. From whence bringest thou this ?

Kundry. From farther hence than thy thought can guess ;
  If this balsam fail,
   Arabia bears
Naught else that can give him ease. —
Ask no farther ! — I am weary.

(She throws herself on the ground.)

A train of ESQUIRES and KNIGHTS appears L., bearing and attending the litter in which AMFORTAS lies stretched out. — GURNEMANZ immediately turns away from KUNDRY towards the newcomers.

Gurnemanz

(while the procession is entering).

He comes : by faithful servants carried. —
Alas ! How can mine eyes have power
To see, in manhood's stately flower,
This sov'reign of the staunchest race
To stubborn sickness made a slave !

(to the ESQUIRES.)

Be heedful ! Hark, your master groans.

(They stop and set down the litter.)

Amfortas

(raising himself slightly).

'Tis well ! - - My thanks ! — Remain awhile. —

Gurnemanz

(ausweichend).

Sorgt für das Bad !

Der erste Knappe

(als er sich mit dem zweiten KNAPPEN dem Hindergrunde zuwendet nach rechts blickend).

Seht dort die wilde Reiterin !

Zweiter Knappe. Hei !
  Wie fliegen der Teufelsmähre die Mähnen !

Erster Ritter. Ja ! Kundry dort.

Zweiter Ritter. Die bringt wohl wicht'ge Kunde ?

Erster Knappe. Die Mähre taumelt.

Zweiter Knappe. Flog sie durch die Luft ?

Erster Knappe. Jetzt kriecht sie am Boden.

Zweiter Knappe. Mit den Mähnen fegt sie das Moos.

Erster Ritter. Da schwang sich die Wilde herab.

KUNDRY stürzt hastig, fast taumelnd herein. Wilde Kleidung, hoch geschürzt ; Gürtel von Schlangenhäuten lang herabhängend : schwarzes, in losen Zöpfen flatterndes Haar ; tief braun-röthliche Gesichtsfarbe ; stechende schwarze Augen, zuweilen wild aufblitzend, öfters wie todesstarr und unbeweglich. — Sie eilt auf GURNEMANZ zu und dringt ihm ein kleines Krystallgefäss auf

Kundry. Hier nimm du ! — Balsam !

Gurnemanz. Woher brachtest du diess ?

Kundry. Von weiter her, als du denken kannst ;
  Hilft der Balsam nicht,
   Arabien birgt
nichts mehr dann zu seinem Heil. —
Frag' nicht weiter ! — Ich bin müde.

(Sie wirft sich auf den Boden.)

Ein Zug von KNAPPEN und RITTERN, die Sänfte tragend und geleitend, in welcher AMFORTAS ausgestreckt liegt, gelangt, von links her, auf die Bühne. — GURNEMANZ hat sich, von KUNDRY absogleich den Ankommenden zugewendet.

Gurnemanz

(während der Zug auf die Bühne gelangt).

Er naht : sie bringen ihn getragen. —
O weh' ! Wie trag' ich's im Gemüthe,
in seiner Mannheit stolzer Blüthe
des siegreichsten Geschlechtes Herrn
als seines Siechthum's Knecht zu seh'n !

(Zu den KNAPPEN.)

Behutsam ! Hört, der König stöhnt.

(Jene halten ein und stellen das Siechbett nieder.)

Amfortas

(der sich ein wenig erhoben).

So recht ! — Habt Dank ! - Ein wenig Rast.

From madd'ning tortured nights
Fair morn to woods invites :
   Sure even me
The lake's pure wave will freshen ;
   My pain will flee
And tortured nights' oppression. —
Gawaine !

First Knight.   Sire, Gawaine waited not :
For, when the healing herb,
Whose gain such toil hath needed,
Did disappoint thy hopes,
He to another search in haste proceeded.

Amfortas.   Unordered ? — May he be requited
For slighting thus the Grail's commands !
O woe to him, whom foes ne'er frighted,
If he should fall in Klingsor's hands !
Let none my feelings henceforth harry :
For him, the promised one, I tarry.
   " By pity ' lightened " —
Was't not so — ?

Gurnemanz.   'Twas so thou said'st to us.

Amfortas.   " The guileless Fool — "
To me he doth unveil him, —
Might I as Death but hail him !

Gurnemanz.   But first behold : accord to this a
trial.
   (He hands him the flask.)

Amfortas
   (regarding it).
From whence this wondrous-looking flask ?

Gurnemanz.   'Twas brought for thee from Araby
afar.

Amfortas.   Who went to win it ?

Gurnemanz.   'Twas she, yon woman wild.
Up, Kundry ! come !
   (She refuses.)

Amfortas.   Thou, Kundry ?
Mak'st me again thy debtor,
Thou restless, fearful maid ? —
   Well then !
Thy balsam I will even try,
In gratitude for thy good service.

Kundry
   (moving uneasily on the ground).
No thanks ! — Ha ha !   What will it help thee ?
No thanks ! — Go, go !   Thy bath !

Nach wilder Schmerzensnacht
nun Waldes-Morgenpracht ;
   im heil'gen See
wohl labt mich auch die Welle :
   es staunt das Weh',
die Schmerzensnacht wird helle. —
Gawan !

Erster Ritter.   Herr, Gawan weilte nicht
Da seines Krautes Kraft,
wie schwer er's auch errungen,
   doch deine Hoffnung trog,
hat er auf neue Sucht sich fortgeschwungen.

Amfortas.   Ohn' Urlaub ? — Möge das er sühnen
dass schlecht er Gralsgebote hält !
O wehe ihm, dem trotzig Kühnen,
wenn er in Klingsor's Schlingen fällt !
So breche Keiner mir den Frieden :
ich harre dess', der mir beschieden.
   „ Durch Mitleid wissend " —
war's nicht so ?

Gurnemanz.   Uns sagtest du es so.

Amfortas.   „ der reine Thor " — — :
mich dünkt, ihn zu erkennen : —
dürft ich den Tod ihn nennen !

Gurnemanz.   Doch hier zuvor : versuch' es noch
mit diesem !
   (Er reicht ihm das Fläschchen.)

Amfortas
   (es betrachtend).
Woher diess heimliche Gefäss ?

Gurnemanz.   Dir ward es aus Arabia hergeführt.

Amfortas.   Und wer gewann es ?

Gurnemanz.   Da liegt's, das wilde Weib. —
Auf, Kundry ! komm ' !   *(Sie weigert sich.)*

Amfortas.   Du, Kundry ?
Muss ich dir nochmals danken,
du rastlos scheue Magd ? —
   Wohl denn !
Den Balsam nun versuch' ich noch ;
es sei aus Dank für deine Treu' !

Kundry
   (unruhig am Boden liegend)
Nicht Dank ! — Ha ha ! Was wird es helfen ?
Nicht Dank !   Fort, fort !   Zum Bad !

AMFORTAS gives the sign to proceed ; the procession disappears **7** towards the valley. — GURNEMANZ, sadly looking after, and KUNDRY still crouching on the ground, remain. — ESQUIRES pass to and fro.

AMFORTAS giebt das Zeichen zum Aufbruch ; der Zug entfernt sich nach dem tieferen Hintergrunde zu. — GURNEMANZ, schwermüthig nachblickend, und KUNDRY, fortwährend auf dem Boden gelagert sind zurückgeblieben. — KNAPPEN gehen ab und zu.

Third Esquire
(a young man).
Hey! Thou there!—
Why liest thou thus like a savage beast?

Kundry. Are not beasts here safe and sacred?

Third Esquire. Aye; but if thou art so,
We know not for certain yet.

Fourth Esquire
(also a young man).
With her enchanted drugs, I ween,
She'll bring destruction soon to our Master.

Gurnemanz. Hm!—Hath she done harm to
ye?—
When all are sore perplext
For ways to send tidings to distant lands,
Where warrior brethren are battling,
Their whereabouts scarcely known—
Who, ere ye are even resolved,
Starts and dashes thither and back,
The charge fulfilling with faith and knack?
She needs ye not, she's nigh you ne'er,
Nought common hath she with you;
But when ye need help in danger time,
She breathes the breath of zeal through your
ranks,
And never wants a word of thanks
If only thus she harm ye,
It need not so much alarm ye.

Third Esquire. She hates us, though.—
See there, how hellishly she looks at us!

Fourth Esquire. 'Tis a Pagan, sure; a sorceress.

Gurnemanz. Yea, under a curse she may have
been:
Here now's her home,—
Renewed become,
That of her sins she may be shriven
From former life yet unforgiven,
Seeking her shrift by such good actions
As advantage all our knightly factions.
Sure she does well in working thus:
Serves herself and also us.

Third Esquire Then is it not surely her fault
So much distress hath come on us?

Gurnemanz. Aye, when she often stayed afar
from us
Then broke misfortune ever in.
I long have known her now;
But Titurel knew her yet longer:
When he yon castle consecrated,

Dritter Knappe
(junger Mann).
He! Du da!—
Was liegst du dort wie ein wildes Thier?

Kundry. Sind die Thiere hier nicht heilig?

Dritter Knappe. Ja! doch ob heilig du,
das wissen wir grad' noch nicht.

Vierter Knappe
(ebenfalls junger Mann).
Mit ihrem Zaubersafte, wähn' ich,
wird sie den Meister vollends verderben.

Gurnemanz. Hm!—Schuf sie euch Schaden
je?—
Wann Alles rathlos steht
wie kämpfender Brüdern in fernste Länder
Kunde sei zu entsenden,
und kaum ihr nur wisst, wohin?—
Wer, ehe ihr euch nur besinnt,
stürmt und fliegt dahin und zurück,
der Botschaft pflegend mit Treu' und Glück?
Ihr nährt sie nicht, sie naht euch nie,
nichts hat sie mit euch gemein;
doch wann's in Gefahr der Hilfe gilt,
der Eifer führt sie schier durch die Luft,
die nie euch dann zum Danke ruft.
Ich wähne, ist diess Schaden,
so thät' er euch gut gerathen?

Dritter Knappe. Doch hasst sie uns.—
Sieh' nur, wie hämisch sie dort nach uns blickt!

Vierter Knappe. Eine Heidin ist's, ein Zauber-
weib.

Gurnemanz. Ja, eine Verwünschte mag sie sein:
hier lebt sie heut',—
vielleicht erneu't,
zu büssen Schuld aus früher'm Leben,
die dorten ihr noch nicht vergeben.
Uebt sie nun Buss' in solchen Thaten,
die uns Ritterschaft zum Heil gerathen,
gut thut sie dann ganz sicherlich,
dienet uns, und hilft auch sich.

Dritter Knappe. Dann ist's wohl auch jen' ihre
Schuld,
was uns so manche Noth gebracht?

Gurnemanz. Ja, wann sie oft uns lange ferne
blieb,
dann brach ein Unglück wohl herein.
Und lang' schon kenn' ich sie:
noch länger kennt sie Titurel:
der fand, als er die Burg dort weih'te,

10

He found her sleeping in this wood,
  All stiff, rigid, like death.
Thus I myself did find her lately,
Just when the trouble came on us
Which yonder miscreant beyond the mountain,
So shamefully did bring about. —
(to KUNDRY).
Hey, thou ! — Hearken and say :
Where wert thou wandering around
When our commander lost the spear ?
(KUNDRY is silent.)
Wherefore didst thou not help us then ?

Kundry. I never help.

Fourth Esquire. She says't herself.

Third Esquire. If she's so true and void of fear,
Then send her to search for the missing spear.

Gurnemanz
(gloomily).
That is quite diff'rent ! —
'Tis denied to all. —
(with deep emotion).
Oh, wounding, wonderful
  and hallowéd spear !
I saw thee swayed
  by th' unholiest hand ! —
(becoming lost in remembrance).
When thus equipped, Amfortas, all too bold one,
  Who could thine arm be staying
  Th' enchanter from essaying ?
While near the walls, from us the king was ta'en :
A maid of fearful beauty turned his brain.
He lay bewitched, her form enfolding,
  The spear no longer holding : —
  A deathly cry ! — I rushed anigh ; —
  But laughing, Klingsor fled before;
  The sacred spear away he bore.
I fought to aid the flying king's returning ;
A fatal wound, though, in his side was burning.
That wound it is which none may make to close.

Third Esquire. Thou knewest then Klingsor ?

Gurnemanz
(to the first and second ESQUIRES who come from the lake).
How fares the king now ?

Second Esquire. Refreshed by 's bath.

First Esquire. The balsam soothes the smart.

Gurnemanz
(after some silence).
That wound it is which none may make to close.

---

sie schlafend hier im Waldgestrüpp',
  erstarrt, leblos, wie todt.
So fand ich selbst sie letztlich wieder,
als uns das Unheil kaum gescheh'n,
das jener Böse dort über'm Berge
So schmählich über uns gebracht. —
(Zu KUNDRY.)
He ! Du ! — Hör' mich, und sag' :
wo schweiftest damals du umher,
als unser Herr den Speer verlor ? —
(KUNDRY schweigt.)
Warum halfst du uns damals nicht ?

Kundry. Ich helfe nie.

Vierter Knappe. Sie sagt's da selbst.

Dritter Knappe. Ist sie so treu und kühn in
  Wehr,
  so sende sie nach dem verlor'nen Speer !

Gurnemanz
(düster).
Das ist ein And'res : —
jedem ist's verwehrt. —
(Mit grosser Ergriffenheit.)
Oh, wunden-wundervoller
  heiliger Speer !
Dich sah ich schwingen
von unheiligster Hand ! —
(In Erinnerung sich verlierend.)
Mit ihm bewehrt, Amfortas, allzukühner,
  wer mochte dir es wehren
  den Zaub'rer zu beheeren ? —
Schon nah' dem Schloss, wird uns der Held
  entrückt :
ein furchtbar schönes Weib hat ihn entzückt :
  in seinen Armen liegt er trunken,
  der Speer ist ihm entsunken ; —
  ein Todesschrei ! — ich stürm' herbei : —
  von dannen Klingsor lachend schwand,
  den heil'gen Speer hat er entwandt.
Des Königs Flucht gab kämpfend ich Geleite
doch eine Wunde brannt' ihm in der Seite :
die Wunde ist's, die nie sich schliessen will.

Dritter Knappe. So kanntest du Klingsor ?

Gurnemanz
(zu dem ersten und zweiten KNAPPEN, welche vom See her kommen)
Wie geht's dem König ?

Zweiter Knappe. Ihn frischt das Bad.

Erster Knappe. Dem Balsam wich der Schmerz.

Gurnemanz
(nach einem Schweigen).
Die Wunde ist's, die nie sich schliessen will ! —

Third Esquire. But look ye now, father, I'd like
    to know :—
    Thou knewest Klingsor : how was that so ?

(The third and fourth ESQUIRES have now seated themselves at GURNEMANZ' feet ; the other two do likewise.)

Gurnemanz. Titurel, the pious lord,
      He knew him well ;
For, when the savage foe with craft and might
    The true believers' kingdom rended,
Anon to him, in midst of holy night
    The Saviour's messengers descended.
The sacred Cup, the vessel pure, unstainéd,
Which at the Last Passover Feast He drainéd, — **I**
Which at the Cross received His holy blood,
With eke the Spear that shed the sacred flood, — **5**
These signs and tokens of a worth untold
The angels gave into our monarch's hold.
A house he builded for the holy things.
    Ye, who their service have attained to
    By paths no sinners ever gained to,
    Ye know 'tis but permitted
    The pure to be admitted
'Mid those the Grail's divinely magic power
With strength for high salvation's work doth
    dower.
He whom you named had therefore been denied:—
Klingsor — however long and hard he tried.
Far in yon valley then he found asylum ;
For over there 'tis rankest Pagan land.
I ne'er found out what sin he had committed ;
Absolved he now would be, yea, holy even.
Unable in himself to stifle thoughts of evil,
    He set to work with guilty hand,
    Resolved to gain the Grail's command ;
But with contempt was by its guardian spurned.
Wherefore in rage hath Klingsor surely learn'd
    How by the damnable act he wrought
    An infamous magic might be taught ;
    Which now he's found : —
The waste he hath transformed to wondrous
    gardens
Where women bide, of charms infernal ;
Thither he seeks to draw the Grail's true wardens
    To wicked joys and pain eternal.
    Those who are lured find him their master :
    To many happens such disaster. —
When Titurel decayed in manhood's power
And with the regal might his son did dower
    Amfortas gave himself no rest,
    But sought to quell this magic pest ;
    The sequel ye have all been told ;
    The spear is now in Klingsor's hold.
Even the holy it can cleave asunder :
The Grail already he counts as his plunder.

(During the above, KUNDRY has several times turned round quickly in angry unrest.)

Dritter Knappe. Doch, Väterchen, sag' und
    lehr' uns fein :
    du kanntest Klingsor, — wie mag das sein ?

(Der dritte und der vierte KNAPPE hatten sich zuletzt schon zu GURNEMANZ' Füssen niedergesetzt ; die beiden anderen gesellen sich jetzt gleicher Weise zu ihnen.)

Gurnemanz. Titurel, der fromme Held,
      der kannt' ihn wohl.
Denn ihm, da wilder Feinde List und Macht
    des reinen Glauben's Reich bedrohten,
ihm neigten sich in heilig ernster Nacht
    dereinst des Heiland's sel'ge Boten :
    daraus er trank beim letzten Liebesmahle,
das Weihgefäss, die heilig edle Schale,
    darein am Kreuz sein göttlich Blut auch floss,
zugleich den Lanzenspeer, der diess vergoss,—
    der Zeugengüter höchstes Wundergut, —
    das gaben sie in uns'res König's Hut.
Dem Heilthum baute er das Heiligthum.
    Die seinem Dienst ihr zugesindet
    auf Pfaden, die kein Sünder findet,
    ihr wisst, dass nur dem Reinen
    vergönnt ist sich zu einen
den Brüdern, die zu höchsten Rettungswerken
des Grales heil'ge Wunderkräfte stärken :
d'rum blieb es dem, nach dem ihr fragt, verwehrt,
Klingsor'n, so hart ihm Müh' auch drob be-
    schwert.
11 Jenseits im Thale war er eingesiedelt ;
    darüber hin liegt üpp'ges Heidenland :
unkund blieb mir, was dorten er gesündigt ;
doch büssen wollt' er nun, ja heilig werden.
Ohnmächtig, in sich selbst die Sünde zu ertödten,
    an sich legt er die Frevlerhand,
    die nun, dem Grale zugewandt,
verachtungsvoll dess' Hüter von sich stiess ;
darob die Wuth nun Klingsor'n unterwies,
    wie seines schmählichen Opfers That
    ihm gäbe zu bösem Zauber Rath ;
    den fand er jetzt : —
die Wüste schuf er sich zum Wonnegarten
    d'rinn wachsen teuflisch holde Frauen ;
dort will des Grales Ritter er erwarten
    zu böser Lust und Höllengrauen :
    wen er verlockt, hat er erworben ;
    schon Viele hat er uns verdorben. —
Da Titurel, in hohen Alter's Mühen,
    dem Sohne nun die Herrschaft hier verliehen,
    Amfortas' liess es da nicht ruh'n
    der Zauberplag' Einhalt zu thun ;
    das wisst ihr, wie es da sich fand :
    der Speer ist nun in Klingsor's Hand ;
kann er selbst Heilige mit dem verwunden.
den Gral auch wähnt er fest schon uns entwun-
    den.

(KUNDRY hat sich, in wüthender Unruhe, oft heftig umgewendet)

Fourth Esquire. Behoves us then that spear
soon to reclaim.

Third Esquire. Ha! he who could would get
both joy and fame.

Gurnemanz
(after a silence).
Before the plundered sanctuary
In pray'r impassioned knelt Amfortas,
Imploring for a sign of safety:
A heav'nly radiance from the Grail then floated;
A sacred phantom face
From lips divine did chase
These words, whose purport clearly could be
noted:—
"By pity 'lightened
A guileless Fool;—
Wait for him
My chosen tool."
(The four ESQUIRES with deep awe repeat the oracular words.)
From the lake come cries and exclamations of the

Knights and Esquires. Woe! Horror!—Hoho!
Up! Who is the culprit?

GURNEMANZ and the four ESQUIRES start up and turn round in
alarm. A wild swan flutters feebly from over the lake, strives to
keep up, and finally sinks dying to the ground. Meanwhile:—

Gurnemanz. What is 't?

First Esquire. There!

Second Esquire. Here—a swan!

Third Esquire. A poor wild swan!

Fourth Esquire. It hath been wounded.

Other Esquires
(rushing on from the lake).
Ha! Horror! Woe!

Gurnemanz. Who shot the swan?

Second Knight
(advancing).
The king esteemed it a happy token,
When over the lake it circled aloft:
Then flew a dart,—

More Esquires
(bringing forward PARSIFAL).
He 'twas! He shot! Here's the weapon.
See this arrow, like his own.

Gurnemanz
(to PARSIFAL).
Is't thou, that dealt this swan its death blow?

Parsifal. For sure; in flight I hit all that flies.

Gurnemanz. This thou hast done? And hast
no sorrow for thy deed?

8

12

Vierter Knappe. Vor Allem nun: der Speer
kehr' uns zurück!

Dritter Knappe. Ha! wer ihn brächt', ihm wär's
zu Ruhm und Glück!

Gurnemanz
(nach einem Schweigen).
Vor dem verwaisten Heiligthum
in brünst'gem Beten lag Amfortas,
ein Rettungszeichen heiss erflehend:
ein sel'ger Schimmer da entfloss dem Grale;
ein heilig' Traumgesicht
nun deutlich zu ihm spricht
durch hell erschauter Wortezeichen Male:—
„durch Mitleid wissend
der reine Thor,
harre sein',
den ich erkor."
(Die vier KNAPPEN wiederholen, in grosser Ergriffenheit, den Spruch)
Vom See her hört man Geschrei und das Rufen der

Ritter und Knappen. Weh'! Wehe!—Hoho!
Auf!—Wer ist der Frevler?

GURNEMANZ und die vier KNAPPEN fahren auf und wenden sich
erschrocken um. — Ein wilder Schwan flattert matten Fluges vom
See daher; er ist verwundet, erhält sich mühsam und sinkt endlich
sterbend zu Boden. — Während dem:

Gurnemanz. Was giebt's?

Erster Knappe. Dort!

Zweiter Knappe. Hier! Ein Schwan.

Dritter Knappe. Ein wilder Schwan!

Vierter Knappe. Er ist verwundet.

Andere Knappen
(vom Se her stürmend).
Ha! Wehe! Weh'!

Gurnemanz. Wer schos den Schwan?

Der zweite Ritter
(hervorkom end).
Der König grüsst' ihn als gutes Zeichen,
als über dem See dort kreis'te der Schwan:
da flog ein Pfeil—

Neue Knappen
(PARSIFAL vorführend).
Der war's! Der schoss! Diess der Bogen!
Hier der Pfeil, den seinen gleich.

Gurnemanz
(zu PARSIFAL).
Bist du's, der diesen Schwan erlegte?

Parsifal. Gewiss! Im Fluge treff' ich was

Gurnemanz. Du thatest das? Und bangt' es
dich nicht vor der That?

The Esquires.   Punish the culprit!

Gurnemanz.   Unconceived of fact!
Couldst thou do murder?   Here in holy forests,
  Whose quiet peace o'erspreads thy path?
The beasts around, didst thou not find them tame?
    Were they not friendly and fond?
    From the branches what warbled the birds to
      thee?
      How harmed thee that goodly swan?
    To look for his mate he flew aloft,
    With her to hover over the lake,
Thus consecrating for us the health-giving bath.
  Thou didst not revere, but lusted for
  A wild puerile shot of the bow.
  He was our joy: what is he to thee?
  Here — behold! — thy arrow struck; —
There stiffens his blood;   hang pow'rless the
      pinions,
  The snowy plumage darkly besplashed, —
  Extinguished his eye; — mark'st thou its look?
  Art thou now conscious of thy trespass?

(PARSIFAL has listened to his words with increasing attention; he now breaks his bow and casts his arrows away.)

Say, boy?   Perceivest thou thy heinous sin?

(PARSIFAL draws his hand across his eyes.)

How couldst thou have acted thus?

Parsifal.   I knew not 'twas wrong

Gurnemanz.   Whence comest th u?

Parsifal.   I do not know.

Gurnemanz.   Who is thy father?

Parsifal.   I do not know.

Gurnemanz.   Who bade thee wander this way?

Parsifal.   I know not.

Gurnemanz.   Thy name then?

Parsifal.   I once had nany,
But now I know not one of them.

Gurnemanz.   Thou know'st not anything?

(aside).
                              A dolt so dull
I never found, save Kundry here.

(to the ESQUIRES who have assembled in still greater numbers).
                              Now go
Nor leave the king in his bath alone! — Help.

(The ESQUIRES lift up the swan reverently and bear it away towards the lake.)

Gurnemanz
                (turning again to PARSIFAL).
Now say!   Nought know'st of all I have asked
      thee;
  Declare then what thou know'st:
  Of something must thou have knowledge.

Die Knappen.   Strafe den Frevler!

Gurnemanz.   Unerhörtes Werk!
Du konntest morden?   Hier im heil'gen Walde,
  dess' stiller Frieden dich umfing?
Des Haines Thiere nahten dir nicht zahm,
    grüssten dich freundlich und fromm?
    Aus den Zweigen, was sangen die Vöglein **dir?**
    Was that dir der treue Schwan?
    Sein Weibchen zu suchen flog der auf,
    mit ihm zu kreisen über dem See,
den so er herrlich weih'te zum heilenden Bad.
  dem stauntest du nicht, dich lockt' es nur
  zu wild kindischem Bogengeschoss? —
  Er war uns hold: was ist er nun dir?
  Hier — schau' her! — hier traf'st du ihn:
da starrt noch das Blut, matt hängen die Flügel;
  das Schneegefieder dunkel befleckt, —
  gebrochen das Aug', siehst du den Blick?
  Wirst deiner Sündenthat du inne? —

(PARSIFAL hat ihm mit wachsender Ergriffenheit zugehört: jetzt zerbricht er seinen Bogen und schleudert die Pfeile von sich.)

Sag', Knab'!   Erkennst du deine grosse Schuld!

(PARSIFAL führt die Hand über die Augen.)

Wie konntest du sie begeh'n?

Parsifal.   Ich wusste sie nicht.

Gurnemanz.   Wo bist du her?

Parsifal.   Das weiss ich nicht.

Gurnemanz.   Wer ist dein Vater?

Parsifal.   Das weiss ich nicht.

Gurnemanz.   Wer sandte dich dieses Weg's?

Parsifal.   Ich weiss nicht.

Gurnemanz.   Dein Name dann?

Parsifal.   Ich hatte viele
  doch weiss ich ihrer keinen mehr.

Gurnemanz.   Das weisst du Alles nicht?

(Für sich :)
                              So dumm wie den
erfand ich bisher Kundry nur. —

(Zu den KNAPPEN, deren sich immer mehre versammelt haben.)
                              Jetzt geht!
Versäumt den König im Bade nicht! — Helft!

(Die KNAPPEN haben den Schwan ehrerbietig aufgenommen, und entfernen sich mit ihm jetzt nach dem See zu.)

Gurnemanz
                (sich wieder zu PARSIFAL wendend).
Nun sag'!   Nichts weisst du, was ich dich frage
  jetzt melde, was du weisst!
  denn etwas musst du doch wissen.

13

Parsifal. I have a mother; Heart's Affliction 13
    she's hight:
The woods and the waste of moorlands were
    our abode.

Gurnemanz. Who gave thee that weapon?

Parsifal. I made it myself,
    To drive the savage eagles from the forest.

Gurnemanz. But eagle-like seem'st thyself, and
    well descended:
    Why did thy mother not teach thee
    Manlier weapons to handle?
         (PARSIFAL remains silent.)

Kundry
(who, still crouching by the wood, has glanced sharply at PARSIFAL,
now breaks in with hoarse tones).

  Bereft of father his mother bore him,
  For in battle perished Gamuret:
  From like untimely hero's death
  To save her offspring, strange to arms
  She reared him a witless fool in deserts.—
    What folly!
        (She laughs.)

Parsifal
    (who has listened with sharp attention).
Aye, and once along the hem of the wood,
  Most noble beasts bestriding,
  Passed by men all a-glitter;
  Fain had I been like them;
  With laughter they galloped away.
Now I pursue; but cannot as yet o'ertake them;
  Through deserts I've wandered, o'er hill and
    dale;
  Oft fell the night, then followed day:
  My bow was forced to defend me
  'Gainst the wolves and mighty peoples.

Kundry
    (warmly).
Yes, caitiffs and giants fell to his might;
The fierce-striking boy brings fear on their
    spirits.

Parsifal. Who feareth me, say?

Kundry. The wicked.

Parsifal. Those who attacked me, were they
    then bad?
       (GURNEMANZ laughs)
Who is good?

Gurnemanz
    (earnestly).
    Thy dear mother, whom thou forsookest,
And who for thee must now mourn and grieve.

Kundry. She grieves no more; for his mother is
    dead.

Parsifal. Ich hab' eine Mutter; Herzeleide sie
    heisst:
  im Wald und auf wilder Aue waren wir heim.

Gurnemanz. Wer gab dir den Bogen?

Parsifal. Den schuf ich mir selbst,
  vom Forst die rauhen Adler zu scheuchen.

Gurnemanz. Doch adelig scheinst du selbst und
    hochgeboren:
  warum nicht liess deine Mutter
  bessere Waffen dich lehren?
      (PARSIFAL schweigt.)

Kundry
(Welche, in der Waldecke gelagert, den Blick scharf auf PARSIFAL
gerichtet hat, ruft mit rauher Stimme hinein).

  Den Vaterlosen gebar die Mutter,
  als im Kampf erschlagen Gamuret;
  vor gleichem frühen Heldentod
  den Sohn zu wahren, waffenfremd
  in Oeden erzog sie ihn zum Thoren —
    die Thörin!
      (Sie lacht)

Parsifal
    (der mit jäher Aufmerksamkeit zugehört).
Ja! Und einst am Waldessaume vorbei,
  auf schönen Thieren sitzend,
  kamen glänzende Männer:
  ihnen wollt' ich gleichen;
  sie lachten und jagten davon.
Nun lief ich nach, doch konnte sie nicht erreichen;
  durch Wildnisse kam ich, bergauf, thalab;
  oft ward es Nacht; dann wieder Tag:
  mein Bogen musste mir frommen
  gegen Wild und grosse Männer.

Kundry
    (eifrig).
  Ja, Schächer und Riesen traf seine Kraft
  den freislichen Knaben fürchten sie Alle.

Parsifal. Wer fürchtet mich? Sag'!

Kundry. Die Bösen.

Parsifal. Die mich bedrohten, waren sie bös'?
      (GURNEMANZ lacht.)
Wer ist gut?

Gurnemanz
    (ernst).
    Deine Mutter, der du entlaufen,
und die um dich sich nun härmt und grämt.

Kundry. Zu End' ihr Gram: seine Mutter ist
    todt.

Parsifal
(in feartul alarm).

Dead? — what, my mother? —- who says so?

Kundry.   I rode along and saw her dying;
Poor fool, she sent thee her blessing.

(PARSIFAL springs upon KUNDRY, raging, and seizes her by the
throat.)

Gurnemanz
(holding him back).

Insensate stripling! Outrage again?—
What harm has she done? She speaks the truth.
For Kundry lies not, and much has seen.

(After GURNEMANZ has released KUNDRY, PARSIFAL stands awhile
as if turned to stone; then he is seized with a violent trembling.)

Parsifal.   I — am fainting!
(KUNDRY has hastily sprung to a brook, brings water now in a horn,
sprinkles PARSIFAL with some, and then gives him to drink.)

Gurnemanz.   'Tis well! Thus has the Grail
directed :
He ousteth ill who doth give for it good.

Kundry
(sadly turning away).

I do no good thing; — but rest I long for.

(Whilst GURNEMANZ is attending to PARSIFAL with fatherly care,
KUNDRY, unperceived by them, crawls towards a thicket.)

But rest, but rest! Alas, I'm weary!—
Slumber!—Oh, would that none might wake me!
(starting timidly).

No! I'll sleep not! — Terror grips me.

(She gives a suppressed cry and falls into a violent trembling; then
she lets her arms drop powerless, and her head sinks low, and staggers
a little farther.)

Vain to resist! The time has come.
Slumber — slumber —: I must.

(She sinks down behind the thicket and is seen no more. A stir is
perceived down by the lake, and the train of KNIGHTS and ESQUIRES
with the litter passes back homewards at back.)

Gurnemanz.   From bathing comes the king again;
High stands the sun now:
Let me to the holy Feast then conduct thee;
For — an thou'rt pure,
Surely the Grail will feed and refresh thee.

(He has gently laid PARSIFAL's arm on his own neck, and, supporting his body with his arm, leads him slowly along.)

Parsifal.   What is the Grail?

Gurnemanz   I may not say:
But if to serve it thou be bidden,
Knowledge of it will not be hidden. —
And lo! —
Methinks I know thee now indeed:
No earthly road to it doth lead,
By no one can it be detected
Who by itself is not elected.

Parsifal
(in furchtbarem Schrecken).

Todt? — Meine Mutter? — Wer sagt' es?

Kundry.   Ich ritt vorbei, und sah sie sterben:
dich Thoren hiess sie mich grüssen.

(PARSIFAL springt wüthend auf KUNDRY zu und fasst sie bei der
Kehle.)

Gurnemanz
(ihn zurückhaltend).

Verrückter Knabe! Wieder Gewalt?
Was that dir das Weib? Es sagte wahr.
Denn nie lügt Kundry, doch sah sie viel.

(Nachdem GURNEMANZ KUNDRY befreit, steht PARSIFAL lange wie
erstarrt; dann geräth er in ein heftiges Zittern.)

Parsifal.   Ich — verschmachte!—
(KUNDRY ist hastig an einen Waldquell gesprungen, bringt jetzt
Wasser in einem Horne, besprengt damit zunächst PARSIFAL, und
reicht ihm dann zu trinken.)

Gurnemanz.   So recht! So nach des Grales
Gnade :
das Böse bannt, wer's mit Gutem vergilt.

Kundry
(traurig sich abwendend).

Nie thu' ich Gutes; — nur Ruhe will ich.

(Während GURNEMANZ sich väterlich um PARSIFAL bemüht, schleppt
sich KUNDRY, von Beiden unbeachtet, einem Waldgebüsche zu.)

Nur Ruhe! Ruhe, ach, der Müden! —
Schlafen!—Oh, dass mich keiner wecke!
(Scheu auffahrend).

Nein! Nicht schlafen!—Grausen fasst mich!

(Nach einem dumpfen Schrei verfällt sie in heftiges Zittern; dann
lässt sie die Arme matt sinken, neigt das Haupt tief, und schwankt matt
weiter.)

Machtlose Wehr! Die Zeit ist da.
Schlafen — schlafen —: ich muss.

(Sie sinkt hinter dem Gebüsch zusammen, und bleibt von jetzt an
unbemerkt. — Vom See her vernimmt man Bewegung, und gewahrt den
im Hintergrunde sich heimwärts wendenden Zug der RITTER und
KNAPPEN mit der Sänfte.)

Gurnemanz.   Vom Bade kehrt der König heim;
hoch steht die Sonne:
nun lass' mich zum frommen Mahl dich geleiten
denn, — bist du rein,
wird nun der Gral dich tränken und speisen.

(Er hat PARSIFAL's Arm sich sanft um den Nacken gelegt, und hält
dessen Leib mit seinem eigenen Arme umschlungen; so geleitet er ihn
bei sehr allmählichem Schreiten.)

Parsifal.   Wer ist der Gral?

Gurnemanz.   Das sagt sich nicht;
doch bist du selbst zu ihm erkoren,
bleibt dir die Kunde unverloren. —
Und sieh'! —
Mich dünkt, dass ich dich recht erkannt:
kein Weg führt zu ihm durch das Land,
und Niemand könnte ihn beschreiten,
den er nicht selber möcht' geleiten.

Parsifal. I scarcely move,—
    Yet swiftly seem to run.

Gurnemanz. My son, thou seest
    Here Space and Time are one.

Gradually, while PARSIFAL and GURNEMANZ appear to walk, the **14**
scene changes imperceptibly from L. to R. The forest disappears; a **15**
door opens in rocky cliffs and conceals the two ; they are then seen
again in sloping passages which they appear to ascend. — Long
sustained trombone notes softly swell, approaching peals of bells are
heard. — At last they arrive at a mighty hall, which loses itself over-
head in a high vaulted dome down from which alone the light streams
in. — From the heights above the dome the increasing sound of chimes.

Gurnemanz

(turning to PARSIFAL who stands spellbound).

Now give good heed, and let me see,
    If thou'rt a Fool and pure,
What wisdom thou presently canst secure.—

At each side in the background a large door opens. From the R. **2**
enter slowly the KNIGHTS of the GRAIL in solemn procession, and
range themselves, during the following chorus, by degrees at two long **14**
covered tables which are placed endways towards the audience, one on
each side, leaving the middle of the stage free. Only cups—no dishes
—stand on them.

The Knights of the Grail. The Holy Supper duly
    Prepare we day by day,
    As on that last time truly
    The soul it still may stay.
    Who lives to do good deeds
    This Meal for ever feeds ;
    The Cup his hand may lift
    And claim the purest gift.

Voices of younger Men

(coming from the mid-height of the hall).

    As anguished and lowly
    His life stream's spilling
For sinners He did offer,
    For the Saviour holy
    With heart free and willing
My blood I now will proffer.
His body, given our sins to shrive,
Through death becomes in us alive.

Boys' voices

(from the summit of the dome).

    His love endures,
    The dove upsoars,
The Saviour's sacred token.
    Take the wine red,
    For you 'twas shed ;
Let Bread of Life be broken.

Through the opposite door AMFORTAS is brought in on his litter
by ESQUIRES and serving brethren : before him march boys who bear a
shrine draped in purple-red cloth. This procession wends to the
center of the background, where, overhung by a canopy stands a raised
couch. On this AMFORTAS is placed ; before it stands an altar-like,
longish marble table, on which the boys place the shrine, still covered. —
    When the song is ended and the KNIGHTS have all taken their
seats there is a long pause and silence. — From the distant back is
heard, from an arched niche behind AMFORTAS' throne, as from a
grave, the voice of old

Parsifal. Ich schreite kaum,—
    doch wähn' ich mich schon weit.

Gurnemanz. Du siehst, mein Sohn,
    zum Raum wird hier die Zeit.

Allmählich, während GURNEMANZ und PARSIFAL zu schreiten
scheinen, verwandelt sich die Bühne, von links nach rechts hin, in
unmerklicher Weise : es verschwindet so der Wald ; in Felsenwänden
öffnet sich ein Thor, welches nun die Beiden einschliesst ; dann
wieder werden sie in aufsteigenden Gängen sichtbar, welche sie zu
durchschreiten scheinen. — Lang gehaltene Posaunentöne schwellen
sanft an : näher kommendes Glockengeläute. — Endlich sind sie in einem
mächtigen Saale angekommen, welcher nach oben in eine hochgewölbte
Kuppel, durch die einzig das Licht hereindringt sich verliert. — Von der
Höhe über der Kuppel her vernimmt man wachsendes Geläute.

Gurnemanz

(sich zu PARSIFAL wendend, der wie verzaubert steht).

Jetzt achte wohl ; und lass' mich seh'n,
    bist du ein Thor und rein,
welch Wissen dir auch mag beschieden sein. —

Auf beiden Seiten des Hintergrundes wird je eine grosse Thür
geöffnet. Von rechts schreiten die RITTER des GRALES, in feierlichem Zuge, herein, und reihen sich, unter dem folgenden Gesange,
nach und nach an zwei überdeckten langen Speisetafeln, welche so
gestellt sind, dass sie, von hinten nach vorn parallel laufend, die Mitte
des Saale frei lassen : nur Becher, keine Gerichte stehen darauf.

Die Gralsritter. Zum letzten Liebesmahle
    gerüstet Tag für Tag,
    gleich ob zum letzten Male
    es heut' ihn letzen mag,
    wer guter That sich freu't,
    ihm sei das Mahl erneu't :
    der Labung darf er nah'n,
    die hehrste Gab' empfah'n.

Jüngere Männerstimmen

(von der mittleren Höhe des Saales her vernehmbar).

    Den sündigen Welten
    mit tausend Schmerzen
wie einst sein Blut geflossen,
    dem Erlösungs-Helden
    mit freudigem Herzen
    sei nun mein Blut vergossen.
Den Leib, den er zur Sühn' uns bot,
er leb' in uns durch seinen Tod.

Knabenstimmen

(aus der äussersten Höhe der Kuppel).

    Der Glaube lebt ;
    Die Taube schwebt,
    des Heiland's holder Bote.
    Der für euch fliesst,
    des Wein's geniesst,
    und nehmt vom Lebensbrode !

Durch die entgegengesetzte Thüre wird von KNAPPEN und die-
nenden Brüdern auf einer Tragsänfte AMFORTAS hereingetragen : vor
ihm schreiten KNABEN, welche einen mit einer purpurrothen Decke
überhängten Schrein tragen. Dieser Zug begiebt sich nach der Mitte
des Hintergrundes, wo, von einem Baldachin überdeckt, ein erhöhetes
Ruhebett aufgerichtet steht, auf welches AMFORTAS von der Sänfte
herab niedergelassen wird ; hiervor steht ein Altar-ähnlicher länglicher
Marmortisch, auf welchen die KNABEN den verhängten Schrein
hinstellen. —
    Als der Gesang beendet ist, und alle RITTER an den Tafeln ihre
Sitze eingenommen haben, tritt ein längeres Stillschweigen ein. — Vom
tiefsten Hintergrunde her vernimmt man, aus einer gewölbten Nische
hinter dem Ruhebette des AMFORTAS, wie aus einem Grabe die Stimme
des alten

The marginal numbers 15 and 3 appear in the center gutter.

Titurel. My son Amfortas ! Art at thy post?
(Silence.)

Shall I again look on the Grail and quicken?
(Silence.)

Must I perish, unguided by my Saver?

Amfortas
(in an outburst of painful desperation).

> Woe's me ! Woe, alas, the pain ! —
> My father, oh, once again
> Assume the office thou !
> Live on ! Live and let me perish.

Titurel. Entombed I live still, by the Grace of
> God ;
> Too feeble am I now to serve Him :
> In works for Him thy guilt efface !—
> Uncover the Grail!

Amfortas
(restraining the boys).

No ! Leave it unrevealed ! — Oh ! —
May no one, no one know the anguish dire
Awaked in me by that which raptures ye !—
What is the wound and all its torture wild,
'Gainst the distress, the pangs of hell,
In this high post — accurst to dwell ! —
Woeful inheritance on me presséd,
I, only sinner 'mid the blesséd,
The holy house to guard for others
And pray for blessings upon my purer brothers !—
Oh, chast'ning — chast'ning dire ! descended
From — ah ! the Almighty One offended.
For grace and for compassion yearning
> My panting heart is riven;
In deepest soul's repentance burning
> By Him to be forgiven.
> The hour is nigh —
The ray descends upon the vessel divine ;—
> The veil is raised,
The sacred stream that in the crystal flows
> With strength and radiant lustre glows ; —
By this delight but filled with anguish sore,
> The heavenly fount of blood
Into my heart I feel to pour ;
My own life current's iniquitous flood
> In delirious flight
Backward within me rushes :
Toward the world where sin has might
With wildest dread it gushes. —
> Again it forces the door
> From which now the stream doth pour,
Here through the wound, — like His 'tis here,
Inflicted by a stroke of that same spear. —

Titurel. Mein Sohn Amfortas? Bist du am Amt?
(Schweigen.)

Soll ich den Gral heut' noch erschau'n und leben ?
(Schweigen.)

Muss ich sterben, vom Retter ungeleitet !

Amfortas
(im Ausbruche qualvoller Verzweifelung)

> Wehe ! Wehe mir der Qual ! —
> Mein Vater, oh ! noch einmal
> verrichte du das Amt !
> Lebe ! Leb' und lass' mich sterben !

Titurel. Im Grabe leb' ich durch des Heiland's
> Huld ;
> zu schwach doch bin ich, ihm zu
> dienen :
> du büss' im Dienste deine Schuld !—
> Enthüllet den Gral !

Amfortas
(den Knaben wehrend).

Nein ! Lasst ihn unenthüllt !— Oh ! —
Dass Keiner, Keiner diese Qual ermisst,
die mir der Anblick weckt, der euch entzückt ! —
Was ist die Wunde, ihrer Schmerzen Wuth,
gegen die Noth, die Höllenpein,
zu diesem Amt — verdammt zu sein ! —
Wehvolles Erbe, dem ich verfallen,
ich, einziger Sünder unter Allen,
des höchsten Heiligthum's zu pflegen,
auf Reine herabzuflehen seinen Segen !—
Oh, Strafe ! Strafe ohne Gleichen
des — ach !— gekränkten Gnadenreichen ! —
Nach Ihm, nach Seinem Weihegrusse
> muss sehnlich mich's verlangen ;
aus tiefster Seele Heilesbusse
> zu Ihm muss ich gelangen : —
> die Stunde naht : —
der Lichtstrahl senkt sich auf das
> heilige Werk ;
> die Hülle sinkt :
des Weihgefässes göttlicher Gehalt
> erglüht mit leuchtender Gewalt ; —
durchzückt von seligsten Genusses
> Schmerz,
> des heiligsten Blutes Quell
fühl' ich sich giessen in mein Herz :
des eig'nen sündigen Blutes Gewell
> in wahnsinniger Flucht
> muss mir zurück dann fliessen.
> in die Welt der Sündenzucht
> mit wilder Scheu sich ergiessen : —
> von Neuem sprengt er das Thor,
> daraus es nun strömt hervor,
hier durch die Wunde, der Seinen gleich,
geschlagen von desselben Speeres Streich

As in our Redeemer, the selfsame place,
  From which with tears of blood burning
The Son of Man wept over man's disgrace
  With sacred pity yearning;
And from which in me, in this sacred mountain,
  While holding high gifts beyond measure,
  — Our redemption's healing treasure —
The hot and sinful blood doth surge,
Ever renewed from my yearnings' fountain,
Which no expiation yet can purge.
       Have mercy! Have mercy!
God of pity, oh! have mercy!
     Take all I cherish,
     Give me but healing,
     That pure I may perish,
     Holiness feeling.
       (He sinks back as if unconscious.)

Boys' voices
       (from the dome).
    " By pity 'lightened,
    The guileless Fool —
    Wait for him,
    My chosen tool."

Knights
       (softly).
   Thus came to thee the fiat.
    Wait on in hope : —
   Fulfil thy duty now !

Titurel's
       (voice).
   Uncover the Grail!

AMFORTAS has again raised himself in silence. The boys uncover the golden shrine, take out of it the "Grail" (an antique
crystal cup) from which they also take a covering and set it before
AMFORTAS.

Titurel's
       (voice).
   The Blessing !

While AMFORTAS devoutly bows himself in silent prayer before
the cup, an increasing gloom spreads in the room.

Boys
       (from the dome).
  " Take and drink my blood ;
  Thus be our love remembered !
  Take my body and eat :
  Do this and think of me ! "

A blinding ray of light shoots down from above upon the cup,
which glows with increasing purple lustre. AMFORTAS, with brightened mien, raises the "Grail" aloft and waves it gently about on all
sides. Since the coming of the dusk all have sunk upon their knees,
and now cast their eyes reverently towards the "Grail"

Titurel's
       (voice).
   Celestial rapture !
How light now the looks of the Lord !

---

15 der dort dem Erlöser die Wunde stach,
  aus der mit blutigen Thränen
der Göttliche weint' ob der Menschheit Schmach
  in Mitleid's heiligem Sehnen, —
und aus der nun mir, an heiligster Stelle,
  dem Pfleger göttlichster Güter,
  des Erlösungsbalsam's Hüter,
das heisse Sündenblut entquillt,
ewig erneu't aus des Sehnen's Quelle,
das, ach! keine Büssung je mir stillt!
       Erbarmen! Erbarmen!
Allerbarmer, ach! Erbarmen!
     Nimm mir mein Erbe,
     schliesse die Wunde,
     dass heilig ich sterbe,
     rein Dir gesunde!
       (Er sinkt wie bewusstlos zurück.)

Knabenstimmen
       (aus der Kuppel).
8 ,, Durch Mitleid wissend,
    der reine Thor :
    harre sein',
    den ich erkor."

Die Ritter
       (leise)
   So ward es dir verkündet,
    Harre getrost;
    des Amtes walte heut' !

Titurel's
       (Stimme).
   Enthüllet den Gral !

AMFORTAS hat sich schweigend wieder erhoben. Die KNABEN
entkleiden den goldenen Schrein, entnehmen ihm den ,, Gral" (eine
antike Krystallschale), von welchem sie ebenfalls eine Verhüllung
abnehmen, und setzen ihn vor AMFORTAS hin.

Titurel's
       (Stimme).
   Der Segen !

Während AMFORTAS andachtsvoll in stummem Gebete sich zu dem
Kelche neigt, verbreitet sich eine immer dichtere Dämmerung in
Saale.

Knaben
       (aus der Kuppel).
I ,, Nehmet hin mein Blut
  um uns'rer Liebe Willen !
  Nehmet hin meinen Leib
  auf dass ihr mein' gedenkt.

Ein blendender Lichtstrahl dringt von oben auf die Schale herab
diese erglüht immer stärker in leuchtender Purpurfarbe. AMFORTAS,
mit verklärter Miene, erhebt den ,, Gral" hoch und schwenkt ihn
sanft nach allen Seiten hin. Alles ist bereits bei dem Eintritte der
Dämmerung auf die Knie gesunken, und erhebt jetzt die Blicke
andächtig zum ,,Grale."

Titurel's
       (Stimme.)
   Oh! Heilige Wonne !
Wie hell grüsst uns heute der Herr !

AMFORTAS sets down the " Grail " again, which now, while the deep gloom wanes, grows paler ; the boys cover it as before and return it to the shrine. — As the original light returns to the hall the cups on the table are seen to be filled with wine, and by each is a piece of bread. All sit down to the repast, including GURNEMANZ, who keeps a place by him for PARSIFAL whom he invites with a sign to come and partake. PARSIFAL, however, remains silent and motionless at the side, as if quite dumbfounded.

(Alternative, during the Supper.)

Boys' voices
(from the height).

Wine and Bread the Grail's Lord changéd
Which at that Last Meal were rangéd,
Through His pity's loving tide
When He shed for you His gore
And His Body crucified.

Youths' voices
(from the middle height).

Blood and Body which he offered
Changed to food for you are proffered
By the Saviour ye revere
In the Wine which now ye pour
And the Bread ye eat of here.

The Knights
first half).

Take of this Bread,
Change it again,
Your pow'rs of body firing ;
Living and dead
Strive amain
To work out the Lord's desiring.

(second half).

Take of this Wine,
Change it anew
To life's impetuous torrent ;
Gladly combine,
Brothers true,
To fight as duty shall warrant.

(They rise solemnly and all join hands.)

All the Knights.   Blesséd Believing !
Blesséd in Loving !

Youths
(from the mid height).
Blesséd in Loving !

Boys
(from the utmost height).
Blesséd Believing !

During the repast AMFORTAS, who has not partaken, has gradually relapsed from his state of exaltation : he bows his head and presses his hand to the wound. The pages approach him ; his wound has burst out afresh ; they tend him and assist him to his litter ; then, while all prepare to break up, they bear off AMFORTAS and the shrine in the order in which they came. The KNIGHTS and ESQUIRES fall in and slowly leave the hall in solemn procession, whilst the daylight gradually wanes. The bells are heard pealing again. —
PARSIFAL, on hearing AMFORTAS' cry of agony, has clutched his heart and remained in that position for some time ; he now stands as if petrified, motionless. When the last knight has left the hall and the doors are again closed, GURNEMANZ in ill humour comes up to PARSIFAL and shakes him by the arm.

AMFORTAS setzt den „Gral" wieder nieder, welcher nun, während die tiefe Dämmerung wieder entweicht, immer mehr erblasst : hierauf schliessen die KNABEN das Gefäss wieder in den Schrein, und bedecken diesen, wie zuvor.— Mit dem Wiedereintritte der vorigen Tageshelle sind auf den Speisetafeln die Becher, jetzt mit Wein gefüllt, wieder deutlich geworden, neben jedem liegt ein Brot. Alles lässt sich zum Mahle nieder, so auch GURNEMANZ, welcher einen Platz neben sich leer hält und PARSIFAL durch ein Zeichen zur Theilnehmung am Mahle einlädt : PARSIFAL bleibt aber starr und stumm wie gänzlich entrückt, zur Seite stehen.

(Wechselgesang während des Mahles.)

Knabenstimmen
(aus der Höhe).

Wein und Brod des letzten Mahles
wandelt' einst der Herr des Grales,
durch des Mitleid's Liebesmacht,
in das Blut, das er vergoss,
in den Leib, den dar er bracht'.

Jünglingsstimmen
(aus der mittleren Höhe.)

Blut und Leib der Opfergabe
wandelt heut' zu eurer Labe
der Erlöser, den ihr preis't,
in den Wein, der nun euch floss,
in das Brod, das heut' euch speis't.

Die Ritter
(erste Hälfte).

Nehmet vom Brod,
wandelt es kühn
zu Leibes Kraft und Stärke ;
treu bis zum Tod,
fest in Müh'n,
zu wirken des Heiland's Werke.

(Zweite Hälfte.)

Nehmet vom Wein,
wandelt ihn neu
zu Lebens feurigem Blute,
froh im Verein,
brüdertreu
zu kämpfen mit seligem Muthe.

(Sie erheben sich feierlich und reichen einander die Hände).

2 *Alle Ritter.*   Selig im Glauben !
Selig in Liebe !

Jünglinge
(aus mittler Höhe).
Selig in Liebe !

Knaben
(aus oberster Höhe).
Selig im Glauben !

Während des Mahles, an welchem er nicht theilnahm, ist AMFORTAS aus seiner begeisterungsvollen Erhebung allmählich wieder herabgesunken : er neigt das Haupt und hält die Hand auf die Wunde. Die KNABEN nähern sich ihm ; ihre Bewegungen deuten auf das erneuerte Bluten der Wunde : sie pflegen AMFORTAS, geleiten ihn wieder auf die Sänfte, und, während Alle sich zum Aufbruch rüsten, tragen sie, in der Ordnung wie sie kamen, AMFORTAS und den heiligen Schrein wieder von dannen. Die RITTER und KNAPPEN reihen sich ebenfalls wieder zum feierlichen Zuge, und verlassen langsam den Saal, aus welchem die vorherige Tageshelle allmählich weicht. Die Glocken haben wieder geläutet.
PARSIFAL hatte bei den verangegangenen stärksten Klagerufe des AMFORTAS eine heftige Bewegung nach dem Herzen gemacht, welches er krampfhaft eine Zeit gefasst hielt ; jetzt steht er noch wie erstarrt, regungslos da. — Als die Letzten den Saal verlassen, und die Thüren wieder geschlossen sind, tritt GURNEMANZ missmüthig an PARSIFAL heran, und rüttelt ihn am Arme.

Gurnemanz. Why standest thou there?
    Wist thou what thou saw'st?

    [PARSIFAL shakes his head slightly.]

Gurnemanz. Thou art then nothing but a Fool!
    (He opens a small side door.)

Come away, on thy road be gone
  And put my rede to use:
Leave all our swans for the future alone
  And seek thyself, gander, a goose.

(He pushes PARSIFAL out and slams the door angrily on him. As
c follows the knights, the curtain closes.)

ACT II.

KLINGSOR's magic Castle. — In the inner keep of a tower open
above; stone steps lead up to the battlemented summit and down into
darkness below the stage, which represents the rampart. Magical imple-
ments and necromantic appliances. — KLINGSOR sits at one side on
the rampart before a metal mirror.

Klingsor. The time has come! —
Lo! how my magic tow'r entices
Yon Fool who neareth, shouting like a child.
A deadly slumber lays its hold on her
  Whose anguish I can chase away. —
    Up then! To work!

He descends somewhat lower, and lights incense, which immediately fills part of the background with a bluish vapor. He then
reseats himself in his former place, and calls towards the depth with
mysterious gestures:

  Arise! Draw near to me!
Thy Master calls thee, nameless woman:
She-Lucifer! Rose of Hades!
Herodias wert thou, and what else?
Gundryggia there, Kundry here: —
Approach! Approach then, Kundry!
Thy Master calls — appear!

[In the bluish light rises the form of KUNDRY. She is heard to
utter a dreadful cry, as if half-awakened from a deep sleep.]

Klingsor. Awak'st thou? Ha!
    To my spell again
Thou succumbest now the time befits.

(The figure of KUNDRY gives forth a sudden shriek of anguish sinking
to a frightened wail.)

Say, where hast thou been roving again?
Fie! There with the knights and their crew,
Where as a brute they regarded thee?
  With me art thou not far better?
When once their chieftain thou hadst allured
    me —
Ha, ha! — the spotless knight of the Grail —
What drove thee again from my side?

Gurnemanz. Was stehst du noch da?
    Weisst du was du sah'st?

    (PARSIFAL schüttelt ein wenig sein Haupt.)

Gurnemanz. Du bist doch eben nur ein Thor!
    (Er öffnet eine schmale Seitenthüre.)

Dort hinaus, deinem Wege zu!
  Doch räth dir Gurnemanz,
lass' du hier künftig die Schwäne in Ruh'.
  und suche dir Gänser die Gans!

Er stösst PARSIFAL hinaus und schlägt, ärgerlich, hinter ihm die
Thüre stark zu. Während er dann den RITTERN folgt, schliesst sich
der Bühnenvorhang.

ZWEITER AUFZUG.

Klingsor's Zauberschloss.

Im inneren Verliesse eines nach oben offenen Thurmes; Stein-
stufen führen nach dem Zinnenrande der Thurmmauer; Finsterniss
in der Tiefe, nach welcher es von dem Mauervorsprunge, den der
Bühnenboden darstellt, hinabführt. Zauberwerkzeuge und nekro-
mantische Vorrichtungen. — KLINGSOR auf dem Mauervorsprunge
zur Seite, vor einem Metallspiegel sitzend.

Klingsor. Die Zeit ist da, —
Schon lockt mein Zauberschloss den Thoren,
den, kindisch jauchzend, fern ich nahen seh'. —
Im Todesschlafe hält der Fluch sie fest,
  der ich den Krampf zu lösen weiss. —
    Auf denn! An's Werk!

Er steigt, der Mitte zu, etwas tiefer hinab, und entzündet dort
Räucherwerk, welches alsbald einen Theil des Hintergrundes mit
einem bläulichen Dampfe erfüllt. Dann setzt er sich wieder an die
vorige Stelle, und ruft, mit geheimnissvollen Gebärden, nach dem
Abgrunde:

  Herauf! Hieher! zu mir!
Dein Meister ruft dich Namenlose:
Ur-Teufelin! Höllen-Rose!
Herodias war'st du, und was noch?
Gundryggia dort, Kundry hier:
  Hieher! Hieher denn, Kundry!
Zu deinem Meister, herauf!

In dem bläulichen Lichte steigt KUNDRY's Gestalt herauf. Man
hört sie einen grässlichen Schrei ausstossen, wie eine aus tiefstem
Schlafe aufgeschreckte Halbwache.

Klingsor. Erwach'st du? Ha!
    Meinem Banne wieder
verfiel'st du heut' zur rechten Zeit.

(KUNDRY's Gestalt lässt ein Klagegeheul, von grösster Heftigkeit
bis zu bangem Wimmern sich abstufend, vernehmen.)

Sag' wo trieb'st du dich wieder umher?
Pfui! Dort, bei dem Ritter-Gesipp',
wo wie ein Vieh du dich halten lässt?
  Gefällt's dir bei mir nicht besser?
Als ihren Meister du mir gefangen —
ha, ha! — den reinen Hüter des Gral's, —
  was jagte dich da wieder fort?

10

Kundry

(hoarsely and in broken accents, as if striving to regain speech).

Ah ! — Ah !
Dismal night —
Frenzy — Oh ! — Fear ! —
Oh, anguish ! —
Sleep, sleep —
Deepest sleep ! — Death !

Klingsor. Some other there has waked thee ? Hey ?

Kundry

(as before).

Yes ! — My curse —
Oh ! Yearning — yearning !

Klingsor. Ha, ha ! — there with the knights unsullied ?

Kundry. I — I — served them.

Klingsor. Aye, aye ! — To make some reparation,
For the arrant wrong thou hast wrought.
They give thee no help ;
All may be purchased,
When I but bid their price ;
The firmest one fails
When thy arms are around him :
And so he falls by the spear,
Which from their chief himself I purloined. —
The most dangerous must to-day be withstood :
Whom sheerest Folly shields.

Kundry. I — will not ! — Oh ! — Oh !

Klingsor. Well wilt thou, for thou must.

Kundry. Thou — never — canst — hold me.

Klingsor. But I can force thee.

Kundry. Thou ?

Klingsor. Thy Master.

Kundry. And by what pow'r ?

Klingsor. Ha ! Because against me
Thine own pow'r — cannot move.

Kundry

(laughing harshly).

Ha, ha ! Art thou chaste ?

Klingsor

(wrathfully).

Why askest that, thou outcast wretch ?

(He sinks into gloomy brooding.)

Awfullest strait ! —
So laughs now the Fiend below,

Kundry

(rauh und abgebrochen, wie im Versuche, wieder Sprache zu gewinnen).

Ach ! — Ach !
Tiefe Nacht —
Wahnsinn ! — Oh ! — Wuth ! —
Oh ! Jammer ! —
Schlaf — Schlaf —
tiefer Schlaf ! — Tod !

Klingsor. Da weckte dich ein And'rer ? Hei

Kundry

(wie zuvor).

Ja ! — Mein Fluch ! —
Oh ! — Sehnen — Sehnen ! —

Klingsor. Ha, ha ! — dort nach den keuschen Rittern ?

Kundry. Da — da — dient' ich.

Klingsor. Ja, ja ! — den Schaden zu vergüten,
den du ihnen böslich gebracht ?
Sie helfen dir nicht :
feil sind sie Alle,
biet' ich den rechten Preis ;
der festeste fällt,
sinkt er dir in die Arme :
und so verfällt er dem Speer,
den ihrem Meister selbst ich entwandt. —
Den Gefährlichsten gilt's nun heut' zu besteh'n
ihn schirmt der Thorheit Schild.

Kundry. Ich — will nicht ! — Oh ! — Oh !

Klingsor. Wohl willst du, denn du musst.

Kundry. Du — kannst mich — nicht — halten.

Klingsor. Aber dich fassen.

Kundry. Du ?

Klingsor. Dein Meister.

Kundry. Aus welcher Macht ?

Klingsor. Ha ! Weil einzig an mir
deine Macht — nichts vermag.

Kundry

(grell lachend).

Ha ! ha ! — Bist du keusch ?

Klingsor

(wüthend).

Was fräg'st du das, verfluchtes Weib ?

(Er versinkt in finst'res Brüten.)

Furchtbare Noth ! —
So lacht nun der Teufel mein',

That once I sought the holier life !
 Awfullest strait !
Irrepressible yearning woe !
Terrible lust in me once rife,
Which I had quenched with devilish strife ; —
 Mocks and laughs it at me,
 Thou devil's bride, through thee ? —
  Have a care !
One his contempt and scorn hath repented ;
The stern one, strong in holiness,
 By whom I once was spurned
  His stock I've ruined :
   Unredeemed
Shall the Relics' curator soon languish ·
 And soon — I feel it —
 I shall possess the Grail. —
  Ha ! ha !
How suited thy taste Amfortas the brave,
Whom to thee in rapture I gave ?

Kundry. Oh ! — Mis'ry — Mis'ry !
Weak e'en he ! Weak — all men !
 By my curse and with me
 All of them perish ! —
 Oh, unending sleep,
 Only release,
When — when shall I win thee ?

Klingsor. Ha ! He who spurns thee setteth thee
  free ;
So try't with yon boy who draws near !

Kundry. I — will not !

Klingsor. Lo, where he climbs to the tow'r !

Kundry. Oh, woe's me ! woe's me !
 Awakened I for this ?
 Must I — must ?

Klingsor
   (who has ascended to the wall).
Ha ! — He is fair, the stripling.

Kundry. Oh ! — Oh ! — Woe is me ! —

Klingsor
   (winding a horn towards the outside).
Ho ! ho ! — My watchmen ! Soldiers !
Heroes ! — Up ! — Foes are near !
  (Increasing clash of weapons heard without.)
Hey ! — How they haste to the ramparts,
 The deluded garrisoners,
To guard their engaging she-devils ! —
 So ! — Courage, courage !
 Haha ! — He is not afraid : —
From bold Sir Ferris he's wrested his weapons ;
And flashes them fiercely now at the swarm. —
  (KUNDRY begins to laugh gloomily.)

dass ich einst nach dem Heiligen rang !
 Furchtbare Noth !
Ungebändigten Sehnens Pein !
Schrecklichster Triebe Höllendrang,
den ich zu Todesschweigen mir zwang, —
 lacht und höhnt er nun laut
 durch dich, des Teufels Braut ? —
  Hüte dich !
Hohn und Verachtung büsste schon Einer
der Stolze, stark in Heiligkeit,
 der einst mich von sich stiess,
  sein Stamm verfiel mir,
   unerlös't
soll der Heiligen Hüter mir schmachten :
 und bald — so wähn' ich —
 hüt' ich mir selbst den Gral. —
  Ha ! Ha !
Gefiel er dir wohl, Amfortas, der Held,
den ich dir zur Wonne gesellt ?

Kundry. Oh ! — Jammer ! — Jammer !
Schwach auch Er ! Schwach — Alle !
 Meinem Fluche mit mir
 Alle verfallen ! —
 Oh, ewiger Schlaf,
 einziges Heil,
wie, — wie dich gewinnen ?

Klingsor. Ha ! Wer dir trotzte, lös'te dich frei ;
versuch's mit dem Knaben, der nah't !

Kundry. Ich — will nicht !

Klingsor. Jetzt schon erklimmt er die Burg.

Kundry. Oh Wehe ! Wehe !
 Erwachte ich darum ?
 Muss ich ? — Muss ?

Klingsor
   (Ist auf die Thurmmauer gestiegen).
Ha ! — Er ist schön, der Knabe !

Kundry. Oh ! — Oh ! — Wehe mir ! —

Klingsor
   (stösst nach Aussen in ein Horn).
Ho ! Ho ! — Ihr Wächter ! Ritter !
Helden ! — Auf ! — Feinde nah' !
  (Aussen wachsendes Getöse und Waffengeräusch.)
Hei ! — Wie zur Mauer sie stürmen,
 die bethörten Eigenholde,
zum Schutz ihres schönen Geteufel's ! —
 So ! — Muthig ! Muthig ! —
 Haha ! — Der fürchtet sich nicht : —
dem Helden Ferris entwand er die Waffe ;
die führt er nun freislich wider den Schwarm.
  (KUNDRY beginnt unheimlich zu lachen)

How ill doth his zeal agree with those sots!
That one's lost an arm — that one his ankle.
 Haha! They waver — they're routed:
With their wounds they are all running home! —
　　What welcome I'll give them! —
　　Truly I wish
That all the rabble of Knights
So might destroy one another! —
Ha! How proudly he stands on the rampart!
His countenance how smiling and rosy,
　　As childlike, surprised
　　On the desolate garden he looks! —
Hey! Kundry!

He turns round. KUNDRY, *who has gone off into more and more ecstatic laughter which at last culminates in a spasmodic cry of anguish, now suddenly vanishes; the bluish light is extinguished; complete darkness reigns in the depths.*

　　What! Gone to work?
Ha, ha! the charm I know full well,
Which ever compels thee to do my behest. —
　　Thou there, babyish sprig!
　　What — though
Wise redes thou hast won —
　　Too young and dull,
Into my power thou'lt fall: —
When pureness has departed,
To me thou'lt be devoted.

He sinks slowly with the whole tower; at the same time the garden rises and fills the entire stage. Tropical vegetation; most luxuriant wealth of flowers; at the back it is bounded by the battlements of the castle wall on to which give sideways abutments of the castle itself (florid Arabian style) with terraces.

On the wall stands PARSIFAL, *looking down on the garden in astonishment. — From all sides, from the garden and from the palace rush in mazy courses lovely damsels, first singly, then in numbers; their dress is hastily thrown about them, as if they had been suddenly startled from sleep.*

Damsels
　　　　(coming from the garden).
　　Here was the tumult; —
　　Weapons, wild exclaimings!

Damsels
　　　　(from the castle).
　　Horror! Vengeance! Up!
　　Where is the culprit?

Several. My beloved is wounded!

Others. Where is my lover?

Others. I wakened alone! —
　　Where hath he fled to?

Still Others. There in the palace? —
　　They're bleeding! Horror!
　　Where is the foe? —
　　There stands he! See! —
　　'Tis my Ferris' sword —
　　I saw't, he took us by storm. —

9

12

Wie übel den Tölpeln der Eifer gedeih't!
Dem schlug er den Arm,— Jenem den Schenkel
　　Haha! — Sie weichen, — sie fliehen:
seine Wunde trägt Jeder nach heim! —
　　Wie das ich euch gönne! —
　　Möge denn so
das ganze Rittergeschlecht
unter sich selber sich würgen! — —
Ha! Wie stolz er nun steht auf der Zinne
Wie lachen ihm die Rosen der Wangen,
　　da kindisch erstaunt
　　in den einsamen Garten er blickt!
He! Kundry!

Er wendet sich um. KUNDRY *war in ein immer extatischeres Lachen gerathen, welches endlich in ein krampfhaftes Wehgeschrei überging; jetzt ist ihre Gestalt plötzlich verschwunden; das bläuliche Licht ist erloschen: volle Finsterniss in der Tiefe.*

　　Wie? Schon am Werk? —
Haha! Den Zauber kannt' ich wohl,
der immer dich wieder zum Dienst mir gesellt. —
　　Du dort, kindischer Spross!
　　Was — auch
Weissagung dir wies, —
　　zu jung und dumm
fiel'st du in meine Gewalt: —
die Reinheit dir entrissen,
bleib'st mir du zugewiesen!

Er versinkt langsam mit dem ganzen Thurme; zugleich steigt der Zaubergarten auf und erfüllt die Bühne völlig. Tropische Vegetation, üppigste Blumenpracht; nach dem Hintergrunde zu Abgrenzung durch die Zinne der Burgmauer, an welche sich seitwärts Vorsprünge des Schlossbaues selbst (arabischen reichen Styles) mit Terrassen anlehnen.

Auf der Mauer steht PARSIFAL, *staunend in den Garten hinab-blickend. — Von allen Seiten her, aus dem Garten wie aus dem Palaste, stürzen wirr durch einander, einzeln, dann zugleich immer mehre, schöne* MÄDCHEN *herein: sie sind in flüchtig übergeworfener Kleidung, wie soeben aus dem Schlaf aufgeschreckt.*

Mädchen
　　　　(vom Garten kommend).
　　Hier war das Tosen,
　　Waffen, wilde Rüfe!

Mädchen
　　　　(vom Schlosse heraus).
　　Wehe! Rache! Auf!
　　Wo ist der Frevler?

Einzelne. Mein Geliebter verwundet.

Andere. Wo ist der Meine?

Andere. Ich erwachte allein, —
　　wohin entfloh er?

Immer Andere. Drinnen im Saale? —
　　Sie bluten! Wehe!
　　Wer ist der Feind? —
　　Da steh't er! Seht! —
　　Meines Ferris Schwert? —
　　Ich sah's, er stürmte die Burg. —

I heard too the master's horn.
  My hero rushed on :
They all assailed him, but each one
Encountered a bloody repulse.
  What boldness ! what virulence !
  All of them fled from him. —
  Thou there ! Thou there !
Why shape for us such distress ?
Accurst, accurst mayst thou be !

(PARSIFAL leaps somewhat lower toward the garden.)

Damsels. Ha ! bold one ! Dar'st thou approach us ?
Why hast thou slaughtered our lovers ?

Parsifal
        (in greatest astonishment).
Ye lovely maidens, had I not to slay them,
When they endeavored to check approach to your charms ?

Damsels. To us camest thou ?
        Sawest thou us ?

Parsifal. I've seen nowhere yet beings so bright :
If I said fair, would it seem right ?

Damsels
        (changing from surprise to merriment).
  Then wilt thou not treat us badly ?

Parsifal. I could not so.

Damsels. But sadly
  What thou hast done has annoyed us ;
  Our playmates thou hast destroyed us.
    Who'll sport with us now ?

Parsifal. That well will I.

Damsels
        (laughing).
If thou art friendly come more nigh.
  Let kindness be accorded,
  And thou shalt be rewarded :
  For gold we do not play,
  But only for love's sweet pay,
  Wouldst thou console us rightly
  Then win it from us, and lightly.

Some have gone into the groves and now return in flower-dresses, appearing like flowers themselves.

The adorned Damsels
        (severally).
Touch not the stripling ! — He's for none but me. —
  No ! — No ! — Me ! — Me !

The other Damsels. Ah, the minxes ! — They've slily adorned them.

(They also withdraw and return similarly dressed).

Ich hörte des Meisters Horn.
  Mein Held lief herzu,
sie Alle kamen, doch Jeden
empfing er mit blutiger Wehr.
  Der Kühne ! Der Feindliche !
  Alle sie flohen ihm. —
  Du dort ! Du dort !
Was schuf'st du uns solche Noth ?
Verwünscht, verwünscht sollst du sein !

(PARSIFAL springt etwas tiefer in den Garten herab.)

Die Mädchen. Ha ! Kühner ! Wag'st du zu trotzen ?
Was schlug'st du uns're Geliebten ?

Parsifal
        (in höchster Verwunderung).
Ihr schönen Kinder, musst' ich sie nicht schlagen ?
Zu euch Holden ja wehrten sie mir den Weg.

Mädchen. Zu uns wolltest du ?
        Sah'st du uns schon ?

Parsifal. Noch nie sah ich solch' zieres Geschlecht :
nenn' ich euch schön, dünkt euch das recht ?

Die Mädchen
        (von Verwunderung in Heiterkeit übergehend).
So willst du uns wohl nicht schlagen ?

Parsifal. Das möcht' ich nicht.

Mädchen. Doch Schaden
  schuf'st du uns grossen und vielen ;
  du schlugest uns're Gespielen :
    wer spielt nun mit uns ?

Parsifal. Das thu' ich gern.

Die Mädchen
        (lachend).
Bist du uns hold, so bleib' nicht fern ;
  und willst du uns nicht schelten,
  wir werden dir's entgelten :
  wir spielen nicht um Gold,
  wir spielen um Minne's Sold :
  willst du auf Trost uns sinnen,
  sollst den du uns abgewinnen.

Einzelne sind in die Läuben getreten, und kommen jetzt, ganz wie in Blumengewändern, selbst Blumen erscheinend, wieder zurück.

Die geschmückten Mädchen
        (einzeln).
Lasset den Knaben ! — Er gehöret mir. —
  Nein ! — Nein ! — Mir ! — Mir !

Die andern Mädchen. Ah, die Schlimmen ! — Sie schmücken sich heimlich.

Diese entfernen sich ebenfalls, und kehren alsbald in gleichem Blumenschmucke zurück.

The Damsels	*Die Mädchen*
(while, as if in merry childish gambols they press round PARSIFAL in mazy figures and softly stroke his face).	(während sie, wie in anmuthigem Kinderspiele, in abwechselndem Reigen um PARSIFAL sich drehen, und sanft ihm Wange und Kinn streicheln).

16

Come! Come!
 Handsome stripling,
  I'll be thy flower!
 Sweetly dancing and rippling
 Bliss unshadowed I'll shower.

Komm'! Komm'!
 Holder Knabe,
  lass mich dir blühen!
 Dir zu wonniger Labe
 gilt mein minniges Mühe.

Parsifal
 (standing in their midst in quiet enjoyment).
 How sweet is your scent!
 Are ye then flowers?

Parsifal
 (mit heit'rer Ruhe in der Mitte stehend).
 Wie duftet ihr hold!
 Seid ihr denn Blumen?

The Damsels
 (still sometimes severally, sometimes together).
 The garden's pride
  And odor we've given.
 In spring time we were riven;
  We here abide,
  Through sunlight and summer,
 To bloom still on each comer.
Oh, be but kind and true,
And grudge not the flowers their due:
If thou wilt not fondle and cherish,
We swiftly must wither and perish.

Die Mädchen
 (immer bald einzeln, bald mehre zugleich).
 Des Gartens Zier
  und duftende Geister
 im Lenz pflückt uns der Meister;
  wir wachsen hier
  in Sommer und Sonne,
 für dich blühend in Wonne.
Nun sei uns freund und hold,
nicht karge den Blumen den Sold·
kannst du uns nicht lieben und minnen,
wir welken und sterben dahinnen.

First Damsel. Unto thy bosom take me!

Erstes Mädchen. An deinen Busen nimm mich!

Second. Thy hot brow, let me soothe it!

Zweites. Die Stirn lass' mich dir kühlen!

Third. Turn thy fair cheek that I smooth it!

Drittes. Lass mich die Wange dir fühlen!

Fourth. Thy mouth give to my kisses!

Viertes. Den Mund lass' mich dir küssen!

Fifth. No, here! 'Tis I am the best.

Fünftes. Nein, mich! Die Schönste bin ich.

Sixth. No, I! I am the sweeter.

Sechstes. Nein, ich! Duft' ich doch süsser.

Parsifal
 (gently repulsing their eager advances).
Ye wild crowd of beautiful flowers,
if I am to play, ye must widen your bowers.

Parsifal
 (ihrer anmuthigen Zudringlichkeit sanft wehrend).
 Ihr wild holdes Blumengedränge,
 soll ich mit euch spielen, entlasst mich der Enge!

Damsels. Why quarrel?

Mädchen. Was zank'st du?

Parsifal. 'Tis your riot.

Parsifal. Weil ihr streitet.

Damsels. We quarrel for thee.

Mädchen. Wir streiten um dich.

Parsifal. Then quiet.

Parsifal. Das meidet!

First Damsel
 (to the second).
Back with you! See, he wants me.

Erstes Mädchen
 (zu dem zweiten).
 Weiche du! Sieh', er will mich.

Second Damsel. No, me!

Zweites Mädchen. Nein, mich!

Third. Me, rather!

Drittes. Mich, lieber!

Fourth. No, me!

Viertes. Nein, mich!

First Damsel (to PARSIFAL).
Thou shunnest me ?

Second.   Flyest me ?

First.   Art with women so wary ?

Second.   Of thy favor chary ?

Several Damsels.   The cold trembler ! see how
he cowers !

Others.   Wouldst see the butterfly wooed by the
flowers ?

First Half.   Fool ! we refuse him !

One Damsel.   I'm willing to lose him.

Others.   We others will choose him.

Others.   No, we ! draw near ! —
No, I — here, here ! —

Parsifal
(half angry, turns away and seeks to fly).
No more ! You'll catch me not !
(From a flowery arbor at side is heard)

Kundry's
(voice).
Parsifal ! — tarry !
The DAMSELS are startled and pause — PARSIFAL stands arrested.

Parsifal.   Parsifal . . .?
So once, when dreaming, my mother called me. —

Kundry's
(voice).
Here bide thee, Parsifal ! —
Where joy and gladness on thee shall fall. —
Ye frivolous wantons, leave him in peace :
Flow'rs soon to be faded,
He came not here for your delight !
Go home, tend the wounded :
Lonely awaits you many a knight.

The Damsels
(tremblingly and resistingly departing from PARSIFAL).
Thus to leave thee, thus to sever —
Alas ! Alas, what pain !
From all we'd gladly part for ever,
With thee but to remain. —
Farewell ! farewell !
Thou fair one, thou proud one !
Thou — Fool !
(With the last words they disappear into the castle, gently laughing.)

Parsifal.   Was all this — nothing but a dream ?

He looks timidly to the side from whence KUNDRY'S voice came.
There is now visible, the branches being withdrawn, a youthful female
of exquisite beauty — KUNDRY, in entirely altered form — on a flowery
couch and in light drapery of fantastic, somewhat Arabian style.

Erstes Mädchen (zu PARSIFAL).
Du wehrest mir ?

Zweites.   Scheuchest mich ?

Erstes.   Bist du feige vor Frauen ?

Zweites.   Magst nicht dich getrauen ?

Mehre Mädchen.   Wie schlimm bist du, Zager
und Kalter !

Andere Mädchen.   Die Blumen lässt du umbuh-
len den Falter ?

Erste Hälfte.   Weichet dem Thoren !

Ein Mädchen.   Ich geb' ihn verloren.

Andere.   Uns sei er erkoren !

Andere.   Nein, uns ! — Nein, mir ! —
Auch mir ! — Hier, hier ! —

Parsifal
(halb ärgerlich sie von sich abscheuchend, will fliehen).
Lass't ab ! Ihr fangt mich nicht !
(Aus einem Blumenhage zur Seite vernimmt man)

Kundry's
(Stimme).
Parsifal ! — Weile !
Die Mädchen erschrecken und halten sogleich ein. — PARSIFAL
steht betroffen still.

Parsifal.   Parsifal . .?
So nannte träumend mich einst die Mutter. —

Kundry's
(Stimme.)
Hier weile, Parsifal ! —
Dich grüsset Wonne und Heil zumal. —
Ihr kindischen Buhlen, weichet von ihm ;
früh welkende Blumen,
nicht euch ward er zum Spiel bestellt !
Geht heim, pflegt der Wunden :
einsam erharrt euch mancher Held.

Die Mädchen
(zaghaft und widerstrebend sich von PARSIFAL entfernend).
Dich zu lassen, dich zu meiden, —
O weh' ! O weh' der Pein !
Von Allen möchten gern wir scheiden,
mit dir allein zu sein. —
Leb' wohl ! Leb' wohl !
Du Holder ! Du Stolzer !
Du — Thor !
(Mit dem Letzten sind sie, unter leisem Gelächter, nach dem Schlosse
zu verschwunden.)

Parsifal.   Dies Alles — hab' ich nun geträumt ?

Er sieht sich schüchtern nach der Seite hin um, von welcher die
Stimme kam. Dort ist jetzt durch Enthüllung des Hages ein
jugendliches Weib von höchster Schönheit — KUNDRY, in durchaus
verwandelter Gestalt — auf einem Blumenlager, in leicht verhüllen-
der, phantastischer Kleidung — annähernd arabischen Styles
sichtbar geworden.

Parsifal
   (still standing aloof).
 Calledst thou me, who am nameless?

Kundry. I named thee, foolish pure one,
   " Fal parsi, "—
  Thou, guileless Fool, art " Parsifal. "
So cried, when in Arabia's land he expired,
Thy father Gamuret unto his son,
Who then the daylight had not greeted:
'Twas by this name he, dying, called thee.
Here have I tarried this but to disclose:
What drew thee here, if not desire to know?

Parsifal. I saw ne'er, I pictured ne'er what here
I see, and which impresses me with awe. —
And bloomest thou too in this flower-garden?

Kundry. Nay, Parsifal, thou foolish pure one!
 Far — far from hence my home is: —
For thee to find me, I but tarried here.
I come from far lands, where I've noted much.
I saw the child upon its mother's breast;
Its infant lisping laughs yet in my ear:
 Though filled with sadness.
 How laughed even then Heart's Affliction,
  When, shouting gladness,
 It gave her sorrows contradiction!
 In beds of moss 'twas softly nested,
 She kisses it till in sleep it rested:
  With care and sorrow
 The timid mother watched it sleeping;
  It waked the morrow
 Beneath the dew of mother's weeping.
 All tears was she, encased in anguish,
 Caused by thy father's death and love:
 That through like hap thou shouldst not languish,
 Became her care all else above.
Afar from arms, from mortal strife and riot,
Sought she to hide away with thee in quiet.
 All care was she, alas! and fearing:
 Never should aught of knowledge reach thy hearing:
 Hear'st thou not still her lamenting voice,
  When far and late thou didst roam?
 Ah! how she did laughingly rejoice
  To welcome thee hastening home!
 When her wild arm around thee was laid,
 Wert thou of kisses so much afraid? —
 But thou didst not behold her pain,
  Her features anguish ridden,
 When thou returnedst not again, ·
  And ev'ry trace was hidden.

Parsifal
   (noch ferne stehend).
 Riefest du mich Namenlosen?

Kundry. Dich nannt' ich, thör'ger Reiner,
   „Fal parsi,“ —
  Dich, reinen Thoren: „Parsifal.“
So rief, da in arab'schem Land er verschied.
dein Vater Gamuret dem Sohne zu,
den er, im Mutterschooss verschlossen,
mit diesem Namen sterbend grüsste.
Dir ihn zu künden, harrt' ich deiner hier:
was zog dich her, wenn nicht der Kunde Wunsch?

Parsifal. Nie sah' ich, nie träumte mir, was jetzt
ich schau', und was mit Bangen mich erfüllt. —
Entblühtest du auch diesem Blumenhaine?

Kundry. Nein, Parsifal, du thör'ger Reiner!
 Fern — fern — ist meine Heimath: —
dass du mich fändest, weilte ich nur hier.
Von weit her kam ich, wo ich viel ersah'.
Ich sah' das Kind an seiner Mutter Brust,
sein erstes Lallen lacht mir noch im Ohr;
 das Leid im Herzen,
  wie lachte da auch Herzeleide,
  als ihren Schmerzen
 zujauchzte ihrer Augen Weide!
 Gebettet sanft auf weichen Moosen,
 den hold geschläfert sie mit Kosen,
  dem, bang' in Sorgen,
 den Schlaf bewacht der Mutter Sehnen,
  ihn weckt' am Morgen
 der heisse Thau der Mutter-Thränen.
 Nur Weinen war sie, Schmerz-Gebahren
 um deines Vaters Lieb' und Tod;
 vor gleicher Noth dich zu bewahren,
 galt ihr als höchster Pflicht Gebot:
 den Waffen fern, der Männer Kampf und Wüthen,
  wollte sie still dich bergen und behüten.
  Nur Sorgen war sie, ach! und Bangen:
  nie sollte Kunde zu dir hergelangen.
  Hör'st du nicht noch ihrer Klagen Ruf,
  wann fern und spät du geweilt?
  Hei! Was ihr das Lust und Lachen schuf,
  wann suchend sie dann dich ereilt!
  Wann dann ihr Arm dich wüthend umschlang,
  ward dir es wohl gar bei'm Küssen bang!
 Ihr Wehe doch du nicht vernahm'st,
  nicht ihrer Schmerzen Toben,
 als endlich du nicht wieder kam'st,
 und deine Spur verstoben:

17

18

For days and nights she waited,
And then her cries abated :
Her pain was dulled of its smart,
And gently ebbed life's tide ;
The anguish broke her heart,
And — Heart's Affliction — died. —

Parsifal
(always earnestly, finally terribly affected, sinks down at KUNDRY's
feet, painfully overpowered).

Woe's me ! Woe's me ! What did I ? Where was I ?
Mother ! Sweetest, dearest mother !
Thy son, thy son must be thy murderer ?
Oh Fool ! Thoughtless, shallow-brained Fool !
Where couldst thou have roved, thus to forget her ?
     Thus, oh, thus to forget thee,
     Faithful, fondest of mothers !

Kundry
(still reclining, bends over PARSIFAL's head, gently touches his forehead, and wreathes her arms confidingly round his neck).

Hadst thou ne'er been distrest,
     Then consolation
Could not have cheered thy breast.
Let now thy bitter woe
     Find mitigation
In joys that Love can show !

Parsifal
(sadly).

My mother, my mother ! Could I forget her ?
Ah ! must all be forgotten by me ?
What have I e'er remembered yet ?
But senseless Folly dwells in me !
(He droops still lower.)

Kundry.   Transgression
When owned is quickly ended !
     Confession
Hath Folly often mended.
Of Love, oh, learn the fashion
Which Gamuret once knew,
When Heart's Affliction's passion
Had fired his bosom through.
     The life thy mother
     Gave thee can smother
E'en death, and dullness too remove.
     To thee
     Now she
Sends benediction from above
     In this first — kiss of Love.
(She has bowed her head quite over his, and now presses her lips
on his in a long kiss.)

Parsifal
(starts up suddenly with a gesture of intense terror ; his looks alter
fearfully, he presses his hands tightly against his heart, as if to
repress an agonizing pain ; finally he bursts out).

Amfortas ! —
The spearwound ! — The spearwound ! —

13

---

sie harrte Nächt' und Tage,
bis ihr verstummt die Klage,
der Gram ihr zehrte den Schmerz,
um stillen Tod sie warb :
ihr brach das Leid das Herz,
und — Herzeleide — starb. —

Parsifal
(immer ernsthafter, endlich furchtbar betroffen, sinkt, schmerzlie
überwältigt, bei KUNDRY's Füssen nieder).

Wehe ! Wehe ! Was that ich ? Wo war ich ?
Mutter ! Süsse, holde Mutter !
Dein Sohn, dein Sohn musste dich morden ?
O Thor ! Blöder, taumelnder Thor !
Wo irrtest du hin, ihrer vergessend ?
     Deiner, deiner vergessend,
     traute, theuerste Mutter ?

Kundry
(immer noch in liegender Stellung ausgestreckt, beugt sich über
PARSIFAL's Haupt, fasst sanft seine Stirne, und schlingt träulic
ihren Arm um seinen Nacken).

War dir fremd noch der Schmerz,
     des Trostes Süsse
labte nie auch dein Herz :
das Wehe, das dich reu't,
     die Noth nun büsse,
im Trost, den Liebe dir beut !

Parsifal
(trübe).

Die Mutter, die Mutter konnt' ich vergessen
Ha ! Was Alles vergass ich wohl noch ?
Wess' war ich je noch eingedenk ?
Nur dumpfe Thorheit lebt in mir !
(Er lässt sich immer tiefer sinken.)

Kundry.   Bekenntniss
wird Schuld und Reue enden.
     Erkenntniss
in Sinn die Thorheit wenden :
die Liebe lerne kennen,
die Gamuret umschloss,
als Herzeleid's Entbrennen
ihn sengend überfloss :
     die Leib und Leben
     einst dir gegeben,
der Tod und Thorheit weichen muss,
     sie beut'
     dir heut' —
als Muttersegens letzten Gruss
     der Liebe — ersten Kuss.
(Sie hat ihr Haupt völlig über das seinige geneigt, und heftet nun ihre
Lippen zu einem langen Kusse auf seinen Mund.)

Parsifal
(fährt plötzlich mit einer Gebärde des höchsten Schreckens auf
seine Haltung drückt eine furchtbare Veränderung aus ; er stemmt
seine Hände gewaltsam gegen sein Herz, wie um einen zerreissenden
Schmerz zu bewältigen ; endlich bricht er aus).

Amfortas ! —
Die Wunde ! — Die Wunde ! —

In me I feel it burning. —
　　　Oh, horror! horror!
　　　Direfullest horror!
It shrieks from out the depth of my soul.
　　　Oh! — Oh! —
　　　Misery! —
　　　Lamentation! —
I saw thy wound a-bleeding: —
It bleeds now in myself —
　　　Here — here!

(Whilst KUNDRY stares at him in wonder and alarm, he continues madly.)

No, no! This is not the spearwound:
Let it gush blood in streams if it list.
Here! — here! My heart is ablaze!
　　The passion, the terrible passion,
　　That all my senses doth seize and sway!
　　Oh! — Love's delirium! —
How all things tremble, heave and quake
　　With longings that are sinful! . . .

　　　　　(terribly quiet).

My frozen glance stares on the sacred Cup: —
　　The Holy One's blood doth glow; —
Redemption's rapture, sweet and mild,
Is trembling far through ev'ry spirit;
But in this heart will the pangs not lessen.
　　The Saviour's wailing I distinguished,
　　The wailing — ah! the wailing
For His polluted sanctuary: —
　　" Recover, save me from
　　The hands that guilt has sullied! "
　　Thus — rang the lamentation
Through my soul with fearful loudness:
　　And I — oh, Fool! — oh, coward!
To wild and childish exploits hither fled.

　　　(He throws himself despairingly on his knees.)

Redeemer! Saviour! Gracious Lord!
What can retrieve my crime abhorred?

Kundry

(whose astonishment has changed to sorrowful wonder, tries tremblingly to approach PARSIFAL).

My noble knight! fling off this spell!
Look up! nor Love's delights repel!

Parsifal

(still in a kneeling posture, gazing blankly up at KUNDRY, whilst she stoops over him with the embracing movements which he describes in the following).

Aye! Thus it called him! This voice it
　　was; —
And this the glance; surely I know it well, —
The eyeglance which smiled away his quiet. —
These lips too, — aye — they tempted him
　　thus; —
　　So bowed this neck above him, —
　　So high was raised this head; —

Sie brennt in meinem Herzen. —
　　　Oh, Klage! Klage!
　　　Furchtbare Klage!
Aus tiefstem Inner'n schreit sie mir auf,
　　　Oh! — Oh! —
　　　Elender! —
　　　Jammervollster! —
Die Wunde sah' ich bluten: —
nun blutet sie mir selbst —
　　　hier — hier!

(Während KUNDRY in Schrecken und Verwunderung auf ihn hin starrt, fährt PARSIFAL in gänzlicher Entrücktheit fort.)

Nein, nein! Nicht ist es die Wunde:
fliesse ihr Blut in Strömen dahin!
Hier! Hier im Herzen der Brand!
　　Das Sehnen, das furchtbare Sehnen,
　　das alle Sinne mir fasst und zwingt!
　　Oh! — Qual der Liebe! —
Wie Alles schauert, bebt und zuckt
　　in sündigem Verlangen! . . .

　　　　(Schauerlich leise).

Es starrt der Blick dumpf auf das Heilsgefäss · —
　　das heilige Blut erglüh't; —
Erlösungswonne, göttlich mild',
durchzittert weithin alle Seelen:
nur hier, im Herzen, will die Qual nicht weicher.
　　Des Heiland's Klage da vernehm' ich,
　　die Klage, ach! die Klage
um das verrath'ne Heiligthum: —
　　,erlöse, rette mich
　　aus schuldbefleckten Händen!"
　　So — rief die Gottesklage
furchtbar laut mir in die Seele.
　　Und ich? Der Thor, der Feige?
Zu wilden Knabenthaten floh' ich hin!

　　　(Er stürzt verzweiflungsvoll auf die Knie.)

Erlöser! Heiland! Herr der Huld!
Wie büss' ich Sünder solche Schuld?

Kundry

(deren Erstaunen in leidenschaftliche Bewunderung übergeht, sucht schüchtern sich PARSIFAL zu nähern).

Gelobter Held! Entflieh' dem Wahn!
Blick' auf! Sei hold der Huldin Nah'n!

Parsifal

(immer in gebeugter Stellung, starr zu KUNDRY aufblickend, während diese sich zu ihm neigt und die liebkosenden Bewegungen ausführt, die er mit dem Folgenden bezeichnet).

Ja! Diese Stimme! So rief sie ihm: —
und diesen Blick, deutlich erkenn' ich ihn. —
auch diesen, der ihm so friedlos lachte.
Die Lippe, — ja — so zuckte sie ihm: —
　　so neigte sich der Nacken. —
　　so hob sich kühn das Haupt; —

So fluttered these locks as though laugh-
ing, —
So circled this arm round his neck —
So softened each feature in fondness, —!
In league with Sorrow's dismal weight,
This mouth took from him
His soul's salvation straight! —
Ha! — with this kiss! —

(With the last words he has gradually risen, and now springs completely up and spurns KUNDRY from him.)

Pernicious one! Get thee from me!
Leave me — leave me — for aye!

Kundry

(in intense grief).

Cruel one! — Ha! —
Felt e'er thy nature
For one fellow creature,
Then feel now my desolation!
Wert thou the Saver,
Thou wouldst not waver,
But with me unite for salvation?
Through endless ages for thee I've waited,
The Saviour — ah, so late!
At whom I scoffed in hate. —
Oh! —
Couldst thou know the curse,
Which through me, waking, sleeping,
Through death and lifetime,
Joy or weeping,
While ever steeled to bear fresh woes,
Endless through my being flows! —
I saw Him — Him —
And — mocked Him! . . .
I caught then His glance, —
I seek Him now from world to world,
Once more to stand before Him:
In deepest woe —
Sometimes His eye doth seem near,
His glance resting on me.
Returns then th' accursed laughter on me, —
A sinner sinks in my embraces!
Then laughter — laughter —,
Weep I cannot;
But only shriek
And rage and wallow
In night and madness never slaked,
From which, repentant, scarce I'd waked. —
Thou for whom, shamed to death, I've bided,
Thou whom I knew and, fool, derided,
Let me upon thy breast lie sobbing,
But for one hour together throbbing;
Though forced from God and man to flee,
Be yet redeemed and pardoned by thee!

Parsifal. Eternally
Should I be damned with thee,

so flatterten lachend die Locken, —
so schläng um den Hals sich der Arm —
so schmeichelte weich die Wange —!
Mit aller Schmerzen Qual im Bund,
das Heil der Seele
entküsste ihm ihr Mund! —
Ha! — dieser Kuss! —

(Er hat sich mit dem Letzten allmählich erhoben springt jetzt vol
lends auf, und stösst KUNDRY heftig von sich.)

Verderberin! Weiche von mir!
Ewig — ewig — von mir!

Kundry

(in höchster Leidenschaft).

Grausamer! — Ha! —
Fühlst du im Herzen,
nur Anderer Schmerzen,
so fühle jetzt auch die meinen!
Bist du Erlöser,
was bannt dich, Böser,
nicht mir auch zum Heil dich zu einen?
Seit Ewigkeiten — harre ich deiner,
des Heiland's, ach! so spät,
den einst ich kühn verschmäht. —
Oh! —
Kenntest du den Fluch,
der mich durch Schlaf und Wachen,
durch Tod und Leben,
Pein und Lachen,
zu neuem Leiden neu gestählt,
endlos durch das Dasein quält! —
Ich sah — Ihn — Ihn —
und — lachte . . .
da traf mich sein Blick. —
Nun such' ich ihn von Welt zu Welt,
ihm wieder zu begegnen:
in höchster Noth —
wähn' ich sein Auge schon nah',
den Blick schon auf mir ruh'n: —
da kehrt mir das verfluchte Lachen wieder.
ein Sünder sinkt mir in die Arme!
Da lach' ich — lache —,
kann nicht weinen:
nur schreien, wüthen,
toben, rasen
in stets erneu'ten Wahnsinn's Nacht,
aus der ich büssend kaum erwacht. —
Den ich ersehnt in Todesschmachten,
den ich erkannt, den blöd' Verlachten,
lass' mich an seinem Busen weinen,
nur eine Stunde dir vereinen,
und, ob mich Gott und Welt verstöss't!
in dir entsündig't sein und erlös't!

Parsifal.
In Ewigkeit
wärst du verdammt mit mir

19

If for one hour
I forgot my holy mission,
  Within thy arms embracing !—
To thy help also am I sent,
If of thy cravings thou repent.
The solace, which shall end thy sorrow,
Yields not that spring from which it flows :
Salvation can'st thou never borrow,
Till that same spring in thee shall close.
Far other 'tis—far other, aye !
For which I saw, with pitying eyes,
That brotherhood distrest and pining,
Their lives tormented and declining,
But who with certain clearness knows
The source whence true salvation flows ?
Oh, mis'ry ! What a course is this !
  Oh, wild hallucination !
In such a search for sacred bliss
Thus to desire the soul's damnation !
	für eine Stunde
	Vergessen's meiner Sendung,
	  in deines Arm's Umfangen !—
	Auch dir bin ich zum Heil gesandt,
	bleib'st du dem Sehnen abgewandt.
	Die Labung, die dein Leiden endet,
	beut nicht der Quell, aus dem es fliesst :
	das Heil wird nimmer dir gespendet,
	wenn jener Quell sich dir nicht schliesst.
	Ein andrer ist's,—ein andrer, ach !
	nach dem ich jammernd schmachten sah,
	die Brüder dort in grausen Nöthen
	den Leib sich quälen und ertödten.
	Doch wer erkennt ihn klar und hell,
	des einz'gen Heiles wahren Quell ?
	Oh, Elend ! Aller Rettung Flucht !
	  Oh, Weltenwahns Umnachten :
	in höchsten Heiles heisser Sucht
	nach der Verdammniss Quell zu schmachten !

Kundry. And was it my kiss
This great knowledge conveyed thee ?
  If in my arms I might take thee,
  'T would then a god surely make thee !
Redeem the world then, if 'tis thy aim :—
  Stand as a god revealéd ;
For this hour let me perish in flame,
  Leave aye the wound unhealéd.
	Kundry.
	  So war es mein Kuss,
	der Welt-hellsichtig dich machte ?
	
	  Mein volles Liebes-Umfangen
	  lässt dich dann Gottheit erlangen !
	Die Welt erlöse, ist diess dein Amt :—
	  schuf dich zum Gott die Stunde,
	für sie lasse mich ewig verdammt,
	  nie heile mir die Wunde.

Parsifal. Redemption, sinner, I offer e'en thee—	*Parsifal.* Erlösung, Frevlerin, biet' ich auch dir

Kundry. Let me, divine one, but love thee ;
  Redemption then should I see.
	Kundry. Lass' mich dich Göttlichen lieben,
	  Erlösung gabst du dann mir.

Parsifal. Love and Redemption thou shalt lack
  not,—
    If the way
  To Amfortas thou wilt show.
	Parsifal. Lieb' und Erlösung soll dir lohnen,—
	  zeigest zu
	  zu Amfortas mir den Weg.

Kundry
            (breaking into a rage).
  Thou—never shalt find it !
  Let the doomed one perish forever.—
    The shame seeker,
    Joy-destitute,
  Whom I have laughed at —laughed at —
    laughed at !
  Ha, ha ! He fell by his own good spear ?
	Kundry
	            (in Wuth ausbrechend).
	  Nie—sollst du ihn finden !
	  Den Verfall'nen, lass' ihn verderben,—
	    den Un-seligen,
	    Schmach-lüsternen,
	  den ich verlachte—lachte—lachte !
	  Haha ! Ihn traf ja der eig'ne Speer ?

Parsifal. Who dared raise against him the holy
  gear ?
	Parsifal. Wer durft' ihn verwunden mit heil'ger
	  Wehr ?

Kundry. He—he—,
  Who puts my laughter to flight :
His curse—ha !—doth lend me might :
For thyself the Spear doth await
If thou dost pity the sinner's fate !—
        Ha ! madness !
    Pity ! pity me, pray !
	Kundry. Er—Er—,
	  der einst mein Lachen bestraft :
	sein Fluch—ha !—mir giebt er Kraft ;
	gegen dich selbst ruf' ich die Wehr,
	gieb'st du dem Sünder des Mitleid's Ehr' !—
	        Ha ! Wahnsinn !—
	    Mitleid ! Mitleid mit mir !

One single hour with me —
One single hour with thee —
    Then, the wished-for
Path thou shalt straightway see !

(She seeks to embrace him : he thrusts her from him.)

Parsifal.   Begone, detestable wretch !

Kundry
        (beats her breast and shrieks in wild frenzy).
Hither ! Hither ! Oh, help !
Seize on the caitiff !   Oh, help !
    Ward all the ways there !
    Ward ev'ry passage ! —
For, fled'st thou from hence, and foundest
All the ways of the world,
The one that thou seek'st
That pathway ne'er shalt thou pass through !
    All paths and courses,
    Which from me would part thee,
Here — I curse them to thee :
    Wander — wander, —
    Thou whom I trust —
Thee will I give as his guide !

KLINGSOR has appeared upon the castle wall ; the DAMSELS also rush out of the castle and seek to hasten toward KUNDRY.

Klingsor
            (poising a lance).
Halt there !   I'll ban thee with befitting gear :
The Fool shall perish by his Master's spear !

He flings the spear at PARSIFAL ; it remains floating over his head ; PARSIFAL grasps it with his hand and brandishes it with a gesture of exalted rapture, making the sign of the Cross with it.

Parsifal.   This sign I make, and ban thy cursed
        magic :
    As the wound shall be closed,
    Which thou with this once clovest, —
    To wrack and to ruin
    Falls thy unreal display !

As with an earthquake the castle falls to ruins ; the garden withers up to a desert : the DAMSELS lie like shrivelled flowers strewn around on the ground. — KUNDRY has sunk down with a cry. To her turns once more from the summit of the ruined wall the departing

Parsifal.   Thou know'st—
    Where only we shall meet again !

(He disappears. The curtain closes quickly.)

Nur eine Stunde mein, —
nur eine Stunde dein — :
    und des Weges —
sollst du geleitet sein !

(Sie will ihn umarmen. Er stösst sie heftig von sich.)

Parsifal.   Vergeh', unseliges Weib !

Kundry
        (zerschlägt sich die Brust, und ruft in wildem Rasen).
Hilfe !   Hilfe !   Herbei !
Haltet den Frechen !   Herbei !
    Wehr't ihm die Wege !
    Wehr't ihm die Pfade ! —
Und flöh'st du von hier, und fändest
alle Wege der Welt,
den Weg, den du such'st,
dess' Pfade sollst du nicht finden !
    Denn Pfad und Wege,
    die mir dich entführen,
so — verwünsch' ich sie dir :
    Irre !   Irre, —
    mir so vertraut —
dich weih' ich ihm zum Geleit' !

KLINGSOR ist auf der Burgmauer heraus getreten ; die MÄDCHEN; stürzen ebenfalls aus dem Schloss und wollen auf KUNDRY zueilen.

Klingsor
            (eine Lanze schwingend).
Halt da ! dich bann' ich mit der rechten Wehr :
den Thoren stell' mir seines Meisters Speer !

Er schleudert auf PARSIFAL den Speer, welcher über dessen Haupte schweben bleibt ; PARSIFAL erfasst ihn mit der Hand und schwingt ihn, mit einer Gebärde höchster Entzückung, die Gestalt des Kreuzes bezeichnend.

Parsifal.   Mit diesem Zeichen bann' ich deiner
        Zauber :
    wie die Wunde er schliesse,
    die mit ihm du schlugest, —
    in Trauer und Trümmer
    stürze die trügende Pracht !

Wie durch ein Erdbeben versinkt das Schloss ; der Garten verdorrt zur Einöde : die MÄDCHEN liegen als verwelkte Blumen am Boden umher gestreut. — KUNDRY ist schreiend zusammen gesunken. Zu ihr wendet sich noch einmal, von der Höhe einer Mauertrümmer herab, der enteilende

Parsifal.   Du weisst—
    wo einzig du mich wiedersieh'st !

(Er verschwindet. Der Vorhang schliesst sich schnell.)

ACT III.

In the Grail's domain. — Open, pleasant spring landscape, with flowery meadows rising towards the back.   At the front is the border of a wood, which extends away R.   A spring, in the foreground, by the wood ; opposite, higher up, a narrow hermitage, built against a rock.   Daybreak. —
GURNEMANZ, now extremely aged, meanly dressed as a hermit, but with the tunic of a Knight of the Grail, emerges from the hut and listens.

Gurnemanz. From thence the groaning cometh. —
    No animal grieves like that ;
And on this, besides, — the holiest day we
    have. —
Methinks I recognize those rueful tones.

A low moaning is heard as of a sleeper terrified by dreams. — GURNEMANZ strides resolutely to a thicket at one side which has overgrown itself : he forcibly tears the brambles asunder, then pauses suddenly.

    Ha ! She — here again ?
    The hedge with its thorns overgrown
    Has been her grave for how long ? —
    Up — Kundry ! — Up !
The winter's fled, and Spring is here !
    Awake, awake to the Spring !
        Cold — and stiff ! —
This time truly I deem she's dead : —
Yet was't her groaning I heard just now ?

(He drags KUNDRY, quite rigid and lifeless out of the bushes, bears her to a grassy mound near, chafes her hands and temples, breathes on them, and does his utmost to relax her stiffness.   At last she revives   She is, just as in the first Act, dressed in the wild garb of a servant of the Grail ; only her complexion is paler, and the wildness has faded from her mien and bearing — She stares awhile at GURNEMANZ.   Then she rises, settles her hair and dress, and goes immediately, like a serving maid, to her work.)

Gurnemanz. Thou crazy wench !
    Hast not a word for me ?
      Are these thy thanks,
      When from deathly slumber
    I have waked thee yet again ?

Kundry
(bows her head slowly : then in hoarse and broken accents murmurs).
    Service . . . service ! —

Gurnemanz
        (shaking his head).
    Now will thy work be light !
We send no errands out since long :
    Simples and herbs
    Must ev'ryone find for himself :
'Tis learnt in the woods from the beasts.

KUNDRY has meanwhile looked about her, and now perceives the hut, and goes within.

Gurnemanz
      (looking after her in surprise).
    How unlike this her step of yore !
    Is this holy morning the cause ?

DRITTER AUFZUG.

Im Gebiete des Grales

Freie anmuthige Frühlingsgegend mit nach dem Hintergrunde zu sanft ansteigender Blumenaue.   Den Vordergrund nimmt der Saum des Waldes ein, der sich nach rechts zu ausdehnt.   Im Vordergrunde, an der Waldseite, ein Quell ; ihm gegenüber, etwas tiefer eine schlichte Einsiedlerhütte, an einen Felsen gelehnt.   Frühester Morgen. —
GURNEMANZ, zum hohen Greise gealtert, als Einsiedler, nur in das Hemd des Gralsritters dürftig gekleidet, tritt aus der Hütte und lauscht.

Gurnemanz. Von dorther kam das Stöhnen. —
    So jammervoll klagt kein Wild,
und gewiss gar nicht am heiligsten Morgen
    heut'. —
Mich dünkt, ich kenne diesen Klageruf ?

Ein dumpfes Stöhnen, wie von einer im tiefen Schlafe durch Träume Geängstigten, wird vernommen. — GURNEMANZ schreitet entschlossen einer Dornenhecke auf der Seite zu : diese ist gänzlich überwachsen ; er reisst mit Gewalt das Gestrüpp auseinander ; dann hält er plötzlich an.

    Ha ! Sie — wieder da ?
    Das winterlich rauhe Gedörn'
    hielt sie verdeckt : wie lang' schon ? —
    Auf ! — Kundry ! — Auf !
Der Winter floh, und Lenz ist da !
    Erwach', erwache dem Lenz ! —
        kalt — und starr ! —
Diessmal hielt' ich sie wohl für todt . —
doch war's ihr Stöhnen, was ich vernahm ?

Er zieht KUNDRY, ganz erstarrt und leblos, aus dem Gebüsche hervor, trägt sie auf einen nahen Rasenhügel, reibt ihr stark die Hände und Schläfe, haucht sie an, und bemüht sich in Allem, um die Erstarrung weichen zu machen.   Endlich erwacht sie.   Sie ist, gänzlich wie im ersten Aufzuge, im wilden Gewande der Gralsbotin ; nur ist ihre Gesichtsfarbe bleicher, aus Miene und Haltung ist die Wildheit gewichen. — Sie starrt lange GURNEMANZ an.   Dann erhebt sie sich ordnet sich Kleidung und Haar, und geht sofort wie eine Magd an die Bedienung.

Gurnemanz. Du tolles Weib !
    Hast du kein Wort für mich ?
      Ist diess der Dank,
      dass dem Todesschlafe
    noch einmal ich dich entweckt ?

Kundry
(neigt langsam das Haupt ; dann bringt sie, rauh und abgebrochen hervor) :
    Dienen . . dienen ! —

Gurnemanz
        (schüttelt den Kopf).
    Das wird dich wenig müh'n !
Auf Botschaft sendet sich's nicht mehr :
    Kräuter und Wurzeln
    findet ein Jeder sich selbst,
    wir lernen's im Walde vom Thier.

KUNDRY hat sich während dem umgesehen, gewahrt die Hütte und geht hinein.

Gurnemanz
      (verwundert ihr nachblickend).
    Wie anders schreitet sie als sonst !
    Wirkte das der heilige Tag ?

Oh, day of mercy unimagined !
No doubt for her salvation
Heaven through me revived
This wretch from deathly slumber.

KUNDRY comes from the hut again ; she bears a water pot, which she takes to the spring. Whilst she waits for it to fill, she looks into the wood, and perceives some one approaching in the distance ; she turns to GURNEMANZ to point him out to him.

Gurnemanz
(peering into the wood).

Who comes towards the sanctified stream ?
In gloomy war apparel—
None of our brethren is he.

KUNDRY withdraws, with the filled pitcher, to the hut, where she busies herself.—GURNEMANZ steps aside in surprise, to observe the newcomer.—PARSIFAL enters from the wood. He is in complete black armor ; with closed helmet and lowered spear he walks slowly forward, his head drooping, dreamily vacillating—he seats himself on the little knoll by the spring.

Gurnemanz
observes him a long while and then approaches somewhat).

Greet thee, my friend !
Art thou astray, and shall I direct thee?
(PARSIFAL shakes his head softly.)

Gurnemanz. And hast thou no greeting for me ?
(PARSIFAL bows his head.)

Gurnemanz. Hey ! — what ? —
If by thy vow
Thou art bound to perfect silence,
So mine remindeth me
Straight to inform thee what is due. —
Here thou art in a holy place ;
No man with weapons hither comes,
With shut-up helmet, shield and spear.
This day, besides ! Dost thou not know
What holy day hath dawned ?
(PARSIFAL shakes his head.)
No? From whence com'st thou then ?
What heathen darkness hast thou left
To hear not that to-day is
The ever hallow d Good-Friday morn ?
(PARSIFAL droops his head still lower.)
Quick, doff thy weapons !
Trouble not this morn the Master,
Who once did free all men from hell,
When bare of defence He bled for us.

PARSIFAL rises, after a further silence, thrusts the spear into the ground before him, lays down his sword and shield before it, opens his helmet and, taking it from his head, lays it with the other arms, and then kneels down in silent prayer before the spear. GURNEMANZ observes him with surprise and emotion. He beckons KUNDRY, who has now come out of the hut.—PARSIFAL raises his eyes, in ardent prayer, towards the spear's head.)

Gurnemanz
(softly to KUNDRY).

Dost know who 'tis ? . .
He who, long since, laid low the swan.
(KUNDRY confirms him by a slight nod.)

Oh ! Tag der Gnade ohne Gleichen !
Gewiss zu ihrem Heile
durft' ich der Armen heut'
den Todesschlaf verscheuchen.

KUNDRY kommt wieder aus der Hütte ; sie trägt einen Wasserkrug und geht damit zum Quelle. Während sie auf die Füllung wartet, blickt sie in den Wald, und bemerkt dort in der Ferne einen Kommenden ; sie wendet sich zu GURNEMANZ, um ihn darauf hinzudeuten.

Gurnemanz
(in den Wald spähend).

Wer nahet dort dem heiligen Quell ?
Im düst'ren Waffenschmucke,
das ist der Brüder keiner.

KUNDRY entfernt sich mit dem gefüllten Kruge langsam nach der Hütte, in welcher sie sich zu schaffen macht.—GURNEMANZ tritt staunend etwas bei Seite, um den Ankommenden zu beobachten.—PARSIFAL tritt aus dem Walde auf. Er ist ganz in schwarzer Waffenrüstung : mit geschlossenem Helme und gesenktem Speer, schreitet er, gebeugten Hauptes, träumerisch zögernd, langsam daher, und setzt sich auf dem kleinen Rasenhügel am Quelle nieder.

Gurnemanz
(betrachtet ihn lange, und tritt dann etwas näher).

Heil dir, mein Gast !
Bist du verirrt, und soll ich dich weisen ?
(PARSIFAL schüttelt sanft das Haupt.)

Gurnemanz. Entbietest du mir keinen Gruss ?
(PARSIFAL neigt das Haupt.)

Gurnemanz. Hei ! — Was ?
Wenn dein Gelübde
dich bindet mir zu schweigen,
so mahnt das meine mich,
dass ich dir sage, was sich ziemt. —
Hier bist du an geweihtem Ort :
da zeiht man nicht mit Waffen her,
geschloss'nen Helmes, Schild und Speer.
Und heute gar ! Weisst du denn nicht,
welch' heil'ger Tag heut' ist ?
(PARSIFAL schüttelt mit dem Kopfe.)
Ja ! Woher komm'st du denn ?
Bei welchen Heiden weiltest du,
zu wissen nicht, dass heute
der allerheiligste Char-Freitag sei ?
(PARSIFAL senkt das Haupt noch tiefer.)
Schnell ab die Waffen !
Kränke nicht den Herrn, der heute,
baar jeder Wehr, sein heilig Blut
der sündigen Welt zur Sühne bot !

PARSIFAL erhebt sich, nach einem abermaligen Schweigen, stösst den Speer vor sich in den Boden, legt Schild und Schwert davor nieder, öffnet den Helm, nimmt ihn vom Haupte und legt ihn zu den anderen Waffen, worauf er dann zu stummem Gebete vor dem Speer niederkniet. GURNEMANZ betrachtet ihn mit Erstaunen und Rührung. Er winkt KUNDRY herbei, welche soeben aus der Hütte getreten ist.—PARSIFAL erhebt jetzt in brünstigem Gebete seinen Blick andachtvoll zu der Lanzenspitze auf.

Gurnemanz
(leise zu KUNDRY)

Erkenn'st du ihn ? .
Der ist's, der einst den Schwan erlegt,
(KUNDRY bestätigt mit einem leisen Kopfnicken.)

For sure 'tis he!
The Fool whom in anger I dismissed?
Ha! by what path aye came he?
That Spear — I recognize!

      (in great emotion).

Oh! — holiest day,
To which my happy soul awakes! —

      (KUNDRY has turned away her face.)

Parsifal
(rises slowly from his prayer, gazes calmly around, recognizes
GURNEMANZ, and stretches out his hand to him in greeting).
    Thank Heaven that I again have found
      thee!

Gurnemanz.   And dost thou know me too?
    Dost recognize me,
So lowly bent by grief and care?
How cam'st thou here? From whence?

Parsifal.   Through error and through suff'ring
    lay my pathway;
May I believe that I have freed me from it,
    Now that this forest's murmur
    Falls upon my senses,
And worthy voice of age doth welcome?
    Or yet — is't new error?
    All's altered here, meseemeth.

Gurnemanz.   But say, where points the path thou
    seekest?

Parsifal.   To him, whose dire complainings
    Once came to me, an awestruck Fool,
    And for whose healing surely
I must believe myself ordained.
      But — ah! —
The wished for path for aye denied me,
    I wandered at random,
Driven ever on by a curse:
      Countless distresses,
      Battles and conflicts
    Drove me far from the pathway;
    Well though I knew it, methought.
    Then hopeless despair overtook me
    To hold the holy Thing safely.
In its behalf, in its safe warding
I won from ev'ry weapon a wound;
      For 'twas forbidden
    That in battle I bore it:
      Undefiled
    E'er at my side I wore it,
    And now I home restore it.
'Tis this that gleaming hails thee here, —
    The Grail's most holy spear.

Gurnemanz.   Oh Glory! Bounteous bliss!
Oh marvel! Beauteous, boundless marvel!

Gewiss 's ist Er!
Der Thor, den ich zürnend von uns wies?
Ha! Welche Pfade fand er?
Der Speer, — ich kenne ihn.

      (In grosser Ergriffenheit.)

Oh! — Heiligster Tag,
zu dem ich heut' erwachen sollt'! —

      (KUNDRY hat ihr Gesicht abgewendet.)

Parsifal
(erhebt sich langsam vom Gebete, blickt ruhig um sich, erkennt
GURNEMANZ, und reicht diesem sanft die Hand zum Gruss).
    Heil mir, dass ich dich wieder finde!

Gurnemanz.   So kenn'st auch du mich noch?
    Erkenn'st mich wieder.
    den Gram und Noth so tief gebeugt?
    Wie kam'st du heut'? Woher?

Parsifal.   Der Irrniss und der Leiden Pfade
    kam ich;
soll ich mich denen jetzt entwunden wähnen,
    da dieses Waldes Rauschen
    wieder ich vernehme,
    dich guten Alten neu begrüsse?
    Oder — irr' ich wieder?
    Verwandelt dünkt mich Alles.

Gurnemanz.   So sag', zu wem den Weg du
    suchtest?

Parsifal.   Zu ihm, dess' tiefe Klagen
    ich thörig staunend einst vernahm,
    dem nun ich Heil zu bringen
mich auserlesen wähnen darf.
      doch — ach! —
    den Weg des Heiles nie zu finden,
    in pfadlosen Irren
iagt' ein wilder Fluch mich umher:
    zahllose Nöthen,
      Kämpfe und Streite
    zwangen mich ab vom Pfade,
    wähnt' ich ihn recht schon erkannt.
    Da musste Verzweiflung mich fassen,
    das Heilthum heil mir zu bergen,
um das zu hüten, das zu wahren
ich Wunden jeder Wehr' mir gewann.
      Denn nicht ihn selber
    durft' ich führen im Streite;
      unentweih't
    führt' ich ihn mir zur Seite,
    den ich nun heim geleite,
der dort dir schimmert hiel und hehr,
    des Grales heil'gen Speer.

Gurnemanz.   O Gnade! Höchstes Heil!
O Wunder! Heilig hehrstes Wunder! —

(After he has somewhat collected himself).

Great knight! If 'twere a curse,
Which drove thee from thy proper path,
   Be sure it has departed.
Here art thou, in the Grail's domain ;
Here waits for thee the knightly band
   Ah ! how they need the blessing,
   The blessing that thou bring'st ! —
Since that first day in which thou camest here,
The mourning, which thou heardest then —
The anguish — sorely has increased.
Amfortas, struggling with his torture,
With the wound that tore his spirit,
Des.red with reckless daring then his death :
No pray'rs, no sorrow of his comrades
Could move him to fulfil his holy office.
In shrouded shrine the Grail has long remained.
   Its sin-repentant warder wishing,
   Since he could perish not,
   While he beheld its light,
   To speed his dissolution,
And with his life to end his bitter sorrows.
The Holy Meal to us is now denied,
   And common viands must content us ;
Thereby hath withered all our heroes' strength :
   Ne'er cometh message now,
Nor call to holy warfare from far countries ;
   Pale, dejected, strays around
The crushed and leader-lacking band of knights.
Here on the woodside lone I hid myself,
   For death with calmness waiting,
To which my old commander has succumbed ;
   For Titurel, my cherished chief,
When he no more beheld the Grail's refulgence,
   Expired, — a man like others !

Parsifal
   (flinging up his arms in intense grief).

   And I — I 'tis,
   Who all this woe have wrought !
     Ha ! what a grievous,
   What a heinous guilt
   Must then my foolish head
   For ever be oppressed with !
   If no atonement, expiation
   My blindness e'er can banish !
   I, who to save men was selected,
     Must wander undirected ;
   All paths of safety from me vanish !

(He is on the point of falling, helplessly. GURNEMANZ supports
him, and allows him to sink down on the grassy knoll. — KUNDRY has
brought a basin of water to sprinkle PARSIFAL with.)

Gurnemanz
   (waving her off.)

   Not so ! —
The holy fount itself

(Nachdem er sich etwas gefasst.)

O Herr ! War es ein Fluch,
der dich vom rechten Pfad vertrieb,
   so glaub', er ist gewichen.
Hier bist du ; diess des Gral's Gebiet,
dein' harret seine Ritterschaft.
   Ach, sie bedarf des Heiles,
   des Heiles, das du bring'st ! —
Seit jenem Tage, den du hier geweilt,
die Trauer, so da kund dir ward. —
das Bangen — wuchs zur höchsten Noth.
Amfortas, gegen seiner Wunde,
seiner Seele Qual sich wehrend,
begehrt' in wildem Trotze nun den Tod :
kein Fleh'n, kein Elend seiner Ritter
bewog ihn mehr des heil'gen Amt's zu walten
Im Schrein verschlossen bleibt seit lang' der
Gral :
   so hofft sein sündenreu'ger Hüter,
   da er nicht sterben kann
   wann je er ihn erschau't,
   sein Ende zu erzwingen,
und mit dem Leben seine Qual zu enden.
Die heil'ge Speisung bleibt uns nun versagt,
   gemeine Atzung muss uns nähren ;
darob versiechte unsrer Helden Kraft :
   nie kommt uns Botschaft mehr,
noch Ruf zu heil'gen Kämpfen aus der Ferne ;
   bleich und elend wankt umher
die Muth- und Führer-lose Ritterschaft.
Hier in der Waldeck' barg ich einsam mich,
   des Todes still gewärtig,
dem schon mein alter Waffenherr verfiel
   denn Titurel, mein heil'ger Held,
den nun des Grales Anblick nicht mehr labte
   er starb, — ein Mensch wie Alle !

Parsifal
   (vor grossen Schmerz sich aufbäumend).

   Und ich — ich bin's,
   der all' diess Elend schuf !
     Ha ! Welcher Sünden,
   welcher Frevel Schuld
   muss dieses Thoren-Haupt
   seit Ewigkeit belasten,
   da keine Busse, keine Sühne
   der Blindheit mich entwindet,
   mir, selbst zur Rettung auserkoren,
   in Irrniss wild verloren
   der Rettung letzter Pfad verschwindet !

(Er droht ohnmächtig umzusinken. GURNEMANZ hält ihn auf
recht, und senkt ihn zum Sitze auf den Rasenhügel nieder. — KUNDRY
hat ein Becken mit Wasser herbeigeholt, um PARSIFAL zu besprengen.)

Gurnemanz
   (KUNDRY abweisend).

   Nicht so ! —
Die heil'ge Quelle selbst

Befitteth more our pilgrim's bath.   **21**
   I ween a mighty feat
   Must he this morning finish,
Fulfil a sacred, mystic duty:
   He should be pure as day ·
   So let his travel stains
Be now completely washed away.

<small>They both turn PARSIFAL gently to the edge of the spring.
Whilst KUNDRY removes the greaves from his legs, and then bathes
his feet, GURNEMANZ meanwhile removing his corselet,—</small>

Parsifal
<small>(asks gently and wearily).</small>
Shall I straight be guided unto Amfortas?

Gurnemanz
<small>(busying himself).</small>
Most surely; there the Court our coming waits.
The obsequies of my belovéd chief,
   Have even summoned me.
The Grail to us will once more be uncovered,
   The long neglected office
   Once more performed before us —
To sanctify the sov'reign father,
Who through his son's great sin has died,
Which he now fain would expiate. —
   'Tis thus Amfortas wills.

Parsifal
<small>(observing KUNDRY with wonder).</small>
   Thou'st washed my feet so humbly: —
This friend besprinkles now my head.

Gurnemanz
<small>(taking water from the spring in the hollow of his hand, and
sprinkling PARSIFAL's head).</small>
Now blessed be, thou pure one, through pure
     water!   **21**
   So may all care and sin
   Be driven far from thee.

<small>Meanwhile KUNDRY has taken a golden flask from her bosom
and poured some of the contents upon PARSIFAL's feet, which she
now dries on her hair, quickly unbound for the purpose.</small>

Parsifal
<small>(taking the flask from her).</small>
Now that my feet thou'st anointed,
My head the friend of Titurel must lave;
For I to-day as king shall be appointed.

Gurnemanz
<small>(empties the flask completely over PARSIFAL's head, rubs it gently,</small> **12**
<small>and folds his hands over it).</small>
   Aye, thus it was foretold me,
   My blessing on thy head: —
   Our king indeed behold we.
     Thou — pure one —·
   Allpitying sufferer,
   Allknowing rescuer!
Thou who the sinner's sorrows thus hast suffered,
Assist his soul to cast one burden more.

---

erquicke uns'res Pilgers Bad.
   Mir ahnt, ein hohes Werk
   hat er noch heut' zu wirken,
zu walten eines heil'gen Amtes:
   so sei er fleckenrein,
   und langer Irrfahrt Staub
soll jetzt von ihm gewaschen sein.

<small>PARSIFAL wird von den Beiden sanft zum Rande des Quelles ge-
wendet. Während KUNDRY ihm die Beinschienen lös't und dann
die Füsse badet, GURNEMANZ ihm aber den Brustharnisch entnimmt,
frägt</small>

Parsifal
<small>(sanft und matt).</small>
Werd' heut' ich zu Amfortas noch geleitet?

Gurnemanz
<small>(während der Beschäftigung).</small>
Gewisslich, uns'rer harrt die hehre Burg:
die Todtenfeier meines lieben Herrn,
   sie ruft mich selbst dahin.
Den Gral noch einmal uns da zu enthüllen,
   des lang' versäumten Amtes
   noch einmal heut' zu walten —
zur Heiligung des hehren Vaters,
der seines Sohnes Schuld erlag,
die Der nun also büssen will, —
   gelobt' Amfortas uns.

Parsifal
<small>(mit Verwunderung KUNDRY zusehend).</small>
   Du wuschest mir die Füsse: —
nun netze mir das Haupt der Freund.

Gurnemanz
<small>(mit der Hand aus dem Quell schöpfend und PARSIFAL's Haupt
besprengend).</small>
Gesegnet sei, du Reiner, durch das Reine !
   So weiche jeder Schuld
   Bekümmerniss von dir !

<small>Während dem hat KUNDRY ein goldenes Fläschchen aus dem
Busen gezogen, und von seinem Inhalte auf PARSIFAL's Füsse ausge-
gossen, jetzt trocknet sie diese mit ihren schnell aufgelösten Haaren.</small>

Parsifal
<small>(nimmt ihr das Fläschchen ab).</small>
   Salbtest du mir auch die Füsse,
das Haupt nun salbe Titurel's Genoss',
dass heute noch als König er mich grüsse.

Gurnemanz
<small>(schüttet das Fläschchen vollends auf PARSIFAL's Haupt aus,
reibt dieses sanft, und faltet dann die Hände darüber).</small>
   So ward es uns verhiessen,
   so segne ich dein Haupt,
   als König dich zu grüssen.
     Du — Reiner.
   mitleidvoll Duldender,
   heilthatvoll Wissender !
Wie des Erlös'ten Leiden du gelitten,
die letzte Last entnimm nun seinem Haupt.

Parsifal

(scoops up some water from the spring, unperceived, bends down to
the kneeling KUNDRY and sprinkles her head).

I first fulfil my duty thus : —
　　Be thou baptized,
　And trust in the Redeemer !

(KUNDRY bows her head to the earth and appears to weep bitterly.)

Parsifal

(turns round and gazes with gentle rapture on the woods and
meadows).

How fair the fields and meadows seem to-day ! —
　　Many a magic flow'r I've seen,
Which sought to clasp me in its baneful twin-
　　ings ;
　But none I've seen so sweet as here,
　These tendrils bursting with blossom,
　Whose scent recals my childhood's days
　And speaks of loving trust to me.

Gurnemanz.　That is Good-Friday's spell, my
　　lord !

Parsifal.　Alas, that day of agony !
　　Now surely everything that thrives,
　　That breathes and lives and lives again,
　　　Should only mourn and sorrow ?

Gurnemanz.　Thou see'st, that is not so.
　　The sad repentant tears of sinners
　　　Have here with holy rain
　　　Besprinkled field and plain,
　　And made them glow with beauty.
　　All earthly creatures in delight
　　At the Redeemer's trace so bright
　　　Uplift their pray'rs of duty.
To see Him on the Cross they have no power :
And so they smile upon redeeméd man,
Who, feeling freed, with dread no more doth
　　cower,
Through God's love-sacrifice made clean and
　　pure :
And now perceives each blade and meadow-
　　flower
That mortal foot to-day it need not dread ;
For, as the Lord in pity man did spare,
　　And in His mercy for him bled,
　　All men will keep, with pious care,
　　　To-day a tender tread.
　　Then thanks the whole creation makes,
　　With all that flow'rs and fast goes hence,
　　That trespass-pardoned Nature wakes
　　　Now to her day of Innocence.

(KUNDRY has slowly raised her head again, and gazes with moist
eyes, earnestly and calmly beseeching, up at PARSIFAL.)

Parsifal.　I saw my scornful mockers wither :
　　Now look they for forgiveness hither ? —

Parsifal

(schöpft unvermerkt Wasser aus der Quelle, neigt sich zu der vo
ihm noch knienden KUNDRY, und netzt ihr das Haupt).

Mein erstes Amt verricht' ich so : —
　　die Taufe nimm,
　und glaub' an den Erlöser !

(KUNDRY senkt das Haupt tief zur Erde und scheint heftig zu weinen.)

Parsifal

(wendet sich um, und blickt mit sanfter Entzückung auf Wald
und Wiese).

Wie dünkt mich doch die Aue heut' so schön ! ··
　　Wohl traf ich Wunderblumen an,
die bis zum Haupte süchtig mich umrankten ;
　doch sah' ich nie so mild und zart
　die Halmen, Blüthen und Blumen,
　noch duftete All' so kindisch hold
　und sprach so lieblich traut zu mir ?

Gurnemanz.　Das ist Char-Freitags-Zauber, Herr

Parsifal.　O weh', des höchsten Schmerzentag's
　　Da sollte, wähn' ich, was da blüh't,
　　was athmet, lebt und wieder lebt,
　　　nur trauern, ach ! und weinen ?

Gurnemanz.　Du sieh'st, das ist nicht so.
　　Des Sünders Reuethränen sind es,
　　　die heut' mit heil'gem Thau
　　　beträufet Flur und Au' :
　　der liess sie so gedeihen.
　　Nun freu't sich alle Kreatur
　　auf des Erlösers holder Spur
　　　will ihr Gebet ihm weihen.
Ihn selbst am Kreuze kann sie nicht erschauen
da blickt sie zum erlös'ten Menschen auf ;
der fühlt sich frei von Sünden-Angst und Grauen
durch Gottes Liebesopfer rein und heil :
das merkt nun Halm und Blume auf den Auen.
dass heut' des Menschen Fuss sie nicht zertritt.
doch wohl, wie Gott mit himmlischer Geduld
　　sich sein' erbarmt und für ihn litt,
　　der Mensch auch heut' in frommer Huld
　　sie schont mit sanftem Schritt.
　　Das dankt dann alle Kreatur,
　　was all' da blüht und bald erstirbt,
　　da die entsündigte Natur
　　heut' ihren Unschulds-Tag erwirbt.

(KUNDRY hat langsam wieder das Haupt erhoben, und blickt
feuchten Auges, ernst und ruhig bittend zu PARSIFAL auf.)

Parsifal.　Ich sah' sie welken, die mir lachten
　　ob heut' sie nach Erlösung schmachten ?

Like blessed sweet dew a tear from thee too
    floweth:
Thou weepest — see! the landscape groweth.

(He kisses her softly on the brow.)
(Distant bells are heard pealing, very gradually swelling.)

Gurnemanz.   Mid-day. —
    The hour has come: —
Permit, my lord, thy servant hence to lead thee! —

GURNEMANZ has brought out a coat-of-mail and mantle of the knights of the Grail, which he and KUNDRY put or PARSIFAL. The landscape changes very gradually, as in the first Act, but from R. to L. PARSIFAL solemnly grasps the Spear and, with KUNDRY, follows the conducting GURNEMANZ. — When the wood has disappeared, and rocky entrances have presented themselves in which the three become invisible, processions of knights in mourning garb are perceived in the arched passages; the pealing of bells ever increasing. — At last the whole immense Hall becomes visible just as in the first Act, only without the tables. Faint light. The doors open again. From one side the knights bear in TITUREL's corpse in a coffin. From the other AMFORTAS is carried on in his litter, preceded by the covered shrine of the Grail. The bier is erected in the middle; behind it the throne with canopy where AMFORTAS is set down.

(Song of the knights during the procession.)

First Train
(with the " Grail " and AMFORTAS).

To sacred place in sheltering shrine
    The Holy Grail do we carry;
What hide ye there in gloomy shrine,
    Which hither mourning ye bear?

Second Train
(with TITUREL's coffin).

A hero lies in this dismal shrine
    With all this heavenly strength,
To whom all things once God did entrust:
    Titurel hither we bear.

First Train.   By whom was he slain, who by God himself
    Once was ever sheltered?

Second Train.   He sank beneath the mortal burden of years,
When the Grail no more he might look on.

First Train.   Who veiled then the Grail's delights from his vision?

Second Train.   He whom ye are bearing: its criminal guardian.

First Train.   We conduct him to-day, for here once again,
      — And once more only —
    He fulfilleth his office.

Second Train.   Sorrow! Sorrow! Thou guard of the Grail!
    Be once more only
    Warned of thy duty to all.

(The coffin is set down on the bier, AMFORTAS placed on the couch.)

Auch deine Thräne wird zum Segensthaue:
    du weinest — sieh! es lacht die Aue.

(Er küsst sie sanft auf die Stirne.)
(Fernes Glockengeläute, sehr allmählich anschwellend.)

Gurnemanz.   Mittag. —
    Die Stund' ist da: —
gestatte, Herr, dass dich dein Knecht geleite! —

GURNEMANZ hat Waffenrock und Mantel des Gralsritters herbeigeholt; er und KUNDRY bekleiden PARSIFAL damit. Die Gegend verwandelt sich sehr allmählich, ähnlicher Weise wie im ersten Aufzuge, nur von rechts nach links. PARSIFAL ergreift feierlich den Speer und folgt mit KUNDRY langsam dem geleitenden GURNEMANZ. — Nachdem der Wald gänzlich verschwunden ist, und Felsenthore sich aufgethan haben, in welchen die Drei unsichtbar geworden sind, gewahrt man, bei fortdauernd anwachsendem Gelaute, in gewölbten Gängen Züge von RITTERN in Trauergewändern. — Endlich stellt sich der ganze grosse Saal wie im ersten Aufzuge (nur ohne die Speisetafeln) wieder dar. Düstere Beleuchtung. Die Thüren öffnen sich wieder. Von einer Seite ziehen die RITTER, TITUREL's Leiche im Sarge geleitend, herein. Auf der andern Seite wird AMFORTAS im Siechbette, vor ihm der verhüllte Schrein mit dem ,, Grale," getragen. In der Mitte ist der Katafalk errichtet, dahinter der Hochsitz mit dem Baldachin, auf welchen AMFORTAS wieder niedergelassen wird.

(Gesang der Ritter während des Einzuges.)

Erster Zug
(mit dem ,, Gral " und AMFORTAS).

Geleiten wir im bergenden Schrein
    den Gral zum heiligen Amte,
wen berget ihr im düst'ren Schrein
    und führt ihn trauernd daher?

Zweiter Zug
(mit TITUREL's Sarge).

Es birgt den Helden der Trauerschrein,
    er birgt die heilige Kraft;
der Gott selbst einst zur Pflege sich gab:
    Titurel führen wir her.

Erster Zug.   Wer hat ihn gefällt, der in Gottes Hut
    Gott selbst einst beschirmte?

Zweiter Zug.   Ihn fällte des Alters tödtende Last,
    da den Gral er nicht mehr erschaute.

Erster Zug.   Wer wehrt' ihm des Grales Huld zu erschauen?

Zweiter Zug.   Den dort ihr geleitet, der sündige Hüter.

Erster Zug.   Wir geleiten ihn heut', denn heut' noch einmal
      — zum letzten Male! —
    will des Amtes er walten.

Zweiter Zug.   Wehe! Wehe! Du Hüter des Heil's!
    Zum letzten Male
    sei deines Amts gemahnt!

(Der Sarg ist auf dem Katafalk niedergesetzt, AMFORTAS auf das Ruhebett gelegt.)

Amfortas. Aye, sorrow! Sorrow! Sorrow for me!—

With you I willingly cry;
Liefer yet would I ye'd give me death,
Atonement light for my trespass!

(The coffin is opened. At the sight of TITUREL's body all burst into a poignant cry of distress.)

Amfortas

(raising himself high on his couch and turning to the body).

My father!
Highest venerated hero!
Thou purest, to whom once e'en angels bended!
I only desired to perish,
Yet—gave thee to death!
Oh! thou who now in heavenly heights
Dost behold the Saviour's self,
Implore him to grant that his hallowed blood,
(If once again here his blessing
He pour upon these brothers)
To them new life while giving,
To me may offer—but Death!
Death—darkness!
Solitary mercy!
Take from me the horrible wound, the poison,
Stiffen the heart so tortured and rent!
My father! I—call thee,
Cry thou my words to Him:
"Redeemer! give to my son release!"

The Knights

(severally, pressing towards AMFORTAS)

Uncover the shrine!—
Do now thine office!
Thy father demands it;—
Thou must, thou must!

Amfortas

(in a paroxysm of despair springs up and throws himself amid the knights, who draw back).

No!—No more!—Ha!
Already is death glooming round me,—
And shall I yet again return to life?
Insanity!
What one in life can yet stay me?
Rather I bid ye to slay me!

(tears open his dress).

Behold me!—the open wound behold!
Here is my poison—my streaming blood.
Take up your weapons! Bury your swordblades
Deep—deep in me, to the hilts!
Ye heroes, up!
Kill both the sinner and all his pain:
The Grail's delight will ye then regain!

All have shrunk back in awe. AMFORTAS stands alone in fearful ecstasy.—PARSIFAL, accompanied by GURNEMANZ and KUNDRY, has entered unperceived, and now advancing stretches out the Spear, touching AMFORTAS' side with the point.

Amfortas. Ja, Wehe! Wehe! Weh' über mich!
So ruf' ich willig mit euch:
williger nähm' ich von euch den Tod
der Sünde mildeste Sühne!

(Der Sarg ist geöffnet worden. Beim Anblick der Leiche TITUREL's bricht Alles in einen jähen Wehruf aus.)

Amfortas

(von seinem Lager sich hoch aufrichtend, zu der Leiche gewandt).

Mein Vater!
Hochgesegneter der Helden!
Du Reinster, dem einst die Engel sich neigten!
Der einzig ich sterben wollte,
dir—gab ich den Tod!
Oh! der du jetzt in göttlichem Glanz
den Erlöser selbst erschau'st,
erflehe von ihm, dass sein heiliges Blut,
wenn noch einmal jetzt sein Segen
die Brüder soll erquicken,
wie ihnen neues Leben,
mir endlich spende—den Tod!
Tod!—Sterben!
Einzige Gnade!
Die schreckliche Wunde, das Gift ersterbe.
das es zernagt, erstarre das Herz!
Mein Vater! Dich—ruf' ich,
rufe du ihm es zu:
Erlöser, gieb meinem Sohne Ruh'!

Die Ritter

(sich näher an AMFORTAS drängend, durch einander).

Enthüllet den Schrein!—
Walte des Amtes!
Dich mahnet der Vater:—
du musst, du musst!

Amfortas

(in wüthender Verzweiflung aufspringend, und unter die zurückweichenden RITTER sich stürzend).

Nein!—Nicht mehr!—Ha!
Schon fühl' ich den Tod mich umnachten,—
und noch einmal sollt' ich in's Leben zurück?
Wahnsinnige!
Wer will mich zwingen zu leben?
Könnt ihr doch Tod nur mir geben!

(Er reisst sich das Gewand auf.)

Hier bin ich,—die off'ne Wunde hier!
Das mich vergiftet, hier fliesst mein Blut.
Heraus die Waffe! Taucht eure Schwerter
tief—tief hinein, bis an's Heft!
Ihr Helden, auf!
Tödtet den Sünder mit seiner Qual:
von selbst dann leuchtet euch wohl der Gral!

Alle sind scheu vor ihm gewichen. AMFORTAS steht, in furchtbarer Extase, einsam.—PARSIFAL ist von GURNEMANZ und KUNDRY begleitet, unvermerkt unter den RITTERN erschienen, tritt jetzt hervor, und streckt den Speer aus, mit dessen Spitze er AMFORTAS' Seite berührt.

Parsifal. One weapon only serves : —
  The one that struck
  Can staunch thy wounded side.

<small>AMFORTAS' countenance is irradiated with holy rapture ; he totters with emotion ; GURNEMANZ supports him.</small>

Parsifal. Be whole, unsullied and absolved !
For I now govern in thy place.
  Oh, blessed be thy sorrows,
  For Pity's potent might
  And Knowledge' purest power
  They taught a timid Fool.
   The holy Spear —
  Once more behold in this. —

<small>(All gaze with intense rapture on the spear which PARSIFAL holds aloft, while he continues in inspiration as he looks at its point.)</small>

  Oh, mighty miracle of bliss ! —
  This that through me thy wound restoreth.
  With holy blood behold it poureth.
  Which yearns to join the fountain glowing,
  Whose pure tide in the Grail is flowing !
  Hid be no more that shape divine :
  Uncover the Grail ! Open the shrine !

<small>The boys open the shrine ; PARSIFAL takes from it the " Grail " and kneels, absorbed in its contemplation, silently praying. The " Grail " glows with light ; a halo of glory pours down over all. — TITUREL, for the moment reanimated, raises himself in benediction in his coffin. — From the dome descends a white dove and hovers over PARSIFAL's head. He waves the " Grail " gently to and fro before the upgazing knights. KUNDRY, looking up at PARSIFAL, sinks slowly to the ground, dead. AMFORTAS and GURNEMANZ do homage on their knees to PARSIFAL.</small>

All

<small>(with voices from the middle and extreme heights, so soft as to be scarcely audible.)</small>

  Wondrous work of mercy :
  Salvation to the Saviour !

<small>(The Curtain closes.)</small>

Parsifal. Nur eine Waffe taugt : —
  die Wunde schliesst
  der Speer nur, der sie schlug.

<small>AMFORTAS' Miene leuchtet in heiliger Entzückung auf ; er scheint vor grosser Ergriffenheit zu schwanken ; GURNEMANZ stützt ihn</small>

Parsifal. Sei heil, entsündigt und gesühnt !
Denn ich verwalte nun dein Amt.
  Gesegnet sei kein Leiden,
  das Mitleid's höchste Kraft
  und reinsten Wissens Macht
  dem zagen Thoren gab.
   Den heil'gen Speer —
  ich bring' ihn euch zurück. —

<small>(Alles blickt in höchster Entzückung auf den emporgehaltenen Speer, zu dessen Spitze aufschauend PARSIFAL in Begeisterung fortfährt.)</small>

  Oh ! Welchen Wunders höchstes Glück ! —
  Die deine Wunde durfte schliessen,
  ihm seh' ich heil'ges Blut entfliessen
  in Sehnsucht dem verwandten Quelle,
  der dort fliesst in des Grales Welle !
  Nicht soll der mehr verchlossen sein :
  enthüllt den Gral ! Oeffnet den Schrein !

<small>Die KNAPPEN öffnen den Schrein : PARSIFAL entnimmt diesem den „ Gral," und versenkt sich, unter stummem Gebete, in seinem Anblick. Der „ Gral " erglüht : eine Glorienbeleuchtung ergiesst sich über Alle. — TITUREL, für diesen Augenblick wieder belebt erhebt sich segnend im Sarge. — Aus der Kuppel schwebt eine weisse Taube herab und verweilt über PARSIFAL's Haupte. Dieser schwenkt den „ Gral " sanft vor der aufblickenden Ritterschaft. — KUNDRY sinkt, mit dem Blicke zu ihm auf, langsam vor PARSIFAL entseelt zu Boden. AMFORTAS und GURNEMANZ huldigen kniend PARSIFAL.</small>

Alle

<small>(mit Stimmen aus der mittleren, so wie der obersten Höhe kaum hörbar leise).</small>

  Höchsten Heiles Wunder :
  Erlösung dem Erlöser !

<small>(Der Vorhang schliesst sich.)</small>